What Difference Does a Husband Make?

Studies on the History of Society and Culture

Victoria E. Bonnell and Lynn Hunt, Editors

What Difference Does a Husband Make?

Women and Marital Status in Nazi and Postwar Germany

ELIZABETH D. HEINEMAN

University of California Press

BERKELEY   LOS ANGELES   LONDON

University of California Press
Berkeley and Los Angeles, California

University of California Press, Ltd.
London, England

First paperback printing 2003

Library of Congress Cataloging-in-Publication Data

Heineman, Elizabeth, 1962– .
 What difference does a husband make? : women and marital status
in Nazi and postwar Germany / Elizabeth Heineman.
  p. cm.—(Studies on the history of society and culture ; 33)
 Includes bibliographic references and index.
 ISBN 0-520-23907-5 (pbk : alk. paper)
 1. Single women—Germany—Social conditions—History. 2.
Marital status—Germany—History. 3. Marital status—Germany—
Psychological aspects—History. I. Title. II. Series.
HQ800.2H45   1999
 305.48'9652—dc21   98-28003

Printed in the United States of America

11 10 09 08 07 06 05 04 03
9 8 7 6 5 4 3 2 1

The paper used in this publication meets the minimum requirements of
ANSI/ NISO Z39.48-1992 (R 1997) (Permanence of Paper). ∞

Contents

Illustrations

Preface

I began this project in the wake of the fortieth anniversary of the end of the Second World War. West Germany was a hothouse of debate about whether Germans had adequately "worked through" the Nazi past. By the time I completed this book, East Germany had ceased to exist as an independent state; the "postwar period"—as defined by the division of Germany and of Europe—was over. Germans had turned their tendency toward tortured self-reflection to contemplating the Stalinist era—and, in circular fashion, to wondering whether West Germany's absorption of East Germany had diverted attention from the still unfinished task of "mastering" the Nazi past.

When I began researching "women standing alone" in Nazi Germany and postwar West Germany, I knew that current questions, especially feminist questions regarding the role of marriage in establishing women's position, drove my inquiry. But I could never have dreamed that contemporary events would shape my study as they have. With the fall of the Berlin Wall, I imagined opportunities to expand an already solid study by adding a consideration of East Germany. Instead, I discovered that my "solid study" rested on shaky foundations. The opening of East Germany taught me as much about Nazi Germany and the Federal Republic as it did about East Germany itself.

The fortieth anniversary of 1945 coincided with the maturation of West German feminist historical writing. It was thus not surprising that the mid-1980s saw a flood of works—both scholarly and popular—revisiting women's roles in the chaotic aftermath of the war. Women standing alone, who confronted daily life without husbands, loomed large in these histories. And for good reason. There were a lot of them, and they played a remarkable role in the struggle for survival as the war was being lost and after the defeat of Nazi Germany.

This image led me to study women standing alone. Dramatic as it was, though, it was clearly limited. Most obviously, it referred to only a few short years: roughly 1943–48. Where had these women come from, and where did they go? I wanted to "fill in" the history of this marginal group. What shaped these women's lives? How did they experience their situations? What was their impact on wartime and postwar Germany?

I also intended to address two larger issues. In the Germanist context, I was concerned with the issue of periodization—to what extent should we understand 1945 as a breaking point? Despite much questioning of the extent to which 1945 represented a "zero hour," especially in matters outside military and high-political history, few people wrote across 1945. There was some influential work proposing that 1942–48 be understood as a discrete period, at least in social history,[1] but 1942–48 is a very short period. Studying it in isolation begs the question of longer-term change and continuity. Furthermore, as a period marked first by the collapse of government, then by an utter absence of central government, 1942–48 is clearly an exceptional period in a century in which the state is so important. By starting the story in peacetime Nazi Germany, taking it through the war, the collapse, the period of occupation, and then through a full decade of the "return to normalcy" of the 1950s, I hoped to get at longer-term issues of change and continuity and also to bring the state back into the business of transgressing the 1945 border.

In the context of feminist scholarship, I wanted to explore the significance of marital status. How strong is the divide between married and single women legally, socially, economically, and in terms of personal identity? What determines how rigid the divide is? I was starting with the proposition that marital status has, through much of Western history, been a basic category of difference for women, in some ways analogous to race, class, and gender.[2] Women's legal personhood—their right to enter into contracts, to own property, to have legal guardianship of their children—has, until recently, depended on marital status. In addition, physical markers such as head coverings and wedding rings, as well as the use of different forms of address (Miss versus Mrs., Fräulein versus Frau), served to make a woman's marital status as immediately recognizable as her sex, her race, or her class. One need have had no interaction with a woman, in person or on paper, without knowing whether she was or had been married.

At the same time, I wanted to enter discussions about the fluidity and the constructed nature of categories of difference—how fixed a category is race, for example? I am a firm believer in the "constructed" nature of such categories, but I also recognize that poststructuralist analysis can be problematic.[3] No matter how much we may understand that the meaning of "female" varies over time or in different societies, for example, most individual women—our historical subjects—describe themselves as "women" without tortured qualifications. But the fluidity of marital status is much more transparent than is the fluidity of race, class, or gender. Most people in the Western world experience more than one marital status in their adult lives: they start out single and become married. Many enter a third state: they become widowed or divorced. Shifting categories of marital status are easily comprehended beyond the individual level as, for example, marriage and divorce laws change. Finally, the same marital status can have more than one meaning at a time: never to have married, for example, might be considered a bit unusual for a childless woman, but it spells real trouble for a bourgeois woman with children. It seemed to me that, by thinking about marital status, we might be able to get over some of the conceptual difficulties around the notion that categories of difference can be at once extremely rigid and extremely flexible. In entering larger discussions of war and gender formation, women standing alone also seemed particularly promising. After all, they were popularly understood to have been "created" by the war.

Whether I defined my work as filling in the history of a marginal group, transgressing the 1945 border, or exploring marital status as a category of difference, the obvious relevance of my work in West Germany was striking. First, I was on to an absolute gold mine of archival material. The existing literature suggested that these women were basically marginalized in the Nazi period and in the 1950s, as governments focused on the "complete family." This assumption proved not to be true. For both the Nazi and the Federal periods, there was a staggering amount of material on such topics as unwed mothers and widows' pensions, indicating that governments paid a great deal of attention to women standing alone. These materials also gave evidence of a great public awareness of them in forms such as constituent letters.

Second, and even more striking, was the popular resonance of my work in West Germany. Whenever the project came up in casual discussion—with professionals, friends, or chance acquaintances—I seemed to have hit a nerve. "Oh, all those women who couldn't marry because of the war, . . . those terrible postwar years, . . . how hard those women worked. . . . The 'women of the rubble' . . . someone really needs to write their story!" The conversation usually ended with my companion offering up an elderly aunt or neighbor as interview subject. Even in the early 1990s, West

Germans clearly remembered the wartime generation of women standing alone, and they still considered them important.

This happy confluence of ample sources and timely questions resulted in my dissertation. In transforming it into a book, my major project would be to add East Germany. Not only were the archives newly opened, but this was a great topic for East Germany. All the elements that had made women standing alone important in the West were even more in place in the East— a greater demographic imbalance, yet harsher living conditions, a greater reliance on women for reconstruction. My plans were for a fairly tidy research project: figure out the parallel story to what had happened in the West—for example, by examining relevant social-policy measures.

My problems began as soon as I stepped off the plane. It quickly became clear that, in East Germany, my project had no popular resonance whatsoever. When I told people I was working on the "women standing alone," they didn't know what I was talking about. To be sure, they understood the technical meaning of the term, but they referred it to the present. "Oh, yes, we have many more single mothers here than in West Germany." The term did not trigger an association with the postwar period or with a particular generation of women left single by the war.

A little concerned but certain there was a "hidden" history waiting to be discovered—after all, everyone was discovering "hidden histories" in East European archives—I plunged into my research. Nothing. Topics that had left mountains of records in West Germany, like the status of unwed mothers and war widows' pensions, seemed to have been nonissues in the East. Instead I found a few isolated scraps about such underwhelming matters as the annual Christmas bonus of twenty-five marks rather than the thirty-five marks married women received.

I was now stuck with a question of an entirely different magnitude than those that had driven my original research. I knew there had been a significant population of women standing alone in East Germany. Why had they not become part of the landscape of East Germany in the 1950s, as the archives informed me; and why were there no recollections of them in the 1990s, as I could see from my conversations? And then, of course, I had to ask the flip side of the question: why had they become so important in West Germany? I could no longer take for granted that their prominence was the "natural" result of the demographic imbalance or the "natural" result of their roles in the years surrounding the collapse of Nazi Germany. I also had to ask new questions about the Nazi era. If Nazi Germany had helped to shape the meanings West Germans attached to marital status, and not just the postwar demographics of marital status, then were there elements of the Nazi experience that had helped to shape the very different meanings marital status had in East Germany?

But East and West Germans' different reactions to my discussions of the women standing alone raised as many questions about the 1990s as they did about the late 1940s and 1950s. When my West German acquaintances recalled "all those women who could not marry because of the war," were they demonstrating a consciousness that had been passed down from the immediate postwar period? Or did their comments reflect the publicity women standing alone received in the mid-1980s, when feminist historians and journalists helped to shape the discourse surrounding the fortieth anniversary of 1945? When my East German acquaintances described the frequency of single motherhood in the East in the 1980s, were they displaying amnesia about the war generation of women standing alone? Or were they revealing that their *first* priority, in the aftermath of 1989, was to reclaim some of what had been positive about the East German experience in light of West Germany's "victory" in the Cold War? These problems will be familiar to oral historians, but they also draw attention to the politically loaded nature of representations of the Nazi era and of East-West German comparisons.

This book represents my attempt to untangle this web of comparative, interlocking histories: to consider three German states and a stateless period; to consider the cultural history of memory, the political history of policy formation, and the social history of lived experience; to consider heads of state and the most humble citizens—and those excluded from citizenship entirely. Many institutions and individuals helped to make it a better book than it otherwise might have been. For research fellowships, I am indebted to the German Academic Exchange Service, the National Endowment for the Humanities (FT-41287–95), the American Philosophical Society, the German Marshall Fund, the American Institute for Contemporary German Studies, the Mowry Fund of the History Department of the University of North Carolina, and the Faculty Research Council of Bowling Green State University. As a James Bryant Conant Fellow at the Minda de Gunzberg Center for European Studies at Harvard University, I benefited from access to remarkable libraries and the luxury of time to read, write, and think. The University of North Carolina and Bowling Green State University provided not only financial support but also environments conducive to serious intellectual work. Countless archivists pointed me in the direction of significant collections, bent regulations concerning lunch-hour closings, and gave me the benefit of the doubt in allowing me to view restricted materials.

This book began as a dissertation under the guidance of Konrad H. Jarausch, who devoted much time and energy to my intellectual development. His critical reading and remarkable fluency in contemporary discussions contributed greatly to this book's breadth. In addition to modeling commitment to feminist scholarship, Judith Bennett modeled stern editing, rendering turgid (or, as she would put it, "Germanic") prose readable. Gerhard Weinberg provided his renowned training in careful archival research and offered something for which his renown should be greater: encouragement in pursuing unorthodox, even professionally risky, questions. From the book's earliest to its final stages, Robert Moeller patiently read and reread, critiqued first drafts and critiqued revisions, suggested further work when new questions begged exploration, and encouraged pulling the plug when the project was done. Donna Harsch brought fresh and thoughtful perspectives to her careful reading of the entire manuscript. Tatyana Dumova and Michael Evans provided invaluable research assistance, and Todd Good and Chad Simpson contributed their skills in indexing. Thanks are also due to Sheila Levine, Laura Driussi, Mary Severance, Pamela Fischer, and Amber Teagle Thompson of the University of California Press.

Many other people contributed to this work by commenting on portions of it, by sharing insights from their own research, or by helping me to work through knotty problems. These include Daphne Berdahl, Doris Bergen, Christiane Eifert, Anna-Sabine Ernst, Dagmar Herzog, Paul Jaskot, Daniel Mattern, Ina Merkel, Maria Mitchell, Kathryn Nasstrom, Susan Pedersen, Christiane Rothmaler, and Johanna Schoen. The Schoen family, Birgit Müller, and Mathias Gross created refuges in Germany, enabling frequent and comfortable research visits. Jayante Singh, Rochelle Haynes, and the staffs at Children's Oasis and Montessori Old West End in Toledo and East End House in Cambridge did the notoriously undervalued work of providing childcare. Without their labors, I would not have a doctorate, much less be the author of a book.

Johanna Schoen and Joshua Schoen Heineman have lived with all this book has entailed, from profound intellectual questions to hard-drive crashes. They provided not only emotional sustenance but also comic relief. This book bears the imprint of my father, a refugee from Nazi Germany, and my mother, an unwilling product of prefeminist bourgeois womanhood. However inadvertently, Herbert and Margaret Andrus Heineman made it urgently necessary for me to confront German history, racism, sexism, and the all too numerous forms of injustice that still define life on earth.

Abbreviations

AA	Arbeitsamt (Employment Office)
AWG	Arbeiterwohnungsbaugenossenschaft (Workers' Building Cooperative, GDR)
BAA	Bundesanstalt für Arbeitsvermittlung und Arbeitslosenversicherung (Federal Agency for Job Placement and Unemployment Insurance, FRG)
BDM	Bund Deutscher Mädel (League of German Girls, Nazi Germany)
BFA	Betriebsfrauenausschuss (Company Women's Commission, GDR)
BRD	Bundesrepublik Deutschland (West Germany)
BVG	Bundesversorgungsgesetz (Law to Aid Victims of War, FRG)
CDU	Christlich-Demokratische Union (Christian Democratic Union: conservative Christian party, FRG)
CSU	Christlich-Soziale Union (Christian Social Union: Bavarian counterpart to federal CDU)
DDR	Deutsche Demokratische Republik (East Germany)
DFD	Demokratischer Frauenbund Deutschlands (Democratic Women's League of Germany, GDR)
DFW	Deutsches Frauenwerk (German Women's Works, Nazi Germany)
FDGB	Freier Deutscher Gewerkschaftsbund (League of Free German Labor Unions, GDR)
FDP	Freie Demokratische Partei (Free German Party: Liberal Party, FRG)
FRG	Federal Republic of Germany (West Germany)

GDR   German Democratic Republic (East Germany)

KPD   Kommunistische Partei Deutschlands (Communist Party of Germany: folded into SED in GDR, remains in FRG)

LAA   Landesarbeitsamt (Provincial Employment Office, FRG)

NSF   NS-Frauenschaft (National Socialist Women's Organization, Nazi Germany)

PHPWB   Public Health and Public Welfare Branch, Office of Military Government (U.S.)

RAD   Reichsarbeitsdienst (Reich Labor Service, Nazi Germany)

RADwJ   Reichsarbeitsdienst—weibliche Jugend (Reich Labor Service for Female Youth, Nazi Germany)

RKZSH   Reichsbund der Kriegs- und Zivilbeschädigten, Sozialrentner und Hinterbliebenen (National League of War and Civilian Wounded, Pensioners and Survivors, FRG)

RSHA   Reichssicherheitshauptamt (Reich Security Administration, Nazi Germany)

SBG   Schwerbeschädigtengesetz (Law for the Severely Wounded, FRG)

SD   Sicherheitsdienst (intelligence and counterespionage service, Nazi Germany)

SED   Sozialistische Einheitspartei Deutschlands (Social Unity Party: Communist-dominated union with Social Democratic Party, GDR)

SPD   Sozialdemokratische Partei Deutschlands (Social Democratic Party of Germany: Social Democrats, FRG)

SS   Schutzstaffel (Elite Guard, Nazi Germany)

STD   Sexually Transmitted Disease

VdK   Verband der Kriegsbeschädigten, Kriegshinterbliebenen, und Sozialrentner Deutschlands (League of War Wounded, War Survivors, and Pensioners of Germany, FRG)

1 Introduction

War, Politics, and Marital Status

Shortly after the Second World War, psychoanalyst Carl Jung reissued his essay on "the woman in Europe." Jung devoted over half his space to the subject of marriage. "Contemporary marriage has become insecure," he found. "And the remarkable thing is that the scapegoat is not the man this time, but rather the *woman*. She is the one projecting doubt and uncertainty. It is no wonder; in postwar Europe there is such an alarming number of unmarried women that it would be almost incredible if there weren't a reaction from every side. Such an amassing of misery has inevitable consequences."[1] Clearly, Jung continued, the experience of single womanhood would change, as the population of unwed women now included not only those inclined to the cloister or the brothel but also millions of "decent women" who were unwed or widowed against their wills. The effects of the demographic imbalance between the sexes would go further, however, radically altering the experience of marriage. This in turn would change partners' understanding of what destroyed a marriage—that is, it would change divorce. Although Jung, like others who wrote on the subject, noted that the institution of marriage had been in a process of transformation for decades if not centuries, he was not alone in claiming that the large postwar population of "women standing alone" cast the problem of marital status for women in an entirely new light. The fact that he had originally written of women in post-World War I Europe hardly made his analysis moot; if anything, it seemed eerily prescient. With the even greater carnage of World War II, Jung's consideration of the effect of a large "surplus of women" on the "woman question" as a whole seemed more relevant than ever.

What kind of single women, what kind of insecure marriages did Jung have in mind? A survey of the female inhabitants of one residence in Darmstadt, a medium-sized city in West Germany, allows us a glimpse into a variety of women and marriages of Jung's day. On the ground floor lived Else.[2] Born in Darmstadt in 1913, she had married a mechanic in 1933 and had borne a child a year later. By the time Else and her son, Bernhard, were bombed out in September 1944, Else's husband had long been away at war. In 1947, Else would learn of his death in a French African prison camp.

Else and Bernhard were evacuated from Darmstadt following the bombings; they returned in July 1945. Less than a year later, they moved to Weisestraße 22, where Else's parents and teenage niece joined them. When her parents died in 1948, Else sublet their furnished room; this was her only source of income. A short engagement dissolved in 1954. After Bernhard moved out in 1955 to marry, Else remained in the apartment, continuing to sublet rooms.

On the next floor lived Gertrud. Born in then-German Silesia in 1922, she fled west in 1945; her hometown would become part of postwar Poland. After two years in the Soviet zone, Gertrud moved to the U.S. zone. She arrived in Darmstadt in January 1948 and found work as a waitress. In August 1949, she married Werner, a divorced grocer who had lost a leg in the war and who brought a two-and-a-half-year-old son into the marriage. The family became the subtenants of an elderly couple at Weisestraße 22.

Together, Gertrud and Werner opened a restaurant. But the marriage was strained, and the couple divorced in November 1953. Werner and his son moved out, and Gertrud's aunt and divorced mother joined her. Both older relatives, refugees from East Germany, worked for Gertrud in the restaurant. The women left Weisestraße in 1958, but Gertrud and her mother continued to share housing.

The apartment above Gertrud's was inhabited by Margarethe, an elderly woman who had never married. In the spring of 1946, Margarethe briefly shared her rooms with her forty-six-year-old sister, Mathilde, and Mathilde's teenage daughter, Lena. Mathilde's husband, Hermann, had had a child with another woman during the war. A former Gestapo officer, he was now awaiting trial in a U.S. detention camp. In 1944, according to Mathilde, the couple had divorced, but the papers had been destroyed in a bombing raid. Destitute, Mathilde now supported herself and Lena as a seamstress.

Mathilde's claim of divorce seems to have stemmed mainly from a desire to avoid scrutiny as the wife of a Gestapo man. When city officials pressed her to file new papers, she refused, and on his release in May 1948, Hermann returned to Mathilde, who by now had moved to a new address. The couple remained together until Mathilde's death in 1957.

In September 1949, Mathilde's old rooms were taken over by Helene, who was born in 1908. Helene's wartime marriage had ended in widowhood; she had remarried in August 1947. Nine months after they moved into Weisestraße 22, Helene and her husband divorced. Shortly thereafter, Kurt, a divorced veteran, moved in. He and Helene began what would become an eleven-year-long cohabitation—the longest relationship under the roof of Weisestraße 22 in the decade and a half following the war.

Both Helene and Kurt were invalids, unable to work, and dependent on small pensions. Thus when the house manager pressured them to leave in 1957, they found that they had little clout in the housing market. The house manager initiated eviction proceedings; Helene sued. The legal battle was cut short when, in late 1961, Helene and Kurt found another apartment. But their happiness was short-lived. Their relationship had turned rocky in the previous couple of years, and in June 1962 Kurt married another woman.

After the Second World War, Germans were painfully aware that the war had robbed masses of young women of their male contemporaries. The first postwar census showed that seven million more women than men lived in occupied Germany.[3] Germans did not have to wait for the census, though, to know that the war had left large numbers of "women standing alone"; they needed only to look at themselves and their neighbors.[4] While the census takers were collecting their data in October 1946, Else was wondering about the fate of her missing husband; Gertrud was a twenty-four-year-old refugee in the Soviet zone, where 70 percent of the population age twenty to twenty-five was female; Mathilde listed herself as divorced; and Helene was a war widow.

Yet as the stories of Else, Gertrud, Mathilde, and Helene indicate, the divisions between married, never-married, divorced, and widowed women were not hard and fast. The women of Weisestraße 22 married, saw their husbands go to war, were widowed, divorced, cohabited, and remarried. Their adult lives were marked by frequent shifts in marital status that would have been unimaginable to their grandparents, and their legal status often played only a minor role in determining their daily experience. The women of Weisestraße 22 would have provided little support for many Germans' belief that the war had condemned a generation of women to lifelong singlehood. They also gave lie to the term "women standing alone." They may have been without husbands, but they lived with children, siblings, parents, landlords, and lovers. To be sure, their histories would have confirmed the sense that the Second World War and its aftermath had radically changed the significance of marital status. But as Jung's analysis suggested, it was hard to separate discussions of women standing alone from discussions of all marital states, their meanings, and the relationships among them.

The Second World War destabilized marital status across Europe, but social and political developments ensured that the large numbers of single women and the changing significance of marital status appeared in especially sharp relief in Germany. Two phenomena particularly shaped the history of mid-twentieth-century Germany. The first was the political turmoil that brought Germans Nazi, communist, and liberal democratic government within the span of a few years. The second was the Second World War: an aggressive, genocidal war that culminated the Nazi project, left Germany in a state of incredible physical devastation, and determined that postwar Germans and governments of German lands would have to devote the bulk of their energies to survival and to reconstruction. These same factors made the mid-twentieth century an extraordinary period for women standing alone and a crucial juncture in the history of marital status. Each of the three political systems attempted to shape marital status and to address women standing alone in unique ways. Preparation for war, war, and recovery from war profoundly influenced the experience of women standing alone and the implications of marital status for all women.

Under what conditions does marital status come to figure as a central determinant of women's position? How do political ideology and public policy shape the significance of marital status for women? What role do demographic, economic, and cultural factors play? This book will argue that, while the war made the experience of women standing alone a dramatic one and caused much public discussion about the changing significance of marital status, state activity played at least as great a role in formulating the meanings of various marital states. Two key observations underlie this thesis. First, even before the war, the Nazi state radically altered the conditions and meanings of various marital states and the experience of single womanhood. Second, although the wartime and postwar dislocations affecting marital status and the population of single women were common to all regions of Germany, marital status came to have different meanings for women in the two postwar states.

In order to understand the significance of these mid-twentieth-century developments, one need only consider the ways marital status had shaped women's circumstances in previous centuries. Since the sixteenth century, some 15 percent of Western populations had typically not married. Among elderly women, single status, usually in the form of widowhood, had been the norm for centuries.[5] Thus the mere presence of a large number of single women was nothing new.

What had changed was the relationship among unmarried, married, divorced, and widowed status. Prior to the twentieth century, the division between women who lived their adult lives as single women and those who lived as married women (until they reached old age) had seemed firm.[6] The medieval division of women into the categories "virgin," "wife," and "widow" paralleled the division of men into those who prayed, those who fought, and those who worked. Cultural conventions made marital status immediately apparent. Head coverings or wedding rings distinguished married from never-married women on sight; titles such as "Miss" and "Mrs." or "Fräulein" and "Frau" distinguished them in writing. One need have no interaction with a woman, in person or on paper, without knowing whether she was or had been married. Furthermore, law codified the existence of distinct types of legal female persons depending on their marital status. Women's marital status determined their right to own property and to enter into contracts as well as their legal relationship with their children. By contrast, men did not take a new form of address on marriage, and although married men wore rings in Germany, physical markers such as these were far less widespread than were physical markers for women. In no Western society did men become different legal persons on marriage.[7] In its legal and social significance, marital status for women resembled other categories of difference, such as race, class, and gender. Women were not born spinsters or wives, as they were evidently born to a class, a sex, and a race—but once they were separated into wives and spinsters as adults, the division seemed clear.

Four aspects of experience, in theory, differentiated married from single life for women. Married women had their own households; single women did not. Single women of the laboring classes worked consistently outside the home; married women did not. Married women had children; single women did not. Married women had emotional and sexual lives based in their families; single women sought friendship elsewhere and delayed sexual activity. These divisions were far from absolute, but they were also not imaginary. They described larger patterns, if not all cases, and they depicted social expectations.

For Germans living at the close of the nineteenth century, the distinction between married and single women appeared alive and well. Although the Civil Code of 1900 granted married women greater legal personhood than had the Prussian Civil Code of 1794, it reaffirmed that women's legal and economic status depended on their marital status.[8] To be sure, there were some concerns about changing marital behavior. In the late nineteenth century, the terms *women standing alone* and *surplus women* gained currency despite a fairly constant marriage rate. In an industrial economy, single women had no function in the urban bourgeois household: although the presence of single women in such families was not new, it was newly troubling.[9] Among the lower social classes, too, evident change was misleading. Property qualifications, which had prevented the very poor from marrying, were mainly abolished in the second half of the nineteenth century; couples that previously would not have been able to wed now did so.[10] But the emergence of an urban proletariat rendered more visible those who did not adhere to bourgeois convention: concentrated in the cities and associated with the strains of industrialization, cohabiting couples and unwed mothers attracted more attention. Furthermore, popular reactions to the feminist movement included the worry that women would reject marriage in order to live an independent life.[11] In combination with concerns about declining birthrates, which had a firmer base in demographic trends (Fig. A.4), the image of the woman standing alone fanned dual fears of population decline and decreasing male authority. The legal, economic, and social divisions between single and married women, however, remained firm.

After the First World War, even these divisions seemed to break down. Statistical yearbooks showed that an ever-increasing proportion of women were married: 34.7 percent in 1907, 39.4 percent in 1925, and 42.7 percent in 1933.[12] Yet this was little comfort in the midst of so many other upheavals. Fifteen percent of men age twenty to forty had died in the war, and the 1925 census showed two million more women than men.[13] Young war widows, struggling to raise children on inadequate pensions, provided graphic evidence of the suffering that could result from a dislocation in marital status.[14] They also challenged popular assumptions about widowhood: these were not elderly women who could enjoy the support of their grown children, however modest that support might be. Germans were further troubled by evident changes in the lives of never-married women. According to popular perceptions, unwed city women had abandoned the sexual innocence that was supposed to distinguish them from married women.[15] Even the implications of marriage had changed radically. A couple that married in 1905 would have nearly five children; marriages entered between 1925 and 1929 produced, on the average, slightly under two children. Divorce was three times more likely in the early 1920s than it had been at the turn of the century (Fig. A.3). Although the birthrate had begun its decline and the divorce rate its rise in the late nineteenth century, both trends accelerated after the First World War, and Germans found these phenomena especially alarming in the general atmosphere of crisis that characterized the Weimar period. Furthermore, the Great Depression brought a new threat to the experience of wifehood. With official unemployment figures of one-third and unofficial unemployment yet higher, Germans could no longer believe that marriage, as a rule, brought a woman access to a male income.

Many of the apparent changes since the late nineteenth century were meaningful only in the context of uniquely bourgeois notions of the significance of marriage. Among the urban proletariat, unwed motherhood and cohabitation had been common all along, and marriage had rarely insulated proletarian women from the need to earn income—even if working-class wives usually earned in the home, while their single sisters went to the factories. Yet the very class specificity of the division between wives and single women made the blurring of these boundaries particularly alarming. Narrowing distinctions between wives and single women suggested proletarianization just as the post-World War I inflation impoverished large segments of the middle class, and just as the Great Depression impoverished the citizenry as a whole.

Germans had to rethink two bourgeois social "truths": first, that when girls grew up, they married, and their lives revolved around their marriage until, at an advanced age, they were widowed or died; second, that the majority who married and the minority who did not had fundamentally different paths of life. Demographic, cultural, and economic changes wreaked havoc on the meaning of all marital states for women, and they made women without men unusually prominent. The instability of maidenhood, wifehood, and widowhood aggravated fears of social disintegration at the same moment a lost war, political collapse, and economic chaos fed worries of national decline.[16] As part of their general longing for order and security, many Germans hoped that the Nazis could reverse this trend with policies favoring marriage, an economic upturn, and cultural renewal.

This book picks up with the Nazis' attempt to do so. The Nazis indeed appeared to restore the centrality of marriage to women's lives. Pro-marriage policies and a recovering economy encouraged women to marry; propaganda reinforced the idea that marriage and motherhood were the central features of an adult woman's life.[17] Rates of marriage rose, and public discussion of women standing alone nearly ceased. Nevertheless, the respite was an uneasy one. The Nazi elevation of the family coexisted awkwardly with approval of extramarital childbearing among the racial elite, eased divorce law, and prohibitions against many marriages. Furthermore, socially and racially acceptable women who remained single fulfilled important political, economic, and military functions.[18] Indeed, the simultaneous "restoration" of traditional housewifery (however illusory) and "emancipation" to fuller participation in public life (however compromised) reflected a larger tension between nostalgia and modernization in Nazi Germany.[19] Finally, the Nazis launched a war that removed some twenty million German men from their homes. For young women in wartime, the distinctions between unwed, married, and widowed status were often more a technical matter than anything affecting their day-to-day lives.[20]

None of Germans' previous experience with single women or with the changing role of marriage in women's lives, however, could prepare them for the situation following the Second World War. The "crisis years" of military collapse and occupation were the heyday of the woman standing alone, and marital status divided women less than ever. With men at war, imprisoned, missing, or dead, women of all marital states relied on their own resources to keep their families out of danger and to make ends meet.[21] Contemporaries marveled at this display of female competence. They also, however, feared that the war might have brought not only political and economic collapse but also the destruction of the smallest cell of social life. Echoing the situation of Weimar, but now even more strikingly, the lessening significance of marital status signaled universal, rather than class-specific, poverty. As men returned and long-awaited reunions proved ridden with conflict, even the reestablishment of marital households did little to reassure Germans about the future of the institution of marriage.

The most intractable problem seemed to be the demographic imbalance: dead men could not be brought back to life. Germans became painfully familiar with graphs—bearing all the authority of their scientific mode of representation—illustrating the "surplus of women" among young adults (Figs. 1 and 2). The implications of the demographic imbalance for women's ability to marry or remarry seemed to need no explanation. Clearly, the war had made it impossible for a large number of women to marry or remarry. Equally clearly, these women standing alone would have to pursue different lives than the married majority.

Appearances, however, were misleading. On the one hand, an unprecedented rate of marriage among men meant that women—even those whose male cohort had been decimated in the war—were as likely to be married in the early 1960s as had been women their age before the war (Fig. A.1).[22]

The war had not condemned an unusually large number of women to life-long singlehood. On the other hand, women who spent their adult lives in a single marriage were less and less a demographic norm. Women like Else, Gertrud, Mathilde, Helene, and Margarethe, who either remained single or moved in and out of marriage, constituted nearly half of Darmstadt's women of the war generation (Figs. B.1 and B.2).[23] Instability in marital status, and not a chasm between a swollen minority of women who stood alone and the majority who lived as wives, was what differentiated members of the war generation from their predecessors.

Thus the story is not a simple one of the demographic effects of the war. Rather, it is also a story of the ways postwar Germans dealt with the perception that a generation of women could not marry or remarry and with changes in all marital states.[24] Here the two postwar German states took very different paths. West German efforts to "reconstruct the (bourgeois) family," complete with stay-at-home wife and mother, meant upholding legal distinctions according to marital status as well as restoring different life-styles for married and single women. Even if the "economic miracle" came later to working-class than to bourgeois families, the restoration of marital status as a central marker for women was associated with embourgeoisement. Indeed, it accompanied increasing working-class aspirations for bourgeois life-styles rather than class conflict. Since they deviated so strikingly from the theoretically normative housewife, single women were considered a major social problem, and they felt marginalized by a society that promoted domesticity for women. Ironically, however, the constant problematization of their status meant that women standing alone had a relatively high profile.

Although the demographic imbalance was greater in East than in West Germany, "surplus women" were not treated as a major social problem by the East German state. By promoting paid labor for married women and devaluing the role of full-time housewife, the German Democratic Republic (GDR) attempted to diminish the extent to which marital status determined women's daily routines and purpose in life. Bolstered by communist ideology, single women in the East had an easier time finding personal rewards in the workplace and in the community than did their counterparts in the West. Legislative innovations, such as equal pay for men and women performing the same work and equal rights for illegitimate and legitimate children, removed legal irritants that, in the West, constantly reminded single women of their second-class status. In a "workers' state," the characteristically bourgeois division between women of different marital states would narrow. But the population resisted the notion that wives and

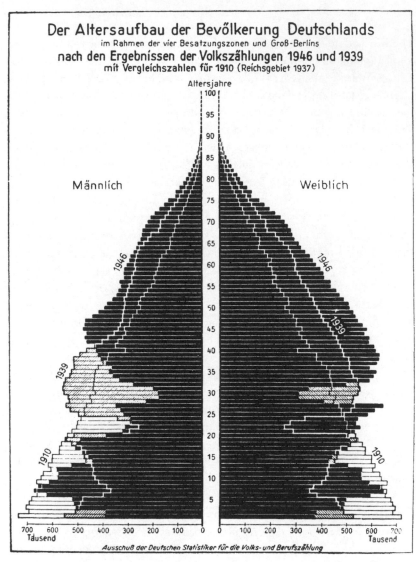

Der Altersaufbau der Bevölkerung Deutschlands
im Rahmen der vier Besatzungszonen und Groß-Berlins
nach den Ergebnissen der Volkszählungen 1946 und 1939
mit Vergleichszahlen für 1910 (Reichsgebiet 1937)

Altersjahre

Männlich

Weiblich

700 600 500 400 300 200 100 0
Tausend

0 100 200 300 400 500 600 700
Tausend

Ausschuß der Deutschen Statistiker für die Volks- und Berufszählung

Figure 1.   "The Age Pyramid of Germany's Population." Graphic representations of the "surplus of women" were ubiquitous in statistical reports starting with the first postwar census in October 1946, and they seemed to require little comment. This misshapen age- and sex- pyramid was published repeatedly and entered the popular consciousness. Note the imbalance of the black bars (representing the 1946 population) between left (male) and right (female) from ages twenty to forty-five. A comparison of the regular 1910 pyramid (white bars) and the irregular 1946 pyramid also reveals a distorted age structure resulting from deaths and reduced births in two world wars, as well as reduced births during the Great Depression. This imbalance had profound implications for future population growth and for the comparative size of the labor force and the dependent population. *Volks- und Berufszählung vom 29. Oktober 1946 in den vier Besatzungszonen und Groß-Berlin: Textteil, 40.*

Figure 2. "Marriagelessness: Women's Fate." With a graph of the sexual imbalance in the background and the sex ratio of the Berlin-Schöneberg district in bold type, the conclusion seemed obvious enough for the designers of this 1946 poster. Courtesy Schöneberg Museum/Archiv, Berlin.

mothers should find their main purpose in the workplace. At least through the 1950s, the experiential divide between married and single women remained firm. Furthermore, marriage rates exceeded those of the old proletariat, as East Germans, like West Germans, associated unwed motherhood and cohabitation with lack of means, and marriage with better times (Fig. A.2). Marital status's power to divide women declined, making East Germany less "bourgeois" than West Germany. The high rates of marriage in East Germany, however, suggested an "embourgeoisement" of the working class in comparison with its habits of the turn of the century.

By 1961, each of the new states had recovered from the immediate postwar crisis, and each had established a distinct political, economic, and social order. At the same time, a new generation had come of age. Whether the war generation of women married or remained single no longer seemed as pressing as had been the case ten or fifteen years earlier. But the notion that marital status did not have a fixed, timeless meaning but rather could be manipulated had become a fact of life: East and West Germans took for granted that their states had opposing family ideologies and policies.

By examining both the role of the state and the social impact of the war in formulating marital status, I hope to push forward a literature that has tended to focus on one or the other but not both. Gisela Bock and Gabrielle Czarnowski, for example, both show that the National Socialist state shaped family formation by regulating entry to marriage and the ability to have children.[25] The social impact of the war, however, is not the subject of either historian's study, and thus these works do not explore the relationship between Nazi intrusions into family life and disruptions due to wartime dislocation. Likewise, Robert Moeller makes clear that the West German "reconstruction of the family" was a matter of public policy, not just a grass-roots "flight into domesticity."[26] Here, the social disruptions of the war provide the context for understanding the political pressures of the 1950s, but they are not a central theme. By contrast, Sibylle Meyer, Eva Schulze, and Barbara Willenbacher make clear the extraordinary social impact of the war and immediate postwar period in shaping women's marital status and understanding of it, but they do not address the interplay between demographic and social change on the one hand and state regulation of the family on the other.[27] Ina Merkel's work brings together the political and the popular culture of the GDR in regard to women and the family.[28] Like the other authors of the postwar Germanys discussed here, however, she gives relatively little consideration to the legacy of Nazi regulation of the family and women's position.

Clearly, part of the challenge is to overcome not only the distinctions between political and social history but also the chronological boundaries that still characterize much of German historical writing. There are good reasons the authors discussed above limited themselves to considering the Nazi period, the Federal Republic of Germany (FRG), the Democratic Republic, or the social historical period 1942–48.[29] Each one of these is complex enough to warrant a full examination. Nevertheless, by adhering to traditional chronological divisions, historians exclude certain questions from their field of vision. The interplay between the pre-1945 state, the post-1949 states, and the social upheavals of 1942–48 is one such question.

An exploration of the period 1933–61, however, does more than raise questions about the relative significance of the turmoil of 1942–48 on the one hand and the political ideologies and public policies of the various German states on the other. It also becomes a comparative history of the Nazi, Communist, and liberal democratic states, their policies, and their ideologies. Three features are central to this comparison.

The first concerns material and demographic conditions. It goes without saying that both East and West Germany were post-World War II societies while Nazi Germany was not, but the implications are worth explicating. The postwar states shared the demographic imbalance resulting from the Second World War, while Nazi Germany's demographic imbalance (resulting from the First World War) was much smaller and concentrated in an age cohort beyond the stage of family formation. Both postwar states needed to respond to the physical and psychological devastation left by the war, a matter that had profound implications for the family, for living conditions, and for labor, paid and unpaid. East and West Germany faced a set of common problems in the formative years of their existence, even if they followed different paths in responding to them. Insofar as demographic and material setting determined the prominence of single women and the significance of marital status, Nazi Germany appears in sharp contrast to the two postwar states.

In another regard, the Democratic Republic stands out. Both Nazi Germany and the Federal Republic promoted gender as a central social category; the Democratic Republic did not. To be sure, the ideological constructs surrounding gender differed in Nazi and in West Germany. In Nazi Germany, gender difference was inextricably tied to race, which was the ideological "ground zero"; the Federal Republic's endorsement of gender as a central social category was not tied to an official racialist ideology.[30] Nevertheless, the centrality of gender in both states contrasts sharply with the situation in the Democratic Republic. The reification of class as the central social category in East Germany did not admit gender as a "companion category," as did the Nazi reification of race. Distinct gender roles beyond those strictly tied to biological difference were understood as derivative, the mere creations of bourgeois society; the achievement of class justice would automatically bring sexual equality in tow. None of the three states acted purely on the basis of ideology, and the ideologies themselves were not always consistent or transparent. Nevertheless, insofar as the ideological centrality of gender shaped the significance of marital status and the situation of single women, East Germany appears in sharp contrast to the other two German states.

The complicated relationship among official ideology, public policy, and unofficial culture points to the third area of comparison. The Nazi and Communist states carefully controlled public discussion regarding political and social questions; in the Federal Republic private citizens, formal organizations, and informal social groups participated much more autonomously in public debates. Not only did the participation of private West German citizens mean that they could have a greater impact on policymaking than was the case in the other states, but it also made for lively, contentious, differentiated public discussion, which shaped West Germans' perceptions of their situation regardless of the specific policies that emerged. This is not to say that the Nazi and Communist states were monolithic entities. Nazi officials could disagree with each other on important issues, as could Communist officials, and opposing views were sometimes aired publicly. Nor did the suppression of civil society in Nazi and Communist Germany equal the elimination of autonomous thought and action within the household, between neighbors, or in social and professional circles.[31] Nevertheless, public debate was constrained and controlled, and unofficial discourse was characterized by the "whispered dialogue, neither completely suppressed nor genuinely public," that Donna Harsch describes.[32] Insofar as the interplay among "official," "public," and "private" created a culture which, among other things, helped to determine the significance of marital status, West Germany appears in sharp contrast to both Nazi Germany and Communist East Germany.

In examining the intertwined histories of marital status and politics, this book will consider both ideology and public policy. Nazism, Communism, and liberal democracy revealed their ideologies in part through programmatic statements and official publications, in part through debates about the issues of the day. This book will consider both. Although ideologies always informed public policy, they were not always fully realized in state actions. Economic calculations, political pressures, and social considerations also contributed to the formulation of public policy. This book will focus on a handful of areas that were particularly crucial in responding to and shaping the changing meaning of marital status and the population of women standing alone. These were marriage, divorce, and illegitimacy law; female labor-force participation; and welfare and pension policy. Except for the stateless years 1945–49, these were matters of national policy, but implementation often occurred locally. This study will thus move between the local and national levels in order to examine both the making and the effects of public policy. In addition to analyzing the effects of ideology and policy on women's material and legal situations, this book will explore the ways both aspects of political life shaped cultural attitudes toward women of varying marital states and women's perceptions of their own situations.

This book will also examine the ways preparation for war, war, and recovery from war influenced women's experience of marital status. It will consider the ways the war shaped patterns of marriage, divorce, widowhood, and motherhood; material factors such as housing, standard of living, and source of income; and determinants of women's daily routines such as workforce participation and the nature of unpaid work. It will also consider popular perceptions of women of varying marital states. The war and its aftermath created new female prototypes, such as the labor-service draftee and the "woman of the rubble"; they also gave new twists to old prototypes, such as the housewife and the sexually delinquent woman. The evolution of this typology influenced the ways Germans thought about marital status for women, which in turn affected the treatment and social position of women of all marital states.

The social effects of the war, on the one hand, and the battles between political ideologies and systems, on the other, fundamentally define the period 1933–61. Nevertheless, many other factors also shaped single women's experience and the meanings of marital status in mid-century Germany. Examining religious life, rural and urban communities, film, or radio would deepen our understanding of this book's subject. In exploring the larger contours of the period, defined by the war and the profound changes in political life, this book aims to provide a framework for further inquiry—not the final word.

This book is arranged chronologically. Certain overlaps, however, reflect the difficulty of neatly periodizing mid-century Germany. Chapters 2 and 3 examine how the Nazi state shaped both legal distinctions of marital status and women's experience of it, first in peace, then in war. Doubling back to the second half of the war, chapters 4 and 5 examine the "crisis years" of military defeat and occupation; here the focus is on the social effects of the war and its immediate aftermath. Chapter 4 considers the events that made 1942–48 the period in which marital status seemed least relevant and the woman standing alone normative, while chapter 5 looks at the rearticulation of marital status via family reunification and popular discussions about women standing alone. Chapters 6 and 7 focus on the ways each of the postwar states attempted to codify the significance of marital status; in order to do so, each dips back into the political history of the military occupation. Drawing on evidence from both Germanys, chapter 8 examines the extent to which material conditions and social pressures divided women according to marital status in the 1950s. The book concludes with a look at the legacy of the three Germanys' distinct treatment of marital status for women in the age of reunification.

2 Housewives, Activists, and "Asocials"

Controlling Marital Status
under Nazism

"One wants to honor the married woman especially. . . . As a woman I can only be pleased by such an attitude by the state," wrote Elisabeth H., an unmarried schoolteacher, to Hitler in 1941. "It is regrettable only," she continued cautiously, "that this conscious honor of one group brings the other group so to speak into discredit. The people judge as follows—I quote the judgment literally, as I once heard it—'Yes, the state wants every woman to marry and have children; it doesn't want single women; it rejects them.'"[1] Long after the demise of the Third Reich, we tend to share Elisabeth's impression of her government's attitude toward single women. The Nazis' vision of women's role, according to stereotype, was *Kinder, Küche, Kirche:* children, kitchen, and church. Women standing alone must have been outsiders.

This stereotype is incorrect. Single women did have a place in the Nazi state and society. More accurately, they had two places. On the one hand, as far as the Nazis were concerned, not all women should marry and have children. Some were undesirable as wives and mothers because of their race, their genetic material, or their conduct. On the other hand, even those who should eventually marry would probably not do so immediately on reaching adulthood. They should not spend the interim in limbo; there was plenty they could do to contribute to the *Volk* only as long as they were single.

Nevertheless, the Nazi leadership did consider the "Aryan," eugenically sound, socially conformist wife and mother to be the ideal woman. As was so often the case, National Socialists cast the matter in black and white terms. Some women absolutely should marry and others absolutely should not (Figs. 3 and 4). For those who should, their lives before and after marriage should be fundamentally different. Nazis did not see marriage as women's only possibility, but they did envision a sharp distinction between married and single status for women.

In the years before Germany became absorbed with total war, ideologues, policymakers, and civil servants hardened the divide between married and single women. This took two forms. First, the Nazis divided women into "desirable" or "valued," on the one hand, and "undesirable" or "unvalued" on the other. Although having a certain number of single women was inevitable, the matter of which women would remain single was too important to be left to chance. Thus the regime attempted to lead fertile Aryan couples with desirable genetic stock and a proper commitment to the Nazi program and the German *Volk* to the altar. It simultaneously aimed to restrict marriages among other segments of the population: non-"Aryans" as well as "Aryans" who were infertile, who might pass on physical or intellectual flaws to their children, or who were considered "asocial" (Fig. 5).[2] When it took this form, hardening the distinction between married and unmarried status meant further marginalizing women standing alone. In fact, it meant putting them at great risk. In Nazi Germany, to be labeled eugenically inferior, non-Aryan, or asocial was dangerous.

Second, the National Socialists attempted to intensify the difference between married and single status for those women whom the regime considered valuable. Like most Germans, National Socialists felt that married women should devote themselves to their households. More unusual was the Nazi philosophy that single, valued women should turn their energies from their families of origin or their preparations for marriage to the *Volk* as a whole. In envisioning an important and unique public role for single women, the Nazis helped to legitimize single status for women who passed racial, eugenic, and social muster.

Many factors conspired to prevent the National Socialists from making either sort of division between married and single status as firm as they might have liked. The difficulty in neatly categorizing women was one such factor. Leading Nazis found their belief in a clear distinction between "valued" and "unvalued" confused especially by unmarried mothers. Was unwed motherhood a way to enable valued women who had not married to produce desirable offspring? Or did the mere fact of unwed motherhood demonstrate a woman's poor social and eugenic qualities, thus making her offspring undesirable? By calling into question the dichotomous categorization of "valued" and "unvalued," unwed mothers also confused the matter of single women's status.

Even where the distinction between "good" and "bad" seemed clear, however, there were serious obstacles to making the division between mar-

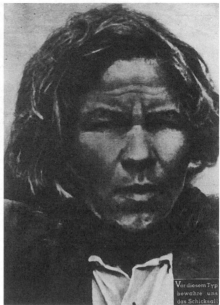

Figures 3 and 4. Nazi eugenic classification. The Nazi racial vision divided women neatly into two types: those who should marry and have children and those who should not. The caption in figure 3 reads, "Women like this should become the mothers of Europe"; that in figure 4 reads, "Preserve us from the fate of this type!" The visual codes emphasize a distinction according to eugenic qualities rather than racial categorization. Courtesy Elefanten Press.

ried and single complete. If the state was going to control access to the institution of marriage, permitting entry to those who passed social and eugenic muster and denying it to others, it would have to research each and every person who wished to marry. The task of ensuring that all valued wives were housewives and all valued single women contributed to the *Volksgemeinschaft* via their paid labor or organizational life presented similar bureaucratic obstacles. Since the regime lasted only twelve years and devoted most of its energies to waging war during its latter years, it was not able to make the distinction between married and single status as firm as it might have liked.

In the years before total war, however, it did make the distinction firmer than it had been previously, with concrete consequences for single women. While not absolute, the state's efforts to control who could marry meant that even before the war began, hundreds of thousands of women remained single against their wills. Involuntary single status was not simply a result

Figure 5.   Nazi warning against "racially-mixed" contact. This sticker advised the recipient: "German girl: Turn the Jew[ish man] away to his black Sarah and Rebekka!" Courtesy Elefanten Press.

of the war; it also resulted from peacetime Nazi policy. And given the punitive nature of public health and welfare services in the Nazi state, to be labeled eugenically or socially inferior was extremely dangerous. Where prolonged singlehood was associated with outsider status on racial, eugenic, or social grounds, the marginality of women standing alone was intensified.

For those whose marriage was considered desirable, the Nazi state's emphasis on public service meant that they would gain different experiences as single women than their older sisters or mothers had. Single women's taste of officially organized agricultural labor or household service was only a pale foreshadow of what they would experience during the war, when much larger numbers would be drafted into the armaments industry and into military auxiliary units. Nevertheless, even in peacetime, women who delayed marriage even a few years began to accumulate different experiences than did those who married quickly. These women were not marginalized; in fact, they gained a new social and political significance and legitimacy. If single women had traditionally been defined by their deficiency in comparison with their married sisters, they were now increasingly understood as a social force in their own right—as long as they were of the correct racial type and as long as they conformed socially and politically. Indeed, such women were among those who would recall peacetime Nazi Germany as the "good old days." As single women, they enjoyed new independence, purpose, and official recognition; but they could also look forward to honors and financial support once they married. Both the present and the future looked bright.

After 1945, the competent, self-sacrificing "woman of the rubble," who performed extraordinary feats during Germany's hour of greatest need, would share the stage with the fraternizer, who, according to reputation, threatened Germany's moral and physical integrity. In some ways, this division echoed a centuries-long dichotomy between madonna and whore; more recently, in the Weimar period, Germans had internalized contradictory images of the struggling war widow on the one hand and the carefree young woman, sexually liberated and unconcerned about her compatriots' sufferings, on the other. Yet the Nazi years intensified the dichotomous interpretation of single womanhood. On the one hand, the campaign against women labeled "asocial" contributed to many Germans' intolerance of women who broke sexual boundaries after the war. On the other hand, Germans—young women included—became increasingly accustomed to the notion that women could perform strenuous, independent, and socially valuable work without men. Women's remarkable efforts following the collapse of Nazi Germany were the culmination of the single woman's journey from nineteenth-century "house daughter" through civic worker in peacetime Nazi Germany and finally military draftee during the second half of the war.

.———.———.

"Marriage must remain unassailable for the race hygienist and German doctor, for only it allows us to realize certain demands in regard to hereditary health and race."[3] To be sure, eugenicists knew that prohibiting marriage among unvalued populations would not guarantee that they would remain childless, any more than encouraging marriage would ensure large families among those whose offspring were desired. They accordingly focused much attention on sterilization and euthanasia.[4] But sterilization and euthanasia did not replace control of marriage for Germans whose offspring were not desired. Rather, genocide, euthanasia, sterilization, restrictions on marriage, and schemes to encourage marriage and childbearing formed a continuum of measures applied according to the perceived threat or promise of particular offspring.[5] The Nazi regime made elimination of its imagined racial enemies a higher priority than eugenic control of the "Aryan" population, thereby doing incomparably more damage to non-"Aryans" than to "Aryans" in the supposed interest of future generations. Among "Aryans" who were singled out for eugenic reasons, victims of the sterilization program suffered more far-reaching consequences than those whose marital behavior the regime attempted to shape. Nevertheless, attempts to shape membership in the categories "married," "single," and "divorced" grew out of the same racialist vision of the future.

The peacetime Nazi government introduced a number of financial incentives to coax healthy, fertile, single "Aryans" into marriage. Most loudly touted were the marriage loans, introduced in June 1933. Upon a couple's application, a newlywed husband could receive an interest-free loan of up to RM 1,000. Twenty-five percent of the loan was forgiven for each child the couple produced. To ensure the desirability of the union, both partners received a physical examination, and the family history of each partner was investigated for eugenic flaws or signs of "asociability." Initially, the law's primary purpose was to reduce male unemployment. Accordingly, the loan was awarded only when the wife had worked or had sought employment prior to her marriage and now withdrew from the labor market. After 1937, the law took on a purely eugenic character, and the woman's employment after marriage played no role.[6] The loans, as well as other financial incentives for childbearing, were financed by increased taxes paid by single people.[7]

In 1938, fully 40 percent of couples marrying received marriage loans. Few of these couples, however, married in order to receive the loan or to reduce their taxes. At most, such measures may have encouraged couples considering marriage to move up the date in order to reap the benefits sooner rather than later. For women who might have continued work after marriage, the loan may have tilted the scales in favor of giving up employment. The improved economy, however, must receive most of the credit for increased marriage rates in the mid-1930s. While 55 percent of twenty-five-year-old women were unmarried in 1933, the proportion had dropped to 44.5 percent by 1939.[8]

More important than loans in affecting marital choice before the war were restrictions placed on certain marriages for eugenic and social reasons. Negative measures aimed at preventing or ending undesirable marriages could be more effective than could programs to encourage desired marriages since a greater degree of compulsion was possible with those whose loyalty was of lesser concern.

In 1938, divorce law was rewritten according to eugenic considerations.[9] Among the new measures was no-fault divorce in cases where the marriage was "fundamentally and irreparably estranged" and where the partners had been separated for at least three years. The courts decided on a case-by-case basis whether the dissolution of a particular marriage was in the interest of the community. Approval was likely if one of the partners (usually the husband) had developed a new liaison from which marriage and children could be expected if the divorce were concluded. A healthy, fertile, "Aryan" woman who had fulfilled her duties as a wife and who wanted to remain married and bear (more) children could end up divorced if the courts felt that more children would result from the husband's new marriage than from his current one.[10] Already in 1938, 15.8 percent of divorces were no-fault divorces; in 1939, the proportion rose to 24.7 percent.[11] The 1938 law also made it possible to divorce a partner because of the partner's characteristics, not just because of guilty behavior or lengthy separation. Mental derangement, infectious or repulsive illness, refusal to reproduce although no serious physiological complications threatened, infertility for reasons other than age or unusual hardship, and Jewish background became grounds for divorce from a non-Jewish German.[12]

Even when divorce was not at issue, political and racial persecution disrupted tens of thousands of marital or potential marital households. The wave of political arrests that followed the Nazi ascension to power overwhelmingly netted men, and the first mass arrest of Jews, following the November 1938 pogrom, targeted men exclusively: thirty thousand of them.[13] Their wives now had full responsibility for their families, even as they were denied most forms of assistance and were subject to neighbors' harassment and police scrutiny. Men's relative ease in emigrating left single women with diminished marriage prospects and left wives awaiting their husbands' call to join them in emigration. For every thousand Jewish men in Germany there were 1,093 Jewish women in 1933, but 1,366 in 1939.[14]

Perhaps of greatest statistical significance were those forbidden to marry. Eugenicists estimated that ten to twenty million Germans (of a population of eighty million after 1938) fell into that category of people whose offspring were not desired.[15] One such woman was Fräulein S. of Bremen. An optical examination revealed that she had a rare disease of the retina which was thought to be hereditary and to cause color blindness. The health department informed her that she could marry only if she were sterilized. After discussion with her fiancé and parents, Fräulein S. consented. Her second application for marriage, made after the operation was completed, was likewise denied. The reason: her fiancé was a presumably fertile man with good eugenic indications; he should not be paired with an infertile woman.[16]

The year 1935 saw the passage of the Nuremberg racial laws, which prohibited marriage between "Aryans" and people of "foreign blood." The same year, the Certificate of Fitness to Marry (*Ehetauglichkeitszeugnis*) was introduced.[17] Couples seeking a Certificate of Fitness to Marry underwent a physical examination, and the health departments researched the applicants' forebears. Because the health departments were not yet up to the task of examining everyone who wished to marry, only applicants for marriage loans and Germans such as Fräulein S., whose supposed physical, eugenic, or moral flaws (or those of family members) were known to the health department or to the social services, were required to present this certificate. Even applicants for a marriage loan could end up with a prohibition to marry or sterilization instead, depending on the results of their physical and genealogical examinations.[18] After the war, an examination was to be required of all couples. Beginning in December 1941, every couple wishing to marry had to present a Certificate of Unobjectionability to Marry (*Eheunbedenklichkeitsbescheinigung*), which required an interview, but no physical exam, at the health department. All applicants for a Certificate of Fitness to Marry, a Certificate of Unobjectionability to Marry, or a marriage loan received marriage counseling, which gave the health department the opportunity to pressure couples whose marriage was undesirable but technically permitted to drop their plans.[19]

Grounds for restrictions on marriage were many. Infectious disease that could affect the health of the spouse or offspring, legal declaration of incompetence, psychological illness, inheritable illness, and Jewish ancestry could justify a prohibition to marry a fertile, eugenically desired German. The eugenic history of applicants' forebears was considered, as were indications of asociability. Health authorities applied labels such as "inheritably" and "psychologically" ill with abandon, basing such judgments as often on observations of relatives as on observations of the clients themselves; meanwhile, the social services displayed great enthusiasm for declarations of legal incompetence.[20] Thus denials of permission to marry on these grounds were common. The vague definition of "asocial" similarly created obstacles for those wishing to marry. For the purpose of denying applications to marry, an individual who displayed one of the following characteristics was considered asocial: criminality, past assignment to reformatory school, promiscuity, feeble-mindedness, insanity, alcoholism, spendthrift tendencies, legal incompetence, avoidance of work, and other unspecified forms of asociability.[21] Starting in 1941, partners who cohabited although they had been denied permission to marry were defined as asocial regardless of the original reason for the rejection of their application.[22]

In Berlin-Charlottenburg, 9 percent of couples announcing their intention to marry between 1934 and 1940 were required to obtain a Certificate of Fitness to Marry. Over half of these (5 percent of the total wishing to marry) were denied permission.[23] Given the imprecise criteria for denying permission, it is likely that the rate of rejection varied greatly from office to office. If Berlin-Charlottenburg's rate was average, however, this would mean that over two hundred thousand couples were denied a Certificate of Fitness to Marry by 1940. In addition, 3.63 percent of individuals applying for marriage loans, or 113,543 people, were rejected nationwide between 1934 and 1941, a large proportion for reasons that were likely also to lead to a prohibition to marry.[24] Sixty percent of applicants for marriage loans who were judged "unfit to marry" between 1935 and 1941 were women.[25]

Although wartime measures undercut the state's ability to control marriage after 1938, the effect of all these examinations was significant. In the summer before the war, the Ministry of the Interior estimated that 30 percent of the population was covered by the laws concerning healthy marriage and marriage loans.[26] Out of a population of some eighty million, ten million were included in the health departments' cross-referenced records in 1942. This figure included four million applicants for marriage loans and an undetermined number of career soldiers and members of the RAD (labor service), SS (Elite Guard), and police and their potential partners, for whom an examination was required. The rest were mainly persons who were on record because of their own or family members' history of asociability, sterilization, institutionalization, and so on. They would be able to wed only if they produced a Certificate of Fitness to Marry.[27]

The state was thus most heavily involved in the marriages of the most and the least desired elements of the population. For those who fell in the middle—people who did not expect to be eligible for a marriage loan but who had no recorded strikes against them—the new regulations introduced an element of self-selection. Well-justified fears that undesired qualities detected in marriage counseling could lead to sterilization, institutionalization, or persecution led many couples to abandon their marriage plans on their own. Reluctance to undergo a physical or gynecological exam may have deterred additional couples.[28] Although few of the criteria for "marital persecution" were technically sex-specific, many were so for practical purposes. Men were rarely described as sexually promiscuous and thus classified as asocial, and the physical examination for the marriage loan sometimes tested women but never tested men for fertility.[29]

Furthermore, the social and economic consequences of not being able to marry were more severe for a woman than for a man. During the prewar period, knowledge of the procedures leading to marriage increased the suspect nature of those who did not marry. Although Nazi leaders were prepared to label as asocial any woman who was capable of producing valued offspring but nevertheless chose not to marry, many Germans were not. To be sure, most may have found a decision against marriage a bit odd, but an "odd woman" might nobly sacrifice personal happiness in order to teach or perform social work. Or she might just not yet have found the right man. As the state denied hundreds of thousands of Germans permission to marry, however, one could no longer be sure that a single woman was single by choice or lack of opportunity. In the 1940s, it became clear that war, and not the Health Department, was the major hindrance to marriage. But in the mid- and late-1930s, when the economy, the sex ratio, and the social climate favored marriage, neighbors might wonder whether a woman who failed to marry had been denied permission, particularly if she had had serious suitors.[30]

.—.—.

Perceptions of asociability and eugenic flaws had a chicken-and-egg relationship with single status: it is sometimes difficult to say which came first. When women were denied permission to marry because of supposed eugenic flaws or asocial behavior, it might be accurate to say that perceptions of their shortcomings "caused" their prolonged single status. Yet the reverse was also true: single status made it more likely that women would attract official disapproval in the first place. Hitler's comments in *Mein Kampf* that women would attain citizenship in the future Reich only upon marriage cast an unambiguous (if impolitic) light on his assumption that single women would have little to offer the new Reich.[31] Healthy, fertile Aryans who chose not to marry could not be full members of the *Volksgemeinschaft*.[32] Like married couples who remained childless, they shirked one of their most important duties to the Fatherland. But this could be changed in the time it took to marry and conceive a child. Other types of asociability associated with single women were considered far more vicious and irredeemable.

During peacetime, party officials and social workers identified asocial women much in the same way as governments and social workers had done before the Nazis came to power. Only one "type" of asocial woman was married: the bad housekeeper who neglected her children.[33] Other "types" were imagined to be, and disproportionately were, single. These were prostitutes, women with sexually transmitted disease, those who had sex prior to marriage or engagement, those who relished evenings dancing or drinking with soldiers, and those who simply struck teachers or social workers as "overly sexual."

The Nazis were not the first to target "asocials." Many vocal physicians and social workers had called for a sterilization law and a probation law, which would limit asocials' freedom of movement, since the 1920s.[34] Such demands, furthermore, built on popular perceptions regarding acceptable and unacceptable behavior. Social ostracism of women perceived as promiscuous preexisted the Nazi regime. In fact, public disgust with asocial men and women aided the Nazis' rise to power, as the party promised to "clean up the streets." The Nazi regime made it neither more nor less respectable for a single woman to be sexually active. It did, however, sharpen the penalties. On the grounds of their "asociability," hundreds of thousands of women were declared wards of the state, were sterilized, and were institutionalized or imprisoned. They were disproportionately single.

This campaign against those labeled asocial was possible because women who misbehaved did not just attract the attention of neighbors. They also attracted the attention of one of the most advanced bureaucracies in the world, a web of public agencies that possessed enormous amounts of information about private persons. Across the Reich, health departments, welfare departments, and the police exchanged information about clients and offenders. Hamburg's "archive of health certificates," established in 1934, is illustrative. By 1936, the archive contained certificates for half of Hamburg's population; on the eve of the war, for over 90 percent. The certificates—which included not only medical histories, but also social workers' comments and information about performance in school, party organizations, professional life, and more—were available to the public health service, the party, the university, and insurance companies.[35]

As the head of Hamburg's Foster Care Office (*Pflegeamt*), Käthe Petersen was well integrated into this system. By 1941, Petersen had taken over legal guardianship of 1,133 "community-foreign and endangered" women.[36] All of Petersen's charges were female, two-thirds were under thirty, and 925 were unmarried when they came under Petersen's supervision. One-fourth of the married women lived apart from their husbands or lived in unhappy marriages; Petersen had divorce proceedings initiated for twenty-nine of her charges. Sterilization and institutionalization were the fates of these overwhelmingly single women. Over half—607—were sterilized while under her guardianship. Many already resided in institutions when they were declared legally incompetent; Petersen had the police locate the remainder for institutionalization.

The majority of her charges, according to Petersen's description, were prostitutes. Others were alcoholics, drug addicts, mentally ill, or "incompetent of life."[37] Some of Petersen's charges would probably have attracted attention even under a less oppressive regime: Anna C., for example, was a long-time prostitute who abused cocaine, morphine, and alcohol, and stole from customers. Others, however, may have stumbled through a difficult phase without lasting damage if they had not fallen into the hands of such a harsh system of social welfare. Hedwig A.'s teachers considered her difficult, stubborn, and untalented, but on leaving school, Hedwig held a series of jobs with employers who had no complaints about her performance. At seventeen, she moved in with an aunt whose son was suspected of pimping. Hedwig began to live an "unsolid life-style," which Petersen attributed to her aunt's influence, and became infected with gonorrhea. Hedwig's mother, still the guardian of the nineteen-year-old, had her institutionalized. When Hedwig reached adulthood, Petersen had herself declared Hedwig's legal guardian and arranged for Hedwig's sterilization. Hedwig was released from the institution the next year and promptly found employment. She received good reports from her employers, showed no evidence of fast living, and was declared legally competent two years later.[38] But her fertility could not be restored as easily as could her legal competence.

The legal definition of "asociability" was fuzzy at best. According to the 1937 Decree Concerning the Preventive Fight Against Crime, an asocial person "show[ed] by an attitude that [was] adverse to the community, if not criminal, that he [did] not want to adapt to the community, . . . that he [did] not want to adapt to the order that is self-evident in a Nazi state."[39] Other attempts at definition usually consisted of examples. The Ministry of the Interior listed as asocial those who had come into conflict with the law, chronically unemployed people who allowed their families to be supported by welfare, those leading disorderly households or not raising their children responsibly, alcoholics, and those leading immoral life-styles or earning their living by immoral means.[40] The Bavarian police named beggars, vagabonds, Gypsies, tramps, the chronically unemployed, idlers, prostitutes, gripers, habitual drinkers, rowdies, psychopaths, the mentally ill, and traffic offenders.[41] Although the terms used to define asocials were mostly sex neutral, the epithet was applied differently to men and women. Women were described as asocial mainly on the basis of their sexual behavior or demeanor, while men earned the term mainly on the basis of criminality, chronic unemployment, or failure to support their families.[42]

When women were labeled asocial because of their heterosexual behavior, they were judged more strictly than were men. The designation of lesbian activity as asocial, however, represented a milder standard than that applied to men. Preexisting law criminalized male but not female homosexuality. In 1935, a panel of jurists sharpened the provisions regarding men but concluded that criminalizing female homosexuality would do more harm than good. Unlike male homosexuals, the majority on the commission concluded, women who experienced lesbian relationships did not usually withdraw their reproductive potential from the population. Whether because of the social and economic pressures to marry or because their lesbian activity had resulted from an adolescent crush or a temporary reaction to a bad experience with a man, as the jurists felt was usually the case, most eventually had children. At the same time, criminalization might result in a flood of false accusations since heterosexual women's customary intimacies with each other might be confused with sexual interactions.[43]

This relatively lenient stance did not mean that lesbianism was desirable but only that it was not usually worth persecuting in isolation. Lesbianism was often, however, associated with other dangers. A jurist who favored criminalization held that lesbian leaders of the feminist movement converted heterosexual women, thus drawing them from their natural inclinations to be wives and mothers.[44] With the destruction of the feminist movement, however, this hardly continued to be a serious concern. Of greater ongoing relevance was the association with prostitution. Opponents and proponents of criminalization alike felt confident that lesbian activity was most common among prostitutes. In this light, however, lesbianism appeared as yet another asocial behavior among an already asocial population; prostitutes' sexual activity with men, which was already criminalized, was more dangerous than was their sexual activity with women.[45] Lesbianism, which was technically a form of asociability, barely figured in images of asocial womanhood in its own right.

Social workers were frustrated by the limits on their powers over asocials, and they lobbied for legislation that would have allowed sterilization on the sole grounds of asociality. Their efforts were in vain, and they remained dependent on physicians for the diagnoses of inheritable disease that would justify sterilization—admittedly, not too burdensome a dependence since public health physicians understood the granting of such diagnoses to be part of their job.[46] A second pet project also failed: a draft Law for the Treatment of People Foreign to the Community (Probation Law), which would have allowed the "indefinite revocation of the personal freedom of the person in need of probation," including "all people . . . who . . . cannot be left to themselves or who are socially dangerous, . . . who, through their own fault or not, cannot or will not fit in with the community."[47]

Despite their protestations of inadequate power, social workers were part of a web of institutions that snared hundreds of thousands of "asocials." A prison sentence could come only from a court of law, and a physician's signature was necessary to order sterilization, but a social worker could assign a client to a workhouse or set the wheels in motion for a removal of legal competence or sterilization. Although the Probation Law never went into effect, the draft's measures found their way into many directives concerning the treatment of asocials.[48] Thus a record with the health or welfare department could lead as quickly to internment and sterilization as could a record with the police.[49]

Approximately half of the 400,000 Germans sterilized against their wills under the Nazi regime were women. Seventy to eighty percent of these were single.[50] "Feeble-mindedness," a psychiatric diagnosis applied to women mainly when their sexual behavior or demeanor was judged abnormal, was the reason for 57 percent of female sterilizations; the second most common diagnosis, schizophrenia, also rested in large part on observations of sexual behavior when applied to women.[51] Public authorities aggressively sought out candidates for sterilization: the Hamburg Foster Care Office expected its social workers to recommend one client for sterilization each week.[52]

Sterilization, often described as the duty of the physically or mentally deficient toward the German people, became a strike against those who submitted to it. Infertility was grounds for rejecting applications to marry fiancés whose offspring were considered desirable, and sterilization often led to institutionalization, as social workers feared sterilized women would become promiscuous since they need no longer fear pregnancy. Assuming that immodest sexual behavior had led to their sterilization and that claims of rape or harassment would thus be received with skepticism, and knowing that no accusations of paternity would result, employers and neighbors sexually exploited women whom they knew to have been sterilized.[53]

Sterilized or not, young women designated as asocial were frequently institutionalized: Petersen sought institutionalization for all her charges. The "feeble-minded" wound up in mental institutions; prostitutes, the chronically unemployed, and those who demonstrated poor work discipline were sent to workhouses.[54] Inpatient hospital care in segregated wings was required for women, but not men, with sexually transmitted disease. Lacking a medical diagnosis or criminal record, women who had been declared legally incompetent were typically sent to residential institutions (*Versorgungsheime*). "Work-shy" women and women who failed to have sexually transmitted diseases treated might be found guilty of criminal offenses and thus imprisoned.[55] Institutionalization not only restricted women's movements (and endangered their health and lives) but also further restricted their ability to marry. Indeed, public authorities saw imprisonment and even execution as elements of reproductive policy.[56] Concentration camps proved the eventual destination of many asocials. Two-thirds of the 110,000 non-Jewish Germans sent to concentration camps by 1943 bore the label "asocial."[57]

In targeting asocials for punitive treatment, the Nazis built on the long-standing desires of many welfare and medical professionals, and they enjoyed the support of much of the German population. Nevertheless, the Nazi regime dramatically raised the stakes for women who did not conform, and single women were far more likely to be seen as nonconformist than were married women. Measures such as forced sterilization and transfer to concentration camps were new under the Nazis, and involuntary institutionalization was carried out on an unprecedented scale. Women who had previously risked social ostracism now faced physical danger.

.———.——.

In only one case did the Nazis consider tampering with the social norms that defined acceptable sexual behavior for single women: that of unmarried mothers. Unmarried motherhood proved to be one of the most difficult points of Nazi population policy. The central figure in the matter—the unwed mother who was a full-fledged member of the *Volk*—was, to most minds, a contradiction in terms. Unwed motherhood was itself an indication of asociability, and if a mother was asocial, then her children were undesirable. A few radicals genuinely did not share the popular association of "unwed mother" with "asocial." But for most Nazi leaders, this was not just a popular association: it was also their own.

In the first season of the war, Deputy Führer Rudolf Hess received a letter from a bereaved woman. The woman's fiancé—like her, an "Aryan" with good eugenic indications—had died at the front, leaving her pregnant and her plans for marriage destroyed. Now she faced approbation as an unwed mother. Hess's supportive response of December 1939 was widely reprinted. "What would it help if a people were victorious but became extinct through the sacrifice for the victory?" A woman who bore and raised eugenically valuable children under such difficult circumstances performed a great service.[58]

Hess's letter was not the first discussion of the importance of nonmarital childbearing.[59] Two months earlier, Heinrich Himmler, head of the SS, had issued an order to the SS and police encouraging them to produce children outside marriage if necessary and assuring them that any eugenically valued children they left behind would receive good care in the event of their deaths.[60] Particularly infamous was the SS's *Lebensborn* program. Beginning in 1936, Himmler established a network of homes to enable racially desired pregnant single women to bear their children in discrete and comfortable surroundings. With the war, he increasingly saw the program as an opportunity to make valued single women available for fertilization by SS men; the resulting children would be adopted into worthy families.[61]

To many minds, it was only a small step from approving a *fait accompli*, as Hess did, to encouraging premeditated extramarital conception, as Himmler did. In fact, however, Hess and Himmler represented two different positions. Himmler genuinely wished to encourage the racial elite to throw off traditional restraints and reproduce outside of marriage. This was a radical attitude, at odds with all previous strains of family politics in modern Germany, and it brought more controversy than policy.[62] Hess, by contrast, took up a cry that had been fairly familiar since the late nineteenth century: improve the situation of the unwed mothers and nonmarital children who would inevitably be present. Hess's angle proved dominant. Nearly all who addressed illegitimacy shared the assumption that there was a natural conflict between the interests of unwed mothers and their children, on the one hand, and families with married parents on the other; nearly all agreed that marital families must take precedence.[63] Even draft legislation aimed at radically improving the legal standing of nonmarital children acknowledged that this could be done only "as far as consideration for marriage and the family allows."[64]

The married couple did not just bring children into the world. It educated them to be good members of the national community, to appreciate the rules of social order, and to understand the leadership principle, whose application started with the parents and extended to the *Führer* himself.[65] Indeed, despite statements to the effect that only the goal of reproduction gave meaning to marriage,[66] partnership between women and men was crucial to the new order. Women's preparedness to risk their lives in childbirth and men's readiness to risk theirs at work or at war could only find true meaning "when they, man and woman, find themselves in a true, genuine, and unconditional community and master life together."[67] To encourage illegitimacy was to trivialize this partnership.

The most common argument against encouraging nonmarital births, however, was that it was bad population policy. A eugenically valued woman raising a child on her own would be careful not to add to her burdens by producing additional children.[68] But more to the point, unwed mothers, according to their detractors, were overwhelmingly of bad genetic, physical, intellectual, and moral stock; their children could be little different.[69] "'Unmarried mothers are not *necessarily* inferior,'" admitted a jurist, quoting a common argument against discrimination against unwed mothers, but "this truism must not blind us to the fact that . . . unwed mothers yesterday and today . . . *are* . . . in the overwhelming majority morally, genetically, and often also physically inferior."[70] If the mother was not deficient, chances were good that the father had provided poor genetic material.[71] If the father remained unknown, he might be a Jew. Even if both parents had provided good genetic material and were known to be "Aryans," the child would still not grow up in that institution that best educated the young: the "complete family." "Considered from the point of view of the *Volksgemeinschaft*, a child's value does not just depend on its blood, on its genetic material, but rather also from the *environment in which the child grows up*; . . . the best environment for the child is the family."[72] Convinced that the "complete family" provided the ideal atmosphere for raising children, jurists and social workers considered nonmarital child-bearing with trepidation. Their suspicion that most unmarried mothers were either mentally or physically deficient or asocial could only add to their fear.

Hess's relatively traditional focus on improving the lot of nonmarital children rather than actively promoting childbearing outside marriage triumphed partly because it corresponded to most social workers' and jurists' gut prejudices about unwed mothers and their children. It also benefited, however, from a lack of agreement among population-policy radicals. In the summer of 1940, the Ministry of Justice completed a draft of legislation that would have resulted in far-reaching improvements in the legal situation of racially acceptable unwed mothers and their children. The draft foresaw full legal equality of legitimate and illegitimate children, including equal claims to the father's property; it increased the mother's privacy; and it made it easier to transfer guardianship of nonmarital children from the state to the mother. Hitler refused to approve the draft, however—largely because he felt it did not go far enough. Unwed mothers, he argued, should automatically be the legal guardians of their children.[73]

With the radicals at the top unable to agree on an overhaul of illegitimacy law, those with more traditional views on illegitimacy continued, by default, to make and implement policy regarding unwed mothers and their children. There was little need to fear that they would promote unwed motherhood. Instead, they proposed improving conditions for nonmarital children. But this was hardly radical. It had been promoted by socialists, feminists, and religious and liberal reformers since the nineteenth century, and it had been incorporated into the Weimar constitution.

People like Hess strayed from tradition only in pondering how fair circumstances would be created for nonmarital children. First, only those who passed racial and eugenic muster would enjoy improved conditions such as equal access to financial benefits. This policy, however, was not what ruffled feathers. Rather, it was Nazi Germany's second digression from tradition. Hess's widely publicized letter embodied the strategy of improving the lot of nonmarital children by denouncing the social discrimination that plagued unwed mothers.[74]

The suggestion that unmarried mothers should escape condemnation went well beyond the traditional demand for better treatment for their children. Religious and conservative bourgeois feminists had tacitly approved social discrimination against unwed mothers by insisting that the innocent child should not be penalized for the mother's poor behavior. That the mother deserved approbation had gone without saying. Nazi leaders' interests were no different from those of most social workers: to prevent abortion, reduce infant mortality, and ensure that nonmarital children not be so disadvantaged that their alienation from the community was inevitable. But only now-taboo movements for social reform, such as socialism and radical bourgeois feminism, had urged an end to social ostracism of unwed mothers and an expansion of the mother's—and not just the child's—legal rights.[75] In fact, Hitler's position that unwed mothers should automatically be the guardians of their children would become the position of the East German Communists and the West German Social Democrats after the war. But arguments favoring acceptance of unwed mothers on grounds of human dignity and a rejection of a sexual double standard had not played in Buxtehude. Hess's attempt to elevate them on the basis of their contribution to the *Volk* proved a similar flop.

Few female Nazis were as flexible about unwed motherhood as even relatively moderate Nazi men, like Hess. Many Nazi women, particularly those in social work, continued to press for improved legal and economic measures for those illegitimate children and unwed mothers who would inevitably exist, and they argued that the children should suffer no social condemnation (while, of course, considering illegitimate birth a symptom of asociability once the child reached adolescence or adulthood).[76] They stopped far short, however, of promoting a change of morals that might make illegitimate motherhood socially acceptable. The flip side of such a moral code, they felt, would be to devalue the "family," an institution that did not include unwed mothers and their children. And it was the family that provided most of them with legal and economic security as well as a well-respected social station.

Policy toward unwed mothers reflected Nazi leaders' mixed attitudes. On the one hand, certain routine forms of harassment were curtailed, and financial benefits for racially acceptable nonmarital children were improved. A small number of unwed mothers could claim a special status as pioneers in the new order. On the other hand, public officials continued to judge the vast majority of unwed mothers to be asocial, and penalties for asociability became ever sharper.

Symbolic measures to improve unmarried mothers' status without improving their material conditions took many forms. High-profile attempts to challenge social prejudices, like Hess's letter, often backfired. But quieter measures eased the daily experience of unwed mothers without attracting much backlash. Starting in May 1937, unwed mothers could use the title "Frau."[77] A decree of January 1938 allowed nonmarital children and their mothers to take the father's name if a planned marriage had been interrupted by the man's death.[78] Information regarding nonmarital births was no longer to be mailed on postcards that all could read, and mothers who bore nonmarital children away from home and returned without their children no longer had to register the children in their hometowns.[79] Such regulations hardly increased the social acceptance of unmarried motherhood. Rather, they increased the social acceptance of certain unmarried mothers by allowing them to pass as married, widowed, or childless. Nevertheless, these innovations protected unwed mothers from unwanted exposure and allowed them to determine the circumstances in which they would reveal their situation.

Some new measures for unwed mothers improved their material status. A tax law of 1938 allowed employed unmarried mothers of racially acceptable children to join divorced and widowed mothers in paying taxes at the lower married women's rate.[80] In 1940, the Labor Ministry dropped its requirement that illegitimate children be so designated in women's working papers, making it easier for unwed mothers to find employment.[81] Nonmarital childbirth ceased to constitute grounds for firing state employees, including teachers, in the mid-1930s, and local and national courts subsequently ruled that unmarried pregnancy was not a legitimate reason to fire a private employee.[82] After some adjustments to the law, nonmarital children of military fathers drew allowances for military dependents and orphans whether or not their fathers, in civilian life, had lived up to their obligations.[83]

Efforts to improve maternal and infant health also benefited unwed mothers who passed racial and social muster. The party's social work organization, Mother and Child, offered the same services to married and to single pregnant women and mothers, with the caveat that "the question of worthiness [would be] checked even more closely" in the case of unwed clients.[84] In the hopes of preventing abortion, the organization offered maternity homes, pre- and postnatal care, and assistance in finding work and housing.[85] In addition to practical aid, clients received affirmation that their contribution to the *Volk* was valued. Women who were admitted to the exclusive *Lebensborn* maternity homes, if they took Nazi rhetoric seriously, could imagine themselves to be in the vanguard of a new racial and moral order.[86]

But the first priority of Mother and Child for unmarried mothers was not to make it easier for them to raise their children alone. It was to enable them to marry. Thus before a social worker sought work or housing for the mother, she sought the same for the father, for lack of housing and secure employment often discouraged men from marrying.[87] The social worker also pressured the father, reminding him of his responsibility to the woman, the child, and the *Volk*.

When Nazi jurists and social workers talked about the undesirable qualities of "most" illegitimate children, they did not mean those who were soon legitimized. And when they disparaged "unwed mothers," they did not mean those who quickly married. Belated marriage was merely a risky variant of premarital conception, which remained common.[88] Mother and Child thus institutionalized the most important factor separating asocial from respectable unwed mothers: the durability of their single status.

About half of nonmarital children born in 1935 were legitimized in early childhood as their parents married or as their mothers married other men.[89] Indeed, despite popular assumptions that the presence of illegitimate children reduced a woman's chances of marriage, unwed mothers in Darmstadt wed at greater rates than did women with no children.[90] The birth of a child often motivated couples to marry, and mothers who had been abandoned by the fathers of their children often felt compelled to seek new partners quickly. Child-free women, by contrast, could afford to wait until a truly satisfactory man came along. Single mothers who wed had a different social and economic standing than those who did not.

Compounding the economic disadvantages of prolonged single motherhood were the dangers of not clearing up any suspicion that one might be asocial. For social workers, illegitimate children were evidence of asociability. If the father was unknown or if a woman had illegitimate children with different fathers, the legal burden of proof was on the mother to demonstrate that she and her children were racially and socially valuable.[91] Since all nonmarital children had official guardians, every such child and every unmarried mother was known to the organs of the state. Guardians' periodic inquiries about the children's well-being meant that all unwed mothers were under routine state surveillance. Minor difficulties in the household were thus far more likely to result in state intervention than was the case in households where only marital children were present. In addition to sterilization and institutionalization, asocial unmarried mothers risked having their children removed from their care.

The party's obsession with race further complicated life for mothers of children whose paternity was not crystal clear. Prior to the Nazi period, the courts' main interest in investigating paternity was to ensure the child's financial well-being. If a man was almost surely the child's father, courts often named him the father even if some uncertainty remained. This practice may have been adequate for determining financial responsibilities, but it was too sloppy for the purpose of establishing racial membership.[92] A draft law assigned an illegitimate child non-Aryan status if there was any possibility that the father was not Aryan.[93] But the planned overhaul of illegitimacy law never took place. Instead, local officials determined nonmarital children's racial membership by measures ranging from pressuring the "paying father" to recognize biological fatherhood to having the National Agency for Genealogical Research (*Reichsstelle für Sippenforschung*) research the case.[94] If an Aryan mother's behavior and the child's appearance aroused no suspicion, the child was to count as Aryan.[95] In the end, however, the mother's behavior often did arouse suspicion—simply because she was an unwed mother.

The extension of many benefits to nonmarital children provided the appearance of a generous attitude, but this appearance was misleading. Like all other benefits of the Nazi state, these depended on the recipient's "race," and if the child's mother failed to establish the child's race satisfactorily, she would have to maintain the child by other means. Unmarried motherhood could bring burdens even more severe than sole responsibility for a child, as bearing a child out of wedlock drew the attention of a harsh system of social services predisposed to distrust unwed mothers. Only a tiny number of women with unassailable racial, eugenic, and social profiles could enjoy the new status the Nazi state promised unwed mothers. Even their status, however, was acknowledged only in like-minded circles. Most of the population took an even dimmer view of women willing to function as "breeding machines" than it did of women whose extramarital pregnancies were accidental.[96] Unmarried women's dread of becoming mothers was confirmed by those charged with preventing them from terminating their pregnancies. Social workers guessed that nearly every unwed, pregnant woman attempted abortion.[97]

.——.——.

Single women may have attracted more than their share of negative attention in the Third Reich, but this does not mean that Nazi leaders viewed all single women with suspicion. Being single was a perfectly natural condition preceding marriage. The Nazis risked unnecessarily alienating potential supporters if they condemned single status out of hand. Besides, the regime could put valued single women to good use; once they married, such women would turn their attention elsewhere.

"Recent times have coined a term that we National Socialist women want to strike out once and for all, for it is as shameful as it is oppressive: the term 'superfluous woman.' In a people on its knees, like the German people, there are no superfluous women!"[98] With these words, Gertrud Scholtz-Klink, the future head of the Nazi women's organization, addressed single women of the World War I generation in 1933. Many had been widowed; others had never married. They had passed their young adulthood in the 1920s, often raising children with widows' pensions and women's wages.[99] Inflation had made a mockery of their already inadequate pensions. With the Depression had come attacks against so-called double earners, a term that cast suspicion on all female workers, whether or not they belonged to two-income households. In short, single women of the World War I generation were among those who had suffered in the series of crises that aided the Nazis' rise to power, and the National Socialists lobbied for their support.[100] Not surprisingly, references to their troubles quickly vanished once the party was firmly established and turned its attention to male unemployment and female fertility. Between 1933 and 1939, Nazi speeches and writings referred to single women of this generation only rarely; when they did, they focused on their sacrifices during the past war, not on their subsequent lives.[101]

Although Nazi leaders rarely publicly appealed to single women's interests after 1933, single women contributed more than their share to Nazi organizational life. As the widow of a Nazi who had died of a heart attack during the excitement of a Nazi rally and as the mother of four children, Scholtz-Klink provided one model for activist womanhood. A never-married woman could not have served as the symbol of German womanhood, but a wife could not have been an exemplary public figure: her first duty would have to have been to her husband.[102]

A broader variety of single women was active in lower-profile positions within the Nazi women's organizations. Single women were overrepresented among the relatively elite *NS-Frauenschaft* (NSF) and the more open *Deutsches Frauenwerk* (DFW). Their overrepresentation was at its greatest within the small cadre of NSF and DFW members who also belonged to the Nazi party.[103] Single women's high rate of participation in organizational life was nothing new: with fewer household responsibilities, they had long had more time for such activity. Indeed, they had formed the solid core of women's groups across the political spectrum since the mid-nineteenth century. The disproportionate number of single women in Nazi organizations thus did not mean that single women were more likely than married women to harbor Nazi sentiments. It did, however, mean that single women more often took on official functions. For single women who sympathized with the Nazi program, the women's organizations offered opportunities to work for the new order without marrying and bearing children. Nevertheless, the regime's reliance on single women was ironic. If all adult, racially approved women had married and devoted themselves to raising children—as they, in theory, were supposed to—the party would have been hard-pressed to keep its women's organizations functioning.

Likewise, the regime relied on single female teachers, nurses, and social workers—like Petersen—to carry out social and racial policy. Female professionals had always been overwhelmingly single; the Nazis' expulsion of wives from the civil service tipped the balance yet more precariously. Typical was Regina Frankenfeld. Born in 1906, Frankenfeld studied home economics, psychology, and pedagogy before becoming a teacher in 1926. An enthusiastic party member since 1932, she left her teaching position in 1934 to advance through the ranks of the Home Economics Division of the Reich Agricultural Board. As coordinator of two thousand home economics advice centers throughout Germany, this professional single woman became the manager of an important service for housewives—the type of service that convinced politically, racially, and socially acceptable Germans of the Nazis' attentiveness to their well-being.[104]

The place of marriage in female youth organizations was similarly ambiguous. The League of German Girls (*Bund Deutscher Mädel*, or BDM) encouraged girls to assume, like Hitler, that "the woman's world, when she is lucky, is the family, her husband, her children, her home."[105] Nevertheless, in encouraging girls to anticipate fulfillment as wives and mothers, the BDM was preaching to the converted. Much more challenging was the task of convincing girls that until they married, they should turn their energies to the *Volk* and to public events rather than to family, friends, and preparation for marriage.[106] The commitment expected of young women in youth organizations, if taken seriously, might leave little room for courtship. The BDM taught an ideal of comradeship with male peers: young people should work chastely side by side for the new Reich.[107] Furthermore, the BDM and the Labor Service for Female Youth (*Reichsarbeitsdienst— weibliche Jugend,* or RADwJ) required thousands of *Führerinnen,* who were of little use if they quickly dropped out to marry or if they allowed courting to take precedence over their political functions (Fig. 6).

As acute as the regime's reliance on single women to perform political functions was its dependence on them in the productive economy.[108] Over 80 percent of German women born in the first third of the twentieth century worked until marriage, and nearly 90 percent of unmarried women aged twenty to twenty-nine worked in 1939.[109] Although an increasing number of wives worked after the turn of the century, married women accounted for only 29.9 percent of the female labor force in 1933.[110]

The Nazi regime, however, could not allow single women simply to constitute the "natural" female workforce. Instead, both unable and unwilling to mobilize middle-class wives and facing a labor shortage after 1936, the regime turned ever more attention to organizing single women's labor. In establishing work programs for single women, economic planners lay the groundwork for one of the most significant factors differentiating single and married women's wartime experiences: the large-scale recruitment of single women to places of work away from their homes.

Before the war, young, single women's labor was harnessed into two programs: the Year of Duty (*Pflichtjahr*) and the RADwJ. Both required that women provide six months or a year of almost uncompensated service prior to taking other employment. Understood as parallels to compulsory military service for young men, these programs provoked little agonizing on the part of policymakers—in stark contrast to wartime discussions regarding the recruitment of married women to the workforce. Nor did they prompt widespread popular objections, although individuals often tried to evade service.[111]

The earliest programs' aim was to introduce teenage girls to agricultural and domestic work in the hope that some would remain in these sectors. In 1934, two varieties of the Year of Duty were introduced: the Land Year (*Landjahr*) and the Household Year (*hauswirtschaftliches Jahr*). While the Household Year was voluntary, girls could be drafted into the Land Year from the time of its inception.[112] In the Land Year, urban teenagers of both sexes went to rural areas, where they lived in barracks and performed agri-

Figure 6. Mixed messages in the Nazi League of German Girls. Most BDM girls received training in housewifely skills, such as checking the cleanliness of shoes, from models of single women's activism. Courtesy Landesbildstelle Berlin.

cultural or craftwork with individual families. The Household Year placed girls in families, where they presumably perfected their housewifely skills. Both programs covered room and board and paid a token sum of "pocket money." In 1936, 19,000 boys and 12,500 girls performed a Land Year; 10,000 girls completed a Household Year.

Only in 1938 did the Year of Duty for girls become a mass program. Starting in February, all single women under twenty-five who sought pink- or white-collar work or employment in textile, clothing, or tobacco production had to complete a Land or Household Year first. In December of that year, the directive was extended to apply to all single women under twenty-five who wished to commence any waged or salaried work.[113] Between February and July 1938, 77,400 young women completed a Year of Duty; 217,000 did so during the same period the following year.[114]

The Reich Labor Service Law (*Reichsarbeitsdienstgesetz*) of June 26, 1935, set the foundations for a draft of all young, single women regardless of their desire for future employment.[115] Although designed in part to prepare a large, trained labor force that could spring into action in case of war, the law was initially little used by the regime. On the eve of the war, the RADwJ numbered only fifty thousand.[116] Still, as of September 1936, labor service was the legal duty of every single woman aged eighteen to twenty-six.

In the meantime, Nazi leaders loudly trumpeted their vision for a purely domestic role for married women, especially for those with children. To be sure, image and reality did not necessarily coincide. The marriage loans, for example, were intended to free up positions for unemployed men and create full-time housewives. In fact, however, the law did little to reduce female employment, which increased by three hundred fifty thousand between 1933 and 1936.[117] To enjoy the law's benefits, wives could not take on salaried or waged work, but they could serve as assistants in family businesses or perform work at home. Women who did give up employment were usually replaced by other women since most performed traditionally female work for female wages.[118] The law was perhaps better suited to influencing the proportion of working women who were single than it was to decreasing women's overall labor-force participation. Yet married women's representation in the female labor force increased from 29.9 percent in 1933 to 33.6 percent in 1939.[119]

Already in 1932, the Weimar Parliament had passed a law enabling the firing of female civil servants whose livelihoods were otherwise ensured, typically by their husbands. Little used during the last months of Weimar, the regulations were reiterated in June 1933 and enforced with all vigor thereafter.[120] A 1937 law required that married female civil servants be fired.[121] Only 1.1 percent of employed women were civil servants, but the message was clear: the state, at the very least, was going to eliminate married women from the ranks of its employees.

With the labor shortage of the late 1930s, these regulations were quietly overturned. Starting in October 1937, a new bride no longer had to give up work in order for her husband to qualify for a marriage loan. Early in the war, the requirement that female civil servants be fired upon marriage was lifted.[122] The government's removal of self-inflicted barriers to married women's participation in the labor force, however, did not amount to active encouragement of their employment.

The 1939 census showed 5.4 million child-free married women but only 948,000 single women who were not working although they were physically fit.[123] Nevertheless, institutions and attitudes of the prewar period set the parameters for the regime's organization of female labor during the war. In giving up its campaign against "double earners," the leadership had cleared the way for married women who worked of their own accord. But with many key figures possessed of incurably cold feet about actively recruiting married women—and especially mothers—the matter ended there. Despite the 1935 Defense Law, which committed the entire female population to labor for the country in case of war, the government increasingly relied on the structures that had been created for exploiting young, single women's labor.[124] From an economic perspective, this could not be a satisfactory solution, for it made the government dependent on a small population of women. But, for all its shortcomings, it had one distinct advantage: it was politically and ideologically feasible.

.——.——.

By shaping both the composition and the experience of the single and married populations in peacetime, the Nazi state gave lie to the postwar myth that the war had "created" the women standing alone. Prewar marriage and divorce laws created hundreds of thousands of women who stood alone, above and beyond the "natural" population of single women. By associating single status with undesirable eugenic or social qualities, the Nazi state transformed the social marginalization of women standing alone into endangerment. At the same time, political and labor organization decreased the marginalization of single women who passed racial and social muster. Rather than remaining socially insignificant until their marriage, they now had unique political and economic roles and a new public presence. Their public activity, however, like unvalued single women's supposed deficiencies, established their difference from married women. Marital status divided women, even as women of all marital states were divided according to racial, eugenic, and social criteria.

The war would radically change both facets of single womanhood, and the defeat would bring about yet more changes. Nevertheless, the peacetime developments were significant in two regards. First, they established institutional structures that would continue to shape the lives of single women as well as the distinction between single and married status. Marriage law, policy toward nonmarital children, and labor organization would profoundly shape women's experience during and even after the war. Second, they socialized both the postwar cohort of women standing alone and the contemporaries who would interact with and judge them. Retrospective writings tended to describe women standing alone as having come from nowhere to help build the new Germany in 1945. But single women did not simply burst onto the scene. Like all Germans, they carried the experience of the Nazi era with them, and those who later commented on them had also known them during the Nazi years.

3 War Wives, Workers, and Race Traitors
Losing Control during War

In many ways, the Second World War created a generation of German women standing alone. Of course, as the previous chapter has shown, many women were kept single against their wills even before the war. Furthermore, the state's promotion of public service meant that young single women who, by Nazi standards, were racially acceptable gained both a new social function and a taste of independence. Nevertheless, wifehood remained normative. Women forbidden to marry were, by definition, outsiders; the single women laboring for the *Volk* would presumably marry.

The war changed all that. First, it chipped away at the state's ability to correlate marital status with racial, eugenic, and social characteristics. The state stepped up its campaign against perceived racial enemies, but it decreasingly enforced measures aimed at preventing unvalued "Aryans" from marrying. Furthermore, regulations easing servicemen's marriage enabled hundreds of thousands of women who would have married anyway to move up the date. Women who would have entered the postwar period unwed were instead married, widowed, or divorced.

Second, the war lessened the gap between the civilian experience of married and single women, as millions of wives encountered daily life without their husbands. One striking outcome was the expansion of the category "asocial woman," usually associated with single women, to include large numbers of wives. Women with husbands at war became potential or real adulterers; large numbers broke not only sexual but also racial and political boundaries as they developed relationships with foreign slave laborers or prisoners of war. In some cases, the war even blurred the legal distinctions between married and single status. "Postmortem marriage" made widows out of women who had never been married. "War brides" did not enjoy full status as wives.

Nevertheless, married status remained important even to wives separated from their husbands. Marriage brought legal privilege, and wives could look forward to their husbands' return. Those who were widowed retained legal and social standing. If, after the war, masses of women who had proven their independence and competence nevertheless longed for marriage and domesticity, their desires can be traced to more than their hopes for security and comfort. Marriage had become a part of the personal and legal identity of hundreds of thousands of women who had never experienced daily married life.

But if social and legal distinctions between married and single women became blurred during the war, an opposite trend was also evident. With the regime bent on preserving a purely domestic role for housewives, economic planners organized single women's labor ever more intently. The regime thus spared not only German women at the expense of foreign labor and middle-class women at the expense of working-class women but also married women at the expense of single women.[1] While allowances for dependents of military men allowed hundreds of thousands of wives to leave the workforce, single women's work not only expanded but changed qualitatively. Most striking was the government's employment of millions of young, single women in the military and affiliated organizations. These women owed official status, adventure abroad, participation in racial crimes, and capture and death to their single status.

Yet even as postwar Germans spoke of the remarkable presence of the women standing alone, the single woman's military (or military-related) experience did not become the stuff of legend. In part, this omission reflected tendencies to portray women as restorative rather than destructive, as well as efforts to restore order in gender relations. But it also illustrated the limitations on single status's potential to become normative. Only when millions of married women shared significant aspects of single women's experience did single women cease to be the "other." Ironically, although postwar Germans often spoke of the extraordinary experiences of women standing alone, they excluded those experiences that were most unique to legally single women.

. —. —.

As men went to war, the social and sexual lives of all women changed dramatically, whatever their marital status. Single women encountered difficulties meeting eligible men and finding time for courtship, but if they overcame these hurdles, they benefited from eased regulations regarding marriage. Marriage, however, had a minimal effect on their daily lives. Those who married men at war continued to live with their parents, and they still spent most of their waking hours with their co-workers. Even women who had married before the war and had set up their own households found their social worlds radically changed if their husbands went to war. If they had left the workplace but had no children, they now returned to work. They had far more contact with other men than had been the case when their husbands had been present. For both married and single women, the opportunities for "licit" sexual activity decreased while those for "illicit" sexual activity increased. The experiential divide between the two groups lessened.

Wartime measures made it easier for couples to marry. Cut-backs in domestic programs made it impossible to carry out physical and genealogical examinations on the massive scale of the prewar period. Thus the transfer of medical personnel to military duty, as well as popular opposition, led to a drop in the number of sterilizations after 1939.[2] Similarly, although examinations of applicants for marriage loans continued, progress toward routine examinations for all applicants for marriage was reversed.

In September 1939 procedures for "war marriages" were outlined. Stipulations regarding age and minimum length of service that normally applied to soldiers wishing to marry were removed, as were the requirements regarding proof of one's genealogy and healthy condition (but not racial pedigree) in most circumstances. With the introduction of "long-distance marriages" that November, prospective husbands and wives could make their declarations of marriage at separate times and in separate places.[3] Forty percent of couples marrying between May 1939 and April 1940—330,000 couples—took advantage of the new provisions.[4]

With the regime concerned about a drop in birthrates as men and women of marriageable age were separated, these measures signaled a shift in emphasis from "quality" to quantity.[5] Indeed, "undesired" elements of the population benefited at least as much as did "desired" elements from the new regulations, particularly the eased requirements regarding proof of genealogy and health. The sudden and temporary jump in marriage rates in the second half of 1939 and 1940 suggests a backlog of couples who had previously been unable to marry.[6] Nevertheless, many couples who concluded war marriages would have been able to marry even under the stricter regulations; war marriage allowed them to move up the date or to avoid burdensome paperwork. The subsequent death of thousands of the husbands meant that many of these marriages would not have taken place if war marriage had not been available.

Women who married men at war led lives similar to those of unmarried women. The partners had often been barely acquainted—if at all—in peacetime, and as spouses they met only for brief periods of military leave. The wives usually continued to live with their families of origin. Unless the husband had supported the wife for a year before their marriage, the wife did not receive the usual state support for dependents of military men; she thus continued to rely on her own labor or her family of origin for sustenance. Those who were subsequently widowed had never known routine married life. Those whose husbands survived confronted a stranger at war's end. "We hadn't even really begun to lead a married life," recalled a woman after her husband's 1946 return from prison camp. "We married in 1943. That was a so-called war marriage, and our son came in '44. It wasn't exactly a well broken-in marriage. Now we were actually together for the first time." Like many couples who had entered war marriages, they soon divorced.[7]

Provisions for war marriages and long-distance marriages had a precedent in the First World War and parallels in other countries. Unique to Nazi Germany were postmortem marriages: marriages between women and already-fallen soldiers. A decree by Hitler in November 1941 authorized "the subsequent marriage of women with fallen military men . . . when serious intent to marry can be proven and no evidence is presented to indicate that this intent was abandoned before death."[8] In theory, the most important factor in judging an application for partners who would have passed the usual requirements was to be the presence or expectation of children. In practice, marriages that would have passed the usual regulations were routinely approved, whether or not a child from the union was present or expected.[9] If the marriage was approved, it was declared to have been concluded on the day preceding the husband's death. Approximately eighteen thousand women became postmortem brides during the course of the war.[10]

Most discussions of "corpse marriages," as they were popularly known, assume that they were introduced in order to make engaged women less hesitant to conceive children. But both the decree and the guidelines were marked "confidential," neither was published before the end of the war, and nowhere was the availability of a postmortem marriage publicized. Rather, local administrators of survivors' pensions explained this option to fiancées of fallen soldiers whose difficulties were known to them.[11] The measure allowed officials to ease the situations of selected women who had become mothers with the expectation of marriage.[12]

Postmortem marriage was a concession to reality. It made widows out of unmarried Aryan mothers who had conceived children when their engagement was firm: women whose illegitimate children did not indicate their asociability. Rather than becoming alienated from the state whose war had taken their fiancés, the fathers of their children, and their financial security, they would be grateful to the state for sparing them the humiliating status of unwed mother, for enabling them to collect a widow's pension, and for granting them the civil rights of a widow, such as a claim to an inheritance.[13] They and their children would remain part of the *Volksgemein-schaft*, and their chances of (re)marriage would presumably improve.

War marriage, long-distance marriage, and postmortem marriage offered only legal status; they did not introduce couples to the daily experience of marriage. Nevertheless, the legal status of marriage was of tremendous demographic and personal significance. Of the three to four million male German military casualties, roughly 40 percent were married.[14] War marriages created wives out of women who, in peacetime, would have remained single; and they created widows out of women who would have become bereaved fiancées or lovers (Fig. 7). A significant portion of this generation had a deep personal stake in the institution and entitlements of marriage without ever having experienced routine married life.

War marriages, long-distance marriages, and postmortem marriages may have lowered the bureaucratic hurdles for marriage, but they could do little to acquaint women and men in the first place. Even before the war, marriage rates among young men dropped, as the reintroduction of the military draft took them away from daily contact with young women.[15] The war deepened this sexual segregation. Some twenty million men served in the armed forces, and nearly half of them had left civilian life by June 1941.[16] Civilian labor service removed another large group. Young women, too, left their homes to perform civilian or military service. Organs of the state thus turned their attention to bringing likely couples together—for example, by sponsoring social events for women and soldiers on leave.[17]

More characteristic of the Nazi state were programs for matchmaking along explicitly eugenic lines.[18] Two wartime initiatives were aimed at bringing valued women and men together. The first, introduced in 1943, targeted severely wounded soldiers whose chances of marriage were poor although they were fertile and of approved eugenic stock.[19] Aiming at a broader clientele was the second program, the letter exchange of the League of German Families (*Reichsbund Deutscher Familien*), which promised to put well-matched men and women in contact with each other.

Few marriages resulted from these programs. Local administrators of the scheme for wounded veterans feared appearing tactless by publicizing the service too aggressively. Since the letter exchange opened only in 1944, it had little time to process the forty thousand letters it collected by

Figure 7.   War marriage. Couples who married during
the war rarely set up households together, and the
partners saw each other only for brief periods of military
leave. Many war brides were widowed or divorced
without ever having experienced the daily routine of
married life. Courtesy Landesbildstelle Berlin.

November of that year. Women investigating matches with wounded veterans often lost interest once they understood what was meant by
"severely wounded." Most female applicants to both programs had a relatively high class background, performed pink- or white-collar work (the
majority were in the female professions), and lived in cities. They had little desire to marry the farmers, small-time artisans, and laborers who made
up the bulk of the male applicants. The wounded veterans, for their part, did
not want to settle for second best (that is, older, physically imperfect, or

uppity because of class background) just because they were wounded. The matchmaking offices were committed to upholding the male prerogative to be choosy, both in order to strengthen the wounded men's self-esteem and in order to establish the proper hierarchy for married life.[20]

Despite their ineffectiveness, the matchmaking service and the letter exchange offer glimpses into single people's attitudes about being single. When male applicants were limited to the severely wounded, female applicants far outnumbered them. Given the already-existing demographic imbalance, however, the fact that the letter exchange had as many male as female applicants is telling.[21] The dearth of applications by war widows was due, according to the organizers of the services, to widows' attractiveness on the marriage market: widows had already proven themselves as wives, housekeepers, and, in some cases, mothers. The predominance of professional and urban women illustrates their continuing difficulty in finding partners, as does the number of poor, rural, and propertyless men. In this context, it is worth noting women's choosiness. Few seriously considered a severely wounded man. The disinterest of men with low class status in women of higher standing was heartily reciprocated. Most significantly, women in their twenties—precisely those who would face the worst demographic imbalance—did not sign up. This does not mean they did not wish to marry, simply that they were not worried enough to go beyond traditional methods of courtship. By contrast, many men in their twenties applied, apparently afraid of missing the boat while at war despite their demographic advantage.[22]

Formal matchmaking schemes had limited reach; efforts to evaluate potential marriage partners had lost their effectiveness with the introduction of war marriage. Nazi ambitions of totalitarian control notwithstanding, most social and sexual interaction would occur outside the state's purview.

Unmarried women could not remain oblivious to the implications of wartime casualties. Those with suitors may have pressed for marriage to ensure some experience of married life, legitimate status for their expected children, and widowed status for themselves in case of their suitors' deaths. Others, however, delayed marriage because of the uncertainties war brought, and there is little indication that those without suitors engaged in much of a scramble to find a partner while there were still men to be had.

Why was there no such scramble if most young women assumed that their future happiness and well-being would depend on marriage? One reason may have been sheer optimism: each woman's assumption that other women and not she would fall victim to the shortage of men. Aside from faith in the future, however, there were many further arguments against wartime marriage. A woman who worked full-time and shared responsibility for the increasingly burdensome housework in her parents' home had little time or energy for men. "This heavy duty, to be there for the whole family, for my mother, my sister, and myself, just didn't leave much time," recalled a woman of her inability to court during the war.[23] Furthermore, while marriage may once have offered relief from work outside the home, it no longer did so. Unwed working women were prohibited from giving up employment upon marriage. Only the care of young children could free a woman of this duty—and responsibility for a child was not necessarily a better deal if the father's life was in danger. Fear of having widowhood follow motherhood, indeed, probably discouraged many who were not already pregnant from marrying.[24]

Finally, just as marriage had ceased to offer relief from the workplace, it was no longer necessary as a means of getting out of the parental home. The BDM had offered girls a sense of independence from their parents; civilian labor and military service now brought millions more out of their parents' homes, often to unfamiliar regions of Germany, sometimes abroad in occupied Europe. Whether or not they liked their work, they no longer needed to marry if they wanted to enjoy a measure of freedom from their parents. If they did still live with their parents, marriage would not bring independence. The establishment of the new household would have to wait until after the war anyway. Since the partners would not be able to live together, marriage's emotional rewards would be diminished; indeed, there was a great danger of growing apart.

Marriage's benefits had dwindled. Marriage still brought an elevated social status, and it guaranteed certain legal benefits, particularly if a child was present or expected. For those deeply attached to a particular man, marriage was of great emotional significance. But it no longer offered freedom from the workplace or independence from the parental household. Young women, especially if they were not pregnant, had good reason to weigh marriage's benefits against the risks of widowhood, pregnancy, and estrangement.

Well over a million women were widowed during the war. In the postwar period, the significance of widowhood would be hotly contested, as the West German state elevated and the East German state downplayed the identity of the war widow. During the war, propaganda and experience alike minimized the significance of widowhood.

As young women faced the loss of suitors and husbands, the Nazi propaganda machine referred them to the brave precedent set by women of the previous generation.[25] But these "sisters of fate" were unequal siblings: the widows of the First World War were now losing their sons. Younger widows could do nothing but admire the incomparably greater sacrifice of their mothers.[26] A model was Annemarie Mölders, whose flying-ace son was killed in action in 1942. Mölders's words were broadcast on radio; reprinted in magazines, newspapers, and schoolbooks; and distributed by the war victims' association in the form of a booklet of consolation. As Mölders told it, her husband had died in the First World War, leaving her with three young sons. She had wished nothing more than to see her sons live in peace; now one lay dead, another was a prisoner of war, and the third was living a precarious existence at the front. She had come to understand, however, "that man stands under a different law than does woman. And . . . it must be so. And . . . it is good so. As long as the world exists, woman will hate war and love the warrior—precisely because the best warrior is also the best man."[27] Nevertheless, mothers of fallen men did not allow mourning to kill their spirits. Rather, Mölders proclaimed, they "want to and must turn back to life; for life needs us as we need life."

If Mölders felt an obligation to life in her advanced age after having lost both a husband and son, younger women could have no excuse for sinking into despair. As a young author wrote, "Indeed the times burden us heavily. . . . But let us take a look back to the generations that preceded us: they had to make *no smaller sacrifice.* . . . Didn't they all begin their paths young and optimistic and wanting to be 'happy'? And didn't they—as we— have to learn to conquer themselves, to practice denial in many areas, and to stand up for something greater than their personal lives!"[28]

If Annemarie Mölders was the ideal war mother, Lina Heydrich was, at least in one respect, an exemplary widow. Her advanced pregnancy not only demonstrated her maintenance of a regenerative sphere to balance her husband's grisly work but also prevented her from attending her husband's burial.[29] Propagandistic references to fallen soldiers' immortality in the form of their children encouraged men to procreate, and they comforted men facing death.[30] A higher birthrate and better morale were the intended results. Similarly, references to a widow's children suggested that her loss was not as great as she might initially have imagined. She still had a highly meaningful mission.[31]

Nevertheless, widows were also needed in the workplace. Thus, caring for the children of the fallen could not be promoted as the best way to recover from loss. Rather, work should be the "remedy" for a widow's sufferings. "In order not to become bitter or unfair in the fate that has befallen me, I need not only a career that will secure myself and my child financially; I need a duty that fulfills me. For to be only a mother—that is unfortunately lost to me."[32] So wrote, ostensibly, a young widow who decided to learn midwifery—after arranging for her mother-in-law to watch her child, an arrangement that provided not only security for her child but also comfort to her husband's bereaved mother.

Thus widowhood and mourning had different meanings depending on the age of the widow. Older widows who now lost sons took on a symbolic role as "social mourners." A military man could rest assured that even if he fell, he would always be the centerpiece of his mother's life. For younger women, widowhood would hurt, but it would not change their mission in life: to serve the *Volk* by raising children and laboring for the war effort.[33] Memories of their husbands might motivate them in their duties as mothers and workers, but these duties had existed before widowhood and dwarfed it in importance.

This propagandistic message confirmed young widows' experience. Although they had written letters and sent packets to the front and although they had looked forward to their husbands' periods of leave, their husbands had ceased to be a part of their daily routines when they had left for war. "My colleagues helped me to get over it, and work went on," recalled a woman of the 1943 death of her husband, to whom she had been married only a year. "And in the business I slowly forgot about it. Not much had changed; after all, we'd only had written contact."[34] Whatever widows' dreams for the future, their current lives consisted of child rearing, working, or both. Widowhood changed only two things: it shattered women's hopes for reduced burdens and emotional comfort when their husbands returned, and it reduced the amount of financial assistance they received from the state. Widows did not need to be told that mourning was an unaffordable luxury. The only point on which representation and experience differed was whether it was the *Volk* or their own families who could not afford it.

At the same time that marriage and widowhood played a less central role in women's daily lives, the unusual social and psychological conditions of war led to an increased amount of sexual interaction that broke both social convention and the law. When the war began, government authorities anticipated a rise in sexually transmitted disease (STD) and illegitimate pregnancy. The picture they found was uneven: in some regions and cities rates rose; in others, they did not.[35] The Ministry of the Interior instructed the police to crack down on street prostitution and reestablish municipal regimentation of prostitution; local health departments were to raid bars and dance halls and test female employees and patrons for STDs.[36] Employees of the health department soon required military protection in at least one major city as raids degenerated into brawls between male customers, including SS and Gestapo men, and health officials.[37] A police decree of March 1940 forbade minors from loitering after dark; from visiting restaurants, movies, or dance halls; and from smoking or drinking in public.[38] Of particular concern to local police were young women who hung around soldiers' quarters. In the winter of 1942, Hamburg health authorities estimated that two-thirds of young women with STDs had been infected by soldiers.[39] Tough legislation, however, could not always solve the practical problems of supervising young women in rapidly changing conditions. Already at the beginning of the war, "endangered girls" claimed to be too busy at work to attend their appointments with social workers. Young women slipped away from their supervisors as bombing raids presented opportunities to disappear.[40] The predominantly female environment enabled lesbian contacts and relationships with women who otherwise lived as heterosexuals.[41] The foster-care offices and health departments, which had long been in the business of checking delinquent young single women, had their hands full.

Married women posed a yet more difficult problem. Although official involvement in the lives of married women was not unheard of, it was less common, as matters between husband and wife apparently regulated themselves. With war, however, husbands might be away for years at a time. When their wives' marital fidelity proved problematic during the war, the matter could not regulate itself. If infidelity was intolerable, the state would have to step in.

The monthly reports of the Hamburg Social Offices give a good sense of the growing concern about military wives' adultery. A July 1940 report regretted "isolated confirmed reports concerning women, . . . that unworthy restaurants are being visited and that the women in part run around nights." By September of that year, the head social worker found "frightening" the number of "wives of military men [who] don't adhere very precisely to marital fidelity." A year later, the report complained that "many women let themselves get mixed up with foreigners, especially Danes." By 1942, the head social worker was concerned about the increasing number of war wives who were pregnant by men other than their husbands.[42]

In analyzing military wives' behavior, Käthe Petersen, Hamburg's head social worker, differentiated among the large majority whose conduct was beyond reproach, asocial wives whose nature had been evident earlier, and the "stumbling and endangered women, who under normal circumstances no doubt would have led an orderly life."[43] Such wives were drawn to infidelity for a number of reasons, Petersen explained. Their generous family allowances made employment unnecessary, leaving them with too much time and money on their hands. Those who did work came under the influence of less-than-upright co-workers. Their husbands' long absences and depressing news about losses at the front led them to seek comfort in human contact. Aware of military men's infidelities, they wondered why they should be held to stricter standards.[44] And public opinion did not uniformly censure adulterous wives. While some condemned adultery as a sign of a too-carefree life-style, others pitied women who passed their best years without their husbands and amidst the hardships of war. Worst of all, husbands' reactions were unpredictable. On the one hand, Petersen felt, husbands who were too understanding failed to deter future adultery. On the other hand, husbands sometimes went overboard and petitioned for divorce or even initiated criminal suits. This was no better; the point of reinforcing the husband's authority was to keep the marriage intact. If the state was going to get involved, it would have to tread a thin line. It would have to make clear that adultery was unacceptable behavior for married women, while discouraging husbands from drawing the conclusion that their wives deserved divorce.

The municipalities, which administered family allowances, took the lead in the first strategy. Lacking instructions for dealing with such cases early in the war, many cities reduced or revoked the family allowances of adulterous wives.[45] In May 1942, the Ministry of the Interior authorized the revocation of the family allowances of wives who demonstrated "dishonorable or immoral conduct" or who neglected their children.[46] Statistics regarding the number of women whose adultery led to the reduction or revocation of their family allowances are not available, but the option was discussed frequently in social work journals.

The Justice Department, for its part, tried to ensure that adultery did not result in a wave of divorce. As things stood, the criminal code's provisions for adultery required that both adulterous parties be sued and that the adultery have led to divorce.[47] In 1942, a new crime was introduced: "insult of husbands at the front." This provision allowed the husband to sue only the interloper, even as the marriage remained intact.[48] In guidelines of 1942 and 1943, however, the Justice Department discouraged suits of any sort, civil or criminal, against either the wife or the interloper.[49] When the husband insisted on pressing charges, the courts were to distinguish between more and less serious incidents of adultery.

Thus organs of the state punished adulterous women by revoking their family allowances, while encouraging their husbands to go easy on them in court. This policy reflected what many felt was the ideal resolution of adultery. The threat of losing income and having the husband informed might result in a quick end to the affair. If it did not, it would be up to the husband to exert a bit of discipline. But the marriage would continue; it did, after all, promise to provide the German *Volk* with children. Only if the marriage would in no case continue—that is, if the husband was dead—did this logic break down. If the husband had fallen, the damage done to his honor by his adulterous wife—not to mention the damage done to the state treasury, which paid a widow's pension—justified a "postmortem divorce," an innovation of March 1943.[50]

The very need to walk this tightrope attested to a simple fact: with husbands at war, young wives' social lives resembled those of single women more than those of married women in peacetime. But even for single women, the war had disrupted older patterns of courtship. Among other things, the war had introduced a new population of potential sexual partners: foreign slave laborers and prisoners of war. Women, married or single, who had "forbidden contact" transgressed not only the limits of acceptable sexual behavior but racial and political boundaries as well. While adultery was a matter for social workers and lawyers, forbidden contact was a matter for the Gestapo.

Starting in the fall of 1939, Polish prisoners and civilians were imported to work for the *Reich*. A few months later, French workers joined them, and Soviets followed starting in the summer of 1941. By August 1944, 7,615,970 prisoners of war and foreign civilians from all over Europe labored inside Germany.[51] A large number of these were women, but, even so, millions of foreign men worked and lived alongside German women. German women and foreign men worked side by side in factories, and foreign men often provided the only adult male labor on farms. In Berlin, nearly half the foreign workers were housed privately with Germans; in some towns the number was well over half. In rural areas, room and board with private families was standard.[52]

Foreign men were a sizable subpopulation in wartime Germany; they were well-integrated into daily life; and they were an important source of social and sexual companionship for German women. By 1942, the SD (intelligence and security service) estimated that foreign laborers had fathered at least twenty thousand illegitimate children born to German women.[53] Children born to women married at the time of conception were legitimate and thus excluded from these figures. Nearly one-quarter of those reported as the source of infection for STDs in one large city in 1943 were foreigners.[54]

German women from all walks of life had relationships with foreign laborers. A seventeen-year-old servant in a candy store developed a relationship with a Pole who worked in a nearby auto shop. A fifty-five-year-old single woman admitted to a fleeting relationship with a Pole twenty years her junior who worked for her brother. Two young widows lived for over a year with French prisoners of war who snuck out of their barracks nightly to join them. A woman with four children whose husband lived at home but worked nights became involved with her Italian subtenant.[55] Women had relationships with foreign workers and prisoners of war for the same reasons they had relationships with German men. They came to like them in daily life; they appreciated their help on their farms or in their businesses; they desired friendship and intimacy; they sought sex; they were pressured or forced into it. But in some cases there were additional motivations. Popular perceptions of French eroticism, as well as their packages of chocolate and coffee from home, made French men appealing.[56] The police were convinced that the very danger surrounding it gave "contact with foreigners a special attraction . . . for many youth."[57] Pity for the malnourished, homesick prisoners they met in the workplace led some women to offer bread or cigarettes, and religious solidarity brought many German and foreign Catholics together.

The SD optimistically reported, early in the war, that the population censured such relationships and supported an official crackdown.[58] Most women were found out only when their neighbors or co-workers denounced them. Villagers took part in the public head shaving and humiliation of women found guilty of forbidden contact.[59]

As the war proceeded, however, neighbors seemed to want less direct involvement in punishment, although they still condemned the crime. In July 1941, the director of the Reich Propaganda Ring reported that the public shaming of women had little effect; by late 1943, the practice had been discontinued.[60] Villagers disapproved of public executions of foreigners convicted of forbidden contact.[61] By the middle years of the war, the SD was forced to admit that much of the public found at least some level of friendly contact unproblematic. Many had difficulty understanding why relationships with allies such as Italians or members of "Aryan" races such as the Dutch deserved censure.[62] A lengthy report of 1943 acknowledged that, particularly in rural areas, where foreigners were admired as good workers, "the strict prohibition on contact with prisoners of war has never been 'internally accepted' by the population." Husbands of accused women often stood behind their wives, and the women themselves did not all fall into the

category of "morally loose women."[63] Denunciations of women for forbidden contact were less often a condemnation of the crime itself than a
weapon in disputes between neighbors or co-workers.[64]

The regime obsessed with racial purity had become the catalyst of an
unprecedented number of relationships between Germans and foreigners.
But it could not do without foreign labor, and it could not provide housing
and round-the-clock supervision for all its foreign workers. It could only
hope to impress on German women the importance of racial purity or, failing that, frighten them into line. Propaganda campaigns, however, were
stymied by an unwillingness to tackle the problem head-on in a public
forum. "Racial purity" and "blood" were tired clichés, incapable of com-
municating fresh urgency. But anything more direct—for example, a discussion concerning "women" rather than "blood"—would constitute an
admission that the situation was out of control.[65]

Besides, it was difficult to put one's finger on the problem. To describe
the racial danger was inadequate; foreign "Aryans" as well as Slavs, south-
ern Europeans, and Jews were off limits. Political arguments did not make
sense if contact with men from Italy and other allied countries was forbidden.[66] Wrapped up in a discourse of racialism and war, Nazi leaders seemed
unable to articulate what was really troubling them: they were, as a nation,
being cuckolded.[67] After 1940, when it was clear that the problem was not
going to go away, an embarrassed silence replaced attempts at education.
Harsh sentences failed to serve as deterrents as they received inadequate
press coverage.[68]

Furthermore, even in the cases considered most objectionable—those
involving a man from a Slavic, enemy nation—there was a way out. If the
man proved "capable of Germanization," he could escape death and even
marry the woman simply by having his racial category changed.[69] The
woman's fate, too, depended on whether her partner proved "capable of
Germanization." If he did, bygones would be bygones; if not, she faced
prison and concentration camp. Needless to say, "Germanization" was an
imprecise science. Eligibility depended not only on the man's appearance
and character, two factors that already left much room for interpretation,
but also on the circumstances of the affair. If the woman was married, a
minor, or a prostitute, his case would not be considered. If the woman was
none of these but was single and pregnant, his case would be processed
extra quickly.[70] "Capability of Germanization" referred not at all to a man's
race and only in small part to his ability to "pass" as a German. Rather, it
concerned the desirability of a pardon for his crime, which in turn depended
on the desirability of a pardon for the woman's crime. With "Germaniza-

tion," local authorities had an outlet when confronted with cases concerning women they wished to save.

The connection between a man's "capability of Germanization" and his lover's marital status is significant. Race alone could not explain the crime; neither could wartime alliances. The parallel between this "national adultery" and adultery within individual marriages was the unarticulated missing link. It was mentioned nowhere in official analyses of forbidden contact; instead, it became critical at key moments after the crime was detected. A married woman who had a relationship with a foreigner found that he was ineligible for "Germanization"; this eliminated her escape route from a severe sentence. If "Germanization" was not at issue or if the application had been rejected, the woman's marital status was considered in sentencing.[71] Although unmarried women were overrepresented among those convicted of forbidden contact, their overrepresentation was much narrower than it was for designations of asociability. While 70–80 percent of sterilized women had never been married, unmarried women accounted for only 45 percent of women sentenced for forbidden contact.[72]

Even when the woman was single, male sexual possessiveness in the face of "national adultery" was evident. The extremely explicit confessions and court testimony reveal a voyeuristic fascination on the part of the male interrogators who forced the confessions from the women.[73] The detailed descriptions of the sexual acts contrast starkly with the formulaic recitations of the racial crime and the utter silence on the political dangers of forbidden contact that appear in the court materials.[74] Women who declared a genuine emotional investment in their foreign lovers were judged especially harshly.[75]

The toxic combination of racial, political, and marital infidelity made forbidden contact a severe crime. Nearly one-fourth of the judgments for political crimes in 1940–41 were for forbidden contact, and the great majority of trials resulted in guilty verdicts.[76] In 1944, there were two to three execution orders daily for Soviet workers alone who had had illegal contact with German women.[77] Up to ten thousand German women per year were sent to concentration camps for forbidden contact.[78] And married women's prominence in the crime testified to an unsettling fact of wartime life: whatever wives' legal status, they did not share daily life with their husbands, and their social and sexual lives often resembled those of single women.

.—.—.

The Nazi regime was better able to maintain the distinction between married and single women in their working lives than it was in their social and sexual lives. It maintained two programs for recruiting female labor to the wartime economy. One aimed at mobilizing the large "reserve" of female labor—mainly married women of the middle classes. The second intensively targeted teenage girls and young, single women. The first never gained the full support of party leaders, was highly unpopular among the people, introduced women to no essentially new experiences, and failed to provide much-needed labor for the war economy. The second was unambiguously promoted by the leadership, raised relatively few objections from the population, had a profound impact on the women concerned, and was at least moderately successful from the regime's point of view.

Even before the war, 88.7 percent of never-married women who were capable of working were doing so. The same could be said of only 36 percent of married, divorced, and widowed women.[79] Married women's employment declined even further as generous allowances for families of military men allowed many to give up their jobs. If there was a "reserve" labor force to be tapped, this was it. Nevertheless, Nazi leaders were both ideologically committed to a domestic role for most married women and fearful of popular objections to compelling housewives to work.

In seeking a way out of this cul-de-sac, economic planners followed a simple logic: it was easier to delay the conferral of the privileges of marriage than to revoke them. Nazi policy thus differentiated between women who were already married and women who married during the war, and it separated wives who had cashed in on the privileges of marriage—that is, who had left employment—from those who had remained in the workforce. For wives who, for economic reasons, had continued to work, this was simply an officially enforced version of old class distinctions. For women who married during the war, however, this was new since it disregarded class distinctions. War brides became a brand of "semimarried" women. They were legally married, but they did not enjoy all the benefits of wifehood, such as a family allowance adequate to replace paid labor and exemption from the civilian labor draft.

The working history of Inge D. illustrates both the limitations and the benefits of wartime marriage. In 1938, Inge, eighteen years old, joined her mother in home production of boxes. Her Land Year had been cut short by illness. In March 1940, she married a man from a well-situated family, and the couple moved to a comfortable apartment. A year later, her husband was drafted. Since the couple had lived together and her husband had supported her financially, Inge drew the full allowance for military wives. Nevertheless, because she was young, fit, childless, and a former worker, she was vulnerable to the employment office's draft, and she was assigned work in an armaments factory. Inge was paid regular wages, but her work was compulsory. Unenthusiastic about producing munitions, Inge remained absent from work. She was charged with sabotage. Like many absentee women, however, she was judged not to be a saboteur—simply lazy. "Since, by virtue of her position as the wife of a military man, the accused is financially secure, she believes she does not need to work." The case against her was dismissed, and Inge now had a legitimate reason not to work: she was pregnant.[80]

When the war began on September 1, 1939, Germany was already suffering a labor shortage, and the sudden expansion of the military draft sharply reduced the supply of male workers. To make matters worse, hundreds of thousands of women left their posts in the early months of the war. Between July 1939 and March 1940, the employment of women (not including family assistants) decreased by 540,000.[81] Poor work discipline further aggravated the problem. Unexcused absences accounted for at least 20 percent of days missed by women in the spring of 1940.[82] Domestic and agricultural workers abandoned their jobs for work that paid more for shorter hours.[83] Penalties for women who exhibited poor work discipline remained nominal throughout the war.[84]

Most of those who left the labor market were wives benefiting from generous support for military dependents. Inadequate support for military dependents in the previous war had contributed to unrest on the home front, and the Nazi leadership was determined not to repeat the mistake.[85] Families of military men serving the Nazi state could receive up to 85 percent of the prewar earnings of their husband-fathers.[86] At the same time, the regime saw no reason to subsidize families that were earning their own keep. Thus any income earned by the wife's waged or salaried work that exceeded one-third of her support was deducted from her allowance.[87]

The consequences of this plan should have surprised no one. As long as wives' earnings had supplemented those of their husbands, many families calculated that the extra income compensated for the reduced time for housework and children. The subtraction of wives' earnings from family allowances, however, meant that wives' wages essentially replaced their husbands' contributions. It was no longer worth wives' while to work outside the home. But family support was intended to keep housewives from being forced to work when the state took their husbands away to war. The framers of the system seem not to have expected employed wives to take advantage of the opportunity to become housewives.

The role of family allowances in decreasing female employment contributed to a contemporary impression that family allowances were a windfall for wives, an impression that remains in the historiography.[88] The program, however, did not benefit all military wives equally. Inequitable family allowances resulted in resentment and, in some cases, genuine hardship.[89]

Only a woman who had lived with her husband before his military service received an allowance calculated as a percentage of his income. Women who married men already in the service received a flat, minimal sum, regardless of the man's former income.[90] Receiving this small allowance rarely worsened the new wife's situation; rather, it meant that marriage did not bring the usual benefit: a male income that might enable one to leave the workplace. Thus while public opinion already condemned war brides, who presumably married for financial gain, the exclusion of most childless war brides from full benefits established in law that they did not deserve full recognition as wives.

In addition to disadvantaging war brides, the system of family allowances handicapped already-married women at the lower end of the income scale and wives of men drafted early in the war, since allowances for men drafted later were calculated on earnings that had increased during the war.[91] Finally, ever-changing regulations and a shortage of office staff created much room for error in the calculations. When skilled personnel were drafted, inexperienced office workers took their place; meanwhile, the caseload exploded. In February 1940, the average family allowance administrator in Chemnitz had 309 cases.[92] The frequent revisions to family-allowance law often remained unpublished.[93] In May 1942, a set of revisions was published: it consisted of over one hundred columns of small print and no concordance to existing law that might assist case workers.[94] Women's complaints that their allowances were smaller than their neighbors' often stemmed from reasonable suspicions that someone had erred in the calculations.

Despite the shortcomings of family allowances, the image of the soldier's wife who had given up work to while away her hours in the café captured the imagination of the public and policymakers alike. When discussions about requiring women to register for employment began in earnest in the spring of 1940, opponents of a blanket exemption for married women drew on the already-familiar notion of the soldier's wife living all too comfortably on her family allowance.[95] The decree that resulted from these discussions, released in June 1941, required recipients of family allowances who had given up employment during the war to return to work. Unless they had had a child in the interim or had another legitimate excuse, failure to take up employment could lead to a reduction in their allowances. A carrot complemented this stick: income earned via waged or salaried work would no longer be calculated against family allowances.[96]

Employment offices ensuingly examined over eighty-two thousand recipients of family allowances. Over four-fifths of them either could not be located or had a legitimate reason not to work, and women's employment did not even regain its prewar levels.[97]

The decree of June 1941 thus did little to increase women's participation in the workforce. It did more to intensify the perception that policies regarding women's work were deeply class-biased. Military wives who had not worked prior to drawing allowances—including many without children and with household servants—continued to be exempt, while women who had worked earlier were vulnerable, even if they had many children. The same was true of the decree of January 1943, which required that all men age sixteen to sixty-five and all women age seventeen to forty-five register for work. Pregnant women and women with one preschool child or two under the age of fourteen were exempt, but working women who fit this description learned that the exemptions did not apply to women already employed.[98] Of the three million who registered by June 1943, only half a million took up full-time work; by the end of the year, half of these had produced medical excuses.[99]

By May 1944, 1.2 percent more women were working than before the war. Women's participation in the U.S. workforce had grown 50 percent, while England had achieved a 50 percent increase by 1943.[100] Germany had fallen far short of tapping its "reserve" of married women's labor. The only effective means of increasing wives' employment had been the denial of full family allowances to war brides. This policy did not bring new women to the workplace; it simply prevented some from leaving.

Conditions for working women worsened considerably during the war. As the working week grew longer and transportation deteriorated, women's time away from home averaged eleven to twelve hours and could reach fifteen or more.[101] Neither shops nor childcare facilities—when available at all—accommodated such working hours. The pay gap for women in industry widened as wages for unskilled female labor declined; few women obtained positions previously designated as men's, and few were able to move into semiskilled or skilled work.[102]

Nevertheless, these hardships did not represent any fundamental change in the nature of women's work. Only in two regards was there qualitative change in the work of women employed via the employment offices. First, employment became life-threatening. Unless they had very small children, working women were prohibited from leaving the cities as millions were evacuated. Single women and war brides, who worked in far greater proportions than did women who had married before the war, stood a disproportionate chance of injury or death in bombing raids. Second, there was a dramatic shift in the economic sectors in which women worked. Office workers' salaries rose while industrial wages declined, and women who took over many traditionally male civil service functions earned the full male wage. Traditionally, domestic servants and agricultural workers seeking better earnings had gone to the factories. Now they turned to the civil service, to office work, and to the military.[103]

Otherwise, married women's work showed more continuity than change. The draft introduced an unprecedented type of compulsion, but it brought to the workplace mainly women who had previously belonged to the working population. That unmarried women would work continued to go without saying except for those who were well situated. Working-class wives resented the draft but were unable to change it. By not awarding war brides full family allowances, the regime enforced continuity in the working lives of women who otherwise would have departed from the labor force. While longer hours increased employed women's burdens, they simply made more difficult the situation of women already juggling household and work responsibilities. Few women were introduced to this conflict by wartime measures.

Unable or unwilling to alter married women's habits of employment, the regime extended its reliance on young, single women. The Year of Duty, the RADwJ, and the Auxiliary War Service (*Kriegshilfsdienst*) required that young single women provide six months or a year of almost uncompensated service. Those who participated were exposed to ways of life and work that remained unknown to their married peers. Often serving far from home, they lived in barracks or with strange families. Noncombatant military service introduced hundreds of thousands to new roles, to a new discipline, and to new dangers. Whether they enthusiastically or reluctantly joined the war effort, women born roughly from 1918 to 1928 who remained single during the war contributed to it more directly than any other group of German women.

The working history of the unwed Elisabeth L. contrasts with that of Inge D., who remained in her comfortable apartment, whose absenteeism was judged mildly, and who was excused from work when she became pregnant. Elisabeth worked for an armaments factory early in the war. In 1941, at the age of twenty-one, she was drafted into the RADwJ. After a short period in the barracks, she became ill and was transferred to her home city of Berlin, where she completed her service as a cook, earned twenty-five pfennig daily, and lived with her parents. Following her six-month stint with the RADwJ,

Elisabeth worked for six months in the Auxiliary War Service in a grenade factory; here she earned one mark per day. She was then drafted into the army. In an army school on the Soviet border, she learned to operate a telex. Her next post was a Berlin suburb, where she received training as a radio operator. Her training complete, she was stationed in Denmark, where she remained ten months. Discouraged by Danish partisan activity and worried about their families in the bombed German cities, Elisabeth and her colleagues expressed doubts about the war. They were sent to the army school in Giessen for disciplinary action. Once there, however, they were simply assigned work on the home front; in the confused conditions of fall 1944, word of their traitorous remarks had not preceded them. As the western front approached, work ceased and Elisabeth was released. She returned to Berlin early in 1945 and was assigned a civilian position as telephone operator. Elisabeth had her first contact with the Soviets at her place of work: one evening, the language spoken on the other end of the phone was Russian.[104]

In September 1939, the quota for participants in the RADwJ was raised from fifty thousand to one hundred thousand. By the middle of the war, 25 to 30 percent of girls from the relevant years of birth worked for the RADwJ.[105] At the same time, young women who wished to enter waged or salaried work continued to perform their Year of Duty: 335,972 in 1940.[106] Both programs assigned tasks mainly in keeping with their original aims: to inculcate in young women an interest in agricultural and domestic work. By responding to a genuine need for labor in these sectors of the economy, however, the programs aggravated the shortage of female labor in industry and offices.[107]

Thus in the summer of 1941, a six-month period in the Auxiliary War Service was added to the half year in the RADwJ on farms or in households.[108] Women spent the second half-year mainly in armaments factories; the armed forces, public transportation, and hospitals also received female workers via the Auxiliary War Service. Two increases in quotas for the RADwJ followed shortly, first to one hundred thirty thousand and then to one hundred fifty thousand. Shortages of housing and supervisors led to delays in reaching these goals and made it impossible to raise them further. Despite this limitation, however, young, unwed women's labor was exhaustively engaged in the war economy. In September 1944, Party Chancellor Martin Bormann acknowledged that finding a hundred thousand women to take over searchlight batteries would not be easy: most women of the appropriate age were already at jobs designated indispensable for the war economy.[109]

If the regime remained too passive in the matter of married women's work, it probably intervened in single women's work more than was good for the economy. Urban teenage girls who might have been effective in offices or in industry proved a nuisance to farmers, and the Year of Duty and service in the RADwJ resulted in a constant rotation of labor that was an irritant to employers.[110] Nevertheless, the Year of Duty and the RADwJ had a tremendous impact on the young women who took part in them. Both programs typically required that young women leave their homes, and it brought them into unfamiliar—and sometimes dangerous—surroundings. It thus represented a much sharper break with the previous experiences of young single working women than did the wartime employment of married and older single women.

The Nazi leadership was adamant that girls and young women in these programs be housed communally if their work took them from their parents' homes. This arrangement would protect them from dangers such as too-close contact with foreign laborers living on the farms or unsupervised evenings in the cities. It would also create opportunities for political education. The difficulty of housing young women communally in rural areas and the relative ease of doing so in cities was a crucial factor in the increasing placement of RADwJ draftees in industry.[111] For many young women, this living situation was a great attraction.[112]

Although most members of the RADwJ performed work on the home front, and although they might have worked in factories or offices in peacetime, young women also labored in the administration of the occupied territories, including the racial reorganization of Eastern Europe. These women could have no doubt about the political nature of their work. Their assignments might include accustoming indigenous ethnic German families to their new privileged status or aiding in *Reichs*-Germans' settlement into the region. It might include the persecution of the native Slavic populations, sometimes as a result of the women's own requests to participate.

Melita Maschmann's history illustrates the opportunities the war presented for a young, single, ideologically committed woman. An activist since joining the League of German Girls in 1933 at age fifteen, she was frustrated by the bureaucratic routine and, in her opinion, mediocre minds she encountered in her work for the League's press and propaganda section. The war opened up a new world to her: the occupied East. The sight of starving, begging Poles left her unmoved, as did her travels through the Lodz ghetto. Instead, she was thrilled by the opportunity to make herself indispensable in a setting that demanded initiative rather than passive obedience to orders from Berlin. As the only female volunteer at the *Ost-*

deutsche Beobachter, the party newspaper, she battled overt hostility on the part of her male colleagues. When she became the first BDM-*Führerin* from Germany in the newly conquered territory of Warthegau, she was charged with organizing ethnic German girls whose inadequacy as the new elite deeply concerned her. In charge of a camp of female RADwJ volunteers, she supervised her group's expulsion of Poles from their ancestral homes and confiscation of their property. Maschmann found such challenges exhausting but exhilarating; she welcomed the opportunity to stretch her limits in the service of the Nazi cause.[113]

Late in the war, tens of thousands of RADwJ conscripts were assigned to military work. They thus joined hundreds of thousands of young women employed directly by the armed services, the Red Cross, and party organizations such as the SS. Childless married women could take on regular employment with these institutions, but military and related work was a much stronger preserve of single women than was civilian employment, and the RADwJ remained a draft of single women only.[114] Military work became a potent symbol of the war's impact on young, single women (Figs. 8 and 9).

Starting in the fall of 1943, women aged twenty to twenty-four in the RADwJ were assigned to service with the air force. A few months later, they began to take over antiaircraft guns and, in the last months of the war, searchlights. Some sixty-eight thousand women in the RADwJ were serving in or training for military capacities at the end of the war.[115]

The RADwJ preferred to assign military work to women who had already completed their regular labor service. This policy guaranteed that the draftees would be accustomed to discipline, and it ensured that the supply of RADwJ conscripts to industry would not be disrupted. It also meant that military service normally followed a year of civilian service—or two years for RADwJ veterans who had also performed a Year of Duty.[116] RADwJ draftees received only short leaves and were subject to having their periods of service adjusted as the military situation demanded. In April 1944, their service was extended to eighteen months, and, in November, their period of service was made indefinite.[117]

Like RADwJ recruits, female military employees' work took them into German-occupied Europe with provisions for only short leaves. Most auxiliaries performed secretarial or communications work; the air force assigned some to such work as searchlight maintenance and, in 1944, to the antiaircraft guns. Nurses and nurses' assistants found work in military infirmaries, and employees of the SS found work ranging from secretarial work to guard duty in concentration camps.[118] The best available statistics indicate that at

Figures 8 and 9. Auxiliary military service. Military-related service was a nearly exclusive preserve of single women and a powerful symbol of their extraordinary roles in wartime. In addition to experiencing the rigors of military discipline (figure 8, left), they found adventure, traveled (figure 9, right), and participated in the domination of the native populations. Courtesy Bundesarchiv.

least six hundred thousand women were regular employees of the armed forces alone; the true number is probably well over one million.[119]

If the Nazi leadership was divided about drafting women for civilian work, it was uniformly apprehensive about military-related service for women. Perhaps embarrassed by the need to draw on women or perhaps fearful of popular opinion, Bormann promoted word-of-mouth recruiting rather than open advertisement.[120] If women did have to perform military functions, their femininity must be preserved, and consideration of sexual difference permeated all levels of operation.[121] Although selection of female SS auxiliaries was considered to be particularly strict, a regional office instructed SS recruiters not to judge too harshly female applicants who were unable to answer such questions as "What does NSDAP stand for?" and "When did the *Führer* come to power?" "In general," the instructions read, "not much can be expected from women in terms of knowledge of politics and contemporary events, and correspondingly one cannot be too hard on failures in these areas." More important were women's answers to "practical" questions, such as "Why do ovens and irons have wooden rather than iron handles?"[122] An inspection of the school where SS auxiliaries were trained resulted in the recommendation that the common rooms be provided with "good pictures of SS men (for the development of the proper feeling for the later choice of a spouse)."[123] Women in military and related organizations were neither to be housed nor to dine with the troops or with male employees, and their social contacts were to be carefully supervised, partly in order to prevent sexual harassment by male colleagues.[124]

Despite the disadvantages of constituting a small female minority in a military culture, there is no evidence that young women resisted service with military organizations or with the party organizations that administered the occupied territories. The RADwJ was a draft, but regular employment with military and party organizations was not. Large numbers volunteered such service either because of their enthusiasm for the cause or because of the promise of adventure and companionship with other young women. Women stationed abroad could feel flattered at having been selected to represent German womanhood. By the time women were drafted for military functions, such as work with antiaircraft guns and searchlights, Germany had been heavily bombed and was fighting a defensive war. Protecting the country from further devastation was a goal with which few quibbled.[125]

Like their male counterparts, women who performed military functions and worked in the occupied territories eventually encountered the dangers of defeat. In early 1945, tens of thousands of female auxiliaries who had been released from their duties raced ahead of the quickly advancing Allies. Men are conspicuously absent from women's recollections at this point; female auxiliaries, ever subordinate to military men pledged to protect them, seem to have been left on their own once collapse was imminent.[126] Instead, small groups of auxiliaries set out on the long and dangerous road home, hoping to avoid capture and find their homes and families intact. Thousands were captured with the liberation of France, and perhaps twenty-five thousand joined the hundreds of thousands of civilian women in the East who were transported into the Soviet Union. There are no figures for casualties among members of the RADwJ and women's auxiliaries.[127]

—·—·—

Seven months after the war ended, a remarkable story appeared in *Sie*, Berlin's largest women's magazine. The piece described the return of a young woman from prisoner-of-war camp. While idealizing the heroine's desire for a return to a feminine sphere, the story included a straightforward admission that the woman had killed. The piece deserves to be quoted at length:

> There lay the street along which she had strode, one long year ago, cheerfully, confidently, even a bit proud of the uniform that revealed to all that she belonged to the German Anti-Aircraft Service (*Flak*); . . . that was once a uniform that made every young girl so endlessly proud . . .
>
> A million eyes still keep the daily watch for "him," the father, the husband, the brother, the friend, but few also discover among the released prisoners—the woman. Do they no longer remember that they met the woman in uniform everywhere, with steel helmet, with backpack, at the searchlight, yes, even at the guns? . . .
>
> At first she was not even upset [upon her capture]; oh, on the contrary, finally it could be proven once and for all that the "weaker sex," too, looked death in the eye. But then the girl looked at the enemy's dead. He was young . . . just like her brother; . . . her brother was also a flier; . . .
>
> Then all at once she wanted to lay aside her uniform, wanted nothing else but to leave, . . . to go home; she wanted to be a girl or a woman, . . . just wanted to cook, sew, play, or . . . oh, it didn't matter what, she just didn't want to kill any more! . . .
>
> From the distance sounds a little evening song, comes closer, fills the silent street for a moment and then moves away. They are young girls, strolling in long rows through the evening and lilting the melody in

amorous melancholy. The woman watches them a long time. They are
so young, like she had still been a year ago—back then, just four
hundred days ago.

If this story weren't extraordinary enough, the author's description of how
she came to write it should give pause for thought.[128] As she recalls, she
was asked to "paint a portrait, the portrait of a woman who is not just
pretty or clever, not just motherly, proud, courageous, or even doubtful, no,
a woman about whom everybody thinks—that could be me!"

The author's choice of an antiaircraft auxiliary worker as Everywoman
provides a striking contrast to most historians' emphasis on the regime's
failure to mobilize women for the war effort. Particularly for younger, single women—those who had been most affected by Nazi socialization and
who would be most affected by the postwar demographic imbalance—
mobilization for the war effort was more than thorough. It involved not
only putting in one's hours in the workplace but also leaving home, living
in barracks, and performing work—including auxiliary military service—
one otherwise would not have performed. It could mean participating in the
explicitly violent aspects of implementing the Nazi racial vision. The story
in *Sie* was unique, however; representations of women's losses and of their
survival work quickly overwhelmed memories of women's contribution to
the war effort. Even during the heyday of the woman standing alone—the
immediate postwar period—*this* woman standing alone was discreetly
overlooked.

Military-related work was not the only aspect of women's wartime
experience that postwar Germans largely ignored. As concerns about sexual promiscuity grew in the postwar period, many Germans would idealize
the Nazi period as a time of sexual order. Alternately, they would blame
Nazi radicalism for increased promiscuity, pointing, for example, to the
Nazis' evident encouragement of illegitimate childbearing. They reflected
little, however, on the wartime history of adultery, illicit sex, and forbidden
contact—that is, a history in which German women risked severe penalties
for straying from the regime's standards.

Military-related experience and the breaking of sexual rules illustrate
war's profound influence on the experience of women. They also suggest
two different ways the Second World War shaped the significance of marital status. The history of women's work points to a profound separation of
women according to marital status. While married women continued their
prior patterns of employment, with their decision to remain in or to depart

from the workforce depending mainly on their class status, young women who remained single experienced a different war. Only for war brides did marriage not bring the traditional freedom to make a decision about employment dependent on the family's financial situation. Even for such women, however, continued employment would mean civilian employment, not the military-related employment that was the experience of a cohort of single women.

The history of sexual misconduct, by contrast, points to a lessening distinction between married and single women. War disrupted the scene of safe female sexuality: the conjugal German home. But one of the basic distinctions between unmarried and married women had been the location of legitimate sexual expression—indeed, whether any sexual expression was legitimate. The removal of husbands as sexual partners profoundly affected the very meanings of "single womanhood," "wifehood," and the relationship between them.

Marital status did not divide women into neat categories of victim and victimizer, loser and beneficiary of Nazism. It did, however, affect the ways women were sometimes implicated in, sometimes damaged by, the Nazi regime. The Nazis' politicization of and incursions into the family make it impossible to speak of the family as a "private" sphere, distinct from the "public" arenas of politics, work, and war. Nevertheless, families did not cease to be important. They continued to shape individuals' relationship to work, military activity, and the state; they sometimes acted as a buffer between the state and the individual. As buffers, they might protect individuals from what was undesirable about the "outside" world—or they might deny individuals access to what was desirable in the "public" sphere. Thus, single women were more vulnerable to the state's campaign against asocials, even if wives came under increasing scrutiny during the war. Single women could much more easily be drafted for dangerous and unpleasant labor than could married women. Single women also, however, had access to new, exciting roles that were still unavailable to most married women. Single women could easily translate their nationalism, their devotion to the Nazi cause, or their simple desire to have an impact on the world around them into a job that was essential to the achievement of Nazi racial goals or a leadership position with a party organization. Wives who wanted to support the war or larger Nazi goals could perform "public" functions such as block warden or denunciator, which could easily be combined with housework. More often, however, they supported their husbands and children in *their* "public" roles. The Nazi regime required both: it needed women to handle antiaircraft guns and to organize female labor, and it needed women to raise the sons and provide comfort to the husbands who pulled the triggers at the front and in the shooting squads.

The war's impact on the significance of marital status was mixed. By removing millions of men, the war greatly reduced the importance of the married couple as a basic social cell of everyday life. Single women had previously stood outside this norm; now the norm itself was unclear. Wives of men at war remained wives, and this status determined their obligations to the labor market and the standards by which their sexual and social lives would be judged. Nevertheless, they confronted daily life without their husbands' companionship, support, or restrictions. Those who married men already at war lived the lives of single women but had the legal and personal identity of wives. After the war, many would continue to live as single women because their husbands failed to return or because divorce followed reunion. But they retained a personal identification with wifehood, and they enjoyed the legal benefits that accrued to widows, divorced women, and wives of missing men. Despite their never having experienced the day-to-day routine of marriage, their personal stake in marriage would help to shape their behavior and attitudes in the 1950s.

4   The Hour of the Women
Survival during Defeat and Occupation

"We need only let the wartime and postwar fates of our families and the families of our friends and acquaintances pass over us, and we will scarcely find *one* woman among them on whom these years did not impose and demand extraordinary things." So began the introduction of *The Woman in Our Time*, published in West Germany in 1954. "There was not only the separation and the tearing apart of families, the dark fears of the air war, evacuation, and loss of the home; there was not only the wartime death of the fiancé, the son, the husband, not only the evacuation from the home-town with all the unspeakable horrors left and right on the refugee trails, the grueling fear for a prisoner of war, the life-destroying wait for a miss-ing man year after year; . . . there was above all the inexorable need to deal with this fate every hour of every day."[1]

By the 1950s, memories of women's sacrifices, sufferings, and exertions in the absence of their men in the mid- and late 1940s had a firm place in German folk memory. Germans lived under different occupation regimes starting in 1945, but they shared most of the elements of daily experience that constitute Germans' memories of the "crisis years." During those years, framed by the 1942–43 defeat at Stalingrad and the western cur-rency reform and establishment of separate states in 1948–49, women experienced bombing raids, evacuation from endangered cities, flight from the East, rape, hunger, residence in badly damaged housing, the search for missing relatives, the scramble for life's basic necessities, and the efforts to clear the streets of rubble by hand. Last-minute call-ups of older and unfit men, the drafting of those previously protected by their civilian positions, and delays in releasing prisoners of war meant that the number of single women was at its height during these years. Popular memories of the "hour of the women" became inseparably intertwined with perceptions of a land of "women standing alone" (Fig. 10).[2]

East and West Germans eventually attached different meanings to women's activities from 1942 to 1948. By the 1950s, West Germans understood the "crisis years" as an era of "forced emancipation" which left women longing for the domestic roles they would subsequently enjoy.[3] In the 1980s, West German feminists offered a revised interpretation: the crisis years had been a "lost opportunity" for emancipation, as women's potential gains fell victim to a reconsolidation of male privilege.[4] In both cases, West Germans described the immediate postwar period as an extraordinary moment sandwiched between the Nazi model of *Kinder, Küche, Kirche* and the domesticity of the West German 1950s.

East Germans more often described movement in a single direction: wartime mobilization under an oppressive regime segued into extraordinary efforts during the postwar crisis, which in turn segued into greater workforce participation, economic independence, and public presence in the Democratic Republic. This last chapter might represent emancipation or it might represent the exchange of one oppressive regime by another; in either case, although the hardships of the immediate postwar period were exceptional, women's expanding functions were not. Instead, the hour of the women was a steppingstone to permanently changed roles for women.[5]

Clearly, the divergent subsequent histories of women in the two states contributed to differing perceptions of the hour of the women. Yet there were crucial regional differences in occupied Germany, even before the institutionalization of different gender roles in the two postwar states. For example, women's position in the paid labor force in the Soviet zone and in the western zones differed radically. In the western zones, efforts to coax women to the workplace alternated with an insistence on the greater importance of employment for veterans and the eventual goal of domesticity for women. Despite the visibility of the "women of the rubble" (*Trümmerfrauen*), who performed the heavy work of cleaning the rubble from Germany's bombed cities, women could recognize a familiar pattern: the use of women as reserve labor in times of labor shortage. In the Soviet zone, by contrast, measures intended to revolutionize women's position in the labor force coexisted with a harsh system of forced labor. Whatever this was—emancipation or bondage—it certainly was not familiar. The changing relationship of women to the labor force dominated public discussions of women in the Soviet zone.

Equally striking was a second difference among the zones: in the western zones, according to popular perception, women "fraternized" with the

Figure 10.   Standing alone. In the immediate aftermath of the war, millions of women of all marital states "stood alone." Marital status became almost insignificant as women's activities pulling their families and German society through the "crisis years" became the stuff of legend. Courtesy Landesbildstelle Berlin.

former enemy; in the Soviet zone, they were raped. This popular opposition was too starkly drawn and reflected a troubling tendency to consider consensual and violent sex two sides of the same coin. It did, however, reflect both the broad sweep of the landscape and Germans' feelings about their conquerors. Not only that—it prompted two distinct ways of thinking about single women's sexual lives. In the Soviet zone, the rapes loomed like an elephant in the living room, indiscussable but crowding out consideration of other aspects of women's sexual experience. In the western zones, fraternization became one of the most-discussed aspects of the occupation, and women's occupation-era experience came to be defined in large part by their sexual behavior.

The history of women standing alone between 1942 and 1948 thus provided crucial building blocks for the ways East and West Germans would think about women and marital status. The disruption of conjugal life might suggest victimhood; it might provide the opportunity for emancipation; or it might set the stage for moral degradation. In any case, these images of women and marital status were highly politicized, articulating a triangular relationship between the two halves of postwar Germany and between each half and the Nazi past.

.——.——.

Women's recollections of the war rarely begin with September 1, 1939. Instead, they open with their husbands' or fathers' departures, and they intensify with Stalingrad and the air war. Women's narratives emphasize their sufferings and losses and downplay their contributions to and rewards from the regime. For this reason, they can be misleading: as Chapter Three noted, nonpersecuted women gained with the outbreak of war. A generous system of family allowances allowed hundreds of thousands of working wives to give up their jobs; the war introduced war booty to the consumer economy; many young, single women found opportunities for travel, adventure, or a role in realizing the Nazi party's aims; and Germany's early successes in the war allowed women as well as men to feel pride in their country's military prowess. The war was begun with an intent to win, and German women stood to gain much by being on the victorious side.

Furthermore, insofar as tales of wartime sufferings are presented as reminders that German "bystanders" were among the victims of the Nazi regime, they distract attention from the tremendous support German men and women lent the regime before it began the war—or, more precisely, before it began to lose the war.[6] Finally, reminders of "Germans'" sufferings rarely force the listener to understand those sufferings in relation to other traumas caused, facilitated, or at least tolerated by the very people who, by losing the war, eventually experienced pain of their own. To the contrary, stories of "Germans'" sufferings tend to displace reminders of the hundreds of thousands of (German) Jews, Communists, and Socialists forced to emigrate before the war; (German) "asocials" and physically and mentally disabled people "euthanized," sterilized, or institutionalized; and (German) criminals and political opponents who withstood torture and spent years in prison or concentration camp, often to die there. They draw attention away from the East European Jewish civilization obliterated by the genocide; the millions of Poles evicted from their homes and villages in order to "Germanize" eastern lands; the tens of millions of Europeans killed in the Germans' aggressive war or imported into the *Reich* as slave labor; the tens of millions who died in German concentration and prisoner-of-war camps; and the hundreds of millions of weakened, displaced, and traumatized survivors of all of these.

Women's retellings of their war experiences conspicuously omit such points, something that has deservedly raised a few eyebrows among women's historians.[7] But they are rarely intentionally disingenuous. Instead, they, like many oral histories, are self-centered reflections on events that demand a broader perspective. Women's recollections of the war focus on the events that most dramatically affected their lives: bombing raids, evacuation, flight, widowhood, rape, and hunger. Whatever the shortcomings of typical "German women's" reflections, those reflections became the basis for the legend of the hour of the women.[8]

And whatever their shortcomings, German women's war stories are indeed dramatic tales, leaving little doubt that their tellers suffered genuine traumas. Of Germany's prewar population of roughly eighty million (including annexed territories), twenty million were removed for military or related service during the war, half of them before the invasion of the Soviet Union in June 1941. The cities hit by bombs and evacuation orders in the second half of the war were inhabited mainly by women, children, and the elderly. Night after night, women woke to the sound of sirens, dressed their children, grabbed their belongings, and ran to the nearest cellar or bunker. After the "all clear" was sounded, and if no damage had been done, they returned home to soothe their children to sleep and salvage what was left of the night for themselves. Germany's city women, even if they and their homes were untouched by bombs, lived the second half of the war with little sleep and shattered nerves.

Millions of German women, however, did lose their homes, members of their families, or their lives. By the end of the war, some 4.11 million apartments were destroyed and millions more damaged; fourteen million people were without homes before refugees added to this number. Perhaps six hundred thousand died in air raids, three-quarters of them civilians.[9] Those who emerged from the bomb shelters to find that their apartments had been hit set about extinguishing the fires, rescuing their surviving belongings, and, if possible, making at least a portion of their apartments livable. If their apartments were uninhabitable, they might move in with relatives, but conditions were cramped. If they worked in the city but had no relatives or friends with extra rooms, they were assigned to live with strangers who had rarely volunteered to share their space.

Beginning in 1943, ten million people, mainly women and children, were evacuated from Germany's cities. But sex did not qualify an adult for evacuation; rather, nonemployed status or responsibility for small children did. Working women without children remained in the endangered cities, as did employed mothers unless their children were very young.[10] Women who had seen their husbands, fathers, or brothers sent into danger now remained in dangerous places themselves as their children departed. Or they accompanied their children, leaving support networks behind and knowing that if their apartments were now hit, they would be unable to salvage their property.

The story of the Darmstadt family F. illustrates the cumulative effects of the separation of marriage partners, bombing raids, homelessness, and evacuation. In 1939, Herr F. was drafted, leaving his wife with their two children: three-year-old Gisela and one-year-old Willy. Frau F. worked as a letter carrier; her mother, who lived nearby, watched the children late afternoons, when the day-care center closed.

In the last years of the war, Frau F. and her children spent many nights in air-raid shelters. On the night of September 11–12, 1944, their shelter was hit. They ran to another, from which they also soon had to flee. Willy's clothes caught fire; as Frau F. beat out the flames, Gisela disappeared. She was never found. With burn wounds, Frau F. and Willy made their way to Frau F.'s sister-in-law, who, like Frau F., her mother, and two-thirds of Darmstadt's population, had been left homeless by the raid. The extended family had been able to save only a few linens and two suitcases full of clothing. The group spent the next three days in the open air and the nights in an air-raid shelter. Then Frau F. took Willy and her mother to relatives in the countryside; Frau F. returned, as required by law, to her post in Darmstadt. She and her sister-in-law were assigned a room in an apartment with several other bombed-out families. With Herr F. at war, Gisela presumably dead, and Willy and Frau F.'s mother evacuated, Frau F. lived out the remainder of the war in Darmstadt.[11]

Women had already learned that they could shoulder the extra burdens of paid work and housework in war. But recovering from bombing raids and evacuating one's family were tasks for which there was no model. Both required the re-creation—not the mere maintenance—of a household; both called for heavy physical labor; both involved entanglements with the bureaucracy to ensure continuation of ration cards, residence permits, family allowances, and other entitlements. If mother and children were separated, evacuation meant maintaining an overview of family members separated by great distances. For many women, these were the episodes through which they first discovered their own capabilities.[12]

Or they discovered their competence as they fled west, ahead of the Soviet army. For some, this was not their first move. Large numbers had moved east to "Germanize" Polish territories (thus forcing Poles onto their own refugee trail a few years earlier); others had been evacuated to the East, out of the range of English and U.S. bombers; another group had been stationed in the East with the *Reich* Labor Service or with military units.

The largest number fleeing the East, however, were natives, now leaving their lifelong homes.

The 4.5 million who fled during the last months of the war and the chaotic period before official transports began in 1946 belonged mainly to female-headed families.[13] With as many possessions as they could carry, they traveled by bicycle, horse-drawn cart, and foot. They faced roads blocked for military use and a crippled system of railroads. As they progressed west, they arrived in badly damaged cities that already had a sizable native homeless population. Their treks often lasted weeks.

Germans fleeing westward wanted to be in a portion of Germany conquered by the Western Allies rather than by the Soviet Union. Germans could reasonably expect a much harsher payback from the Soviets than from the Western Allies. Germans' recent conduct in the East, however, was only one of many factors contributing to women's fears of the coming Soviet conquest. German stereotypes of semi-human peoples of the East had a centuries-long history, and the Nazi party had made portrayals of "Red Hordes," "Tartars," "Huns," and "Asiatics" part of its racial and political vocabulary. As the war drew to a close, depictions of Soviet brutalities, and specifically of rape, became an important tool in urging Germans to fight to the last breath.[14]

As the first refugees brought news west, they confirmed Germans' worst fears. "Everyone knew already, everyone had already heard, that the Russians raped a lot of women, etc., and that the Americans, they would hand out chocolate."[15] Germans' expectations of gentle treatment by the Western Allies were sometimes disappointed, but their fears of particularly brutal experiences in the East would be validated. Estimates of the numbers of rapes at the hands of Soviet soldiers range widely, from the tens of thousands to two million. Whatever the precise numbers, rape was a common experience for women in eastern parts of the old *Reich*, and fear of rape was universal.[16] Confronted with the conquering armies, German women were left largely to their own devices. When German men were present, they were rarely able to provide any defense, and they sometimes seemed all too eager to trade women's safety for their own.[17]

Women's immediate reactions to rape varied widely. For some, it was one problem among many: a horrible episode, but so were many other events of those weeks.[18] For others, rape was an earth-shattering experience. The fact that rape was often accompanied by shooting—either of the victim, of others with her, or simply reckless shooting into the air—meant that women had to fear rape as a mortal danger and not "just" as a painful and traumatic episode. Some families and fiancés reacted with disgust even as women returned tattered and bleeding; others felt but could not express their sympathy.[19] Where internal injuries, sexually transmitted disease, or pregnancy resulted, women's feelings of lasting damage were confirmed.[20]

Bombings, flight, and rape: these experiences, and not work for the war economy or for Nazi organizations, constituted the "home front" recalled by German women who did not suffer persecution. Many had surprised themselves with their capabilities and were proud to have saved their families and some possessions. And they were relieved the war was over—no more bombs, and their husbands, if they still lived, would be coming home soon. In the meantime, though, they still faced a brutal struggle for survival.

.——.——.

Even before the war, Frau P. had not had an easy life.[21] Born to an unwed mother, she grew up in a children's home. She became a household servant and had relationships with two men, each of whom left her when she became pregnant. At twenty-six, she married a house painter; two more children followed. Her husband was drafted in 1941 and fell in 1944. Frau P. and her four children were evacuated to the East. After the war they returned with only the clothes on their backs. Now, back in Berlin, Frau P.'s real nightmare began.

Every room in her apartment had been badly damaged; none was weatherproof. Surrounded by ruins, the apartment could be entered only by climbing through a hole in the wall. During the first winter, the children spent weeks in bed to avoid freezing, and the second winter was worse. The pipes burst repeatedly, sending water throughout the apartment. Before Frau P. could bail out the rooms, the water froze. The family retreated to the warmest room, a tiny, windowless nook that could be heated to twenty-five degrees Fahrenheit. For five weeks Frau P. used a gas flame as auxiliary heat—until the gas was cut off because the household had exceeded its ration. Frau P. and her oldest son collected wood in the forest; as this became impossible because the boy had no winter clothing for the excursions, the family turned to its furniture. By the end of the winter, the household of five possessed three beds, a table, and a kitchen cabinet.

The family often finished its rations by the tenth of the month, and its winter supply of potatoes froze and thus became inedible in January 1947. Frau P.'s in-laws, who lived on the land, twice sent potatoes, but the shipments never arrived, and Frau P. expended much time, effort, and money in unsuccessful efforts to trace them. Welfare payments were cut from RM 135 to RM 100 in the fall of 1946; Frau P. supplemented the family's income with part-time janitorial work. After the fall of 1946, the family's total income was RM 130 per month. Rent was RM 40, leaving RM 90 for other expenses. A kilogram of flour on the Berlin black market cost RM 80.[22]

Frau P. wanted to support her family, and she felt like a beggar at the welfare office. She thought remarriage might ease her situation but had no time to meet men and, in any case, feared finding herself pregnant and abandoned once more. Under the strain of her hopeless situation, she lost her composure easily. This embarrassed her, so she steered away from all social contact. Her one comfort was that she could, in the end, prevent further decline. Suicide was still within her means.

Frau P.'s situation was extreme but illustrative. Germans faced unmanageable shortages of housing, fuel, and food. Women who had survived bombings, flight, and rape now faced the task of keeping themselves and their families alive in Germany's wasteland.

Germans had suffered housing shortages since industrialization. In 1933, after extensive Weimar-era building projects, one in twelve households still had no apartment of its own.[23] Wartime bombings had wreaked havoc on this already inadequate stock. In the three western occupation zones, 45 percent of the prewar housing stock had been either destroyed or severely damaged.[24] Yet the population grew as refugees poured in: by 1949, refugees constituted one-quarter of the population of the Soviet zone.[25] In North Rhine-Westphalia, 41 percent of households lived as subtenants.[26] A study of 154 Berlin households in the winter of 1946–47 showed 30 percent living in rooms under forty-one degrees and another 30 percent in rooms from forty-two to fifty degrees Fahrenheit.[27] Fifty percent of all apartments in the Soviet zone were smaller than thirty-five square meters, and only 20 percent had more than fifty square meters.[28] Hundreds of thousands lived in refugee camps, in bunkers, and in train stations.

The prospects for eating were no more rosy than were the prospects for finding shelter. In mid-May 1945, housewives and the unemployed in Berlin could claim a daily ration of 300 grams of bread, 400 grams of potatoes, 30 grams of grain, 20 grams of meat, and 7 grams of fat.[29] The housewives' ration card, the lowest in all zones, was alternately nicknamed the "ascension pass" and the "ticket to the graveyard."[30] Rations declined through the first two years of the occupation, and full rations were often unavailable. In the summer of 1946, holders of the lowest ration cards in the Soviet zone received 738 to 961 calories daily.[31] In November of that year, the average weight for women in U.S.-occupied Hessen was 93.5 pounds; men, whose health had worsened in prisoner-of-war camps, weighed an average of 92.3 pounds.[32] Children's essays on "my most beautiful day" were shocking enough to warrant publication in Hamburg's major weekly: "My most beautiful day was my birthday, when I could sleep all alone in a bed." "My most beautiful day was recently, when I got a pair of wood sandals from our shoemaker." "My most beautiful day was the day my brother Friedrich died. Since then I have a coat and shoes and socks and a knit vest."[33]

Feeding and clothing families and keeping them warm was women's work. Eighty-five percent of women who responded to a survey in Berlin in January 1947 had dependents.[34] They had none of the familiar resources for attending to their households. Women normally turned their husbands' incomes, their own incomes, or pensions into food, clothing, and heat for their families. Now many were widowed, and husbands in prisoner-of-war camps sent no money. The Allies had eliminated family allowances and war widows' pensions because of their militaristic connotations. The armaments factories and military offices where women had worked were closed, and those who had employment brought home useless currency. Their bank accounts were frozen, and many of their material possessions had been lost to bombs or flight. With few means for obtaining basic necessities and with those necessities in short supply anyway, women almost literally had to make something out of nothing in order to feed their dependents.

Their success in doing so made this the "hour of the women." Women hauled wood from forests and stole coal from trucks, bartered with farmers, stood in endless lines before shops, and tended gardens. They repaired clothing late into the night, gave part of their meager rations to their dependents, learned to make bread from acorns and soap from ash, and tried to keep the peace among short-tempered, overcrowded, starving family members. In 1947, a Leipzig newspaper sang the praises of such women in maudlin, but not entirely unrealistic, tones:

> Women of all social classes are out there, riding and walking for hours, undernourished and overtired, a day's work still ahead of them when they come home exhausted late afternoons. And when that too is done, when the children are long in bed, then they lay their aching heads in their hands, think of the man who is perhaps still in prison, worry about feeding their loved ones in the coming winter, and can comfort themselves with only one thought: they've done what they could![35]

The black market became the most prominent symbol of unorthodox but socially acceptable survival strategies. Perhaps 85 percent of Berlin's population was active on the black market in 1947, and black markets flourished in all German cities.[36] Unlike after-hours mending, black-market transactions took place in public spaces and were illegal. Unlike prostitution, however, they did not involve sex. Although Germans resented the black market's big profiteers, who were usually male, they did not condemn the black market as a whole. If it had not been for the black market, consumers would not have had access to many essential goods. Women occasionally came under unique criticism for allowing their offspring to witness their black-market activity or for sending their children to steal or barter, but in general contemporaries attached little stigma to women's illegal but nonsexual survival strategies.[37] This was in part because the boundaries between legal and illegal activity were so fleeting. For most, black-market activity was an extension of housework. In order to mend their families' clothes, women might seek out needles on the black market; if scraps of fabric were left over after the mending, they might be transformed into a doll that could be exchanged for a hat.

Such transactions were unauthorized, but with official distribution mechanisms utterly inadequate, they ensured that Germans' health did not deteriorate even further than it did. Dependent on the underground economy to feed the working population but simultaneously struggling to bring order to the economy, occupation authorities pursued inconsistent policies. By raiding centers of black-market activity, they hoped to capture major speculators and their stocks; minor players, such as the woman trading a doll for a hat, were also picked up.[38] The police confiscated the contents of the backpacks women carried from their bartering trips to the countryside, but municipal officials often welcomed the importation of food to the cities. With food a burning political issue, ruling parties sometimes tried to curry favor with the electorate by officially tolerating unauthorized economic activity.[39]

Unlike illicit sexual activity, black-marketeering and unauthorized bartering did not become skeletons in women's closets; they were simply facts of life. Women who used such strategies recalled their success with pride, even if their actions were illegal. "How I ran to all ends of the earth to get that one room, how I struggled under the load while bartering for food in the countryside, how my mother and I sewed night and day, just to get a bit of flour or sugar—it was all utterly exhausting. But I felt good doing it. I felt very strong. I had to care for my children and my mother—and I did."[40]

Occupation authorities, however, were not pleased. The problem was not so much the unauthorized transactions, as long as they remained small-scale. The problem was that while women devoted much energy to the underground economy, they seemed uninterested in helping to rebuild the legitimate economy. This lack of interest was of little concern to families and neighbors, who agreed that survival must take precedence. But it aggravated both occupation authorities and German bureaus of labor.

Immediately after the war, many women wanted legitimate work but could not get it. With the closing of state, party, and military offices, women lost their clerical positions; now municipalities and employers sought heavy laborers to rebuild the cities and revitalize the mines. Employers, anticipating the return of veterans, fired women who still had work.[41] Many women's husbands did not immediately return, however, and those who did were often unable to work. Few of the forms of state support that had allowed some women to stay away from the workplace were available. In the Soviet zone in the winter of 1945–46, there was one "women's position" for every fourteen women seeking jobs.[42]

As the months rolled by and the economy sunk ever deeper into chaos, however, even employed women found themselves unable to make ends meet. Rations, inadequate in any case, were often unavailable. Women needed to supplement them by barter or with goods purchased on the black market, where the Reichsmark they earned was almost worthless. Furthermore, time spent at work was time away from bread lines and the forests where one might scrounge for firewood or mushrooms. "I can't afford to work—I have to feed my family," went the joke.[43] Large numbers of women quit work or gave up their search for it, convinced that their energies were better spent elsewhere. Women, who had accounted for 35.2 percent of the employed before the war, composed only 28.3 percent of the labor force in the U.S. and British zones in 1947, despite their great demographic majority.[44]

Women's discovery that the underground economy had more to offer than the legitimate economy coincided with employers' discovery that they still needed female labor. Preemptive firings of women turned out to have been premature since large numbers of men languished in prison camp, and those who returned were often unfit for work or disqualified from their former positions because of their Nazi background.[45] Certain critical sectors of the economy, such as agriculture, had always relied heavily on female labor. This was no time to be hounding women from the workplace. Occupation authorities resolved to draw on the "reserves" of women who, according to directives in all four occupation zones, were required to register at the employment offices.[46] But registration was no cure-all. In addition to exemptions based on age or physical disability, women could be excused because of household responsibilities.[47] Those who could not claim exemption often avoided registration entirely. The time freed up for the underground economy more than made up for the foregone ration card and the need to duck the military police, who periodically demanded that Germans show their papers. With part of the potential female workforce legally exempt and another portion evading registration, the labor exchanges had few women to draw on. Registered female unemployment in the British zone in the fall of 1947 was under 1 percent.[48]

Official responses to this problem differed according to visions of women's employment in the longer term. In the western zones, efforts to bring women into the labor force were tempered by two assumptions. The first was a general principle: that women's employment was desirable only as long as the economy required it. When this was not the case, women should perform unpaid labor for their families, and men should enjoy greater privileges in the labor market. Although some heirs to the socialist and liberal feminist traditions contested this assumption, their voices were weak, especially as they softened their statements in order to separate themselves from developments in the Soviet zone.[49] The second assumption regarded the application of this principle to the historical moment. Western economic authorities believed that the return of men from prison camp would quickly render female labor superfluous.

For both ideological and practical reasons, women in the western zones experienced a fair degree of continuity in their working lives. As had been the case during the war, the need for female labor resulted in recruitment drives and even some compulsion. But all this recruitment was half-hearted: it conflicted with the conviction that women's most important role was in the household, and it conflicted with expectations about women's role in the labor market in the long term. The result was contradictory and inconsistent treatment. On the one hand, women's legal responsibility to the labor market was limited: there would be relatively little compulsion. On the other hand, employment offices resented women who withheld their labor, and punished women perceived as slackers.

In the Soviet zone, economic planners operated from different assumptions. First came general principles. Equal rights for women, particularly as workers, belonged to the communist and socialist visions. Regardless of the sexual division of labor in their own families; regardless of their lack of interest in having women occupy leadership positions; regardless of the fact that the political system they helped to shape had little respect for equality between the governed and the governors—even male functionaries in the Social Democratic and Communist parties had internalized Bebel's, Engels's, and Lenin's writings on the economic liberation of women under socialism. There was a practical angle to this: Communists hoped to improve their poor standing among women and to enlarge the labor force by enhancing women's workplace rights. But this was a principled political position, not a purely opportunistic one. Reminders of women's equal rights on the labor market, whatever the state of the economy and whether or not they could rely on a husband for support, appear in talks and papers never intended for public consumption.[50]

The second factor distinguishing the Soviet from the western zones was the understanding of the historical moment. As Soviet occupation authorities and East German economic planners saw it, the shortage of male labor would be a long-term problem; the return of prisoners of war would ease it only a bit. Furthermore, the shortage of male labor was not concentrated in positions that could be quickly filled by unskilled women. None of those concerned with reconstructing the East German economy believed that temporarily drawing on a "reserve" of female labor would solve the woes of the labor market. In official publications, in public assemblies, and in closed-door sessions, labor officials insisted that women would have to become a permanent part of the entire labor force at all levels.[51] The sense of urgency about utilizing women's labor brought with it a commitment to increasing their vocational skills, which implied improved status. In combination with the Soviets' resolve to make the Germans pay at least part of the price of the Soviet recovery, however, it also contributed to the large-scale use of women as forced laborers.

Authorities in all four zones introduced mandatory labor for former Nazis and their dependents. Despite the later heroization of the women of the rubble, contemporaries knew that those performing this undesirable work were often assigned to it because of their Nazi histories. Beyond this, while mandatory registration in the western zones constituted compulsory labor, the regulations brought a relaxation of the inequities that had plagued the Nazi system. Age limits alone—and not previous work experience—determined who must register, and exemptions for women with family responsibilities were more generous. Thus the mere fact of prior employment no longer condemned a working-class woman with young children to the factory floor (or the rubble heap); instead, middle-class women who had not worked previously but had fewer household responsibilities were to take their place. In practice, bourgeois women found ways to avoid employment if they so desired, but so, often, did working-class women, and this had been far from the rule under the Nazis.

Other programs in the western zones also seemed harsh on the surface but brought a relaxation of compulsory labor. In order to supply agricultural and domestic workers, some states directed the revival of the Year of Duty.[52] Labor offices were to return to their original professions agricultural and domestic workers who had performed other work during the war, even though their war work was often more skilled and better-paid.[53] It is not clear, however, whether the labor offices followed such instructions. The reintroduction of a year of service attracted virulent protest, and there is no evidence that it was ever implemented.

In contrast, forced labor was a fact of life for tens of thousands of women in the Soviet zone, and although it was certainly no harsher than the Nazi system of slave labor, it targeted a different group of people. To the German women affected, it represented a new experience.

Compulsory labor in the Soviet zone fell under many rubrics. The mildest was the labor office's draft, which German women had known under the Nazis and to which West German women were also vulnerable. Since there was a labor shortage, women usually had some choice of positions, even if some had no choice about whether to work. The Allied Control Council, however, also permitted the labor offices to assign persons to specific positions against their will. Distinct from measures regarding punitive labor, this order accounted for 12.7 percent of assignments in the Soviet zone in July 1947.[54]

Other forms of involuntary labor were considerably harsher. In addition to capturing approximately twenty-five thousand female military personnel, the Soviets rounded up hundreds of thousands of German civilians in the last months of the war and transported them to labor camps inside the Soviet Union. In locations where the military draft had made men of working age scarce, women in their late teens constituted the majority of those deported.[55] "The abducted" (*die Verschleppten*), as they came to be known, lived, labored, and, in large numbers, died in terrible conditions. The impoverished Soviet Union was unable to feed even its own population and was ill-equipped to do more for prisoners. Germans had been imported explicitly to repair the damage done by their own country and thus elicited little sympathy, and labor camps for Germans expanded a gulag system that had hardly been gentle even to Soviet citizens. Nevertheless, these women saw themselves neither as prisoners of war nor as political prisoners, and they were struck by the randomness of their fate in having been rounded up.[56]

For those who avoided the transports, the uranium mines on the East German-Czechoslovak border became the most potent symbol of forced labor in the Soviet zone.[57] Germans were better informed about the abysmal working and housing conditions than they were about the dangers of radiation, but this information was enough to ensure that precious few volunteered. The labor offices, ordered by the mines' Soviet administration to provide tens of thousands of workers, utilized the draft. But few experienced miners or even strong men were available, and word of demands for new workers sent potential recruits fleeing westward. As a result, the labor offices drafted men who had no experience in mining or even of heavy labor, men who were physically unfit, men who had been rounded up in black-market raids or caught trying to cross the border, and, by the end of 1948, at least twenty thousand women.[58] Making the false claim that forced labor for all women was Communist policy, West German reports published lurid descriptions about the use of women in the uranium mines.[59] Even more sober research, however, reveals not only horrible working and living conditions but also severe compulsion. Workers were jailed or deprived of their already meager rations if their supervisors felt they were not working hard enough. Labor offices hunted down and returned workers who escaped, whether those workers had originally come as conscripts, criminals, or volunteers.[60]

But if the stick in the Soviet zone was harder, the carrot was also sweeter. In August 1946, the military government announced equal pay for equal work. The occupation authorities banned sexual discrimination in education, and they removed almost all the prohibitions against women in certain types of employment.[61] East German economic planners insisted that they intended a radical transformation of women's paid labor from unskilled, subordinate work in typically "female" positions to skilled work in all areas of endeavor. Not only would public officials remove legal barriers; they would also promote higher training for women, the entry of women into nontraditional fields, and women's assignment to positions with increased responsibility (Fig. 11).

By contrast, measures to improve the status of working women in the western zones were half-hearted at best. Shortly after the Soviet military government decreed equal pay for equal work, the Allied Control Council released a directive *permitting* equal pay for equal work.[62] Few employers in the western zones leapt at the opportunity to raise women's wages. Limiting themselves to a far milder extension of rights than applied in the Soviet zone, employers and labor offices in the western zones preferred to rely on the equally mild level of compulsion they could exert to bring women to the workplace.

The divergent fates and symbolic uses of the women of the rubble highlight the differences in women's labor in the Soviet and western zones.

Figure 11. Focusing on labor. In the Soviet zone, the image of women standing alone was strongly shaped by the efforts to increase female participation in the labor force. This feature article emphasizes that laboring women will benefit from the new order, which brings equal pay for equal work, health care, and expanded vocational training. It urges a vote for the SED's National Front coalition in upcoming local elections. *Neue Berliner Illustrierte* 2/30 (1946).

Rubble clearance was not an occupation women enthusiastically entered in any zone. Lacking volunteers, occupation authorities assigned to the job former members of Nazi organizations as well as dependents of those implicated.[63] When this policy did not provide an adequate labor pool, the same authorities turned to a system of mandatory labor among the general population. Some women volunteered for the task, not for the poor pay but for the better ration cards they received as heavy laborers. However mixed their motivations, women set to the tedious, heavy work of moving, cleaning, and sorting building material for reuse—the first step of Germany's physical reconstruction. Women of the rubble peopled the streets of many German cities; they constituted 5 to 10 percent of employed women in Berlin.[64]

All four zones shared this striking visual image, but there the similarities ended. According to law, women were prohibited from entering apprenticeships that might have allowed them to advance in the construction industry. This law was strenuously enforced in the western zones; in the Soviet zone the prohibition was lifted. In the western zones, labor offices replaced women with men as quickly as possible; in the Soviet zone, labor offices actively recruited women for training that would prepare them for a lifetime of employment in construction.[65]

In addition, recollections of the women of the rubble served different purposes in East and West German official culture in the 1950s. As the woman of the rubble became a symbol of reconstruction in West Germany, she seemed to belong to a world light years away from the economic miracle. She was a heroic figure, but a figure of yore—no woman in her right mind would want to return to such labor. The contrast between her hard labor and the domestic comforts of the 1950s symbolized the remarkable distance West Germans had traveled since the "rubble years."[66]

In East Germany, the woman of the rubble was likewise a heroic figure—but she represented the brave new world, not a thankfully bygone era. In 1952, when official West German publications were using images of women clearing rubble in East Germany as anti-Communist propaganda, the GDR's National Building Program (*Nationales Aufbauprogramm*) presented similar images positively in its recruiting posters and in the scarf worn by participants.[67] In part, East Germany's use of this affirmative image reflected the fact that, in 1952, it still had more rubble to clear than did West Germany. But it also characterized the contrast between the western assumption that heavy, dirty work for women could only be an emergency measure, and the eastern attitude that women's entry into male professions was part of a positive transformation of women's work.[68]

In June 1948, the three western zones, already unified for most administrative and economic purposes, introduced a new currency, the *Deutschmark* (DM). Later that month, the Executive Committee (*Parteivorstand*) of the Socialist Unity Party (SED) released a two-year plan for the Soviet zone, initiating a planned economy to begin in 1949. Both halves of Germany began a transition from the provisional economy of the occupation to long-term economic structures. An adjustment of women's place in the labor force would be part of this process.

In the case of the future West Germany, this transition meant a reversal of directions. When the DM was introduced in June 1948, labor became more expensive, and employers cut back. In a position to be more selective, employers finally implemented their stalled plans to reduce their female work force.[69] Even women who had worked only sporadically or not at all prior to currency reform, however, suddenly needed legitimate work. Their skills on the black market had become useless, and those who had managed to live on savings could do so no longer.

Women thus flooded the labor exchanges. In North Rhine-Westphalia, there were 46.3 female applicants for every 100 openings in June 1948; a month later, there were 122.7.[70] When they could not find work, women applied for unemployment compensation. Their applications were considered by the very people they had so frustrated over the preceding years by claiming exemptions from employment or by failing to register. Now, the labor offices had the upper hand.

Three days after the currency reform, the Central Office for Labor of the combined western zones released a decree concerning applicants for unemployment compensation who had previously avoided employment. "During a time when every productive hand was most urgently needed . . . in order to satisfy the need for labor for the most urgent, life-essential work, these people defrayed their costs by business that was partly dark, partly damaging to the legitimate economy. . . . Whoever can give no adequate explanation for the fact that he withheld himself from the labor market in the past will probably not be able to be seen in the future as available for work without further consideration."[71] This was a critical point: those not classified as "available for work" were not eligible for placement through the employment offices, nor were they eligible for unemployment compensation if they found no work.

The decree was technically sex neutral (despite the generic "he"), but provincial officials understood it to refer to women. The Minister of Labor in North Rhine-Westphalia singled out young women who had previously claimed that they could not work because they were needed in their parents' households.[72] In Hessen, single mothers, home workers, and women over fifty were eligible for unemployment compensation only if they had worked prior to currency reform.[73] While women who had been employed prior to June 1948 were pushed out of work, those who had not been employed were denied assistance in finding work and unemployment compensation when their circumstances changed. In August 1948, 30.6 percent of registered unemployed but only 14.7 percent of recipients of unemployment compensation were female.[74] West German women's refusal to act as a reserve labor force during the "crisis years" became a weapon in denying them equal rights after the crisis was resolved.

In the western zones, the legacy of the occupation period for employed women was a negative one. As concern for the family brought hostility toward women's employment in the 1950s, women who wanted paid work had to contend with institutional memory as well. One of the guiding principles of labor exchanges and unemployment offices, as they shifted to the DM economy, was that women who had avoided employment during the "hunger years" were suspect. And women came out of the occupation era with no legal structures, such as a guarantee of equal pay for equal work or a removal of prohibitions from traditionally male jobs, that could help them to articulate a claim to better treatment.

The East German transition over 1948 represented less a change of direction than an intensification of efforts and a smoothing out of rough edges. As was the case in the western zones, unemployment—especially female unemployment—rose with currency reform.[75] But with economic planning, women did not become surplus labor; rather, they became more necessary than ever. The two-year plan called for 250,000 new workers, mostly women; it mandated the expansion of childcare facilities and the integration of women into training programs. The February 1949 guidelines of the Commission on the Economy outlined the systematic replacement of male by female workers—concurrent with the systematic replacement of female by male workers in the West.[76] The point in the Soviet zone was not to give women preference over men; rather, it was to increase female employment while freeing up men for heavier tasks such as mining.[77] While female workers in the western zones were welcomed only in fields that were undesirable for men,[78] women in the Soviet zone were explicitly urged to move into men's positions.

At the same time women were gaining increased access to the labor market, the most coercive elements of the pre-1949 period were fading from view. They did not disappear: the Soviets continued to demand additional labor for the uranium mines well into the 1950s, and many of the "abducted" did not return until years later. But as East Germans took control of ever-greater parts of the economy, those sectors administered directly by the Soviets became less the rule, more the exception. Compulsion in the economy of the Democratic Republic was, by and large, gentler, more bureaucratic: the withholding of pensions, for example, to compel war widows to work.

What were East German women to make of their role as workers, which their rulers seemed bent on transforming? Was paid labor a privilege that had been unfairly reserved for men? Or was it a burden for which men, thankfully, had been primarily responsible? Women had long been aware of the ambiguities of their marginality as workers. On the one hand, employed women had long been frustrated by their poor pay, their exclusion from vocational training, and the fact that men had first crack at most jobs. On the other hand, recent history had reminded women that marginalization from the labor force could be a relief. The labor draft had weighed

heavily on single and working-class women during the war, and the preva-
lence of forced labor in the Nazi economy had demonstrated just how
undesirable the role of worker could be. Indeed, the very women who had
been sheltered from mandatory employment by the Nazi ideals of *Kinder,
Küche, Kirche* were among those most familiar with forced labor: slave
laborers from occupied Eastern Europe had become agricultural workers
and domestic servants in their households.

The Soviet occupation drove home the extremes of this ambiguity to
masses of East German women in their own working lives. Equal pay for
equal work was no longer some pie-in-the-sky goal; suddenly it was policy. Furthermore, the SED asserted the need to overcome job segregation
and women's lack of training, which did even more than separate wage
scales did to depress women's earnings. At the same time, forced labor was
no longer the lot of some despised "others." Now it was the lot of "ordinary" German women. Women's mixed feelings about paid labor were
turning into the profound schizophrenia that would characterize the first
decades of the Democratic Republic. And the public discussion of women's
work in the Soviet zone, neatly divided between the glowing reports produced in East Germany and the horror stories propagated in the West,
reflected this tension.

. —— . —— .

The divergent effects of the occupation on women's sexual worlds were just
as striking as the differences between East and West German women's position in the labor force. While memories (and continuing threats) of rape
permeated the atmosphere in the Soviet zone, fraternization and prostitution created a new sexual culture in the western zones, especially the British
and U.S. zones. Both contributed to sexual conservatism in the 1950s, but
the overtones of this conservatism owed significant differences to the legacy
of the occupation. In East Germany, popular sexual conservatism deplored
not only the perceived sexual radicalism of Communist ideology but also
the demonstrated sexual danger of Communism's Soviet representatives.
West Germans, too, criticized what they interpreted as Communist sexual
immorality, but they also responded to their own occupation-era history.
West German women's perceived waywardness in the late 1940s resulted
in pressures on women to demonstrate their sexual conformity.

Despite the popular contrast between rape in the Soviet zone and
fraternization in the western zones, upheavals in women's sexual lives
transcended zonal boundaries. Marital infidelity and premarital sex had

increased during the war. As the bombing raids and the situation at the front worsened, delaying sexual gratification seemed ever less sensible, and many sought out pleasure amidst fear and danger.[79] As the wartime emergency segued into the postwar emergency, short-term liaisons between Germans continued to be a source of comfort, pleasure, and support.[80] Financial insecurity, physical disability, and lingering questions about the whereabouts of spouses caused many couples to cohabit or extend their courtship rather than to marry.[81] Finally, both material need and the search for companionship brought women into relationships with members of the occupation forces. "Sure, the shortage of men was great after the war, but many found comfort. . . . With the Americans, there were of course economic considerations as well, stockings and so on, you know."[82] But the appeal was not limited to the Americans: with occupation troops of all nationalities, including the Soviets, German women found alliances that offered both material relief and emotional satisfaction.[83]

Nevertheless, memories and the continuing threat of rape served to minimize discussion of consensual relationships between German women and Soviet soldiers. If German women who chose U.S. or British men attracted accusations of disloyalty, "fraternizers" in the Soviet zone had all the more reason for secrecy. The rapes did not just mute discussion of consensual relationships, however; they also created an environment in which fewer such relationships probably occurred. Women in the Soviet zone had extraordinary fears to overcome if they were to consider dating an occupation soldier. Even aside from the history of rape, prejudices against Slavs and Asians meant that social pressures against involvement with Soviet men were considerable.

Furthermore, the opportunities for contact shrunk with time. In the interests of enabling Germans to learn through personal contact of the advantages of the Soviet system, the Soviets, unlike the Western Allies, never had a nonfraternization policy. Soviet soldiers and German women had no legal barriers to overcome—even if they did have personal barriers. But the continuing rapes had a disastrous effect on Germans' impressions of the Soviets.[84] Furthermore, Soviet authorities sensed that, rather than impressing Germans with the advantages of socialism, contact was teaching their own men about the attractions of a bourgeois life-style. With the disadvantages of contact outweighing the hoped-for advantages, the Soviets increasingly separated their troops from the civilian population. Starting in the summer of 1947, Soviet troops were moved to tightly controlled compounds. By the end of the occupation era, they were effectively cut off from contact with civilians.[85]

This isolation penalized Soviet troops more harshly than it did German civilians, but the contrast with the western zones was nevertheless striking. Sexual contacts between Germans and western soldiers increased over the course of the occupation, and the culture of fraternization became well established. Indeed, it was replenished in the 1950s by men and women too young to have been in such relationships during the era of occupation.[86] By contrast, sexual contact between Germans and Soviet soldiers was suppressed within a couple of years. There would be no "second-generation" camp followers, and there would be no further dating or inter-marriage to remind Germans of the earliest days of such relationships. This lack of contact, as well as the history of rape, prevented memories of fraternization from becoming prominent in East Germans' recollections of the occupation.

Although all the western zones contrasted markedly with the Soviet zone, the U.S. zone stood out. Sexual relations with Americans represented in microcosm West Germans' mixed feelings about their new friendship with the West. Already in the Weimar era, many Germans had feared that U.S. consumer goods and cultural exports threatened German traditions. The extraordinary allure of this threat—U.S. exports had found enthusiastic markets—had made it all the more dangerous.[87] And although the Nazis had railed especially hard against U.S. culture, fear of Americanism was hardly limited to Nazi circles. To Christian conservatives, U.S. influence threatened to undermine a desperately-needed return to tradition and piety.[88] Fraternization demonstrated the extent of the danger: the promise of material gain and disregard for traditional sexual mores demoralized German men, brought disease, and exposed children to illicit relationships.

Yet preventing U.S. influence would be an uphill battle. Not only did the Americans have all the money as well as political control in their zone, but there was tremendous demand, on the German side, for things American. This was hardly limited to fraternizers' legendary desire for stockings. American cigarettes, to name only one item, were not only a treasured luxury item but also black-market currency, which meant that everybody wanted them. Furthermore, Germans often came to like the GIs who gave their children chocolate, tipped generously, and projected an openness, innocence, and optimism that contrasted so refreshingly to the environment from which Germans were now emerging. Young women's interest in men who could offer relief from both hunger and depression was in keeping with many Germans' genuine attraction to Americans.

When the Americans lifted their prohibition of fraternization on July 15, 1945, a lively social culture featuring young German women and U.S.

soldiers began to flourish.[89] By December, most U.S. veterans of the war—many of whom still had some reservations about Germans—were released from their duties. They were replaced by young men with no wartime experience, little bitterness against Germans, and eagerness for adventure. Contact with German women became a routine part of their lives. Army investigators estimated in 1946 that 50 to 90 percent of U.S. troops "fraternized" with German women; one in eight married men had entered a stable relationship in Germany.[90]

Tens of thousands of German women married occupation soldiers and thus cemented personal bonds between German and foreign families.[91] Relatives and friends of women who dated Allied soldiers often supported the relationships. Not only did they share in the material benefits, but they felt these women's youth had been unfairly snatched from them—and they often agreed that the healthy, emotionally sound foreigners contrasted favorably with the available German men.[92] If their daughters had the opportunity to emigrate from Germany's bombed landscape to a land of plenty, parents could only rejoice.

Yet German women hoping to marry their U.S. suitors confronted bureaucratic obstacles, and they risked having their lovers lose interest or use army regulations to hide their own lack of seriousness.[93] They also faced neighbors' skepticism regarding the nature of the relationship. Even sympathetic observers typically put respectable words the couples used to describe themselves—words like "fiancé" and "engaged"—into quotation marks. The press and social workers routinely characterized women who claimed to be engaged to occupation soldiers as prostitutes.[94]

Although families often shared in the excitement of their daughters' courtships, few Germans who were not involved in relationships with occupation soldiers considered them anything other than prostitution. And there was an enormous amount of prostitution. A small number of women belonged to the dying profession of licensed prostitution. Because of the desperate conditions, the ranks of "wild" (unlicensed) prostitutes grew tremendously.[95] The large majority of women popularly identified as prostitutes, however, did not see themselves as such. They were simply women who received gifts or material support from their suitors. Since gift giving was a traditional part of the most respectable courtships, however, the popular distinction between casual prostitutes and nonprostitutes lay in the national identity of the man, not in the fact of material exchange.[96] Relationships between Germans were not suspect unless the man paid cash for sex. Relations between German women and Allied soldiers, by contrast, were suspect even if the couple was engaged and the support took the form of payment of joint household expenses.

Graffiti, anonymous handbills, and even public hair-cutting threatened "faithless" German women.[97] In many ways, these women's offense seemed even graver than that of women who had had "forbidden contact" during the war. Foreign laborers and prisoners of war had typically been coreligionists, they had shown themselves to be hard workers and had often been integrated into German families, and they had maintained a certain level of subservience. In any case, they had been white and Christian. Occupation soldiers included thousands of Jews, and black GIs attracted attention out of all proportion to their representation among fraternizers.[98] The main economic function of occupation soldiers seemed to be as profiteers from the black market. And they were anything by subservient. Occupation soldiers' economic advantage, as well as their frequent racial difference, made it tempting to claim that sexual relationships with them must be prostitution.

To be sure, some contemporaries pleaded for a generous treatment of these "prostitutes" in light of the hard times.[99] Yet the discourse surrounding fraternization guaranteed that nearly everyone could feel offended by German women who dated occupation soldiers. They insulted German manhood; they endangered German womanhood. They mocked the sufferings of victims of war, and they sullied the honor of the German nation. Whether a woman collected payment or not, she prostituted her nation and her sex.

For German men returning wounded, emotionally scarred, and hungry from war or prison, the sight of German women with the former enemy could be bitter. Some forty years after the end of the war, a man recalled a discussion with an occupation soldier: "A Negro said, 'The German soldier fought for six years, the German woman only five minutes!' That's how it was from beginning to end. I was ashamed."[100] Others who had suffered during the war and its aftermath also resented these women's apparent privilege. The policy of reserving penicillin for those infected with STDs angered Germans who felt others were more deserving of the drug.[101] Germany's umbrella social work organization calculated the cost of treating STDs in Hessen in 1947 and informed its members that the sum could have paid the pensions of 17,800 war widows and orphans for a year.[102]

As German women seemed to mock the sufferings of veterans and victims of war, many contemporaries concluded that young women were sullying what they still felt was the good name of the German people. A twenty-two-year-old student and former Nazi wrote of fraternizers in 1946, "Have the German people no honor left? . . . One can lose a war, one can be humiliated, but one need not dirty one's honor oneself!"[103] Like many of her contemporaries, this young woman felt that the sexual conduct of many of her peers—and not the previous regime—had cost the nation its honor.

By offending German men, victims of war, and the nation, fraternizers endangered the reputation of all German womanhood. Thus while German men resented women who fraternized, nonfraternizing women tried to separate themselves from the phenomenon of fraternization. And Germans who wished to ostracize fraternizing women received assistance from an unexpected quarter: the Allies themselves. With widespread sexual contact came an epidemic of STDs. The program implemented by the Allies to control the epidemic routinely trampled the civil liberties and dignity of young women. In doing so, it confirmed the "otherness" of the women it swept up.

In August 1946, STD rates among U.S. soldiers stationed in Germany were ten times the 1939 armywide rate and growing.[104] The epidemic cost the occupation vast numbers of personnel hours, made a mockery of the notion of military discipline, and resulted in bad press back home. The Americans, like the other Allies, took control of STDs into their own hands.[105]

In order to reduce infection among their own troops, military authorities relied on measures ranging from "moral instruction" through distribution of condoms to revocation of off-duty passes and even courtsmartial.[106] Articles in *Stars and Stripes* warned soldiers about the dangers of contact with German women. A comic in the same paper featured "Veronica Dankeschön" (Veronica Thank-you-very-much), a young German woman whose handbag bore her initials: VD (Fig. 12).[107] In at least one command, prominently displayed photos of infected women helped to guide soldiers in their selection of dates, and the military issued passes— quickly dubbed "bed passes" in German slang—which identified uninfected women eligible to enter U.S. clubs.[108] Soldiers in Berlin filed by diseased civilians in order to view syphilis's effects.[109]

More important for the larger German population, however, were the measures intended to reduce what the Americans called the "indigenous reservoir" of disease. Aside from encouraging people to seek examination and treatment voluntarily, there were three important methods of location and treatment: routine examination of certain population groups, source tracing, and vice raids.[110] All of these methods overwhelmingly affected

OCCUPATION   **By Shep**

"Sarge, I'd like to have ya meet the sweetest little gal in Deutschland—
Miss Veronica Dankeschön."

Figure 12. Focusing on sex. In the western zones, the image of women standing alone was strongly influenced by a highly sexualized atmosphere in which mass prostitution, STDs, and fraternization were widely discussed. In this cartoon from *Stars and Stripes,* German women are equated with venereal disease; their Nazi background is apparent, linking political with sexual guilt. Courtesy *Stars and Stripes.*

women. Targeted for routine examination were registered prostitutes and, depending on region, female food workers and hotel personnel.[111] In theory, all people seeking treatment for an STD were to report their sexual contacts, and the Health Department then investigated these contacts. In practice, women were traced more conscientiously than were men, and women named as sexual partners of occupation troops were handled more urgently than were women named as contacts of Germans.[112]

Vice raids, however, were the most public, the most controversial, and the most fear-inspiring means of locating infected women. Typical of the occupation era was the period from February to July 1947 in the state of Hessen: 6,719 people were picked up in raids of dance halls and bars; 99 percent were female.[113] Normally, women accompanied by their husbands were immediately released; all other women were legally designated as "strongly suspected" of carrying infection. This legal designation allowed the police to send women for involuntary examination and, if necessary, inpatient treatment.[114]

Women who had been accused of no crime were thus held against their wills; their presence at a raided establishment cost them rights of movement that people who had been accused of no crime normally enjoyed, even during the military occupation (but not under the Nazis). A woman of twenty-three, happy that the wartime prohibition on dancing had been lifted, visited a club with her mother and friend only to end the evening in an assembly-line gynecological examination: "Well, before we could look around, there was a truck outside. . . . 'All girls out of the dance bar, all onto the truck, get on, on to the Health Department.' That was really bad; they were handled like hookers there. . . . You could hardly go dancing without running a risk; . . . you couldn't enjoy the fact that you could go dancing again after so many years."[115] Allied health authorities calculated that only 18.2 percent of people apprehended as contacts and through vice raids were infected.[116] Despite several episodes that were embarrassing to the Americans—a raid in Coburg netted the mayor's daughter and the wives of many prominent businessmen, for example—vice raids remained routine occurrences.[117]

As a result of sex-specific methods of locating patients, women were far more likely to be treated against their wills than were men. In early 1947, 52.1 percent of female but only 6.6 percent of civilian male patients in Hessen were being treated involuntarily.[118] Women undergoing compulsory treatment were normally placed in segregated STD units in hospitals, and provincial laws allowed transfer to an institution or prison if this was considered necessary to prevent further spread of infection. Female patients thus missed work, left their dependents hanging, and had a hard time preventing their families from learning that they were infected. German men, including those receiving compulsory treatment, typically received outpatient care.[119]

Over 9 percent of Berlin women aged nineteen to twenty and over 7 percent of those aged twenty-one to twenty-five were reported as infected in early 1947.[120] Nevertheless, women had no monopoly on STDs in the civilian population. Sex-specific methods of locating civilian patients created an imbalance in the reporting of infection, and women's majority among the infected approximated their majority in the population. By the end of the 1940s, men accounted for half the civilian cases, which meant that their rates of infection were higher than women's.[121] The STD program focused on civilian women not because they were sicker than men but because they were the traditional target of German efforts and because they were the most obvious source of infection to occupation soldiers. The reduction of the transient population, the introduction of penicillin, the reunion of couples, and women's lessening need to turn to prostitution—and not measures such as vice raids—brought a dramatic decline of STDs in the late 1940s.[122]

The Military Government oversaw the program of STD control, but Germans executed most of its measures. German and military police carried out raids jointly, German public health clinics and hospitals conducted exams and administered treatment, and German physicians passed names of infected women to military authorities. Some doctors objected to the routine violations of patient confidentiality or held that compulsion was bad medicine.[123] For the most part, however, German medical professionals found the Allies' measures reasonable. The future head of the Ministry of the Interior's Health Division recalled with anger in 1950, "As the Allies' drastic measures against the VD problem developed and the official explanations came, not a single German doctor or any of the West German medical societies turned against them. . . . In the entire area of the three western zones no medical voice was raised to warn or to slow things down or to protest. . . . On the contrary, like toadstools in a warm rain, the medical demands sprang up, one after the other, for force, more force, and yet more force."[124]

Social workers, too, demanded "force, more force, and yet more force." Social work organizations renewed their old call for a probationary law that would punish chronically unemployed men, women carrying STDs, and transients of both sexes. They achieved greater success under the occupation government than they had under the Nazis. In Bavaria, a 1946 decree allowed the institutionalization of young women "who contribute to the spreading of VD by their life-style and thereby constitute a danger to public health, or who are otherwise wayward."[125] In demanding an increased role in the fight against STDs, social work organizations cited the need to humanize a system dominated by doctors and police.[126] Yet the recent history of the social work profession and the failure to denazify it gave little reason to assume that social workers would be any less punitive.[127]

Most of the objections to the trampling of civil liberties came from the U.S. side. Higher-ups worried that the STD program was making Germans skeptical of U.S. ambitions to teach them about civil liberties. They occasionally took their subordinates to task for conducting raids without adequate evidence that those rounded up were likely to be infected.[128]

Not surprisingly, women caught up in the raids resented the assumption that they were infected. "What purpose does all this have?" asked a young woman who was overheard by a reporter. "The really sick ones will be on their guard against the police, and those of us who are healthy will lose our last sense of decency if we are handled like this. Have we no right to enjoyment? We haven't all lost our morals!"[129] Irritated as they may have been, however, such women were unlikely to protest publicly and thereby acknowledge that they had been picked up.[130]

More vocal objections to the program came from a few German feminists. "Old feminists"—women who had been active in the pre-1933 feminist movement—quickly noted parallels with the situation that had moved them to demand reform in STD and prostitution control earlier in the century.[131] But "old feminists" commanded little respect in the postwar world: they seemed to belong to another age. When Agnes von Zahn-Harnack, an "old feminist," protested to a woman's magazine that Munich authorities were considering reintroducing municipal control of prostitution, a presumably younger woman retorted that Zahn-Harnack was misapplying the rules of a long-gone era. "What in normal times was an insult to women's equal human rights with men is today a self-defense of all decent powers to keep the concept 'woman' pure."[132]

The battle to combat STDs and control prostitution had taken on a meaning beyond its original purpose. Harsh measures might curb the epidemic, but just as significantly they allowed "decent powers" to restore the purity of the concept "woman."[133] Widespread illicit sex had threatened the reputation of German womanhood; the attack on fraternization and the program to combat STDs helped to restore the distinction between "good girls" and "bad girls."

Indeed, with German women criticized for threatening the nation's honor, those who did not want to be mistaken for the wrong type of woman would do more than condemn bad behavior. They would also make sure their own reputations were beyond criticism, and they would support political and social movements that vowed to restore women's good name. "Women's public face is in danger!" warned a 1946 pamphlet addressed to women and girls from the CDU (Christian Democratic Union, a conservative political party), citing divorce, the STD epidemic, public obscenity, and juvenile criminality. "Neither poverty nor need can justify casually giving up one's most valuable possessions: honor, purity, and decency!" Women and girls who agreed were urged to work with the CDU to restore marriage and the family and to honor women and girls.[134] For German women emerging from the sexual turbulence of the occupation era, family, marriage, and conservative politics offered to restore not only material comfort but also womanly honor.

Fraternizers and prostitutes, for their part, faced immense pressure to change their behavior. Even in normal times, single women risked their reputations if they were sexually active, but they hurt no one else unless they spread disease. In the late 1940s, they bore far greater burdens. According to the discourse of the day, they broke the hearts of returning German men; they took bread out of the mouths of orphans; they disgraced the supposedly good name of the German nation; and they endangered the reputation of all German womanhood. Harsh STD control measures confirmed this social judgment by denying women civil liberties, not because of criminal behavior or even because they carried disease but on the basis of their appearance at disreputable establishments. Sex outside respectable settings might be a humiliating way to earn a living, a form of escape, a good time, or part of a loving relationship, but the price was high. Women were well advised to put these episodes behind them as the postwar crisis subsided.

Sexual relationships with Allied soldiers symbolized one of the most important contrasts between life in eastern and western Germany: the antagonistic relations with the Soviets on the one hand, the far more complicated relations with the Western Allies on the other. While rape became a metaphor for the Soviet Union's treatment of eastern Germany (at least in western accounts), fraternization symbolized the ambiguous appeal of western—especially U.S.—culture, financial support, and political models. On the one hand, West Germans coveted U.S. goods, enjoyed friendships with Americans, and were glad to have U.S. protection from the Soviets. On the other hand, Germans feared for their cultural distinctiveness, despised fraternizers, and eagerly sought national sovereignty.[135]

But the different cultures of the occupation era did not just symbolize later relations; they also helped to establish them. The rapes turned many a potential Communist sympathizer against the Soviet Union. They even created banal logistical problems to recruitment as, for example, women avoided evening assemblies because they feared assault.[136] Good personal relations between German civilians and U.S. occupation soldiers, by contrast, achieved precisely what Soviet authorities had hoped casual contact would achieve in the eastern zone. Masses of West Germans became sold on the "American way of life" (or the British or, to a lesser degree, the French way of life), not necessarily because they admired or even cared about U.S. political principles but because they developed warm personal bonds with individual Americans. But just as fury at the symbolic rape of East Germany by the Soviet Union coexisted with the silencing of women who had suffered real rape, so did the figurative "love affair" with the Americans coexist with condemnation of the German women who entered literal love affairs with Americans.

.——.——.

"The war had many faces," explained a Berlin woman over forty years after the end of the war. "On the one hand is the respect for the Berlin women of the rubble; on the other hand, women experienced things about which no one wanted to speak. We were front soldiers, undertakers, objects of revenge, and objects of lust in one person."[137] And the array of images of women during the "crisis years" went yet further. It included survivors of bombing raids, refugees, prostitutes, fraternizers, black-marketeers, and forced laborers. With the institutions and rules of "normal life" gone, there seemed no limit to the unexpected roles women might inhabit.

Yet even as daily life seemed hopelessly chaotic, prolonged singlehood, hunger, and military occupation imposed new structures on everyday life. Women learned a remarkable degree of self-sufficiency as they pulled through trying situations without male assistance. In later years, women's family lives and dependence on men would become the subject of ideological and legal battles, but women's memories of the "crisis years" would also shape their experience of marital status in the 1950s.

The hour of the women, however, did not lend itself to simple conclusions about the significance of marital status for women. On the one hand, it demonstrated that marital status really did not make much of a difference. Whether a woman was unwed, married, divorced, or widowed, she faced a brutal struggle for survival. On the other hand, it demonstrated that marital status was everything. The years that most German women considered their most traumatic were those when they were without men. The difference between misery standing alone and comfort at the side of a husband seemed all too obvious.

The distinctions between the Soviet and western occupation zones also bore heavily on the meaning of marital status. No zone had a monopoly on any part of occupation-era life, but some aspects loomed larger in the western zones, others in the Soviet zone. In the Soviet zone, the taboo nature of rape muted discussion of women's sexual activity, while the contrast between equal rights in the labor force and the use of women as forced laborers pushed the question of women's role as workers into the foreground. In the western zones, efforts to ensure that women's recruitment to the labor force would be temporary took much of the punch out of discussions of a new economic role for women. At the same time, the spirited culture of fraternization meant that there would be much talk of women's sexual lives.

But how would all this affect marital status? Paid labor for women and sexual promiscuity were hardly new topics. However inaccurately, Germans traditionally thought of them in connection with single women. Once women married, neither the world of productive labor nor the danger of promiscuity seemed as relevant. It was not yet clear whether this would change. For the moment, marital status did not determine whether a woman had to support herself, and East German economic planners seemed to envision a permanent transformation of women's workforce participation regardless of marital status. Whether the link between marital status and workforce participation would remain broken in the longer term, however, was still open to question. In the western zones, it was clear that women of all marital states were engaging in illicit sexual behavior, but there was no telling yet whether this phenomenon would outlast the present moment of crisis. Determining the durability of occupation-era shifts in the significance of marital status would be a central concern of both German states.

5 Marriage Rubble

The Crisis in the Family,
Public and Private

"The family fragment dominates the hour," acknowledged a Berlin journalist in 1946. "But the idea of the family as a basic formation—that is, as an imaginary space which one can restore and fill—seems to have remained alive."[1] In the aftermath of the war, Germans were deeply impressed by women's ability to pull their families through on their own. Nevertheless, they hoped that women would need to exert such efforts only temporarily. Certainly most women scrounging to feed their dependents and heat their apartments would have preferred to share the burdens of daily life. To be sure, some missing and imprisoned men would never return; not all widows could expect to remarry; and many unwed women would have to remain single. But although demographic realities might mean that many families could not be reconstituted, the "idea of the family" seemed unthreatened. If anything, the family's "imaginary" nature contributed to its appeal. In the midst of hardship, it was easy to idealize an imaginary family life.

As men returned and familial conflict became almost the order of the day, this idealization became difficult to uphold. "Family fragments" had not seriously threatened the privileged place of the nuclear family because they were presumably inferior. Discord within "complete" families was a more serious matter. Husbands' return shattered many women's hopes that the restoration of their families would provide relief. At the very least, men's return meant more work. Frequently, it also meant marital strife, and divorce quickly followed many reunions. Unmarried, divorced, and widowed women, observing the chasm that now seemed to separate men from women, had reason to reconsider their desire for marriage. While men's absence had not shattered the ideals of marriage and the nuclear family, men's presence frequently did.

The futures of innumerable families were in doubt. Even excluding the inevitable problems facing those who had married in haste during the war, wrote a contributor to a West German social work journal in 1949, "there still remains a mountain of marriage rubble [*Ehetrümmer*] caused by completely reasonable people. Ruins are a general phenomenon. Just as concretely as they lay on the street corners, so are they present inside people."[2] Millions of Germans faced a "crisis in the family," and these private crises might prove even more crippling than the physical destruction. In the words of a correspondent to the Soviet zone's women's magazine, *Die Frau von heute* (The woman of today), "It has been clear to us all for a long time that our external reconstruction will remain a half-measure if internal [reconstruction] . . . does not accompany it hand-in-hand. And here I have great fears."[3]

The "crisis in the family," however, was not purely private. It also raised questions about the family as an institution. Was the restoration of the family in its prior form crucial to the renewal of civil society? Or did the current crisis provide an opportunity to rethink an institution whose shortcomings were now laid bare? As individuals faced crises in their own families, so did the press discover a crisis in the institution of the "family."

Women's magazines became the major popular forum for discussion of the family and women's issues. In December 1945, *Sie* (She) began publication in Berlin. Supervised by the western authorities, it printed weekly runs of some 125,000. Two months later, the inaugural issue of *Die Frau von heute* appeared; this was the major women's magazine in the Soviet zone and, later, the Democratic Republic.[4] In March 1948, *Constanze* (a woman's name) entered the scene. Addressing a national readership, it quickly became West Germany's largest women's magazine.[5] In a publishing culture that reflected a jubilant freedom from Nazi constraints—albeit tempered by occupation censorship, particularly strict in the Soviet zone—authors in these and smaller publications penned daring pieces about alternatives for women destined to remain single. They composed critical analyses of the legal codification of "family" and "marriage," and they questioned the appropriateness of older codes to contemporary conditions.

The "crisis in the family" thus referred to personal dramas, to popular discourse, and to the law; it transgressed zonal boundaries. As wide-ranging as it was, however, it would not prove permanent. Many crises in the family would find private resolution. Women who, during the occupation, rejected traditional models of marriage (or marriage altogether) often reconsidered later. Men's recovery from physical and emotional wounds made them more pleasant companions. In the occupation-era economy, men were often a burden, but in the 1950s, a male wage enabled a level of material comfort inaccessible to women living on their own. Thus women who chose singlehood or rejected bourgeois marriage during the occupation did not necessarily continue to do so. In both halves of Germany, marriage rates rose, the age of first marriage dropped, divorce and illegitimacy declined, and married mothers steered away from full-time employment during the 1950s.

Nevertheless, the occupation-era crisis in the family had lasting consequences. Some women who chose not to marry during the occupation had lost their opportunity by the time they desired marriage. For others, the added years of independence made marriage even less appealing in the 1950s than it had been earlier. Although the division of labor in marriages of the 1950s resembled that of the 1930s, the distribution of power did not: wives played a far greater role in making family decisions than they had a generation earlier.

If changing circumstances affected individuals' marital behavior, popular representations of marriage and of single women shaped public attitudes. Daring discussions of single women, particularly characteristic of western publications, quickly disappeared as a backlash set in. The tone was set for the social ostracism of women living outside traditional family constellations in West Germany in the 1950s. The debate about the institution of marriage, by contrast, continued into the 1950s. As the East German government codified the Marxist critique, West Germany grappled with the implications of constitutionally mandated sexual equality for the family within an anti-Marxist framework. Many Germans on both sides of the border felt that Soviet law was being foisted on East Germany, and West German conservatives portrayed even their internal critics as "foreign." Nevertheless, the discussions of the immediate postwar period made clear that socialist and feminist blueprints for revamping the family had deep roots in Germany—and that, even after twelve years of Nazi rule, broad sectors of German society were conversant with these critiques.[6]

.——.——.

Frau A.'s story is representative of many from postwar Berlin. Her husband had been drafted in 1942 and imprisoned in 1945. When her story was recorded in 1948, she was still awaiting his return. She lived with her three children in a dark and badly damaged basement apartment that, until recently, had had as its only entrance a kitchen window. Only the kitchen could be heated during the winter of 1946–47, and that room only to forty-three to forty-five degrees Fahrenheit. Frau A. had a poorly paying janitorial position; the family lived mainly on the earnings of the oldest son, an unskilled laborer. The second son, a boy of twelve, had lost a leg in a trolley accident.

Although she often came close to despair, Frau A. never lost hope entirely. "As soon as my husband is back, things will get better for us," she told her interviewer. Her faith in a better future enabled Frau A. to make the best of a bad situation. Despite the filth surrounding the apartment, she kept her family's rooms immaculately clean, and flowers on the kitchen table lent a note of cheer to the family's main gathering place.[7]

In the grim circumstances of Germany's "crisis years," many women found strength in the promise of their husbands' return. Frau A.'s material situation was not considerably better than that of Frau P. (see Chapter Four), but Frau A.'s flowers provide a striking contrast to Frau P.'s thoughts of suicide. One important difference: Frau A. anticipated her husband's return; Frau P. was a widow. While Frau P. could envision no end to her miserable predicament, Frau A. could.

Women whose husbands were missing or imprisoned eagerly awaited the day when their husbands would relieve them of their burdens. Widowed, unmarried, and divorced women might also dream of rescue in the form of a man, but the expectation was far more visceral for women who already (or still) had husbands. They recalled the division of labor, the material comfort, and the emotional satisfaction of their prewar partnerships. Conflicts were either forgotten or seemed to pale in comparison with present hardships. Those who had married during the war looked forward to the belated beginnings of married life.[8]

Wives, like parents, siblings, and children of men who had been at war, grasped at whatever scraps of information they could obtain about their men. Women who had addresses for their husbands sent letters and packages. If their husbands had been imprisoned by the Western Allies and were on German soil, they might even visit. A few particularly brazen women arranged men's escapes.[9] Women who had no news of their husbands consulted the stars and fortunetellers, lavished gifts on fraudulent "greeting-carriers" (*Grußbesteller*) who claimed to have seen their husbands, and clung to rumors of secret camps in Siberia from which prisoners could send no mail.[10] They flooded the train stations when returning prisoners were expected, displayed posters with photos and details of the last known whereabouts of their husbands, and hoped that one of the returning men might have news. In the Soviet zone, they let officials know at public assemblies that information about missing men would greatly increase their trust in the SED.[11] For at least fifteen years after the end of the war, West German women placed ads in veterans' newspapers, hoping that their husbands' former comrades would contact them. Wives and mothers of missing and imprisoned men constituted the target audience for countless articles about conditions in the camps, and social work and religious organizations addressed their emotional and pastoral needs.[12]

The release of prisoners of war was a delicate political issue across occupied Germany. German officials in all four zones pressed for the release of prisoners of war, arguing that this would improve morale, stabilize families, and aid the economy. By the end of 1946, the Western Allies had released most of their prisoners. At the end of 1948, however, when the Western Allies had freed the last of their prisoners, the Soviet Union officially acknowledged nearly half a million still in its camps. Still, the Soviets did not ignore the issue. In 1946, the SED, closely associated with the Soviet occupation, lobbied for women's votes by expressing its understanding of the "spiritual burdens" of relatives of men still imprisoned and by claiming credit for negotiating the release of 120,000 men.[13] By the end of 1949, the USSR declared that it had released all prisoners except convicted war criminals. Nevertheless, the Western Allies, the West German government, and East and West Germans were certain that many more— possibly millions—languished in Soviet camps well into the 1950s.[14] Since there was no accurate count of war dead, even wildly inflated estimates seemed plausible. Wives of "missing" men could not know whether their husbands had been killed in action but listed as missing in the Wehrmacht's attempts to hide the extent of its casualties; whether their husbands had been captured but had subsequently died in prison; or whether their husbands were still alive somewhere in the Soviet Union.

In practical terms, it mattered little where such a wife resided: she had no power to gain her husband's release or even to find out whether he was alive or dead. In political terms, however, it made a great difference. In West Germany, dependents of men who might still be imprisoned became symbols of victimization at the hands of the Soviets and thus reminders of the superiority of the western alliance. The constant reiteration of Soviet guilt in not repatriating prisoners of war also helped to displace thoughts of German guilt.[15]

In the Soviet zone, women who suspected their husbands might still be in prison camps were politically destabilizing. Even when it was campaigning for votes in mid-1946, the SED alternated its expressions of sympathy for dependents of men still imprisoned with reminders that the current suffering was the fault of Hitler and the Nazis, not the Soviet Union.[16] A few years later, the SED turned its blame to West German "anti-Soviet agitation" (*antisowjetische Hetze*), which, in the words of an official history, "did not shy away from abusing the feelings of wives and mothers whose husbands and sons had not returned from the war and from scrupulously feeding false hopes."[17] East German women, however, remained unconvinced that western propaganda was responsible for their suspicions that their husbands might still be alive. Well into the 1950s, the conviction that the Soviets were lying about the prisoners of war—like fears of rape—undercut the SED's attempts to win influence among women.[18]

As the occupation authorities arrested an overwhelmingly male group of Germans suspected of Nazi activity, they created a new type of woman standing alone. Indeed, men who had been deemed indispensable to the state or economy had been spared military service. Their wives had thus enjoyed the unusual luxury of their husbands' presence during the war. Now, however, those men were called to account for their activities under the previous regime.

In the western zones, denazification featured large-scale amnesties, short sentences, and the release of former Nazis considered valuable for reconstruction.[19] The ironically nicknamed "Ivory Snow Certificate" (*Persilschein*), which declared that its bearer had, at most, been a "fellow traveler," benefited not only those released to resume their careers but also their dependents. West German families of men who had contributed to the Nazi state gained much by escaping thorough denazification—even as quick denazification seemed to make a mockery of the sufferings of families that had been broken by Nazi persecution and aggression.

If western denazification minimized the significance of Nazi crimes, then the eastern variant eased the task of those who wished to claim German victimhood. Occupation authorities imprisoned hundreds of thousands of East Germans without formal charges and without family notification. The Soviets and the SED claimed that these were Nazis and saboteurs of the occupation; most Germans were convinced that the roundups were a Stalinist-style purge of real or imagined opponents. In fact, the arrests claimed many types of Germans: adults who had played a significant role in the previous regime, teenagers accused of membership in the largely mythical Nazi "Werewolf" organization, and potential opponents of the SED and Soviet occupation such as large property owners and leaders of the SPD (Social Democratic Party) and bourgeois parties.[20] The fact that former Nazi concentration camps now became camps for opponents of the Communists and the fact that one-third or more of those interned died in captivity lent a particularly grisly tone to the phenomenon. Prisoners typically disappeared without a trace, and their families' attempts to gather information elicited only a stony silence.[21]

In addition, the Soviet authorities imported thousands of East German workers into the Soviet Union.[22] Most were rounded up at their homes or places of work and transported with no warning. Almost all were male. While draftees could occasionally arrange to take their families with them, others were unable even to notify their families of their departures. These men, however, were workers—indeed, highly skilled scientists and technicians—and not prisoners. In theory, their pay was to be transferred to their families' German bank accounts, they were to be able to vacation in Germany, they belonged to pension plans. These promises often went unfulfilled, and their wives filed hundreds of complaints with the Ministry of Labor.[23] Unlike wives of men listed as "missing" or wives of men arrested during the occupation, however, these women usually knew of their husbands' whereabouts. Furthermore, they were able to bring their grievances to the authorities without provoking either flat denials of the situation or the response that their husbands must have been war criminals. Nevertheless, they did not know whether and when their husbands would return.

Far more women in the Soviet zone lost their partners during the occupation than was the case in the western zones. Women whose men were absent, however, shared much regardless of the zone in which they lived and regardless of the circumstances of their husbands' absence. In all four zones, waiting was popularly portrayed as a female experience, although parents and children—and not just wives—suffered because of men's absence.[24] In all four zones, however, writing letters to imprisoned husbands, carrying posters at train stations, and petitioning public officials were only brief interruptions from women's most pressing tasks: finding food and fuel, going to work, repairing their apartments, mending their children's clothes. Short of arranging an escape, women could do nothing to hasten men's release. They could only try to keep afloat and hope for a better life after their men returned.

Men also awaited reunions with great anticipation. The life of a soldier had little to recommend it anymore, and the lot of a prisoner of war had never been an enviable one. To be sure, those who had served early in the war had often enjoyed the role of conqueror. The occupied lands' wealth had been theirs for the taking, and conquered people's subservience could be flattering. The great majority of military men, however, had experienced the last years of the war on the eastern front, where hunger, cold, and inadequate supplies had been the order of the day. They had seen countless comrades killed in hopeless battles, and most had fought the final months fully aware that the war was lost.

Those who were imprisoned by the Soviets and later told their stories in the West often claimed that incarceration in the USSR had been even worse than the war itself. Eleven million Germans landed in prisoner-of-war camps, 3.2 million of them in the Soviet Union. One-third of those in the Soviet Union died during captivity.[25] For some, the experience of imprisonment by the Soviets made discussion of German concentration and prison camps irrelevant or downright sacrilegious. But even those who acknowledged Germany's unique guilt bore scars from their own time in prison camp.

Thoughts of home could be a great comfort to prisoners. But just as women lived with uncertainty about their husbands' fates, men often did not know whether their families had survived the bombing raids and the flight west. A former prisoner recalled his two years in a Soviet camp with five thousand men: "The worst was the hunger, that was the absolute worst; . . . and the second worst was the uncertainty. Do you still have parents, a mother? Is your wife still alive? Do you still have an apartment? Are they all dead? Will you even make it home?"[26] While women often learned of their husbands' survival from comrades who had been freed earlier, men usually had to wait longer—at least until postal connections were established—to learn their families' fates. Unless they heard that their families had perished, men fantasized about the emotional release, the physical comfort, and the new purpose that their families would provide upon their release.

When prisoners of war had doubts about their future happiness, their misgivings usually coalesced around one frightening possibility: that their wives or fiancées had found new lovers. A few knew of their wives' infidelities, and some tried to initiate divorce proceedings even before their release.[27] Most, however, simply lived with uncertainty. Wives involved with new men knew they would face a dilemma if and when their husbands returned.

Neither wives nor husbands anticipated that they would face problems much more complicated than infidelity. But the years apart had significantly changed both partners. Women recalled strong, capable husbands who had been a source of emotional comfort, and such men no doubt would have provided much relief. But the men who returned were weak and sick; they were often physically incapable of work, had lost their positions because of denazification, or had slipped a few rungs in their career ladders; and their shattered psyches left them unable to offer emotional comfort. Remembering their husbands' management of family affairs, women expected men to help solve the enormous problems facing their house-holds. Men's years in the military and in prison, however, had taught them to follow orders, not to grasp the initiative or deal creatively with unex-pected dilemmas.[28]

Women, too, had changed in ways that neither sex really anticipated. Husbands who had fingered photos of their smiling, prettily dressed wives returned to starving, haggard women clad in rags. Men suffering from a loss of individuality in the military and in prison camp had longed for a return to their families, where they had been indispensable. A poem in a popular East German newspaper encouraged this hope: "Until recently I was still Private Schmidt, / a gray drop among gray waves. / . . . / Today I am 'Pappi' and authority. / Little Katrin trusts me unreservedly. / I am a god."[29] But the good news that a man's family had survived implied the unsettling conclusion that it had managed without him. Women whose independence and competence had increased gradually often failed to rec-ognize the cumulative effect of their transformation. Although they wanted to share their burdens, a return to the dependence and submission that had frequently characterized their prewar marriages was unthinkable to them. Having long forgotten those days, they learned with incredulity that such memories constituted their husbands' ideal of married life.

While neither sex anticipated the difficulties they would confront upon reunion, men faced additional handicaps. Prisoners of war were rarely informed of conditions inside Germany. In addition to the wives they had left years earlier, they dreamed of the wealthy, orderly, and comfortable surroundings they recalled from their civilian days. All knew of the bomb-ing raids, and some had seen bombed towns while on leave, but most were unprepared for the extent of physical destruction. They were even less pre-pared for the implications of this destruction: that mere survival required constant struggle. The psychological state of the nation, too, was unset-tling. Veterans' wartime experience had extended until their release from prison camp, and many recalled this last chapter as the most harrowing. Yet they returned to a society determined to put the war behind it, instead focusing almost obsessively on the present and future.

Women were better informed about the problems they would face when their men returned. Although official descriptions of prison camps were unrealistically rosy (with the exception of western reports on Soviet camps), most Germans skeptically expected the worst. The press covered the diffi-culties veterans faced in their reintegration into civilian society, and women witnessed the return of neighbors' sons and husbands before their own came back.[30] Furthermore, reunion would take place on what had been women's territory. Gaps in women's comprehension of prison camp made it difficult for them to understand their husbands, but they did not interfere with women's understanding of their own surroundings. Men's ignorance about postwar Germany was an ignorance about the society in which they would have to live.

German women had no more grown up expecting to live in a land of ruins than had German men. But they had adjusted: they had had to if they wanted their families to survive. Much as women looked forward to sharing their burdens, by the time men returned, it was clear that survival did not depend on men. Men would both enjoy this situation as a privilege and resent it. In countless families, men would decline to shoulder their share of the work and at the same time bristle under their wives' mastery of the situation. Other couples would simply discover that they had grown apart. Marital conflict and a wave of divorce resulted. Men's return would not mean a smooth return to the peaceful conjugal life of memory. Instead, it would reveal a deep crisis in the family.

·——·——·

When we left Frau F. at the end of the war in chapter 4, she was living with her sister-in-law and many others in one of Darmstadt's few inhabitable apartments. Her husband had been at war since 1939, and she had become a mail carrier. A bombing raid had claimed her apartment, her belongings, and her daughter, and she had subsequently arranged the evacuation of her mother and her son, Willy.

When the Americans entered the town where Willy and his grandmother were quartered, they requisitioned the house in which the evacuees lived. After a nine-day trek back to Darmstadt, the boy and his grandmother were denied permission to move into the overcrowded city. Frau F. successfully battled the municipal authorities, and Frau F.'s mother and son joined her and her sister-in-law in a single room with two beds. A few months later, the Americans requisitioned this room too; the family moved into a basement room not intended for habitation.

In fall 1945, Herr F. returned, uninjured but nervous and starving. Minor inconveniences caused him to lose his temper, and he was a chain smoker, an expensive habit as cigarettes became black-market currency. He took up work—Frau F. had given hers up—and thus received the best ration card in the family. Frau F. gave him twice as much fat and meat as his ration card entitled him to, but Herr F. complained that he received too little. Although he worked steadily for the next several years, the household's income remained inadequate.

Three months after her husband's return, Frau F. had a miscarriage. In the following two years, Frau F. had two children; each time, she was ill during the entire pregnancy. Two attempts at abortion damaged her health but failed to end yet another pregnancy. Her strength drained, she faced enormous household tasks. The three small children were often ill and slept erratically; Willy did poorly in school and got along with none of the household's adults; and her husband physically abused Willy. Exhausted by 8 P.M. daily, Frau F. nevertheless avoided going to bed until her husband was asleep: he wanted sex but refused to use a condom. If she succeeded in avoiding his advances, he became angry. He screamed at her often, and only her mother and sister-in-law prevented him from beating her. Although she often contemplated divorce, she feared initiating proceedings in the face of her husband's opposition.[31]

Like so many other German women, Frau F. had shouldered new burdens during her husband's absence. She had taken on paid work, managed her household, organized the evacuation of her son and mother, and tangled with the authorities in order to bring them back to Darmstadt. She had also faced great hardships: she had lost her daughter, her belongings, and her apartment. But her husband's return proved anything but a relief. The sociologist recording her story noted that Frau F. had aged prematurely, not only following the disappearance of her child and the loss of her home but especially with the numerous pregnancies, the additional work, and the violent tensions that her husband's return brought.

Reunification with a husband was part of millions of women's experience in the late 1940s. In the third quarter of 1945, the victorious Allies officially held 8,699,732 German prisoners of war. About 40 percent were married.[32] By the end of that year, over half had been released. In 1946, almost two million returned home; in 1947, another million; and in 1948, eight hundred thousand, including the last prisoners held by the Western Allies. In 1949, the Soviets released nearly half a million prisoners, and in 1950 another twenty-two thousand; 28,711 officially remained in Soviet camps after 1950.[33]

The release of prisoners of war did not mean that all surviving men returned home. Hundreds of thousands were held for denazification or political intimidation. Over one million were listed as "missing" in 1950; these included 16 percent of all West German men aged twenty-five to twenty-nine and 14 percent of those aged thirty to thirty-nine.[34] Finally, about eight hundred thousand German civilians (probably more than half women) were transported to the Soviet Union at the end of the war. Even men who were released did not all return to their families; some preferred to start new lives elsewhere.[35] Still, millions of women were reunited with their husbands in the late 1940s.

After their emotional initial reunions, partners often discovered that their distance was great. "I didn't want to believe that he had changed so much, that he even treated his relatives differently than before," recalled a woman of her reunion with the man whom she had married during the war. "I constantly tried to figure out what I could do to find him again."[36] The longer the separation had been, the greater the estrangement: men who had spent many years in prison camp were often emotionally unreachable.[37]

Women who had been raped often found that this fact alienated their husbands. Many men doubted that their wives had done all they could to resist.[38] Even those who had no such doubts often felt their wives' value had declined. "He was so shocked at what I had lived through that he said he needed time to think about it. He couldn't say how he would decide. This was such a serious matter, it actually sufficed to terminate a marriage."[39] In fantasizing about their return home, men had imagined a place where they could forget the war. News that their wives had been raped ruined this imaginary idyll. Rape not only amplified the shame of men's defeat but also placed the war and the victor permanently in the marital bed.

Expecting little sympathy, adulterous women preferred to hide their deeds if they could.[40] Sometimes, they could not. Husbands returned to find new men living with their wives, or they found children they could not have conceived. Women with children from adulterous relationships often found themselves forced to decide between their husbands and their children.[41] Even if no children had resulted, however, women's infidelities often proved intolerable to their returning husbands.[42] But men, too, were vulnerable. When wives' new bonds proved stronger than their attachments to their long-absent husbands, men's fantasies of reunion with a loving family disintegrated before their eyes.[43]

If the years apart had weakened wives' and husbands' emotional bonds, many fathers and children had never had such bonds. Fathers returned to children they had never met or had known only years earlier. Their wives had often tried to maintain the fathers' presence in their children's lives, introducing rituals such as saying goodnight to a photo of the father.[44] Nevertheless, fathers were distant figures to children who had lived without them for years. A woman who was fourteen when her father returned recalled that this event "was entirely uninteresting for me; he could have stayed away; . . . he'd been away for six years; . . . he was, so to say, superfluous for us."[45] Young children often failed to recognize their fathers; they called them "uncle" or asked who the strange man was.[46] Fathers anticipating children's excitement upon their return were stung by such reactions. Older children frequently found their fathers' return disruptive. They had taken on great responsibilities, working the black market, collecting food and fuel, and acting as their mothers' confidantes.[47] With their fathers' return, they lost rank.

Fathers, for their part, often found the symbiosis between their wives and children intimidating. "I always had the feeling that I was confronting a unit: mother and children," recalled a veteran. "They were really intimate with each other, and I came as a stranger to it all."[48] Seeking reassurance that they were not superfluous to family life, many men concluded that stern male authority was the missing link. They thus sought to restore their families and to find a niche for themselves by taking on the role of disciplinarian.[49] Children, however, failed to appreciate their fathers' claims to authority. They had witnessed their mothers' remarkable efforts, and they knew that they, as children, had been indispensable to the family's survival. Their fathers, as far as they could tell, had done nothing but lose a war; they returned unable to work but demanding the lion's share of the rations.[50] In the words of a woman whose father returned in 1948, "He had nothing resembling personal authority, but he sure could give orders. He was an expert at that!"[51]

Children whose fathers did not return were jealous of classmates whose fathers were present, and they fantasized about the lives they would enjoy if their fathers returned.[52] Fathers and children who were reunited often managed to achieve some sort of peace, even if closeness remained rare. But veteran fathers' relationships with their children were rarely simple, and this tension compounded marital strains. Jealousies for mothers' attention pitted fathers against children; disputes about children's upbringing resulted in strife between parents.

Hunger made matters worse. Men often failed to understand the severity of food shortages and longed, after their experience of hunger in prison camp, to eat their fill. Although women routinely cut their rations and those of their children short in order to increase their husbands' helpings, men accused their wives of cheating them of their rations. Stories of men eating in one sitting the week's rations for the entire family, hiding CARE packages for themselves, and even slaughtering livestock to eat away from the eyes of their families dot wives' and children's memories of the hunger years.[53]

Housing proved a similar bone of contention. Many women had survived recent years in extended-family households. Such households were crowded and tense, but they also provided emotional support and enabled a division of labor.[54] Returning men, however, unambiguously experienced such arrangements as cramped and the presence of other adults as a factor contributing to their own superfluity. Wives, dependent on their female relatives' help, fought to maintain such households, while husbands argued for a quick move to a private apartment. Although the housing shortage usually decided the issue in the wife's favor—at least in the short run— men's discontent led to conflict.[55]

Food shortages, cramped quarters, emotional distance—although these created tensions, women rarely held their husbands responsible for them. Women were far more critical of their husbands' refusal to contribute what they judged to be men's fair share of the work. Men were often unable to return to their position as breadwinner: they were wounded or sick, their firms had closed or had no openings, or they were excluded from their professions because of their Nazi histories. When men did find employment, they often had to settle for work of lower status than their former occupations had awarded, and their earnings constituted only an insignificant contribution to the household's subsistence. Yet few men, even if unemployed or earning useless currency, considered it appropriate to share the housework. "Of course women should continue to do needlework," remarked a bus driver—whose earnings could not have supported a family at the time of the interview—"or are we men supposed to darn our socks ourselves?"[56]

Understanding of their husbands as long as they were incapacitated, wives often lost patience when fit husbands refused to contribute what they could. Remarking on men's unwillingness to adapt to new circumstances, Walther von Hollander, best-selling novelist and author of advice books, described "passive men" who "sit . . . there and complain about fate. . . . They are so busy contemplating the unjustness of contemporary life . . . that they have no time or strength left over to help justice a little on its way. They aren't even able to establish justice in their own families by relieving their wives of at least part of the burdens of daily life."[57] Wives were no more sympathetic. "I cleared rubble and did my work as a housewife and mother, but my husband didn't want to do his work—for example, collecting wood," recalled a woman whose husband was unemployed. "When I said, 'We're going to freeze, go get a tree stump,' then he went against his will or not at all. And . . . when I stand there in hard times and try to make a meal out of nothing, . . . stand in line for hours, keep the apartment clean, keep him clean, wash his dirty underwear, then I can certainly expect that he do his men's work! I'd rather be alone. I got a divorce."[58] Women's dissatisfaction extended beyond the division of labor to include men's claims to authority. Aware of their own role in ensuring their family's survival, women saw little reason for submission. Those who did want their husbands to take charge were often disappointed: their husbands, weak, unemployable, and conditioned by years of military subservience, were rarely able to do so.[59]

Men returned to a world in which their skills had lost their value and their authority had been usurped. A Berlin man recalled his feelings of superfluity upon his return: "She'd done it all without me. When I came back, I didn't know whether she would still need me at all."[60] Torn between the desires to take charge and to be compensated for their sufferings, men wanted both to reclaim their leading role and to be pampered.[61]

In many ways, men were genuinely incompetent in the postwar order. They did not know the value of items on the black market; their skills were useless in the current economy; they did not know how their children had matured. In other ways, their apparent incompetence stemmed from a refusal to accept changed circumstances. They found household tasks demeaning, or they resisted taking orders from their wives. If they found employment, they felt they had grounds for authority despite the inadequacy of their wages. If they could not find work, they sought prestige in the family to compensate for their lost social status. Men's disappointment in their inability to make themselves indispensable expressed itself in sullenness and irritability, adding to wives' emotional work. Among women's duties was boosting their husbands' egos—not an easy task when husbands correctly estimated their value to have declined. "Konstantin," a pseudonymous East German author, urged women to stop looking so grumpy and instead smile more. Women, unlike men, had the capacity to look cheerful even in terrible circumstances, and men—"the weaker sex, in this regard"—were counting on women to keep their spirits up.[62] In an article entitled "Man as Ballast," Hollander wrote more critically of this expectation: "I know a great many women who devote their entire energy to making sure their husbands don't notice the helplessness and humiliation of their situations."[63]

Despite strains, millions of couples readjusted to married life. Partners forgave each others' infidelities or learned to live with unforgiving spouses; they found new common ground for intimacy or settled for emotionally distant relationships. Wives rarely freed themselves from sole responsibility for housework, but they gained a voice in making significant family decisions. Even families that survived intact were deeply affected by the period of separation and the renegotiation of terms for conjugal life.[64]

Hundreds of thousands of couples, however, divorced. In 1948, 88,374 West German couples divorced—an 80 percent increase over 1946.[65] The raw numbers were misleading: since civil cases had rarely been heard after

1943, there was a great backlog of petitions that could be processed only after the judicial system began to function again.[66] In addition, 42 percent of couples who divorced in 1947–48 had married during the war.[67] While contemporaries wrung their hands at the instability of wartime marriages, the obvious conclusion that the "divorce boom" would peter out once hastily concluded wartime marriages were dissolved seems to have been of little comfort. Furthermore, the "divorce boom" was mirrored by a "marriage boom": the marriage rate of 1947 exceeded that of 1938, and the rate continued to rise until 1950.[68] Nevertheless, the wave of divorces aggravated concerns about the future of the family, especially as women appeared increasingly willing to end their marriages. Before the war, men had sued for divorce nearly three times as often as had women. In 1949, women and men sued equally often.[69] Women were increasingly judged to bear a share of guilt for divorce, which disqualified them from alimony, yet divorced women favored a liberalization of divorce laws more often than did other women.[70] Divorce without alimony appeared preferable to continued marriage.

Men's behavior and spousal incompatibility did not just lead to a large number of divorces. They also made many single women think twice about marrying. "There is a whole group of women who consider things coolly and objectively and who, under the given conditions, have no fear of answering the question whether they will marry and have a family," wrote a reader of the Berlin women's magazine *Sie.* "They say with conviction 'no' and are nevertheless happy."[71] How did these women "consider things coolly and objectively"? They observed the marriages around them. "I've become skeptical because of the large number of divorces," declared a young woman who did not wish to marry.[72] At a 1948 reunion of a girls' school, the married classmates advised their unmarried friends not to wed.[73]

Women's hesitations about marriage stemmed not only from their observations of marriage and divorce, however, but also from their negative impressions of eligible men—a theme West German women's magazines covered with relish. The very shortage of men, according to more than one author, was making men into less desirable companions. "He sits satisfied on his throne as a precious, rare object and lets the best offer be presented to him," wrote a contributor to *Constanze* in 1948. "That his character hardly improves as a result of this excessive and uncritical pampering is a fact that will not be debated here."[74] Men's inability to adjust to postwar conditions prompted disdain. A woman described men in the postwar world: "This is how the men are: passive, impractical, helpless. Take whatever there is and don't ask where it comes from. Not to mention their stubborn rigidity, to which we're already accustomed. Frightful."[75] With tongue-in-cheek generosity, Hollander predicted that such men would eventually reassume some worth, "for in simpler circumstances they are, after all, to a certain extent useful."[76] But most women had been trained to seek a husband who was their superior. Now they suspected that few men were even their equals—even if they were "to a certain extent useful." Even women with more tact often returned to the theme of the disappointing men they had known. "Once in a while I looked around to see if there wasn't a good, trust-worthy man to marry. But I discovered none," recalled a woman wist-fully in a 1960 book. "I had the impression that the men had changed greatly since the war; I found them—and still find them to this day—almost primitive mentally, rather inflexible, and little differentiated from one another."[77]

Men's working lives, too, had ceased to impress many women. Women who had joined the labor force did not just gain economic independence. They also learned, to quote Hollander, "that men's work is, on the average, quite boring but hardly as strenuous as the grumpy and worn-out husband claimed upon coming home evenings."[78] They thus lost any sense of awe they might have had about the mysterious male world of the workplace—and with it some of their sense of awe about men.[79]

Furthermore, women's existing families often took priority. Women whose suitors offered marriage on the condition that they give up their children—including the orphans of their fallen husbands—rarely jumped at the opportunity. "I often had the chance to remarry," wrote a correspon-dent to *Die Frau von heute* in response to a reader whose fiancé wanted her to give her son to her parents. "To be sure, I would have gained a husband, but my two small children would not have gained a father. I . . . would give up a hundred men before I would give up one of my children. . . . If a man wants you to give away your child for his sake, then he is not worthy of your love."[80] Men who did not insist on starting fresh households had to qualify not only as good husbands but also as good fathers—and perhaps as good sons or brothers. As a young widow who lived with her mother and son explained, without irony, "It's very difficult to find exactly the right man for three people."[81] Even when suitors and other family members were willing, prospective wives had hesitations about altering their deli-cately balanced lives. A 1952 characterization in *Die Frau von heute* could have applied five years earlier: "If one asks [single mothers] why they do not marry again, then they say, 'As it is, when we come home, we're with our children; we can devote our couple of free hours to them. If we married, we would also have to take care of our husbands.'"[82]

Finally, women decreasingly saw marriage as a prerequisite to sexual companionship. "You can get by without a husband," explained a Berlin woman. "I mean, you don't have to go out and buy a cow just because you want a little milk."[83] Given recent memories of "forbidden contact," and in light of the uproar about fraternization, women who chose German partners and remained reasonably discreet may have escaped some of the criticism that otherwise accompanied nonmarital sexual relationships.

As the "marriage boom" indicates, women hardly swore off marriage. But they had reason to approach it with caution. In the words of a contributor to *Constanze*, "In our days of marriage crises, countless women have learned that marriage is the embodiment of happiness only in rare cases."[84] Indeed, occupation-era marriages proved as fragile as war marriages.[85] Women drew a variety of lessons from the "crisis." Those who married often had lowered expectations of intimacy or raised expectations of autonomy. Others became less inclined to risk disappointment in the first place.[86] Whether they remained married, divorced, married anew, or stayed single, they did so with a changed understanding of their own capacities and changed expectations of men and marriage.

.—.—.

Just as few women doubted the value of their marriages until their husbands returned, so were observers' concerns about the future of the institution of the family delayed. Women anxiously awaiting their husbands' return, widows mourning their lost husbands, and single women worrying about their chances for marriage all indicated the esteemed position of the "complete family." If many women were destined to remain single and if others ended their wartime marriages, this was the inevitable result of war. It implied no danger for the family as an institution.

But published discussions surrounding single women, marital status, and the future of the family quickly took radical directions. The lively sexual culture in the western zones was matched by daring discussion of single women's sexual lives. While West Germans grew concerned about concrete evidence of divorce, illegitimate childbearing, and cohabitation, they also responded to abstract discussions of unlikely options such as bigamy and short-term marriage. This discourse surrounding single women, as much as single women's actual behavior, made single women seem dangerous to the institution of the family.

The Soviet zone did not see such risqué published discussions of single women's sexual lives. East Germans did, however, share in another radical discussion: one concerning the institution of marriage itself. Noting that marriage made wives legally and economically dependent, critics across occupied Germany held that women's demonstrated competence proved that the institution of marriage was hopelessly outdated. And Germans did not have to look far to find cogent analyses of what was wrong with marriage. Since the nineteenth century, socialists and communists had held that bourgeois marriage had been created to protect men's property. According to this analysis, the double standard by which women's but not men's adultery was severely penalized and in which women were uniquely vulnerable in case of divorce was adequate evidence that pious words about love and commitment were simply a veil hiding the economic nature of the relationship. Bourgeois feminists, including many members of the Weimar parliament, had criticized the discrepancy between liberal ideals of equal rights and wives' disadvantage in family law. Alternately, they had argued that women's unique role as mothers made their legal subordination in the family particularly galling. Marxist and feminist critiques of marriage quickly appeared in women's magazines in all four zones. In the Soviet zone, the Marxist critique became the basis for family law, and those alarmed by it soon had a much more formidable opponent than correspondents to women's magazines. But in the western zones, criticism of the bourgeois institution of marriage led many to rush to defend an institution that was hardly endangered.

The first postwar months saw a brief discussion of a "crisis in the family" that proved to be a pale foreshadow of what was to come later. Here the culprit was the Nazi regime. After recounting admittedly exceptional stories about children who had denounced their parents, the first issue of *Sie* described the regime's larger effects on the family: "What was routine in the relationship between children and their parents was that the young people had 'service' [in the Hitler Youth or the League of German Girls]. . . . They came [home] to eat and to sleep."[87] An early issue of the Soviet zone's *Neue Berliner Illustrierte* featured an article on those who had been prohibited from marrying for racial reasons, although publicity about the woman standing alone took no notice of Jewish women who stood alone because their families had been killed.[88] In any case, within a few months, discussions of the Nazi past had all but disappeared from women's magazines in the western zones. In the Soviet zone reminders of Nazi crimes remained common, but discussion of the family increasingly focused on the codification of the institution under bourgeois law.

But the minimal coverage of the Nazi regime's effects on the family was as much a failure to problematize the family as it was an avoidance of themes related to Nazism. Women's magazines, at least, did not find the large numbers of "incomplete families" and single women particularly troubling. They acknowledged women's hopes for their men's return: the first two issues of *Sie* featured lead stories on "The Great Reunion" and "The Great Wait." Likewise, the inaugural issue of *Die Frau von heute* featured a story on reunions of wives and their husbands; even advertisers latched onto the theme.[89] Nevertheless, discussion of families unselfconsciously integrated the stories of "complete" and "incomplete" families. Articles on single women rarely focused on preparations for marriage; instead, taking single status as a given, they discussed work, child rearing, friendships, and sexuality for single women.

West German women's magazines frankly accepted illegitimate childbearing. Often using essentialist language regarding motherhood as the true purpose of women's lives, journalists, interview subjects, and readers all decried the notion that unwed women should be denied the "right to children."[90] Sociologists and journalists argued that unwed mothers and their children should be considered families: in current parlance, "incomplete families" included only those headed by divorced or widowed parents.[91] Denominational social work organizations reported with great alarm that unwed women, seeing childlessness as yet another form of deprivation, gladly bore children.[92]

Abortion statistics, however, suggest that single women preferred not to exercise their "right to children." Illegitimacy rates peaked in 1946, when few children were likely to have been the result of careful thought. A physician long involved in population policy estimated in 1949 that there was one abortion per 2.2 live births; in 1945 there had been one for every 3.3 live births and in 1942 only one for every 20. Single women who wanted to bear children in the midst of hunger and uncertainty remained exceptional, and the mass rapes prompted a temporary (if not always official) loosening of abortion restrictions.[93] At the same time they promoted tolerance for unwed mothers, contributors to women's magazines pondered ways to enable "surplus women" to bear children within marriage. With "short-term" marriage, for example, women could bear legitimate children with the understanding that the marriage would subsequently be dissolved without a divorce proceeding.[94] Despite single women's fears of bearing children outside marriage, however, the discussion of willed illegitimacy suggested to contemporaries that single women saw nonmarital childbearing as liberating.

Women's magazines covered divorce with equal openness. *Sie*'s sequel to "The Great Reunion" and "The Great Wait" was "The Great Decision," which examined options for estranged couples.[95] In articles with titles like

"A Dangerous Phrase between Spouses: 'For the Children's Sake' . . ." *Constanze* urged readers to divorce rather than prolong painful marriages.[96] Regarding marriages of emotionally distant partners, *Constanze* remarked, "Those who divorce faster have more from life!" and expressed admiration for women who extricated themselves: "We . . . want to bow down before the women who—despite the legal codes, which stand on the side of the men—muster up the courage and the strength to end marriages gone awry."[97] *Die Frau von heute* cited Engels's declaration that "if only marriages founded on love are morally sound, then likewise only those in which love continues," and ran short stories describing divorce as a step toward devotion to a new love.[98]

But unwed motherhood and divorce were tame in comparison with some of the other suggestions for meeting single women's needs, especially in West German magazines. After making quick work of suggestions that single women take comfort in religion and after satirizing men's outrage at fraternizers, Hollander turned to business in his series "On the Theme: Surplus of Women." Many women had no illusions about men, wrote Hollander, and had sworn off marriage entirely. They faced problems combining employment and housework, but, more important, their sexual needs would have to be acknowledged. "The days when a woman uncomplainingly dried up into an old maid, a sexless being, are gone and will not come back."[99] The state would have to revise laws prohibiting cohabitation and allowing hotels to inspect guests' marriage licenses. And since the few immature, unsophisticated, single men would prove inadequate for the masses of worldly, experienced, single women, liaisons between single women and married men were inevitable. In a show of solidarity for their single sisters, wives should tolerate their husbands' affairs, or, better yet, wife and mistress should become friends and enjoy an open relationship with their shared man.

Men's enthusiasm for such solutions exceeded women's, as a female columnist for *Constanze* dryly noted: "There are, after all—so comfort the men with supposedly saintly concern—so many possibilities [for single women]: either as the girlfriend of a married man or as an independent personality, completely wrapped up in her profession, going her 'courageous' way (with occasional affairs naturally— . . . for health's sake, in order to guard against neuroses and hysteria)."[100] But female columnists, too, discussed alternatives such as open marriage, short-term marriage, and marriages made contingent on the birth of the first child.[101]

East German publications remained silent on single women's sexual lives. On the rare occasions when *Die Frau von heute* took up issues in which sex was an inescapable subtext, such as the STD epidemic, the articles appeared in somber blocks of print, without the photos or sketches that ordinarily attracted the reader's attention—indeed, which typically claimed more space than did the text.[102] Although it promoted reform of illegitimacy law, the East German magazine did not discuss intentional nonmarital childbearing—which implied intentional nonmarital sex—as a way for women to fulfill their "natural desires" for children. Instead, *Die Frau von heute* ran fictionalized accounts of women who satisfied such cravings by taking in orphans or their husbands' extramarital children.[103] Only years later did *Die Frau von heute* find an acceptable way of presenting explicitly sexual themes: in the 1950s, it ran photos of camp followers and "exotic dancers" in West Germany as a warning that sexual degradation accompanied capitalism and the U.S. military presence.[104]

Single women's sexual lives, however, were not the only subject at issue. Bigamy, adultery, eased divorce, short-term marriage, and a "right to children" outside marriage did not just promise solutions for single women; they also threatened the institution of marriage. The challenge culminated in writings that shifted attention from problems facing single women to problems facing the theoretically privileged wife. "The bourgeois institution of marriage was built upon a basic premise: providing [for the wife]," wrote a reader of *Sie,* but " . . . today it is more commonly the man who flees into marriage in order to be 'provided for.' . . . Does marriage still have the same meaning for the woman that it once had?"[105] Once the discussion turned to property and the division of labor, *Die Frau von heute* was on firmer ground. Like West German magazines, it suggested that wives' employment would alter the balance of power in marriage; it criticized male privilege in family law; and it objected to the exclusion of nonmarital children from rights to their fathers' property.[106] Generally declining to quibble about distinctions between Marxist and non-Marxist feminist analyses, women's magazines east and west hammered away at the ways marriage systematically disadvantaged women. The occupation-era discussions of the relationship between propertied interests, male privilege, and marriage law suggest that the path taken later by East Germany was not simply an unpopular "revolution from above" or foreign import. Even if the Soviet authorities and the SED censored *Die Frau von heute,* they could not exert this sort of control over the West German magazines. The widespread criticism of the "bourgeois family" in print across occupied Germany indicates that such criticism enjoyed a popular resonance.

Indeed, public-opinion polls conducted in the western zones revealed a considerable tolerance for alternatives to the nuclear family. Only 3 percent of respondents to a 1950 poll in the Darmstadt area felt that the mother of an illegitimate child should be condemned. In the city 41 percent and in the countryside 31 percent said they would accept cohabitation in some or in all circumstances.[107] A 1948 poll in Hamburg and Schleswig-Holstein posed the question "Is 'free love' immoral?" In response, 61 percent answered no, and an additional 10 percent were undecided.[108]

No pollster asked Germans what they thought about lesbianism, and no journalist broached the subject. The social and sexual culture of the occupation, combined with memories of Weimar-era lesbian life, however, enabled a brief flowering of a Berlin lesbian subculture. "[In] 1945 after the war . . . all the clubs were reopened and we were free again, after Hitler had vanished from the scene," recalled a Berlin lesbian who could recall the culture of the Weimar years; "one club after another sprang up . . . it was wonderful."[109] Outside the traditional mecca of Berlin, the demographic imbalance helped to protect unwed women from scrutiny, making the late 1940s a brief interlude between the Nazi era and the repressive 1950s. Enthusiastic discussions about households in which women shared resources and housework enabled lesbian couples to cohabit without raising suspicion of a sexual relationship.[110]

Indeed, discussions of housing also revealed acceptance of other types of nonmarital households. Single women's traditional options had been continued residence with parents; subtenancy, often without kitchen or laundry facilities; or dormitories designed for young, childless, working-class women. Now, many pushed for new living arrangements for single women. A Berlin social worker favored apartment complexes for single, childless women; attached orphanages would enable each woman to "adopt" a child, thus meeting both the children's and the women's emotional needs.[111] Readers of *Constanze* suggested communal housing with day-care facilities for single mothers.[112]

Smacking of segregation for single women, such proposals may hardly sound revolutionary. But to suggest special housing for permanently single women was to acknowledge that singlehood was not necessarily a temporary station on one's life course. Furthermore, it was to recognize this population as worthy of the enormous investment that building projects required. "After all, single people . . . in particular make their energies available for reconstruction," insisted a correspondent to *Die Frau von heute*.[113] A home, like a child, was a woman's natural calling, and single women should have the right to exercise this calling.[114]

In the years immediately following the end of the war, women's magazines suggested a remarkable dismantling of privilege based on sex and marital status. Children, housing, even, according to the western magazines, sexual satisfaction—all should be available to single women. At the same time, even the institution of marriage was due for some rethinking. Married women, like their single counterparts, were living in a new era; they should not be bound by laws from a bygone world.

Nevertheless, there were contrary streams in the women's press. Popular discussions of such topics as divorce and single women's sexual lives indicated not only pity and acceptance but also fear. If tensions upon men's return revealed crises in many individual families, then the blunt discussion of alternatives for unhappy spouses and for single women helped to fan fears of a crisis in the institution of the family. Few Germans were prepared to abandon the institution of marriage. To the question "Do you consider the institution of marriage necessary or obsolete?" 90 percent of respondents across West Germany and West Berlin answered "necessary" in 1949.[115] And while Germans sympathized with single women's desire for children and some unwed couples' need to cohabit, adultery, bigamy, and eased divorce prompted strenuous objections.

Fears for the institution of marriage and fears for women's position went hand in hand. Appreciative commentary on the hour of the women referred at least as much to women's success in nurturing their families as to their visibility clearing rubble. Divorce, nonmarital childbearing, fraternization, and cohabitation signaled increased autonomy for only some women. For many more, it endangered a new-found status. A married woman protested to *Sie* that all the admiring coverage of single women devalued wives: "One gets the impression that every married woman is characterized as 'the little woman,' completely devoid of intellect, simply by the fact of her being married."[116] Not surprisingly, wives protested the apparent promotion of adultery. Wives bore heavy burdens, they argued: if single women wanted to share the pleasures of their husbands, then they could help with the housework those husbands created as well. Ending estranged marriages would be preferable to making them adulterous.[117]

Fears of juvenile delinquency further aggravated concern for the family. Children and teenagers, scarred by bombing raids, flight, the death of family members, and the loss of a political ideology became not only mothers' helpers but also vagrants, prostitutes, and thieves. And the social services that had served them were in shambles. When school opened in October 1945, only 70 percent of children attended, yet they created a teacher-student ratio of 1:84.[118] Firings of teachers associated with the Nazi party left an aging teaching force: in November 1946, elementary school teachers averaged fifty-eight years.[119] The Hitler Youth no longer structured young people's free time, and social workers faced a flood of physically and emotionally displaced youth.

Thus it seemed all the more urgent that families meet children's needs. Yet the relatively egalitarian relationships between mothers and children, which often proved highly functional during the crisis years, attracted little comment.[120] Instead, contemporaries regretted the absence of male authority.[121] In the western zones, social workers and criminologists seldom discussed the role of material need or traumas such as flight in creating youthful offenders. They considered the effects of the Nazi regime only slightly more often. Most commonly, they calculated the number of "fatherless" youthful offenders.[122] Publications in the Soviet zone noted more frequently the effects of Nazism and war, but they, too, indicated that "complete families" would go a long way toward solving the problem.[123]

Single mothers, who otherwise enjoyed the deepest sympathies of women's magazines, came in for a severe written beating when the subject of delinquent youth arose.[124] In an article entitled "Mothers without Love," Else Feldbinder described a social worker's daily rounds. The "mothers without love," all single, included several who traded the family's ration cards for cigarettes and alcohol and one who procured for her daughters. Combining women's magazines' usual cynicism about men with a much rarer critical tone toward women, Feldbinder concluded, "What most deeply disturbs us these days is that it is no longer the man who drinks or gambles away his meager earnings in order to forget his misery—rather, the unrestrained desire for pleasure and forgetting is surfacing among women."[125] Feldbinder's harsh language toward mothers contrasts strikingly with her sympathetic words for women picked up in vice raids.[126]

By the end of the decade, western women's magazines increasingly promoted restorative solutions to the crisis in the family. Two months after advising that "those who divorce faster have more from life!" in January 1949, *Constanze* suggested quite a different tack: "Instead of Divorce, a Kiss of Reconciliation!"[127] Later that year, *Constanze* ran a four-part series by a judge who explained that few complaints constituted grounds for divorce; he posed the question "Does One Really Have to Divorce Right Away?" and reminded his readers that "No Marriage Is Made in Heaven!"[128] Divorce, like adultery and single motherhood, appeared less a hard-nosed solution to postwar conditions and more a threat to the institution of the family.

On the heels of its series on divorce, *Constanze* ran the first of the genre that would characterize West German women's magazines in the 1950s: the instructional article on how to catch a husband. The reader was advised to seek out men on their own territory; to avoid being a fashionable bore, a helpless child, or a masculine buddy; and to care for her appearance, demonstrate her knowledge of housewifery, and mother her suitors. Most of all, she should pursue the goal of marrying with all requisite urgency. "Begin all this good and early. Don't let lovely fairy tales, your career path, or anything else hinder you from being on the lookout for the right partner and from meeting him halfway."[129]

Suggestions that women shift their focus from their jobs to the man hunt did not displace serious discussions of single women's circumstances overnight. Nevertheless, the transformation was anything but subtle. Rather than considering options for women who would remain single, West German women's magazines increasingly advised single women to enter a competition for a husband that many would have to lose. Readers with a continuing interest in the situation of single women would have to turn to the much smaller women's magazines of the unions and the Social Democratic Party.[130]

The desire to resolve the crisis in the family was also strong in East Germany, and *Die Frau von heute*, too, increasingly promoted marriage and discouraged divorce. Although the magazine discussed radical changes in illegitimacy and marriage law in 1949–50, it subsequently referred far more often to the betterment of wives' status than to the improved lot of unwed mothers and their children.[131] *Die Frau von heute* continued to hold that, in a socialist society, divorce was preferable to maintaining an estranged marriage for purely economic reasons, but it increasingly insisted that divorce should not be taken lightly.[132] *Die Frau von heute*, like *Constanze*, offered single women tips on how to attract men—although the tips differed. In a fictionalized letter, "Rudolf" informed "Liselott" that his ideal mate would not be a superficial woman interested mainly in pleasure and appearances. Instead, she would be knowledgeable, would have a well thought-out world-view, would be able to discuss serious things, and would push herself to achieve.[133] Responding to popular concern that maternal employment would produce neglected children, the magazine ran frequent articles concluding that employed women were superior mothers.[134] The ideal women of East and West Germany would differ, but both would be well placed to catch a mate, both would value marriage, and both would be good mothers. Both would restore the stability of the institutions of family and marriage.

At the same time *Die Frau von heute* encouraged marriage, however, it also left open the possibility that stability did not depend on marriage. Starting in 1948, the magazine frequently excluded information about women's marital status. Portraits of politically active women or of model workers described their families of origin, their wartime experience, their current work, and, often, their attachment to their children. Readers curious about a featured woman's marital status, however, would be frustrated. Had the children been born outside marriage? Had widowhood preceded the woman's leap into activism or a new working life? Was the divorced heroine living proof that a woman need not cling to a failed marriage? Was the woman a model socialist wife, sharing household duties and outside interests with her husband? With remarkable frequency, this information was simply omitted.[135]

Die Frau von heute aimed to communicate that marriage—even in a new form—was only one element of a better future for women. Political commitment and willingness to labor were equally important. Yet the reader, schooled to inquire first into women's family situations, might subvert this effort by interpreting women's activity in light of their marital status. Only by eliminating this information entirely could *Die Frau von heute* shift the focus from discussions of marriage, important in their own right, to discussions in which women's marital status was simply not relevant. Both Germanys would work to "restore the family" in the 1950s, but the extent to which this restoration defined women would differ.

.———.———.

Charlotte Kettner felt that single women, herself included, were caught in a no-win situation. As she explained in a letter to *Sie,* single women were surrounded by men eager to confirm their attractiveness via workplace flirtations. Once the women reciprocated their interest, however, the men decided to be faithful to their wives after all. In the meantime, the men's wives had caught wind of the situation and assumed the single women had initiated the flirtation. The single woman was left with no sexual satisfaction, a tense working relationship, and the enmity of the man's wife.[136]

Kettner illustrated both the opportunities and the dangers of single womanhood during the immediate postwar years. Even if she would not initiate a relationship with a married man, she might engage in one. Her co-worker was, after all, attractive, and she had daily contact with him. But she was vulnerable. Family, neighbors, and co-workers would blame her for threatening a marriage. Her suitor could terminate the relationship at will and retreat to his family, and he outranked her at work.

This mixture of opportunity and danger characterized single women's situation in the years after the war. Many single women scanned the families and the men they knew, considered their own situations, and decided against marriage. Or they decided they would marry only if they lucked upon an atypical man who would not threaten their autonomy or family ties. Women's increased confidence, combined with what seemed the reduced appeal of men and marriage, led many to conclude that divorce or singlehood was no catastrophe. It also led many to reject some of the traditional conditions of singlehood: sexual abstinence and childlessness.

But women's enthusiasm for alternatives such as singlehood and unwed motherhood was qualified. Many rejected marriage because men, in their present state, seemed mainly to create new burdens. In different circumstances, with better partners, the question might be reopened. In accepting unwed motherhood, most were expressing support for friends, sisters, and neighbors in a bind rather than revealing their own plans. And in their desire to marry, single women might well see other women as competitors, not comrades. "Women who have already had a husband should consider the fact that thousands of others haven't had one. It's not fair that one woman marries more than once and others not at all."[137] Some men bitterly noted women's interest in occupation soldiers, but others experienced an embarrassment of attentions as women directed their hopes for intimacy at the few available German men.[138]

Few single women desired changes in social mores more radical than sympathy for single status and unwed motherhood. If they had relationships with married men, they hardly wanted to broadcast their deeds with the unlikely expectation that wives would welcome their husbands' philandering. Drastically altering the institution of marriage—or abolishing it altogether—seemed either irrelevant or downright counterproductive. Wives, not single women, were the ones complaining about marriage. And most single women did want to marry—even if only under conditions that, at the moment, were unrealizable. Nevertheless, the mere promulgation of radical ideas in the West German press suggested to many contemporaries that the large numbers of competent, confident single women indeed constituted a threat to the family.

Criticism of the institution of marriage did not indicate popular rejection of the institution. Rather, it extended a discussion that had deep roots in Germany and which was now renewed by women and men, married and single. Just because criticisms of bourgeois marriage now seemed particularly timely, however, did not mean that they were uncontested. To the contrary: the revamping of family law would prove controversial in both Germanys.

Legal reform, however, still lay in the future. For the moment, the issue was the larger significance of marital status, not the specific conditions of each marital state. Starting in the late 1940s, both East and West German publications recommended marriage, but they did so in different ways. *Constanze* recommended marriage over other goals for women. *Die Frau von heute* recommended it over other marital states. In the emerging West German discourse, marital status played a definitive role: all other questions regarding women would have to be considered in the context of marital status. In the East German culture which *Die Frau von heute* helped to shape, marital status would be important but not definitive: in some aspects of women's lives, marital status would simply not be relevant. As the two postwar states loudly dueled over family law, this subtler matter attracted little comment. Yet unarticulated differences regarding the significance of marital status for women shaped family law, labor policy, and personal identity for East and West German women.

6 Restoring the Difference
The State and Marital Status
in West Germany

"Equal rights in marriage and the family are an entirely different matter than equal rights in social and working life."[1] The West German constitution guaranteed sexual equality in 1949; five years later, parliamentarian Helene Weber distinguished between the rights of a woman and the rights of a wife. She was not alone. Women's roles during the crisis years constituted a powerful argument for ending men's legal privilege, while social upheavals brought a desire to restore an order in which the family, complete with subordinate wife, seemed to have provided comfort and security. To affirm women's rights seemed a way of repudiating Nazi misogyny. But to create a protected, domestic sphere for women might be equally important. Not only Nazism, looming in the recent past, but also Communism, looming on the present border, seemed to interfere with the family and demand hard and dangerous labor from women. These tensions resulted in a remarkable shift in the significance of marital status: while legal distinctions according to marital status had always been important in their own right, in West Germany in the 1950s they briefly replaced legal discrimination according to sex.

The state alone did not shape the significance of marital status. Economic conditions, neighbors' attitudes, the media, and memories of earlier family life, to name just a few factors, all helped to form West Germans' perceptions and experiences of marital status. Nevertheless, the state was the arbiter of law, the dispenser of enormous sums of money, and the subject of intense interest by the news media. Public policy was thus the forum where debates concerning women and marital status were most clearly articulated.

These debates shaped the material, legal, and social significance of all marital states. The most heated questions concerned wives: should women continue to become different legal persons upon marriage, and should wife-hood imply an exclusive focus on the household? Motherhood's connection to marital status was also at issue: should unwed mothers have the same legal relationship to their children as did married mothers? Other aspects of single women's lives were at stake: their material circumstances and the shape of their daily routines—whether structured around employment or around housework—depended on women's wages, widows' pensions, alimony, and paternal support for nonmarital children. Through the 1950s, the relationships of marital status, motherhood, employment, and legal standing were matters of intense public debate.

Even aside from their legal and material ramifications, these discussions served to problematize marital status constantly. Although the German population had grown up with the understanding that a woman's marital status was central to her identity, the years of war and military occupation had raised questions about this assumption. During the crisis years, know-ing exactly how a woman was getting by was more informative than know-ing whether she was married. West German policy debates of the 1950s, however, helped to restore the centrality of a woman's marital status. Per-haps most remarkably, they helped to create a popular perception that the war generation of women standing alone constituted a distinct social group with a significance that outlived the crisis years. As developments in East Germany would demonstrate, demographic imbalance and shared experi-ence of survival without men's help did not make a durable common iden-tity for women standing alone inevitable. West German policy debates thus did more than shape the material and personal circumstances of women of all marital statuses: they also reestablished women standing alone as a dis-tinct social group.

But single women were defined almost exclusively by their outsider sta-tus in the early Federal Republic. Unlike the Nazi state, which offered young single women, as a group, a role in shaping the new order via their activism; unlike the Democratic Republic, which elevated working women—a cate-gory that included most single women—into pioneers of its new order; the Federal Republic offered no ideological base on which single women could understand themselves to be significant. West German political discourse offered single women one way to establish a legitimate public identity: they might argue—as did war widows raising their fallen husbands' children—that they at least resembled housewives. In addition, an elite, activist soror-ity succeeded in leaving a mark on West German state and society. But if single women, whether prominent or ordinary, wanted to understand them-selves to have a significant role in building the new West Germany, they would have to identify this role themselves. Political players varied in their treatment of single women, but whether they vilified or pitied them, in one regard their message regarding single women was uniform: women standing alone were a legacy of the dismal past, not a key to a brighter future.

.—.—.

"What is politics?" asked Anna Haag, a Stuttgart activist, in 1946. Many women feared politics, acknowledged Haag, and for good reason. Politics, especially in the years leading to 1933, had not remained a battle of ideas; rather, it had become a war employing "everything that was not nailed down." Now it was "up to us women to show how political meetings must run! . . . For it concerns nothing less than the shaping [*Gestaltung*] of our earthly life."[2] In the early years of the military occupation, many women echoed Haag's call. The Third Reich had been a "men's state" (*Männerstaat*), bringing death and destruction.[3] Now women's majority gave them a unique opportunity, while their feminine sensibility gave them a unique responsibility: to replace a politics of destruction with a politics of nurturing.

When the Western Allies began to shape new political structures and to permit Germans to organize politically, it appeared that women might gain a more prominent role. Having removed Nazi functionaries, the military governments appointed female mayors and administrators; women were well represented on town councils. Furthermore, many grass-roots women's organizations emerged, some under the aegis of the occupier, some independent.[4] Some were explicitly partisan; others focused on meeting women's immediate needs but understood that such matters as the distribution of food were political.[5]

Politics, however, was to remain a male preserve in West Germany. With the revival of political parties and the reestablishment of a complex bureaucracy, old networks and credentials, dating from the Nazi, Weimar, or even imperial period, regained their importance. Neither a claim to a pacifist sensitivity nor a familiarity with the economics of the household counted for much in the halls of Bonn. When the provincial legislatures of the three western zones chose sixty-five delegates to compose a "basic law" for a new West German state, they sent only four women. Of the members of the first Bundestag, 7 percent were female, and, in a land in which joining a political party was a sign of serious commitment, women constituted only about 15 percent of party members in the 1950s.[6] Women's caution about entering the world of politics did not change overnight, nor did most men's and women's greater trust in men to run their political affairs. Elfriede Nebgen, one of many who criticized the "men's state" in print, did not conclude her analysis with a call for more women in politics. Rather, she urged men not to forget women when the former regained their place in political life.[7]

Younger women were especially scarce in political life. Even in the earliest postwar days, when women inhabited many city halls, activists noted young women's disinterest with consternation. In this regard young women hardly differed from young men. Socialized by the excitement of a mass movement, they had subsequently been sorely disappointed by politics. Small, democratic grass-roots efforts were alien to them and had to compete with the demands of daily life. Young women entered the postwar period with experience in the labor service or in auxiliary military organizations, not with the social work and legal backgrounds that had served as an entrée to politics for a few women in the Weimar era.

By contrast, a small but significant number of middle-aged and older women recalled both their own earlier activism and an environment that had enabled serious discussion of issues important to them. They were better equipped than their daughters to become a pioneering minority in the Federal Republic. Gabriele Strecker, a CDU activist, recalled her delight at meeting Maria Probst: forty-seven when she entered the Bundestag in 1949, Probst, a widowed mother of two, was a refreshing contrast to many aging female representatives, who had been born as early as the late 1870s.[8]

Strecker was worried about a generation gap, but younger women had reason to thank middle-aged and older women who, after decades of struggle and, often, personal hardship, inserted themselves into the political process.[9] One of Germany's first female Ph.D.s, Marie-Elisabeth Lüders had organized social services for women and children during the First World War. A member of the Weimar parliament, she had championed feminist issues such as family law reform and deregimentation of prostitutes. Imprisoned for four months in 1937, bombed out of her Berlin home, she celebrated her sixty-seventh birthday in the summer of 1945—and promptly got back to work. Like many heirs of Germany's bourgeois feminist movement, she found a political home in the liberal Free Democratic Party (FDP), which she represented in the Berlin city council until she joined the Bundestag in 1953. Until her retirement in 1961, she untiringly championed a feminist agenda, bringing a sharp mind and a lifetime of experience to the task.

In the 1950s, a small band of women like Probst and Lüders held elected office, led women's sections of federal and state ministries, assumed judgeships, and used their positions in nongovernmental organizations to lobby the government. They often disagreed on issues relating to women, but in this they reflected the population of women at large. And the Federal Republic was a democracy. Unlike their predecessors in the Nazi state and their contemporaries in East Germany, these women's positions did not depend on their adherence to a party line in a single-party state. Although the institutions of the West German state posed formidable obstacles to women's active participation, those who managed to breach the walls were free to employ their powers of persuasion to shape policy.

Politically active women were overwhelmingly single. In the third Bundestag (1957–61), Lüders was among the 60 percent of women, compared with 8 percent of men, who were unwed or widowed and without children. Nineteen percent were married but child-free; only 21 percent had children, and these children were no longer small.[10] In other branches of government, in professional groups that petitioned the state, in religious and social work organizations, and in women's sections of the unions, the story was no different. Strecker, who personally urged elderly women to leave politics since she found their image embarrassing, described single women's overrepresentation and its corollary—a token presence for women overall—as natural.[11] A wife and mother of two children born in the 1930s, she felt that few could follow her path. Political women took for granted that most women were unavailable for political activity, even as they criticized their parties and institutions for erecting roadblocks before the few who were able to enter public life. Political women—mainly middle-aged and older, single, child-free or with grown children, with unusual educational and professional backgrounds—understood themselves to be an elite minority. They did not envision political institutions that enabled wives and mothers or women overburdened by daily routines to participate in numbers proportionate to their part of the population. But they took seriously their duty to represent such women, and they understood that, as a tiny minority, they would have to work hard to address such women's interests. Their skill and persistence ensured that women's issues made it onto the agenda, and their voices were prominent on all sides of debates concerning women's issues.

.—.—.

In 1948–49, the Parliamentary Council drew up a constitution for a new, West German state. The Parliamentary Council included equal numbers of representatives from the SPD and from the Christian Democratic Union/Christian Social Union (CDU/CSU) coalition. Claiming a Christian rather than a nationalist conservatism, the CDU/CSU simultaneously distanced itself from socialism, communism, and Nazism; identifying itself as "democratic" and "social," it distanced itself from the antirepublicanism of most of the conservative Weimar parties. Representing an attempt to overcome the confessional divides that had wracked German politics since

Bismarck's time, the CDU/CSU inherited much of the electorate of the old Center Party, the voice of political Catholicism (and a backbone of the Weimar Republic). It also, however, attracted bourgeois Protestants whose antipathy to socialism and liberalism had led them to vote for antirepublican parties during Weimar. The SPD had adopted reformist socialism in the late nineteenth century. Following the First World War, the revolutionary left had formed a separate Communist Party (KPD), and the SPD had become a mainstay of republicanism while remaining anathema to anti-Marxists. Also represented in the Parliamentary Council were many smaller parties, most notably the liberal FDP, the rump Center Party, and the KPD. The Parliamentary Council reflected the varied political and social landscape that had produced the lively debates discussed in Chapter Five.

It is thus not surprising that the Basic Law, which resulted from the deliberations, ensured that marital status would remain a matter of contention for years to come. The Basic Law guaranteed equal rights regardless of sex and special protections for marriage and the family; it denied equal rights to children regardless of legitimacy status. All these provisions were controversial, and the extent to which marital status defined a woman was a question lurking behind all of them.

Arguing in the Parliamentary Council that the Basic Law should guarantee sexual equality, Social Democrat Elisabeth Selbert did not just insist, as had many feminists in the late nineteenth and early twentieth centuries, that women's distinct contribution as wives and mothers warranted improved legal standing. Rather, she pointedly referred to women in positions in which marital status was irrelevant: "The woman who, during the war years, stood atop the rubble and replaced men at the workplace has a moral right to be valued like a man."[12] Regardless of women's unique roles as wives and mothers, Selbert assumed that recent experience had rendered moot old arguments against equal rights for the entire female sex.

She was mistaken, both in her assumption that the justice of equal rights was too obvious to deny and in her assumption that sexual equality was a basic principle, preceding more specific discussions of wifehood. Even her sole female colleague in the SPD delegation, Frieda Nadig, initially suggested a more gradual approach that would allow legislators time to revise marriage and family law.[13] Other representatives were less concerned about leaving adequate time to revamp family law than they were with the prospect that family law might reflect sexual equality in the first place. With the notion of equality within marriage the clear sticking point, the Council's main committee defeated the provision for equal rights in December 1948.

The West German public, which otherwise showed little interest in the proceedings of the Parliamentary Council, reacted vehemently. Their letters often reflected their sense that sexual equality was a matter of principle, prior to the regulation of family life by the Civil Code. "Whoever in the Parliamentary Council has the courage to oppose equal rights for women with moth-eaten arguments from the previous century seems to have had the luck to have slept through or dreamt away recent years," remarked one correspondent dryly. "*De facto* equality for women has long been achieved—it is hindered only by antiquated [legal] paragraphs—and the rational and sensible men who do not need to draw their superiority from the Civil Code see in this development—despite the red herrings of the right to determine [the family's] place of residence and family name— only relief and simplification."[14] The Parliamentary Council reconsidered. When the Basic Law finally emerged, it included in Article 3 Paragraph 2 an unqualified guarantee of legal equality for men and women.

Compared with the idea of sexual equality, the notion that the state should protect the family was uncontroversial. Somewhat more open to debate was the precise relationship between family and marriage. For the conservative Christian parties, marriage preceded the family. The draft of the CDU/CSU read, "Marriage is the form of communal living between man and woman sanctioned by law. It forms the basis of the family. Marriage and family and the rights and duties associated with it stand under the protection of the Constitution."[15] Social Democrats, like the Communists, argued for consideration of families that differed from the CDU/CSU's vision. Citing the demographic imbalance, Nadig insisted that, "we must take into account that in the future we will have a mother-family"—that is, a family established by a parent-child bond rather than a spousal bond.[16] Christian conservatives took issue with Nadig's chronology: female-headed households, they felt, were the legacy of an unfortunate past; they should not form the basis of discussions about the future. Nevertheless, when the matter advanced to the main committee, Theodor Heuss, leader of the FDP and future president of the Federal Republic, voted with Social Democrats to remove the first two sentences of the CDU/CSU's draft. This excision left a principled expression of support for the family and marriage with no explanation of the precise relationship between the two institutions. Article 6 Sentence 1 of the Basic Law read, "Marriage and family stand under the special protection of the public order [*staatlichen Ordnung*]."

In considering children born outside marriage, however, it was impossible to evade judgment on the primacy of marital status. Consistent with their position in the Weimar period, Social Democrats and Communists pushed for an unequivocal statement that legitimacy would not affect children's legal status. Christian conservatives in the CDU, CSU, and the small Catholic Center Party objected. Granting nonmarital children equal rights would not only threaten the protected place of the family, which, according to their definition, was preceded by marriage. It would also ill serve the children, who could overcome their disadvantage only if the state took over some of the powers parents otherwise exercised.[17]

Although the sentence technically concerned the rights of children, the debate quickly turned to evaluations of mothers. Citing her social work experience, the Center Party's Helene Wessel held that "a number of unwed mothers—this is not a judgment, simply a question of the real conditions—are not at all capable of taking over legal guardianship." Selbert disagreed, urging her colleagues to "recall that, today, not just women and girls from the lowest classes, from the proletarian classes, or perhaps women and girls who do not understand the responsibility of motherhood, are unwed mothers. From Youth Bureau reports, I know that many daughters of the highest circles belong to the group of unmarried mothers today." Selbert's reminder that the daughters of the CDU, CSU, and FDP, and not just the daughters of the proletarian SPD and KPD, might become unwed mothers might have been in part a strategic move. With this reminder of the changing profile of single mothers, however, she implicitly conceded the point that the exercise of parental authority by single mothers—but not by married couples—depended on social evaluations of them. Only the Communist representative to the main committee challenged the premise that an inferior position for young, unwed, working-class mothers and their children might be warranted.[18] The question was now out in the open. Women might have rights equal to men's, but did this mean that marital status could have no bearing on those rights? And to what extent should legal distinctions depend on social evaluations of appropriate behavior for women according to marital status?

The parties initially split as they had on sexual equality, with a narrow majority opposing the SPD's position.[19] But while popular outrage prompted parliamentarians to reconsider women's equality, no public outcry on behalf of nonmarital children and their mothers ensued. Article 6 Sentence 3 of the Basic Law repeated the Weimar Constitution's pledge of equal "conditions for . . . illegitimate children's . . . physical and spiritual development and social status." It did not guarantee legal equality.

The implications of marital status were still ambiguous. On the one hand, the ideal of sexual hierarchy within the family was no longer powerful enough to deny the entire female sex legal equality. On the other hand, marriage and the family still warranted special protections, and marital status still determined the legal standing of mothers and their children. With one in three households headed by a woman in 1950, with nearly 20 percent of urban children in female-headed households in the early 1950s, with one in ten children born outside marriage in 1950, and with married couples struggling with the ramifications of women's increased independence, questions about the significance of marital status were not going to go away.[20]

.——.——.

After 1949, the government faced the task of bringing the Civil Code in line with the new Basic Law. In force since 1900, the Civil Code, which among other things regulated family life, contained countless provisions that violated women's equal rights. In revising the Civil Code, the Bundestag confronted the subject that had lurked beneath the controversy concerning equal rights for women: the legal status of wives. It also reopened the matter of unwed mothers and their children. In the end, the parliament reconfirmed the division of women according to marital status.

The Parliamentary Council gave the government three and a half years to revise the Civil Code. If the law was not revamped by March 31, 1953, the equal rights clause of the Basic Law would go into effect, automatically making many provisions of the Civil Code unconstitutional. The task of revising the Civil Code was an enormous one, and the first Bundestag promptly found a way of bringing it down to size. It limited its view to those portions of the Code that concerned the legal relationship between married couples. Ignoring issues such as women's educational and employment opportunities, differential pay scales, divorce law, and illegitimacy law, the Bundestag instead debated wives' obligations in their households, the property rights of married women, and decision-making powers within the family.[21] Women's equality was redefined as a question about wives; single women were out of the picture.

The first Bundestag, elected in 1949, illustrated the diversity that continued to characterize West German political life. No single party held more than one-third of the seats. A narrow coalition of the CDU/CSU and FDP formed a government, but the SPD was the largest single party, and smaller parties (not including the FDP) occupied 20 percent of the seats. Although the makeup of the Bundestag promised many fundamental disagreements, at least as notable were the areas in which the major (and most of the minor) parties tacitly agreed. Although the Social Democrats' opposition status surely contributed to the Bundestag's disinterest in workplace issues for women, Social Democrats were as inclined as conservatives to turn their attention first to women's roles as wives and mothers. When Selbert had argued for women who had "stood atop the rubble and replaced men at the workplace," she drew on popular images of women's "forced emancipation" in Germany's most desperate hour. If women had been compelled to shoulder equal burdens, they should enjoy equal rights. But the burdens had been heavy, and they contrasted sharply with memories of the prewar Nazi years, which Germans who had not suffered persecution recalled as the best period of the twentieth century.[22] Among other things, full employment, good male wages, and favorable demographics had enabled women to marry, to have children, and to devote themselves to their households during those years. In improving women's situation, the new state's task would be to recapture this environment (minus the racial ideology and aggressive nationalism with which it had been linked), not to enhance the nondomestic roles that Germans associated with hard times.

Social Democrats had been moving away from classical Marxism's views on women since the late nineteenth century. Thinkers such as Engels, Bebel, and Lenin had held that women's full participation in the labor market was the key both to their own emancipation and to the development of marriages between equals. The Communists still challenged the assumption that nondomestic roles were undesirable for women, but they were a marginal presence in the first Bundestag and had no seats whatsoever after 1953. The fact that Communists now ruled East Germany made it all the more necessary for the West German SPD to distance itself from the more radical elements of its nineteenth-century heritage. Throughout the 1950s, the major parties displayed a solid consensus around the notion that the ideal role for a woman was that of housewife and mother.

To be sure, Social Democrats and feminists within the FDP differed from most of the CDU/CSU on the need to create favorable conditions for those who could not realize this ideal: single mothers, women whose husbands earned little or were disabled, women who sought purpose in work since the demographic imbalance denied them marriage. Social Democrats and bourgeois feminists also disagreed with Christian conservatives about the legal status of women who did fulfill the ideal role. Christian conservatives contended that the housewife, while morally and socially equal to the husband, was legally subordinate; their opponents insisted that a wife's moral and social equality must go hand in hand with legal equality. The notion that female fulfillment was tied to a single marital state, however—that of marriage—remained nearly unquestioned.

The focus on wives in their family roles was thus not surprising. Advocates of women's rights argued that recent experience had shown the legal infantilization of wives to be not only unfair but impractical. Wives who had maintained their husbands' businesses single-handedly during the war had no claim on the property—including that acquired solely by their own labors—if their husbands subsequently divorced them.[23] Wives who had deposited their wartime earnings into their husbands' bank accounts had been unable to withdraw money to care for their families during the postwar crisis. Wives had pulled their families through the crisis years by taking on employment, supervising evacuations, and managing hair-raising flights westward. Yet once their husbands returned, these wives had no legal voice in making decisions regarding their own employment or their families' place of residence.

These proved to be compelling arguments for wives' rights. Parliamentarians agreed to make joint ownership of property the norm and to allow both partners to dispose of their own wealth. They revoked the husband's ability to forbid or order his wife's employment, and they struck his sole right to make decisions concerning the common life of the family, such as where it should live.

For these provisions to become law, however, the Bundestag had to resolve a question that proved much stickier: who would have ultimate decision-making power in matters concerning the children? Conservatives argued that someone must have the final say—and that the father should be that someone. The opposition, mainly Social Democrats and inheritors of the bourgeois feminist tradition within the FDP, insisted that such a solution violated women's equal rights. The government and Bundestag were unable to resolve the matter by their deadline, and the equal-rights clause went into effect without a revised Civil Code.

Parliamentary elections in the fall of 1953 awarded the CDU/CSU a simple majority. The victory was less a referendum on policy regarding women and the family than a vote of confidence on the country's economic progress and westward orientation in the Cold War. Nevertheless, Social Democrats who had hoped to capitalize on women's frustration with the CDU/CSU's resistance to equal rights were disappointed: women voted for the Christian conservative parties in even greater proportions than did men.[24] The new conservative consensus would remain solid until the late 1960s.

Proponents of a traditional family policy received a further boost with the creation of a Ministry of Family Affairs in 1954 and the appointment of Franz-Josef Würmeling as its head. Outspoken in his belief that paternal authority was ordained by god, Würmeling understood his job to be the protection and promotion of large, stable families whose members recognized the immediate authority of the husband and father and the ultimate authority of the deity. By producing abundant children, according to Würmeling, such families ensured West Germany's future. They also provided security not only against the intrusions of a totalitarian state, whether Communist or Nazi, but also against a liberal-inspired decline into individualism, materialism, and secularism. Other types of households—childless couples, couples with only one or two children, singles, unwed partners, unwed mothers and their children—at best left their members vulnerable to the dangers of the modern age (Fig. 13). At worst, they owed their very existence to the influence of such principles as individualism and socialism and, embodying such principles, threatened to infect the larger society.[25]

Christian conservatives disagreed with Social Democrats and liberals on the ideal of legal equality within the family, but, even more fundamentally, they disagreed on the relationship between the family and political principles of any type. According to organized Catholicism, in particular, the family was a prepolitical organization. As an organic whole, it acted as a harmonious unit on the social stage.[26] Wives' equality with their husbands was a moral equality, unrelated to secular law. The Basic Law's provision of equal rights, however, was a political language. It had no more place in the family than any other political language.

Proponents of wives' equality argued that if Christian conservatives wished to remove secular politics from the family, they might start with those provisions in the Civil Code that fixed paternal authority in law. While Christian conservatives saw the family as a prepolitical organization, Social Democrats and liberals understood equal rights to be natural rights, prepolitical in their own way. Laws governing family organization would have to adhere to this most basic principle. Not to be outdone in distancing themselves from Nazism and Communism, Social Democrats warned that to prescribe relations within the family was to follow totalitarian practice.[27]

Within the CDU/CSU, religiously inspired social conservatism coexisted with fiscal conservatism. When support for a Christian moral order threatened to be expensive, arguments for a small public sector usually prevailed.[28] More often, however, the two visions complemented each other. In 1957, the Bundestag passed a new law that ended husbands' authority over wives and granted wives considerable property rights but which also upheld the man's role as legal representative for the family and paternal authority over the children. In a common instance, the wife, having learned the hard way that marriage did not ensure a woman's well-being, wanted her daughter to receive vocational training; the husband felt that such

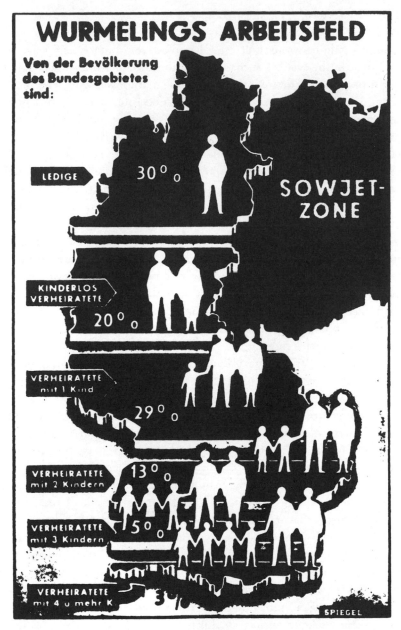

Figure 13. "Würmeling's Working Field." This graph, published in 1954 in West Germany's major weekly, illustrated the family status of West Germany's population. Explicitly focusing on the small number of children per family and large number of singles, the graph also makes some implicit points. Married couples who cross the line that should divide them from singles—by remaining child-free—are a matter of concern; single people who cross the same line by having children are invisible entirely. Courtesy *Der Spiegel*, 15 September 1954.

training would be wasted since the daughter would marry and leave the workforce. In the event of such a conflict, the father's word was decisive— even if the daughter desired training and the mother was willing to finance it from her own earnings. Only a high court decision in 1959 struck down legal inequality within marriage.[29] Even this decision, however, left intact the "housewife marriage." Women, according to law, contributed to marriage by running the household and caring for children; men contributed their paychecks. Such recognition of the value of housework was significant: husbands could not claim, upon divorce, that their wives had contributed nothing to the marriage and thus had no claim to property. Nevertheless, the legal codification of the "housewife marriage" was limiting. Wives' right to seek employment no longer depended on their husbands' agreement—but it did depend on their continued ability to perform their household duties. The legal divide between single and married women had narrowed, but it had not closed.[30] Indeed, with sexual discrimination now technically forbidden, marital status had gained new significance. In the meantime, single women had been defined out of the decade's key debate concerning women's rights.

Although the Parliamentary Council had not made nonmarital children the legal equals of marital children, the Basic Law still required a reform of legitimacy law. The Civil Code's provisions for unwed mothers and their children conflicted both with the requirement that illegitimate and legitimate children enjoy equal conditions and with the stipulation of women's equality. But if lawmakers could not agree on wives' rights within marriage and if they could agree to postpone other aspects of legal reform necessary to realize women's equality, they could certainly take their time when it came to nonmarital children. Throughout the first decade of the Federal Republic's history, lawmakers steered clear of illegitimacy law.[31]

Religious and social work organizations, however, devoted a great deal of attention to the matter. Care for unwed mothers and their children had traditionally been an important component of their work, and they had debated the legal and social implications of illegitimacy for decades. With the revival of organizations that either had been banned or had operated with greatly reduced autonomy during the Nazi years, social workers returned to an old question: what was the best way to improve the situation of illegitimate children and their mothers?[32] In keeping the discussion alive through the 1950s, social work organizations set the terms of the debate that would later be joined by legislators.

Three questions formed the core of the dispute. First, should nonmarital children be the legal relatives of their fathers? If so, they would bear the father's name and have the same claim to financial support and inheritance as the fathers' legitimate children. This option would clearly challenge the privilege of the family, if "family" included only groupings founded upon marriage.[33] Indeed, it promised trouble for wives and marital children. Wives hardly relished the thought of having to divide their family's often meager resources yet further in order to ensure that their husbands' illegitimate children received the same level of support as their own children. And the threat was not only material. Wives who suspected their husbands' infidelities often feigned ignorance, at considerable cost to their dignity, in order to ensure family harmony. To be forced to recognize their husbands' illegitimate offspring would be to shatter a fragile peace.

The second question concerned the establishment of paternity. Should a man's claims that a woman had had relations with more than one man during the period of conception continue to disqualify a mother's suit for child support?[34] Finally, did women's equality entitle unmarried mothers to full parental authority? At present, every illegitimate child was assigned an official guardian (a *Vormund* from the Youth Bureau) at birth. Unwed mothers could apply for legal guardianship of their children, but they were still supervised by the Youth Bureau. An unmarried mother could gain full parental powers (*elterliche Gewalt*) only by adopting her own child. By contrast, married and divorced mothers had parental authority over their legitimate children, which was abrogated only in the case of disagreement with the father—and then the father, not the state, had decision-making powers. Widows had full parental authority unless they remarried, in which case the late father's other surviving relatives gained an interest.

In the debates surrounding the Basic Law, denominational social work organizations had argued alongside Christian conservative parties that legal equality would hurt nonmarital children. Such children, lacking the social, economic, and psychological security of a male-headed family, needed the special protections provided by a state-appointed guardian. "Different things must be handled differently," insisted Elisabeth Zillken, general secretary of the Catholic Caritas from 1916 to 1958, summing up the argument that formulaic legal equality could hurt society's weaker members.[35] Those who insisted on full parental authority for unwed mothers demanded equal rights for women at the cost of children's well-being.

Workers' Welfare, a branch of the SPD until 1947, constructed its proposals for illegitimacy law on different premises. Historically associated with the party that had led the fight for both women's and nonmarital children's rights, it saw no natural conflict between them. Furthermore, while denominational organizations feared that the provision of equal rights for nonmarital children would hinder the attainment of equal conditions, representatives of Workers' Welfare argued that equal conditions depended on equal rights.[36]

Social reformers' interest in illegitimacy law was not infectious. Much to the frustration of activists on both sides, the Bundestag showed no inclination to improve the conditions for nonmarital children's development. In October 1958, the Constitutional Court ordered the Bundestag to do so. The Bundestag responded by considering that aspect of illegitimacy law most closely tied to women's rights: unwed mothers' legal relationship to their children.

Christian conservatives, supported by the religious social work organizations, Würmeling's ministry, and the professional association of guardians, argued against expanding unwed mothers' legal authority. They reiterated that the system of guardianship had been carefully built over decades in order to meet the special needs of nonmarital children. These needs had not changed simply because women as a sex were now the legal equals of men as a sex.[37] The parliamentary minority seconded the Workers' Welfare position that parental authority must be automatic for legally competent, adult, unwed mothers. The Youth Bureau's sole role should be to ensure that the children received the financial support they were due.[38] Jurist Maria Hagemeyer accused the government of withholding the constitutional rights of unwed mothers on the basis of a bigoted assessment of their capabilities. Hagemeyer was well placed to oppose conservatives' insistence that improved status for unwed mothers and their children was part of a Communist program for the destruction of the family. As the author of an officially commissioned, scathing attack on East German family law, Hagemeyer demonstrated that support for unwed mothers and their children could go hand in hand with opposition to Communist family politics.[39]

The government offered a draft law in which official guardians would continue to be assigned to every nonmarital child. Mothers, however, could apply not only for guardianship but also for full parental authority. In such cases, the courts might leave to the Youth Bureau the job of pursuing fathers for financial support.[40] Unwed mothers would retain the burden of proof in demonstrating their competence to be anything other than the caregiver for their children (to have *Sorgerecht*). Not one member of the Bundestag's Committee for Family and Youth supported the proposal that unwed mothers automatically receive the full parental authority that came with marriage.[41] The government's draft was adopted, essentially unchanged, in the Law to Revise Family Law of August 11, 1961.[42]

Although the legal implications of illegitimacy had been debated for decades, the postwar reconsideration of family law established a new framework for such discussions. While parliamentary debates on women's equality reached an impasse over the possibility of a conflict of interest between wife and husband, the question of illegitimacy was dominated by the specter of a conflict of interest between mother and child. "This question concerns less the mother's interests in equal rights than the legal and protective interests of the child," explained a member of the Committee for Family and Youth, expressing the assumption that the law could guarantee one or the other but not both.[43]

The debate on parental authority, however, revealed a curious reversal of positions. When considering marriage law, Christian conservatives had seen the family as a whole in relation to the state: the state must not treat family members as atomized individuals. Social Democrats and many liberals had countered that women's rights must be protected even if this meant the family did not speak with a uniform voice. When it came to nonmarital children, Social Democrats and liberals argued a convergence of mothers' and children's interests: to award mothers full parental authority was to improve conditions for their children. Accusing Christian conservatives of inserting the state, in the form of an official guardian, into a private relationship, they held that unwed mothers should represent their children on the social stage. Christian conservatives, by contrast, presented the possibility—indeed, in their eyes, the likelihood—of a conflict of interest between mother and child. To award mothers full parental authority was to infringe on their children's rights to conditions equal to those enjoyed by marital children; to guarantee nonmarital children equal conditions would require limiting unwed mothers' rights. Children's interests as individuals were paramount, and, not recognizing nonmarital mother-child dyads as families, Christian conservatives did not see them as units that properly stood between the state and the individual.

Nevertheless, the two discussions were not mirror images of each other. In marriage law, Christian conservatives supported the reduction of an adult's legal autonomy; in illegitimacy law, Social Democrats favored parental authority over a minor. In marriage law, Social Democrats and liberals envisioned the possibility of a conflict of interest between partners; in illegitimacy law, Christian conservatives considered a conflict of interest between mother and child to be the norm. Perhaps most significantly, though, the parties did not frame the question in parallel terms. Discussions of marriage pitted Christian conservative language regarding the family as a prepolitical unit against a liberal language of individual rights.

In debates regarding illegitimacy law, Christian conservatives claimed to protect the rights of children, but Social Democrats and feminists did not counter with language emphasizing the unity of the family—the present analysis notwithstanding. Demands to recognize "mother families," audible in 1948, were not now reiterated. Rather, Social Democrats and bourgeois feminists countered with language concerning women's rights. But with children the weaker party, this was a losing strategy. When "the family" entered the debate, it was not the "mother family" of occupation-era discussions. Rather, it was the marital family of the father, which, Christian conservatives pointed out, would be disrupted if nonmarital children could make increased claims on their fathers. In discussions of nonmarital children's rights vis-à-vis their fathers, Christian conservatives preserved their mantle as defenders of "the family."

Still, conservatives were better able to slow the pace of change than to turn back the clock. Despite a concerted campaign by confessional organizations, the Bundestag declined to revoke the Nazi-era innovation of no-fault divorce after three years' separation. Opponents of no-fault divorce emphasized the lot of wives who had upheld their end of the marriage contract, did not wish to divorce, and were left with responsibility for children and no alimony (which required an assignment of guilt).[44] Nevertheless, they could not expect to gain the ear of the Left: the SPD and most bourgeois feminists believed, as they had in Weimar, that estranged partners should be able to end their marriage without a demonstration of guilt—even if they abhorred the Nazis' racialist promotion of no-fault divorce. Opponents of no-fault divorce were more surprised by the CDU/CSU's failure to take up the matter.[45] But even though most Christian conservatives objected to divorce in principle, the CDU/CSU was too preoccupied with bigger battles to include divorce in the debate over the Civil Code.[46]

Besides, the matter had a greater symbolic than practical significance. No-fault divorce accounted for only 8.8 percent of divorces at the height of the "divorce boom" in 1948 and 8.6 percent of divorces in 1956, and divorce for any reason was rare in the 1950s.[47] Conservative judges could do as much as new legislation to ensure that divorce was not too easy.[48] In a near-final draft of the 1961 Law to Amend Family Law, the CDU/CSU finally slipped in a proposed reform of no-fault divorce; the FDP, SPD, and the courts promptly objected, insisting that any change to divorce law would require full debate.[49] But even this proposal did not suggest eliminating no-fault divorce; rather, it would have strengthened the right of the party being sued to contest the procedure. In 1958, the right to contest no-fault divorce had been raised in only about 160 cases.[50]

In revising family law, conservative legislators strenuously resisted allowing women to enter marriage without surrendering some of their rights. Furthermore, they reaffirmed that mothers' relationship to their children depended on their marital status. Still, these decisions hardly reflected a restorative consensus about the significance of marital status. Even Christian conservatives were willing to let no-fault divorce stand. By keeping wives' rights on the table, Social Democrats and bourgeois feminists set the stage for the high court's 1959 decision overturning paternal authority. Likewise, proponents of legal equality for unwed mothers and their children forced continued discussion of the matter. As had been the case with the reaffirmation of paternal authority in 1957, the 1961 confirmation of unwed mothers' and illegitimate children's legal disadvantage proved short-lived. The language used by the opposition became the basis for the new Illegitimacy Law of 1970. With this law, illegitimate children became the legal relatives of their fathers, and unwed mothers gained automatic parental authority over their children. The official guardian was replaced by an official trustee, whose sole duty was to pursue paternal support.[51]

In 1961, however, the Illegitimacy Law was still a thing of the future. While the highest court had forced the Bundestag to recognize spousal equality, the Bundestag refused to make unmarried mothers' legal relationship with their children parallel that of married, widowed, or divorced mothers. Likewise, wives' legal equality with their husbands did not imply legal equality with single women: wives' right to take on employment depended on their ability to perform their household functions simultaneously; single women encountered no such restrictions. Legal distinctions according to marital status had always been significant in their own right, but in the 1950s they began to substitute for the now-forbidden discrimination according to sex.

. —— . —— .

Despite the Bundestag's reduction of equal rights to matters concerning relationships within the family, women's employment could not be ignored entirely. The Bundestag, however, focused almost exclusively on the intersection of women's employment with marriage and motherhood. Even discussions of female labor served to reinforce the significance of marital status.

During the Parliamentary Council's debates on sexual equality, Social Democrats, Communists, and women of other parties had demanded a guarantee of equal pay for equal work. Facing resistance from key committee members, however, proponents of equal pay agreed simply to have the record show that the Parliamentary Council understood the equal-rights clause to imply equal pay.[52] Employers continued to utilize differential wage scales, and women who sued found that, in the courts' view, equal rights did not necessarily imply equal pay.[53] In 1955, the Federal Labor Court finally ruled that the Basic Law forbade separate men's and women's wage scales. However, the Court helpfully added, it would be appropriate to reward "light" and "heavy" work differently. Taking the hint, employers, with the unions' agreement, developed new job classifications which, unsurprisingly, concentrated women in "light" work.[54]

The Bundestag's disinterest in discriminatory wage scales did not reflect a lack of concern about women's paid labor; rather, it indicated apathy toward women's issues that were not simultaneously "family" issues. When women's paid labor became wives' or mothers' paid labor, it became interesting indeed. In the early 1950s, the Bundestag debated measures to protect expectant and nursing mothers, to minimize married mothers' employment by paying their husbands "money for children," and to bar wives from the civil service.

While maternity leave had a long history in Germany, women had been guaranteed full pay during their leave (six weeks before and six after delivery) only since 1942. Because this Nazi-era law included racial criteria, the Allies had suspended it in 1945. In 1952, representatives from all parties supported a new, nonracialist Law for the Protection of Mothers. The law also prohibited the firing of a pregnant woman unless she exhibited reprehensible behavior or unless keeping her on the payroll would endanger the business.

How did nonmarital pregnancy figure into these protections? Employers sometimes claimed that women who became pregnant outside marriage displayed reprehensible behavior and thus could be fired. The local officials who adjudicated contested firings rejected this claim, although the Labor Ministry noted that teachers and employees of institutions for youth might be held to stricter standards. Indeed, the law's particularly tight prohibition against firing a pregnant woman who relied primarily or exclusively on her own earnings offered a useful counterbalance to employers' prejudice against unwed mothers.[55]

The parliamentarians who framed the law hardly considered unwed motherhood ideal, but the Law for the Protection of Mothers was not about ideal situations. In an ideal situation the pregnant woman would quit work entirely, and her husband would support the family. The Law for the Protection of Mothers aimed to improve the health of children born to parents who could not meet this ideal. To discriminate against unwed mothers would be counterproductive: infant mortality of nonmarital children was twice that of marital children.[56] This was one area where the West German government hoped to narrow the gap between married and single women.

Not so in the case of "money for children" (*Kindergeld*), which was designed to address the seeming injustice whereby a father of four struggled to make ends meet on the same wages as a young single man.[57] In theory, this extra money might correct gender inequities as well. Rather than utilizing separate men's and women's wage scales on the assumption that men supported dependents and women did not, money for children could allow the single mother's income to reflect her responsibilities while ceasing to reward single, childless men simply for being male. Money for children might also ease the situation of single mothers who scrambled between household duties and part-time or irregular employment. But money for children also promised to reinforce the gendered division of labor. If the father of four received money for children, then his wife would not have to seek employment.

Whether money for children would assist working women or reinforce the housewife ideal would lie in the details of the program. The deliberations of the early 1950s pitted the interests of the "complete family," characterized by a breadwinning father and a housewife mother, against the needs of female-headed households. Holding that a normal male wage should support a wife and two children, the CDU/CSU proposed legislation that would begin payments with the third child. The CDU/CSU bill attached money for children to the (usually male) wage, rather than making payments to the mother for her use in managing household affairs. The legislation would thus reward the families who produced numerous offspring, and it would reinforce a dependent role for wives.

The SPD, along with middle-class feminists, social workers, and unions, agreed that large families with an income-generating father and a housewife mother were ideal. Indeed, the SPD insisted that its proposal to make payments directly to mothers would recognize the unique value of housework. The SPD, however, also sought to make money for children available to families that did not meet the ideal. Female-headed households rarely had more than two children, and if the theory that a male wage supported two children often broke down in practice, a female wage did not, even in theory, support dependents. Furthermore, many single mothers did not earn regular wages but instead pieced together a living from pensions, casual or home work, and welfare payments. Thus, the SPD held, payments should start with the first or at least with the second child; eligibility should not be limited to waged and salaried workers; and workers excluded in the bill, including domestic workers, should be included.[58]

These proposals, however, failed to gain a majority, and the CDU/CSU version became law in 1954.[59] Single mothers and their children lived more poorly than "full families," but few would receive money for children. In 1955, roughly 8 percent of children qualified their parents for money for children; few had single mothers.[60] An estimated thirty thousand children who had two or more older siblings were ineligible because their parents were domestic servants, pensioners, and so on.[61] Unlike the Law for the Protection of Mothers, money for children was not designed to improve the circumstances of the most needy children. Rather, it was to reward "complete families" with regularly employed husbands, dependent wives, and several children. Both by excluding most single mothers and by compounding married mothers' dependence, money for children hardened the symbolic and material divide of marital status.

No public policy, however, illustrated the effort to discriminate on the basis of marital status as blatantly as did the exclusion of wives from the civil service. The Nazis' strict prohibition on married women's employment in the civil service had been relaxed during the war. Although the U.S. Military Government and SPD officials favored discontinuing the clause after the war, public-sector employers instead resuscitated it, firing married women with the expectation of hiring demobilized men.[62]

There was little doubt that the equal-rights clause of the Basic Law would invalidate the "marriage bar." With the implementation of the equal-rights clause postponed until 1953, however, it was up to the federal, state, and municipal governments to decide whether they would conform to the spirit of the law before it became mandatory. The answer was a resounding no. A provisional Federal Personnel Law of November 1949 allowed (but no longer required) the dismissal of female civil servants upon marriage, and representatives of the CDU/CSU persistently attempted to insert such a clause into the permanent Civil Service Law, which was debated from 1951 to 1953. Despite Helene Weber's (CDU) claim that this clause would serve the interests of single women, who should not have to compete for employment with women whose husbands could ensure their well-being, the aims were clearly to mandate housewifery for at least some women and to increase employment opportunities for men. Of particular concern were men who had been civil servants under the previous regime but had been displaced because their agencies had closed, because they had fled the East, or because they had undergone denazification. In the meantime, federal agencies continued to fire not only female civil servants but also female salaried employees upon marriage.[63] In the end, though, both the rhetoric and the legal provision of equal rights proved too potent to ignore. Doubting that the courts would uphold the clause and fearful of a public outcry against such crude discrimination, an unusually large number of CDU/CSU representatives broke party ranks to defeat the proposal.[64]

The legislative record concerning women's employment and marital status was mixed. The final rejection of the marriage bar and the protection of unwed mothers in the Law for the Protection of Mothers indicated a hesitation to discriminate explicitly on the basis of marital status. The continued firing of married women in public service and the granting of money for children to dependent wives but not to employed mothers, however, illustrated the continuing urge to reward housewifery. Most conspicuously, the lengthy debates over the intersection of employment with marriage and motherhood contrasted starkly with the disinterest in reforming unequal pay and job segregation, which ensured poverty for almost all women relying on their own labor. A 1960 book called poor pay—and not concerns about maternity leave or competition with married women—"the central theme of professional life" for single women.[65] But although working wives and mothers attracted much concern, working women in general were of little interest. If even efforts to achieve equal compensation or access to vocational training attracted so little interest, employed, single women would have difficulty claiming anything more—such as positive recognition of their contribution to reconstruction.

The encouragement of housewifery hardly served the needs of employed wives, with or without children. But it was a double-edged sword for single working women. Excluded from programs designed to assist the "complete family," they also suffered workplace discrimination because of the assumption that women were or would soon be housewives. Indeed, discrimination in hiring, pay, training, and promotion were intimately tied to expectations regarding women's roles as wives and mothers.

Opponents of equal pay for equal work argued on grounds flexible enough to cover women of all marital states. Single women needed less pay because they, in the imagination of employers, supported no dependents; married women, because their earnings supplemented their husbands'. But the largest portion of the pay gap was due to women's inability to rise above unskilled, entry-level positions.

Age limits for training and employment assumed that women would work only a few short years between school and marriage. Adult women were entirely excluded from most vocational training, and women were considered too old for salaried work at surprisingly tender years. In May 1954, 51.5 percent of unemployed female salaried employees were considered to be unemployed because of their advanced ages. Nearly one-third of them had not yet reached forty.[66] Women could have little hope that their government would challenge age discrimination: the federal ministry charged with addressing the problem turned down applicants for typing positions because they exceeded the cut-off age of twenty-five.[67] A 1959 study by the Rationalization Board of the German Economy—hardly a hotbed of feminist activism—described a vicious cycle. Firms refused to train or promote women because they assumed women would leave the workplace upon marriage. By the time employers were convinced that certain women would remain, they found these women too old for training. Women who did obtain credentials learned from their employers that they lacked other qualities necessary for promotion: comfort with authority or an innate concern for the "big picture" of the firm's operations. Knowing their chances of promotion were slim even if they gained credentials, women showed little interest in training when it was offered. They thus confirmed employers' suspicions about their lack of ambition.[68]

The result was job segregation according to sex. Only 20 percent of female school-leavers could find an apprenticeship in the early 1950s, largely because girls were limited to a handful of traditionally female occupations.[69] Segregation was vertical as well as horizontal: in North Rhine-Westphalia in 1951, only 4 percent of female salaried employees were ranked at the highest of three salary grades; 20 percent of men had this rank. At the bottom of the scale were 78 percent of the women but only 37 percent of the men.[70] And with job segregation came an enduring pay gap. Female industrial workers narrowed theirs a bit, earning 59 percent of men's wages in 1950 and 61 percent in 1960. Female salaried employees, however, lost ground, earning 65 percent of men's salaries in 1950 but only 58 percent in 1960.[71]

While earning inferior pay, single women paid high taxes and reaped substandard benefits. Single, childless women belonged to the least favorable tax classification in a system built around deductions for dependents, and they paid into all employee-benefit programs.[72] These payments constituted a transfer of income from single women to men and their families, who paid proportionately less into the system but reaped more from it. Pension funds denied survivors' benefits to the dependent parents and siblings single women often supported. Single women's payments into retirement funds instead financed payments to the dependents of their married male colleagues. Even women supporting children rarely saw a return on their contributions. Eighty-five percent of women who paid into retirement funds stopped work because of invalidism before they became eligible for their pension.[73] Those who worked until retirement drew a pension equaling a fraction of their already-low salaries. In 1960, despite a major overhaul of the social-insurance system three years earlier, 97 percent of retired female waged workers and 68 percent of former female salaried employees drew pensions that left them below the poverty line.[74] Widows of male workers often did better.[75]

If a woman desired economic security, she was better off marrying (provided she could protect herself from divorce and widowhood) than working for pay. Women who reached marrying age in the 1950s were probably only dimly aware of inequities in employee-benefit programs and taxation, but they knew what their wages and their chances of promotion were. Few would have claimed that they married for material reasons. Marriage seemed the normal thing to do, and young women imagined the emotional rewards provided by a husband and children. But by the late 1950s material comfort seemed a natural part of this picture. It was not a natural part of the picture of life independent of marriage.

Despite the poor pay and lack of recognition, single women often found purpose in their work. They felt valued by their employers—although they might have liked to have seen their paychecks reflect their value a little better—and they participated in the common project of rebuilding West Germany.[76] Women also enjoyed the social contacts, the change of pace, and the sense of accomplishment that work brought.[77] "I had the feeling, and I still have the feeling, that I'm doing things right because I committed myself to my work," recalled an unmarried woman who eventually became a supervisor in a large industrial firm. "It didn't fall into my lap—I really worked for it."[78] In addition to personal satisfaction, women who worked full-time and consistently might gain confirmation from the institutionalized subculture of the women's sections of the unions. Women's sections' periodicals and assemblies provided an antidote to Bonn's systematic rejection of the possibility that women's labor had any meaning beyond the danger it posed to their children. In addition to lobbying for material and legal concessions, this subculture legitimized a life-style in which employment was part of a multifaceted experience.[79] Participation in a union or in a professional organization both contributed to women's feelings of satisfaction and gave them a language to understand employment as a positive part of women's experience and not just a burden.

But this was a small subculture. The vast majority of employed women belonged to no union or professional organization and read no working woman's magazine. Isolated from circles that applauded the contributions of employed women, they instead heard constant claims that housewifery alone gave women fulfillment. Parliamentary debates, after all, were the stuff of the nightly news. Employed women understood the importance of their paychecks, and they might enjoy employment's social and emotional rewards. But they would be hard put to gain recognition for the larger social and economic significance of their labor.

.—.—.

War widows attracted a tremendous amount of attention in the early Federal Republic. In addition to making a dent in the state's treasury, they personified the limits of attempts to restore a "complete family" in which the ideal marital status, motherhood status, and division of labor formed a seamless whole. Widows had no husband to support them, so they did not fit the wife/homemaker/mother model. But since they often had their own households and children, they did not fit the stereotype of the single, child-free, fully employed woman. In trying to make sense of this awkward category of womanhood, legislators revisited familiar themes, such as female employment, motherhood, and the value of full-time housewifery. Not surprisingly, war widows found it easier to articulate claims that would enable them to approach the housewife ideal than to argue for a place in the labor force.

Discussion of war widows, however, took on a unique character. Marriage law, illegitimacy law, and women's employment were the subject of parliamentary debate, position papers, and legal decisions. Discussion of war widows entered such realms as popular literature and the boulevard press. And for good reason: when the public thought about war widows, they did not think only about jobs and children; they also thought about sex and war. Defined by an event in their past, war widows' present lives persistently erupted into West German consciousness. War widows were the subject of scandal, and, as such, they played a unique role in keeping women standing alone in the public consciousness.[80]

Since Allied-administered pension programs had excluded able-bodied widows, most Germans saw war widows as doubly victimized: first by the war, then by the Military Government.[81] By quickly attending to "victims of war," the young Federal Republic demonstrated that it protected "ordinary Germans" better than Military Government had. The creation of a nationwide system of pensions was critical to the new state's establishment of legitimacy. The 1950 Law to Aid Victims of War was the Federal Republic's first major piece of social legislation, and it constituted the second largest item in the state's budget. It covered over four million wounded veterans, widows, orphans, and dependent parents; its provisions directly or indirectly affected a fifth of the population. In short, aid to "victims of war" constituted the bedrock of the West German welfare state in the 1950s. By 1954, nearly 1.2 million women were entitled to benefits as war widows.[82]

The Law to Aid Victims of War was passed years before a law that made payments to selected victims of Nazism, and with far less controversy.[83] It both responded to real needs and made clear that "victims of war"—rather than other victims of the recent past—would receive the first attentions of the new state. An early draft disqualified those whom the denazification courts had judged to be compromised, but the clause was struck.[84] Even as they eliminated potentially inflammatory references to the SS and to the Nazi party within the text of the law, parliamentarians made clear that the law covered members of both. The denazification courts might strip pension rights from a German convicted of crimes in connection with the Nazi regime, but the Law to Aid Victims of War excluded no one on the basis of complicity in the crimes of the previous regime.[85]

When the young Federal Republic debated the Law to Aid Victims of War in 1949–50, war victims' associations insisted that all war widows must receive pensions. The Labor Ministry agreed, and its draft awarded benefits to all war widows. Like pensions for orphans and wounded veterans, these would be awarded on a two-tiered system. All beneficiaries would receive a basic allowance, and those who were needy would receive a supplementary allowance to bring their income up to certain minimum levels. In the face of the Finance Ministry's objections to the high costs of the proposed legislation, however, the Labor Ministry agreed to the indefinite suspension of payments to able-bodied widows under the age of forty who had no legally recognized war orphans.[86] It rejected deeper cuts proposed by the Ministry of Finance, including the suspension of payments to the lightly disabled. The amended draft was submitted to the Bundestag.

The arguments for and against pensions for the lightly wounded and for young, able-bodied, orphanless widows were similar. On the one hand, both groups consisted of people who could get by without pensions if need be. Given financial constraints, it seemed reasonable to trim back expenditures that were not necessary for survival.[87] On the other hand, even the lightly wounded and young, able-bodied, orphanless widows had suffered genuine losses. A "light wound" might be the loss of a hand, a foot, or an eye. The death of a husband was hardly an insignificant matter, even for a widow capable of employment. Nevertheless, arguments for young, employable widows without orphaned children proved less persuasive than did those for the lightly wounded. Perhaps most significantly, these widows constituted a much smaller voting bloc. According to a committee member's estimate, about 80,000 widows fell into the category under discussion. By contrast, 661,000 veterans were classified as lightly disabled.[88]

In addition to their lower numbers, young, able-bodied, orphanless widows faced another disadvantage: popular doubts about the seriousness of their marriages. Many had married during the war and had not set up marital households. Instead, they had continued to live with their parents and to work for pay and, according to the German Party's Margot Kalinke, "now continued to live as they had earlier and nevertheless received a considerable subsidy from the state."[89] Kalinke and Erich Mende of the FDP referred to abuses of marriage laws during wartime, playing on popular stereotypes of women who wed soldiers in order to reap state aid.[90] Even those who protested such defamation felt pressed to admit that if young widows had continued employment and if they had no children by their late husbands, their situation differed little from that of women who had never married.

In the end, the lightly wounded fared considerably better than did young, able-bodied, orphanless widows. The Committee for Questions concerning Victims of War and Prisoners of War increased basic allowances for the lightly wounded to DM 15 for the 30 percent and DM 20 for the 40 percent disabled.[91] Able-bodied, orphanless widows under forty (Type I widows) would be eligible for a basic allowance of DM 20 per month, but their benefits would be suspended indefinitely.[92] The remaining widows (Type II) would collect a basic allowance of DM 40; if they were needy, they could collect a supplementary allowance. Neither the lightly wounded nor Type I widows would be eligible for supplementary allowances.[93] The committee's version of the bill became law in October 1950.

In designing this pension scheme, the government divided war widows according to the degree to which their marriages seemed to warrant official recognition. Type I widows constituted something of a category of "lightly widowed women." Withholding benefits from young, fit, orphanless widows, lawmakers questioned whether these women had truly been wives. And by awarding only nominal pensions and withholding even those until August 1953, legislators helped to ensure that Type I widows would, in the future, live similarly to never-married women—that is, they would have to support themselves.

In establishing benefits for Type II widows, lawmakers similarly constructed both a past and a future for them. Older widows had presumably been married longer. If they were younger but had had children with their husbands, their marriages had likewise shaped their lives. Like the severely wounded, Type II widows were considered to have suffered a severe loss and to be genuinely handicapped in earning their own livings. Their pensions thus acknowledged their past marriages and their present loss. But the allowances were also to shape their futures: they were to "enable . . . [them] . . . to carry on their households and support them in the raising and educating of their children."[94] Making explicit that benefits for widows were intended to create full-time housewives, the CSU's Maria Probst argued that "the orphan-child, who has already lost its father, may not also lose its mother" to the workplace.[95] In the future, these widows should resemble wives—and not just any wives but housewives.

The law thus created a schematic divide between widows who resembled married women and those who did not, and it established that the state's basic role in maintaining widows' families would be to provide a pension. By replacing the husband's income, the state aimed to re-create some of the most important distinctions between single women and wives. Wives but not single women were financially dependent, and wives but not single women shaped their days around their household duties.

In theory, at least. In fact, pensions were too low to replace a male income. Without guaranteeing adequate income, the Bundestag could no more create a housewife-widow than it could a housewife whose husband was still alive. But while working wives often felt apologetic for leaving housewifery, war widows felt they had a claim to government assistance in supporting themselves.

Immediately after the war, widows often sought work or vocational training. "For my part, I would participate in any vocational training if it gave me the prospect of an independent existence," wrote a fifty-year-old widow in 1947.[96] Recognizing widows' desire to work and sensing an untapped labor force, some states assisted widows in training for and finding work. States that did so in the late 1940s often achieved great successes, despite high female unemployment following the currency reform.[97]

The federal government, however, was much less helpful to widows who sought employment. The small size of pensions even for Type II widows meant that few could survive on them alone. But outside income, unless very small, resulted in significant cuts to the pension. The pension structure thus penalized a decision to seek well-paying work or training that would lead to a good job. Widows could usually take on part-time, ill-paid work without having it affect their pensions. The stereotypical war widow was a part-time cleaning woman.

The Law to Aid Victims of War included provisions for (re)integrating victims of war into the working world, but widows' place in these plans was unclear. Although there were implementation guidelines for improving employment opportunities for the wounded, their children, and orphans, there were none for widows.[98] Local welfare and employment offices thus assumed they were not to aid widows in their working lives.[99]

The Law to Aid Victims of War promised that a separate law would regulate the creation of jobs and work protections for survivors and the wounded. Three years later the Bundestag passed the Law for the Severely Wounded (*Schwerbeschädigtengesetz*, or SBG) of June 16, 1953. During the composition of the law, arguments regarding vocational assistance for war widows were laced with reservations.[100] The first draft extended assistance only to childless widows, and later drafts included widows only up to age fifty since on reaching that age they could draw a full supplementary allowance and would presumably no longer need paid employment.[101] Employment offices protested that including widows would endanger the placement of the severely wounded.[102] Even war victims' associations, which had demanded assistance in widows' job placement since Weimar, warned that orphans should not lose their mother to the workplace.[103] The largest war victims' association cautioned that the government was about to introduce obligatory labor for war widows, although there was no reason to think that the government was considering any such thing.[104]

With such questions about the virtue of assisting widows in finding work, legislators passed the new law. The SBG required employers to hire a certain percentage of severely wounded, depending on the size of the firm and the branch of industry. The severely wounded were to enjoy preferential treatment in public-sector hiring; they would be protected against layoffs; and employment offices were to place them in appropriate positions and, if necessary, provide job training. Paragraph 8 extended most of these benefits to war widows, regardless of age or motherhood status, with certain qualifications. Firms could include widows in their quotas only if no severely wounded veteran was available for the position the widow filled, and, even then, a position filled by a widow counted as only half a position against the quota.[105]

The Committee for the Welfare of the War Wounded and Survivors authored the implementation guidelines for the SBG.[106] The Subcommittee for Survivors' Welfare included women who understood widows' need for employment, and it produced remarkably far-reaching guidelines.[107] They required that employment offices aggressively seek positions for war widows by making widows' availability and skills known to employers. Employment offices were to help women compensate for disadvantages such as advanced age, reduced strength, and irregular employment histories, and they should assist in finding childcare. All training programs for orphans and wounded veterans were to be open to widows.[108]

The implementation of the guidelines, however, lay in the hands of the Federal Institute for Job Placement and Unemployment Insurance and the local employment offices. Unlike the Subcommittee for Survivors' Welfare, these bodies had no fundamental commitment to widows' well-being. At best, the placement of widows took low priority. But the situation was usually worse. Employment offices exhibited hostility to the entire program, which they felt threatened the employment of the wounded in the interest of widows who, in their opinion, needed no help. The law stipulated that employers count against their quotas only widows who otherwise could not be placed and that the placement of widows was not to endanger the placement of the wounded. Employment offices enforced these measures with a gusto that far outstripped their enthusiasm for fulfilling other stipulations of the law, such as those requiring that they provide vocational training for widows. Few followed the Subcommittee's recommendation to set up a special placement office for war widows, and widows often remained unaware that they had a claim on occupational assistance.[109]

Only a handful of widows gained employment via the SBG. By May 1956, slightly over 1 percent of the 333,465 positions filled as a result of the law were filled by widows and wives of unemployable veterans. Quotas were only 64.3 percent filled, indicating that positions available to wounded veterans were hardly threatened by the hiring of widows. Annual reports concerning the implementation of the law contain no information whatsoever regarding the placement of widows after 1953.[110]

But employment offices' resistance was not the only reason the SBG offered widows no meaningful assistance. Even if it had been aggressively implemented, the law was too little, too late to be of much use. By the time employment offices received the implementation guidelines, nearly nine years had passed since the war's end. Widows who had considered taking up work or learning new skills after the war had either done so, or if they had not, their lives had long since taken different directions. "Much as I welcome the opportunity to promote war widows' vocational training via financial help," wrote a welfare officer in Bremen, "I nevertheless believe that the point that was chosen for the presentation of such an opportunity . . . was really too late to meet a genuine need."[111]

Enabling war widows to find a secure place in the working world was antithetical to the goal of making widows approximate wives. Although the small pensions made it necessary for most to seek employment, the implementation of the SBG undercut attempts to help them find well-paying, rewarding work. Like wives, widowed mothers should work only to tide their families over in times of crisis. Insecure, dead-end work was fine for this purpose. If this policy also hurt child-free widows, this was of no more concern than other areas of women's working lives, such as poor pay and job segregation, that did not bear directly on their roles as wives and mothers.

.—.—.

In order to fulfill the wifely ideal, widows would have to be more than full-time caretakers of their children. They would also have to be faithful wives to their husbands. But while the Law to Aid Victims of War created a forum for discussing widows' work, it provided no guidelines for dealing with their sexual activity. Given the temporary loosening of sexual mores in the mid-1940s, the inadequacies of the law would soon become apparent. Widows' present infidelities—in the form of "wild marriages" or "uncle marriages," the popular terms for nonmarital cohabitation—and their past infidelities, as evidenced by the resulting children, prompted explosive discussions about the state's role in supporting war widows.

Widows were not necessarily expected to retain lifelong fidelity to their deceased husbands. They might remarry. A war widow who remarried gave up her claim on the state to fulfill her deceased husband's financial responsibility. Shifting from the figurative role of the husband to that of the father, the state paid a "marriage settlement" to the war widow—something akin to a dowry.

Aside from this lump sum, the couple was expected to rely on the husband's income. But in many cases this income was too small. The partners might decide that if it meant losing the widow's pension, they could not afford to marry. Or the woman might decide that she could not afford to marry. If her new marriage ended in divorce or widowhood, she could only renew her claim as a war widow in rare circumstances. Thus many couples opted to live together without marrying. Pension policy implicated the state in couples' decisions for cohabitation.

"Wild marriage" had fed occupation-era concern about the family. Still, many had interpreted wild marriages as a symptom of unusually difficult times.[112] As the postwar emergency subsided, though, the tenacity of the practice truly alarmed contemporaries. The press typically quoted an estimate of one hundred thousand such relationships in the mid-1950s.[113]

Although any cohabiting couple might face disapproval, war widows in wild marriages endured special criticism because of their unique cultural significance and the frequent presence of children (who, according to stereotype, called the man "uncle"). Reflecting tensions between married and single women and making note of the special insult to war widows' late soldier-husbands, a women's organization wrote to Würmeling in 1955:

> The war widows are the worst practitioners of concubinage; they take women's husbands, above all the husbands' money, move them into their apartments . . . and live as if married. These women don't think about marriage at all, because they certainly don't ever want to lose their 'well-earned pension,' which they acquired through the death of their fallen husbands. . . . One can scarcely attribute a pronatalist interest to these extramarital relationships, for these concubines want everything, only no children. . . . Only by persecuting concubinage can the family be secured once again, and only with such measures can the irresponsible conduct of frivolous war widows toward their sisters be laid at their own doorsteps.[114]

One of West Germany's most prominent authors, Heinrich Böll, published a novel that was considerably more tactful but nevertheless impressed on readers the unhappy lot of a child whose war-widowed mother had a lover but no plans for marriage.[115]

Despite such worries, there were indications that wild marriages were changing. In the immediate postwar period, many couples had considered their relationships temporary, destined to break up as life returned to normal. Cohabitants in the 1950s often perceived their relationships as permanent. Emphasizing her semblance to a wife, a forty-eight-year-old widow described her domestic partnership: "If he should no longer be with me, I would have to go early to my grave because we are one heart and soul in joy and in sorrow just like husband and wife, and we have also committed ourselves to goodness of deed and a solid, honest, Christian course of life."[116] Like many other pairs, this couple could not afford to marry but took what steps it could to legitimize its relationship.[117]

Neighbors and relatives often viewed cohabitants as respectable people trapped by pension law. "The State Makes the Merry Widows," read a 1953 headline that proved representative of editorial opinion.[118] Only 46 percent of respondents to a 1955 poll disapproved of war widows who cohabited in order to preserve their pension.[119] Human-rights organizations, social welfare groups, feminists, churches, war victims' associations, and concerned citizens petitioned the government to ease war widows' remarriage. Measures might include continuation of the widows' pension upon remarriage, reinstatement of the pension if the second marriage ended, increasing half orphans' pensions to the level of full orphans when their mothers remarried, or a higher marriage settlement.[120]

Würmeling's ministry argued that such revisions would endanger the sexual hierarchy and material dependence that should characterize marriage: "The purpose of a widow's pension is to provide, for the duration of the widowhood, economic compensation for the loss of the husband as breadwinner. When the widow enters a new marriage, the purpose of the aid falls away. It corresponds to the natural order of our society that, with the establishment of marriage, the husband regularly takes over financial responsibility for his wife."[121] As single women, noncelibate widows seemed a far cry from the "deserving widows" who were the intended recipients of pensions. As wives, they desired an unfitting degree of financial independence. Rather than trusting their husbands to make ends meet, they wanted to bring their own income into the marriage; they even seemed to be planning for the eventual breakup of the union.

The Bundestag, however, represented a wider spectrum of opinion on this matter than did the CDU/CSU-led ministries, and continued public uproar led the Bundestag to revise the law in 1956.[122] The marriage settlement was raised from DM 1,200 to DM 1,980, and further revisions in 1957 and 1960 brought it to DM 5,000. The revisions also made it easier to reactivate the pension should the new marriage end. Cohabiting widows' success in obtaining improved benefits contrasted strikingly with the hostile response to widows' pleas for assistance in finding work. Widows who sought employment had no leg to stand on, but even disreputable sexual behavior did not, in the end, invalidate a claim for assistance in realizing the housewife ideal.

By the early 1960s, as the numbers and visibility of wild marriages decreased, so did their place in public discussion. Several developments, in combination with the changes in the Law to Aid Victims of War, eased marriage in the late 1950s. High employment rates and good wages lessened couples' dependence on widows' pensions. Improvements in other pension plans provided better incomes to potential husbands who were themselves pensioners as as well as to widows who drew benefits from their deceased husbands' or their own previous employment.[123] Other wild marriages ended not with legal marriage but with death or separation. The disabled and sick were probably overrepresented in wild marriages because of their reliance on pension income. But the same ill health that made paid work and thus marriage impossible often meant premature death as well.[124] Women who had spent several years in one wild marriage often emerged cautious about repeating the experience. Men, too, may have shown a declining interest, preferring other women to war widows, who were advancing in years and often had half-grown children.

Although improved benefits were intended to coax cohabitants to marry, they also encouraged couples not living together to wed before establishing a household. Lawmakers could rest assured that among the beneficiaries would be many truly "deserving" widows. The same was not true of another controversial group of pensioners. These were children who were "legitimate in appearance only" [*scheineheliche Kinder*] and their mothers. "Apparently legitimate" children were born within marriage but were not the offspring of their mothers' husbands—in other words, they had resulted from adultery. Since the marriage of a woman and a man at war, imprisoned, or missing remained legally intact until the man was officially declared dead, children born years after the last meeting of the child's mother and her husband could be legitimate. If their mothers' husbands had died in the war or had been declared missing, they had the status of, and received the benefits of, war orphans. The Federal Bureau of Statistics estimated in 1955 that there were twenty thousand "apparently legitimate" children passing as war orphans.[125]

The administrative guidelines to the Law to Aid Victims of War instructed pension offices to initiate suits to have such children declared illegitimate.[126] The state's right to challenge a child's legitimacy in the public interest had been created in 1938, with the intention of clarifying "apparently legitimate" children's racial status.[127] In July 1952, however, the government released a draft law which would revoke this right. The notion that the public could have an interest in a child's legitimacy when no member of the family did was now considered to be Nazi in character. The draft specifically noted that financial considerations could not justify giving the state this power.[128]

The Ministry of Labor, responsible for the implementation of the Law to Aid Victims of War, scrambled to get "apparently legitimate" children off the rolls before the new law went into effect. It instructed pension offices to threaten mothers with challenges to suspicious children's legitimacy if the widows pursued their applications for orphans' pensions. This strategy, however, failed to intimidate adequate numbers of mothers. The Ministry of Labor urged district attorneys, the Ministry of Justice, and state departments of justice to initiate challenges to such children's legitimacy, but these bodies objected, noting that such actions would be contrary to the spirit of the impending legislation.[129] Unable to faze the mothers or to gain the cooperation of the judicial system, pension offices had missing husbands declared dead.[130] This, however, was a time-consuming procedure and addressed only a portion of the cases. Finally, the Ministry of Labor proposed a revision to the Law to Aid Victims of War. Pension offices would be empowered to revoke "apparently legitimate" children's allowances without having the children declared illegitimate or the husbands dead. The Bundestag approved the revision in 1953.[131]

Although public moneys were at stake, the Ministry of Labor insisted that "less financial than ethical reasons speak against a child's exploiting a formal legal situation in order to draw a pension as the result of the death of a man who is not the child's father."[132] Ethical objections, however, concerned more the mother than the child. Children did not "exploit the formal legal situation"; rather, their mothers did, by applying for orphans' pensions for their children. Just as widows' pensions were understood as benefits for half orphans, who should not have to "lose" their mothers to the workplace, so were half orphans' pensions simultaneously benefits for their mothers, who would have to raise their children by other means if orphans' pensions were not forthcoming. And women who had conceived children while their husbands were at the front, missing, dead, or in prison camp should not benefit from their children's ability to draw a pension.

Furthermore, the mother might gain undeserved status for herself. To be classified as a Type II widow, a young, able-bodied widow had to have responsibility for a legally recognized war orphan and not simply for a child. This was not because war orphans incurred greater expenses than did other children. Rather, it reflected the sentiment that widows raising their fallen husbands' children should enjoy a special status. The Minister of Labor held that denying adulterous widows the favorable classification "might be even more important than the denial of the orphan's pension."[133] Where missing or deceased husbands could not discipline adulterous wives, the state could.

The persistent scandals about war widows were not conscious attempts to clarify the meaning of widowed status. The uproar about wild marriages explicitly addressed the jarring possibility that the state penalized marriage, and it reflected concerns about children's moral development. Likewise, the desire to revoke "apparently legitimate" children's pensions exposed fears that the state rewarded adultery. In both cases, widows' illicit sexual activity provoked unease at the connection between presumably honorable death on the battlefield and presumably dishonorable sexual behavior.

Nevertheless, the scandals drew attention to a real ambiguity in widows' marital status. If widowed mothers were supposed to be like wives, devoting themselves to household and children and supported by a male income (in this case, a pension), then what was one to make of many widows' desire to share a household and a bed with a man, just like wives did? Were widows to be married in their economic and working lives but single in their sexual and emotional lives? What was the relationship between their past as wives and their present lives as single women? A joke neatly summed up the absurdities of confusing past with present, a husband's memory with his physical presence. A widow took her newborn to court to make sure her papers were in order. "How can you have a newborn?" asked the incredulous judge. "Your husband has been dead for three years!" "Yes, he's dead," replied the woman, unclear about the source of the judge's confusion, "but *I'm* still alive!"

As long as widows were popularly imagined as elderly women, implicitly nonsexual but with a full emotional life behind them, this discrepancy did not seem particularly troublesome. The large number of young war widows combined with the evident loosening of sexual mores during and after the war, however, suddenly exposed the problem. Marital status did not just determine property rights, legal authority, and children's legitimacy. It also established which living arrangements and sexual bonds were acceptable. Improved stipulations for remarriage turned widows into wives and thus relieved this ambiguity. Higher marriage settlements did not, however, answer the more basic question of what heterosexual living arrangements and sexual relations were permissible for single women.

One thing, however, was clear: discussion of women's illicit sexual activity, especially in combination with reference to men's wartime sacrifices, would get people's attention. But scandal was not inevitable. Rather, it occurred under conditions specific to the Federal Republic. First, pensions for victims of war gave West German widows' infidelities public importance. Unfaithful widows did not just insult their late husbands and endanger their children's morals. They also cost the taxpayer. Further, they mocked the identity of "victim of war," which the Law to Aid Victims of War had invested with official significance. Second, the democratic form of government made it worth people's while to voice their objections to the law by repeatedly identifying the objectionable behavior the law promoted. Third, a market-driven press encouraged the constant reiteration of racy issues, while an uncensored press enabled it. East German widows also broke their vows of fidelity, and they also raised children of adultery. But they received no public assistance, and their cuckolded husbands, in the state's eyes at least, were perpetrators of war, not victims. If "adulterous" or cohabiting widows had drawn pensions in East Germany, neither the government nor the press would have allowed popular objections to develop into sustained public expressions of outrage. In addition, the East German press was squeamish about reiterating the theme of sex. In West Germany, however, scandals surrounding war widows' sexual lives kept the war generation of women standing alone in the public consciousness.

Family law, illegitimacy law, widows' pensions, measures for working women, opportunities for women in political life—all served to reinforce the significance of marital status in the early Federal Republic. Still, the process was not a straightforward one. Those who hoped to reaffirm the legal subordination of wives had to contend not only with the parliamentary opposition but also with the Basic Law and the Constitutional Court. Inheritors of the socialist and liberal feminist traditions advocated for nonmarital children and their mothers. War widows forced a reconsideration of how closely female-headed households could be expected to approximate the "complete family." The marriage bar was no longer tolerable, and, as Chapter Eight will show, ever-increasing numbers of wives worked for pay. Although single women remained both socially and legally marginal in the 1950s, those who held that the wife must remain utterly distinct from women of other marital states were never able to rest easy.

Nevertheless, advocates of the uniqueness of wifehood won the day. Although wives gained property rights and a role in making family decisions, their legal authority over their children and the conditions under which they could seek employment remained different from those of single women. In order to enter the socially and economically privileged status of wife, a woman had to relinquish rights other adults took for granted. At the same time, unmarried mothers and their children had inferior status. In this regard, wives retained privilege, and single women were defined by their otherness.

The division of widows into those who resembled wives and those who did not speaks volumes about the West German government's urge to achieve clarity in women's marital status. Several litmus tests served to separate wifelike widows from those who resembled unwed women: Were children present? Had the widow's marriage been an adequately significant influence in her life? Was she a housewife? Did she meet the moral standards expected of a wife and mother? Whether they resembled wives determined both widows' material benefits and their symbolic recognition. Furthermore, by working to preserve housewifery for widows, pension policy encouraged an identity based on the past marriage. Even after its termination, marriage continued to define a woman.

The importance of widows' resemblance to wives, however, also pointed to a larger reality. With the "reconstruction of the family" one of West Germany's great social projects, single women had to seek improved conditions on grounds on which they were, by definition, outsiders. Most single women were not wifelike widows who could promise that, with better pensions, they would live as housewives. Instead, they were women who needed better pay and access to vocational training. In West Germany, however, these were hard demands to articulate. Even when it turned its attention to women's employment, the Bundestag could think of little other than the relationship between women's labor and their marital and motherhood status.

The legislative results of the Federal Republic's consideration of marital status were mixed. Wives gained some rights but were denied others. Unwed mothers' status changed little, but the groundwork was laid for radical reform only a decade later. Some widows' prior status as wives was called into doubt, while others were able to approximate the position of wife even though no husband was present. Explicit discrimination against married women in the workplace was rejected. Yet the assumption that marriage was desirable for all women, and housewifery for all wives, justified inferior treatment for all women in the workplace—even with sexual discrimination technically banned.

Regardless of the resolution of specific legal questions, the centrality of marital status was reaffirmed. Whether the Bundestag would meet its deadline for reconciling wives' status with women's equal rights; whether widows' pensions should penalize remarriage; whether unwed mothers should have full authority over their children; whether single mothers should get money for children—this was the stuff of headlines, and dinnertable conversation, throughout the 1950s. West Germans could not help but conclude that marital status was crucially significant for women.

7 Narrowing the Difference
The State and Marital Status in East Germany

"You are the State!" proclaimed a women's magazine in the Soviet zone, *Für Dich*, in 1947. Acknowledging that women's heavy burdens made it difficult for them to engage in politics, the journal nevertheless urged women to become full participants in the new, democratic order. To be sure, different women had different levels of understanding for this task: "The unmarried, childless woman still shows the greatest understanding for it because she, through her work, comes more closely into contact with her environment. But the mothers find themselves more than fulfilled by their husbands and children and believe that they can, in good conscience, leave politics to the men."[1]

If the West German polity defined the housewife as normative and the woman standing alone as problematic, the opposite was true in the East. The reasons were in part ideological. As comfortable as they may have been with male privilege, the new East German leaders had been schooled in classic Marxist writings which had described domesticity as a form of slavery for women. Indeed, East German writings often drew parallels between the exploitation of the worker in capitalism and the exploitation of the wife in bourgeois marriage.[2] Many Communists had also absorbed images of emancipated women under socialism during their years of exile in the Soviet Union, where female tractor drivers and diggers of antitank ditches were the stuff of legend. Female emancipation was clearly to be found in the productive sphere. East German leaders would devote much energy to the emancipation, as they understood it, of married women; for the time being, however, women standing alone seemed closer to its realization. The majority of married women were housewives, and an even larger majority of single women were engaged in production. If the politically enlightened portion of the working class formed the vanguard of the class revolution, women standing alone formed the vanguard of the revolution in sexual hierarchies.

The struggle for political legitimacy and economic recovery also led the new regime to feel more comfortable with single than with married women. East German leaders expected women standing alone, familiar with the inequities of the marketplace, to support the "workers' and peasants' party" more readily than housewives, who might feel threatened by communism's perceived sexual radicalism and disdain for the nuclear family. Furthermore, women standing alone contributed desperately needed labor to reconstruction; wives mainly avoided employment.

To be sure, the divisions between married and single women were no more crystal clear in the East than they were in the West. Most significantly, the East German leadership hardly wanted women to abandon marriage; they did not consider the employed, politically active, single woman to be the ideal. Married women provided invaluable (and free) assistance to husbands and children, and they bore offspring much more readily than did single women. Ideally, women would marry, have children, work for pay, and be politically active—all at the same time.

But this ideal would not be realized overnight. For the time being—and that meant for the critical years of economic reconstruction and establishment of political legitimacy—married and single women had fundamentally different patterns of labor-force participation and political engagement. According to Minister of Justice Hilde Benjamin, only 18.3 percent of wives in families consisting of husband, wife, and children were employed in 1956.[3] The East German government's challenge would be to shape the behavior of married women to approximate more closely that of single women—and not vice versa. Explaining East Germany's inability to reform marriage law in the 1950s, Benjamin later recalled that "developments were not yet mature. . . . The normative woman, whose rights we wished to establish, was the employed woman."[4] Wives had yet to become normative.

The East German state shaped the significance of marital status in ways strikingly different from the western case. Two institutions were particularly important in this process. The first were mass organizations charged with organizing various subpopulations, such as youth, women, and labor. The second was a new body of family, labor, and pension law. Mass organizations and the law affected women's material circumstances; they also propagated an official discourse that problematized housewives and normalized employed women, who ideally would include women of all marital states but who in fact were overwhelmingly single.

These institutions had a complicated relationship with the populations whose behavior and consciousness they were intended to influence. In many regards, they were divorced from popular consciousness and social norms. While ideology trumpeted the working wife and mother and while the law supported her, families that included wife, husband, and children adhered to a familiar sexual division of labor in the 1950s. Furthermore, as men returned from prisoner-of-war camps, and as new families were formed, women standing alone—and not married women—felt isolated.

Nevertheless, the official culture of the Democratic Republic was influential. If a new ideology and new institutions neither reflected an already-achieved social revolution nor brought it about overnight, they did become part of the public discourse. They helped to determine which topics would be discussed and which would not, and they shaped the vocabulary and the terms of the discussion. In voicing claims in ways that seemed most promising in the East German context, women of all marital states emphasized certain parts of their identities while leaving others less fully articulated.

In the 1960s, the social revolution propagated for women began to see results. More married mothers worked full-time and continuously, and young women increasingly received vocational training, preparing for a lifetime rather than an interim period of employment. By the end of the Democratic Republic's history, women's working lives no longer differed significantly according to their marital histories.[5] Wives' social and emotional lives also underwent remarkable change. Like their single counterparts and unlike housewives, they had extensive social networks, emotional lives, and feelings of identity based on their workplace.[6]

This did not mean that marriage became insignificant in the Democratic Republic: marriage rates in East Germany exceeded those in West Germany throughout the period of separate states. Marriage continued to bring economic benefits, such as a second income; women also hoped that with marriage they would have two emotionally rewarding "homes": one with family and one at work. But the changes in married women's relationship to the workplace meant that the difference in life-style between married and single women—and thus the significance of marital status—was far narrower in the East than it was in the West. This was a genuine social revolution.

In explaining the turning point in this revolution—the 1960s—East German writings tended to emphasize a new cohort's maturation.[7] The East German government took credit for having raised women who took a lifetime of employment for granted, who understood that motherhood and employment could be combined, and who benefited from vocational training, legal protections, and social programs. This was correct as far as it went, but it suggested that socialization was destiny. Implicitly, since the older generation had been shaped by bourgeois society, fundamental change for it had never been possible. The emphasis on generational turnover minimized the changes experienced by the older generation since they did not result in new behavior in the marketplace. But even if married and single women's labor-force participation differed in the 1950s, women's understanding of the significance of marital status was changing.[8]

.——.——.

When members of the German Communist Party (KPD) set up operations in the Soviet occupation zone, they knew that the Soviet Union had certain conditions for the kind of polity that would emerge. They did not know, however, that they were laying the groundwork for a single-party dictatorship in half of a divided Germany. The KPD and the Soviet occupation forces had no intention of letting other political programs triumph over theirs—but they hoped that Communism would rule by virtue of popular appeal. In the spring of 1945, there was reason for optimism on this point. The KPD had been the third largest party, after the Nazis and the Social Democrats, in all German elections between 1930 and 1933; after 1933, it had been the party most identified with resistance. The SPD, which had claimed a large electorate from the late nineteenth century through the Weimar era, shared much philosophically with the Communists, despite the parties' history of competition for the left-wing vote. Between August 1945 and April 1946, membership in the KPD and SPD more than doubled to some 1,280,000 with the KPD growing faster than the SPD.[9]

In the spring of 1946, the KPD and Soviet authorities, fearful of the still-greater popularity of the SPD, forced a merger of the KPD and SPD, arguing that divisions within the Left had led to the catastrophe of 1933. The new party was called the Socialist Unity Party (SED). The merger was a risky move. On the one hand, the combined following of the old SPD and KPD constituted a far stronger political force than the nearest contender. On the other hand, the elimination of the old, proud SPD and the heavy-handed domination of the new party by the Communists alienated precisely the voters the move was intended to recruit.

If the costs of the merger became clear in hindsight, however, leaders of the SED hoped that the electorate would demonstrate that Germans in the Soviet zone approved of such a unified Left. But many of the changes since 1933 were to the Communists' disadvantage.[10] Thousands of Communist leaders had been killed by the Nazis, and those who had survived in exile had not shared the experiences of the German population. A significant portion of the Communists' electoral following, too, had fallen victim to Nazi repression or to the war. Among those who had not earlier been Communists or Socialists, anti-Communist feeling had been hardened both by Nazi propaganda and by the war. Harsh Soviet occupation was chipping away at support among many who had Communist sympathies. Finally, the demographic profile of the electorate had changed. Young men, traditionally the most attracted to revolutionary ideologies, were in short supply. Women, more religious, less connected to the factory floor, and raped in large numbers by the occupation forces who backed the SED, formed the large majority of the adult population.

The first major test of the SED's popularity would be a referendum in Saxony, the Soviet zone's largest and most heavily industrialized province. On July 16, 1946, voters would decide whether to confiscate firms belonging to former Nazis and war criminals. The owners would receive no compensation, and the firms would become public property. Although many of the prior owners had been killed or imprisoned or had fled to the West anyway, the referendum was an important step in formalizing the nationalization of industry.

Some 60 percent of the electorate was female, and the SED was concerned, certain that, "in elections in the past, women had almost always been a reserve for [the] reaction[ary Right]."[11] The party's worries about female voting behavior and its strategies for meeting the challenge reflected considerations of marital status. Past efforts to rally women, according to SED strategists, had focused on a narrow group: those who were already politically enlightened.[12] Two types of women belonged to this category. The first recognized the relevance of proletarian politics because of their experience as workers. Not all female workers fit into this category, however. Those who expected to work for pay only temporarily rarely engaged in workers' politics. Mothers who continued working were too overburdened for politics. Only child-free women who expected to remain single slowly came to identify with the workplace rather than with the household. On the basis of this workplace identification, they might develop a commitment to working-class politics. Clearly, this had always been a small group of women, and although the numbers of single women was now unusually high, most either had children, had an on-and-off relationship with the workplace, did not see their single status as permanent, or all three.

The second group of women traditionally attracted to Communism were wives and daughters of Communist men. In the past, as the SED understood it, the KPD could at least expect daughters and wives of Communists to follow their men's leads. Since many of these wives were not employed and many of the daughters did not maintain their own households, they had time for politics. But now the fathers and husbands were gone. Fewer women were politicized by male relatives, and women who might have engaged in radical politics when they could share the burdens of daily life now had other priorities.

In other words, most married women (and women who intended to marry) had found their identity in the home and were thus out of the KPD's reach. Men's absence meant that the one route the KPD had had to some of these women—their Communist fathers and husbands—was now blocked off. During the Weimar period, the KPD had appealed to women outside their roles as workers and dependents of Communists: the party had led the campaign for reform of abortion law. But with abortion now entangled with the issue of Soviet rape, with a new pronatalism that reflected concern over the size of the labor force, and with the Soviet Union's own turnaround from a lenient to a restrictive abortion policy in 1936, the SED declined to capitalize on this legacy.[13]

Some political strategists favored making a virtue out of necessity by focusing their efforts on women standing alone. "We should take advantage of all energies that are not claimed first and foremost by families. There are millions of women today who . . . cannot form a family. . . . [I]f we now need women for administration and for leading roles, then I believe we can lean first of all on . . . these women, [who] are not handicapped by other tasks."[14] But 44 percent of eligible voters in Saxony described themselves as housewives.[15] Victory would depend on winning over these women.

The SED, having inherited a key debate from the old KPD, was deeply divided over the matter of paying special attention to women's issues.[16] Much of the male leadership, opposed to "women's politics," limited itself to promises of workplace rights and offers of material relief, such as improved rations, on the eve of elections.[17] By contrast, the local women's commissions (*Frauenausschüsse*), technically nonpartisan but in fact dominated by the SED, favored active campaigning among housewives. In addition to organizing more than a thousand assemblies, they prepared radio programs, short films, brochures, and speeches emphasizing the SED's concern for such matters as food supplies and shoes for children. They rethought tactics poorly suited to attracting female voters, such as denouncing religion and blaming women for Hitler's election.[18] Most important, they abandoned Communists' traditional focus on the workplace and engaged in a door-to-door effort in residential areas.[19]

The Saxon referendum passed by a margin of over three to one and became one of the GDR's founding myths. Barely a year after the collapse of the Nazi state, the referendum demonstrated overwhelming popular support for a move backed by the SED and, as the SED cast it, for the SED itself. Although the women's commissions had received little official support, their willingness to target housewives almost certainly played a role in the referendum's success.[20]

The SED fared worse in direct competition with other political parties, and it continued to have special problems attracting women. Although it did well in some communal elections, the SED suffered an embarrassing defeat in Berlin elections in October 1946. It responded by ignoring the results of the election and declining further opportunities to prove its popularity at the ballot box. The era of meaningful electoral politics in the Soviet zone was over.

Attempts to win legitimacy at the ballot box were brief, but they occupied the first, formative months of the party's history, and they required that the SED think seriously about housewives. The conclusion: housewives would be difficult to win over. To be sure, the female and male leadership drew different lessons from this conclusion. While SED women organized direct appeals to housewives, the male leadership seemed to write housewives off, assuming that they would never be part of the SED's constituency. Both approaches, however, recognized that the SED had a "housewife problem."

Given the challenges posed by housewives, other women attracted relatively little concern. They seemed a more natural constituency of the SED, and even the male leadership could easily imagine ways to reach them. Directives ordering equal pay for equal work and ending discrimination in education, vocational training, and employment, for example, promised to attract employed women. Thus even before the first two-year plan called for hundreds of thousands more women in the workplace, the SED learned to consider housewives problematic and other women potential assets. The SED would not, in the future, need to worry about housewives' electoral strength. Nevertheless, it would need to work harder to weave them into the fabric of the "New Germany" than would be the case with women standing alone. The end of the SED's attempts to win elections did not mark the end of its efforts to win over the citizenry.[21] The party leadership could not realize its ambitious plans without assistance from the population, and the effort to win votes segued into a campaign of political integration. As this campaign began, party leaders knew that single women played a disproportionate role in the political life of the zone.[22] The greater difficulty would be to integrate wives.

The main tools in the campaign of political integration were the mass organizations, which were to extend party influence to people who were not politically engaged. In its use of mass organizations, the SED continued to problematize housewives, almost always married, and to reveal a relative comfort with women standing alone. The Democratic Women's League of Germany (DFD) focused largely on the "housewife problem." Employed, mainly single women, by contrast, were assigned the task of whipping industrial management and another mass organization, the Free German League of Unions (FDGB), into shape.

Starting in the summer of 1945, women's organizations began to form in the Soviet zone, just as they did in the western zones. Despite women's reputation for political apathy, women's assemblies were often well-attended, as speakers addressed such pressing issues as food supplies, the return of prisoners of war, and abortion law.[23] In August, the Central Berlin Women's Commission was founded, and, in October, the Military Government ordered the establishment of women's commissions across the zone.[24] The women's commissions united to form the zone-wide DFD in March 1947. By this time, some two hundred thousand women already belonged to approximately seven thousand local DFDs; in September of that year, the membership of the zonal DFD was 242,000.[25]

Although the local DFDs were dominated by the SED and counted "political education" among their tasks, their agendas reflected efforts to balance the SED's plans with women's needs. They promoted equal rights and equal pay for equal work, which were part of the SED platform. They also organized sewing centers and kindergartens. They campaigned, successfully, for improved rations for housewives and pregnant women and for wives of missing and imprisoned men to gain access to their husbands' bank accounts. They claimed partial credit for the release of some 120,000 prisoners held in Soviet camps and, to the annoyance of occupation authorities, continued to petition for the release of prisoners of war.[26] Most significantly, considering the DFD's future, they addressed women's interests as workers as well as their interests as mothers and wives, and they organized women at workplaces as well as in residential neighborhoods.[27]

With the consolidation of the party and the move toward a centralized government, however, the reach of the DFD was sharply reduced. In early 1949, the DFD was placed under the direction of the *Politbüro*, and DFD groups based in workplaces were disbanded. Henceforth, the DFD was to focus on organizing housewives and female assistants in family businesses. The aims were twofold: to increase the numbers of female workers and to recruit women for unpaid positions in state and party organizations.[28] Employed women clearly did not need to be coaxed to the workplace, and, for purposes of political education and recruitment, they were within the grasp of the FDGB. Workplace activism not only would divert the DFD's energies but was antithetical to work with housewives, as it would identify the DFD with the sort of class-based politics that presumably alienated housewives.[29] The official mass organization for women in the GDR was for and about married women.[30]

Until 1953, the DFD's leader was Elli Schmidt, a model of female political engagement in a state that hoped to bring wives out of the household.[31] An "Old Communist" who had been active prior to 1933, Schmidt had continued her work illegally in Nazi Germany before fleeing abroad. After working underground in several European cities, she settled in Moscow, where she transmitted radio broadcasts to Germany. She returned to Berlin after the victory of the Soviet Union and immediately began organizing women. She had not sacrificed marriage and motherhood to activism nor, even temporarily, politics for marriage and motherhood. Her husband, too, had been a Communist activist, and their underground work had sometimes required that they live separately. She had borne two children during critical years of her work: one as an emigrant in Moscow, a second amidst the rubble of Berlin in the summer of 1946.

Despite Schmidt's extraordinary background, correspondents to her office often expressed their sense that Schmidt was a woman who understood "real life." Having discovered someone in a high place who they felt would understand them, they discussed their situations with a frankness unusual in interactions with party functionaries. Schmidt's responses were informative and individualized; only when she received inquiries about prisoners of war in the Soviet Union did she have an assistant sign a form letter blandly stating that only war criminals were still imprisoned.[32] But Schmidt could rarely offer genuine help; most correspondents' requests concerned matters that were beyond the control of the DFD.

Answering correspondence was an important function. A poor response could alienate the petitioner and those with whom she discussed her correspondence; a good response sent the message that the state was responsive to its citizenry. In serving this function, the DFD did not differentiate between married and single women. Likewise, the legal section of the DFD drafted and commented on laws of interest to all women. When the DFD demanded more and better consumer goods, it spoke for housewives, but women juggling employment with housework were at least as inconvenienced by shortages.

Nevertheless, the DFD's most important function, and the one with which the public most associated it, was work among housewives—even as the proportion of members who described themselves as housewives declined.[33] The goal was "to form a new image of the person [*Menschenbild*], especially with the nonemployed women and the women from the middle classes. The particular concern of the DFD [is] to involve nonemployed women in ever greater numbers in the solution of economic tasks."[34] Emblematic were the widely publicized "Housewives' Brigades," which, late in the decade, acquainted (or reacquainted) housewives with the workplace on a part-time basis (Fig. 14).[35] But there were many other ways a housewife could help to build the New Germany. The DFD enlisted parents' (mainly mothers') cooperation in the work of the schools, and it offered short courses combining practical guidance on housework with political education.[36]

The DFD's explicit relevance to women standing alone was thus limited. The DFD's role in shaping single womanhood in East Germany first becomes clear when its activities are contrasted with contemporaneous developments in the Federal Republic. While a loud official discourse idealized housewives and problematized single and employed women in West Germany, an equally prominent official discourse in the East problematized the housewife and idealized the working woman. With housewives a "problem group" targeted for integration by the DFD, employed women, who were disproportionately single, were the implied norm against which housewives were measured.

To be sure, the East German ideal was the working wife and mother. In the 1950s, however, the state was far less proactive in promoting marriage and motherhood than it was in promoting women's employment. The GDR upheld restrictive abortion laws, courts granted divorces reluctantly, and housing policies privileged married couples.[37] None of these phenomena, however, was particularly innovative; none lent itself to bold pronouncements about the socialist state's new path. Indeed, the SED's stands on divorce and abortion represented a reversal of the positions of the Weimar-era KPD. Institutions promoting marriage and, especially, motherhood in a distinctly socialist fashion, such as universal childcare, would wait until future decades. In the 1950s, while the state built new institutions to bring wives to the workplace, it promoted marriage and motherhood mainly by declining to dismantle existing policies.

But single employed women were not just unproblematic beings who performed their functions smoothly and were thus left alone. Constituting the vanguard of the revolution in sexual roles, they could push along more reluctant elements. In the 1950s, these included populations and institutions that, in theory, should have identified most closely with socialist goals: working men, unions, and worker-owned firms.

The party's reliance on women to revolutionize the workplace developed erratically and was marked by the leadership's own attachment to male privilege. Although the political elite loudly trumpeted equal pay for equal work and the banning of discrimination in employment and training, the party subsequently did little to improve working women's situation. In late 1948, the FDGB shut down its women's sections. The official explanation: the union as a whole should be responsible for working women, and since "equal rights for women [had] . . . been achieved in principle," a special women's section was no longer necessary.[38] The claim that sexual equality had been achieved was, to say the least, premature, and the party leadership criticized the FDGB for its action (without, however, ordering a reversal).[39] For employed women, however, the FDGB's facile claim had profound consequences. Just as the DFD was banished from the workplace, employed women lost their advocates within the FDGB. There was no institution left to champion the interests of working women.

If the SED expected the FDGB to address employed women's problems, it would be sorely disappointed. By the end of the 1940s, the Military Government and the SED had promulgated many measures promoting women at the workplace. The two-year plan for 1949–50 called for extensive recruitment and training of female workers. An additional order opened trades previously closed to women, with the exception of a small number considered too hazardous.[40] But the Military Government's wish was not managers', unions', or working men's command. Management dodged the implementation of equal pay for equal work, declined to hire women for positions for which they were supposed to be actively recruited, and fired "double earners." Master tradesmen in traditionally male trades accepted only male apprentices; employment offices passed over older girls in favor of younger boys for training programs. Men on the shop floor refused to train women to work beside them, sabotaged women's work, and denied assistance in situations where men routinely helped each other.[41] Without the women's sections, the FDGB proved strikingly unconcerned about the lot of working women, instead dragging its feet on measures that might threaten its disproportionately male membership. Female unionists described the male leadership's inattention to legal stipulations regarding the promotion and integration of women as "criminal."[42]

But the party had not introduced measures promoting women at the workplace as a publicity stunt. The two-year plan for 1949–50 required 250,000 new workers. Most of these would have to be women. The first five-

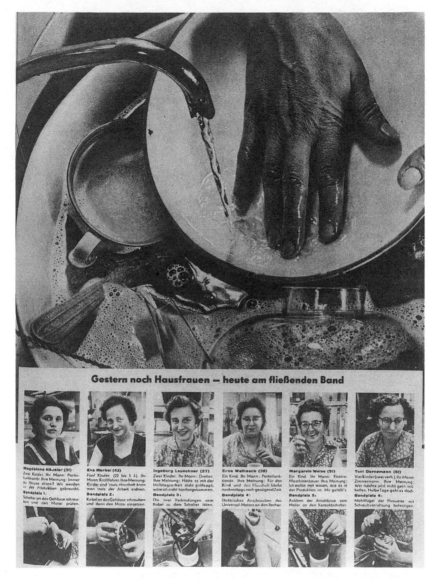

Figure 14. "Yesterday still housewives—today on the assembly line." The East German state attempted to lessen the division of women into single workers and married housewives. During the 1950s, however, married mothers with able-bodied husbands continued to avoid full-time, continuous paid labor. *Neue Berliner Illustrierte* 15/31 (1959).

year plan, which covered the years 1951–55, foresaw a labor force expanded by 890,000 and an increase in women's representation from 37 percent to 42 percent, including growth from 33.3 percent to 42 percent in worker-owned industries.[43] If the political leadership was to realize its economic goals, it would need to revolutionize women's position in the labor force.

Needless to say, employed women also had reason to be dissatisfied with their situation. Unlike employed women in the West, however, they did not have to convince themselves that their government was wrong if they were to be right in expecting better treatment. Working women in the East knew that their demands were consistent with official policy—even if they were at odds with male working culture.

The SED and employed women thus shared an interest in improving women's position at the workplace. In the summer of 1952, the Politbüro recommended that women form commissions at their places of work.[44] The Company Women's Commissions (*Betriebsfrauenausschüsse*, or BFAs) were elected by the women of each firm, and membership was independent of party or organizational affiliation.[45] Like the mass organizations, the BFAs were to address women's needs and provide political education. By the end of 1957, there were 15,681 BFAs with 85,651 members, and additional women turned to the BFAs for help although they were not members.[46]

The party leadership relished the possibility that the BFAs would end the plant-level resistance to women's work and training that hindered economic progress. It repeatedly claimed that, in disputes between a BFA and management or the FDGB, it could be assumed that the BFA was in the right.[47] Of course, if the party's authority had been definitive, it would not have needed BFAs to make the FDGB and management obey the law in the first place. Furthermore, party backing was inconsistent. While the *Politbüro* claimed that women's equality was a matter of principle, at the plant level, the SED and FDGB—which after all was a branch of the party—were far more attuned to working men's culture than to socialist theory. Nor was the party, even at the highest levels, as generous with material support as it was with principled statements. Unable to get their hands on public moneys supposedly set aside for the purpose, for example, BFAs relied on volunteer labor to build childcare facilities.[48]

The BFAs were not able to revolutionize the workplace. The BFAs had to explain labor law not only to employees but also to managers and shop-level union leaders, who seemed to have remained intentionally ignorant of women's rights.[49] Initially hostile to the BFAs' incursion into union territory, shop-level FDGBs quickly determined that the creation of the BFAs had relieved them of any responsibility to address women's complaints.[50]

BFAs struggled to get firms to fulfill their legal obligation to develop plans to promote women's work—never mind to follow through on those plans.[51] BFAs that forced management and the union to admit women to training programs then had to fight equally hard to get firms to hire the women for the positions for which they were now qualified.[52] Ten years after the BFAs' inauguration, employed women faced many of the same problems they had in 1952: segregation into poorly paying occupations and low ranks; inadequate childcare facilities; and a grueling second shift aggravated by shoddy housing, shortages of consumer goods, and sole responsibility for housework.

The BFAs did not create equality for women at the workplace, but they helped to break the resistance of management, working men, and the FDGB to a permanently increased female presence. By the 1960s, women were visible even in traditionally male-dominated sectors of the economy. Further increasing women's usefulness to the economy would require extensive state investment in childcare and education for women, tasks that were beyond the reach of the BFAs.[53] The BFAs were accordingly folded into the shop-level unions in 1965.

For a decade and a half after the collapse of the Nazi state, married and single East German women continued to behave differently on the labor market. The SED thus felt nervous about the political tendencies of housewives, who were out of the party's reach, and comfortable with employed women, who belonged to a world in which the party had a presence. Indeed, the party felt so comfortable about employed, mainly single, women that it counted on them, via the BFAs, to achieve party goals at the level of the individual firm. At the same time, the DFD tried to make married women more like single women by recruiting wives to the workplace and by bringing housewives into contact with the party. Both in the brief era of electoral politics and in the longer era of work through mass organizations, the SED exhibited different attitudes about housewives on the one hand and employed, usually single, women on the other. The aim, however, was to narrow the distinction.

.—.—.

The East German state, like the Federal Republic, emerged in an era of concern about the family. High illegitimacy and divorce rates, large numbers of war widows, and geographic mobility had profoundly disrupted families in the Soviet zone. While the Federal Republic used family and pension law to restore a nuclear family with a clear sexual division of labor, the Democratic Republic took a different approach. Spurred by economic and ideological considerations, East German leaders used family law and pension policy to narrow the gap between women within and women outside nuclear families. Some of their innovations had immediate, material effects. Others had less direct consequences, instead shaping popular perceptions of the significance of marital status.

Already during the Soviet occupation, far-reaching measures concerning women and the family were introduced. As in the West, special pensions related to military activity, including those for war widows and orphans, were eliminated. In the East, however, they were never reintroduced. Provincial constitutions established equal rights regardless of sex or legitimacy. As a concession to the CDU, which still operated with some degree of independence, some of these constitutions, like the SED's first draft constitution for the new Republic, required that discriminatory laws be overturned in the future. When the GDR's Constitution was released in October 1949, however, it declared all such laws immediately void.[54] The Law for the Protection of Mothers and Children and the Rights of Women of September 27, 1950, reaffirmed the abolition of discrimination according to sex or legitimacy.[55]

East German laws went through multiple drafts; hundreds of thousands of East Germans discussed them at public assemblies; and they required guidelines for implementation and adjustments to existing law.[56] It would be a gross exaggeration to say that because of the dictatorial nature of the state, orders were simply given from above, without prior or subsequent discussion. Nevertheless, the SED leadership was in agreement about certain basic principles. Why debate whether a socialist state should ban discrimination on the basis of sex or legitimacy? Foundational texts such as Engels's *The Origin of the Family, Private Property, and the State* had shown that such distinctions were simply structures to protect capital; the Soviet example confirmed Communists' position on these matters. The gap between theoretical formulations and most male Communists' assumption of male privilege was, for the purposes of promulgating law, entirely irrelevant. Ordinary East Germans might disagree with some of these basic principles, but further discussion was pointless.

Thus the very issues that prompted prolonged debate in the West— equal rights for women, the timing of the implementation of equal rights, the legal status of unwed mothers and their children, separate wage scales, war widows' pensions—had been resolved with a few strokes of the pen in East Germany by the fall of 1950. The precise measures introduced in the GDR had far-reaching significance, but just as important in understanding the contrast to the West was the relative quiet regarding so many issues crucial to single women. While policy debates kept women standing alone in West German headlines through the 1950s, the quick official resolution of these same issues mediated against such a development in the East.

Partly as a result, East Germans did not maintain as strong a sense of women standing alone as a problematic social group resulting from the war as did West Germans—although the demographic imbalance was greater in the East than in the West and although all East Germans knew many single women in their midst. Similarly, subgroups of single women, particularly war widows, lacked the institutional framework that enabled their counterparts in the West to develop a cohesive public identity. Widowhood continued to play a great role in women's emotional lives, but its official, public significance was greatly diminished.

The relatively low profile of women standing alone in East Germany cut two ways. On the one hand, it reflected the fact that single women in the East—like women in general—faced less blatant discrimination than did their counterparts in the West. On the other hand, the theoretically more egalitarian environment may have made areas of continued discrimination all the more troubling. Single women's protests against inequitable treatment expressed bitterness at the failure of the socialist state to live up to its promise.

Furthermore, single East German women, like all East Germans, evaluated their situation in light of the information they received about the West and against their memories of the prewar period. Women of proletarian background, especially, might feel lucky to be in East Germany: their chances of obtaining vocational or even professional training, filling skilled positions, and enjoying the security of guaranteed employment were greater than they would have been a generation ago and greater than they would now be in West Germany. But for many material privation seemed especially harsh in comparison with memories of the mid-1930s and images of the booming West. Although both Nazi Germany and the Federal Republic had their economic losers as well as winners, fantasies were usually selective, and there *was* ample evidence of genuine prosperity for many in both societies. Finally, those who suffered from political repression in East Germany—who experienced state harassment or violence or whose loved ones did—might grant that the Nazis had been yet more repressive or might long for the days when they had been beneficiaries rather than victims of a repressive regime, but in any case they knew that they would suffer less in West Germany.

Although the West German debates concerning women standing alone had no parallel in the East, East German women experienced radical changes in family, labor, and pension law. Two of the quickest issues to be resolved were equality of the sexes and the legal status of unwed mothers and their children. The law would forbid discrimination; case closed. To Western accusations that the East German state thus undermined the family, the East German leadership responded in kind. "The reactionary powers . . . claim that our new family law endangers the family, and their latest slogan is, 'The woman belongs in the home,'" declared a member of the DFD secretariat. "But the people who make these demands are, strangely enough, the same people who, both yesterday and today, especially love to use the woman as a cheap source of labor."[57] Support for the "full family" and for other household constellations was "no contradiction; it [had] much more to do with two essential aspects of socialist family policy," explained two prominent commentators on family law in the early 1970s. "The 'logic' of the Rule of the Exploiters [*Ausbeuterordnung*], according to which the protection of marriage must be attached to discrimination against single—especially unmarried—mothers, has always been foreign to the working class and the socialist state."[58]

Some of the most important developments were changes in married women's status. Attempts to make the married woman more independent made her more like a single woman—in legal and economic terms, if not in her emotional life—and thus made the single woman less a deviant from a distant norm.

The East German Constitution declared all laws violating sexual equality invalid. Although the 1950 Law for the Protection of Mothers and Children and the Rights of Women promised that the Justice Ministry would produce a new draft family law by the end of the year, the draft did not materialize until 1954. It was widely publicized, circulated, and discussed in public forums; it was then abruptly withdrawn without explanation. In 1955 and 1956, many of the draft's measures reappeared in the form of decrees.[59] A comprehensive family law was not passed until 1965.

Until the release of the 1955 and 1956 decrees, broad areas of family life thus fell outside any body of law. Portions of the Civil Code that had violated sexual equality were invalid, but no new measures had replaced them. As questions arose, they wound their way through the courts. During the first half of the decade, clarifying the implications of sexual equality for the family became a major preoccupation of the East German judiciary.[60]

The high court affirmed wives' ability to act independently of their husbands. Wives were not obligated to keep house, and they could perform paid work of their choice regardless of their husbands' desires. Property acquired during the marriage, including income earned by an employed husband while the wife performed housework, belonged to both partners. Wives were not required to share their husbands' residences if training or employment opportunities elsewhere beckoned.[61]

In ruling that housework and earned income were equally legitimate contributions to a household, the court indicated that it did not intend to force wives into employment. Nor would it support husbands who sought to pressure wives to work despite the women's insistence that housework constituted a full-time job. Nevertheless, the court clearly intended to eliminate barriers to wives' employment. When West German commentators described in apocalyptic terms the "disintegration of the family" under socialism,[62] East German jurists countered that a marriage that hindered the wife from developing her interests and talents was hardly the kind of marriage a socialist state should support—never mind impose. In a typical potshot at West German ideals of family life, President Otto Grotewohl declared, "When people say that women's honor is injured by their integration into the production process, then I'd like to say: one can impose nothing more dishonorable on a woman than to expect her to be her husband's unpaid maid."[63] Legal commentators and the courts insisted that socialist law demonstrated increased respect for marriage by separating it from crass material considerations, by turning it into a partnership of equals, and by allowing estranged partners to divorce even if no "guilt" was involved.[64]

Still, in permitting the wife to live apart from her husband for reasons other than incompatibility or the husband's professional or military obligations,[65] the High Court blurred an important distinction between single and married women. The admittedly few wives who lived apart from their husbands for professional reasons were no longer automatic candidates for the designation of "guilty party" in a divorce case. Instead, they became a legally recognized category of women standing alone.[66]

New thinking on marriage most directly affected wives, but it also profoundly shaped the situation of single women. On the one hand, women standing alone theoretically ceased to suffer in comparison with the dependent housewife since efforts were being made to eliminate housewives' dependence. On the other hand, women no longer had to choose between legal independence and marriage. Marriage's economic and social benefits had come at a price, and a small minority of women had found this price too high to pay. Now they would no longer need to trade legal rights for the emotional and financial rewards of marriage.[67] Wives might still have to battle their husbands for independence—but they would not have to battle the state. A motivation for not marrying was eliminated.

If the courts did not intend to force wives to work, the issue quickly became fuzzy in the case of divorced women. Divorce was rare in the GDR in the 1950s. Despite theoretical writings favoring easy divorce and despite early Soviet legislation allowing quick divorce at the request of one partner, the Soviet family law of 1936 had sharply restricted divorce.[68] Millions of abandoned women and children had constituted a social crisis, and by the time the Communists were in control of East Germany, the lesson had long since been learned. The GDR retained no-fault divorce, which Weimar-era Social Democrats and Communists had championed before the Nazis had introduced it. In practice, however, East German courts granted divorce reluctantly.[69] West Germany maintained precisely the same uneasy truce in the 1950s: it declined to eliminate no-fault divorce, but would-be divorcees encountered hostile judges.

East Germany, however, took a different path in determining the implications of divorce once approved. From the late 1940s through the mid-1950s, a debate on alimony raged in the highest legal circles.[70] On one side were those who argued that if women no longer suffered discrimination in earning a living, then men need no longer be burdened with indefinite responsibility for their ex-wives. In fact, ex-wives who expected to be maintained rather than support themselves—and help to build the new state—were selfish and lazy. The High Court's declaration, in 1951, that divorce did not give women "a *carte blanche* to lead a life of idleness by speculating on her ex-husband's obligation to support her" was widely quoted in East German attempts to defame women who requested alimony—and in West German attempts to defame East German family law.[71] Limiting alimony to a period of transition was in the ex-wife's interests, according to opponents of lifelong alimony. Alimony encouraged women to remain attached to a failed marriage, and it made them continually vulnerable to their ex-husbands. A complete break would enable ex-wives to build a new, independent existence.[72] If marriage was no longer to be the old bourgeois institution designed for the material maintenance of the wife, then divorce certainly should shed this character.

Among those who found this too harsh was Hilde Benjamin, who in 1954 became Minister of Justice. Quite simply, Benjamin wrote, this position "gives rise to the impression that equality has alrea en achieved."[73] New Constitution or not, a woman of middle age pent years or even decades in a marriage was rarely equipped to pport herself. Such a woman had grown up in an era when vocational training was denied her or when she could sensibly have considered it unnecessary since her husband would support her. If she had worked before her marriage, she had long since lost her job skills. Her opportunities for decent employment were slim. But more was at risk than fairness if courts too brutally refused women alimony. Popular support for equal rights might rise or fall with the issue. "Legal civic equality cannot be permitted to be a Damoclean Sword for women who can no longer use their newly acquired rights; they may not, in the name of equality, be denied what little they have. . . . Precisely the endangering of their material existence in case of divorce—I know this from more than one letter—causes many women to reject an equality that, in their calculation, endangers their existence and brings them rights that they can no longer use."[74]

It is difficult to know how this debate affected routine court decisions. Appeals courts and legal commentators frequently noted the special circumstances of women from "old marriages." Even the High Court decision that accused women of seeking a "*carte blanche* to lead a life of idleness" found that, "on the other hand, the demand to work may not be schematically applied. . . . Older women . . . who could reasonably believe that, by marrying, they had secured their existence for the rest of their lives . . . can no longer, in case of divorce, make use of their equal rights at the workplace."[75] Nevertheless, appeal courts' frequent need to reiterate the difference between "schematic" and "real" equality suggests that local courts shared the popular assumption that women's equality implied the denial of alimony. Furthermore, local judges assumed that the denial of alimony was consistent with demands for an increased female workforce, and they were often ideologically committed to radical change.[76]

The trend was toward strict limitation of alimony. The 1955 decree confined support in most cases to one or two years, during which the ex-wife was to find employment or obtain vocational training. Further support was restricted to cases where the ex-wife was physically incapacitated and the ex-husband had adequate means to support a second household.[77]

These limitations had both a material and a symbolic impact on divorced women. In material terms, they denied divorced women an important source of income. More accurately, they denied these women a claim to a source of income. Even in states where divorced women could expect alimony awards, such as Nazi Germany and the Federal Republic, payment was often too sporadic or too small to replace an earned income. Thus, the symbolic impact was probably even greater. Younger, able-bodied, child-free women were able to earn their own livings, and there were few popular objections to the requirement that such women support themselves. But if they were older or had children, divorced women appeared to be, and felt themselves to be, victimized by their government.[78]

Compounding the sense of victimization were changes in pension and welfare law. The state was no more interested in enabling widows to remain housewives than it was in encouraging divorced women to do so. It had even less desire to award special prestige to those whose husbands and fathers had died in the Nazis' war.

Instead, a different group of widows enjoyed privileged status: those who had lost their husbands or domestic partners to the fight against fascism or to Nazi persecution. The inclusion of domestic partners constituted a recognition of nonmarital relationships, which was particularly important because resistance fighters or those being persecuted might have endangered their lovers by marrying them. Such widows received numerous benefits, including pensions far more generous than those available to any other type of widow.[79] But the designation "Victim of Fascism" (later, "Persecutee of the Nazi Regime") was highly politicized. The elevation of this category helped to articulate East Germany's understanding of its relationship to the Nazi era, as was the case with the Federal Republic's programs to assist "victims of war" and former civil servants. Equally significant, the admission of individuals to this category depended on political considerations. Although racial and religious persecutees were eligible for the designation, the model "victim of fascism" had been persecuted on political grounds. Furthermore, recipients had to demonstrate that they had maintained a "flawless antifascist democratic attitude" since 1945.[80] In other words, they had to support the new state and the SED fully.

East Germans quickly came to regard victims of fascism as an insiders' club of Communists who awarded themselves hefty benefits.[81] Given this popular attitude, widows who qualified gained more materially and politically than socially from the honor. In any case, partly because of the strict political test, their numbers were tiny. In East Germany, not including Berlin, fewer than five thousand widows received such pensions in December 1953.[82]

Much more deserving, in popular opinion, were women whose husbands had died in the war. With the initial abolition of all pensions related to military activity, war widows relied on a combination of public assistance and the survival tactics described in chapter 4.[83] Starting in October 1946, women who had previously drawn war widows' pensions could join plans for widows of civil servants, which, in accordance with occupation authorities' hostility toward those who had enabled the Nazi state to function, were none too generous.[84] In July 1948, the [East] German Commission on the Economy released a decree that guided assistance to victims of war from that time forward. This order ensured that both the symbolic significance and the material conditions of war widows in the East would be very different from those in the West.

The 1948 decree folded assistance to victims of war into the work of the social-insurance offices. This move was part of a larger plan to create a unified insurance system out of the existing crazy quilt of separate schemes, each with its own regulations and bureaucracy, which discriminated against members of the lower social classes.[85] Nevertheless, it raised alarm among western advocates of victims of war, who felt it insulting to require victims of war to appear at the same offices and be subject to the same measures as "ordinary" pensioners.

East German victims of war may also have preferred the dignity of a unique pension scheme, but they had a bigger problem on their hands: the meager provisions of the 1948 decree. The maximum a wounded veteran could draw, including supplements for dependents, was DM 90 per month; the most frequent award was DM 50. A household of survivors—widows and orphans—could draw no more than DM 80 per month. There was no marriage settlement. Most seriously, few widows would receive a pension at all. Not only were survivors of members of the Nazi party and its affiliated organizations excluded, but pensions were available only to survivors who were incapable of paid work. For a widow under sixty to gain this status, she had to have one child under the age of three, two under the age of eight, or be an invalid. Invalidity was defined as a long-term physical condition that prevented her from earning one-third of the earnings an able-bodied worker.[86] In April 1947, only slightly more than a hundred thousand World War II widows in the Soviet zone qualified. As their children grew older, their numbers declined further.[87]

The SED employed two arguments against improving war widows' pensions. First, the party wished to undermine the notion that veterans, civil servants, and their survivors deserved special treatment. Why should a wounded veteran or an invalid civil servant receive DM 90, as many petitioners demanded, when the victim of an industrial accident had to make do with DM 40 or 50? "We now have the situation that social insurance [for ordinary workers] can improve and that—for the first time in German history—former civil servants and victims of war pull up the rear. Until now it was the other way around: the working person pulled up the rear and came up short, while the 'heroes' of the battlefield and the civil servants were privileged."[88] This was a simple matter of class justice. Second, war widows' pensions left women vulnerable to militaristic appeals. A party functionary cautioned, "We must explain to women why we do this: in order that women don't say, 'If war comes and my husband doesn't return, then I'll be taken care of by the state.' Then one is a little less willing to have a new war."[89] The claim that working-class draftees and civil servants enjoyed equivalent privileges was as unfair as the implication that a widow's pension could bring women otherwise opposed to war to support it. Nevertheless, in the context of the socialist critique of fascism and amid accusations that the western bloc was preparing for a new war, these were useful arguments against special war widows' pensions.

While fairness and pacifism justified eliminating special status for war widows, a more general and practical argument applied to those capable of working for pay. These women were needed in the labor force, and the number of people paying into social-insurance plans was inadequate to support so many pensioners. Communists had historically demanded improved social programs, but when they took power in East Germany, they faced a declining ratio of workers, who paid into social programs, to pensioners, who drew from them. The declining birthrate and flight west were key culprits, and pronatalist measures, including strict restrictions on abortion, were designed partly to reverse the trend.

But if more babies promised a larger working population in twenty years, working women promised both to create more workers and to reduce the number of pensioners now. Jenny Matern, a prominent figure in labor and welfare policymaking, made the connection explicit: "The 250,000 additional laborers [for the economic plan for 1950] can in large part be drawn from the healthy female welfare recipients and pensioners who are capable of work. . . . Let's change the situation whereby they and their children live off a minimal sum that has to be raised by the working people. If they work too, the number of welfare recipients will shrink; they will pay taxes and contribute to pension plans; and, by doing so, they will make it possible to help the remaining elderly and invalids more than is now possible."[90] The new social-insurance scheme eliminated pensions to all able-bodied widows without young children, not just war widows.[91] Even those deemed incapable of paid work collected pensions only if they drew no pension from their own prior employment and only if their husbands had provided most of their subsistence.[92]

Insurance authorities sought to convince women that these measures did not represent a worsening of their circumstances. Since women no longer faced discrimination in the labor market, they would earn their own, larger pensions. Elderly women would do better under socialism than they would in the capitalist West. There, discrimination against women left them dependent on widows' pensions that were not only smaller but vulnerable to their husbands' changing fortunes—not to mention to divorce.[93]

Lacking pensions, widows might turn to welfare, but the news here was grim as well. Starting in 1953, welfare and unemployment offices were to screen out female applicants capable of employment, applying the even harsher restriction that responsibility for young children did not constitute inability to work; only physical disability did.[94] Doctors', local courts', and welfare offices' attempts to undermine pension and welfare law testify to the unpopularity of these measures.[95] Doctors affirmed the complete invalidity of patients who were only partially disabled or who had difficult household situations. Courts awarded pensions to partially invalid women who could not find work in their towns. Welfare offices continued to consider the presence of young children in awarding benefits.[96] Higher offices and courts, however, cracked down. A directive of February 1953 required that widows undergo regular examinations by a commission of doctors appointed for this purpose.[97] Provincial courts determined that partially disabled widows' inability to find work did not make them eligible for a pension, nor did a combination of a moderate disability and responsibility for several children above the age of eight.[98]

No doubt widows still slipped through the cracks. The doctors' commissions, which also examined recipients of disability pensions, were too swamped to evaluate clients particularly critically, and welfare offices continued to aid women who were technically ineligible for assistance.[99] Nevertheless, the writing was on the wall. If a woman's husband was willing to support her during his lifetime, that was fine, but the state was not going to pick up the ball after his death. Widows, like workers or veterans, could collect pensions if they were incapacitated, and they could get some relief during their children's youngest years. They might apply for welfare, where the same rules applied to them as applied to other women. But the mere fact of a prior marriage would bring no special privilege. In January 1954, only 59,369 women drew war widows' pensions; an additional 386,347 drew widows' pensions from the main plan for workers and employees.[100] Welfare and unemployment compensation aided even fewer women. In 1954, welfare was the primary source of income for 139,666 female heads of household (including one-person households).[101] In December 1953, only 22,073 women (and 1,938 men) received unemployment compensation.[102] Public assistance and pensions, when awarded, were tiny. A study in 1954 revealed that the main food of welfare recipients was potatoes; noodles, produce, and jams were unaffordable luxuries, and recipients counted on churches and neighbors to provide clothing.[103] Widows' pensions averaged only DM 10 per month more than welfare, and half orphans and children of welfare recipients received virtually identical support.[104]

Widows in both Germanys lived poorly and needed either to seek employment or family members' assistance. In the West this situation betrayed the ideology that widows, unless they were young and child-free, should be able to be housewives. In the East it was the fulfillment of an ideology that able-bodied women, with the possible exception of mothers of small children, belonged in the workforce. While the early German Democratic Republic did not realize this ideal for wives of able-bodied men, pension law enabled the state to apply it to widows, just as limitations on alimony made it a reality for divorced women.

East Germans, however, interpreted restrictions on widows' pensions as something quite different from female emancipation. More often, they regarded it as akin to forced labor. Indeed, it is hard to exaggerate the unpopularity of the pension policy. Popular dissatisfaction with similar policies at the provincial level had concerned those attempting to rally the women's vote in the earliest years of the occupation. By the time zonal consistency was achieved in 1948, the vote was irrelevant, but complaints continued.[105] To this day, East Germans are quick to point to what they recall as the elimination of war widows' pensions as evidence of the difficult lot of women after the war—particularly in contrast to what they imagine to have been the case in the "Golden West."

But East Germans' dissatisfaction did not refer just to widows' material deprivation. In the case of war widows, it also reflected a bitterness about the lack of recognition—indeed, the defamation—of people most East Germans saw as innocent victims of war. East Germans regarded pension policy as the crudest sort of victors' justice, whereby the victors not only rewarded their friends and punished their enemies but also rewrote history to buttress their claims to virtue. Although the East German population included many who had been persecuted under the previous regime and many who had opposed Nazism, it included more who, at the very least, had enjoyed Nazism's early successes and had obediently waged war when their government had instructed them to do so. For them, East German pension policy turned outcasts and saboteurs into heroes by calling them victims of fascism; it turned victims of war into villains, condemning them to poverty and labeling them accomplices of Nazism. Denied symbolic recognition by their government, East German war widows instead symbolized the chasm between official and popular narratives of recent history.

Considering the far-reaching impact of the denial of widows' pensions, however, objections—in the form of letters to officials or comments at assemblies—were extraordinarily rare. Women attempted much more seriously to get action on issues that, in sheer material terms, were much less significant. War widows and their defenders understood that the matter of a special status was closed. There was no point in lobbying for women whose husbands had died trying to eliminate Communism and who had caused unprecedented suffering in the Soviet Union.

Other widows did not face the impossible task of defending the manner in which their husbands had died, but their state's ideology did not make it easy to build a case for support. Widows could not protest being denied their "natural calling" as housewives since official culture recognized no such natural calling. They could not argue that they had already suffered enough and should be spared having to take up paid work; the state was trying to get all women to make precisely this adjustment. Reminders that children were involved were likewise of little help—even married women were supposed to be learning that their children could do well in nurseries, in preschool, and in after-school care. Widows resented the restrictions on pensions, just as divorced women resented the restrictions on alimony. But there was no use fighting such developments by emphasizing the common ground shared by widows and wives. As the utility of emphasizing this common ground was eliminated, widows' reference to their past marriages was increasingly limited to their personal and social lives.

In seeking to improve their circumstances by formulating a public identity, women standing alone stood more to gain by emphasizing their equivalence to married women in the workplace. Despite single women's overrepresentation in the labor force, they faced legal disadvantages vis-à-vis married women. To be sure, single mothers enjoyed one significant privilege: first dibs on childcare. With only 6.3 places for every thousand children up to age three in 1950, 60 in 1955, and 106 in 1961, childcare resources were rationed to those who needed them most.[106] But this advantage did not make single mothers better off than wives. In the 1950s, wives who worked had no children, grown children, or relatives to watch their children. Mothers with husbands but without childcare simply did not work for pay unless they faced dire circumstances. Single mothers with preferential access to childcare enjoyed an advantage only over single mothers without preferential access to childcare.

When employed single women compared themselves to their married colleagues, they saw ample evidence of discrimination. In its effort to attract married women to the factory floor, the government offered them special benefits.[107] Single women, painfully aware that households with two employed adults already enjoyed a better standard of living than did their own households, responded bitterly.

In a 1955 letter to the Volkskammer, two widows made no mention of the pensions they certainly would have drawn if they had lived in the West, but they had a litany of other complaints: (1) Widows under fifty with no minor children were in the highest tax class, but married women were taxed less, even if they also had no children. (2) When an employed wife was hospitalized, she received "household money" to pay her rent, although she shared expenses with her husband. When a widow, who bore all the costs of her household herself, stayed in the hospital, she received the much lower "pocket money," which covered only food. (3) Child-free single women got a Christmas bonus of only DM 25; married women got DM 35, although their households also benefited from the husband's bonus. (4) A single employed mother whose adult son lived at home got no paid monthly "housework day," but if that son married, his wife did— although the housework was much more strenuous for the older woman and although the mother would probably do a portion of the newlyweds' housework. The authors of the letter understood the reasons for these policies, but they bristled at the indignity of such discrimination. "These are hardships that we women standing alone do not deserve. When our children are no longer our legal financial responsibility, we are stamped as 'single,' although these children still belong to our households and the mother still has to do the bulk of the work in keeping them up. We understand very well that the married woman is needed in the workforce in our German Democratic Republic, but we still don't think it's right that double earners should be given such advantages."[108]

The tenor of these women's letter is typical. If widows raised barely a peep—officially, at least—about the denial of their pensions, and if divorced women resigned themselves to life without alimony, single women were anything but shy in protesting workplace inequities. "What ever happened to equal rights?" a single woman asked in a letter regarding her Christmas bonus to none less than the President of the Republic.[109] "Those are such utterly *bourgeois tendencies*!" fumed another, upon learning that women living in domestic partnerships with men would no longer receive a paid housework day.[110] A workplace survey concluded that "single working women with their own households decisively reject the argument that one must provide married women with special motivations or concessions in order to bring them into the production process. They say, 'Just because we're forced to earn our own livings, we're penalized.'"[111]

The most volatile issue was the housework day. In one of the Nazis' typically fruitless efforts to tempt wives into the wartime economy, a 1943 ordinance had granted employed women with their own households one unpaid day off per month to do housework. The ordinance did not specify which women were considered to have their own households, but it instructed firms to err on the side of generosity.[112] Ordinances of the Soviet Military Government continued the housework day and added pay but did not clarify the matter of which women had their own households.[113] A 1952 ordinance finally defined "women with their own households." All wives and women with male domestic partners fell into the category, as did single women with children under the age of fourteen.[114] A 1953 revision enabled single mothers of children up to sixteen to take a housework day if those children were in school or in vocational training. At the same time, it disqualified women in domestic partnerships.[115] Single mothers of older children still had no housework day; women in domestic partnerships lost theirs. And while widows who were denied pensions found no sympathy in official circles, the opposite was true for women claiming workplace rights. The BFAs, the revived women's section of the FDGB, the women's section of the Central Committee of the SED, and the DFD all took an interest in single women's eligibility for the housework day.

One reason the housework day attracted such attention was that there was no serious discussion of housework itself. Early Soviet promises of collectivized laundries and kitchens found no echo here. Even with canteens at work and childcare facilities, there was no question that the private household would remain the primary sphere of reproduction and consumption. Yet even as they called on women to join the labor force, the East German leadership did not challenge women's sole responsibility for housework. Late in the decade, popular magazines began to suggest that men might spend more time with their children, and International Women's Day often brought light-hearted stories of men, dressed in aprons, recognizing their wives' year-long work by serving them a cup of coffee.[116] No one, however, proposed a fundamental redistribution of housework.

And if domestic work would remain women's work, it would also remain hard work. Economic planners directed most resources to heavy industry, leaving women to search long and hard for consumer goods, to make items by hand, and to perform labor-intensive work rather than use machines. The DFD took note of women's burdens in the household, but its demands for increased production of consumer goods got it nowhere. The steel mill, not the diaper factory, was the icon of socialist industry, and to ease housewives' work would be to reward precisely those who refused to contribute their labor to building socialism. In addressing women's household duties, the male leadership focused almost exclusively on childcare: responsibility for children, after all, made it literally impossible to take up paid work, while grueling housework simply made for an exhausting double burden. Nevertheless, the state was far less active in promoting childcare than its rhetoric might suggest. The first five-year plan mandated the creation of sixty thousand spaces in residential children's homes (children's delicate health was threatened by the long daily commutes required for day care) and forty thousand day-nursery places. The budget, however, set aside only half the requisite funds for the nursery places, and no money at all for the residential spots.[117]

With no serious discussion of either redistributing or easing domestic labor, the housework day gained a significance out of all proportion to its potential for lightening women's burdens. As a benefit that presumed full-time employment, it was the most promising forum for gaining some relief for some women performing laborious housework.

In 1953, the women's section of the FDGB and the Ministry of Labor proposed legislation to extend the housework day to more single women.[118] By 1956, the women's section of the Central Committee was arguing to the Central Committee that special concessions for married women were obsolete, suggesting instead a paid housework day for women with children under eighteen and for women over fifty, regardless of marital status.[119] In 1959 and 1960, the FDGB and its women's section recommended several amendments to the law based on analyses of hundreds of petitions it had received.[120]

Only the sustained protests of single women motivated so many people in high circles to pursue the housework day. Nevertheless, their efforts failed. The official reasons for denying the housework day to more single women were threefold. First, it would reduce productivity, which could not be in the interests of single women, who, like everyone else, stood to benefit from an improved economy. Second, the more effective solution to single women's "double burden" was the expansion of facilities like day-care centers and public laundries, which was supposedly well underway.[121] Finally, the housework day was a characteristically backward, German institution. In the USSR, where sexual equality had been achieved, men and women shared housework equally; why, one might just as well petition for a housework day for men![122] The real, albeit unofficial, reason for refusing to extend the housework day was that it was not necessary. Whether or not special benefits were still required to coax married women into the workplace, such benefits were clearly superfluous in the case of single women.[123]

Single women achieved greater success when their needs corresponded to the financial interests of the state. This was the case with care for sick children. Childcare facilities in the 1950s were crowded, unsanitary, under-equipped, and staffed by ill-trained personnel. With poor health character-izing the country as a whole, especially in the first half of the decade, nurs-eries and preschools became quick transmission sites for such deadly diseases as measles and diphtheria.[124] Yet single mothers had little choice but to bring their contagious children. If the government wanted to change this situation, it had two options: build an extensive network of facilities for contagious children or enable their mothers to stay home with them.[125] Allowing mothers to stay home was cheaper. Starting in January 1956, sin-gle mothers could draw 90 percent of their pay for up to four weeks a year to care for sick children.[126]

The results of complaints regarding other areas of discrimination were mixed. The stakes in the matter of the Christmas bonus were low, and in 1953 funds were redistributed so single mothers (but not child-free single women) got the same bonus as married women.[127] In 1957, single women over forty entered a more favorable tax classification.[128] Single women's demands for household money during hospital stays, however, got them nowhere.

All these were clear cases of discrimination. Nevertheless, in comparison with the discrimination faced by single working women in the West, whose earnings were determined by sex-specific pay scales until 1955 and who faced legal barriers to vocational training and promotion, a Christmas bonus and a monthly housework day seem trivial. As a plant-level SED official noted in reference to the Christmas bonus, however, "It's not a mat-ter of the DM 10—it's a matter of the basic recognition and treatment of women standing alone."[129] In a polity that not only trumpeted sexual equality but also held up the independent single woman as a model to be emulated by married women, even minor indignities stung.

Yet if these forms of workplace discrimination paled in comparison with those in the West, they also paled, in their sheer material effects, in com-parison with the denial of widows' pensions and alimony to these same women. A monthly pension or alimony payment would have been worth far more than a day's wages—that is, more than the monetary value of a housework day. Equal rights did not embolden women standing alone to protest all policies that hurt them. Rather, it defined specific grounds on which single women could expect improved treatment, and it eliminated others.

Although East German women used a generic rhetoric of equal rights, their pursuit of workplace rather than family issues indicates a nuanced understanding of their state's political culture. Sexual equality referred first and foremost to the sphere in which class hierarchies were to be eliminated: the productive sphere. The workplace was fruitful ground for protesting inequities, whether they be between workers and management, men and women, or married and single women. To be sure, sexual equality affected the family, and party leaders and jurists challenged legal inequities in this arena. But equality in the family was derivative of larger notions of equality, which always referred back to the sphere of production. Women could argue for consideration of their domestic roles if that consideration would aid progress in the workplace: the housework day, for example, presumed paid labor. There was no point, however, in arguing for consideration of women's domestic duties if those duties would replace paid labor. In the West, proponents of widows' pensions argued that women who had lost their husbands should not be forced to exchange their place at the stove for a place on the assembly line. Such an argument was a nonstarter in the East, and it was hard to find an effective substitute. Indeed, when tackling purely domestic issues, East German women sometimes adopted workplace analogies, perhaps because such rhetoric was more promising than was western-style language regarding the sanctity of a separate family-based role. "Every employed person who has faithfully performed his duty (twenty-five, thirty, or forty years) is honored and respected, receives bonuses and recognition," noted thirty women in a complaint about the lot of wives whose husbands decided unilaterally for divorce. "Only we wives get a kick and are treated like a used-up old maid."[130]

While western women standing alone found it difficult to articulate workplace claims but could make a case to approach ideals of domesticity, the reverse was the case in the East. As a result, marriage in the East increasingly had an immediate significance only—that is, its significance ended with the marriage itself. Widows' and divorced women's position was less ambiguous in the East than it was in the West, where such women occupied an awkward place between married and single status. With no hope of retaining some residual glow of married status and with that glow somewhat dimmed anyway, at least in official culture, widows and divorced women turned their attention more fully to their present lives as single women. All single women, in turn, could insist not only on their rights but also on their legitimate social identity as workers. But for widows and divorced women, all these rights came, quite literally, at a price: the loss of crucial sources of income.

.——.——.

In the 1950s, West German warnings about the collapse of the family under Communism and East German declarations of the achievement of sexual equality were equally far-fetched. In those areas where the East German leadership did achieve real change, the effect was to worsen single women's material conditions (contrary to East German claims) without, however, changing the situation for "complete families" in any notable way (contrary to West German claims). Women could not obtain the job skills and childcare to which they were legally entitled as quickly as they could lose their alimony and widows' pensions. Furthermore, legal discrimination against women standing alone was not eliminated. The East German leadership introduced special benefits to coax housewives to the workplace, and single working women took note. Like their counterparts in the Federal Republic, women standing alone in the East felt like second-class citizens.

Nevertheless, the contrast with West Germany was striking. While women standing alone, dependent on their own work for subsistence, had to battle separate wage scales in the Federal Republic, in the East they turned their attention to such matters as a paid day off for housework. The scale of the problem, at least in legal terms, was incomparably smaller in the East than it was in the West.

Furthermore, the locus of the discussion was different in East and West. In the Federal Republic, the major debates concerned the family. How should widows' families approximate "full families"? What should the legal standing of unwed mothers and their children be? Should women give up rights upon marriage? These were important questions, but they were played out on a territory on which single women, by definition, were outsiders. It was up to single women to demonstrate that they could measure up to standards set by married women—a task that was doomed from the start. In the Democratic Republic, the major legal issues concerning the family were resolved with dispatch. Wives and husbands would have equal legal standing; there would be no discrimination on the basis of legitimacy; women would reap little material benefit from their past marriages. The continuing debates in the East concerned the workplace, and this was single women's turf. The declaration of equality in the workplace brought fewer immediate rewards than subsidies to preserve a domestic role would have. But while western single women attempting to approximate married women had to adopt an apologetic tone appropriate to pretenders, eastern single women asserting their rights in the workforce could do so with greater confidence.

East German single women's evident advantage in legal standing and in the terms of discourse did not mean economic or social equality. Equal pay did not bring material comfort to women trapped in unskilled positions or performing domestic chores in decrepit housing. An end to legal discrimination on the basis of legitimacy meant neither an end to social discrimination nor adequate economic resources to raise children. But married women's situation was changing too. Marriage to an able-bodied man and motherhood still usually meant relief from paid work. Becoming a housewife, however, no longer brought official praise. The economic advantage of marriage no longer survived the marriage itself. And the advantages of a husband's income came with some of the same qualifications as did equal pay for women: in an economy of shortage, genuine comfort was out of the reach of most households. The gap between married women and women standing alone had not closed. But it was narrowing.

8 What's the Difference?

Marital Status and Everyday Life
in the Reconstruction Germanys

In its introductory chapter, this book inquired about the relationship between politics and ideology on the one hand and the social upheavals of war on the other. Both helped to determine the position of single women and the significance of marital status, and throughout the mid-twentieth century both were in flux. Germans experienced Nazism, Communism, and liberal democracy; they passed through peace, war, and recovery from war. Germans had every opportunity to contrast ideologies, public policies, and social settings.

Yet at no point was the temptation to compare greater than in the 1950s. Communism and liberal democracy existed simultaneously, separated only by a border that was not yet sealed but which represented the global conflict of the Cold War. The recovery in the West earned the nickname "economic miracle," but this was also a time of rebuilding in the East, and Germans on both sides of the border could ask themselves which half would provide greater security. Material conditions and the psychological and demographic aftereffects of war, as much as ideological battles and policy decisions, would determine the effects of marital status on a woman's experience. And while the ideological and legal implications of marital status in the two states contrasted sharply, the material and psychological distinctions were not as clear.

According to stereotype, four factors differentiated married and single women's experience: living environment, workforce participation, motherhood, and emotional life. Married women had their own households; single women did not. Single women earned their own livings; married women did not. Married women had children; single women did not. Married women had emotional lives based in their families; single women had to look elsewhere. Although none of these divisions held up hard and fast, neither were they arbitrary. They described likelihood, if not certainty, and they described social expectations.

By these measures, the impact of marital status was remarkably similar in East and West Germany in the 1950s. To be sure, the social climate differed. Most notably, pressures against working mothers, a category which included most single mothers, were more severe in the West than in the East. But this did not alter the fact that women of different marital statuses lived different lives; rather, it affected the social implications of those differences. In both Germanys, marriage rates rose, age of marriage dropped, and illegitimacy rates declined. In both Germanys, married mothers remained distant from full-time labor while single women sought employment. In both Germanys, single women sublet rooms and lived on meager incomes, while wives enjoyed a modicum of economic security. In both Germanys, wives' social and emotional lives centered on their families, while single women, overlooked or even feared by the married majority, sought friendships elsewhere. As Chapters Six and Seven have noted, the contrasting ideologies and policies of the two Germanys led West Germans but not East Germans to problematize women standing alone. As this chapter will show, however, the relationship between marital status and daily routine was another matter entirely. Here, the two Germanys shared more than either state cared to admit.

.——.——.

The 1946 census had shown a "woman surplus" of seven million in occupied Germany. By 1950 it was only three million in West Germany and two million in East Germany. Over the next decade, the demographic imbalance remained roughly constant, but the number of single women continued to decline. Most notably, the proportion of single women among young women shrank (Fig. A.1).[1] The average age of marriage for women dropped over two years in West Germany and over three years in East Germany between 1949 and 1960.[2]

More surprisingly, even those whose male cohort had been decimated in the war were as likely to be married in 1960 as had been women their age before the war—thanks to an unprecedented rate of marriage among men (Fig. A.1).[3] One-third of women born 1915–25 were single in 1950; by the early 1960s, three-quarters were married.[4] Popular perceptions notwithstanding, the demographic imbalance created by the war did not condemn a generation of women to singlehood. Nor were the social and ideological shifts of the postwar period enough to change the next generation's desire to marry.

The "surplus of women" had surprisingly mild effects on the raw numbers of married and single women. But it had a dramatic influence on single women's life-style. Single women were more often widowed or divorced and less often unmarried than they had been before the war (Fig. A.1), and more of them had dependents. They were no longer overwhelmingly never-married, childless women whose incomes supplemented their fathers'. Millions now headed households, supported dependents, or did both.

While the return of prisoners of war reunited countless couples in both Germanys, the flight west created a new, specifically East German type of woman standing alone: the "widow of flight from the Republic" (*Republiksfluchtwitwe*). Eastern Germans released from prison camps located in the western zones sometimes simply stayed in the West. Refugee families split up, as wives eager to settle remained in the Soviet zone, while husbands pressed forward. Until 1948, although women outnumbered men in the general population, far more men than women relocated from East to West Germany.[5] After 1948, more women than men moved west, but men remained overrepresented in light of the overall demographic imbalance.[6] By the time the Berlin Wall was built in 1961, 3.5 million East Germans had gone to the West. Among men, bachelors were overrepresented, but abandoned wives had a tremendous symbolic significance (Fig. 15).[7] It was impossible to enforce their husbands' financial responsibilities, but wives and children thus abandoned were ineligible for welfare, lest the state reward flight by relieving men of their duty to support their families.[8] The result was impoverished women who resented both their husbands and the state.

"Widows of flight from the Republic" aside, the larger pattern of household organization was similar in East and West Germany. Married women, by and large, shared independent households with their husbands, and such households constituted the large majority. Single women who headed households faced unusual problems finding living quarters and even making ends meet. Indeed, marital status divided women more convincingly than did residence on one side of the border or the other. On both sides of the border, single women had a hard time getting by while most married women put the struggles of the crisis years behind them.

The most visible sign of German reconstruction was the transformation of a landscape of rubble into millions of housing units. West Germany built three million units between 1951 and 1956.[9] Between 1955 and 1959, 270,000 apartments were built or restored to habitability in the GDR.[10] West Germany's reconstruction thus proceeded much more quickly than did East Germany's, but over the course of the decade millions in both

Figure 15. Family abandonment and the flight west. An official East German display from 1960 protesting "The Enticing Away of Citizens of the GDR." Men's higher rates of westward flight created a specifically East German, and highly politicized, variant of women standing alone. Courtesy Landesbildstelle Berlin.

states moved into apartments more modern and comfortable than those they had inhabited before the war.

Single women, however, rarely shared the good fortune of their married peers. Throughout the decade, the single woman living in a sublet room remained an enduring stereotype. In the early years, subtenancy was hardly reserved for single women: according to a legal correspondent in *Die Frau von heute*, the majority of employed East Germans lived as subtenants in 1951. Indeed, the housing shortage often prevented "complete families" from living together.[11] In a typical case, an East German couple that married in 1948 could not find an apartment together until 1952. With their three children, they moved into their tiny abode: a kitchen and bedroom totaling thirty-two square meters. When the husband was drafted into the police five months later, he was required to move into the police barracks in a different section of the country; he visited his family on weekends. When the wife recorded her story in 1953, she was not optimistic about finding an apartment in the town where her husband was stationed.[12]

Even at this early date, however, subtenancy was more common for single women heading their own households than for married women, and never-married women were very unlikely to head their own households (Figs. B.3, B.4). As new housing was built, the overall level of subtenancy declined dramatically, especially in West Germany.[13] Rates of subtenancy among single women, however, remained high. Of West German women born between 1925 and 1929 who lived alone in 1960, 65 percent were subtenants, and 54 percent of those born between 1920 and 1924 who lived alone were subtenants, as were 9 percent of West German households consisting of a single parent and children.[14]

Subtenants lacked the security of a lease; they lived in substandard conditions; and they endured irritating scrutiny. In 1960, 43 percent of West German subtenant households lived in apartments with a bath, and only 63 percent of main tenants who had a bath allowed their subtenants to use it. Of subtenant households 43 percent had access to a kitchen, usually only during restricted hours.[15] Landlords harassed female subtenants who had male guests, who spent nights away, or who returned home late at night.[16] According to *Constanze*, one in ten West German relationships between main tenants and subtenants ended in court. But subtenants in both Germanys tolerated much harassment rather than take their complaints to the authorities and risk provoking their landlords' wrath.[17]

Single women who owned or rented their own apartments—often having inherited them from their late husbands—were prominent on the other side of the subtenancy equation, as rental income supplemented inadequate earnings or pensions.[18] Despairing of single women who sublet rooms, East German housing offices pressured or forced such women to relinquish their apartments to "complete" families and skilled laborers and to accept smaller units or subtenancy for themselves.[19] Whether subtenants, leaseholders, or property owners, single women rarely found privacy at home (Fig. B.6).

Women's organizations petitioned their governments to consider single women's housing needs. "Do not forget the woman standing alone! She also needs her own apartment! Build small apartments!" demanded the women's section of the umbrella union for West German salaried employees.[20] In the view of both governments, however, the housing problem of single women would solve itself with time, as the women aged.[21] Families, too, lacked housing—and while the "surplus women" of the war generation would die out, families would not. There was little point in creating permanent structures for a temporary phenomenon.

Housing and family policies went hand in hand in the 1950s. Already during the occupation, the East German publication on social welfare repeated a refrain common since the nineteenth century: that decent apartments would lead to healthier families and thus a healthier *Volk*.[22] On both sides of the border, housing officials agreed that cramped living conditions prevented couples from marrying, made them hesitate to have children, caused tensions that could lead to divorce, and exposed children too early to sex. A speech by Paul Lücke, chair of the West German Bundestag's Committee for Reconstruction and Housing, demanded, "Protect the Family! Build Homes Suited for the Family!"[23] Calling childless households and those with only one child "egoistical," Family Minister Franz-Joseph Würmeling asked whether they, with their majority of 82 percent, should be permitted to deny "living space" to the families who "carr[ied] our future": the 7 percent with three and more children.[24] A public-opinion poll—which presumably included an accurate representation of "egoists"—revealed that West Germans considered the housing shortage a greater threat to the family than the standard of living, moral dangers, unemployment, or adultery.[25]

Reflecting this concern about family housing, building projects offered little to single women. The first West German Law Regarding the Construction of Housing, passed in 1950, focused almost exclusively on housing for families.[26] Of publicly financed housing units built in Hessen in the 1950s, 91 percent had three or more rooms (not including kitchen and bath); only 1.1 percent were one-bedroom and studio apartments.[27] Estimating that, at the then-present rate of construction, it would take seventy-five years to meet the needs of single women, the Housing Ministry's new Division on Women demanded increased consideration of the needs of single women in the second housing law, debated in 1955.[28] The Christian Democratic majority, however, rejected even a mention of single-person households prior to the law's final paragraphs, arguing that more prominent placement would be contrary to the intent of the program.[29] The Second Housing Law, subtitled Law for Construction and Family Homes, gave special consideration to war widows with at least two children and low-income individuals and families. Otherwise, it made no provisions for households that varied from the "complete family."[30]

East Germany inaugurated its major construction programs in the winter of 1953–54 with the establishment of Workers' Building Cooperatives. These *Arbeiterwohnungsbaugenossenschaften* (AWGs) allowed employees of a single firm to pool financial resources and labor to build new housing units, with additional funding provided by the state. Members would own their apartments. AWGs quickly dominated construction, accounting for nearly 50 percent of new units in 1959.[31] Membership, however, was out of the reach of most single women. AWGs excluded not only all who were not full-time laborers but also employees of smaller enterprises, agricultural laborers, and family assistants, all of whom were disproportionately female.[32] The financial burden was prohibitive for women with no male income. A model contract required that each member contribute DM 2,500.[33] With incomes well below the 1955 monthly average of DM 432, women were hard put to meet such financial obligations. Furthermore, single women, whose evenings and weekends were cluttered with housework, found it impossible to contribute the several hundred hours' work required of members.[34] In theory, other members could participate in "solidarity actions" and contribute surplus hours to members strapped for time. In practice, most AWGs either systematically excluded single women or simply found them unable to meet the conditions of membership.[35] Even if more single women had been members, however, they would only have been eligible for studio and one-bedroom apartments unless they had several children. Yet during the first four years of AWG construction, not one East Berlin AWG built a one-bedroom or studio apartment.[36]

Those excluded from public building programs could try the free market or seek the assistance of municipal housing offices. In both Germanys, private landlords resisted renting to children, to people with low incomes, and to single women, who were often assumed to be sexually promiscuous and thus undesirable neighbors.[37] Women standing alone who could not count a landlord among their personal acquaintances thus turned to the public housing offices.

Single East German women trying this route confronted their state's prioritization of applicants for housing. The Soviet zone's Housing Law of 1946 rewarded former resistance fighters, skilled workers, and families "rich in children." Subsequent legislation rewarded those who had distinguished themselves as "activists" in the workplace and dependents of the "productive intelligentsia."[38] Few single women belonged to any of these categories. The 1950 Law for the Protection of Mothers and Children and the Rights of Women instructed housing offices to give priority to single working mothers and to employed mothers of several children, but municipal housing offices largely ignored this proviso.[39] Indeed, while single women rarely qualified for housing, they often qualified for state-ordered eviction. Housing offices removed welfare recipients (usually single women with their children) in order to move workers closer to job sites.[40] If a larger apartment was inhabited by two or more small households—for example, if a main tenant with two children occupied one room of a two-room apartment, and a subtenant and her child the other—the apartment was officially underoccupied. Housing officials might requisition it for reassignment to a "complete" family.[41] Some West German municipal housing offices, for their part, turned away single childless women entirely, and single mothers did little better.[42] Faced with insufficient numbers of larger apartments for "complete" families and couples planning to have children, housing offices assigned them scarce one-room apartments so they could at least move out of subtenancy or the parental home.[43]

The best route to an apartment was still marriage. For those who did not wed, continued residence with one's family of origin remained common. Some 63 percent of unmarried Darmstadt women ages twenty to fifty lived with adult family members in 1950 (Fig. B.6). In West Germany as a whole, nearly 1.5 million unmarried children over the age of twenty-five lived with their parents in 1957; the large majority were probably women.[44]

These women bore heavier burdens than had the stay-at-home daughters of the turn of the century, who had performed housework in exchange for continued financial support or who had contributed their wages to a family purse that also included others' earnings. In 1950, female heads of West German households supported 2.4 million people above the age of fifteen, compared with 1.8 million children.[45] A West German organization of female Catholic clerical workers reported that 40 percent of their single members above age twenty-eight supported dependents, usually adults.[46] Such households often practiced a division of labor similar to that in "complete families." Especially if the father was deceased or incapacitated, the younger woman typically worked for pay while her mother kept house. "I had to support my mother, . . . who had lost all financial means . . . ," recalled a childless West Berlin woman. "Naturally, she keeps my things in order, shops, cooks—takes care of the entire household. That is a welcome relief for me."[47] Single women's mothers were also an important source of childcare. Relatives, most often a grandmother, cared for over half of West German children under six with fully employed mothers in 1962.[48] Even in East Germany, the building boom in childcare facilities was still a thing of the future, and relatives, usually the mother's mother, picked up the slack.[49] *Die Frau von heute* approvingly published letters such as that of a single mother of three who explained that her mother watched the children while she, the correspondent, not only studied but pursued political activities.[50]

Single women often saw caretaking as an opportunity to repay old debts. As a war widow who lived with her child and her mother explained in the late 1950s, "I'd like to make a nice life for her [the grandmother]; for she had it very hard earlier on."[51] Yet relationships between single women and adult relatives were not always symbiotic. Families rarely questioned arrangements whereby single daughters supported elderly parents while married siblings' incomes, no matter how much larger, were exempt since they "had their own families." Families that considered it unacceptable for mothers to combine paid work with care for children expected fully employed single daughters to nurse sick, frail parents.[52] Supporting parents reduced the time, money, and geographic mobility available for courting, marriage, and professional advancement.[53] The West German SPD women's magazine described such women as having "all the burdens of the head of household—but none of the rights."[54]

No one thought to quantify the number of households where a single woman supported dependent parents or siblings, and few turned any attention to the problems facing such households.[55] Single women who supported children were another matter entirely. In West Germany, approximately 16 percent of children lived in households headed by a woman in 1950.[56] By 1957, this figure had declined to 11 percent, but female-headed households still represented 18 percent of those with children.[57] In 1959 East Germany, approximately 5 percent of households consisting of two to four people, including 8.2 percent of two-person households, housed only one adult, most often the mother of the child or children present. These figures understate the number of single mothers: they include only those lucky enough to have their own households.[58]

Discussions of single motherhood were inseparable from discussions of maternal employment. Single mothers' need to divide their time between their children and the workplace, in their detractors' view, made good mothering impossible. The notion that employment made single women inferior mothers depended on single mothers' implied opposite: married women who were full-time housewives. Married mothers, who benefited from their husbands' income, presumably devoted their full attentions to their children.

When considering public opinion regarding women's employment—and especially maternal employment—it is tempting to assume that Germans, steeped in the tradition of the *Hausfrau*, saw the full-time housewife as normative. Germans would thus naturally applaud the West German promotion of housewifery; East German policies encouraging the employment of wives and mothers, by contrast, would have been uniformly unpopular.

Germany, however, had many traditions; the *Hausfrau* was only one of them. Millions had personal recollections of employed mothers even prior to the Nazi period. Some of the women they recalled had been single; others had been married to men who earned too poorly to support families alone.[59] Poverty rather than preference might have led such mothers to seek employment; still, women had been juggling motherhood with employment for a long time, and the overwhelming majority of them had raised perfectly average children.

More than personal experience confirmed that employment for mothers might be tolerable. Socialists and bourgeois feminists, in demanding improved working conditions for women, had acknowledged that laboring women were often also mothers. The Law for the Protection of Mothers, which included provisions for maternity leave, had acknowledged maternal employment; individual firms' occasional provision of childcare did the same.[60] Bourgeois feminists, governments, and, increasingly, socialists had insisted that housewifery was ideal, but they tacitly suggested that other arrangements could also work if only the right conditions were created. The Second World War and the crisis years had expanded Germans' experience with maternal employment. They had also shown that even if the *Hausfrau* were ideal, refusing to consider other alternatives only made matters worse when that ideal could not be realized. Millions of women had had to pull their families through hard times without the benefit of vocational training, which had been denied them because of the assumption that they would devote their adult lives to household tasks.

As the two new states were founded, the majority of Germans almost certainly felt that a full-time housewife was the ideal mother. The further implications of this basic understanding, however, were open to debate. If the housewife was ideal, was maternal employment unthinkable? Or was it simply a slightly less desirable second choice? Should public policy and social pressure penalize maternal employment in order to ensure that the greatest possible number of mothers fulfill the housewife ideal? Or should they improve the climate for employed mothers, thus narrowing the gap between ideal and less-than-ideal? With such questions open and with Germans drawing on a wide variety of experiences, there was room for a broad range of opinion regarding mothers' relationship to the labor force. East and West Germany developed policies and, eventually, cultures that differed radically in their approach to maternal employment. Both drew on some preexisting strands in public opinion and experience; both suppressed others. Neither Germany upheld a clear, uniform tradition, just as neither broke cleanly with the past.

Married women's representation in the female labor force increased in both Germanys. Between 1950 and 1962, married women's representation among employed West German women increased from 36 to 50 percent. In 1950, one-quarter of married women above age twelve worked for pay; by 1962, the proportion had risen to one-third.[61] The booming economy could absorb all the labor it could get, and young families found that two incomes gained them access to the consumer goods of the economic miracle. Not only were more married women working, but so were more married mothers of small children. Indeed, the number of married mothers performing waged or salaried work increased by 324 percent between 1950 and 1962.[62] In 1957, nearly one-third (30.1 percent) of West German wives with one to three children under the age of three were employed. The same proportion of married West German women whose children were all over the age of six (but still lived at home) worked for pay. Contrary to stereotype and the experts' advice, wives thus did not make employment contingent on their children's entry into school: if they had, fewer mothers of young children but more mothers of older children would have been in the workforce. Widows' behavior makes the point even more strikingly: 60 percent of widows with children only under six, but 34 percent of those with older children, were employed. Younger widows rarely drew a full pension, and their relatively good health enabled paid labor As they aged, their pensions improved and their health declined, and this was reason enough to leave the workforce—even as their children required less attention.[63]

The trend in East Germany was similar. Wives already formed half the female labor force in 1950; still, only 36 percent of married women aged eighteen to fifty, compared with 63 percent of single women, were employed.[64] Only 14 percent of women living with husbands and children performed paid work, and six years later the proportion had risen only to 18.3 percent.[65] When rationing ended in 1958, however, food became more expensive, and the increasing availability of consumer goods gave couples more to gain by having a second income.[66] By 1960, 56.7 percent of wives of employed husbands worked for pay.[67] In 1964, 74 percent of wives aged eighteen to fifty were employed, as were 54 percent of married mothers.[68]

Clearly, from the outset, it was more common for women, including married women, to work for pay in East than in West Germany. Still, it is difficult to arrive at a clear statistical picture and even more difficult to pinpoint a reason for divergent patterns of female labor-force participation. In fact, demographics probably explain much of the difference. The "shortage of men" left by the war was considerably greater in East than in West Germany, and it was concentrated among young adults.[69] Because a smaller proportion of the working-age population was male in the GDR, firms were less able to satisfy their need for workers simply by drawing on the available men. Furthermore, a higher proportion of women—including married women, whose husbands might have fled west or been imprisoned during the Soviets' occupation-era roundups—had to fend for themselves in the East than was true in the West.

It is also important to note the limitations of statistical categories. By including only women age eighteen to fifty, for example, the East German report on the proportion of wives who worked for pay in 1950 excludes older women, who were far less likely than younger women to be employed regardless of marital status. The West German figures give a different impression of wives' employment partly because they include older women. Furthermore, neither the East nor the West German statistics differentiate between full-time, consistent work and part-time or irregular work; the raw numbers are thus misleading. Single women, including single mothers, far more often worked full-time and continuously than did married women.[70]

Two things are clear. First, it was more common for women, including married women, to work for pay in the East than in the West, even if we must be cautious about interpreting or even measuring the phenomenon. Second, despite this difference, the trend in both states was similar. Over the course of the decade, ever more wives and mothers worked for pay. The increasing proportion of employed wives and mothers constituted an important backdrop for discussions of single mothers. In West Germany, it provided the context for a public discourse which confused concerns about single mothers with concerns about employed mothers. In East Germany, those who controlled the public discourse welcomed the increasing employment of wives and mothers. In this context, the fact that most single women divided their time between workplace and children seemed less problematic.

Pensions, public assistance, and alimony had traditionally reduced some single mothers' dependence on earned income. Only 32 percent of divorced and widowed women in the Darmstadt sample lived mainly from their own earnings in 1950; nearly 50 percent had a pension or public assistance as their primary source of income (Fig. B.5). In 1961 West Germany, over 70 percent of widowed mothers and nearly 40 percent of divorced mothers of children under six lived mainly from a pension, public assistance, or alimony.[71] In East Germany, however, tight restrictions on pensions, welfare, and alimony meant that single mothers relied almost exclusively on their own earnings.

Pensions and welfare, however, were mixed blessings, providing lower incomes than did employment. The average West German two- to three-person household living from pensions or public assistance had a monthly income of DM 190 in 1953. For these households, the "economic miracle" consisted of eating slightly more butter and meat, fewer potatoes, and less black bread.[72] In East Germany, pensions and welfare payments were even smaller in comparison to average earned income than was the case in West Germany.

Even with regular employment, however, female-headed households subsisted on low incomes. East German law prohibited separate wage scales for men and women, but women remained clustered in unskilled, low-paying occupations.[73] In West Germany, separate wage classifications for men and women remained legal until 1955, and there was little effort to increase women's vocational skills. Over 90 percent of West German female salaried employees—who earned better than wage workers—reported incomes too low to cover essentials in 1952.[74]

Sole responsibility for their households caused considerable strain for single mothers in both Germanys. Social pressures, however, differed. In West Germany, single mothers' numbers were reported with great alarm, and researchers spent thousands of hours evaluating their children. The research and the public debates typically conflated concerns about the father's role (how necessary was his presence?) with those about the mother's role (was it harmful for her to divide her attentions between the home and the workplace?). West German writings overwhelmingly concluded that children needed both fathers and full-time, stay-at-home mothers; on both counts, single mothers came up short. In East Germany, by contrast, there was little public discussion of single mothers per se. East German debates about single mothers were largely subsumed under discussions of women in the labor force, and powerful institutions such as the media and the mass organizations insisted that mothers and children alike benefited from maternal employment.

In neither Germany did official culture serve as a blueprint for public opinion. West German single mothers might be pleased with their accomplishment and their children's development, while East German housewives might remain convinced that their arrangement was superior to any other. Nevertheless, public discussions of mothers, employment, and, in West Germany, fathers, were so passionate that they constituted an inescapable backdrop for individuals' evaluations of their own and their neighbors' situations.

West German single mothers had every opportunity to feel insecure, even if they observed no particular problems with their children. The popular media hammered away the message that men and women had distinct characters, each of which was indispensable to raising healthy children; children of single mothers were labeled "damaged by their environment."[75] Advice books listed the many mistakes single mothers could make in their attempts to make up for the missing father. Such mistakes ran the gamut of parental behaviors and attitudes; conscientious readers could not help but recognize elements of themselves in such catalogues of errors.[76]

The 1950s saw a flood of studies claiming to demonstrate that illegitimate children and those from "incomplete families" were overrepresented in reformatory school and in prison. In a typical report, a court officer wrote that 19.4 percent of youth convicted of crimes in 1950 "had no father." Even more alarming was a survey he cited concerning youth convicted of crimes in a single city between 1946 and 1949. Only one-third came from families the author could describe as "healthy." Social work journals repeated like a mantra the finding that two-thirds of students in reformatory schools came from "incomplete families."[77]

Such statistics were misleading. In 1950, 16.3 percent of children under fifteen lived in households headed by women, and additional "fatherless" children lived in households headed by grandfathers or uncles. If such children constituted 19.4 percent of young offenders, they were barely overrepresented, if at all.[78] The 1946–49 study defined as "unhealthy" not only all "incomplete" families but also those where the father had been absent for a significant period because of prison or work—an enormous part of the general population in the immediate aftermath of total war.[79] Assignments to reformatory school reflected in large part the disproportionate scrutiny of "fatherless" children.[80]

If West German professional literature presented such statistics as proof of the inadequacy of "mother-families," the effect was only exaggerated in popular literature. Such literature hopelessly confused concerns about mothers' employment (the partial absence of the mother), single mothers (the total absence of the father), and households where the father showed little interest in his children. Conclusions that were alarming but impervious to anything other than deconstructive analysis resulted: "Approximately 82 percent of all delinquent youth, youth who are picked up by the police, and youth who go to criminal court come from marriages that are either divorced or estranged, overburdened with careers, or entirely uninterested in the child."[81]

The popularization of such findings helped to fuel popular sentiment against working mothers. A 1963 survey in West Germany indicated that 90 percent of women—employed and nonemployed, mothers and nonmothers, married and single—felt that working mothers should give up their jobs. Women who had combined motherhood and employment reported in later interviews that they believed the two to be mutually exclusive. Such internalized convictions about the price children paid for their mothers' employment resulted in feelings of guilt.[82] And employed mothers who felt guilty hesitated to gain the skills that might bring them a better paycheck and their children greater security. For a woman to seek promotion suggested that her job was important to her—perhaps more important than it should be, considering that she had needy children at home.

Defenders of single and employed mothers, for their part, cited more positive research findings. Such research often shifted the focus from the failures to success stories, finding, for example, that children of single mothers performed unusually well in placement tests.[83] Sympathetic observers felt that children of employed mothers benefited from their early lessons in shared responsibility for housework as well as their mothers' broader horizons.[84] Some pointed to growing criticism of fathers' lack of involvement with their children to argue that children of single mothers weren't missing much.[85]

These studies were much less widely publicized than those that confirmed the dangers of single motherhood and maternal employment. As a result, their methodologies, and sometimes even their origins, are harder to trace, and their results more difficult to evaluate. It also means that, reliable or not, positive research findings could do little to shape public attitudes toward single or employed women and their children, and they could do little to boost such mothers' confidence. Instead, mothers who scanned newspapers and popular journals learned that their children had a greater than average chance of becoming delinquent or criminal. Neighbors and teachers drew similar conclusions and interacted with these mothers and their children accordingly.

In East Germany, there was barely a peep—publicly, at least—about single mothers. In keeping with official priorities, social scientists focused their research on the workplace. In vivid contrast to West Germany, few sociological studies of the family were published before the 1970s.[86] As a result, we now have far less information about East than West German households in the 1950s, but equally significant were the effects of this silence in the 1950s. West Germans constantly heard about research regarding children in female-headed households; East Germans did not. Instead, East Germans were bombarded with research regarding the workplace. East Germans compared their family situations with those of their neighbors, but debates about the importance of the father did not define the very texture of life in East Germany as they did in West Germany. Even professionals addressing juvenile criminality rarely expressed special concern about children of single mothers.[87] When the popular media, on rare occasion, turned their attention to men's role in the household, it was to suggest that husbands relieve their employed wives of some of the housework.[88] If fathers were important to their children (and not just husbands to their wives), this fact rarely found its way into print.[89] Women's magazines advised a simple remedy for single mothers concerned about their children's development: enroll the children in the Pioneers or in a socialist summer camp.[90] East German single mothers, unlike their West German counterparts, did not live in a culture saturated with pronounce-ments about the dangers of raising a child without a father—even if most East Germans assumed that a father was desirable.

There was, however, lively public discussion about employed mothers in East Germany. The East German state unambiguously promoted women's employment. How this principle would affect the frequency of maternal employment and its relationship to marital status, however, would depend on the finer points of public policy. Furthermore, the social climate for sin-gle and married mothers, employed and not, would depend on the sympa-thies and tensions between official discourse and popular sentiment.

By sharply restricting welfare, widows' pensions, and alimony, the East German state made clear that it did not aim to enable single mothers to be full-time housewives. At the same time, by giving single mothers preferred access to childcare, and by indicating that it would encourage but not force wives to join the labor force, it acknowledged that married mothers might well be housewives. East Germans resented the denial of pensions, alimony, and welfare to single women, but for practical purposes the state confirmed what had long been a de facto distinction anyway: married mothers worked at home or at most took on part-time or occasional employment; single mothers were far more active in the labor force.

The debate in East Germany was thus more clear than was the debate in West Germany: it did not confuse the issue of the absent father with that of the employed mother, nor was it fundamentally at odds with practice. It achieved this clarity, however, by focusing entirely on women's employ-ment and ignoring questions about fathers' role. The silence on fathers did not mean that East Germans ceased to assume that children benefited from a man in the house. Nor did it mean that East German single mothers did not miss the male income and the relief that even a lopsided division of household duties brought.

Throughout the decade, employment continued to differentiate married and single women in East Germany. Women with employed husbands could afford not to work full-time for pay, and single mothers had preferred access to the few childcare spots available. Wives' adherence to a home-based role, however, reflected cultural as well as material considerations. Married women, their husbands, and others whose opinions mattered usu-ally felt that if a mother could afford to devote herself to her children, she should do so. "None of my children went to a nursery," recalled a woman whose first child was born in 1953. "I couldn't have reconciled that with my understanding of maternal duties."[91]

Still, although the demographics of women's employment in East Germany resembled those in West Germany, the social climate differed. The mainly single mothers who had to earn their children's keep avoided the relentless criticism that characterized the social atmosphere in the West. Wives who joined the labor force enjoyed official praises. Most families preferred to have mothers home with their children when possible, but mothers who felt that employment would benefit them and their children could claim a legitimate voice.

The debate about married mothers' employment did not pit a monolithic state, promoting full-time labor-force participation, against a monolithic public, favoring housewifery. Rather, all sides wrestled with a variety of opinion. Official publications aggressively battled the notion that children suffered when their mothers went to work. They were careful, however, to present much of the discussion in the form of readers' forums and letters to the editor. Readers thus saw "ordinary people" rather than party functionaries make the common arguments in favor of maternal employment: that working mothers' wider horizons benefited their children, that their children shared in household duties earlier, that their children learned about the importance of contributing to larger social tasks, and that mothers had as great an interest in a quick recovery as anyone else. "Sure, there's plenty to do at home," acknowledged a woman who worked at a cement factory, "but where is the cement for Berlin supposed to come from if we women just want to stand over the stove?" Her sons were perfectly capable of getting themselves ready for school, and they had dinner waiting when their parents returned from work.[92] Women's magazines, however, also noted dissenting voices, such as the reader who inquired, "Is it really so ideal when the children only have their mother for a short time in the morning and the evening, just because the mother loves her career over everything else and is proud of her success?"[93] Editorial staffs naturally selected letters that supported their own positions (or that provided obvious fodder for criticism), but there is no reason to doubt the sincerity of the many correspondents who provided such material. Public opinion, and coverage of it, was divided.

If East German citizens disagreed about the virtues of paid work for married mothers, party leaders were likewise divided over valuing it more than other functions such women might perform. The economic plans of the late 1940s and 1950s required increased female labor-force participation, but much could be achieved simply by eliminating the pensions, alimony, and welfare payments that maintained hundreds of thousands of women without male support. Opening up opportunities for school-leavers would enable women unencumbered by children to contribute more. Wives of able-bodied men raised more complicated problems. Childcare facilities were woefully inadequate even to meet the needs of single mothers, which not only made institutional childcare unpopular but also created genuine health hazards.[94] Why make matters worse by further burdening such facilities with children whose mothers could stay home to watch them?

In addition, nonemployed mothers could perform many crucial services. They could watch the children of employed mothers. They could contribute to their husbands' work. They could participate in party organizations, which threatened to create a triple burden for women working full-time and caring for children and household.[95] And lest anyone assume that if employment broadened women's horizons, then housewives must be inferior mothers, official publications hastened to note that modern housewives' party activity and vocational training made them quite different from the sheltered bourgeois housewives of yore. Indeed, in the mid-1950s, *Die Frau von heute* published sharp rebukes to those who ridiculed or shamed housewives in the name of socialism.[96]

During the 1950s, the state-controlled East German media spoke to those who found employed or single mothers equal to housewives, and they spoke to those convinced that only a full-time married mother would do. They also spoke to those—quite possibly the majority—who felt that a married housewife was ideal but that other arrangements could also work. The diversity of public opinion eased the task of those hoping to create a climate favorable to the variety of roles women would be asked to fill.

Through their publications and assemblies, party officials developed a new prototype: the proletarian, uneducated woman who emerged from the war with children but no husband, who would have been without prospects under capitalism but who now gained vocational training, employment, and recognition for her party work.[97] In her press release celebrating the fourth anniversary of the Law for the Protection of Mothers and Children and the Rights of Women, Käthe Kern, director of the Mother and Child Section of the Ministry of Health, celebrated one such woman. "At the All-German Women's Congress . . . Rosemarie Gutermuth, single mother of a ten-year-old child from Cottbus, explained, 'For the last two and a half years I have studied at the vocational school at Cottbus. I was a simple construction worker and obtained credentials as a master shaft builder [*Schaftmeisterin*]. My company, the Bauunion Stalinstadt, delegated me to attend university. I receive a three-hundred mark stipend from the state. As a construction engineer, I will contribute to the great construction projects of our government.' In these few words, the fundamental transformation of the position of women in the GDR finds expression."[98] Gutermuth tells a story in which her firm and the government enabled her to translate hard work into upward mobility and service to the state; her role as mother is beside the point. But Kern's framing is also significant. The GDR has brought a "fundamental transformation" of women's role not only by enabling a woman to rise from unskilled worker to engineer in a male-dominated field but also by enabling her to do so while raising a child alone—and then to appear prominently as a single mother at a national congress.

Party publications and pronouncements remained uniformly quiet on one subject: childbearing outside marriage. Newspapers and magazines ran glowing features about the promotion of women in the workplace and the provision of childcare and prenatal care. On equal rights regardless of legitimacy, they ran dry summaries of the new law.[99] This relative quiet not only reflected many party leaders' discomfort with unwed motherhood but also helped to minimize backlash among those uncomfortable with the prospect of a radical shift in sexual mores.

The situation was precisely the opposite of that in Nazi Germany. There, the state did little to improve the legal or material situation of unwed mothers and their children, but the aggressive attempt to revolutionize sexual mores had provoked public backlash. Now, in East Germany, the state banned legal and economic discrimination while refraining from loudly trumpeting the overthrow of bourgeois morality, at least in this regard. This restraint did not stop West German critics from describing the new law in apocalyptic terms. It did, however, help unwed mothers—most of whom would rather not have been in this state anyway—avoid unwelcome attention as the beneficiaries of the destruction of a widely respected sexual order.

Intentional or not, this minimization of negative attention had significant ramifications. Combined with legal equality regardless of legitimacy, preferred access to childcare, and increased acceptance of maternal employment, it helped to create an environment in which pregnant, unwed women seem to have felt less compelled to marry or seek abortion than was the case in West Germany. East German rates of illegitimacy hovered between 13.1 and 13.3 percent from 1951 to 1957. Although they subsequently dropped to 9.5 percent in 1964, West German births outside marriage were already nearly this low (9.73 percent) in 1950, and they declined every year until they reached 4.99 percent in 1964 (Fig. A.5).[100] The never-married Liesbeth Mühle was no doubt exceptional in becoming a "Hero of Labor" and receiving the Karl Marx Order while raising five children starting in 1946, but her emphasis on East Germany's distinct social climate is nevertheless telling. "For my children it went without saying that I was alone, that there was no man there, that they had only the mother. They grew up without inner conflict. . . . Perhaps that's very immoral for the West, to be single and have five children. But I can only emphasize: to do it requires courage and a lot of love."[101] Her words contrast starkly with those of a West German unwed mother: "I am treated like someone who has committed a murder."[102]

Germans began the decade with mixed attitudes about single motherhood. Some on both sides of the border were immutably opposed to it and to maternal employment; others firmly believed that employment benefited mothers and children alike and felt that, aside from securing children's financial well-being, fathers had little role to play. The largest group probably exhibited some flexibility, even if they did not consider all options equally good. In this environment, public discourse could strongly influence the social climate for mothers who were single, employed, or both; it could help determine the significance the public attached to women's marital status. In West Germany, public discussions came down forcefully on the side of the full-time married mother, nearly silencing discussion of the possibility that single, usually employed, mothers might also do a good job. Both motherhood and employment should separate married from single women, and the combination of motherhood, employment, and single status would be particularly toxic. Social penalties against single mothers and against working mothers were accordingly severe. In East Germany, public discussions noted the virtues of both maternal employment and housewifery, and they remained silent on whether fathers were necessary for children's well-being. A woman could find public confirmation for many combinations of employment, motherhood, and marital status.

Starting in the 1960s, pressures on East German housewives to become full-time workers increased. East German officials worked as hard to eliminate the dependence of women's employment on their marital and motherhood status as West German officials had worked to enforce this dependence in the 1950s. Emblematic of the shift were the first and second commentaries to the Family Law of 1965. The first, from 1965, reiterated the legitimacy of the housewife's contribution; the second, from 1967, declared housewifery a sign of a "backward consciousness."[103] Ironically, though, during the 1950s, the tightly controlled East German public discourse tolerated a wider variety of roles for women than did the officially uncensored public discourse of the West.

.——.——.

Single women were marginalized from patterns of sociability that presumed membership in a created family or at least in a couple. A 1959 book on single women published by a West German Protestant press captured the sense of exclusion well. "The unmarried woman lives, for the most part, as a subtenant in a furnished room, or she has a small apartment where no one awaits her when she comes home from work. No one is there who looks forward to seeing her, there is no one there for whom she longs."[104] In the popular imagination—and in many single women's experience—to have lost or never to have created a family left a gaping emotional void.

In contrast to the lonely, pitiful spinster was the bachelorette: the worldly woman conversant in workplace and social issues, who had money for clothing and leisure, whose apartment was free of screaming children and smelly diapers—who, in short, was more attractive to men than their own wives. In West Germany, speculation about single women's sexual lives, combined with fears about consumerism and materialism, made the bachelorette a frightening figure. In East Germany, the notion that single women's wider world not only emancipated them but also increased their appeal to men provided an argument against an exclusive housewife role.

Neither stereotype did justice to the social and emotional lives of either married or single women. Marriage neither guaranteed emotional fulfillment, as the counterimage of the pitiful spinster implied, nor sentenced women to mind-deadening drudgery, as envious descriptions of the bachelorette suggested. Singlehood neither meant a carefree existence nor condemned women to loneliness. In fact, most women, whatever their marital status, worked hard and had significant personal relationships. Nevertheless, their emotional and social lives did differ. Single status both required and enabled friendships of a sort married women were unlikely to maintain.

Just as the difficult years of the 1940s had bound single women tightly to their families, so had hardship encouraged deep ties among friends. "Really good friendships formed during this time because each person was in part dependent on the help of the other," recalled a widow decades later. A single woman who retained close ties to family and to friends explained, "I had the simple luck always to have had wonderful friendships, my whole life long. . . . We went through thick and thin together, after the war as well, as everything was built anew. The need, the need bound people together."[105] Single friends often became integrated into each others' lives to a degree uncommon among married friends. Pairs of single friends set up household or took vacations together; groups formed circles in which male friends, when they appeared on the scene, could find no place.[106]

Indeed, single women's exclusion from couple- and family-oriented social circles made workplace friendships particularly important to them.[107] Single women were far more likely than were married women to become active in unions or other workplace associations, thus extending their commitment to their workplace beyond that necessary to earn a paycheck, identifying more strongly with the social task of rebuilding, and developing deep bonds with their activist colleagues.[108] Those without dependents who required care evenings might attend adult education courses, an activity that particularly attracted women of higher class standing or educational level.[109]

Yet most single women had sole responsibility for their households if they lived alone or with their children only, and they provided care for elderly or disabled relatives if they did not. They had little free time. When the DFD studied the leisure activities of Leipzig women in 1956, it found that single mothers "[broke] out of the circle of their homes" yet less often than other working women. Even those without dependents spent most of their leisure time at home and alone, "feel[ing] their solitude especially strongly on Sundays and holidays."[110]

There is some evidence, particularly for East Germany, of the emergence of a new type of wife: the woman who married a co-worker, remained employed, and whose marriage became both a domestic and a workplace partnership.[111] Nevertheless, marriage usually meant less opportunity for social life outside the family—not necessarily because of housework, which single women also performed, but because of husbands' possessiveness. A war widow said of her frequent participation in West Berlin women's clubs, "If my husband were to come down from heaven one day, he would say, 'No, that's not my wife.' I couldn't live with him any more either, couldn't even imagine it. For he'd say afternoons, 'What now—no lunch on the table again,' and then evenings, 'The wife is out again.' . . . I certainly would have been at home more, . . . and the circle with which one associates at home really is narrower."[112] The DFD study found that few housewives pursued cultural interests or were organizationally active, even though they had more free time than employed women. The housewives felt that they "remained behind the times, because their husbands made little effort to enable them to take part in the life of the larger society."

The apparent naturalness of mutual support among single women meant that close friendship and cohabitation rarely raised suspicions of lesbianism. The West German Constitutional Court upheld the criminalization of male but not female homosexuality in 1957, finding that women were more inclined to abstinence, friendship, and sacrifice than to the "purely sexual" relationships supposedly characteristic of male homosexuals.[113] Legal sexual equality must not prohibit recognition of difference; and *this* difference made it difficult to distinguish homosexual women from those who engaged in physical and emotional, but not sexual, intimacies. As had been the case in 1935, when a panel of Nazi jurists had decided against criminalizing female homosexuality, widespread recognition of women's close friendships helped to protect lesbians from prosecution.

Yet the 1950s hardly constituted a golden age of lesbian life. Lesbians' safety was due more to their ability to pass as heterosexual women with characteristically intimate friendships than to an acceptance of female homosexuality. "We are forced to play-act, to lead a double life, and to fear the discovery of our inclination," wrote a woman in 1951, "because we would be treated every bit as much as outcasts as our male comrades are. . . . Perhaps," she added hopefully, "things are better in Hamburg than in the little Swabian town where I've landed."[114] Despite their lower profile, lesbians, like gay men, faced unemployment if discovered and were vulnerable to blackmail.[115]

Secrecy made it difficult to find partners or even to find any affirmation of lesbian existence. Much had been written in a sympathetic vein about homosexuality between the turn of the century and 1933, but most of this material had been purged from libraries under the Nazis. What remained was mainly in private collections, and those too young to recall Weimar-era lesbian life encountered hostile references to homosexuality if they encountered any at all.[116] The first East German book on homosexuality appeared in 1963; it discussed only men, and ensuing publications barely acknowledged homosexuality among women.[117] The only West German lesbian journal known to have existed in the 1950s published poems and short stories, historical pieces, and pin-up photos; it sought to rally its readers politically and to enable women to find kindred spirits. Its readers' letters attest to lesbians' isolation, but *Wir Freundinnen* was not able to solve the problem: it folded after a few issues. "Twenty years ago," said a West German lesbian in a 1977 interview, "we were still doing everything pretty much in the dark and in great fear. . . . They could spit at you or throw stones or insults, which they did often enough; . . . one had no support anywhere. One was really on one's own."[118]

Given this atmosphere, the number of women who acknowledged lesbian sexual experience in a survey of sexual attitudes and behavior (the Friedeburg survey) was surprisingly large: 5 percent said their first sexual experience had been with a female friend, and 4 percent of unmarried women said they were sexually active in lesbian relationships. The true number was probably larger: 30 percent of unmarried women did not say whether or how they were sexually active, the largest "no response" rate in the entire survey.[119]

Most women who lived together, danced together, and vacationed together, however, were not homosexually active. Their emotional bonds were no less central to their lives for not being sexual. Friendships with other single women became ever more important as single women were marginalized in the couple-oriented society of the 1950s. Peers felt uncomfortable with divorced and widowed women's grief, and circles of couples felt they could include single women only if they could invite a corresponding number of single men—odd numbers of place settings were so awkward.[120] But the reasons for single women's exclusion were often much less innocent. Interviews, contemporary accounts, advice books, magazine articles, and even declarations of war victims' organizations, all point in one direction: married women's fears about adultery.[121]

Although the single woman with her own apartment, disposable income, and plenty of free time was a rarity in the 1950s, her image was prominent in West Germany. Women's magazines' advice on how single women might most tastefully furnish their studio apartments presented women who had put material deprivation behind them. Furthermore, these women seemed to have declared their emotional as well as economic independence: they had home and hearth even without a husband. If anything, their living quarters meant privacy, not loneliness.[122]

The simultaneous allure and threat of such wealth and independence made the sexually active single woman a prominent figure in the West German media.[123] One of the decade's best-known single women was Rosemarie Nitribitt. When the twenty-four-year-old prostitute was found strangled in her apartment in 1957, she left DM 120,000, furs, jewelry, and, most famously, a Mercedes 190 SL with red leather seats. The fact that her (unnamed) clients included members of Frankfurt's financial and industrial elite helped to explain her success and added to the fascination with the never-solved murder. The episode proved worthy of a novel, a movie, and breathless treatment by the boulevard press.[124] But the commodification of Nitribitt's death seemed to confirm the lesson of her life: consumerism threatened conservative virtues such as self-sacrifice and modesty, and the threat was sexual as well as material. While most women struggled with unheated rooms and hungry children, Nitribitt lived in a luxurious apartment, and no children claimed her evening hours. Wives labored for their families, even at the cost of their own health and beauty, but the business-suited icons of the economic miracle left their wives home to run around with less burdened women like Nitribitt.

West Germans knew that Nitribitt was exceptional and that the media description of luxuries—whether they be Mercedes, vacations in Italy, or studio apartments—was not a literal depiction of West Germans' life-style. Nevertheless, the image of single women with independent incomes, no dependents, smart apartments, and an abundance of attention from men could be frightening to married women. Wives with children, no income, and emotional lives built around their families were terribly vulnerable to fears that they might be left alone.

East German wives' worries demonstrated that no scandal sheets were necessary to stoke those fears. "There are few jobs here," wrote a rural woman to *Die Frau von heute*. "Many men work elsewhere. There, in the firms, there are always women willing to take husbands from their wives, fathers from their children. If it comes to divorce, the husband will at most have to pay child support. But for the woman over forty-five, who already has difficulty finding a job in the city, what is she to live from on the land, where there are only occasional opportunities for earning money?"[125] In response to fears of adultery, the magazine's editorial staff and several correspondents articulated a familiar theme with a new twist: wives' employment and party activity would not just aid reconstruction and their own emancipation but also help them to hold onto their husbands.[126]

Husbands, for their part, gave their wives cause for concern. According to the Friedeburg survey, 23 percent of married men admitted to extramarital sex, and 70 percent said it was acceptable in some circumstances.[127] Data about extramarital sex of earlier generations and of East Germans are not available, but popular perceptions of sexually needy and promiscuous single women, combined with men's own experiences of promiscuity during the war, may have made men of this generation quicker than their elders had been to try to seduce female colleagues. Numerous warnings to single women in advice books and women's magazines about "unhappy husbands" claiming to need "comfort" suggest that the phenomenon was hardly uncommon.[128]

Single women protested accusations of adultery, but they were not necessarily celibate. Only 28 percent of unmarried women questioned for the Friedeburg survey said they had never had sex with a man.[129] But single women did not always seek marriage, even if they had suitors. They alternately thought their partners unsuitable for marriage, favored somewhat looser relationships, or preferred to remain single if the alternative was to

break up their lovers' marriages. Many single women described their relationships with men as preferable to, not the next-best thing to, marriage. A
West German divorced woman had a long-term relationship with a man
but never wanted to live with him or marry him. "If one does it when one
is young, then it might work . . . but not when one has reached a certain
age and when one has already lived alone a couple of years. Then there's a
certain self-sufficiency and independence."[130]

Public concern about single women's sexual activity hid many other
varieties of single experience. Many were not able to find partners although
they would have liked to. Some considered only "serious" suitors—that is,
those with whom marriage was a possibility. Women's hopes for marriage
were often dashed as their lovers fled or decided against divorcing their
wives. Many women expressed frustration with men's apparent interest in
quick sex or material gain. A widowed East German mother wished to
remarry, noting that "my son is growing, and so are the concerns that
would be easier for two to handle." Her conscientious reading of personal
ads, however, had made her cynical. "'She' offers herself with a flawlessly
furnished apartment, dowry, property, marriage into a good family, etc.;
'he' seeks a cultured woman, a good mother for his children but preferably
without her own, but she should bring some property."[131] To respond, she
concluded, would not be worth the price of a stamp.

This situation led some women to a genuine bitterness about their lot in
life. Edith, born to a bourgeois family in the early 1920s, spent most of the
war performing compulsory labor. During the war, she turned down a proposal because of class differences she felt to be insurmountable. Her father
died in the war, and she left her mother behind in order to flee west. After
a period of wandering, she fell in love with a divorced man. A devout
Catholic, she turned down his offer of marriage, and he died shortly thereafter from war wounds. Another lonely period as a subtenant of hostile
landlords followed, and then she fell in love with a doctor. The two planned
to marry. "Instead this relationship turned into the worst disappointment
of my life, and I haven't gotten over it till this day," she admitted in an
interview three years later, apparently too distressed even to describe the
precise origin of her disappointment. "Since then I have been alone
again. . . . This damned war—it took my best years and cost the men their
lives."[132] Even those who chose singlehood might miss sexual intimacy.
"People think I'm 'bitter,'" reported a woman who had turned down two
offers of marriage. "It's not so. I just see through everything very quickly,
especially men." Nevertheless, although she still occasionally saw one of
the men with whom she had been seriously involved, she felt pangs of

loneliness. "It is so difficult to do without intimacy and love. It is all terribly difficult."[133]

Nevertheless, a large number of single women seemed to have little trouble dispensing with sex. Only 47 percent of female respondents to the Friedeburg survey felt that heterosexual sex was necessary for their happiness.[134] Such responses may well have resulted partly from social pressures discouraging women from enjoying sex, but for a woman not to need sex could be liberating. Both marriage and risky nonmarital liaisons were less necessary. Widows and divorced women, in particular, often felt that their years of marriage had provided them with sufficient sexual activity.[135] "I would very much like to have a good man for a friend, but as a woman I don't need a man any more," reported a widow who had had many offers of marriage. Her close relationship with her mother and her daughter and her religious faith created a satisfying life for her.[136]

In neither Germany did single women form a cohesive subculture, but they did have patterns of social life that differed from those of most Germans. They formed networks at the workplace and in political and nonpolitical organizations. They had a variety of liaisons with men—some shorter, some longer; some more and some less serious. They had friendships and romantic ties with other women, and they had rewarding relationships with their families. Although many faced difficult periods, single women often led full emotional lives. "I must say, I have actually never known boredom or loneliness," recalled a divorced woman who was close to her family and friends and had a long-term male lover.[137]

Married couples and younger people, however, knew little about the social lives of this generation of single women. Few younger women could imagine emotional satisfaction outside of marriage. "Young girls today show, almost without exception, an aversion to dealing in any way whatsoever with the possibility of unmarried status," wrote the author of a West German book on single women.[138] The result was a remarkable number of married minors. In 1960, 30 percent of West German women marrying for the first time and 37 percent of all East German brides were not yet twenty-one.[139] Young women's rush into marriage was unnerving even to many who believed that marriage was the only road to female happiness. Premature marriages disproportionately ended in divorce, and girls who feared being unpopular and thus remaining single were easily pressured into sex.[140] Still, younger women took messages about the undesirability of single status to heart. "I'm actually very afraid of marriage," admitted a young interview subject in the late 1950s. "But I believe in the old saying, 'The early bird catches the worm!' [*Jung gewagt, ist halb gewonnen!*]"[141]

Whether it delivered or not, marriage promised emotional satisfaction according to a formula. The emotional rewards of singlehood followed no such neat pattern and thus remained invisible. As the author of a 1960 book on single women said of the large majority of younger women who married, "They have chosen a well laid-out path instead of the many adventuresome detours that can easily become dangerous escapes."[142] Single women's lives followed no simple pattern; they were improvised as circumstances required. They contained both risks and rewards unknown to women who built their lives around marriage.

.—.—.

In both East and West Germany, marital status continued to determine the contours of women's lives in the 1950s. Single women lived in subtenancy or with their parents; wives lived with their created families. Single women clung to subsistence on women's wages or pensions; married women had access to a male income. Single women avoided having children; married women took childbearing for granted. Single women had ill-recognized social and illicit sexual lives; married women had clear social and sexual scripts.

These larger trends, however, did not intersect with social perceptions of appropriate behavior in a uniform, predictable manner. In this regard, the two Germanys began to differ significantly in the 1950s—even as both drew on existing strands of popular thought. In the 1950s, West Germany reaffirmed conventions that had assigned wives socially approved motherhood and single women socially approved employment. Clear boundaries between women of different marital states were reestablished, after marital status's power to divide women had receded in the mid-1940s. Some women deviated from the models prescribed for their marital state in the 1950s, but they paid social penalties. In East Germany, already-existing strands of tolerance of maternal employment and single motherhood were given official sanction. Such pressures suggested a blurring of social boundaries between women of different marital states, above and beyond the blurring of experiential boundaries that had characterized the war and its immediate aftermath. In the 1950s, most East German women made childbearing and employment dependent on marital status, but they did so because of economic and emotional rewards; the social penalties for crossing the line were becoming milder.

Opposing ideologies and policies had not yet produced two states in which marital status had profoundly different implications for women's life courses. Only the near elimination of pensions and alimony in East

Germany and the retention of both in West Germany had such sweeping ramifications in the 1950s. These policies affected only divorced and widowed women, whose divergent fates in the two states were a harbinger of things to come for all women. The emergence of different social conventions, however, affected women of all marital states. West Germans knew that marital status should divide women, even if it did not always do so. East Germans knew that marital status did not have to divide women, even if it usually did.

EPILOGUE
Who's More Emancipated?
*Feminism, Marital Status, and the
Legacy of War and Political Change*

When the former East and West Germany became a single state in the fall of 1990, the newly enlarged Federal Republic had a population of 80 million. Of these, 16.5 million had lived in the Democratic Republic in 1988, 61.5 million were West Germans. Nearly 12 million were sixty-five and older and thus had reached adulthood during the Nazi period or earlier; an additional 4.4 million, age sixty to sixty-five, had reached adulthood during the period of military occupation. Germany's population included those who had formed families prior to the Second World War, those who had come of age in the midst of the war and its aftermath, and those who had first begun to think of how they would live their adult lives after the dust had settled. The younger generations had been shaped by developments of the 1960s and 1970s, such as the extension of social benefits in East Germany and the West German feminist movement. It is no wonder that, in the 1990s, opinions about the place of marital status in women's lives were still divided.

In 1992, the feminist journal *WeibBlick* published an article entitled "Farewell to the Feminist Paradise: On the Difficulties of the Coming Together of East and West [German] Women." Although the author did not use the term *standing alone*, impressions of women standing alone on the one hand and women who shared their daily lives with men and children on the other were clearly of deep significance to East and West German feminists. "At every opportunity we reconfirm that we have trouble getting along. We continually renew our prejudices about each other: Western women are arrogant, think they know it all, hate children and men, are dogmatic and intolerant. Eastern women are conformist, middle-brow mommies, fixated on men and not the least bit radical. We consider the respective 'others over there' to be less emancipated and independent than we are."[1]

West German feminists were accustomed to the notion that women had to make a choice between marriage and motherhood, on the one hand, and professional and political engagement on the other. To be sure, they objected to the need to make this choice: they lobbied for childcare facilities, for example, which would enable women to combine motherhood and career. But they lived in the real world, not in some utopia. West German feminists who had come of age in the 1970s and 1980s had often accepted single status and childlessness (or at least postponement of marriage and childbearing) as a condition of their professional and political engagement. Although there were exceptions, most women seemed either to be wives and mothers or to be professionals and perhaps political activists.[2] West German feminist activists had made the choice for full engagement in professional or political life, and, according to their cultural codes, women who were wives and mothers had decided against such lives. When West German feminists muttered about "conformist, middle-brow [East German] mommies" who were "fixated on men," they took for granted that one could not be a conformist mommy who devoted a great deal of attention to men and simultaneously be politically and professionally engaged. East German women must be less emancipated than West German women.

East German feminists had grown up in quite a different culture. They took for granted that women combined marriage and motherhood on the one hand and professional and, perhaps, political life on the other. To be sure, their situation was not ideal. Their men picked up a greater share of the housework than did West German men, but they still did not do half of it; the quadruple burden of political engagement, paid work, childcare, and housework was heavy.[3] An extensive network of social benefits made it possible to juggle motherhood and employment even when no man was present, but it was taken for granted that women had full responsibility for the children, with predictable results for women's ability to rise to positions of genuine authority. Still, to be able to combine marriage and motherhood with political and professional activity and to be able to move in and out of marriage without having it fundamentally change one's activities in the "public" sphere seemed natural. If a woman remained unattached to men or refrained from having children, it could not be because men and children would prevent her from being professionally or politically active. It must be because she really disliked men and children. Or it must be because the unfortunate woman lived in another world—say, West Germany—that forced women to make a choice. West German women must be less emancipated than East German women.

The East and West German women who engaged in these disputes grew up in the postwar world. They were not the women examined in previous chapters of this study; they were their children. By the time East and West Germany became a single state in 1990, Germans' experience of and attitudes toward marital status had been shaped by significant developments of the period following 1961. West Germans were influenced by the post-1968 feminist movement, East Germans by the extraordinary expansion of social benefits such as childcare and maternity leave in the 1970s. Furthermore, in both states, rates of divorce and childbearing outside marriage had climbed since the 1960s; women in both Germanys had greater access to contraceptives and abortion than had been the case for their mothers; and maternal employment had increased dramatically, even if to a lesser degree in the West than in the East.[4] Nevertheless, East and West German women's experiences of and attitudes toward marital status in the 1990s had much deeper roots than the changes of the previous generation.

The extent to which a woman's marital status should determine her fate had been contested at least since the feminist movements of the late nineteenth century. Despite their mutual hostility, both socialist and bourgeois feminists had objected to the legal infantilization of wives. Both had insisted that, for better or for worse, singlehood did not guarantee childlessness any more than marriage guaranteed distance from the labor force. State and society would have to see to the needs of women who gave lie to the bourgeois ideal of a perfect separation of wives-mothers-homemakers from spinsters-nonmothers-workers. The First World War and the social and economic crises of the Weimar period intensified the sense that marital status might not divide women particularly neatly. World War I widows, despite their honorable status, might live as poorly as unwed mothers. "New women" might be sexually active prior to marriage but postpone childbearing once married. Wives might have to support themselves and their families as their husbands joined the ranks of the unemployed.

Responding in part to this insecurity, the Nazis intervened in the implications of marital status for women. They aimed neither to restore a mythical and perfect separation of women by marital status nor to make marital status a matter of emotional significance only. Rather, the National Socialists lessened some areas of distinction, strengthened others, and changed the meanings of some marital statuses while preserving their uniqueness. By mobilizing young, unwed women politically, the National Socialists demonstrated that even if marriage and motherhood were paramount, the years prior to marriage did not have to be a waiting period, devoted to courting and saving money for the new household. Single women could serve a much larger purpose. At the same time, while preserving the ideological sanctity of housewifery for wives, the National Socialist state chipped away at its edges, making war brides vulnerable for the labor draft and emphasizing the value of labor for war widows. Both of these phenomena—enhancement of single women's public role and policies limiting the extent to which marriage "insulated" a woman from the labor force—would also shape the meaning of marital status for women in postwar East Germany. At the same time, the Nazis transformed the longstanding cultural division of women into marriageable and unmarriageable, socially acceptable and asocial, into legal categories with profound ramifications. After the war, the Federal Republic would reject both the extraordinarily punitive aspects and the racial base of the Nazi division of women by marriageability. Nevertheless, the Nazis' reinforcement of divisions according to marital status linked the less consequential distinctions of pre-Nazi and postwar West German society.

When postwar Germans pondered the impact of the Nazi era on women and marital status, however, they thought not of legal innovations but rather of men's death in the war. Ironically, the central "truism" for postwar Germans—that wartime deaths condemned a significant portion of a generation of women to stand alone—was not true. Single women rarely stood alone; instead, they shared their households, their finances, and their emotional lives with parents, siblings, children, lovers, and friends. In any case, by the early 1960s, women of the war generation were as likely to be married as had been women their age before the war. They might have spent a significant, and particularly trying, period of their lives alone, but the remaining men married in such numbers that no more women were consigned to lifelong singlehood than had been the case for previous generations.

More accurate was Germans' perception that, in the upheaval of defeat and military occupation, marital status mattered less than it had in "ordinary" times. In women's need to fend for themselves, in their responsibility for children, in their activity clearing rubble, marital status was simply irrelevant. The implications, however, were anything but clear. All could agree that the times and conditions were traumatic, but was the restoration of marriage's definitive role for women central to overcoming the trauma? Or was a new model of womanhood, independent of marital status and more competent than ever, waiting to bloom once the worst was over?

Long-simmering questions about the place of marital status in women's lives were now associated with burning issues: the legitimacy of German culture and identity, Germany's continuing existence in the Cold War, and the physical recovery of Germany's starving and homeless population. As the two postwar Germanys constructed different meanings for marital status, they drew on longstanding debates about the centrality of marriage for women; they responded to their interpretations of what had been most sinister about Nazism; and they addressed the pressing social and economic problems of the immediate postwar period. Feminists' conflicts about marital status in the 1990s, in other words, had only their most visible roots in the distinct cultures of East and West Germany on the eve of reunification. Their deeper roots were in the longer-term instability of the meaning of marital status for women and in postwar impressions of the impact of Nazi rule and total war on the institution of marriage and on the place of women standing alone. These factors set the stage for East and West Germany to treat women standing alone and marital status in such different fashions.

Already in the 1950s, East Germany began to narrow the gap between women of different marital states. This trend was in keeping with the socialist critique of the bourgeois family, which applied in special measure to Nazi family policy; it was also in keeping with the pressing tasks of economic reconstruction and political integration. Finally, it was consistent with official narratives of the recent past. Only a fine line separated the notion that marital status was critical to women from the notion that single women were somehow deprived—and if women were deprived of marriage because of the war, they might be understood as victims. According to official ideology, this was nonsense. The victims had been the German Communists (upon the Nazi ascension to power) and the Soviet Union (upon its invasion by Germany). Minimizing the significance of marital status to women helped to shift attention from victims of war to victims of Nazism.

Initially, the lessening significance of marital status in East Germany had a material impact mainly on divorced and widowed women, who learned that, aside from its emotional legacy, a marriage's significance did not outlive the marriage itself. Otherwise, the narrowing of the gap was mainly ideological in nature. East Germans heard the message that motherhood and full-time labor might be acceptable for women of all marital states—even if, in practice, marital status still usually divided women into mothers and nonmothers, full-time, permanent workers and part-time, temporary, or nonworkers. The clear official preference for employed over nonemployed women gave single women an important rhetorical strategy. East German single women aiming to improve their conditions could fume about the "bourgeois tendencies" reflected in the denial of the housework day to employed, cohabiting women. West German single women who wished to improve their circumstances via better widows' pensions could only beg their government to recognize that they and their cohabitants were "one heart and soul in joy and in sorrow just like husband and wife."[5] Rhetorical legitimacy did not translate directly into political clout: West German widows got improved pensions; East German cohabiting women did not get their housework day back. Nevertheless, East German single women's insistence on recognition in their own right contrasted strikingly with West German single women's efforts to emphasize their resemblance to wives. The expansion of vocational training for women in the 1960s and of social services in the 1970s, which eradicated much of the remaining material significance of marital status, would validate the rhetorical groundwork laid in the 1950s.

In a different manner, the cultural consensus of the Federal Republic's first decade defined the terms of feminists' later revolt against it. In the 1950s, West German law and culture reinforced distinctions according to marital status. West Germans thereby emphasized their difference from Nazism and Communism, both of which were understood to undermine the family. They also put distance between themselves and the traumatic conditions of the immediate postwar period. During good times—the Imperial period, the mid- to late 1930s, West Germany's economic miracle—marital status was a key determinant of women's status and daily experience. Bad times—Weimar, the Second World War, the immediate postwar period, the present moment in East Germany—were associated with a decline in marital status's power to divide women. Furthermore, if a reduced chance of marriage (or remarriage) was a serious blow to women, then the large number of women left single by the war was evidence of German victimhood. Claiming German victimhood did not imply a defense of Nazism, but it was in keeping with official and popular narratives of a war that Hitler started but all Germans lost. The notion that marital status was of central importance to women, and that single women had thus suffered a great loss, was essential to the development of this narrative.

The division of West German women according to marital status was far from perfect in practice, as many single women were mothers and many wives labored for pay. Nevertheless, the ideal of a sharp division was unmistakable. Furthermore, the two alternatives were clearly ranked. Women should desire wifehood, motherhood, and distance from the labor force; single status, childlessness, and a strong identification with the workforce seemed an undesirable alternative. When feminists rebelled a generation later, they objected to the need to choose, but, just as much, they rebelled against the presumed inferiority of a decision for career and against husband and children. Why should all women be expected to desire marriage and motherhood? Might not some want to devote themselves to professional or political work instead? Strongly socialized by the presumed superiority of the "marriage package" (marriage, children, housewifery), feminists insisted on the possible desirability of the "singles' package" (no marriage, no children, career). This strategy did not exclude the possibility of dismantling the "packages" altogether and working to enable women to combine marital, motherhood, and employment statuses more flexibly. Nevertheless, the either-or model with which postwar West Germans grew up strongly shaped the feminist movement.

Despite the distinctions between East and West Germany, the mid-twentieth century also brought some changes that transcended the East-West divide. The Nazi mobilization of young women and the struggle for survival during the "crisis years" not only invested single status with new meaning but also socialized a whole generation to an unaccustomed level of "public" activity. This socialization affected women's later experience of all marital states. Perhaps most significantly, however, the war ushered in a new era where fewer women than ever would enter adulthood, marry, and remain married until they died or were widowed in old age. During and immediately after the war, widowhood and family separation meant that millions of women deviated from this script. In ensuing decades, young widows became rarer, but rates of divorce rose. Quite simply, women were no longer neatly divided between wives and spinsters—but this change had begun with the First World War and intensified greatly with the Second. The explosion of divorce rates a generation later was just the most recent chapter in a century of change. Young widowhood and the "illegitimacy boom" meant that mid-century wives had no monopoly on motherhood; when their children reached adulthood, steadily increasing illegitimacy and divorce rates had the same effect. Single women had begun to lose their corner on the female labor market early in the century. With the exception of a dip in West German wives' employment in 1950, marriage decreasingly meant full-time domesticity throughout the century. A married West German mother of 1961 was less likely to be fully employed than was her East German counterpart—but she was more likely to be employed than her grandmother had been.

Women standing alone have ceased to be the "others" as they were a century ago, but single women are quick to note that they do not quite fit into a couple- and family-oriented society. Marital status no longer neatly prescribes women's motherhood and employment status—but neither is it irrelevant to their fate as mothers and as employees. And it has not lost its symbolic potency: in the era of reunification, political cartoonists portrayed the "marriage" of East Germany (poor, female, with clinging children) and West Germany (rich, male, now burdened with additional dependents). The metaphor may have been even more apt than it appeared on the surface: the wife, but not the husband, would lose her independent identity and legal existence. Women's marital status is a profound cultural marker; it has striking material ramifications; and it is laden with political significance. Marital status no longer defines women as sharply as it did early in the century, but it has undergone only an incomplete revolution.

Appendix A:
Statistics from Published Reports

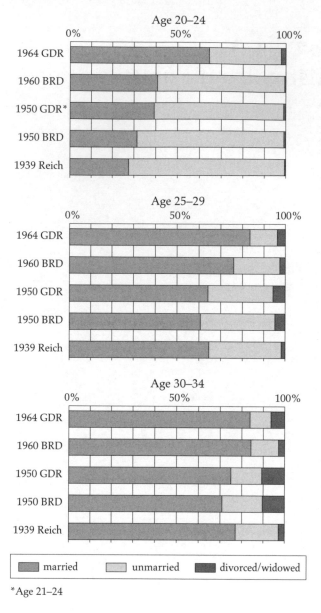

Figure A.1.   Marital status by age cohort. (Source: Census data.)

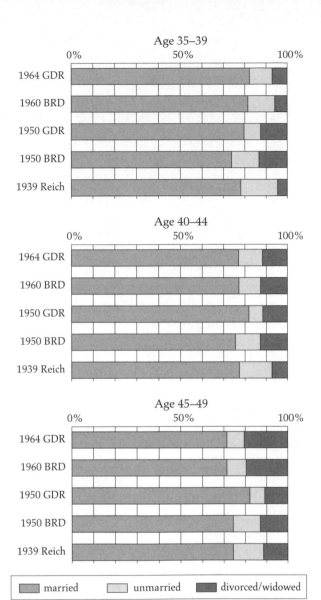

Age 35–39

	0%	50%	100%
1964 GDR			
1960 BRD			
1950 GDR			
1950 BRD			
1939 Reich			

Age 40–44

	0%	50%	100%
1964 GDR			
1960 BRD			
1950 GDR			
1950 BRD			
1939 Reich			

Age 45–49

	0%	50%	100%
1964 GDR			
1960 BRD			
1950 GDR			
1950 BRD			
1939 Reich			

◼ married   ◻ unmarried   ◼ divorced/widowed

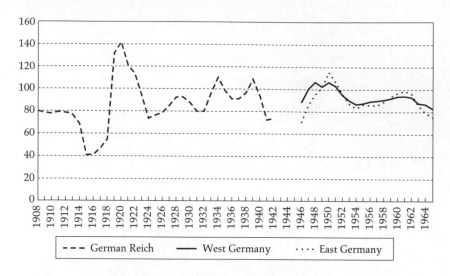

Figure A.2. Marriages per ten thousand residents. First World War and Nazi-era figures exclude annexed territories. (Data sources: *SJ-DR, SJ-BRD, SJ-DDR.*)

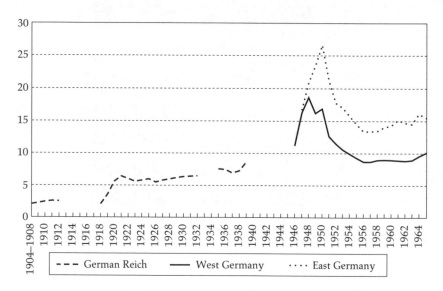

Figure A.3. Divorces per ten thousand residents. 1946–49 figures for both Germanys exclude Berlin, with its higher divorce rates. First World War and Nazi-era figures exclude annexed territories. (Data sources: *SJ-DR, SJ-BRD, SJ-DDR.*)

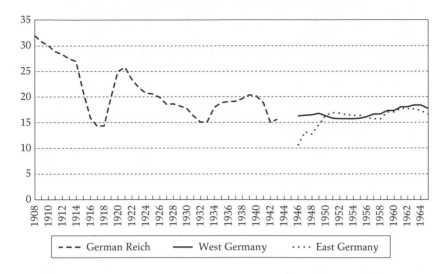

Figure A.4. Births per thousand residents. First World War and Nazi-era figures exclude annexed territories. (Data sources: *SJ-DR, SJ-BRD, SJ-DDR.*)

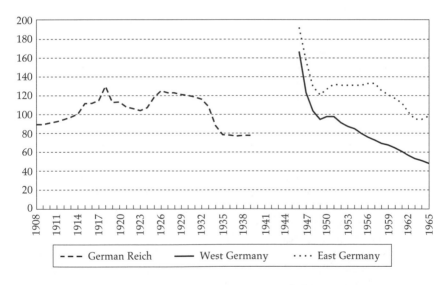

Figure A.5. Nonmarital births per thousand births. Reich and East Germany 1946–49: live and still births. West Germany and East Germany 1950–65: live births. First World War and Nazi-era figures exclude annexed territories. (Data sources: *SJ-DR, SJ-BRD, SJ-DDR.*)

Appendix B: The Darmstadt Study

METHODOLOGICAL NOTES

The Darmstadt study was based on a sample of 734 women born between 1900 and 1930 who were registered residents of Darmstadt for at least one six-month period between 1945 and 1955. The Stadtarchiv Darmstadt (Bestand ST 23/12—Jüngere Melderegistratur) holds approximately 400,000 registration cards for residents; the cards are divided into 1,254 boxes. I examined the first fifty cards of every tenth box, selecting women born between 1900 and 1930 who were listed as the main registrants or as the wives of the main registrants (but not as children of main registrants). This yielded 734 cases. Further information was gathered from the Jüngere Melderegistratur by tracing the women under both their married and maiden names, where relevant, and by locating the registration cards of their parents, husbands, and children. Privacy restrictions mandated that I collect data only through 1960.

The registration cards yielded information about births, deaths, religion, marriages, childbearing, refugee status, movement into and out of Darmstadt, and changes of residence while in Darmstadt. Information on immigrants to Darmstadt was less complete than that for native Darmstadt women. Children who had moved out of the parental household or who had died before their mothers arrived in Darmstadt, for instance, may not have appeared on their mothers' registration cards. Information regarding women's occupations at the time they registered proved not to be useful since there was no information about how long a woman practiced her occupation or what sort of work a woman listed as a "housewife" formerly performed. Municipal address books filled in occasional gaps in the information provided by the registration cards.

Women who were in Darmstadt at the time of the census of October 1950 were traced further in the questionnaires filled out for that census; the questionnaires are held by the Hessisches Hauptstaatsarchiv (Abteilung 920—Statistisches Bundesamt Wiesbaden, Volkszählung). Among women presumably living in Darmstadt in October 1950, about 80 percent could be located on the census forms for the addresses listed on the women's registration cards. Approximately 10 percent could be located at different Darmstadt addresses; the remainder could not be located.

The census forms yielded information on home ownership, tenancy and subtenancy, cohabitants, and principal sources of income. The language of the forms encouraged respondents to identify their households as independent households even in many cases where the economic and spatial relationship was one of subtenancy in a shared apartment. In cases where other evidence pointed to subtenancy, I classified residents accordingly, but the information provided by this study on subtenancy may not be fully reliable.

The data were processed using PC SAS version 6.04 and Excel version 5.0.

THE RESULTS

The Darmstadt study presents a longitudinal analysis of the marital histories of a constant group of women. It complements Figure A.1, which offers periodic "snapshots" of the marital status of the entire female population. Figure A.1 illustrates the high proportion of women who were married in the 1960s, giving lie to the impression of a generation of women fated to single status because of the war. Figures B.1 and B.2, however, reveal that this did not constitute a return to prewar patterns. A large proportion of those who were wives in 1960 were on their second or third marriages (some of those whose second marriage ended by 1960 had entered a third marriage), and the proportion of second or third marriages among all marriages was higher among younger than among older women. Instability in marital status, rather than permanent single status, differentiated the war generation from previous generations.

Figures B.1 and B.2 also illustrate local variations on a national theme. Even if subsequent marriages are taken into account, a larger proportion of the female population was single in Darmstadt than was the case in the FRG as a whole. In its higher rates of divorce and larger number of never-married women, Darmstadt, a mid-sized city of approximately 100,000, resembled other urban environments.

Figures B.3 through B.6 shed light on the ways marital status shaped women's lived experience. Although the distinctions in lived experience according to marital status reflect larger patterns, here, too, local conditions are important. With the city approximately 60 percent destroyed in the war, the pressure on the housing stock was particularly severe; single women, always last in line for housing, would have special difficulties establishing their own households in such an environment.

Figures B.3 through B.6 illustrate the variety of divisions among women according to marital status. The ability to rely on another member of the household for financial support and to live only with one's created family separated married women from all single women (Figs. B.5, B.6). But widows, divorced women, and wives had strikingly similar patterns of residence (Figs. B.3, B.4). The differences between "ever-married" and "never-married" women reveal that some privileges of marriage outlasted the marriage itself. The GDR would utilize pension and alimony policy to challenge this phenomenon.

In Darmstadt, only a bare majority of women born 1900–25 married and stayed married until they reached age fifty-one of until 1960, whichever came first (Fig. B.1). Because the youngest in the sample were only thirty-five in 1960, even this chart exaggerates the likelihood of long-term marriage: an additional number of women would divorce or be widowed before they finished their fiftieth year.

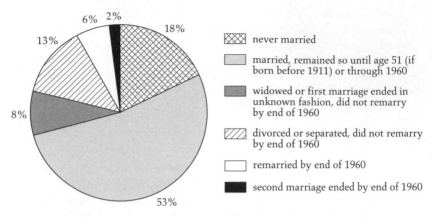

Figure B.1. Marital histories of Darmstadt women born 1900–1925.

The war had a tremendous impact on women's marital histories (see Fig. B.2). Women born before 1910 were significantly more likely than women of later cohorts to live most of their adult lives as married women since younger women were the peers of the large majority of men who served in the Second World War.

Women born 1910–14 married at about the same rate as women born in the previous decade, but their marriages were considerably more likely to end in divorce or widowhood. Women born 1915–19 married in greater numbers than had their elders since they entered marrying age in the late 1930s and early 1940s, when marriage rates were high. Many of these marriages, however, did not survive the strain of war, and an extraordinarily high divorce rate complemented a large number of bereavements. Although this cohort had the highest rate of marriage, it also had the lowest rate of long-term marriage.

Women born 1920–24 entered marrying age when their male peers were already at war or had already fallen. By the end of 1960, an unusually large proportion of these women had still never married.

The large majority of unwed women were dependents of another member of the household; an additional 6 percent were live-in housekeepers or residents of institutions (Fig. B.3). Only about 20 percent of wives, widows, and divorced women were dependents of another member of the household (other than the husband).

Half the unwed women who headed their own households were subletters (Fig. B.4). Over half of wives, widows, and divorced women who headed their own households (alone or with husbands) rented their homes, but subletting was common even among these women.

The large majority of wives were financially dependent on another member of their household, usually their husbands (Fig. B.5). Nearly half of widows and divorced women lived primarily from pensions or public assistance, but a third lived by their own earnings. The overwhelming majority of unwed women lived from their own earnings.

Only 11 percent of widowed and divorced women and 1 percent of unwed women lived alone or exclusively with their created families (Fig. B.6). Only one-quarter of

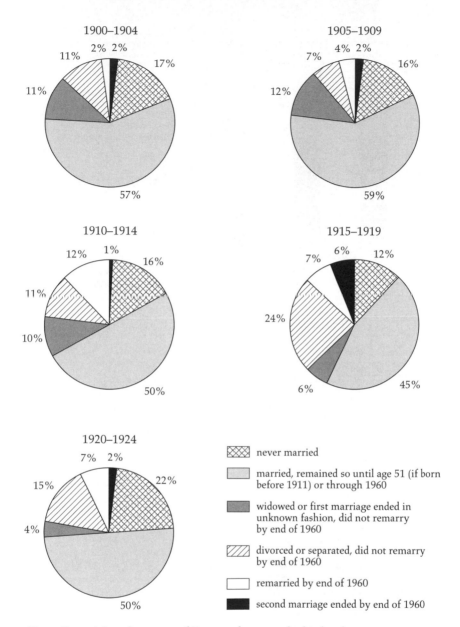

Figure B.2.   Marital patterns of Darmstadt women by birth cohort.

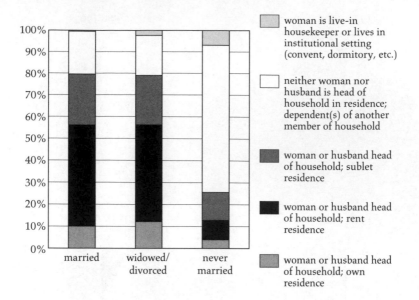

Figure B.3. Residence of Darmstadt women born 1900–1930, October 24, 1950.

Figure B.4. Residence of Darmstadt women born 1900–1930 who were heads of household or whose husbands were heads of household, October 24, 1950.

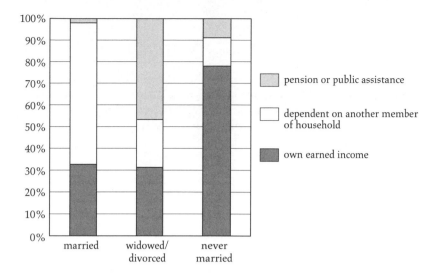

Figure B.5. Primary source of income of Darmstadt women born 1900–1930, October 24, 1950.

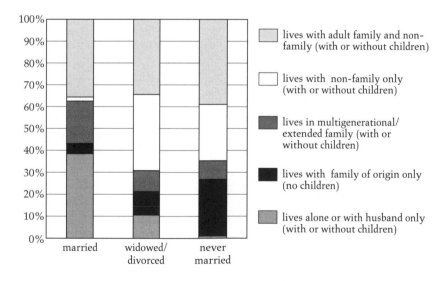

Figure B.6. Cohabitants of Darmstadt women born 1900–1930, October 24, 1950.

unwed women resided with only their families of origin; roughly one-quarter of them and one-third of divorced and widowed women had only nonrelatives as cohabitants, their own children excepted. By contrast, nearly 40 percent of wives lived alone or exclusively with their created families. Nevertheless, residence with nonrelatives was common for women of all marital states: over one-third of wives and roughly two-thirds of single women lived with people to whom they were not related.

Notes

Abbreviations used in the notes can be found in the List of Abbreviations in the front of the book and in the lists of archival collections and journals at the beginning of the Bibliography.

PREFACE

1. Most importantly, Broszat, Henke, and Woller, eds., *Von Stalingrad zur Währungsreform.*

2. The literature on categories of difference is substantial; for examples of feminist writing on difference, see Gordon, "On 'Difference'"; Brown, "'What Has Happened Here'"; Lerner, "Reconceptualizing Differences among Women."

3. The classic statement of feminist historical deconstruction is Scott, "Gender"; see also her *Gender and the Politics of History* and Riley, *Am I That Name?* For an early theoretical discussion, see Alcoff, "Cultural Feminism versus Poststructuralism." Especially useful for the interplay of racial, sexual, and class constructions is Higginbotham, "African-American Women's History and the Metalanguage of Race."

CHAPTER 1: INTRODUCTION

1. Jung, *Die Frau in Europa*, 17–18.

2. This address was chosen at random from the hundreds of Darmstadt residences administered by the city. A comparison with records of other such houses indicates that this building had a typical variety of residents. The address as well as the names have been changed to protect residents' privacy. Jüngere Melderegistratur, Bestand ST23/12, SA-D; Hausakten des Städtischen Wohnungsamtes Darmstadt, Bestand ST26.41 Nr. 2/182, SA-D.

3. Grebing, Pozorski, and Schulze, *Die Nachkriegsentwicklung in Westdeutschland*, vol. A, *Die wirtschaftlichen Grundlagen*, 19; Barthel, *Die wirtschaftlichen Ausgangsbedingungen der DDR*, 54. These numbers exclude occupation soldiers.

4. I adopt the definition for "women standing alone" of Meyer and Schulze, who differentiate between "married women whose husbands were present in the family" and

"women standing alone, who confronted everyday life without a husband"; *Auswirkungen des II. Weltkrieges auf Familien,* 190.

5. On the proportion of the population marrying, see Hajnal, "European Marriage Patterns in Perspective." On medieval widowhood, see Mirrer, ed., *Upon My Husband's Death.*

6. For this reason, "independent women" or "spinsters" appear as a distinct social group in literature concerning Western Europe and the United States in the nineteenth and early twentieth centuries. Vicinus, *Independent Women;* Jeffreys, *The Spinster and Her Enemies;* Meyerowitz, *Women Adrift;* Chambers-Schiller, *Liberty a Better Husband.*

7. On the role of marital status in determining men's citizenship in nineteenth-century Britain, however, see McClelland, "Rational and Respectable Men."

8. Hubbard, *Familiengeschichte,* 49ff.; Frevert, *Frauen-Geschichte zwischen bürgerlicher Verbesserung und neuer Weiblichkeit,* 132–34; Vogel, "Property Rights and the Status of Women in Germany and England."

9. Dollard, "A Tool of Social Reform," 4–22; Greven-Aschoff, *Die bürgerliche Frauenbewegung in Deutschland 1894–1933,* 46; Frevert, *Frauen-Geschichte,* 117ff.

10. Frevert, *Frauen-Geschichte,* 80–83.

11. See, for example, Baumann, *Protestantismus und Frauenemanzipation in Deutschland,* 204–16.

12. Grossmann, *Reforming Sex,* 221, n. 30.

13. Ibid., 6.

14. Hausen, "The German Nation's Obligations to the Heroes' Widows of World War I."

15. Grossmann, "The New Woman and the Rationalization of Sexuality in Weimar Germany"; Usborne, "The New Woman and Generation Conflict." See Roberts, *Civilization without Sexes,* 149–211, on popular perceptions of single women in interwar France.

16. Grossmann, *Reforming Sex;* Bessel, *Germany after the First World War,* 220–53.

17. Although *Kinder, Küche, Kirche* is still the popular stereotype of women's lives under Nazism (at least, outside Germany), historians of women have, from the beginning, examined women's other roles in Nazi Germany, most notably that of the worker. Winkler, *Frauenarbeit im "Dritten Reich";* von Gersdorff, *Frauen im Kriegsdienst 1919–1945;* Mason, "Women in Germany, 1925–1940"; Frauengruppe Faschismusforschung, ed., *Mutterkreuz und Arbeitsbuch;* Tröger, "The Creation of a Female Assembly-Line Proletariat"; Rupp, *Mobilizing Women for War.*

18. Koonz, *Mothers in the Fatherland;* Stephenson, *The Nazi Organization of Women;* Reese, "Straff, aber nicht stramm—herb, aber nicht derb."

19. See Reese, "The BDM Generation," and Clemens, "'Die haben es geschafft, uns an unserem Ehrgeiz zu packen . . . ,'" on the "modernizing" effects of the League of German Girls. For summaries of the modernization debate more generally, see Roseman, "National Socialism and Modernisation"; Frei, "Wie modern war der Nationalsozialismus?"

20. Meyer and Schulze, *Wie wir das alles geschafft haben;* Meyer and Schulze, *Von Liebe sprach damals keiner.* See also Fishman, *We Will Wait.*

21. In addition to Meyer and Schulze's work and numerous local studies, see Horbert and Spindler, *Wie wir hamsterten, hungerten und überlebten;* Stolten, ed., *Der Hunger nach Erfahrung;* Freier and Kuhn, eds., *"Das Schicksal Deutschlands liegt in der Hand seiner Frauen."*

22. In 1939, 84.9 percent of men age thirty-five to thirty-nine were married; in 1950, the figures were 84.5 percent for West Germany and 83.7 percent for East Germany (not including East Berlin). In 1960, by contrast, 91.6 percent of West German men of this age group were married. In 1964, the East German figure was 93 percent, not including residents of institutions. *SJ-DR* (1941–42): 24; *SJ-BRD* (1962): 47; *SJ-DDR* (1955): 19; *Haushalte nach Art, Größe, und Gebiet*, 300.

23. Methodological details of this study, which I performed in 1990–91, appear in Appendix B. Privacy restrictions stipulated that I collect data only through 1960, which meant that the youngest women in the sample were only thirty-five at the end of the study. These figures thus actually overestimate the number of women who lived all their middle years as wives. Many younger women's marriages would end in divorce or widowhood before they reached age fifty but, if prior trends continued, few of those whose marriages ended would remarry, and few of those who had not married by the age of thirty-five would do so.

I was unable to perform a comparable study in an East German city. The higher rate of divorce in the German Democratic Republic, however, means that movement in and out of marriage was yet more common there than in the Federal Republic (Fig. A.3).

24. For an interesting parallel, see Bessel, "The 'Front Generation' and the Politics of Weimar Germany." Bessel argues that battles over policy toward veterans after World War I, more than the experience of war itself, created a popular perception of a unified "front generation" and that this perception, flawed as it was, had a tremendous political and social impact.

25. Bock, *Zwangssterilisation im Nationalsozialismus*; Czarnowski, *Das kontrollierte Paar*; Czarnowski, "'The Value of Marriage for the *Volksgemeinschaft*.'"

26. Moeller, *Protecting Motherhood*; Moeller, "Protecting Mother's Work"; Moeller, "Reconstructing the Family in Reconstruction Germany."

27. Meyer and Schulze, *Wie wir das alles geschafft haben*; Meyer and Schulze, *Auswirkungen des II. Weltkrieges*; Meyer and Schulze, *Von Liebe sprach damals keiner*; Willenbacher, "Zerrüttung und Bewährung der Nachkriegs-Familie."

28. Merkel, *. . . und Du, Frau an der Werkbank*; Merkel, "Leitbilder und Lebensweisen von Frauen in der DDR."

29. On the use of the social historical period 1942–48, see Broszat, Henke, and Woller, eds., *Von Stalingrad zur Währungsreform*. On change and continuity over 1945 in the writing of East German social history, see Kaelble, Kocka, and Zwahr, "Einleitung," 9–15; Niethammer, von Plato, and Wierling, *Die volkseigene Erfahrung*. For West Germany, see Niethammer, ed., *"Hinterher merkt man, daß es richtig war, daß es schiefgegangen ist"*; Niethammer and von Plato, eds., *"Wir kriegen jetzt andere Zeiten"*; Niethammer, ed., *"Die Jahre weiß man nicht, wo man die heute hinsetzen soll."*

30. See Bock, "Racism and Sexism in Nazi Germany," and Koonz, *Mothers in the Fatherland*, for different yet powerful analyses of the ways in which gender difference was intrinsic to the fulfillment of racial goals in Nazi Germany. On the centrality of gender difference in the early Federal Republic, see Moeller, *Protecting Motherhood*.

31. Treatments of a domestic life shaped but not fully controlled by the Nazi dictatorship include Peukert, *Inside Nazi Germany*; Kershaw, *The "Hitler Myth"*; Niethammer, *"Die Jahre."* On the "totalitarianism" debate and the relationship between political and social history in the GDR, see the essays in Bessel and Jessen, eds., *Die Grenzen der Diktatur*; "Totalitäre Herrschaft und totalitäres Erbe"; Kocka, "Eine durchherrschte Gesellschaft." On the "public sphere" in bourgeois society, see Habermas, *The Structural Transformation of the Public Sphere*; see also Fraser, "Rethinking the Public

Sphere," and Davis, "Reconsidering Habermas, Gender, and the Public Sphere: The Case of Wilhelmine Germany."

32. Harsch, "Society, the State, and Abortion in East Germany, 1950–1972," 56.

CHAPTER 2: HOUSEWIVES, ACTIVISTS, AND "ASOCIALS"

1. Elisabeth H. to Hitler, 8 January 1941, 15.01/27419, folio 214–22, here 214, BAP.

2. Nazis would have referred to the first type as "valuable" or "desirable" and the latter types as "nonvaluable" or "undesirable." I will use the terms "valued," "desired," "unvalued," and "undesired."

3. Arthur Gütt et al., *Blutschutz- und Ehegesundheitsgesetz: Gesetze und Erläuterungen* (Munich, 1936), 25, quoted in Czarnowski, *Das kontrollierte Paar*, 62.

4. See, for example, Stämmler, *Rassenpflege im völkischen Staat*, esp. 91–100.

5. See, for example, the continuum described by W. Scheurlen of the Reichsgesundheitsamt, quoted in Czarnowski, *Das kontrollierte Paar*, 173.

6. Gesetz zur Verminderung der Arbeitslosigkeit vom 1. Juni 1933 (*RGBl* I 323–39); 3. Änderungsgesetz vom 3. November 1937 (*RGBl* I 1158).

7. Verordnung über die Gewährung von Kinderbeihilfen an kinderreiche Familien vom 15. September 1935 (*RGBl* I 1160); Mühlfeld and Schönweiß, *Nationalsozialistische Familienpolitik*, 193; Sachse, *Siemens, der Nationalsozialismus und die moderne Familie*, 131; Klinksiek, *Die Frau im NS-Staat*, 88; Einkommenssteuergesetz vom 16. Oktober 1934 (*RGBl* I 1065); Vermögenssteuergesetz vom 16. Oktober 1934 (*RGBl* I 1052). Unwed mothers and unmarried people over the age of fifty-five did not have to contribute to the marriage-loan fund.

8. For twenty-one-year-olds, the numbers were 87.9 percent and 81.1 percent; for thirty-year-olds, 29.3 percent and 21.5 percent. "Familienstand der Bevölkerung," *WS* (1940): 522–58, here 523.

9. Gesetz zur Vereinheitlichung des Rechts der Eheschließung und der Ehescheidung im Lande Österreich und im übrigen Reichsgebiet vom 6. Juli 1938 (*RGBl* I 807ff.), discussed in Wolf, Lücke, and Hax, *Scheidung und Scheidungsrecht*, 78ff.; Mühlfeld and Schönweiß, *Nationalsozialistische Familienpolitik*, 93–94; König, *Die Frau im Recht des Nationalsozialismus*.

10. If the new relationship had produced children, the courts were particularly likely to approve the divorce. The same law reduced the ex-husband's duty to support his former wife if his support payments inhibited his ability to remarry and have children in a second marriage. Contemporaries noted that women were harder hit than men by the new clause. Klinksiek, *Die Frau*, 81; Heddy Neumeister, "Die Berufslage der geschiedenen Frau," *Die Frau* 47 (July 1940): 305–7.

11. Wolf, Lücke, and Hax, *Scheidung*, 210.

12. These proved of far lesser statistical significance than the measure regarding estrangement. Czarnowski, "Value," 104–10.

13. Koonz, *Mothers in the Fatherland*, 374.

14. Milton, "Women and the Holocaust," 301; see also Kaplan, *The Jewish Feminist Movement in Germany*, 186–87.

15. Czarnowski, *Das kontrollierte Paar*, 136.

16. Schmacke and Güse, *Zwangssterilisiert—Verleugnet—Vergessen*, 90–91. On marriages of infertile people, see "Ehevermittlung für 'Minderwertige,'" *Deutsches*

Ärzteblatt, 8 February 1941, reprinted in Schmacke and Güse, *Zwangssterilisiert*, 91–92; Harmsen, *Eheschließung Sterilisierter;* "Verweigerte Ehen—verhüteter Nachwuchs," *Mainfränkische Zeitung*, 25 March 1939, 62.03/4885, folio 8, BAP.

17. The Gesetz zum Schutze des deutschen Blutes und der deutschen Ehre vom 15. September 1935 (*RGBl* I 1146) prohibited "racially" mixed marriages; the Gesetz zum Schutze der Erbgesundheit des deutschen Volkes vom 18. Oktober 1935 (*RGBl* I 1246) prohibited marriages between "Aryan" Germans from whom unhealthy offspring were feared. See the summary of these measures in Czarnowski, "Value," 100–103.

18. Czarnowski, *Das kontrollierte Paar*, 173–86. Applicants for a loan became more self-selecting as they learned of the dangers of a reckless application.

19. Klinksiek, *Die Frau*, 75; Czarnowski, *Das kontrollierte Paar*, 128.

20. Meister and Langholf, "'Zweckmäßige Asozialenbehandlung'"; Rothmaler, "Die Sozialpolitikerin Käthe Petersen zwischen Auslese und Ausmerze."

21. Czarnowski, *Das kontrollierte Paar*, 165.

22. RSHA to Kriminalpolizei(leit)stellen, 25 October 1941, R58/473, folio 136, BAK; Schmacke and Güse, *Zwangssterilisiert*, 89; Czarnowski, *Das kontrollierte Paar*, 197; Kranz and Koller, *Die Gemeinschaftsunfähigen*, 55.

23. "Erb- und Rassenpflege in der Praxis: Ein Bericht der erbbiologischen Poliklinik in Berlin-Charlottenburg," *Hamburger Fremdenblatt*, 14 January 1941, Sozialbehörde I GF 00.11, Sta HH.

24. Czarnowski, *Das kontrollierte Paar*, 224–26.

25. Ibid., 224. Statistics broken down by sex for applications for Certificates of Fitness to Marry are not available. The partner who had not been denied a certificate could marry another partner.

26. 30 June 1939, RMdI IV b 2340/39 II/1075 a betr.: Inkrafttreten des Par. 2 des Ehegesetzes, 352–53 Medizinkollegium II U 52-00, Sta HH.

27. Czarnowski, *Das kontrollierte Paar*, 136–50, 169ff.

28. Ibid., 127ff., 205ff.; "Eheberatung ohne Schrecken," *Der Angriff*, 8 December 1937, 62.03/4885, folio 57, BAP.

29. Bock, *Zwangssterilisation im Nationalsozialismus*, 401–10.

30. On such suspicions during the war, see Magnussen, "Krieg und Kriegsfolgen vom Standpunkt der Rassen- und Bevölkerungspolitik," 154.

31. Hitler, *Mein Kampf*, vol. 2, 79. Hitler added that employed unmarried women could be given citizenship on a selective basis. None of these anticipated restrictions on female citizenship was ever implemented.

32. See, for example, Stämmler, *Rassenpflege*, 64.

33. On asocial wives, see Weyrather, *Muttertag und Mutterkreuz*, 85–124.

34. Harvey, "Die Jugendfürsorge in der Endphase der Weimarer Republik"; Dickinson, *The Politics of German Child Welfare*, 198–99, 208; Bock, *Zwangssterilisation im Nationalsozialismus*, 80–94; Kaupen-Haas, *Der Griff nach der Bevölkerung*; Grossmann, *Reforming Sex*, 70–75; Usborne, *The Politics of the Body in Weimar Germany*, 148–55; Weindling, *Health, Race and German Politics between Unification and Nazism, 1870–1945*, 383–93, 450–57; Peukert, *Grenzen der Sozialdisziplinierung*.

35. Rothmaler, "Die 'Volksgemeinschaft' wird ausgehorcht und 'wichtiges Material der Zukunft' zusammengetragen," 109–10.

36. Petersen, "Sammelvormundschaft für gemeinschaftsfremde und gefährdete Frauen." For more on Petersen, see Rothmaler, "Die Sozialpolitikerin Käthe Petersen."

37. Petersen, "Sammelvormundschaft," 38.

38. Ibid., 58–59.

39. Hepp, "Vorhof zur Hölle: Mädchen im 'Jugendschutzlager' Uckermark," 192. See also 25 June 1942 (Folge 45) Partei-Kanzlei (II B 4 / Beitrag 597) (Abschrift), NS25/1055, folios 155–57, BAK.

40. Bock, *Zwangssterilisation im Nationalsozialismus*, 365.

41. Scherer, *"Asozial" im Dritten Reich*, 55.

42. Bock, *Zwangssterilisation im Nationalsozialismus*, 401ff.

43. Detailed discussion of these debates can be found in Schoppmann, *Nationalsozialistische Sexualpolitik und weibliche Homosexualität*, 95–109. See also Kokula, "Lesbisch leben von Weimar bis zur Nachkriegszeit"; Schoppmann, *Zeit der Maskierung*, 11–31.

44. Klare, "Zum Problem der weiblichen Homosexualität." See also Alice Rilke's rejoinder, "Homosexualität der Frau und die Frauenbewegung," *Deutsches Recht* 9 (1939): 65–68.

45. Schoppmann, *Nationalsozialistische Sexualpolitik*, 208–14.

46. Scherer, *"Asozial,"* 120. Physicians usually found their asocial clients to be either feeble-minded or schizophrenic.

47. Hepp, "Vorhof," 193; Deutscher Gemeindetag III 2508/39 Beigeordneter Schlüter to the Vorsitzenden der Arbeitsgemeinschaft für Wohlfahrtspflege, 9 June 1939, R36/921, BAK.

48. For example, Vfg. Nr. VII/105 betr. Behandlung Asozialer, 29 March 1938, reprinted in Scherer, *"Asozial,"* 207ff.; Bock, *Zwangssterilisation im Nationalsozialismus*, 366; Hepp, "Vorhof," 193. Both draft laws are in R22/943, BAK.

49. Meister and Langholf, "'Zweckmäßige Asozialenbehandlung'"; Niederschrift über die Sitzung der Vorsitzenden der Arbeitsgemeinschaften für Wohlfahrtspflege im Deutschen Gemeindetag am 20. September 1940, R36/922, folios 18–19, BAK. Particularly important in bringing young women under police supervision were the Gesetz zur Bekämpfung der Geschlechtskrankheiten vom 18. Februar 1927 (*RGBl* I 61), the Polizeiverordnung zum Schutze der Jugend vom 9. März 1940, and the Polizeiverordnung zum Schutze der Jugend vom 10. Juni 1943 (*RGBl* I 349).

50. Bock, *Zwangssterilisation im Nationalsozialismus*, 238, 424–46. Statistics on men's marital status are not available.

51. Ibid., 400–402. For men, the diagnosis "feeble-minded" typically referred to a failure to earn a living; other diagnoses, in order of frequency, were epilepsy, manic-depressive disease, alcoholism, deafness, blindness, physical deformation, and St. Vitus's Dance (303).

52. Scherer, *"Asozial,"* 79.

53. 4 May 1937, Hermine Bäcker, Aussprache über die Lage der evangelischen Gefährdetenfürsorge in Boppart am 29. April 1939, ADW, CA/GF 1353/10a2, ADW-IM; Bock, *Zwangssterilisation im Nationalsozialismus*, 393.

54. In Hamburg, "vocationally weak" or "vocationally immature" girls were placed in residential institutions, while boys were placed in closely supervised positions but lived at home. "Ertüchtigung berufsschwacher und berufsunreifer Jugendlicher in Hamburg," *DVöpF* 23 (March 1942): 46–47.

55. Käthe Petersen, "Arbeitsbesprechung über Gegenwartsfragen der Gefährdetenfürsorge," *DVöpF* 23 (January 1942): 18–20, here 19; Zürn, "Von der Herbertstraße nach Auschwitz," 93.

56. Magnussen, "Krieg und Kriegsfolgen," 160.

57. Bock, *Zwangssterilisation im Nationalsozialismus*, 364; Scherer, *"Asozial,"* 111; 31 May 1945, Stadtgesundheitsamt an den Herrn amtierenden Bürgermeister, Az 7104/21 Bd. 1, FMAG, SA-F.

58. "Rudolf Heß an eine unverheiratete Mutter," *Westdeutscher Beobachter*, 24 December 1939, 62.03/4549, folio 46, BAP.

59. The German term *unehelich* has the same colloquial usage, complete with derogatory overtones, as the English *illegitimate*, although it translates more literally to *nonmarital*. A proposed reform of 1940 used the term *natural*.

60. 28 October 1939, Himmler: SS-Befehl für die gesammte SS und Polizei, reprinted in Klinksiek, *Die Frau*, 153; 10 January 1940, Reichsminister des Innern, R43 II/1286 Bd.8, BAK.

61. Klinksiek, *Die Frau*, 96; Wiggershaus, *Frauen unterm Nationalsozialismus*, 85; Mühlfeld and Schönweiß, *Nationalsozialistische Familienpolitik*, 149ff.; Winkler, *Frauenarbeit*, 145.

62. According to Bock, only about eight thousand women bore children at *Lebensborn* maternity homes; *Zwangssterilisation im Nationalsozialismus*, 129. Frevert gives a figure of twelve thousand; *Frauen-Geschichte*, 230.

63. For a rare attack on this position, see Heinrich Webler, "Verdient das uneheliche Kind öffentliche Hilfe?" *Deutsche Jugendhilfe* 32 (October-November 1940): 109–14, esp. 114.

64. Quoted in Schubert, "Der Entwurf eines Nichtehelichengesetzes vom Juli 1940 und seine Ablehnung durch Hitler," 3.

65. Mühlfeld and Schönweiß, *Nationalsozialistische Familienpolitik*, 10; Klinksiek, *Die Frau*, 83.

66. See, for example, Hitler, *Mein Kampf*, vol. 1, 275.

67. Fritz Sauckel, "Gedanken über Mutterschaft und Familie," *Neues Volk* 9 (August 1941): 7. See also Hitler, Rede auf der Frauenkundgebung in Nürnberg, Reichsparteitag der Arbeit 1937, reprinted in *Frauenschaffen* (1937): 4–5.

68. Schmidt-Klevenow, "Das uneheliche Kind in der Volksgemeinschaft"; Klinksiek, *Die Frau*, 94.

69. For studies claiming to demonstrate this point, see Hans Georg Schulze, "Soziale und erbbiologische Verhältnisse unehelicher Kinder," *ABB* (July 1940): 129–44; Wilhelm Lange, "Der erbbiologische Wert der unehelichen Mütter mit drei und mehr unehelichen Kindern," *Volk und Rasse* 12 (1937): 277–79, cited in Klinksiek, *Die Frau*, 94.

70. H. Vellguth, "Ledige Mütter und Familienmütter im Nationalsozialistischen Staat," *Deutsche Justiz* 96 (1934): 1643–44, here 1643; emphasis in original. See also Bock, *Zwangssterilisation im Nationalsozialismus*, 126–27.

71. "Richtlinien für die Beurteilung der Erbgesundheit," ADW, CA/GF 2122/5 III, ADW-IM; Magnussen, "Krieg und Kriegsfolgen," 152–53.

72. Schmidt-Klevenow, "Das uneheliche Kind in der Volksgemeinschaft," 149; emphasis in original. See also Magnussen, "Krieg und Kriegsfolgen," 156.

73. Schubert, "Der Entwurf"; see the documents collected in Schubert, *Das Familien- und Erbrecht unter dem Nationalsozialismus*, 509–713.

74. See also Schmidt-Klevenow, "Das uneheliche Kind in der Volksgemeinschaft," 148–49; "Moral—kritisch betrachtet," *Das schwarze Korps*, 31 August 1944, 62.03/7137, BAP; Rosenberg, *Der Mythos des 20. Jahrhunderts*, 592–93; Picker, *Hitlers Tischgespräche im Führerhauptquartier*, 297.

75. Hagemann, *Frauenalltag und Männerpolitik*, 176–95.

76. See, for example, Guida Diehl, "Die Unverbrüchlichkeit der Gottesgesetze," *Neulandblatt* 25 (15 January 1940): 10ff.; Gertrud Bäumer, "Die Hauptfragen des Unehelichenrechts," *Die Frau* 47 (August 1940): 337–39.

77. Decrees of the Ministry of the Interior, 24 May 1937 (*RMBliV*, 885), 4 July 1940 (*RMBliV*, 3370), 24 June 1941 (*RMBliV*, 1181). Women who had participated in the

Lebensborn program had the unique privilege of being able to list their marital status as "married." 14 December 1942, Reichsführer SS und Chef der deutschen Polizei C-Vu R R III 3078 III/IV/42, 15.01/27419, folio 240, BAP; 14 May 1940, Alice Rilke, Abt. Leiterin DAF, an den Reichsführer SS und Chef der deutschen Polizei (Abschrift), 15.01/27419, folio 234, BAP; 19 January 1942, RMdI (Eckelberg) an den Reichsführer SS und Chef der deutschen Polizei, 15.01/27419, folio 236, BAP.

78. A. Petmecky, "Annahme des Vaternamens unehelicher Kinder und Namensänderung der Mutter," *Die Frau am Werk—DAF* (June 1940), 62.03/7137, folio 28, BAP. Applications were turned down if the couple would not have received permission to marry, if the fallen man had contested his fatherhood, or if the man had been married, which would mean that the new "Frau Schmidt" and her child would be confused with the widow "Frau Schmidt" and her children. See the many applications in 15.01/27439 Bd.I–II, BAP.

79. "Meldung von unehelichen Geburten," *Berliner Börsen-Zeitung*, 22 November 1937, 62.03/4885, folio 65, BAP.

80. "Lohnsteuererleichterung für ledige Mütter," *Der Freiheitskampf*, 16 February 1938, 62.03/7139, folio 15, BAP.

81. "Vermerkung unehelicher Kinder im Arbeitsbuch," *Die Frau am Werk—DAF* (June 1940), 62.03/7137, folio 27, BAP.

82. Erwin Gerlach, "Außereheliche Mutterschaft kein Kündigungsgrund," *Völkischer Beobachter* (Wiener Ausg.), 22 November 1938, 62.03/7137, folio 87, BAP; Amtsgerichtsrat Dr. Bertin, "Kündigung wegen Ausserehelicher Mutterschaft," *Deutsches Arbeitsrecht* (January 1939), 62.03/7137, folio 85, BAP; "Stärkerer Schutz für uneheliche Mütter," *Kölnische Zeitung*, 19 November 1941, 62.03/7139, folio 1, BAP; "Der Gehaltsanspruch bei Schwangerschaft außer der Ehe," *Soziale Praxis* 51 (February 1942): 79–80.

83. "Auszug aus dem Tätigkeitsbericht des Gauamtes für Kommunalpolitik des Gaues Kurhessen für den Monat Oktober 1941," NS25/1172, folio 99, BAK.

84. Hauptamt für Volkswohlfahrt, "Hilfswerk 'Mutter und Kind' 1935/36," R36/1395, folio 14, BAK.

85. Vorländer, *Die NSV*, 62, 67–68, 258, 261; "Heime für ledige werdende Mütter," *DVöpF* 21 (March 1940): 53–55; "Fürsorge für die ledige Mutter und das uneheliche Kind im Hilfswerk 'Mutter und Kind,'" *Die Frau* 47 (June 1940): 287–88. By 1938, Mother and Child claimed to reach 23 percent of all pregnant women in Hamburg; "Fürsorge für werdende Mütter," *DVöpF* 19 (November 1938): 353–54.

86. Bock, *Zwangssterilisation im Nationalsozialismus*, 128–29.

87. Amt für Volkswohlfahrt, "Arbeitsplan für die Durchführung des Hilfswerkes 'Mutter und Kind'" (n.d. [1934]), ADW, BP I 219, ADW-IM; also in R36/1394, folio 14, BAK; "Das Problem der ehelosen Mutter," *Berliner Tageblatt*, 11 November 1937, 62.03/7141, folio 1, BAP.

88. In the mid-1950s, about 40 percent of West German first children born within marriage were conceived before marriage; these numbers represented a moderate decline from previous decades. "Der Zeitabstand zwischen Eheschließung und Geburt des ersten Kindes," *WS* (1958): 214–16.

89. Groth, *Kinder ohne Familie*, 32–33.

90. Darmstadt study (see Appendix B).

91. Richtlinien für die Beurteilung der Erbgesundheit vom 18. Juli 1940 (*MBliV*, 1519).

92. Gesetz über die Änderung und Ergänzung familienrechtlicher Vorschriften und über die Rechtsstellung der Staatenlosen vom 12. April 1938 (*RGBl* I:380–84);

Verordnung zur Durchführung vom 23. April 1938 (*RGBl* I 417); "Begründung," *Deutsche Justiz* 16 (1938): 619; "Die Anfechtung der Ehelichkeit," *Berliner Börsen-Zeitung*, 10 May 1938, 62.03/4890, folio 10, BAP; "Teilreformen im Familienrecht," *DVöpF* 19 (July 1938): 206–9. Nazi courts sometimes resorted to ruling that a man "counted" as the father for purposes of financial support rather than ruling that he was the father. "Klage auf Feststellung der Vaterschaft," ed. Dr. H[einrich] Webler, *Rundbrief des deutschen Jugendarchivs* 12, Sondernummer (19 September 1936): 130, R36/1443, BAK; Redöhl, "Der Abstammungsnachweis bei unehelichen Kindern"; 19 December 1936, Jugendamt für den Kreis Bückeberg (19 493) to the Deutschen Gemeindetag Provinzialdienststelle Hannover, R36/1443, BAK; 19 May 1937, Deutscher Gemeindetag (6014/36) to the Landrat, Jugendamt Bückeberg, R36/1443, BAK.

93. Draft law by Rudolf Bechert and Friedrich Cornelius, discussed in *Deutsches Recht* 4 (1934): 422; Klinksiek, *Die Frau*, 95; Schubert, "Der Entwurf."

94. Redöhl, "Der Abstammungsnachweis"; "Abstammungsnachweis des unehelichen Kindes," *Die Frau am Werk* (May 1939), 62.03/7137, folio 76, BAP.

95. More rigorous requirements were enforced for entitlements, such as children's allowances and orphans' pensions. "Die Kinderbeihilfe in ihrer neuesten Form," *Soziale Praxis* 50 (1941): 192–94; "Versagung der Kinderbeihilfe," *Soziale Praxis* 50 (1941): 452–53; 22 January 1945, Deutscher Gemeindetag, Vermerk (III 60/45), R36/1440 Bd. II, BAK; "Feststellung der blutmässigen Abstammung nach dem Tode des angeblichen Erzeugers," *DVöpF* 22 (February 1941): 31–32.

96. Frevert, *Frauen-Geschichte*, 231; Koonz, "The Fascist Solution to the Woman Question in Italy and Germany," 524.

97. "Fehlgeburten," *DVöpF* 21 (July 1940): 132–36, here 135; Grossmann, *Reforming Sex*, 149–53; Czarnowski, "Frauen als 'Mütter der Rasse.'"

98. "Rede der Gaufrauenschaftsleiterin Frau Scholtz-Klink, Gehalten auf der Delegiertentagung sämtlicher badischer Frauenverbände in Karlsruhe am 21. Juni 1933," reprinted in Scholtz-Klink, *Die Frau im Dritten Reich*, 486ff., here 494–95.

99. Hausen, "The German Nation's Obligations."

100. On pre-1933 Nazi campaigns for women's support, see Koonz, *Mothers in the Fatherland*, 19–124.

101. "Unsere Kriegerhinterbliebenen," *Deutsche Kriegsopferversorgung* 2 (October 1933): 17–18, BAP Library; Horst von Metzsch, *Schlummernde Wehrkräfte*, quoted in "Die unbekannte Soldatenfrau," *Die Frau* 43 (January 1936): 232, and discussed in Else Feissel, "Die unbekannte Soldatenfrau," *MV* 5 (March 1936); Frances Magnus von Hausen, "Der Krieg als Erinnerung und Mahnung," *Die Frau* 41 (August 1934): 641–44.

102. Koonz, *Mothers in the Fatherland*, xxvii–xxviii; compare the fate of Paula Siber, 171–72. On the Nazi women's organizations, see Stephenson, *The Nazi Organization of Women*. On the difficulty of balancing activism with a family-oriented image in the pro-Nazi German Christian movement, see Bergen, *Twisted Cross*, 119–41.

103. Twenty-seven percent of members of the DFW were single at the time they joined the organization. Single women comprised 33 percent of the more selective NSF and 38 percent of NSF and DFW women who also belonged to the Nazi party. These statistics are taken from a systematic sampling of 750 members of both organizations from approximately 3.5 million forms concerning women's admission to the organizations. Because some forms did not request information about organizational membership outside the NSF and DFW, the actual number of party members may have been larger. The forms listed "unmarried," "married," and "widowed" but not "divorced" as options under "marital status." Aufnahme-Erklärungen für die NS-Frauenschaft/Deutsches Frauenwerk, BDC.

104. Owings, *Frauen*, 387–411.

105. "Reden des Führers am Parteitag der Ehre 1936," quoted in Klinksiek, *Die Frau*, 23.

106. Mühlfeld and Schönweiß, *Nationalsozialistische Familienpolitik*; Reese, *"Straff, aber nicht stramm,"* 62, 71; Möding, "'Ich muß irgendwo engagiert sein—fragen Sie mich bloß nicht, warum.'"

107. Reese, *"Straff, aber nicht stramm,"* 45; Mühlfeld and Schönweiß, *Nationalsozialistische Familienpolitik*, 143.

108. Historians have so taken for granted the division of the female labor force according to marital status that leading studies of women's labor during the Nazi period have failed to problematize it. Mason at least comments on the phenomenon; "Women in Germany, 1925–1940," 1: 93; 2: 11–12. Only Sachse makes the distinct consideration of married and single women's labor a central point of her analysis; *Siemens*, 213ff.

109. Hofmann and Kersten, *Frauen zwischen Familie und Fabrik*, 191; Mason, "Women," 2: 11.

110. Mason, "Women," 2: 11. This number includes wives who worked in family businesses, often for no pay.

111. On this point, see also Tobin and Gibson, "The Meanings of Labor," 308–11.

112. Lüders, "Die Dientspflicht der Frau," 1353–1355; "Der Pflichtabend im Juli," 220; and Karin Magnussen, "Pflichtjahr und Bevölkerungspolitik," *Soziale Praxis* 51 (June 1942): 247–54.

113. "Der Pflichtabend im Juli," 222; Lüders, "Die Dientspflicht der Frau," 1355; Winkler, *Frauenarbeit*, 57–58.

114. Winkler, *Frauenarbeit*, 57–58.

115. Lüders, "Die Dientspflicht der Frau," 1351.

116. Winkler, *Frauenarbeit*, 85; von Gersdorff, *Frauen im Kriegsdienst*, 68; 14 January 1936, "Besprechungsniederschrift des RuPrMdI an den Herrn Reichsfinanzminister," R2/4524, BAK, reprinted in von Gersdorff, *Frauen im Kriegsdienst*, 280–81.

117. Moers, *Frauenerwerbsarbeit und ihre Wirkungen auf die Frau*, 25. Because of the even greater rise in male employment, however, women's representation in the workforce declined from 29.3 percent in 1933 to 24.5 percent in the first half of 1936.

118. Mason, "Women," 1: 94.

119. Mason, "Women," 2: 11. Since census takers recorded family assistants—the most common type of employment for married women—more carefully in 1939 than in 1933, these statistics may exaggerate the increase in wives' employment. Mason, "Women," 2: 6.

120. Winkler, *Frauenarbeit*, 49–52; Gesetz zur Rechtstellung der weiblichen Beamten vom 30. Mai 1932 (*RGBl* I 245); Gesetz zur Änderung von Vorschriften auf dem Gebiete des allgemeinen Beamten-, des Besoldungs- und des Versorgungsrechts vom 30. Juni 1933 (*RGBl* I 435); Deutsches Beamtengesetz vom 26. Januar 1932 (*RGBl* I 39).

121. Erlaß des Reichsfinanzministers, reprinted in *Frau am Werk* 2 (1937): 703, and cited in Winkler, *Frauenarbeit*, 57.

122. Verordnung über Maßnahmen auf dem Gebiet des Beamtenrechts vom 20. Mai 1940 (*RGBl* I 732).

123. Winkler, *Frauenarbeit*, 61.

124. Wehrgesetz vom 21. Mai 1935 (*RGBl* I 609–80). This was strengthened by the 1. Durchführungsanordnung zur Verordnung zur Sicherstellung des Kräftebedarfs für

Aufgaben der Reichsverteidigung vom 13. Februar 1939 (*RGBl* I 206); and by 2 June 1939, Erlaß des RAM: Dienstverpflichtung von Ehefrauen, R41/159 Bd. I, BAK, reprinted in von Gersdorff, *Frauen im Kriegsdienst,* 294. According to Winkler, *Frauenarbeit,* 62, this decree was published on July 2; by September 1939, only fifty thousand women had been conscripted via these provisions (61–62, 85). See also von Gersdorff, *Frauen im Kriegsdienst,* 49–50, 294.

CHAPTER 3: WAR WIVES, WORKERS, AND RACE TRAITORS

1. The lengthy discussions among policymakers concerning the recruitment of women for the war economy have been covered in detail elsewhere; they will not form the subject of this chapter. See Winkler, *Frauenarbeit;* von Gersdorff, *Frauen im Kriegsdienst.*

2. Bock, *Zwangssterilisation im Nationalsozialismus,* 234; Ganßmüller, *Die Erbgesundheitspolitik des Dritten Reiches,* 45–46.

3. The publication of banns was also waived. 3. Verordnung zur Ausführung des Personenstandsgesetzes vom 4. November 1939 (*RGBl* I 2163); Magnussen, "Krieg und Kriegsfolgen," 153; Czarnowski, *Das kontrollierte Paar,* 178.

4. Magnussen, "Krieg und Kriegsfolgen," 154. "Eheschließungen, Geburten und Sterbetafel im 1.Vierteljahr 1940," *WS* (1940): 243–45, reports 185,000 in the old Reich until the end of March 1940.

5. Essner and Conte, "'Fernehe,' 'Leichentrauung' und 'Totenscheidung.'"

6. Figure A.2. For official concerns about undesired marriages taking place via the provisions of war marriages and long-distance marriages, see Boberach, ed., *Meldungen aus dem Reich,* 606, 1269, 4270–71.

7. Meyer and Schulze, *Wie wir das alles geschafft haben,* 52–53.

8. 6 November 1941, RMdI, Abschrift an die Aufsichtsbehörden der Standesbeamten, 15.01/27457, folio 1, BAP; see also related correspondence in Schubert, *Das Familien- und Erbrecht,* 914–59. Not all local officials waited for Hitler's initiative; see Monatsbericht für April 1941, Gauleitung Kurhessen, Amt für Kommunalpolitik, Gau Kurhessen, Bd. 2 Tätigkeitsberichte des Gauamtes, Hauptamt für Kommunalpolitik NS25/258, folios 177–78, BAK.

9. Among completed applications that were neither rejected because the man was missing rather than dead nor withdrawn, 91 percent involving children or pregnancy were approved, compared with 89 percent of those without children or pregnancies and 38 percent where it was not clear whether a child was present or expected. Just over half of the postmortem marriages involved a pregnancy or a child from the union. Because of privacy protections, my calculations were based on a single file of 231 case records, which, according to the archivists at the Bundesarchiv-Potsdam, is typical of the 106 files of its kind. 15.01/27515–27620, esp. 27517, BAP.

10. This figure assumes that 15.01/27517, BAP, with 171 approved cases, is average. The number may be higher: the Ministry of the Interior claimed that twenty-five thousand cases awaited processing already in the spring of 1943. Essner and Conte, "'Fernehe,'" 214. For earlier (and much lower) estimates, see 33. Tagung des Länderrats in Stuttgart, 6 July 1948, B141/2202, BAK; Ministry of Justice, Begründung zu dem Entwurf eines Gesetzes über die Rechtswirkungen einer nachträglichen Eheschließung, August 1950, B141/2203, BAK.

11. 12 January 1942, OKW an die Wehrkreiskommandos usw. (Abschrift), 15.01/ 27458, folio 64, BAP. Word of mouth, however, ensured that many segments of the population became aware of postmortem marriages; Boberach, *Meldungen*, 6390–94.

12. Special privileges for select unwed mothers coexisted with a worsening situation for most. Civil suits were put on hold if one of the parties was drafted, and starting in October 1942 no proceedings to establish fatherhood could be brought against members of the military. Until 1941, even illegitimate children with established paternity had no claim to a family allowance except in extraordinary circumstances. If the acknowledged father fell, the mother had to present the father's birth certificate and working papers in order to prove her child's eligibility for an orphan's pension; it was difficult to establish paternity after a man's death. Hildegard Goetting, "Die Arbeit der Amtsvormundschaft im Kriege," *Deutsche Jugendhilfe* 31 (November-December 1939): 233–36; 31 December 1942, Deutscher Gemeindetag Provinzial-Landstelle Ostpreussen (PLS-OP) (1148/1942 Akt Z:1210/4), R36/1439 Bd. I, BAK; "Feststellung der blutmäßigen Abstammung nach dem Tode des angeblichen Erzeugers," *DVöpF* 23 (February 1942): 31–32; Verordnung über Maßnahmen auf dem Gebiete des bürgerlichen Streitverfahrens vom 1. September 1939 (*RGBl* I 656); Verordnung zum Schutz von Wehrmachtsangehörigen in bürgerlichen Rechtsstreitigkeiten vom 13. Oktober 1942 (*RGBl* I 604); Heinrich Webler, "Dienst in der Wehrmacht—ein Freibrief für ledige Väter?" *Deutsche Jugendhilfe* 32 (1940–41): 124–25; Amtsgerichtsrat Hellbach, "Unterhaltsklagen außerehelicher Kinder gegen Soldaten im Kriege," *Deutsches Recht* 10 (1940): 191ff.

13. 15 June 1943, RMdI (Frick) to the höheren Verwaltungsbehörden der Standesamtsaufsicht, B149/12027, folios 2–5, BAK. See also König, *Die Frau im Recht*, 128ff.; 20 March 1945, RMdI I Sta R to the höheren Verwaltungsbehörden der Standesamtsaufsicht, 15.01/27457, folio 26, BAP.

14. "Die standesamtlich beurkundeten Kriegssterbefälle und gerichtlichen Todeserklärungen in den Jahren 1939 bis 1954," *WS* (1956): 302–4, 298* (Tabellenteil).

15. "Familienstand der Bevölkerung," *WS* (1940): 522–28, here 523.

16. "Deutsche Kriegsverluste," *SJ-BRD* (1960): 78.

17. Wiggershaus, *Frauen unterm Nationalsozialismus*, 21.

18. Dr. Gronau, "Rassenhygienische Ehevermittlung, Ziel und Weg," *Zeitschrift des nationalsozialistischen Ärztebundes*, 1 July 1939, 62.03/4885, folio 7, BAP.

19. Correspondence of 1943 in R36/1215, BAK; "Die Lebensgefährtin: Vermittlungsstelle für Schwerkriegsversehrte," *Berliner Börsen-Zeitung*, 4 November 1942, 62.03/5672, folio 26, BAP.

20. See the many newspaper reports of the services in 62.03/4887, BAP; 12 July 1944, RdErl. d. RMdI, "Mitwirkung der Gesundheitsämter bei den Briefzentralen des Reichsbundes Deutscher Familien und Förderung der Eheanbahnung," R36/1215, BAK.

21. It is possible that the letter exchange simply exaggerated the number of male applicants. This practice, common among postwar private matchmaking services, was intended to encourage female clients.

22. "Wie sind die Heiratsaussichten?" *Die innere Front*, 14 September 1944, 62.03/4887, folio 11, BAP.

23. Be., Meyer and Schulze Interview Collection, Institut für Soziologie—TU-Berlin, 18–19.

24. See, however, Moeller, *Protecting Motherhood*, 20, on older working women's perception that younger women "got off the hook" by having children.

25. Anna Götting, "Einsatzarbeit!" *Deutsche Kriegsopferversorgung* 8 (November 1939): 6, NSD 54/2, BAK; von Schell, "Gedanken zum Muttertag"; Alfred Dick, "Die

NSKOV im Einsatz für den Sieg: Grosser Kriegsappel im Berliner Sportpalast," *Deutsche Kriegsopferversorgung* 11 (June–July 1943):1–6, NSD 54/2, BAK.

26. "Dank an die ältere Mitarbeiterin," *Nachrichtendienst der Reichsfrauen-führung* 11 (September 1942): 124–25; Anna Hahn-Kolb, "Muttertag 1944: An die Mütter der Helden!" *Nationalsozialistische Kriegsopferversorgung* 12 (April–May 1944): 3–4, BAP Library; "Mit neuem Lebensmut zurück," *Die innere Front (NSK)*, 24 July 1942, 62.03/5548, folio 11, BAP; Deschinger, "Eine schöne Woche," in Straßner, ed., *Frauen an der Front*, 8–15.

27. "Schicksale aus zwei Weltkriegen: Eine Frau und Mutter, ein Kamerad von 1914/18 und Kriegervater sprachen zu uns," *Deutsche Kriegsopferversorgung* 11 (December 1942–January 1943): 9–10; "Gebt euren Toten Heimatrecht . . . ," *Nachrichtendienst der Reichsfrauenführung* 12 (April 1943): 46–47; Wittrock, *Weiblichkeitsmythen*, 248ff.; Baird, *To Die for Germany*, 227–28.

28. Schell, "Gedanken zum Muttertag," 57; emphasis in original.

29. Baird, *To Die for Germany*, 215. On the significance of women's role in maintaining this balance, see especially Koonz, *Mothers in the Fatherland*, 385–420. Reinhard Heydrich headed the intelligence and counterespionage service (SD), the Gestapo, the Reich Security Administration (RSHA), and the Protectorate of Bohemia and Moravia; he organized the *Einsatzgruppen* that performed mass executions of Jews in the eastern territories; and he presented the implementation plan for the final extermination of Europe's Jews at the Wannsee conference in January 1942. Later that spring, he was assassinated by the Czech resistance; an entire Czech village was razed and its inhabitants were either murdered or sent to concentration camp in reprisal.

30. Baird, *To Die for Germany*, 220.

31. For a particularly maudlin portrayal, see "Der Einsatz," in Straßner, *Frauen an der Front*, 22–25.

32. "Eine tapfere Frau," in Straßner, *Frauen an der Front*, 18–20; see also "Verwundete und Hinterbliebene. Die Arbeit als Heilfaktor," *Münchner neueste Nachrichten*, 31 May 1943, 62.03/5548, folio 7, BAP; "Das grosse nationalsozialistische Erholungswerk für Kriegsopfer," *Deutsche Kriegsopferversorgung* 11 (June–July 1943): 11; "Trauer und Trost," *Nachrichtendienst der Reichsfrauenführung* 12 (November 1943): 157–59.

33. Baird, *To Die for Germany*, 234; 25 April 1944, NSDAP Kreis Untertaunus NS-Frauenschaft—Die Kreisfrauenschaftsleiterin, 483/2793, folio 45, HHA. For a rare portrayal of a young widow as a mourner, see "Auch einer von Stalingrad," *Die Frau* 50 (April–June 1943): 120–21.

34. Unruh, *Trümmerfrauen*, 132.

35. Himmler, "Bericht zur innenpolitischen Lage," 22 November 1938, R58/145, folio 23, BAK; Niederschrift über die Sitzung der Vorsitzenden der Arbeitsgemeinschaften für Wohlfahrtspflege im Deutschen Gemeindetag am 20. September 1940, R36/922, folio 13, BAK; Protokoll: Arbeitstagung der Arbeitsgemeinschaft für sittliche Volkserziehung am 18. November 1940, ADW, CA/GF 2122/2 IV, ADW-IM.

36. RMdI Erlaß vom 8. September 1939, discussed in Besprechung beim Herrn Oberbürgermeister vom 23. Oktober 1939, Az 7104/2 Bd. 1, folio 211, FMAG, SA-F; 9 September 1939, RMdI Pol.S-Kr. 3 Nr. 2217/39 to the Landesregierungen u.a., R22/1515, folios 6–7, BAK; Verordnung zur Änderung des Gesetzes zur Bekämpfung der Geschlechtskrankheiten vom 21. Oktober 1940 (*RGBI* II 1459); Bock, "'Keine Arbeitskräfte in diesem Sinne.'"

37. Besprechung beim Herrn Oberbürgermeister vom 23. Oktober 1939, Az

7104/2 Bd. 1, folio 211, FMAG, SA-F; 2 December 1939, "Wichtige Eingänge aus dem Geschäftsbereich des Stadtgesundheitsamts," Az 7104/2+20+21 Bd. 1, FMAG, SA-F, and subsequent correspondence.

38. Discussed in Boberach, *Meldungen*, 1075. The order was expanded on June 10, 1943. On youthful rebellion and the official response, see Peukert, *Inside Nazi Germany*, 145–74.

39. Hepp, "Vorhof," 199; see also 19 December 1940, Abschrift des höheren SS- u. Polizeiführers beim Bayerischen Staatsminister des Innern u.a. to the Reichsjugendführer Artur Axmann, NS25/1114, folios 29–33, BAK; Protokoll: Arbeitstagung der Arbeitsgemeinschaft für sittliche Volkserziehung am 18. November 1940, ADW, CA/GF 2122/2 IV, ADW-IM.

40. "Gefährdetenfürsorge der Inneren Mission im Jahre 1943," ADW, CA/GF 1417/261, ADW-IM; Schwester Walpurgis Mentzel, "Das Heim im Bunker," in "Rundbrief der Referate Kinder- und Jugendfürsorge am Deutschen Caritasverband," Advent 1946, 21, 319.4 A II, 50 Fasz. 3, DCV.

41. Kokula, "Lesbisch leben," 159. See also Schoppmann, *Zeit der Maskierung;* Fischer, *Aimee und Jaguar.*

42. See the reports reprinted in Ebbinghaus, ed., *Opfer und Täterinnen*, 113, 121, 125.

43. Käthe Petersen, "Das Verhalten der Frauen von Eingezogenen," Sozialbehörde Hamburg, Betreuung von Soldatenfrauen 1943–46, Sozialbehörde I EF 70.24, Sta HH, reprinted in Ebbinghaus, *Opfer und Täterinnen*, 137–42, here 137.

44. Official pressure on men to uphold their marital vows was rare. Martin Semmler, "Ein Manneswort über die Treue," *Neues Volk* 9 (March 1941): 24ff.; 6 April 1942, Reichsführer-SS u. Chef der deutschen Polizei (III/121/4Lg), R43 II/512 Bd. 4, BAK.

45. 16 October 1941, Deutscher Gemeindetag Dienststelle Bayern-Ostmark Nr. 4852 an den Deutschen Gemeindetag, R36/2600, BAK; Aktenvermerk über die Arbeitsbesprechung der Vorsitzenden der Arbeitsgemeinschaften für Wohlfahrtspflege des Deutschen Gemeindetages am 15 April 1942 in Berlin, R36/922, BAK.

46. Friedrich Albrecht, "Neuerungen im Familienunterhalt," *Wiener Völkischer Beobachter*, 17 June 1942, R36/2600, BAK. On implementation, see Vermerk [to the Kreisstellenvorsteherbesprechung, 1 July 1943], Stadt Fürsorgeamt Frankfurt/Main, 34 Bd. 17, folio 207, FLS, SA-F; Fischer-Defoy, Rundverfügung 12 vom 21. August 1943, Stadt Fürsorgeamt Frankfurt/Main, 34 Bd. 18, folio 14, FLS, SA-F; Dr. Suren, RMdI V f 180/43—7900—Bescheide des RMdI in Familienunterhaltssachen, 5 April 1943, Stadt Fürsorgeamt Frankfurt/Main, 35, folios 9–10, FLS, SA-F.

47. Vermerk, 18 May 1940, R43 II/644 Bd. 3, folios 42–43, BAK; OKW (14 f WR (I/1,2)—NR 1921/41; RK 14210B), R43 II/644 Bd. 3, folios 46–47, BAK.

48. "Ehebruch mit Soldatenfrauen," *Kölnische Zeitung*, 27 September 1941, 62.03/4886, BAP; "Ehrenschutz für Frontsoldaten," *Hamburger Fremdenblatt*, 5 July 1942, 62.03/4887, folio 92, BAP. Although this order was discussed in the press, it was, according to Essner and Conte, never actually released; "'Fernehe,'" 216.

49. November 1942 [sic], RMdJ (4052—III a2 2224), R43 II/1544a Bd. 21, folios 68–70, BAK; March 1942 [sic], RMdJ (4052—III a2 446.43) (copy), R43 II/1544a Bd. 21, folios 72–73, BAK. Neither of these copies of the guidelines has a complete date; it is possible that these were only drafts that were never completed or distributed.

50. Essner and Conte, "'Fernehe,'" 216–18.

51. Herbert, *Fremdarbeiter*, 11. See also Homze, *Foreign Labor in Nazi Germany.*

52. Boberach, *Meldungen*, 4953–57.

53. Boberach, *Meldungen*, 3200. In the same year, Himmler reported that German men shared responsibility for 1.5 million pregnancies in the occupied East. Bock, *Zwangssterilisation im Nationalsozialismus*, 400.

54. Referat A 11 "Für die Pressekonferenz; Betr.: Geschlechtskrankheiten," 3 January 1945, R18/3755, BAK. This figure may underestimate the true number of foreigners who were the source of infection since admitting to sex with a foreigner was dangerous.

55. In order, Hepp, "Vorhof," 198; correspondence regarding the case of H. L., RSHA Abt. IV St.3/803, folios 32–61, BAP; Steffens, "Die praktische Widerlegung des Rassismus," 196; Boberach, *Meldungen*, 3202.

56. Herbert, *Fremdarbeiter*, 122; Boberach, *Meldungen*, 5198–5200, 6139–47.

57. Hepp, "Vorhof," 199; see also Boberach, *Meldungen*, 5340.

58. Boberach, *Meldungen*, 638, 822.

59. Der Reichsführer-SS und Chef der deutschen Polizei S I V 1 Nr. 861 VI/39-176-7-SDB.StGB, 31 January 1940, R58/1027, folio 115, BAK; "Bericht über Fragen und Probleme, die durch den Arbeitseinsatz polnischer Kriegsgefangener und polnischer Zivilarbeiter entstanden sind," Aufgestellt durch die Abt. IIH (Berichts- und Informationswesen) July 1940 Bd. II, NS5 I/323, BAK.

60. Herbert, *Fremdarbeiter*, 126; Boberach, *Meldungen*, 6139, 6146.

61. Herbert, *Fremdarbeiter*, 128–29; Correspondence of early 1941 regarding case of G. G. and M. K., RSHA Abt. IV St.3/803 folios 81–147, BAP.

62. Boberach, *Meldungen*, 3201; Meldungen aus dem Reich #325, 12 October 1942, R58/176, folio 94, BAK; Herbert, *Fremdarbeiter*, 126.

63. Boberach, *Meldungen*, 6142, 4316–18. For a different evaluation, see Boberach, *Meldungen*, 3201.

64. Herbert, *Fremdarbeiter*, 122–24; Gellately, *The Gestapo and German Society*, 227ff.; Steffens, "Die praktische Widerlegung des Rassismus," 194.

65. Herbert, *Fremdarbeiter*, 80; "Halte Dein Blut rein!" *Neues Volk* 8 (September 1940): 4–5; Reichsfrauenführung Abt. Recht und Schlichtung, Rundschreiben Nr. F18/4, 26 February 1941, 230 NS-Frauenschaft folios 168–69, BDC; Reichsfrauenführung: Rundschreiben "Schulungslehrgang für Gaujugendgruppenführerinnen vom 23.2.–2.3.41 in der Reichsschule II der NS-Frauenschaft, Berlin-Wannsee," NS-Frauenschaft 44/36, BAK.

66. Geheime Staatspolizei, Staatspolizeistelle Frankfurt/Main, 15 February 1943, 483/3259, folios 76–90, HHA; RMdJ (4052—III a2 2224), November 1942, R43 II/1544a Bd. 21, folios 68–70, BAK.

67. See also Herbert, *Fremdarbeiter*, 126.

68. Steffens, "Die praktische Widerlegung des Rassismus," 185; Boberach, *Meldungen*, 678, 6143. German men who had contact with foreign female laborers went unpunished, and the foreign women rarely ran into trouble (for forbidden contact, at least) unless they became pregnant. Stephenson, "Triangle: Foreign Workers, German Civilians, and the Nazi Regime," 349–50.

69. 13 June 1942, RSHA (IV D 1 b—138/40 II), NS2/293, BAK; Geheime Staatspolizei, Staatspolizeistelle Frankfurt/Main, 15 February 1943, 483/3259, folios 76–90, HHA; Herbert, *Fremdarbeiter*, 79.

70. 9 February 1944, Rasse- und Siedlungshauptamt-SS (RA C2 a7—Vo/Sch 11/44), NS2/295, BAK.

71. Boberach, *Meldungen*, 6139–47; 15 January 1943, Der Generalstaatsanwalt, Kassel (313b—1.21), R22/956, BAK; Bormann #RK 15953B to Lammers, 13 November 1942, R43 II/1544a, BAK.

72. Complete statistics for women convicted of forbidden contact are unavailable,

and this figure refers to a small sample. Of 153 available files on women imprisoned in the Frauenstrafgefängnis Frankfurt-Höchst, 33 were sentenced for forbidden contact; 15 of these were single. Abt. 409/6, HHA.

73. Reichsführer-SS Tgb.-Nr. RF/B, 28 August 1942, R58/1027, folio 269, BAK.

74. Judges also considered details of the sexual activity in sentencing. Judgment against E. F., 9 November 1944, Abt. 409/6 1944 Gefängnisbuch 516/44; judgment against M. S., 15 January 1945, Abt. 409/6 Gefängnisbuch 361/44, HHA.

75. Steffens, "Die praktische Widerlegung des Rassismus," 194–97. To have been raped was, in theory, less offensive. Although German women were sentenced for having been raped by foreigners, judges pointed to the fact of the rape in explaining their supposedly mild sentences. See, for example, judgment against C. L., 12 June 1942, Abt. 409/5 Gefängnisbuch 314/42, HHA.

76. Herbert, *Fremdarbeiter*, 123; Steffens, "Die praktische Widerlegung des Rassismus," 185.

77. Herbert, *Fremdarbeiter*, 248.

78. Bock, *Zwangssterilisation im Nationalsozialismus*, 439.

79. Winkler, *Frauenarbeit*, 61–62, 85; von Gersdorff, *Frauen im Kriegsdienst*, 49–50, 294.

80. Szepansky, *Blitzmädel—Heldenmutter—Kriegerwitwe*, 50–53.

81. Mason, "Women," 2: 19. Between October and December 1939, the number of employed women decreased by nearly three hundred thousand; Winkler, *Frauenarbeit*, 92.

82. They accounted for 6 to 8 percent of days missed by men. Rü IVd Notiz für die am 17.5.40 stattfindende Besprechung über Löhne und Arbeitsbedingungen der Frauen, RW19/2162, BAF.

83. RAM Va 5103/6005/41 g RR Dr. Hamann, 21 August 1941, R41/162 Bd. II, BAK, reprinted in von Gersdorff, *Frauen im Kriegsdienst*, 342–44.

84. RAM, "Betr. Bekämpfung der Disziplinlosigkeit in den Betrieben," 22 November 1941, RW19/940, BAF. See also Wiggershaus, *Frauen unterm Nationalsozialismus*, 76–77; Sachse, *Siemens*, 236; Winkler, *Frauenarbeit*, 96ff.

85. On family support in the First World War, see Guttmann, *Weibliche Heimarmee*, 64–66; Daniel, *Arbeiterfrauen in der Kriegsgesellschaft*, 169–83.

86. For a family with two children, the family allowance equaled 73 to 75 percent of the man's earnings. In England, the figure was 38 percent; in the United States, 36 percent. Winkler, *Frauenarbeit*, 179.

87. Starting in May 1940, earnings of up to two-thirds the level of support were not deducted. Ibid., 106.

88. See, for example, ibid., 102.

89. *Familienunterstützung* was created in 1936; its name was changed to *Familienunterhalt* in June 1940; Gesetz über die Unterstützung der Angehörigen der einberufenen Wehrpflichtigen und Arbeitsdienstpflichtigen vom 30. März 1936 (*RGBl* I 327–34). Both terms translate literally to "family support." Family allowances were based on civilian income and sent directly to families, while "war pay" (*Kriegsbesoldung*) was based on military rank and paid to the man. Since families of men of low rank did better with allowances, this was the more popular program for married servicemen. "Kriegsbesoldung oder Familienunterhalt?" *Deutsche Allgemeine Zeitung*, 17 June 1944, R36/2600, BAK.

90. See also a revision of January 1940, discussed in "Neue Bestimmungen über den Familienunterhalt," *Soziale Praxis* 49 (15 February 1940): 123–25; "Die Kriegsehe und weitere Neuerungen im Familienunterhaltsrecht," *DVöpF* 21 (March 1940): 45–47.

91. 7 March 1940, Oberbürgermeister, Offenbach, R43 II/1282c, folio 80, BAK; Stimmungsbericht zum Thema Familienunterhalt, Sozialbehörde I, VG 30.72, Besonderer Bericht der K.d.L. und Oberfürsorgerinnen über Verhalten und Stimmung der Familienunterhaltsberechtigten (Kreisdienststellenleiter) 1940–41, Sta HH, reprinted in Ebbinghaus, *Opfer und Täterinnen*, 120; Auszug aus dem Tätigkeitsbericht des Gauamtes für Kommunalpolitik des Gaues Sachsen für Januar-Februar 1943, NS25/1173, folio 46, BAK; 8 April 1941, Hauptamt für Kommunalpolitik to the Stellvertreter des Führers, NS25/1015, folios 274–75, BAK; 18 February 1941, NSDAP Gauleitung Kurhessen Amt für Kommunalpolitik to the Zentralamt für Kommunalpolitik, NS25/1015, folios 236–38, BAK.

92. "Ergebnisse einer Rundfrage des Wohlfahrtsamtes der Hauptstadt der Bewegung vom Februar 1940 über Familienunterhalt in 19 Großstädten," Stadt Fürsorgeamt Frankfurt am Main, 146, folios 33–34, FLS, SA-F.

93. 27 October 1941, Gemeinschaftsführender Direktor Knorr, Oberbürgermeister München Deutscher Gemeindetag Dienststelle Bayern-Ostmark Nr. 5001 to the Deutschen Gemeindetag, R36/2600, BAK.

94. 26 May 1942, Stadtrat Dr. Plank, Beigeordneter Nürnberg, to the Deutschen Gemeindetag, R36/2600, BAK; 26 May 1942, NSDAP Gauleitung Franken Amt für Kommunalpolitik to the Zentralamt für Kommunalpolitik, NS25/1173, folio 75, BAK. That fall, the press of the Deutsche Gemeindetag advertised the publication of 130 forms for use in administering family allowances. Deutscher Gemeindetag—Verlagshaus, 7 October 1942, Stadt Fürsorgeamt Frankfurt am Main, 37, FLS, SA-F.

95. Generalbevollmächtigter für die Reichsverwaltung, 9 May 1940, R43 II/652 Bd. 1, BAK; 23 April 1940, Regierungspräsident Niedersachsen, R41/158 Bd. 1, BAK, reprinted in von Gersdorff, *Frauen im Kriegsdienst*, 308–10.

96. 20 June 1941, Reichsmarschall des Großdeutschen Reichs usw., R43 II/652 Bd. 1, BAK. The income of contractors (usually home workers), independent businesswomen, and women who maintained their husbands' businesses continued to be calculated in full against their allowance. This policy encouraged them to close their businesses and take up waged or salaried work, which was more likely to serve the war effort.

97. Of the recipients, 293 refused to return to work and thus had their support cut; 97 took up work after seeing their allowances reduced. 2 October 1941, RMdI to the Reichsmarschall des Großdeutschen Reichs usw. (V f 1016/41—7900), R43 II/652 Bd. 1, BAK.

98. Erlaß des Führers über den umfassenden Einsatz von Männern und Frauen für Aufgaben der Reichsverteidigung vom 13. Januar 1943, R43 II/652a, BAK (reprinted in von Gersdorff, *Frauen im Kriegsdienst*, 375–77); Verordnung über die Meldung von Männern und Frauen für Aufgaben der Reichsverteidigung vom 27. Januar 1943 (*RGBl* I 67). For tightening of the exemptions, see Winkler, *Frauenarbeit*, 146; von Gersdorff, *Frauen im Kriegsdienst*, 55.

99. Winkler, *Frauenarbeit*, 135–36.

100. Ibid., 123, 176, 201.

101. Verordnung zur Abänderung und Ergänzung von Vorschriften auf dem Gebiet des Arbeitsrechts vom 1. September 1939 (*RGBl* I 1683); Winkler, *Frauenarbeit*, 90–91, 160–61, 181; König, *Die Frau im Recht*, 182–83; Verordnung über den Arbeitsschutz vom 12. Dezember 1939 (*RGBl* I 2403ff.); Anordnung über die Mindestarbeitszeit für den öffentlichen Dienst vom 10. April 1942 (*Reichsarbeitsblatt* II, 297).

102. Winkler, *Frauenarbeit*, 126, 151, 154, 202–4; Moers, *Der Fraueneinsatz in der Industrie*, 77; "Arbeitseinsatz der Frau," *Die werktätige Frau* 6 (June-July 1941): 77ff., reprinted in von Gersdorff, *Frauen im Kriegsdienst*, 332–33.

103. Winkler, *Frauenarbeit*, 123, 164, 170.

104. Szepansky, *Blitzmädel*, 92–98.

105. September 1944, Vermerk über eine Besprechung im Reichsfinanzministerium: Verstärkter Einsatz des RADwJ bei der Luftwaffe, R2/4550, BAK, reprinted in von Gersdorff, *Frauen im Kriegsdienst*, 439–40.

106. Winkler, *Frauenarbeit*, 89–90; Kleiber, "'Wo ihr seid, da soll die Sonne scheinen!,'" 210.

107. Winkler, *Frauenarbeit*, 129.

108. Führererlaß JK über den weiteren Kriegseinsatz des weiblichen RAD, 29 July 1941 (*RGBl* I 463); correspondence concerning this decree in R43 II/518a, BAK; von Gersdorff, *Frauen im Kriegsdienst*, 68; Winkler, *Frauenarbeit*, 131.

109. 27 September 1944, Bormann to Goebbels, R43 II/666c, BAK.

110. Boberach, *Meldungen*, 2965–67, 4136–41; Winkler, *Frauenarbeit*, 130, 153.

111. von Gersdorff, *Frauen im Kriegsdienst*, 69.

112. Szepansky, *Blitzmädel*, 47.

113. Maschmann, *Fazit*. See also Harvey, "'Die deutsche Frau im Osten.'"

114. General demographic figures for female military employees are not available, but a list of 145 air force auxiliaries in western France in the winter of 1942–43 includes only fifteen married women, three widows, and one divorced woman. One married woman and one widow were among fifty-nine air force auxiliaries in Brussels. Communication of the District Air Force Commando XI Verw. A 10 a (3) Az. 26 a 18, 27 February 1943, RL14/7, BAF; Lt. Wilhelm Gahlen, "Erfahrungsbericht über den Einsatz von LN-Helferinnen," to LN-Funkhorch-Regiment West, 15 December 1942, RL14/7, BAF. For a useful summary of women's work in the military and in the Red Cross—but not in the SS—see von Gersdorff, *Frauen im Kriegsdienst*, 60–77. On the SS Female Auxiliary Corps, see Seidler, *Frauen zu den Waffen?* 175–202; records in NS32 II, BAK.

115. von Gersdorff, *Frauen im Kriegsdienst*, 69–70.

116. 27 September 1944, Bormann to Goebbels, R43 II/666c, BAK; Winkler, *Frauenarbeit*, 132; 31 October 1944, der Beauftragte für den Vierjahresplan usw. to die Reichsbevollmächtigten für den totalen Kriegseinsatz usw., R43 II/666c, BAK. Late in the war, young women were assigned military work before completing their civilian service. Szepansky, *Blitzmädel*, 47.

117. von Gersdorff, *Frauen im Kriegsdienst*, 69–70; 5 November 1942, RAD—die Führerin des Bezirkes XV Nordmark, RH55/75, BAF.

118. von Gersdorff, *Frauen im Kriegsdienst*, 61–66; Seidler, *Frauen zu den Waffen?* 175; Wiggershaus, *Frauen unterm Nationalsozialismus*, 97–103. Most regular employees stationed outside Germany were over twenty-one years old. OKW (Keitel), "Rückführung von Wehrmachtshelferinnen aus Beschäftigungsstellen ausserhalb des Reichsgebietes," 20 July 1944, NS6/vorl. 347, BAK, reprinted in von Gersdorff, *Frauen im Kriegsdienst*, 429. For a sympathetic portrayal of a concentration-camp guard, see Owings, *Frauen*, 313–41.

119. von Gersdorff, *Frauen im Kriegsdienst*, 73–74. von Gersdorff's figures for the army date from the beginning of the war; the ranks of female employees grew considerably after that. Her figures for other branches of the armed services date from later in the war, but none of her figures account for a turnover of personnel, and she does not consider party organizations such as the SS and SD.

120. 24 August 1943, Rundschreiben des Leiters der Parteikanzlei, Einsatz und Werbung von Flakwaffenhelferinnen, NS6/vorl. 342, BAK, reprinted in von Gersdorff, *Frauen im Kriegsdienst*, 411.

121. 5 September 1944, Befehl des OKW: Stellung der Frau in der Wehrmacht, NS6/vorl. 351, BAK, reprinted in von Gersdorff, *Frauen im Kriegsdienst*, 441–42; Merkblatt, "Verhalten der Helferinnen des Heeres im Falle der Gefangennahme," 1943, MGFA/DZ Box 18/69 39502/62 [BAF], reprinted in von Gersdorff, *Frauen im Kriegsdienst*, 374.

122. Der Rasse- und Siedlungsführer "Süd" to the Führer der SS-Ergänzungsstelle VII SS-Obersturmbannführer Püchl, 13 December 1944, NS32 II/70, folios 15–16, BAK.

123. SS-Oberführer und Kommandeur von Dufais, SS-Nachrichtenschule 'Oberehnheim,' to the Chef des Fernmeldewesens beim RFSS and Chef der deutschen Polizei, 7 June 1943, NS32 II/3, folio 4, BAK. See also Oberstabsarzt Dr. Driest, "Richtlinien über Menschenführung in der Truppe" [1944], MSg2/177, folios 14–15, BAF.

124. OKH, "Betr. Fürsorge für die weiblichen Gefolgschaftsmitglieder in den besetzten Gebieten," 18 December 1941, RH36/227, BAF; 17 June 1942, Reichsminister der Luftfahrt and Oberbefehlshaber der Luftwaffe, RL19/330, folio 74, BAF; 6 June 1941, OKW 589/41 g AWA/W Allg. (II), MGFA/DZ L III 114, BAF, reprinted in von Gersdorff, *Frauen im Kriegsdienst*, 333–34; Oberstabsarzt Dr. Driest, "Richtlinien über Menschenführung in der Truppe" [1944], MSg2/177, folios 14–15, BAF; Kommandantur Seelager Sophienwalde über Konitz to the Reichsschule-SS Oberehnheim/Elsaß, 21 August 1944, NS32 II/111, folio 5, BAK; "Das Verhalten der Luftwaffenhelferin," lecture delivered October 1944, DAF—Amt Luftwaffe—Luftgaudienststelle Münster, NS5 I/219, BAK.

125. Owings, *Frauen*, 266–83; Szepansy, *Blitzmädel*, 240.

126. For a rare and unflattering portrayal of German military men at this moment, see Szepansky, *Blitzmädel*, 97.

127. See Seidler, *Frauen zu den Waffen?* 163–74; 27 November 1944, OKW, Erlaß betr. Rechtzeitige Rückführung des weiblichen Wehrmachtsgefolge, MGFA/DZ III W 89, BAF, reprinted in von Gersdorff, *Frauen im Kriegsdienst*, 467–68. In 1950, 6,024 women were classified as "severely wounded" (over 50 percent reduced working capacity) as a result of injuries sustained while they were in the Wehrmacht. Neither women with milder wounds nor those who had died or had regained their working capacity by 1950 are included. It is not clear whether female members of the RADwJ serving in military capacities are included. Hudemann, *Sozialpolitik im deutschen Südwesten zwischen Tradition und Neuordnung 1945–1953*, 527.

128. Margot Mertens, "Die Wandlung," *Sie* 1/7 (January 1946): 3.

CHAPTER 4: THE HOUR OF THE WOMEN

1. Oppens et al., eds., *Die Frau in unserer Zeit*, 11; emphasis in original.

2. Meyer and Schulze also argue that singlehood was normative in this period and became exceptional only as men returned from war; *Wie wir das alles geschafft haben*, 12. See also Delille and Grohn, *Blick zurück aufs Glück*, 16.

3. For a classic formulation, see Schelsky, *Wandlungen der deutschen Familie in der Gegenwart*.

4. Schubert, *Frauen in der deutschen Nachkriegszeit*, vol. 1, *Frauenarbeit 1945–1949*; Kuhn, "Die vergessene Frauenarbeit in der deutschen Nachkriegszeit."

5. Tobin and Gibson, "The Meanings of Labor"; *Geschichte des DFD*.

6. See the tellingly titled collections edited by Rosenthal and Grote, "*Als der Krieg kam, hatte ich mit Hitler nichts mehr zu tun": Zur Gegenwärtigkeit des "Dritten Reiches" in Biographien* ["When the war came, I had nothing more to do with Hitler": On the presence of the "Third Reich" in biographies], and Niethammer, "*Hinterher*

merkt man, daß es richtig war, daß es schiefgegangen ist": Nachkriegs-Erfahrungen im *Ruhrgebiet* ["In hindsight, one sees that it was right that it didn't work out": Postwar experience in the Ruhr].

7. See especially Koonz, *Mothers in the Fatherland;* Bock, "Die Frauen und der Nationalsozialismus"; Gravenhorst and Tatschmurat, eds., *TöchterFragen;* Grossmann, "Feminist Debates about Women and National Socialism"; von Saldern, "Victims or Perpetrators?"

8. Heineman, "The Hour of the Woman."

9. Ruhl, ed., *Unsere verlorenen Jahre,* 70, 74; *The United States Strategic Bombing Survey: Overall Report (European War)* (September 30, 1945), 92–93, reprinted in *The United States Strategic Bombing Survey.* Statistics on the extent of damage and the number of dead vary considerably.

10. The qualifications for mothers wishing to leave the cities were repeatedly tightened. Beauftragte für den Vierjahresplan, der Generalbevollmächtigte für den Arbeitseinsatz, Schnellbrief (VIa 5550/726), 21 September 1943, R43 II/651d, Bd. 8, BAK; Beauftragte für den Vierjahresplan, der Generalbevollmächtigte für den Arbeitseinsatz, Abschrift zu VIa 5558/223, May 1944, R43 II/651d, Bd. 8, BAK; Beauftragte für den Vierjahresplan, der Generalbevollmächtigte für den Arbeitseinsatz, Schnellbrief (VIa 5558/374), 25 August 1944, R43 II/651d, Bd. 8, BAK.

11. Baumert, *Deutsche Familien nach dem Kriege,* 209–10.

12. Meyer and Schulze, *Auswirkungen des II. Weltkriegs,* 213ff.

13. In April 1946, the U.S. Military Government estimated that no more than 20 percent of current arrivals belonged to "family units with employable male heads"; *Monthly Report,* 9 (20 April 1946): 21. By the summer of that year, adult women constituted 45 percent of the refugees in the Soviet zone; men, 22 percent; and children, 33 percent. 18 June 1946, Jenny Matern, Deutsche Verwaltung für Arbeit und Sozialfürsorge in der SMAD, Abschnitt Wohnung und Siedlung, to the SMAD Abt. Die Arbeitskraft, DQ2/4000, BAP. The sexual imbalance was greatest in the Soviet zone; see Barthel, *Die wirtschaftlichen Ausgangsbedingungen,* 53–55; Reichling, *Die Heimatvertriebenen im Spiegel der Statistik,* 15, 52–53.

14. Joseph Goebbels radio address, delivered on February 28, 1945, in Heiber, ed., *Goebbels-Reden,* vol. 2, *1939–45,* 431–32; *Der Panzerbär,* 27 April 1945, quoted in Schmidt-Harzbach, "Eine Woche im April," 23.

15. Tröger, "Between Rape and Prostitution," 106. See also Meyer and Schulze, *Wie wir das alles geschafft haben,* 61ff.

16. The highest estimates appear in Sander and Johr, eds., *BeFreier und Befreite,* 60; more conservative figures appear in Kuby, *Die Russen in Berlin 1945,* 305–18. On the difficulty of quantification and contextualization, see especially Grossmann, "A Question of Silence"; also Naimark, *The Russians in Germany,* 69–140. On rapes in the western zones, see Frevert, *Frauen-Geschichte,* 246–47.

17. For reports of the dangers men faced in defending women from rape, see *Dokumentation der Vertreibung der Deutschen aus Ost-Mitteleuropa,* vol. I/1, *Die Vertreibung der deutschen Bevölkerung aus den Gebieten östlich der Oder-Neiße,* 65E. For reports of men's unwillingness even to try, see Schmidt-Harzbach, "Eine Woche"; Kuby, *Die Russen,* 305–18; Tröger, "Between Rape and Prostitution," 104; Schmidt-Harzbach, "Doppelt besiegt"; Meyer and Schulze, *Von Liebe sprach damals keiner,* 83; Hörning, "The Myth of Female Loyalty," 29.

18. See, for example, *Eine Frau in Berlin,* 81, 144, 271; Schmidt-Harzbach, "Eine Woche," 39–42; Meyer and Schulze, *Auswirkungen des II. Weltkriegs,* 227.

19. See especially Sander and Johr, *BeFreier und Befreite*, 16–17; Fr., Meyer and Schulze Interview Collection, Institut für Soziologie—TU-Berlin, 42.

20. On abortion following the rapes, see Grossmann, *Reforming Sex*, 193–99; Naimark, *The Russians*, 97–101, 121–25.

21. Thurnwald, *Gegenwartsprobleme Berliner Familien*, 337–47.

22. Meyer and Schulze, *Wie wir das alles geschafft haben*, 189.

23. 2 May 1947, Deutsche Verwaltung für Arbeit und Sozialfürsorge in der SMAD, Abschnitt Wohnung und Siedlung, "Die Entwicklung der Wohnungslage in Deutschland," DQ2/4000, BAP.

24. Ruhl, ed., *Frauen in der Nachkriegszeit 1945–1963*, 11.

25. They accounted for 18.1 percent of the population in the U.S. zone, 15.9 percent in the British, and 3 percent in the French. von Plato and Meinicke, *Alte Heimat—neue Zeit*, 25–26.

26. "Not und Hilfe," *NB*, 1 September 1948, 1.

27. Thurnwald, *Gegenwartsprobleme*, 44.

28. 20 September 1946, Jenny Matern, Deutsche Verwaltung für Arbeit und Sozialfürsorge in der SMAD, "Vorläufige Zusammenstellung der Wohnraumverteilung innerhalb der sowjetischen Besatzungszone," DQ2/4000, BAP; Faber, *Die Wohnungswirtschaft in der sowjetischen Besatzungszone*.

29. Meyer and Schulze, *Wie wir das alles geschafft haben*, 91.

30. On housewives' rations, see Gries, *Die Rationengesellschaft*, 93–107; Schubert, *Frauen*, 45.

31. Gries, *Die Rationengesellschaft*, 102–3.

32. Monthly Narrative Report for Land Hessen, November 1948 (translation), Medical Division, Ministry of the Interior, Hessian State Ministry, Abt. 649 8/59-1/11, HHA.

33. Reprinted in Berger and Müller, eds., *Lebenssituationen 1945–48*, 63.

34. "Wie leben Sie?" *Sie* 2/1 (5 January 1947): 3.

35. 13 May 1947, *Leipziger Volkszeitung* Nr. 183/1947, 4, quoted in Gries, *Die Rationengesellschaft*, 109.

36. Meyer and Schulze, *Wie wir das alles geschafft haben*, 100–101. See also Gries, *Die Rationengesellschaft*, 107–18, 204–23, 299–309.

37. For example, Gries, *Die Rationengesellschaft*, 307. See, however, Baumert, *Jugend der Nachkriegszeit*, 90; Maria Dornow, "Von Frau zu Frau: Ein wichtiges Teilgebiet unseres Rundfunks," *Sie* 2/1 (15 January 1947): 6.

38. In the U.S. zone, women arrested for any reason were tested for STDs; men were not. Co. Milford T. Kubin, Chief Public Health Branch, IA&C Division, to Provincial Offices of Military Government, 5 August 1947, AG 726.1, Box 347, Dec. file 1947, Adj. Gen. Office, RG260, NA-Suitland; Leiby, "Public Health in Occupied Germany 1945–49," 154.

39. Gries, *Die Rationengesellschaft*, 107–45, 204–49, 299–322.

40. Meyer and Schulze, *Von Liebe sprach damals keiner*, 172.

41. Ruhl, *Verordnete Unterordnung*, 47–48; Hinze, "Die Eingliederung der Frauen und weiblicher Jugendlicher in das Arbeitsleben."

42. "Die Arbeitsmarktlage in der sowjetischen Besatzungszone," *AS* 1 (1946): 50–51; *Monthly Report . . . : Manpower, Trade Unions and Working Conditions*, 20 September 1945, 6; *Monthly Report*, 20 December 1945, 16; "Arbeitsmarktlage und Wiederaufbau gesehen am Beispiel Frankfurt am Main," *DVöpF* 1 (September-October 1946): 24.

43. Thurnwald, *Gegenwartsprobleme*, 18; "Stenographische Niederschrift über die Frauenkonferenz am 4. November 1946," IV 2/1.01/22, folio 32, SAPM-DDR-BA.

44. Schubert, *Frauen*, 75–76.

45. E. Beck, "Die berufliche Gliederung der Bevölkerung in der sowjetischen Besatzungzone," *SP* 3 (1948): 99–100.

46. Starting in the summer of 1945, zones and provinces introduced requirements for the registration of potential laborers. Allied Control Council Decree 3 of 30 April 1946 (*Official Gazette of the Control Council for Germany* 30 April 1946: 131–33) created uniform regulations: the mandatory registration of men from fifteen to sixty-five and of women from fifteen to fifty.

47. Exemptions varied according to zone and province but in general became more liberal over the course of the occupation.

48. 10 January 1948, Präsident LAA Hamburg to the Herrn Präsidenten des Zentralamtes für Arbeit in der britischen Zone (Abschrift), Lemgo, LAA-NW 239, folios 32–35, NRW. For the Soviet zone, see Willy Donau, "Arbeitskräfte und Arbeitskraftreserven," *AS* 2 (1947): 407–10; Obertreis, *Familienpolitik in der DDR 1945–1980*, 41.

49. See the documents in Schubert, *Frauen*, 218–34. Moeller, *Protecting Motherhood*, gives a good sense of SPD women's concern not to seem too "radical" (and thus too close to the East Germans) in the 1950s.

50. 16–17 May 1946, Funktionärinnen-Konferenz, Friedel Malter, IV 2/1.01/3, folios 97–99, SAPM-DDR-BA; 26 October 1948, Landesregierung Sachsen—Ministerium für Arbeit und Sozialfürsorge—Hauptabteilung Arbeit—to the AA, DQ2/2072, BAP; 5 October 1949, Hilde Benjamin, Deutsche Justizverwaltung der sowjetischen Besatzungszone, to the Deutsche Wirtschaftskommission Hauptverwaltung Arbeit und Sozialfürsorge, DQ2/2072, BAP. Internal correspondence also reveals practices contrary to approved procedures. See, for example, 23 February 1949, Landesregierung Sachsen-Anhalt, Minister für Arbeit und Sozialpolitik—AA/Se. Ia/5-1390-Ra. to the Deutsche Wirtschaftskommission, DQ2/2072, BAP; Karl Gries, "Wettbewerb zur Unterbringung von Frauen und Schwerbeschädigten in Arbeitsverhältnisse," *AS* 4 (1949): 271–72; 19 October 1949, Willy Donau to Hilde Benjamin, DQ2/ 2072, BAP.

51. This message permeates the official journal of the office that would eventually become East Germany's Ministry for Work and Social Welfare, Arbeit und Sozialfürsorge. See, for example, "Die Arbeitsmarktlage in der sowjetischen Besatzungszone," *AS* 1 (1946): 50–55; Hinze, "Die Eingliederung"; Fritz Bohlmann, "Arbeitermangel und seine Beseitigung," *AS* 1 (1946): 169–70. See also "Stenographische Niederschrift über die Frauenkonferenz an dem 4. November 1946," IV 2/1.01/22, folios 3–20, SAPM-DDR-BA.

52. Schubert, *Frauen*, 62–64, 105–7, 173–74. For a noncompulsory variant, see 18 April 1946, Präsident des LAA Württemberg-Baden Heinz #137 to the AA, Abt. 460 AA Taubersbischofsheim 21, GLK.

53. 9 January 1946, Präsident LAA NRW to the AA, LAA-NW 239, folio 8–10, NRW; May 1946 LAA Rdvfg. /46 (Entwurf) to the AA, LAA-NW 239, folio 416, NRW.

54. Neither a breakdown according to sex nor comparable figures for the western zones are available. Compulsory assignments accounted for only 5.6 percent of assignments in the Soviet zone a year later. W[illy] Donau, "Arbeitsvermittlung—nicht Arbeitseinweisung," *AS* 4 (1949): 386–87.

55. Nawratil estimates the total numbers of deportees at nine hundred thousand;

Die deutschen Nachkriegsverluste unter Vertriebenen, Gefangenen und Verschleppten,
46–52. For an estimate of eight hundred thousand, see 27 October 1955, letter of unclear
origin, III 7d-3621 Tbg Nr. 7521/55 to the Herrn Staatssekretär des Bundeskanzleramtes, B150/7080, BAK.

56. Moser, *Bald nach Hause;* von Plato and Meinicke, *Alte Heimat,* 209–47. See
chapter 5 on political prisoners interned on East German soil.

57. Naimark, *The Russians,* 235–50.

58. Slightly over twenty thousand women worked in the uranium mines at the end
of 1948; this figure does not include women who had worked there previously but left
or those who would be assigned in later years. Naimark, *The Russians,* 245.

59. Langer, "In letzter Konsequenz . . . Uranbergwerk!" Indeed, since the strenuous work of mining impressed contemporaries more than the dangers of radiation, West
German reports made much of East German women's labor in mines in general. See, for
example, Haas and Leutwein, *Die rechtliche und soziale Lage der Arbeitnehmer in der
sowjetischen Besatzungszone,* 78–80.

60. Naimark, *The Russians,* 238–48.

61. SMAD Befehl #253, 17 August 1946, reprinted in Schubert, *Frauen,* 315; Gesetz
zur Demokratisierung der deutschen Schule vom 31 Mai 1946, reprinted in part in Bartel, ed., *Die Deutsche Demokratische Republik auf dem Wege zum Sozialismus.* On the
specific importance of equal pay for equal work for single women, see "Umfrage zum
Befehl der Sowjetischen Militäradministration," *FD* 2 (1946), quoted in Merkel, *. . . und
Du,* 28; *Die Frau und die Gesellschaft,* 158; Kreisfrauenausschuß Döbeln to alle
öffentlichen Dienststellen und ihre Betriebsvertretungen (n.d., [1947]), DQ2/2072, BAP;
W. Häusler, "Die Frau in der Verwaltung," *AS* 2 (1947): 115–16; Alfred Schmidt, "Arbeits-
reserven—woher nehmen?" *AS* 2 (1947): 162–63; Hinze, "Die Eingliederung"; Edith
Hinze, "Grundsätzliches zur Eingliederung der Frauen und weiblichen Jugendlichen in
das Arbeitsleben," DQ2/1571, BAP.

62. Allied Control Council Supplement to Directive 14, 13 September 1946,
reprinted in Schubert, *Frauen,* 314–15, permitted exceptions to the wage freeze in order
to bring women's pay up to men's. See Ruhl, *Verordnete Unterordnung,* 64–67, and Schubert, *Frauen,* 312–22, for failed efforts to mandate equal pay in the western zones.

63. Meyer and Schulze, *Wie wir das alles geschafft haben,* 70; Gimbel, *A German
Community under American Occupation,* 58. The prohibition on women's work in construction was lifted by Allied Control Council Law 32 of 10 July 1946 (*Official Gazette
of the Control Council for Germany* 31 July 1946:166), but women's work clearing rubble predated this law.

64. Meyer and Schulze, *Wie wir das alles geschafft haben,* 95.

65. Contrast Ruhl, *Verordnete Unterordnung,* 37–41, 124–25, on the western
zones, with the Soviet zone pamphlet "Was wird aus Dir? Laß Dich umschulen für einen
Facharbeiterberuf!" published in August 1947 by the Deutsche Verwaltung für Arbeit
und Sozialfürsorge, DQ/2072, BAP.

66. Heineman, "The Hour of the Woman," 374–80.

67. *Arbeiten, arbeiten, arbeiten!; Geschichte des DFD,* 124–25; "Stein auf Stein,"
in *Gerda Müller freut sich auf ihr Kind.*

68. See also Merkel, *. . . und Du,* 31–47; Merkel, "Leitbilder und Lebensweisen,"
363–65.

69. Ruhl, *Verordnete Unterordnung,* 116–27; *Frauen in der Nachkriegszeit,*
72–106; Garner, "Public Service Personnel in West Germany in the 1950s," 52–63.

70. Schubert, *Frauen,* 103; *Monthly Report,* July 1948, 3–4, 79–80.

71. 23 June 1948, Erlaß des Zentralamtes für Arbeit, discussed in 10 July 1948, Der Arbeitsminister des Landes NRW—Hauptabt. LAA—Rdvfg. 311/48, Abt. 940/176, HHA. Unemployment compensation was not limited to those who had lost their jobs. New job seekers were also eligible if they could not find employment.

72. 23 June 1948, Erlaß des Zentralamtes für Arbeit, discussed in 10 July 1948, Der Arbeitsminister des Landes NRW—Hauptabt. LAA—Rdvfg. 311/48, Abt. 940/176, HHA.

73. This requirement violated the legal provision that women who were willing and able to work only half time or only at home could claim unemployment compensation if no half-time or home work was available; 10 September 1948, Der Präsident des LAA Hessen, Dienstanweisung 17/48 (Entwurf), Abt. 940/176, HHA. See also 5 January 1949, Der Präsident des LAA Hessen, Dienstanweisung 6/49 (Entwurf), Abt. 940/164, HHA; "Amtliches Protokol: Richtlinien des Zentralausschusses für Arbeitslosenfürsorge," 7 June 1949, Abt. 940/164, HHA; 31 May 1952, Präsident des LAA Hessen to the Herrn Präsidenten der BAA, Abt. 940/164, HHA; 1 September 1948, der Leiter des AA Offenbach, der Magistrat der Stadt (Fürsorgeamt), der Landrat des Kreises (Fürsorgestelle) Offenbach/Main, Vereinbarung, Abt. 940/164, HHA; 2 July 1948, Präsident des LAA Württemberg-Baden, Abt. 460 AA Tauberbischofsheim 15, GLK; "Abgrenzung des Personenkreises der Arbeitslosenfürsorge bei Frauen," *DVöpF* 4 (1949): 52–53. For an uncharacteristic East German discussion of disqualifying women with household responsibilities from unemployment compensation, see Gerhard Ott, "Die Arbeitsmarktlage in Groß-Berlin seit dem Zusammenbruch," *AS* 2 (1947): 4–6.

74. *Monthly Report,* August 1948, 75, 77.

75. Barthel, *Die wirtschaftlichen Ausgangsbedingung,* 59–62. East and West German unemployment figures are not comparable. West Germany excluded from its statistics many women who desired employment, while East Germany classified as "available for work" many women who did not desire employment. East Germany also reclassified women formerly listed as "family assistants" as members of occupational groups, so when they were no longer needed in their husbands' or fathers' businesses, they appeared in unemployment statistics.

76. 1 February 1949, Deutsche Wirtschaftskommission für die sowjetische Besatzungszone, Rundschreiben Nr. 227, DQ2/2072, BAP.

77. 8 August 1949, Willy Donau, Deutsche Wirtschaftskommission, "Bericht über den Stand der Frauenbeschäftigung," DQ2/2072, BAP; 15 June 1947, Deutsche Verwaltung für Arbeit und Sozialfürsorge der sowjetischen Besatzungszone in Deutschland—IB—Kr./Gro., DQ2/2072, BAP; Edith Hinze, "Grundsätzliches zur weiblichen Nachwuchspolitik," *AS* 2 (1947): 113–15.

78. On June 30, 1949, 70 percent of the positions listed for women in the employment offices were for domestic help and traditionally female areas of agriculture; Schubert, *Frauen,* 105.

79. Schimmel, "Der Einfluß des Zweiten Weltkrieges auf die Prostitution in Berlin"; "Gestaltwandel der weiblichen Gefährdeten," Vermerk, 22 April 1960, ADW, CAW 572, ADW-IM; Oppens et al., *Die Frau in unserer Zeit,* 36; Uthart Richter, "Sexual-wissenschaftliche Betrachtungen über Umsiedler 1945 bis 1948," *ZHGK* 5 (December 1948): 485–89.

80. Difficult times, however, made relationships with men a low priority for some. Bohne, *Das Geschick der 2 Millionen,* 93–94, 176; Sander and Johr, *BeFreier und Befreite,* 86; Fr., Meyer and Schulze Interview Collection, Institut für Soziologie—TU-Berlin, 42.

81. See, for example, Bohne, *Das Geschick*, 99, 173ff.

82. Oe., Meyer and Schulze Interview Collection, Institut für Soziologie—TU-Berlin, 29. See also Thurnwald, *Gegenwartsprobleme*, 147.

83. Naimark, *The Russians*, 92–97.

84. Ibid., 116–21.

85. Ibid., 93–97.

86. Höhn, "GIs, Veronikas and Lucky Strikes."

87. Peukert, *The Weimar Republic*, 99, 174–81.

88. Höhn, "GIs"; Fehrenbach, "The Fight for the 'Christian West'"; Poiger, "Rock 'n' Roll, Female Sexuality, and the Cold War Battle over German Identities."

89. See also Gimbel, *A German Community*, 49ff.

90. "To Tell or Not to Tell Is Query of Worried Home-Bound GIs," *SS*, 28 June 1946, 3; "Yank-Fraulein [sic] Romances Seen Ruining Occupation," *SS*, 24 June 1946, 8.

91. By the end of 1947, 2,262 German women had married occupation soldiers. *Sie* 3/1 (4 January 1948): 1; "Unhaltbare Ehen," *Der Weg zur Seele* 2 (September 1950): 30, SF. By the mid-1950s, the number had risen to over seven thousand per year in the Federal Republic; "Eheschließungen der Deutschen und Ausländer 1952 bis 1957," *SJ-BRD* (1959): 48. Women who emigrated as fiancées rather than as wives were not included in these figures. Between 1944 and 1950, 150,000–200,000 women from continental Europe married U.S. servicemen; this figure includes women who married after arriving in the United States; Shukert and Scibetta, *War Brides of World War II*, 2. Emigration did not ease the "surplus of women," as male emigrants outnumbered female emigrants; "Aus- und Einwanderung," *SJ-BRD* (1955): 69.

92. Kreuzer, *Prostitution*, 222; Thurnwald, *Gegenwartsprobleme*, 197; U. Torrel, "Auf ihren Schultern . . . ," *Sie* 1/15 (17 March 1946): 6; Ewald Gerfeldt, "Sozialbiologische Wandlungen der Geschlechtskrankheiten," *ZHGK* 5 (November 1948): 437–45, here 439; Else Feldbinder, "Mütter ohne Liebe: Einen Tag Unterwegs mit der Jugendfürsorgerin," *Sie* 1/54 (15 December 1946): 2.

93. The U.S. Army banned marriages between servicemen and German women until December 1946; the first such marriages took place in March 1947. Even then, the army confronted couples wishing to marry with considerable obstacles. Shukert and Scibetta, *War Brides*, 144–46, 159–61; Unruh, *Trümmerfrauen*, 31.

94. See, for example, "Die Bekämpfung des Dirnenunwesens (3. Sitzung des Fachausschußes II des Deutschen Vereins für öffentliche und private Fürsorge)," in *Nachrichtendienst des DVöpF* 8 (1953): 356–65; Kreuzer, *Prostitution*, 222, 333; Höhn, "GIs," ch. 3.

95. In 1946, there were about one hundred thousand "secret" prostitutes in Berlin. Before the war, there had been forty-five hundred licensed and fifteen thousand unlicensed prostitutes. Schimmel, "Der Einfluß," 7. See also Bock, "'Keine Arbeitskräfte in diesem Sinne'"; Kreuzer, *Prostitution*, 221; March 1948, "Bordelle in Hamburg," NL151/181, BAK; Karl Friedrich Schaller, "Die Verdienstmöglichkeiten und Lebensunterhaltungskosten der Prostituierten," *ZHGK* 4 (February 1948): 129–34.

96. Kreuzer, *Prostitution*, 218.

97. "Veronica Dankeschoen Gets Notices in German Papers," *SS*, 1 August 1946, 8; *Monthly Report . . . : Public Safety*, 20 October 1945, 1; *Monthly Report*, 20 October 1945, 6; *Monthly Report*, 20 December 1945, 5; 10 December 1945, E. K. Neumann, Chief Public Safety Officer, US HQ Berlin District & HQ 1st Airborne Army, file dec. 014.13 fraternization, Box 15 dec. file 1945–46, Adj. Gen. Office, RG260, NA-Suitland; Shukert and Scibetta, *War Brides*, 126–27.

98. Höhn, "GIs."

99. "Andere Zonen—gleiche Probleme," *Sie* 1/54 (15 December 1946): 2; Schimmel, "Ein Blick in die Prostitution der Nachkriegsjahre"; Bericht über die Jahrestagung 1949 des Verbandes der Mitternachtsmission Deutschlands vom 7.–10. Januar 1949, ADW, CAW 561, ADW-IM; Thurnwald, *Gegenwartsprobleme*, 146.

100. Niethammer, *"Hinterher merkt man,"* 31.

101. Resolution of the Socialdemocratic Women of Heidelberg, folder 10 VD Staff Studies, Box 551 Records of Chief, Med. Aff. Section, PHPWB Branch, CAD, RG260, NA-Suitland; 23 February 1946, letter by Col., IGD, F. J. Pearson to Chief of Staff, Decimal 700 Germany, 30 June 1945–11 December 1946, Box 133 5BT Classified Dec. file 1946, Secretary General Staff, ETO, RG332, NA-Suitland.

102. "Werden die Mittel zur Bekämpfung der Geschlechtskrankheiten richtig verwendet?" *DVöpF* 3 (1948): 161–63. See also Ziskoven, "Sozialpädogogische Maßnahmen zur Bekämpfung von Geschlechtskrankheiten," 3. In a striking East German parallel, a poster informed civilians that STDs cost "the people" (*dem Volke*) six million marks per year, and with twice that sum Dresden could be rebuilt. Foto-Archiv Nr. 2513, Deutsches Hygiene-Museum, Dresden.

103. Thurnwald, *Gegenwartsprobleme*, 156. See also "Ein Wort an die Frauen und Mädchen," *Evangelisches Gemeindeblatt für Württemberg* 18 (5 May 1946) (Abschrift), ADW, CAW 384, ADW-IM; "Betr. Grundlagen der Volkswartbundarbeit," *Volkswartbund* (November-December 1947): 5.

104. 12 June 1946, War Department, Adj. Gen. AGAM-PM 726.1 (5 June 1946) A, Dec. file 726 v.I 1946, box 406, Adjutant Section, ETO RG332, NA-Suitland. In August, the rate was 305 per 1,000; that is, at the present rate of infection, 30.5 percent of men would be infected within the course of a year. "New Drive Set as VD Mounts," *SS*, 21 August 1946, 1. In some areas, the rate was considerably higher; "Strict Garrison Life Urged for ET [European Theater] as VD Rate Soars," *SS*, 26 April 1946, 1.

105. In January 1948, the Military Government returned public health to German authority but kept STD control under Allied supervision; *Monthly Report* 31 (January 1948): 29.

106. For example, 23 April 1946, Headquarters USFET AG 726 GAP-AGO, Classified dec. file 700 v.II 1946 (2 January 1946–3 January 1947), box 133 (5BT), Secretary General Staff, ETO, RG332, NA-Suitland.

107. "Drifting Frauleins [sic] Pose Problem," *SS*, 20 July 1946, 5. On Veronica Dankeschön, see Zumwalt, *The Stars and Stripes*, 141–43. The character appeared in *Stars and Stripes* with the initials "VD" on 9 and 20 July 1946 and without the name or initials in many other editions. The name "Veronika Dankeschön" quickly entered East as well as West German slang. "Top Secret," *NBI* 8/23 (June 1952): title page.

108. "28th Constabulary Fights VD with Bulletin Board Photos," *SS*, 21 July 1946, 1; "McNarney Sets Rules on Passes for Frauleins," *SS*, 10 July 1946, 1, 8; "USFET Preparing New Plan to Screen Fraulein Guests," *SS*, 1 September 1946, 12. Sixteen months after passes were introduced, the routine check of applicants' health records was rescinded as a violation of privacy; 14 November 1946, Theodore Popovich, Chief, VD Control, PHPWB, IA&C Division, to Branch Chief, folder 6 VD Reports, Field Trips, Box 550 Records of the Chief, Medical Affairs Section, Dec. file, CAD, RG260, NA-Suitland.

109. "VD Victims Exhibited to Soldiers in New Type Berlin Lectures," *SS*, 25 July 1946, 1.

110. On voluntary treatment, see "Im Kampf gegen die Geschlechtskrankheiten—Kampaign [sic] vom 15. Juli–15. August [1946]," Abt. 649 8/59-3/1, HHA; *Monthly Report*, 20 May 1946, 19–20.

111. Lt. Col. G. H. Garde, Adj. Gen., to Commander in Chief, European Command, 23 June 1947, AG 726.1, Reports and Programs against Venereal Disease, Prostitution, and Sex Vices, Box 347, Dec. file 1947, Adj. General's Office RG260, NA-Suitland; "Bericht über die gemeinsame Tagung der Nordwestdeutschen und Hamburger Dermatologengesellschaft vom 2.–4. April 1948 in Hamburg," *ZHGK* 5 (July 1948): 43ff.; "Neue landesrechtliche Bestimmungen zur Bekämpfung der Geschlechtskrankheiten," *DVöpF* 2 (December 1947): 137; "Aufstellung eines Gesamtprogramms der Bekämpfung der Geschlechtskrankheiten," *DVöpF* 3 (1948): 105–7.

112. "Geschlechtskrankheiten," Monthly Reports of the Statistisches Landesamt NRW, November 1945–June 1948, Staatsbibliothek Berlin; Albert Schweizer, Director, CAD OMG-Bavaria to Dr. Carl Kofferath, Bav. Min. Interior, Bav. Health Dept., VD Control Section, 20 January 1949, folder 3 Ven. Dis. 1949, Box 549 Records of the Chief, Med. Aff. Section, PHPWB, CAD, RG260, NA-Suitland; "Bericht über die gemeinsame Tagung der Nordwestdeutschen und Hamburger Dermatologengesellschaft vom 2.–4. April 1948 in Hamburg," *ZHGK* 5 (July 1948): 43ff.; Leiby, "Public Health in Occupied Germany," 163–65.

113. Monthly Narrative Reports February-July 1947, Boxes 565–566 Health Reports, PHPWB, CAD, RG260, NA-Suitland. During that period, about eighteen thousand new cases of civilian STDs were registered in Hessen.

114. See, for example, Feldbinder, "Zwischen Tanzbar und Gesundheitsamt."

115. Fr., Meyer and Schulze Interview Collection, Institut für Soziologie—TU-Berlin, 45–46. See also Feldbinder, "Zwischen Tanzbar."

116. Leiby, "Public Health in Occupied Germany," 164.

117. Deputy Military Governor Frank A. Keating Report, 12 June 1947, AG 726.1, Box 347, Dec. file 1947, Adj. Gen. Office, RG260, NA-Suitland. For another embarrassing incident, see Samuel Camerata, Base Surgeon, HQ Straubing Air Base to CO Straubing Air Base, 26 November 1946, file dec. 700 Public Health v.II 2 January 1946–3 January 1947, Box 133 (5BT) Classified dec. file 1946, Sec. Gen. Staff, ETO, RG332, NA-Suitland.

118. Dr. Böhler, Med. Abt., Min. des Innern, to OMG-H, Public Health Division, 17 April 1947, Quarterly Report on Venereal Diseases for the First Three Months of 1947 (translation), Abt. 649 8/60-1/7, HHA.

119. "Abänderung des RG zur Bekämpfung der Geschlechtskrankheiten in Groß-Hessen," *DVöpF* 1 (1946): 28–29; Kreuzer, *Prostitution*, 53, 65; Ziskoven, "Sozialpädagogische Maßnahmen," 5–6.

120. Else Feldbinder, "Die Kurve steigt," *Sie* 2/22 (1 June 1947): 5. The rates per ten thousand West German population for both sexes for gonorrhea and syphillus, respectively, were: 1946: 51.7 and 20.35; 1947: 40.13 and 25.43; 1948: 28.84 and 21.35; 1949: 21.42 and 13.39; 1950: 15.69 and 8.75; *Gesundheitswesen*, 41.

121. Winfried Schimmel, "Über die Entwicklung der Geschlechtskrankheiten und ihre Probleme in den Nachkriegsjahren," Referat anläßlich der 1. Vollversammlung der Gesellschaft zur Bekämpfung der Geschlechtskrankheiten, Landesverband Berlin (n.d. [by 1950]), SF. In some states, the female rate of infection briefly exceeded the male rate of infection; "Geschlechtskrankheiten," in *Gesundheitswesen*, 41.

122. See, however, Weiß, *Das Gesundheitswesen in der sowjetischen Besatzungszone*, 37–38. Weiß notes that although penicillin was not available in the Soviet zone, STD rates there declined 75 percent between 1946 and 1948. In a rare moment of West German admiration for the Soviets' disregard of civil liberties—the desire to crack down on sexually promiscuous women seems to have outweighed even the temptation to find fault with Soviet methods—Weiß credits the Soviets' use of compulsion rather

than the improved social circumstances. On the STD campaign in the Soviet zone, see also Dinter, "Die Seuchen im Berlin der Nachkriegszeit 1945–1949," 533–96; "Gefahren der Strasse," *Fvh* 1/20 (December 1946): 8.

123. Hans Holzamer, "Ist die namentliche Meldepflicht ein Gewinn oder ein Verlust im Kampf gegen die Geschlechtskrankheiten?" *ZHGK* 4 (January 1948): 40–43; Dr. Böhler, Medizinalabt. Minister des Innern, Großhessisches Staatsministerium, to OMG-H, Public Health Branch, 31 August 1946, Abt. 649 8/59-3/1, HHA; Dr. Böhler, "Bericht über die Besprechung eines Gesetzentwurfes zum Kampf gegen die Geschlechtskrankheiten durch Arbeitserziehung," 18 April 1947, Abt. 649 8/60-1/7, HHA.

124. 27 June 1950, Franz Redeker to the Ob.Reg.u.Medizinalrat Dr. Koch (BIM), B142/466, BAK. See also "Für eine vorurteilslose Beurteilung der G-Krankheiten!" *NB* 2/2 (1 February 1946): 2; V. Lundt, "Weiterer Beitrag zur Resozialisierung weiblicher Geschlechtskranker," *Der öffentliche Gesundheitsdienst* 12 (August 1950): 169–74. German officials and doctors faced penalties if they failed to follow Allied policy but not if they expressed objections to it. "Four Powers Act to Curb Berlin VD: New Controls Go into Effect in All Zones," *SS*, 28 June 1946, 8.

125. "Bayerische Verordnung über die Unterbringung verwahrloster Frauen und Mädchen," *DVöpF* 1 (1946): 25–27. See also "Aus einer Begründung zum Entwurf einer VO zum Schutze der gefährdeten Jugend," *DVöpF* 1 (1946): 46–47; "Arbeitserziehung arbeitsscheuer und verwahrloster Jugendlicher," *DVöpF* 1 (1946): 56–58; Ebbinghaus, "Helene Wessel und die Verwahrung."

126. Beschlüsse von der Tagung des Hauptausschusses, 22 August 1948, in Vöhl, III 7/a, AW; [Luise Jörissen], "Gedanken über sozial-pädagogische Aufgaben im Kampf gegen die Geschlechtskrankheiten" [December 1947], 319.4 D I5e Fasz. 2, DCV; December 1948, Katholische Arbeitsgemeinschaft für Volksgesundung, Nachrichten, 319.4 D II, 4 Fasz.1, DCV; "Stand der Vorarbeitung für eine einheitliche Regelung der Bekämpfung der Geschlechtskrankheiten," *DVöpF* 4 (1949): 136–39.

127. The social work profession did not suffer even the temporary disruptions of denazification that struck the medical profession. Hans Muthesius, who a few years earlier had initiated the planning for a concentration camp for youth, authored the position paper on STD control for the western zones' umbrella social work organization; "Aufstellung eines Gesamtprogrammes der Bekämpfung der Geschlechtskrankheiten," *DVöpF* 3 (1948): 105–7. See also social workers' opposition to the U.S. Military Government's abolition of workhouses; "Aufhebung der gesetzlichen Bestimmungen über das Arbeitshaus (amerik.Zone)," *DVöpF* 4 (1949): 36–37. For rare challenges to social workers' claim to more humane methods, see "Vorbeugende und nachgehende Fürsorge als Maßnahmen der Bekämpfung der Geschlechtskrankheiten," *DVöpF* 4 (1949): 133–36; 9 February 1948, Marie Elisabeth Lüders an Prof. Dr. Gustav Hopf, NL151/171, BAK.

128. Lt. Col. G. H. Garde, Adjutant General, to Director OMG-Bavaria, 7 January 1948, AG 726.1, Box 347, Dec. file 1947, Adj. Gen., RG260, NA-Suitland; Lt. Col. G. H. Garde, Adjutant General, to Commander-in-Chief, European Command, 24 December 1947, AG 726.1, Box 347, Dec. file 1947, Adj. Gen. Office, RG260, NA-Suitland; Change #1, Annex #10 to Operational Directive #1, Operational Procedure U.S. Constabulary, Military Government and German Police Agencies (n.d. [April-May 1947]), folder 7 VD Directives, Box 550 Records of Chief, Med. Affairs Section, PHPWB, CAD, RG260, NA-Suitland.

129. Feldbinder, "Zwischen Tanzbar."

130. Ziskoven, "Sozialpädogogische Maßnahmen," 5; Dr. Josef Hormann, Domkapitulat, Augsburg, to Bavarian Ministerpräsident Dr. Hans Erhard, 8 April 1947, Box 347, Dec. File 1947 726.1, Adj. Gen. Office, RG260, NA-Suitland.

131. Since the late nineteenth century, feminists had demanded an end to municipal control of prostitution and an STD program that did not single out prostitutes. A law of 1927 met both demands. For references to the earlier campaign in the current context, see 9 February 1948, Marie Elisabeth Lüders to the Berliner Frauenbund, NL151/171, BAK; 9 February 1948, Marie Elisabeth Lüders to Prof. Dr. Gustav Hopf, NL151/171, BAK; von Zahn-Harnack, "Wieder doppelte Moral?"; Agnes von Zahn-Harnack, Leserbrief, *Sie* 2/15 (13 April 1947): 4. A 1953 law (Gesetz zur Bekämpfung der Geschlechtskrankheiten, *BGBl* I 700ff.) restored the regimentation and registration of prostitutes.

132. von Zahn-Harnack, "Wieder doppelte Moral?"; Margot I. Schwager, Leserbrief, *Sie* 1/51 (24 November 1946): 4.

133. See also 18 February 1948, Prof. Dr. Gustav Hopf to Marie Elisabeth Lüders, NL151/171, BAK; Franz Redeker to Ob.Reg.u.Medizinalrat Dr. Koch (BIM), 27 June 1950, B142/466, BAK; 6 August 1947, Elisabeth Zillken to Fr.Dr. Maria Schlüter-Hermkes, 319.4 D I, 5e Fasz. 2, DCV.

134. Electoral Brochure, Christian Democratic Union, Büren District (n.d. [1946]), 319.4 D I, 5a Fasz.1, DCV.

135. Heineman, "The Hour of the Woman," 380–88.

136. Naimark, *The Russians,* 129–40.

137. Sander and Johr, *BeFreier und Befreite,* 86.

CHAPTER 5: MARRIAGE RUBBLE

1. Torrel, "Auf ihren Schultern . . . ."
2. "Eheberatungsstelle in Hannover," *NB* 3 (1 March 1949): 3.
3. "Die Aussprache," *Fvh* 2/11 (June 1947): 18–19.
4. In the same year, *Für Dich* began publication in the Soviet zone. In 1950, *Die Frau von heute* absorbed *Für Dich.* In 1963, *Die Frau von heute* changed its name to *Für Dich.*
5. On the West German magazines, see Seeler, "Ehe, Familie und andere Lebensformen in den Nachkriegsjahren im Spiegel der Frauenzeitschriften," 92–95. On *Die Frau von heute* and *Für Dich,* see Merkel, *. . . und Du.*
6. Marxist critiques stretched back as far as Friedrich Engels, *The Origin of the Family, Private Property, and the State,* first published in 1884, and August Bebel, *Die Frau und der Sozialismus,* published in 1879. Bourgeois feminist critiques included Dittmar, *Das Wesen der Ehe,* and Stritt, "Rechtskämpfe."
7. Thurnwald, *Gegenwartsprobleme,* 232ff., esp. 235; see also the story of Frau W., 358ff., esp. 362.
8. Meyer and Schulze, *Von Liebe sprach damals keiner,* 161–62; Meyer and Schulze, *Auswirkungen des II. Weltkriegs,* 262–63.
9. von Krockow, *Die Stunde der Frauen,* 262–70; Stolten, *Der Hunger nach Erfahrung,* 49.
10. von Krockow, *Die Stunde,* 234–39; Lehmann, *Gefangenschaft und Heimkehr,* 119–21; 2 December 1949, Marga Schmidt, Frauenabt. [SED Parteivorstand], Bericht, IV 2/17/11, folios 99–100, SAPM-DDR-BA. Many Germans imprisoned in the Soviet Union indeed were unable to write home—not because it was forbidden but because of a severe shortage of postcards. "Zapiska M. Suslova A. Zhdanovu ob uluchshenii organizatsii perepiski voennoplennykh, nakhodiaschchikhsia v SSSR, 5 avgusta 1946 g," in Bonvech et al., eds., *SVAG,* 59–60. Thanks to Tatyana Dumova for her translation of this and other documents from this collection.

11. 13 January 1948, SED Landesvorstand Groß-Berlin to the ZS der SED, IV 2/2.027/35, folio 179, SAPM-DDR-BA; 13 and 18 October 1948, Zentralsekretariat der SED—Frauensekretariat to the Kreisleitung der SED, Greifswald, IV 2/17/11, folios 31–32, SAPM-DDR-BA; 14 October 1950, Auszug aus dem Tätigkeitsbericht von August 1950, [DFD] Kriesverband Eckertsberg, 29 August 1950, IV 2/17/11, folios 13–14, SAPM-DDR-BA; 2 December 1949, Bericht, Frauenabt. [beim Parteivorstand der SED], IV 2/17/11, folios 99–102, SAPM-DDR-BA.

12. Lenka von Körber, "Zurück aus der Kirgisensteppe," *Sie* 1/19 (14 April 1946): 4; "Aus der Praxis—für die Praxis" *NB* 3/10 (1 June 1949): 5–6; Käthe Kern, Vortrag, Bundeskongress, 28–29 May 1948, IV 2/17/26, folios 284–93, SAPM-DDR-BA.

13. Käthe Kern, "Frauen überwinden die Not," radio address, 6 August 1946, IV 2/17/26, folios 13–16, SAPM-DDR-BA; Elli Schmidt, "Frauen denkt daran!" *Neues Deutschland*, 1 September 1946, NY4106/4, folio 141, SAPM-DDR-BA; Elli Schmidt, "Unsere Aufgaben zur Gewinning der Frauen bei den Gemeindewahlen," 20 October 1946, NY4106/4, SAPM-DDR-BA; Entschliessung angenommen auf dem Gründungskongress des DFD, 9 March 1947, reprinted in *Dokumente der revolutionären Arbeiterbewegung zur Frauenfrage 1848–1974*, 160–61; Resolution des II. Parteitages der SED zur Frauenfrage, 24 September 1947, reprinted in *Dokumente*, 162–63.

14. Böhne, *Die deutschen Kriegsgefangenen in sowjetischer Hand*; Smith, *Heimkehr aus dem zweiten Weltkrieg.*

15. Moeller, "War Stories."

16. Käthe Kern, "Frauen überwinden die Not," radio address, 6 August 1946, IV 2/17/26, folios 13–16, SAPM-DDR-BA; Elli Schmidt, "Frauen denkt daran!" *Neues Deutschland*, 1 September 1946, NY4106/4, folio 141, SAPM-DDR-BA; Elli Schmidt, Flugblattentwurf für Berlin, October 1946, NY4106/4, folios 271–87, here 284–85, SAPM-DDR-BA.

17. *Geschichte des DFD*, 86. See also "Kriegsgefangenenfrage—Vermißtenproblem," *Suchzeitung* 9/4 (June 1950), DY55/V278/2/73, SAPM-DDR-BA.

18. See note 11. In August 1948, a delegation of the DFD (Democratic Women's League of Germany) visited Soviet prison camps; its report was intended to put to rest the notion that prisoners suffered wretched conditions; Wittwika, *Was ich mit eigenen Augen sah*. For continuing challenges in the 1950s, see 9 January 1953, Fr. Gerber, DFD, to the DFD-Ortsgruppe Steinfurt, DFD/BV540, folio 37, SAPM-DDR-BA; 3 February 1955, llse Thiele to A. H., DFD/BV557, folios 126–27, SAPM-DDR-BA.

19. See, for example, Niethammer, *Entnazifizierung in Bayern.*

20. Estimates for the number of prisoners range from 120,000 to 240,000. The overwhelming majority were adult men. Fricke, "'Kampf dem Klassenfeind,'" 184–85; Fricke, *Politik und Justiz in der DDR*; Naimark, *The Russians*, 376–91; Gräfe and Ritscher, "Die Speziallager in der Sowjetischen Besatzungszone"; Krüger and Finn, *Mecklenburg-Vorpommern 1945 bis 1948 und das Lager Fünfeichen*; Kilian, *Einzuweisen zur völligen Isolierung.*

21. 17–21 June 1947, Bericht Langney über die Frauenarbeit in den Kreisen, IV 2/17/51, folios 267–70, SAPM-DDR-BA; DFD Kreisorganisation Fürstenberg/Oder to Elli Schmidt, DFD/BV554, folio 15, SAPM-DDR-BA; Kilian, *Einzuweisen*, 95–98; Krüger and Finn, *Mecklenburg-Vorpommern*, 55; Gräfe and Ritscher, "Die Speziallager," 118; Bordihn, *Bittere Jahre am Polarkreis*, 21.

22. Naimark, *The Russians*, 207–28.

23. See the extensive correspondence in DQ2/1589–90, BAP.

24. In addition to wives, magazines often featured daughters and mothers—but

rarely sons and fathers—anticipating men's return. "Und 1946? Was wir uns wünschen," *NBI* 1/8 (December 1945): 2–3; "Suchkarte Trenkner," *NBI* 3/8 (February 1947): 3–5.

25. Soviet soldiers captured by the Germans had stood an even slimmer chance of survival. Of 5.7 million prisoners, 3.3 million are known to have died in captivity; the fate of an additional large number is unknown. Lehmann, *Gefangenschaft*, 10. Prisoners who returned to East Germany more often portrayed the conditions of imprisonment as characteristic of hard postwar times but hardly comparable to combat. Compare Lehmann, *Gefangenschaft*, to von Plato and Meinicke, *Alte Heimat*, 145–46, 193.

26. Meyer and Schulze, *Von Liebe sprach damals keiner*, 84.

27. Hemsing, "Der Heimkehrer und seine Ehe," 205; Carl Speitkamp, "Scheidung von Kriegsgefangenen-Ehen," *Jugendwohl* 29 (September-October 1948): 21–22.

28. Baumert, *Deutsche Familien*, 145; Meyer and Schulze, *Von Liebe sprach damals keiner*, 106; "Heimkehrer-Ehen"; Hemsing, "Der Heimkehrer," 200.

29. "Aus 'Schütze Schmidt' wird wieder 'Pappi,'" *NBI* 2/10 (March 1946): 16. "*Vor kurzem war ich noch der Schütze Schmidt, / ein grauer Tropfen zwischen grauen Wellen./ . . . / Heut bin ich 'Pappi' und Autorität. / Katrinchen schenkt mir unbegrenzt Vertrauen. / Ich bin ein Gott.*" The poem also reminds men that they will now have to watch their language and their manners.

30. Meyer and Schulze, *Von Liebe sprach damals keiner*, 129; Leber, "Der Heimgekehrte"; "Über die Brücke des Verstehens," *Fvh* 1/21 (December 1946): 4.

31. Baumert, *Deutsche Familien*, 209–12.

32. "Die standesamtlich beurkundeten Kriegssterbefälle und gerichtlichen Todeserklärungen in den Jahren 1939 bis 1954," *WS* (1956): 302–4. Of those registered as missing, 47.6 percent were married, but since married men were more likely to be registered than were single men (who had no wives to register them), a disproportionate number of single missing men probably escaped detection. "Im Bundesgebiet vermißte Wehrmachtsangehörige," *WS* (1950): 153–55.

33. Meyer and Schulze, *Von Liebe sprach damals keiner*, 253–54.

34. "Im Bundesgebiet vermißte Wehrmachtsangehörige," *WS* (1950): 153–55.

35. See Chapter Eight.

36. Meyer and Schulze, *Von Liebe sprach damals keiner*, 162; also Unruh, *Trümmerfrauen*, 142.

37. Meyer and Schulze, *Von Liebe sprach damals keiner*, 169.

38. See, for example, Sander and Johr, *BeFreier und Befreite*, 43.

39. Meyer and Schulze, *Von Liebe sprach damals keiner*, 134; also Ha., Meyer and Schulze Interview Collection, Institut für Soziologie—TU-Berlin, 58ff. For a more sympathetic husband, see "Heimkehrer-Ehen."

40. Meyer and Schulze, *Von Liebe sprach damals keiner*, 134.

41. "Keine Ehe wird im Himmel gelebt!" *Constanze* 2/21 (October 1949): 10; Luise Frankenstein, "Uneheliche Kinder von Ausländischen Soldaten mit besonderer Berücksichtigung der Mischlinge," July 1953, B153/345-1, folios 250–90, here 280, BAK; Klaus Eyferth, "Gedanken über die zukünftige Berufseingliederung der Mischlingskinder in Westdeutschland," *NB* 13/5 (1959), n.p., Abt. 940/136, HHA; Wilhelmine Hollweg, "Ohne Ansehen der Rasse . . . ," *Deutscher Paritätischer Wohlfahrtsverband—Nachrichten* 5 (June 1955): 2–3, B153/342, folios 248–49, BAK; Jonny Prei, "Das Kind aus jenen Tagen," *Fvh* 2/24 (December 1947): 27; "Anfechtung der Ehelichkeit nur imlaufe eines Jahres," *Fvh* 12/13 (March 1957): 21. For a fictional representation, see Maschmann, *Das Wort hieß Liebe.*

42. See, for example, "Heimkehrer-Ehen."

43. See, for example, Niethammer, von Plato, and Wierling, *Die volkseigene Erfahrung*, 356–62.

44. Meyer and Schulze, *Von Liebe sprach damals keiner*, 76, 144, 192ff.; Bruns, *Als Vater aus dem Krieg heimkehrte*, 24, 51, 58–59; Roberts, *Starke Mütter—ferne Väter*, 49–51. See also the interesting parallels in families of French prisoners of war in Fishman, *We Will Wait*, 143–45.

45. Zu., Meyer and Schulze Interview Collection, Institut für Soziologie—TU-Berlin, 29.

46. Meyer and Schulze, *Von Liebe sprach damals keiner*, 28, 76; Bruns, *Als Vater*, 27, 100–101; "Ein 'fremder Mann' wird 'Pappi,'" *NBI* 2/10 (March 1946): 16.

47. Meyer and Schulze, *Von Liebe sprach damals keiner*, 99; Meyer and Schulze, *Auswirkungen des II. Weltkriegs*, 244; Thurnwald, *Gegenwartsprobleme*, 126, 312; Bruns, *Als Vater*, 57–60.

48. Meyer and Schulze, *Von Liebe sprach damals keiner*, 148. See also Baumert, *Deutsche Familien*, 132.

49. Meyer and Schulze, *Auswirkungen des II. Weltkriegs*, 274; Bruns, *Als Vater*, 29, 61–62, 101.

50. Thurnwald, *Gegenwartsprobleme*, 97, 150; Zu., Meyer and Schulze Interview Collection, Institut für Soziologie—TU-Berlin, 29; Bruns, *Als Vater*, 97, 104; "Ein 'fremder Mann' wird 'Pappi,'" *NBI* 2/10 (March 1946): 16.

51. Bruns, *Als Vater*, 91.

52. Ibid., 118–20, 136–37, 150, 177. See also the fictionalized account in Böll, *Haus ohne Hüter*.

53. Gries, *Die Rationengesellschaft*, 203; Bruns, *Als Vater*, 22; Meyer and Schulze, *Auswirkungen des II. Weltkriegs*, 247–48; Meyer and Schulze, *Von Liebe sprach damals keiner*, 32, 115–16; Baumert, *Deutsche Familien*, 146; "Die Aussprache," *Fvh* 3/7 (April 1948): 18.

54. On tense relations in overcrowded households, see "Probleme in der Sprechstunde," *Fvh* 2/10 (May 1947): 8–9; "Die Aussprache," *Fvh* 2/10 (May 1947): 18–19; "3 Parteien in einer Küche," *Fvh* 1/9 (June 1946): 4–5. Memories of "communities of women" are occasionally idyllic; see Niethammer, von Plato, and Wierling, *Die volkseigene Erfahrung*, 365–66.

55. Meyer and Schulze, *Auswirkungen des II. Weltkriegs*, 147–48, 282–83; Meyer and Schulze, *Von Liebe sprach damals keiner*, 76.

56. "Zwölf Männer und die Frau von heute," *Fvh* 1/4 (April 1946): 16–17.

57. von Hollander, "Der Mann als Ballast."

58. Meyer and Schulze, *Wie wir das alles geschafft haben*, 53. See also Meyer and Schulze, *Von Liebe sprach damals keiner*, 120; Meyer and Schulze, *Auswirkungen des II. Weltkriegs*, 267.

59. Baumert, *Deutsche Familien*, 133; Meyer and Schulze, *Auswirkungen des II. Weltkriegs*, 262–63; Thurnwald, *Gegenwartsprobleme*, 369.

60. Meyer and Schulze, *Von Liebe sprach damals keiner*, 132.

61. Baumert, *Deutsche Familien*, 145; Thurnwald, *Gegenwartsprobleme*, 199.

62. Konstantin, "Sie flechten und weben," *Fvh* 1/7 (May 1946): 1. See also Leber, "Der Heimgekehrte."

63. von Hollander, "Der Mann als Ballast."

64. See Meyer and Schulze's excellent discussions of adjustments in "complete" West Berlin families; *Von Liebe sprach damals keiner*, passim, and *Auswirkungen des II. Weltkriegs*, 283–302. See also Baumert, *Deutsche Familien*, 134–35.

65. See divorce figures in Figure A.3.
66. Wolf, Lücke, and Hax, *Scheidung*, 212.
67. Ewald Gerfeldt, "Lebensform und Ehekrise," *Soziale Welt* 3 (October 1951): 7–17, here 14.
68. After 1950, the numbers and rates of marriages declined; in 1953, the rate of marriage in both Germanys dropped below the prewar level, and it remained relatively low after that (Fig. A.2). In the immediate postwar period, young women were underrepresented among those marrying. In 1939, 40.4 percent of women marrying in Hessen were between the ages of twenty and twenty-four; in 1946, only 29 percent of women marrying fell into this range. Baumert, *Deutsche Familien*, 29.
69. "Die Ehescheidungen im Bundesgebiet seit 1946"; Thurnwald, *Gegenwartsprobleme*, 202.
70. Men had borne sole guilt for 44.6 percent of divorces in 1939; women had borne sole guilt in only 15.5 percent of cases. In the western zones in 1948, men's share of sole guilt had fallen to 34.1 percent, while women's had risen to 23.9 percent. "Die Ehescheidungen," 292; Baumert, *Deutsche Familien*, 173. On the 1946 reform of marriage and divorce law, which undid the Nazis' racial provisions, see Wolf, Lücke, and Hax, *Scheidung*, 86ff.; "Änderungen des Eherechts durch den Kontrollrat," *DVöpf* 1/3 (November 1946): 34–36; Klaus Tipke, "Die Unterhaltsansprüche der vor dem 1.3.1946 geschiedenen Ehegatten," *Zeitschrift für das Fürsorgewesen* 5 (15 December 1953): 370–71.
71. Hilde Schneider, Leserbrief, *Sie* 2/31 (3 August 1947): 4. See also Dora Bier, "Die glückliche Alleinstehende," *WF* 3 (October 1948), quoted in Seeler, "Ehe, Familie," 108–9.
72. "Nur nicht heiraten!"; also Elfriede Klein, Leserbrief, *Sie* 4 (20 November 1949): 4.
73. "Nur nicht heiraten!"; also Thurnwald, *Gegenwartsprobleme*, 201; Walther von Hollander, "Mann in der Krise (II)," *Constanze* 1/2 (March 1948): 15.
74. Prollius, "Ein Königreich für einen Mann?" See also von Hollander, "Zum Thema" (2/50); Alexander Pauly, "Ehe man Ehefrau wird, gilt der Rat: Sehen Sie die Männer richtig an!" *Constanze* 2/23 (November 1949): 20–21.
75. Quoted in von Hollander, "Der Mann als Ballast."
76. Ibid.
77. Bohne, *Das Geschick*, 100. See also Erika Engelbrecht, Leserbrief, *Sie* 3/6 (8 February 1948): 4.
78. Walther von Hollander, "Mann in der Krise," *Constanze* 1/1 (March 1948): 3, 22, here 3.
79. Schmidt, "Im Vorzimmer," 194ff.
80. "Die Aussprache," *Fvh* 3/6 (March 1948): 24. The original reader's query appears in "Die Aussprache," *Fvh* 3/4 (February 1948): 19. See also Luise Frankenstein, "Uneheliche Kinder von Ausländischen Soldaten mit besonderer Berücksichtigung der Mischlinge," typescript, July 1953, B153/345-1, folios 250–90, BAK, here 262, 280. For an exception, see "Probleme in der Sprechstunde," *Fvh* 2/10 (May 1947): 8–9.
81. Meyer and Schulze, *Auswirkungen des II. Weltkriegs*, 305. See also Schmidt, "Im Vorzimmer," 195–96; Bohne, *Das Geschick*, 98, 173ff.
82. "Wie mein Vorschlag gefallen hat," *Fvh* 7/23 (June 1952): 18.
83. Oe., Meyer and Schulze Interview Collection, Institut für Soziologie—TU-Berlin, 29.
84. Prollius, "Ein Königreich." See also Walther von Hollander, "Die alleinstehende Frau von vierzig Jahren," *Constanze* 2/3 (February 1949): 11; von Hollander, "Mütter ohne Männer"; von Hollander, "Ein zweites Mal nicht!"

85. Of 4,109 divorces in Hamburg in 1951, 1,203 were of war marriages and 1,628 of postwar marriages. "Kriegsehen," *Mitteilungen der Evangelischen Frauenarbeit in Deutschland,* 20 October 1952, 5, SF.

86. Be., Meyer and Schulze Interview Collection, Institut für Sozialfragen—TU-Berlin, 24. See also many testimonies in Bohne, *Das Geschick,* esp. 95, 98, 151, 176.

87. Bergner, "Möblierte Mütter," *Sie* 1/1 (December 1945): 2. See also Agnes von Zahn-Harnack in *WF* 2 (February 1946), quoted in Seeler, "Ehe, Familie," 97.

88. "Die nicht heiraten dürften," *NBI* 2/1 (January 1946): 6–7. On the German presses' blindness to Jewish survivors in the immediate postwar period, see Stern, "The Historic Triangle," 209.

89. "Das große Wiedersehen," *Sie* 1/1 (December 1945): 2; Hanns Schwarz, "Das große Warten," *Sie* 1/2 (January 1946): 2; Leber, "Der Heimgekehrte"; "Kluge Frauen finden einen Weg!" advertisement for Karl Brandt Chem.-Pharm. und Kosm. Fabrik, *NBI* 2/26 (August1946): 10.

90. "*Sie* blickt in die Welt," *Sie* 2/18 (4 May 1947): 3; Hildegard Liepe, Leserbrief, *Sie* 3/1 (4 January 1948): 4; "Nur nicht heiraten!"; Thurnwald, *Gegenwartsprobleme,* 323, 330; Lund, "Möchten Sie 'auf Zeit' verheiratet sein?"; Moeller, *Protecting Motherhood,* 76–79; Seeler, "Ehe, Familie," 102–13.

91. von Hollander, "Mütter ohne Männer"; Baumert, *Deutsche Familien,* 47; Petra Lund, "Man kann sich nur darüber wundern . . . ," *Constanze* 1/12 (August 1948): 3.

92. "Erfahrungen aus der Arbeit einer Vikarin in Frauenkliniken, auf Grund eines Berichtes bei der Geschäftsführerkonferenz der Inneren Mission am 10. Juli 1946," ADW, CAW 384, ADW-IM; 24 August 1948, Hermine Bäcker to Asta Rostger, ADW, CAW 391A, ADW-IM; "Bericht über die Arbeitstagung über Grundfragen der Gefährdetenfürsorge," 18–21 June 1946, ADW, CAW 571, ADW-IM; "Vom Dienst der evangelischen Mütterhilfe," (n.d., [1951]), ADW, CAW 391, ADW-IM.

93. Excerpt from April 20, 1949, report of Protestant women's work in Germany, ffm #9, ADW, BP 220/42 Bd. 1, ADW-IM. The physician was Hans Harmsen. See also "Not und Hilfe," *NB* 2 (15 April 1948): 1. On abortion in the immediate aftermath of the war, see Grossmann, *Reforming Sex,* 189–212.

94. Lund, "Möchten Sie"; also Riebe, "Das Dilemma der sieben Millionen."

95. Ruemelin, "Der grosse Entschluß," *Sie* 1/3 (February 1946): 2; also "Die Frau von heute gibt Auskunft," *Fvh* 1/2 (March 1946): 20.

96. "Nur der Kinder wegen . . . ," *Constanze* 1 (October 1948): 3.

97. "Tut Scheiden weh?" *Constanze* 2 (January 1949): 3–4, here 3.

98. "Worte, die uns Wege weisen," *Fvh* 1/1 (February 1946): inside title page; Marianne Jahn, "Der blaue Leopold," *Fvh* 1/2 (March 1946): 26. See also the reader's query on how to divorce her imprisoned husband in order to marry her new love: "Die Aussprache," *Fvh* 3/5 (March 1948): 24.

99. von Hollander, "Zum Thema" 2/49.

100. Prollius, "Ein Königreich." See also "Mir reicht's!" *Constanze* 1 (December 1948): 7.

101. Petra Lund, "Darf man Ehen stören?" *Constanze* 2/6 (March 1949): 3; Lund, "Möchten Sie"; see also Riebe, "Das Dilemma."

102. "Gefahren der Strasse," *Fvh* 1/20 (December 1946): 8; "Im Spiegel des Tatbestandes," *Fvh* 1/21 (December 1946): 26. "Der Versuchung entzogen," *Fvh* 3/2 (January 1948): 7, includes photos of formerly promiscuous women looking tidy after a period in a workhouse. *Neue Berliner Illustrierte,* intended for an audience of both sexes, ran more frequent illustrations of such themes; "Die Geissel der Nachkriegszeit," *NBI* 3/38 (1947): 4–5; "Verlorene Jugend?" *NBI* 4/4 (1948): 4–5.

103. Hilde Buse-Grundschöffel, "Das fremde Kind," *Fvh* 1/19 (November 1946): 23; Ursula Herold, "Himmelschlüssel," *Fvh* 3/6 (March 1948): 27.

104. Jan Koplowitz, "Schluß mit der Entwürdigung der Frau: Kämpft gegen die amerikanische Lebensweise in Westdeutschland," *Fvh* 7/11 (March 1952): 4–5; Jan Koplowitz, "Schaufenster der Entwürdigung," *Fvh* 7/12 (March 1952): 8–9. East German publications also blamed the "American life-style" for West German divorces; see the series "Zum Entwurf des neuen Familiengesetzbuches," *Fvh* (July-September 1954).

105. Hilde Schneider, Leserbrief, *Sie* 2/31 (3 August 1947): 4.

106. "Die berufstätige Ehefrau unter der Lupe," *Fvh* 1/15 (September 1946): 7; "Die Frau von heute gibt Auskunft," *Fvh* 1/2 (March 1946): 20; "Vereinte Herzen— getrennte Güter," *Fvh* 1/19 (November 1946): 26–27; "Die Aussprache," *Fvh* 3 (February 1948): 18; "Haushalt und Ledigensteuer," *Fvh* 3/5 (March 1948): 24; "Wir protestieren," *Fvh* 3/7 (April 1948): 18–19; Kern, "Unsere eigene Sache. . . ."

107. Baumert, *Deutsche Familien*, 174, 176.

108. Seeler, "Ehe, Familie," 118.

109. Kokula, "Lesbisch leben," 160.

110. von Hollander, "Zum Thema" 2/49; Hilde Pfann, Leserbrief, *Sie* 3/38 (19 September 1948): 4; Esther Harding, "Frauenfreundschaften," *WF* 1 (November 1949): 16–17, 43–45.

111. Meta Kaasch, Leserbrief, *Sie* 1/24 (19 May 1946): 2; Hilde Pfann, Leserbrief, *Sie* 3/6 (8 February 1948): 4; "Wir rufen zur Diskussion," *Fvh* 2/2 (January 1947): 4–5; Karl Jagodzinski, "Neue Ziele der Wohnungspolitik," *AS* 3 (1948): 185.

112. "Kann vor Sorgen nicht einschlafen!" *Constanze* 1 (October 1948): 5, 11. See also Hilde Marks, Leserbrief, *Sie* 2/43 (26 October 1947): 4; "Gefällt Ihnen mein Vorschlag?" *Fvh* 7/14 (April 1952): 18; "Wie mein Vorschlag gefallen hat," *Fvh* 7/23 (June 1952): 18.

113. "Die Aussprache," *Fvh* 2/21 (November 1947): 18–19.

114. Lia Scholz, Leserbrief, *Sie* 3/7 (15 February 1948): 4; Meta Kaasch, Leserbrief, *Sie* 1/24 (19 May 1946): 2; Helene Beer, "Töchter und kein Mann: 80 Jahre Lettehaus," *Fvh* 1/4 (April 1946): 2–3. See also "Die Wohnung der berufstätigen Frau," *AS* 2 (1947): 244; "Die Wohnung der berufstätige Frau," *AS* 3 (1948): 151–52. Little such housing was ensuingly built in either Germany.

115. Baumert, *Deutsche Familien*, 180.

116. Else Rothärmel, Leserbrief, *Sie* 2/51 (21 December 1947): 4; see also "Die Aussprache," *Fvh* 3/4 (February 1948): 18; "Die ganz und gar glückliche Ehe," *Constanze* (October 1949), quoted in Seeler, "Ehe, Familie," 100–101.

117. Dita Pflug, Leserbrief, *Sie* 3/1 (4 January 1948): 4; Ingeborg Goldbeck, Leserbrief, *Sie* 3/4 (25 January 1948): 4; Thomas Fabricius, Leserbrief, *Sie* 3/4 (25 January 1948): 4; von Hollander, "Ein zweites Mal nicht!"; Schreiner, "Es geht um den Mann."

118. *Monthly Report . . . : Education and Religion* 3 (20 October 1945): 4.

119. *Monthly Report* 17 (1–30 November 1946): 18.

120. Sociologists sometimes proved the exception; see, for example, Thurnwald, *Gegenwartsprobleme*, 98, 105, 212.

121. [Banner], *Sie* 1/55 (22 December 1946): 1.

122. For example, Karl Peters, "Die Kriminalität und Verwahrlosung der Waisen und Halbwaisen," *Jugendwohl* 29 (November-December 1948): 3–4; Gerhard Nätebus, "Juvenile Criminal Law—Reform?" *Start Berlin* (29 August 1947) (translation), Abt. 649 8/64-2/1, HHA; Schimmel, "Der Einfluß."

123. "Die Früchte aus Nachbars Garten," *Fvh* 1/7 (May 1946): 27; "'Acht Tage

Verachtung' oder ein neues Leben liegt vor ihnen," *Fvh* 1/11 (July 1946): 8–9; Gisela Jagodzinski, "Schuljugend und Wohnverhältnisse," *AS* 2 (1947): 149–50.

124. For example, Torrel, "Auf ihren Schultern"; Maria Dornow, "Von Frau zu Frau," *Sie* 2 (5 January 1947): 6; Marion Sehmsdorf, Leserbrief, *Sie* 1/24 (19 May 1946): 2; "Kleine 'Schieber'—Grosse Gefahren," *Fvh* 1/7 (May 1946): 26. For an exception, see "Auf der schiefen Ebene . . . und auf der richtigen Bahn," *NBI* 2/26 (August 1946): 4–7.

125. Else Feldbinder, "Mütter ohne Liebe," *Sie* 1/54 (15 December 1946): 2.

126. Feldbinder, "Zwischen Tanzbar und Gesundheitsamt," 9.

127. "Statt Scheidung ein Versöhnungskuß!" *Constanze* 2/5 (March 1949): 4–5.

128. Alexander Pauly, "Ich mußte viele Ehen scheiden," *Constanze* 2/17 (August 1949): 12–13; "Warum heiraten wir eigentlich?" *Constanze* 2/18 (September 1949): 14–15; "Muß wirklich gleich geschieden sein?" *Constanze* 2/20 (September 1949): 12; "Keine Ehe wird im Himmel gelebt!" *Constanze* 2/21 (October 1949): 10.

129. Alexander Pauly, "Ehe man Ehefrau wird . . . ," *Constanze* 22 (October 1949): 7.

130. See *Frauenstimme*, the women's magazine of the Deutsche Angestellten Gewerkschaft; *Frauen und Arbeit*, of the Deutsche Gewerkschaftsbund; *Gleichheit*, of the SPD.

131. See the series "Zum Entwurf des neuen Familiengesetzbuches," *Fvh* 9/28–33 (July-September 1954); Kern, "Unsere eigene Sache"; "Die nächste, Bitte," *Fvh* 6/2 (January 1951): 22; "Die Frau von heute ist der Meinung . . . ," *Fvh* 6/42 (October 1951): 2; "Die nächste, Bitte," *Fvh* 6/14 (April 1951): 22; Fritz Niethammer, "Inwieweit hat sich die rechtliche Stellung des nichtehelichen Kindes gebessert?" *Fvh* 7/12 (March 1952): 21. See also the column "Hier spricht der Jurist," *Fvh* (beginning October 1951).

132. "Wir wollen offen darüber sprechen," *Fvh* 8/9 (February 1953): 11; "Zum Entwurf des neuen Familiengesetzbuches," *Fvh* 9/36 (September 1954): 10; Ruth von Saher, "Ehen die gerettet wurden," *Fvh* 11/33 (August 1956): 6–7.

133. "Meine liebe Liselott," *Fvh* 3/4 (February 1948): 7. See also "Kann auch eine Frau einen Heiratsantrag machen?" *Fvh* 6/38 (September 1951): 10, which advises women to meet potential mates by joining a party organization.

134. See, for example, "Die Frau von heute gibt Auskunft," *Fvh* 1/2 (March 1946): 20; also Chapter Eight.

135. "Wir sprachen mit Frauen vom DFD," *Fvh* 3/5 (March 1948): 18–19; "Mein Tag gehört dem Frieden," *Fvh* 6/36 (September 1951): 9; "Mein Werkzeug—Meine Drehbank—Mein Betrieb!" *Fvh* 6/38 (September 1951): 13; "Frauen die uns helfen werden," *Fvh* 7/16 (April 1952): 6; "In dieser Woche besuchten wir Edith Baumann," *Fvh* 9/32 (August 1954): 2.

136. Charlotte Kettner, Leserbrief, *Sie* 3/4 (January 1948): 4.

137. The quote may be apocryphal; quoted in Schreiner, "Es geht um den Mann."

138. The reputation of the local occupation forces—whether as suppliers of chocolate or as rapists—may account for at least part of the discrepancy. Compare Niethammer, von Plato, and Wierling, *Die volkseigene Erfahrung*, 362; Niethammer, *"Hinterher merkt man,"* 31.

CHAPTER 6: RESTORING THE DIFFERENCE

1. Helene Weber, quoted in *Gesellschaftspolitische Kommentare* 6/7 (1 May 1954): 9ff., reprinted in Ruhl, *Frauen in der Nachkriegszeit*, 179–85, here 184.

2. Anna Haag, "Frau und Politik," speech of 24 March 1946, reprinted in Freier and Kuhn, *"Das Schicksal,"* 158–59.

3. References to the *Männerstaat* were frequent; see, for example, Elfriede Nebgen, *Frauen gestern und heute* (Berlin, 1946), excerpted in Freier and Kuhn, *"Das Schicksal,"* 162–64; Strecker, *Überleben ist nicht genug,* 53; Bäumer, *Der neue Weg der deutschen Frau,* 24.

4. Rupieper, "Bringing Democracy to the Frauleins."

5. Freier, "Frauenfragen sind Lebensfragen—Über die naturwüchsige Deckung von Tagespolitik und Frauenpolitik nach dem Zweiten Weltkrieg"; Harsch, "Public Continuity and Private Change?"

6. Kolinsky, *Women in Contemporary Germany,* 209, 222.

7. Nebgen, *Frauen gestern und heute,* in Freier and Kuhn, *"Das Schicksal,"* 164.

8. Strecker, *Überleben,* 104.

9. See the many sketches of female activists in Moeller, *Protecting Motherhood.*

10. Kolinsky, *Women,* 225.

11. Strecker, *Überleben,* 110–13.

12. Parlamentarischer Rat, Hauptausschuß, 17. Sitzung, 3 December 1948, 206–7, PA, quoted in Moeller, *Protecting Motherhood,* 51. On nineteenth-century feminism's emphasis on motherhood, see Allen, *Feminism and Motherhood in Germany 1800–1914.*

13. Moeller, *Protecting Motherhood,* 50.

14. *Hessische Nachrichten,* 24 January 1949, reprinted in Späth, "Vielfältige Forderungen nach Gleichberechtigung und 'nur' ein Ergebnis: Artikel 3 Absatz 2 GG," 147; see also Böttger, *Das Recht auf Gleichheit und Differenz,* 191–214.

15. Parlamentarischer Rat, Hauptausschuß, 43. Sitzung, 18 January 1949, Z5/50, folio 931, BAK.

16. Quoted in Feuersenger, *Die garantierte Gleichberechtigung,* 50. For the SPD's formulation of marriage and the family, see Parlamentarischer Rat, Ausschuß für Grundsatzfragen, 29. Sitzung, 4 December 1948, Z5/35, folio 1181, BAK; for the KPD's formulation, which made no mention of marriage whatsoever, see Parlamentarischer Rat, Hauptausschuß, 43. Sitzung, 18 January 1949, Z5/50, folio 947, BAK.

17. See, for example, Parlamentarischer Rat, Hauptausschuß, 43. Sitzung, 18 January 1949, Z5/50, folios 944, 951, BAK.

18. Parlamentarischer Rat, Hauptausschuß, 43. Sitzung, 18 January 1949, Z5/50, in order folios 952–53, 941, 955, 960, BAK.

19. Heuss initially supported equal rights regardless of legitimacy. His change of heart probably doomed the clause to defeat. Parlamentarischer Rat, Ausschuß für Grundsatzfragen, 29. Sitzung, 4 December 1948, Z5/35, folio 1150, BAK; Parlamentarischer Rat, Ausschuß für Grundsatzfragen, 30. Sitzung, 6 December 1948, Z5/35, folios 1114, 1119, BAK.

20. *Statistik der BRD* 35/8: 28–32; *Statistik der BRD* 35/9: 78; Gerhard Bomhoff, "Die Folgen des zweiten Weltkrieges für unsere Jugend," *NB* 13 (1959): 117–18.

21. For more detailed discussion of legal reforms concerning marriage, see Moeller, *Protecting Motherhood,* 76–108.

22. Rausch, "Politisches Bewußtsein und politische Einstellungen im Wandel."

23. If the husband was the guilty party in the divorce, the wife might argue for alimony or a divorce settlement. Both, however, presumed a priori male ownership of property. If the women bore a share of the guilt or if the divorce was no-fault, the ex-wife had no claim on any of the property defined by law as her husband's. For pleas for

reform, see Josepha Fischer-Erling, "Das heutige Scheidungsrecht—ein Gesetz gegen die Frau," *Die katholische Frau* 5/3 (March 1952): 10, SF; "Zwanzig Jahre umsonst gearbeitet!" *Constanze* 4/16 (August 1951): 20–21.

24. Bremme, *Die politische Rolle der Frau in Deutschland.*

25. For Würmeling's language on single people and couples with few children or none, see *VdBT,* 2. Wahlperiode, 15. Sitzung, 12 February 1954, 488–93; "Grundlage der Gesellschaft ist die Familie," *BPIB* 21 (November 1953): 1851–54. On Christian conservatives' concerns about materialism and secularism, see Mitchell, "Materialism and Secularism"; Dickinson, *The Politics,* 264–73.

26. On differences between organized Protestantism and organized Catholicism on related matters, see Dickinson, *The Politics,* 244–83.

27. Moeller, *Protecting Motherhood,* 87, 97.

28. See, for example, conflicts between Würmeling and fiscal conservatives over "money for children"; ibid., 109–41; Ruhl, *Verordnete Unterordnung,* 156–75.

29. Moeller, *Protecting Motherhood,* 204–9.

30. Women also continued to relinquish legal rights over their bodies upon marriage. Husbands had a right to sex with their wives regardless of the wives' desires. The legal provision of the "housewife marriage" was discarded in 1977. Kolinsky, *Women,* 49–51.

31. For greater detail on illegitimacy law, see Heineman, "Complete Families, Half Families, No Families at All."

32. On institutional continuities, see Dickinson, *The Politics,* 244–45.

33. Elisabeth Zillken, "Zur Abänderung des Unehelichenrechts" (typescript, n.d. [1950–52]), 319.4 E VII, 3 Fasz. 9: 1949–61, DCV; Walter Becker, "Vorschläge zur Neugestaltung des Rechts des unehelichen Kindes," *WF* 7 (August 1952): 29–31.

34. Walter Becker, "Zur Frage der Neuordnung des Unehelichenrechts" (typescript, n.d. [1949–50]), attached to letter to Elisabeth Zillken, 20 March 1950, 319.4 SKF E VII, 3 Fasz. 7: 1949–55, DCV; Elisabeth Zillken, "Zur Abänderung des Unehelichenrechts" (typescript, n.d. [1950–52]), 319.4 E VII, 3 Fasz. 9: 1949–61, DCV.

35. Elisabeth Zillken, "Zur Abänderung des Unehelichenrechts" (typescript, n.d. [1950–52]), 319.4 E VII, 3 Fasz. 9: 1949–61, DCV. See also Becker, "Zur Frage der Neuordnung des Unehelichenrechts" (see note 34); Beitzke, Webler, Deutsches Institut für Vormundschaftswesen, September 1958, to the Mitglieder des Rechtsausschusses des Bundestages, B141/15643, BAK; "Vorläufige Stellungnahme der Zentrale des katholischen Fürsorgevereins für Mädchen, Frauen und Kinder e.V., Dortmund, zu dem Entwurf eines Gesetzes zur Vereinheitlichung und Änderung familienrechtlicher Vorschriften," B141/15643, BAK.

36. Christa Hasenclever, "Zur Reform des Unehelichenrechts," *NB* 7 (October 1953): 1–3; "Debatte um das Unehelichenrecht," *NB* 5 (July 1951): 7.

37. Kurzprotokoll, 17. Sitzung des Ausschusses für Familien- und Jugendfragen, Bundestag, 4 February 1959, III/394A 1 #11, folio 17/9, PA; Groth, *Kinder ohne Familie.* On the history of guardianship, see Dickinson, *The Politics.*

38. Protokoll: Konferenz eines Unterausschusses des Fachausschusses Jugendwohlfahrt am 14. und 15. November 1959 in Frankfurt, AW.

39. Maria Hagemeyer, "Zum Familienrechtsänderungsgesetz," *IF* 7/12 (1958) (Abschrift), B141/15643, BAK; Der Präsident des Landgerichts in Göttingen to the Herrn Oberlandesgerichtspräsidenten in Celle, 8 April 1959, B141/15641, BAK; Hagemeyer, *Der Entwurf des Familiengesetzbuches der "Deutschen Demokratischen Republik."*

40. Oberlandesgerichtsrat Dr. F. J. Finke, "Zum neuen Entwurf eines Gesetzes zur

Vereinheitlichung und Änderung familienrechtlicher Vorschriften," *EF* 5 (1958): 353–58.

41. Stenographisches Protokoll, 3. Sitzung des Unterausschusses Familienrechtsänderungsgesetz des Rechtsausschusses am 23. September 1960, B141/15644, BAK; Ausschuß für Familien- und Jugendfragen, Ausschußdrucksache 16, 15 April 1959, B141/15643, BAK.

42. Boehmer, *Die Teilreform des Familienrechts durch das Gleichberechtigungsgesetz vom 18. Juni 1957 und das Familienrechtsänderungsgesetz vom 11. August 1961,* 60–64.

43. Bericht des Ausschusses für Familien- und Jugendfragen zu Drucksache 530: Entwurf eines Gesetzes zur Vereinheitlichung und Änderung familienrechtlicher Vorschriften (n.d. [late 1959]), B141/15644, BAK.

44. Bosch, *Familienrechtsreform.*

45. 5 November 1959, Evangelische Kirche in Deutschland to Herrn BMJ, B141/15645, BAK.

46. Moeller, *Protecting Motherhood,* 85–86. For the debate in general, see B141/15645–46, BAK.

47. Wolf, Lücke, and Hax, *Scheidung,* 210.

48. For a summary of significant decisions regarding divorce, see Walther J. Habscheid, "Die Rechtssprechung zu den Folgen der Eheauflösung," *EF* 6 (1959): 317–24.

49. For the introduction of the amendment, 3 March 1961, Stenographisches Protokoll, 10. Sitzung des Unterausschusses Familienänderungsgesetz des Rechtsausschusses, B141/15647, BAK. For sample objections, Ruth Tangemann, "Änderung des Eherechts durch die Hintertür?" *Freie Demokratische Korrespondenz,* 18 May 1961, JG 12/38: 5–8, B141/15647, BAK; 8 May 1961, Landgerichtsrat Stüben, Landesjustizverwaltung Hamburg 3400–1c/3 to Herrn BMJ, B141/15647, BAK; 26 April 1961, Stenographisches Protokoll, 147. Sitzung des Rechtsausschusses des DBT, B141/15648, BAK.

50. Wittrock, Auszug aus dem Kurzprotokoll der 152. Sitzung des Rechtsausschusses des 3. DBT vom 8. Juni 1961, B141/15648, BAK. The 1977 reform of family law eased no-fault divorce further; Kolinsky, *Women,* 49–54.

51. Hasenclever, *Jugendhilfe und Jugendgesetzgebung seit 1900,* 208–9. The law did not create full legal equality; see Berghahn and Fritzsche, *Frauenrecht in Ost und West Deutschland,* 168–70.

52. Ruhl, *Verordnete Unterordnung,* 221–24.

53. Maria Schulte Langenforth, "Frauenlöhne und Grundgesetz," *Bundesarbeitsblatt* (1953): 74–76.

54. Moeller, *Protecting Motherhood,* 152–53; Ruhl, *Verordnete Unterordnung,* 275–79.

55. Ruhl, *Verordnete Unterordnung,* 327; Moeller, *Protecting Motherhood,* 162–73.

56. *SJ-BRD* (1952): 32, 44.

57. The following is drawn from Moeller, *Protecting Motherhood,* 109–30; Moeller, "Reconstructing the Family"; Ruhl, *Verordnete Unterordnung,* 156–75.

58. Alfons Montag, "Unverantwortliche Kindergeld- und Altrentengesetze," *Frankfurter Rundschau,* 16–17 October 1954, B153/758, folio 166, BAK.

59. Gesetz über die Gewährung von Kindergeld und die Errichtung von Familienausgleichskassen, 1954 (*BGBl* I 333–40).

60. "Sozialrecht noch verworrener," *Vorwärts,* 14 July 1955, B153/758, folio 17, BAK.

61. "Noch 136 000 unerledigte Kindergeld-Anträge," *Westfälische Rundschau,* 24 May 1955, B153/758, folio 34, BAK.

62. Ruhl, *Frauen in der Nachkriegszeit,* 74–77, 89–91; Garner, "Public Service Personnel," 54.

63. Garner, "Public Service Personnel," 55.

64. Ibid., 59.

65. Bohne, *Das Geschick,* 55.

66. "Zur Berufsnot der älteren Angestellten," *IF* 3 7–8 (1954): 18–19; "Zum Problem: 'Ältere Angestellte,'" *FB* 2/2 (1952): 1; "Für die älteren Angestellten," *FB* 4/2 (1954): 5; "Noch einmal: Die älteren Angestellten," *FB* 4/5 (1954): 5–6; "Das Problem 'Ältere Angestellte,'" *FB* 8/5 (1958): 34; "Zu alt fürs Vorzimmer?" *FB* 10/10 (1960): 67; "Keine Chance für ältere Frauen?" *Constanze* 6/3 (February 1953): 24–25; Maria Tritz, "Vermittlungsfähigkeit arbeitsloser Frauen," *FB* 3/5 (1953): 3.

67. "So geht es nicht, Herr Bundesminister!" *FB* 5/3 (1955): 21–22; see also "Zusätzliche Einstellung von arbeitslosen älteren Angestellten," *FB* 4/12 (1954): 4.

68. Rationalisierungs-Kuratorium der deutschen Wirtschaft, ed., *Frauenarbeit,* 14–25. See also Bohne, *Das Geschick,* 39ff.

69. Käthe Mahrt, "Die Berufsnot der weiblichen Jugend," *Bundesarbeitsblatt* 3 (1953): 468–69. Boys who wished to enter vocational training did so as a matter of routine.

70. Christa Morawe, "Die Lage der älteren weiblichen Angestellten," *Bundesarbeitsblatt* 5 (1955): 274–77; Garner, "Public Service Personnel," 60–62.

71. Figures for salaried employees exclude those earning over DM 600 per month (mainly men) and employees under the age of twenty (mainly women); this makes the gap look artificially narrow. *SJ-BRD* (1952): 412, 433; *SJ-BRD* (1963): 497, 506.

72. Hedwig Matuschek, "Auswirkungen der Steuerreform," *FB* 8/9 (September 1958): 1–2; "Kommt die 'Steuerstrafe' für Ledige?" *FB* 7/12 (December 1957): 83–84; "VWA protestierte gegen Junggesellensteuer," *FB* 9/9 (September 1959): 61; Margot Kalinke, "Sollen wir Frauen allein die Lasten tragen?" *FB* 4/7–8 (July-August 1954): 1–5. For a similar discussion regarding public housing, see "Wohnungsbau für alleinstehende berufstätige Frauen," *IF* 5/2 (February 1956): 7–8; "Bauen wir in Deutschland richtig?" *FB* 10/5 (May 1960): 34; 14 January 1956, Verband der weiblichen Angestellten to the Bundesminister für Wohnungsbau, B134/3497, BAK.

73. "Wann kommt die Sozialreform?" *FB* 5/11 (November 1955): 75–78, here 76.

74. Moeller, *Protecting Motherhood,* 131.

75. Hildegard Bleyler, "Die berufstätige Frau in der Sozialversicherung," *FB* 6/4 (April 1956): 27–28; Margot Kalinke, "Werden die Frauen wieder vergessen?" *FB* 6/10 (October 1956): 70–71.

76. Schmidt, "Im Vorzimmer," 192ff., 214.

77. Bohne, *Das Geschick,* 41ff.; Hofmann and Kersten, *Frauen zwischen Familie und Fabrik,* 26–27; Kolkmann and Schlißke, *Mütter allein,* 193; Wirtz, *Die Witwe,* 135.

78. Sch. interview, Institut für Geschichte und Biographie—Fern-Universität Hagen; see also Bohne, *Das Geschick,* 55.

79. See *Frauenstimme,* the women's magazine of the Deutsche Angestellten Gewerkschaft; *Frauen und Arbeit,* of the Deutsche Gewerkschaftsbund; *Gleichheit,* of the SPD.

80. For greater detail on war widows, see Heineman, "Complete Families";

Tumpek-Kjellmark, "From Hitler's Widows to Adenauer's Brides." For a more detailed examination of the role of media scandal in formulating perceptions of women and sexual danger, see Walkowitz, *City of Dreadful Delight.*

81. "Victims of war" were eligible for welfare and for pensions provided to those who had been injured, widowed, or orphaned for other reasons, such as industrial accidents. The Western Allies subsequently relaxed this prohibition, and individual states developed a variety of military-related pensions. A federal law of March 1950 allowed for consideration of hardship cases. Gesetz zur Verbesserung von Leistungen an Kriegsopfer vom 27. März 1950 (*BGBl* 77).

82. Gesetz über die Versorgung der Opfer des Krieges (Bundesversorgungsgesetz) vom 20. Dezember 1950 (*BGBl* 791). For detailed examinations of the Law to Aid Victims of War, see Diehl, *The Thanks of the Fatherland;* Hudemann, *Sozialpolitik.* For statistical overviews of beneficiaries of the law, see Schönleiter, *Die Kriegsopferversorgung; Die Leistungen der Bundesrepublik Deutschland auf dem Gebiet der Kriegsopferversorgung 1.4.1950– 31.12.1956* (Bonn, n.d. [1957]); "Kriegsopferversorgung 1950–1977" (pamphlet, RKZSH, n.d. [1977]), ZSg1-156/8(1), BAK.

83. On payments to victims of Nazism, see Goschler, *Wiedergutmachung.* A law assisting those who had lost their homes or property to bombing raids or to flight from the East was also passed early and with little controversy.

84. Bundestag proceedings of 13 September 1950 (84. Sitzung), VdBT 1950: 3176, 3178; Bundestag proceedings of 19 October 1950 (93. Sitzung), VdBT 1950: 3442.

85. Niethammer, *Entnazifizierung;* Garner, "Public Service Personnel."

86. The term *orphan* referred generically to "full orphans," who had lost both parents, and to "half orphans," who had lost one parent.

87. See also Franke and Bazille, eds., *Das tapfere Leben,* 20–21; Inge Gerth, "Zur sozialen Lage der Kriegerwitwen," *Sozialarbeit* 7 (1958): 152–56, here 155.

88. On widows: Verhandlungen des (26.) Ausschusses für Kriegsopfer- und Kriegsgefangenenfragen des Deutschen Bundestages über das Bundesversorgungsgesetz, 107D, I/87A, Lfd. 10, PA. On veterans: Diehl, *The Thanks,* 228.

89. Stenographisches Protokoll (Abschrift), 32. Sitzung des Ausschusses für Kriegsopfer- und Kriegsgefangenenfragen, 28 September 1950, I/87A, Bd. 2, p. 61, PA.

90. Stenographisches Protokoll (Abschrift), 37. Sitzung des Ausschusses für Kriegsopfer- und Kriegsgefangenenfragen, 11 October 1950, I/87A, Bd. 2, pp. 19, 21, PA. In fact, wartime provisions awarded only token amounts to women who had not lived with or been supported by their husbands and who had no marital children; see chapter 3.

91. Diehl, *The Thanks,* 231.

92. They began to collect pensions in August 1953, by which time their numbers had declined to about thirty-eight thousand. Schönleiter, "Zweites Gesetz zur Änderung und Ergänzung des Bundesversorgungsgesetzes."

93. Able-bodied widows age forty to fifty who cared for an orphan received a reduced supplementary allowance; disabled widows and those over fifty received the full supplementary allowance. Periodic revisions to the law raised the pensions.

94. *Drei Jahre Landeswohlfahrtsverband Hessen, 1953–56,* 51.

95. Maria Probst, "Die Stellung der Christlich-Sozialen-Union zur Kriegsopferversorgung," draft article for *Festschrift Bayern-Kurier* (n.d. [late October 1955]), NL219/16, BAK.

96. L. Degner, Leserbrief, *Sie* 2/1 (5 January 1947): 4; see also Julianne Frieser, "Die Frau von Heute," *Wille und Weg* (September 1949): 80.

97. Der Arbeitsminister des Landes Nordrhein-Westfalen—Hauptabt. LAA (Iid—

5340), Vermerk: Vermittlung von Kriegshinterbliebenen, 17 August 1950, LAA-NW 237, folios 133–37, NRW; Präsident des LAA Württemberg-Baden #506/49 to the AA, 1 December 1949, Abt. 460 AA Tauberbischofsheim 18, GLK; Präsident des LAA Württemberg-Baden #108/49 to the AA, 7 March 1949, Abt. 460 AA Tauberbischofsheim 18, GLK; LAA Baden-Württemburg (Der Präsident—Ia 5350 A/320) to Herrn Präsident der BAA, 15 June 1954, B119/2967, BAK.

98. Pars. 25–27, BVG. Social welfare was regulated mainly by the 1951 Grundsätze über Voraussetzung, Art und Maß der öffentlichen Fürsorge; the paragraphs concerning occupational assistance to victims of war were coincidentally Paragraphs 25–27.

99. "Berufsförderung für Kriegerwitwen," *VdK Mitteilungen* 4 (July 1954): 310–11; "Die Hauptfürsorgestellen, ihre Aufgaben und ihre Tätigkeit," Landeswohlfahrtsverband Hessen—Hauptfürsorgestelle (n.d. [1953]), Abt. 508/3195, HHA; "Bericht über die Tätigkeit der Hauptfürsorgestelle Kassel im Rechnungsjahr 1951," Abt. 508/3195, HHA.

100. Deutscher Städtetag to the Bundesministerium für Arbeit (copy), 20 June 1950, B106/10726, BAK; Der Geschäftsführer des Bundesausschusses der Kriegsbeschädigten- und Kriegshinterbliebenen-Fürsorge im Bundesministerium des Innern, Übersicht der Gesetzentwürfe und Stellungnahmen zur zukünftigen Gestaltung des SBG, 12 April 1951, B106/10745, BAK.

101. Bundesministerium für Arbeit (II b 4—2380.1), Entwurf eines Schwerbeschädigtengesetzes, 9 October 1951, B119/1726, BAK; Begründung des Gesetzes über die Beschäftigung Schwerbeschädigter (Schwerbeschädigtengesetz) (n.d. [probably draft of January 1952]), B119/1726, BAK.

102. 28 November 1952, LAA (IIe 3—5340.10) Vermerk, LAA-BR 1134/587, folio 14, NRW; Begründung des Gesetzes über die Beschäftigung Schwerbeschädigter (Schwerbeschädigtengesetz) (n.d. [probably draft of January 1952]), B119/1726, BAK.

103. "Hinterbliebenenkonferenz des VdK in Bad Godesberg," *VdK Mitteilungen* 1 (September 1951): 224–25; Der Staatssekretär des Bundeskanzleramtes (7—81003—669/52) to the Bundesministerien für Arbeit, des Innern, und der Finanzen, 15 March 1952, B149/16571, BAK; "Frauenarbeit im Blickfeld der Fürsorge," *DVöpF* 3 (April-May 1948): 84–86; "Wir fordern Arbeit für die Hinterbliebenen," *Wille und Weg* (August 1948): 68; "Hinterbliebenen-Konferenz des Reichsbundes in Hamburg," *Reichsbund* (August 1952): 4; Ursula Alter, "Mit der Sicherung von Arbeitsplätzen ist uns nicht gedient," *Wille und Weg* (June 1952): 87.

104. Max Wuttke, "Stellungnahme des Sprechers des VdK, Hauptgeschäftsführer Max Wuttke, zum Entwurf des Gesetzes über die Beschäftigung Schwerbeschädigter," delivered to the Bundestag Ausschuss der Kriegsbeschädigten- und Kriegshinterbliebenen-Fürsorge on June 27, 1952, B119/2965, BAK; Max Wuttke, "Hinterbliebenenversorgung und Hinterbliebenenarbeit" *VdK Mitteilungen* 2 (1952): 531–38, here 534.

105. Der Geschäftsführer des Bundesausschusses der Kriegsbeschädigten- und Kriegshinterbliebenen-Fürsorge im Bundesministerium des Innern, Übersicht der Gesetzentwürfe und Stellungnahmen zur zukünftigen Gestaltung des SBG, 12 April 1951, B106/10745, BAK.

106. "Förderung und Hilfe für Kriegsopfer," *BPIB* 38 (25 February 1954): 311–12.

107. The subcommittee included Elisabeth Selbert, Maria Detzel, in charge of survivors' welfare for the VdK, and Frau K. Vollnberg, who had a similar position with the Reichsbund. Ergebnis-Protokoll über die Sitzung des Bundesausschusses der Kriegsbeschädigten- und Kriegshinterbliebenenfürsorge am 18. Februar 1954, B149/7272, BAK; Ergebnis-Protokoll über die Sitzung des Bundesausschusses der Kriegs-

beschädigten- und Kriegshinterbliebenenfürsorge am 22. Juni 1955, B149/7272, BAK; Vermerk über die gemeinsame Sitzung der Arbeitsausschüsse Soziale Fürsorge und Hinterbliebenenfürsorge des Bundesausschusses der Kriegsbeschädigten- und Kriegshinterbliebenenfürsorge am 25. Juni 1958, B149/7273, BAK; Ergebnis-Protokoll über die Sitzung des Bundesausschusses der Kriegsbeschädigten- und Kriegshinterbliebenenfürsorge am 26. Juni 1958, B149/7273, BAK.

108. "Richtlinien des Verwaltungsrates der BAA über die Bildung bes. Vermittlungsstellen für Schwerbeschädigte sowie Witwen und Ehefrauen der Kriegs- und Arbeitsopfer vom 17. Dezember 1953," B149/16516, BAK; "Allgemeine Verwaltungsvorschriften des Verwaltungsrates der BAA über die bevorzugte Arbeitsvermittlung der Witwen und Ehefrauen der Kriegs- und Arbeitsopfer vom 14. Mai 1954," *Die Praxis* 7 (June 1954): 180–82; Max Wuttke, "Das Schwerbeschädigtengesetz in der praktischen Durchführung," *VdK Mitteilungen* 5 (1955): 77–83.

109. LAA Nordrhein-Westfalen, Rdvfg. 225/55 to the Herrn Direktoren der AA, 28 July 1955, LAA-NW 234, folios 202–8, NRW; LAA Nordrhein-Westfalen, Rdvfg. 144/54 (Id 2/54) to the Herrn Direktoren der AA, 5 May 1954, LAA-NW 235, folios 266–68, NRW; BAA, Ref. ORR Dr. Schwarz, to the Präsidenten der LAA, 22 July 1953, B119/2967, BAK; Auswertung der Erfahrungsberichte der AA über die Betreuung von Witwen und Ehefrauen der Kriegs- und Arbeitsopfer, Stand 30. August 1954, LAA-NW 235, folios 274–80, NRW; "Mehr Berufsförderung für Kriegerwitwen," *Reichsbund* (July 1957): 11; "Kriegerwitwen sind zu bevorzugen!" *Die Fackel* (April 1955): 10.

110. BAA, Auswertung der zahlenmässigen Ergebnisse der Anzeigen gemäss Par.11 SBG nach dem Beschäftigtenstand vom 1. November 1955 (Stand der Bearbeitung der Anzeigen am 15. Mai 1956), B106/10727, BAK; *Die Beschäftigung Schwerbeschädigter*, 5.

111. Der Senator für das Wohlfahrtswesen, Bremen (Degener) (412—04—05/10) to the Bundesminister des Innern, 16 July 1955, B106/10683, BAK. See also Niederschrift über die Hauptversammlung der Arbeitsgemeinschaft der Deutschen Hauptfürsorgestellen am 10.–11. September 1954 in Bremen, B149/7272, BAK; Auswertung der Erfahrungsberichte der AA über die Betreuung von Witwen und Ehefrauen der Kriegs- und Arbeitsopfer, Stand 30. August 1954, LAA-NW 235, folios 274–80, here 280, NRW.

112. Schulze, "Überlegungen zum Problem der 'Onkelehen.'"

113. For example, Marie-Elisabeth Lüders, "Gesetzliche oder 'freie' Ehe?" *WF* 7 (June 1952): 24–25. The origin of the estimate of one hundred thousand is unclear. West Germany's population in the mid-1950s was roughly fifty million.

114. Die Niedersächsische Frauenvereinigung to Franz-Joseph Würmeling, 10 November 1955, B153/1113, folios 134–35, BAK.

115. Böll, *Haus ohne Hüter*.

116. L. K. to Würmeling, 18 February 1955, B153/1113, folio 54, BAK.

117. Couples with children often had their offspring declared legitimate. The pair discussed here, like others, considered seeking a church that would recognize their situation as a "moral emergency" and exercise its right to perform a ceremony independent of a state-sanctioned marriage. See "'Onkel-Ehen': Stellungnahme zu einer kirchlichen Trauung vor der standesamtlichen Eheschliessung," *BPIB* 43 (4 March 1955): 359; Dr. Albrecht Röder, "Die Witwenrente," *Frankfurter Allgemeine Zeitung*, 20 December 1955, B153/1113, folio 139, BAK; Wolfgang Schrieber, "Das Problem der Onkelehen," *Die Praxis* 9 (April 1956): 158–60; "Neues Rentengesetz gegen 'Onkelehen' in Österreich," *Bonner Rundschau*, 1 July 1954, B149/1881, folio 77, BAK.

118. "Der Staat macht die lustigen Witwen," *Der Mittag*, 3–4 January 1953, 15,

B149/1881, folio 15, BAK. This file contains numerous clippings illustrating editorial support for improved provisions.

119. Forty-three percent found it understandable; the remainder did not know or said "it depended." Noelle-Neumann and Neumann, eds., *The Germans*, 66.

120. From private citizens, see letters to the Labor Ministry, B149/1881, BAK. From human-rights groups: Deutsche Liga für Menschenrecht to the Bundesministerium für Familie, 20 March 1956, B153/1113, folios 178–79, BAK. From social-welfare groups: Protokoll der Sitzung des Fachausschusses Jugendwohlfahrt in Bonn am 4. Februar 1955, AW; Schulze, "Überlegungen." From feminists: Ruth Tangemann, "Onkel billiger als Vati," *Das Frauen-Journal* 9 (1956): 13. From war victims' associations: "Erleichterung der Eheschliessung von Kriegerwitwen," *VdK Mitteilungen* 4 (January 1954): 38–39. From the Catholic church: "Denkschrift der katholischen Bischöfe Deutschlands zu den Fragen der 'Rentenkonkubinate,'" 25 February 1955, *EF* 3 (1956): 33. On the Protestant synod, Kolkmann and Schlißke, *Mütter allein*, 105.

121. Bundesministerium für Familie und Jugend (F3—6401—B) to Herrn Bundestagsabgeordneter Rainer Barzel (draft), 30 January 1959, B153/1113, folios 245–47, BAK.

122. 5. Novelle zum BVG, 1 April 1956. For summaries of the revisions, see Waldemar Schönleiter, "Fünftes Gesetz zur Änderung und Ergänzung des Bundesversorgungsgesetzes," *Bundesversorgungsblatt* (1956): 100–102; W[aldemar] Schönleiter, "Fünftes Gesetz zur Änderung und Ergänzung des Bundesversorgungsgesetzes," *BPIB* 130 (17 July 1956): 1291–92; Helmut Ziem, "Erstes Neuordnungsgesetz zur Reform des Kriegsopferrechts," *Sozialarbeit* 9 (1960): 289–93.

123. Moeller, *Protecting Motherhood*, 130–33. Statistics regarding the marriage of partners in wild marriages are not available. Of children born outside marriage in 1952, 25 to 30 percent were legitimized by the time they were six; many of these were probably born to cohabitants who later married. Groth, *Kinder ohne Familie*, 28.

124. On widows' poor health and high mortality, Freudenberg, *Die Sterblichkeit nach dem Familienstand in Westdeutschland 1949/1951; BPIB* 82 (3 May 1960): 798. On disability among men, Hudemann, *Sozialpolitik*, 528.

125. Dr. Fürst, Statistisches Bundesamt—der Präsident (VII K 04/03), 21 March 1955, B141/15635, BAK.

126. "Verwaltungsvorschriften Nr. 1 Abs. 2 zu Par. 45 BVG," cited in Ministry of Labor (IV b 3—1599/52), ORR Dr. Bürger to Herrn Bundesminister für Arbeit, 3 June 1952, B149/1876, folios 92–93, BAK.

127. Gesetz über die Änderung und Ergänzung familienrechtlicher Vorschriften und über die Rechtsstellung der Staatenlosen vom 12. April 1938 (*RGBl* I 380).

128. Familienrechtsgesetz (Entwurf) vom 15. Juli 1952, discussed in Ministerium für Justiz Dr. Bülow (3470/4–12 554/52) to Herrn Bundesminister für Arbeit, 23 July 1952, B149/1876, folio 96, BAK; Bundesminister für Justiz (3400/3–11 048/53) to Herrn Bundesminister für Arbeit Anton Storch, 21 April 1953, B149/1876, folios 114–15, BAK. See also "Aus der Fürsorgepraxis," *DVöpF* 4 (June 1949): 150–52.

129. Bundesministerium für Arbeit (IV b 3—1599/52) ORR Dr. Bürger to Herrn Bundesminister für Justiz, 3 June 1952, B149/1876, folios 92–93, BAK; Bundesminister für Arbeit (IV), Vermerk: Betrifft: Versorgung scheinehelicher Kinder nach dem BVG, 10 February 1953, B149/1876, folios 108–9, BAK.

130. Bundesministerium für Arbeit (IV b 3—1599/52) ORR Dr. Bürger to Herrn Bundesminister für Justiz, 3 June 1952, B149/1876, folios 92–93, BAK.

131. Bundesministerium für Arbeit (IV b 2—1793/53) RR Dr. Wilke to Herrn Bun-

desminister für Justiz Thomas Dehler, 14 April 1953, B149/1876, folios 112–13, BAK. The measure did not pass without opposition, as some expressed concern for "apparently legitimate" children who had resulted from rape. Der Präsident des Bundesrates to Herrn Bundeskanzler (copy), 27 March 1953, B153/345-II, folios 555–57, BAK; Schriftlicher Bericht des Ausschusses für Kriegsopfer- und Kriegsgefangenenfragen (26. Ausschuss) über den Entwurf eines Zweiten Gesetzes zur Änderung und Ergänzung des BVG—Drucksache #4493, 17 June 1953, B153/345-II, folios 574–82, here 575, BAK; Kabinettsache (I A 6 1605–2417 A), Betr: Entwurf eines Zweiten Gesetzes zur Änderung und Ergänzung des BVG; hier: Entwurf einer Stellungnahme der Bundesregierung zu den Änderungsvorschlägen des Bundesrates, 17 April 1953, B153/345-II, folios 571–73, BAK.

132. Bundesminister für Arbeit (IV), Vermerk: Betrifft: Versorgung scheinehelicher Kinder nach dem BVG, 10 February 1953, B149/1876, folios 108–9, BAK. On financial interests, see Parlamentarischer Rat, Hauptausschuss, 43. Sitzung, 18 January 1949, Z5/50, folio 944, BAK.

133. Schönleiter, "Zweites Gesetz," 1378.

CHAPTER 7: NARROWING THE DIFFERENCE

1. "Der Staat bist du!" *FD* 2/16 (1947): 1, reprinted in Merkel, *. . . und Du,* 69.

2. For example, Horst Büttner, "Die Rolle des Arbeitsrechts bei der Verwirklichung der Gleichberechtigung der Frau," *NJ* 8 (1954): 628–32, here 628; Schlicht, *Das Familien- und Familienverfahrensrecht der DDR,* 33.

3. Benjamin, "Wer bestimmt in der Familie"; see also Obertreis, *Familienpolitik in der DDR 1945–1980,* 70.

4. Benjamin, "Die Kontinuität in der Entwicklung des Familienrechts der Deutschen Demokratischen Republik," 735.

5. Kohli, "Arbeit, Lebenslauf und soziale Differenzierung," 40.

6. Hampele and Naevecke, "Erwerbstätigkeit von Frauen in den neuen Bundesländern—Lebensmuster unter Druck"; Dölling, "Between Hope and Helplessness."

7. Merkel, *. . . und Du,* 67ff., 93; Aufruf des ZK der SED zum 10-jährigen Bestehen der Frauenausschüsse in der Industrie und Landwirtschaft, im Handel und Verkehrswesen, in der Institution und Verwaltung, Berlin, 1 November 1961, reprinted in *Dokumente,* 254–57, esp. 255; Thesen des ZK der SED zur Vorbereitung des 8. März, Berlin, January 1960, reprinted in *Dokumente,* 234–50, esp. 248; *Die Frau und die Gesellschaft,* 189.

8. On the importance of the founding years for the establishment of a distinct East German culture, see Mühlberg, "Überlegungen zu einer Kulturgeschichte der DDR," 70.

9. Naimark, *The Russians,* 274, 283; Weitz, *Creating German Communism, 1890–1990,* 327–40.

10. Weitz, *Creating,* 280–310.

11. *Die Frau und die Gesellschaft,* 156; see also Otto Grotewohl's comments, 16–17 May 1946, Funktionärinnen-Konferenz, IV 2/1.01/3, folios 7–9, 16, SAPM-DDR-BA.

12. Notes of meeting of Frauensekretariat [of the SED], 31 May 1946, NY4145/49, folios 1–8, here 5, SAPM-DDR-BA.

13. Grossmann, *Reforming Sex,* 78–106, 189–212; Harsch, "Society, the State, and Abortion"; Goldman, *Women, the State and Revolution.*

14. 16–17 May 1946, Funktionärinnen-Konferenz, IV 2/1.01/3, folios 123–24,

SAPM-DDR-BA. For an opposing view, see J[enny] Matern, "Die Frau in der Sozialpolitik," *AS* 2 (1947): 109–10.

15. *Die Frau und die Gesellschaft,* 157.

16. Weitz, *Creating,* 220–30.

17. Gries, *Die Rationengesellschaft,* 108, 121–26; Naimark, *The Russians,* 130.

18. *Geschichte des DFD,* 61; 16–17 May 1946, Fuktionärinnen-Konferenz, IV 2/1.01/3, folios 63, 222, SAPM-DDR-BA; Elli Schmidt, "Unsere Aufgaben zur Gewinnung der Frauen bei den Gemeindewahlen," NY4106/4, folios 288–90, here 288, SAPM-DDR-BA. For an example of an SED appeal to women blaming them for the election of Hitler, see Entschliessung der 1. Delegiertenkonferenz der Frauenausschüsse über die Bestrafung der Kriegsverbrecher und für die Sicherung des Friedens, 14 July 1946, reprinted in *Dokumente,* 155–56. For more positive appeals to women, see Elli Schmidt, "Frauen, denkt daran!" *Neues Deutschland,* 1 September 1946; "Eure Sorgen sind unsere Sorgen!" draft election pamphlet, October 1946, NY4106/4, folios 274–87; Leitfaden für die Mitgliederversammlungen zur Behandlung der Fragen des Volksentscheids, 27 May 1946, reprinted in *Um eine ganze Epoche voraus,* 129; Erklärung des Landesfrauenausschusses Sachsen zum Volksentscheid über die Übergabe von Betrieben von Kriegs- und Naziverbrechern in das Eigentum des Volkes, 1 June 1946, reprinted in *Dokumente,* 153–54; "Aufruf des Landesfrauenausschusses von Sachsen zum Volksentscheid, 1. Juni 1946," reprinted in *30 Jahre volkseigene Betriebe,* 96–97.

19. Notes of meeting of Frauensekretariat [of the SED], 31 May 1946, NY4145/49, folios 1–8, here 5, SAPM-DDR-BA; *Die Frau und die Gesellschaft,* 157; *Geschichte des DFD,* 61–62; Elli Schmidt, "Unsere Aufgaben zur Gewinnung der Frauen bei den Gemeindewahlen," NY4106/4, folios 288–90, here 289, SAPM-DDR-BA; 16–17 May 1946, Funktionärinnen-Konferenz, IV 2/1.01/3, folios 21–23, 57, SAPM-DDR-BA; Elli Schmidt at Berliner Funktionärskonferenz, 10 September 1946, NY4106/4, folios 147–61, here 151, SAPM-DDR-BA.

20. With few exceptions, official histories of the referendum omit mention of concerns regarding the housewives' vote or even the women's vote. See, for example, *Zur Wirtschaftspolitik der SED,* 109–19; *30 Jahre,* 5–27. Not only the SED but also the Liberal and Christian Democratic parties of the Soviet zone urged a positive vote.

21. For continuing concerns about the difficulties of reaching housewives for purposes of political education, see H. Ulbricht et al., "Probleme der Frauenarbeit," *Arbeitsökonomik* 7 (1963), quoted in Koch and Knöbel, *Familienpolitik der DDR im Spannungsfeld zwischen Familie und Berufstätigkeit von Frauen,* 46–47. On the East German leadership's continuing need to win popular support, see Kopstein, *The Politics of Economic Decline in East Germany, 1945–1989.*

22. Records of organizational membership or attendance at party functions rarely include information on marital status. A rare exception is the data collected concerning attendance at week-long political-education courses for women run by the FDGB (Free German League of Unions), which show married women participating at low rates. Beteiligung der Frauen an der Schulungsarbeit des FDGB, FDGB-Berlin 1657, SAPM-DDR-BA; Zusammensetzung der 3. Frauenschule in Buch, 12–17 July 1948, FDGB-Berlin 1657, SAPM-DDR-BA; Fragebogen über die Zusammensetzung der 4. Frauenschule September 1948, FDGB-Berlin 1657, SAPM-DDR-BA.

23. Berichte der Frauenleiterin, Kreis Brandenburg, IV 2/17/51, SAPM-DDR-BA; SED-Frauengruppe Teltow to the SED-Frauensekretariat, 15 June 1947, IV 2/17/51, folio 262, SAPM-DDR-BA. See also reports of other assemblies in the same file.

24. Aufruf des zentralen Berliner Frauenausschusses, 4 September 1945, IV

2/17/55, folio 000 [sic], SAPM-DDR-BA; 30 October 1945, SMAD-Befehl #80 über die Organisierung der antifaschistischen Frauenausschüsse, discussed in Obertreis, *Familienpolitik*, 34.

25. *Die Frau und die Gesellschaft*, 161. For the official history of the DFD, see *Geschichte des DFD*; for a more distanced history of the early years, see Gerda Weber, "Demokratischer Frauenbund Deutschlands," in *SBZ-Handbuch*, 691–73.

26. Elli Schmidt, "Die Arbeit der Frauenausschüsse," address to unidentified Berlin audience (n.d. [February 1946]), NY4106/4, folios 12–17, SAPM-DDR-BA; Käthe Kern, "Frauen überwinden die Not," radio address, 6 August 1946, VI 2/17/26, folios 13–16, SAPM-DDR-BA; Elli Schmidt, "Die Aufgaben der deutschen Frauen zur Erhaltung des Friedens," speech to the Arbeitstagung der Frauenausschüsse, 7–8 December 1946, NY4106/4, folios 375–94, SAPM-DDR-BA; 16–17 May 1946, Funktionärinnen-Konferenz, IV 2/1.01/3, folios 280–83, SAPM-DDR-BA.

27. Überblick über die Entwicklung des DFD in der Sowjetzone: Fr. Maria Weiterer, Referat, Bundesausschuß-Sitzung, 3– 4 October 1947, DFD/BV95, folios 42–63, here 49, SAPM-DDR-BA; *Geschichte des DFD*, 79; Hildegard Schikowski, Geschäftsbericht, Bundesausschuß-Sitzung, 27 February 1948, DFD/BV95, folios 140–58, here 150, SAPM-DDR-BA; Protokoll der 1. Bundesausschußsitzung, 27 February 1948 [sic; 2. Bundesausschußsitzung] in Berlin, DFD/BV95, folios 173–79, here 176, SAPM-DDR-BA.

28. Hampele, "Arbeite mit, plane mit, regiere mit—Zur politischen Partizipation von Frauen in der DDR," 298; Obertreis, *Familienpolitik*, 36–37.

29. Walter Ulbricht, "Verbesserungen der Organisationsarbeit der SED. Aus Referat und Schlußwort auf der Organisationskonferenz der SED, 7. und 8. Juni 1949," in Ulbricht, *Zur Geschichte der deutschen Arbeiterbewegung*, vol. 3, 471–518, here 514–15.

30. Until the end of the GDR's existence, East Germans popularly understood the DFD to be a married women's organization. In directing me to sources, archivists often informed me that the DFD was for married women; women standing alone belonged to the FDGB.

31. In the political shake-up that followed Stalin's death and the strikes of June 17, 1953, Schmidt belonged to a faction critical of Ulbricht. She was dismissed and replaced by Ilse Thiele, who remained at the head of the DFD until the end of the GDR's history.

32. See, for example, DFD-Ortsgruppe Steinfurth to Elli Schmidt, 17 December 1952, and Elfriede Gerber's response, 9 January 1953, DFD/BV540, folios 36–37, SAPM-DDR-BA. If the DFD reported critical correspondents to other offices, these files do not indicate that.

33. *Geschichte des DFD*, 77; 7. Bundesvorstandssitzung des DFD, 21–22 March 1951, DFD/BV110, folio 62, SAPM-DDR-BA; Fridl Levin, Stenographische Niederschrift, IV. Bundeskongress des DFD in Berlin, 16—19 May 1952, DFD/BV16, folio 277, SAPM-DDR-BA. One year after the founding of the DFD, over 60 percent of members were housewives and assistants in family businesses; the statistical yearbook describes 59 percent as housewives in 1947. *Geschichte des DFD*, 77; *SJ-DDR* (1956): 131. After the early years, recorded statistics fluctuated wildly from year to year. According to the statistical yearbooks, slightly fewer than 30 percent were housewives in 1955; the proportion rose to 44 percent in 1959, then dropped to 34.3 percent in 1960. *SJ-DDR* (1956): 131; *SJ-DDR* (1960–61): 157. Internal correspondence describes 40 percent of members as housewives (and 16 percent as party members) in 1956. Soziale Entwicklung [des DFD] vom 1.1.1951—1.1.1956, IV 2/17/89, folio 435, SAPM-DDR-BA; Rechenschaftsbericht der Abt. Org.-Instr.-Kader, DFD/BV29, folios 108–34, here 109, SAPM-DDR-BA.

34. *Die Frau und die Gesellschaft*, 184. For additional official portrayals of the DFD as an organization for housewives, see Grußadresse des Zentralkommittees der SED zum 10-jährigen Bestehen des DFD, Berlin, March 1957, reprinted in *Dokumente*, 213–15, esp. 215; *Handbuch der Deutschen Demokratischen Republik*, 145–53.

35. Obertreis, *Familienpolitik*, 149–50; *Geschichte des DFD*, 154; Merkel, . . . *und Du*, 84; D. Schulz, "Die Hausfrauen wollen nicht abseits stehen," *AS* 14 (1959): 520–21.

36. For a report on such activities, see Rechenschaftsbericht der Abt. politische Massenarbeit (n.d. [for the period 1954–57]), DFD/BV29, folios 26–65, SAPM-DDR-BA.

37. On abortion, see Harsch, "Society, the State, and Abortion"; on divorce, see below; on housing, see chapter 8.

38. Obertreis, *Familienpolitik*, 37.

39. Schubert, *Die Frau in der DDR*, 56ff. For public criticism by Ulbricht, see Walter Ulbricht, "Verbesserungen der Organisationsarbeit der SED," in Ulbricht, *Zur Geschichte*, vol. 3, 514–15.

40. See chapter 4.

41. Clemens, "Frauen helfen sich selbst: Die Betriebsfrauenausschüsse der fünfziger Jahre in kulturhistorischer Sicht," 131–42; 16–17 May 1946, Funktionärinnen-Konferenz, IV 2/1.01/3, folio 35, SAPM-DDR-BA; Protokoll der Arbeitskonferenz des FDGB-Bundesvorstandes über Fraueneinsatz, 13 June 1951, Halle/Saale, DY34/2105, SAPM-DDR-BA; *Die Frau und die Gesellschaft*, 170; Benjamin et al., eds., *Zur Geschichte der Rechtspflege der DDR 1945–1949*, vol. 1, 312; SED-Provinzialverband Mark Brandenburg Abt. Frauen, Rundschreiben Nr. 3 of 27 May 1946, IV 2/17/51, folio 73, SAPM-DDR-BA.

42. Herta Zimmer, Referat zur Konferenz über die Verbesserung der Gewerkschaftsarbeit unter den Frauen, IG Bergbau, 22 November 1952 in Halle, DY34/21507, SAPM-DDR-BA; 9 January 1952, Erna Dyballa to Zentralvorstand der Gewerkschaft Land und Forst, DY34/23744, SAPM-DDR-BA. See also 15 February 1951, Pressestelle des FDGB—Artikeldienst—#38, DQ2/3804, folios 302–7, BAP; 13 December 1951, Erna Dyballa, notes on Besprechung im Zentralkommittee, 12 December 1951, DY34/24181, SAPM-DDR-BA; "Vorschläge," Konferenz zur Verbesserung der Gewerkschaftsarbeit unter den Frauen, FDGB, 26 September 1952, DY34/21148, SAPM-DDR-BA (the same document can be found in DQ2/3804, folios 43–50, BAP); Walter Ulbricht, Referat und Schlußwort auf der 2. Parteikonferenz der SED, 9—12 July 1952, reprinted in *Dokumente*, 194–95.

43. Koch and Knöbel, *Familienpolitik der DDR*, 44–48.

44. Beschluß des Politbüros des ZK der SED vom 8. Januar 1952, reprinted in *Dokumente*, 192; Hampele, "Arbeite mit, plane mit, regiere mit," 292–93; Merkel, . . . *und Du*, 87. Shortly thereafter (September 1952), the FDGB reintroduced women's sections; Schubert, *Die Frau in der DDR*, 58–60.

45. In 1957, 26 percent of members belonged to the SED. Clemens, "'Die haben es geschafft,'" 62–63.

46. Clemens, "Frauen helfen sich selbst," 116–17; *Die Frau und die Gesellschaft*, 177–78.

47. Clemens, "Frauen helfen sich selbst," 111; Obertreis, *Familienpolitik*, 82; "Fordert in jedem volkseigenen Betrieb Frauenausschüße!" *Fvh* 7/28 (July 1952): 8–9; 2. Parteikonferenz der SED, July 1952, quoted in *Dokumente*, 185; "Die Rolle der Frau im neuen Deutschland," aus der Rede auf der Tagung der Frauenausschüsse des Landes Thüringen, 28 May 1952, in Ulbricht, *Zur Geschichte*, vol. 4, 340–51.

48. Clemens, "Frauen helfen sich selbst," 127–30.

49. Ibid., 118.

50. *Die Arbeiterin* (1960), 372, quoted in Clemens, "Frauen helfen sich selbst," 139; 25 October 1956, FDGB-Bundesvorstand-Frauensekretariat, "Information für alle Sekretariatsmitglieder," DY34/23744, SAPM-DDR-BA; 3 January 1958, Frauensekretariat, "Einschätzung der Empfehlungen der Zentralvorstände und Fachministerien zum Abschluß des BKV 1958," DY39/86/5568, SAPM-DDR-BA.

51. Obertreis, *Familienpolitik*, 87; 21 October 1953, Ministerium für Arbeit, Stand und Ergebnisse der Einbeziehung der Frauen in die Produktion und der Förderung der Frauen, DQ2/3804, folios 80–86, here 84–85, BAP. The guidelines were published by the Deutsche Wirtschaftskommission für die sowjetische Besatzungszone as Rundschreiben Nr. 227, 1 February 1949.

52. Clemens, "Frauen helfen sich selbst," 132–42.

53. On the division between the 1950s, when the emphasis was on increasing the representation of women in the workforce, and the 1960s and 1970s, when qualifications and childcare attracted a great deal of attention, see Merkel, "Leitbilder und Lebensweisen," 371.

54. Obertreis, *Familienpolitik*, 33; *Die Frau und die Gesellschaft*, ⁻⁶ₒ.

55. Gesetz über den Mutter- und Kinderschutz und die Rechte der Frau vom 27. September 1950 *(GBl* 1037–41). In a telling symbolic gesture, Section I of the law concerns "Special Assistance for Mothers Standing Alone"; the law turns to "Marriage and Family" only with Section II. For evidence that local officials did not honor the provision of equal rights regardless of legitimacy, see "Die Nächste, Bitte!" *Fvh* 6/2 (January 1951): 22. On the earlier history of the Law for the Protection of Mothers, see Bajohr, *Die Hälfte der Fabrik*, 298–309; Hagemann, *Frauenalltag*, 189–90. The 1965 Family Law replaced the morally loaded term *illegitimate* with the more purely descriptive designation "children whose parents have never been married to each other."

56. The 1950 law underwent the most extensive discussion prior to its release; see, for example, 18 August 1948, Entwurf: Gesetz zum Schutze der Mutterschaft, DQ2/3887, BAP; 29 November 1949, Entwurf: Gesetz zum Schutze von Mutter und Kind, DQ2/3887, folios 70–73, BAP; Vorschläge der DFD zur Förderung der Frauen, 7 March 1950, IV 2/17/30, folios 22–25, SAPM-DDR-BA; Protokoll Nr. 7 der Sitzung des Politbüros des ZK am 5. September 1950, IV 2/2/107, SAPM-DDR-BA; 24 April 1950, Entwurf für das Gesetz zur Förderung der Frau, IV 2/17/30, folios 82–89, SAPM-DDR-BA; Nathan, "Zur Neugestaltung des Familienrechts"; "Zur Neugestaltung des Familienrechts," *NJ* 3 (1949): 242–45.

57. Wilhelmine Schirmer-Pröscher, Stenographische Niederschrift über den 3. Bundeskongress des DFD, 21–24 April 1950, DFD/BV11, folios 69ff., here 75, SAPM-DDR-BA.

58. Anita Grandke and Jutta Gysi, "Die Familien- und Bevölkerungsentwicklung als Sache der ganzen Gesellschaft," *SR* 22 (1973): 55–68, here 65. See also Kuhrig and Speigner, "Gleichberechtigung der Frau," 67; Verordnung über Eheschliessung und Ehescheidung vom 24. November 1955 *(GBl* I 849ff.); Eheverfahrensordnung vom 7. Februar 1956 *(GBl* I 145). See also Richtlinien des Obersten Gerichtes vom 1. Juli 1957, *NJ* 11 (1957): 441; Verordnung über die Annahme an Kindes statt (1956) *(GBl* I 1326).

59. For the official explanation for the withdrawal of the 1954 draft, see Benjamin, "Die Kontinuität," 735. On the 1954 draft and the extensive discussion of it, see *Neue Justiz* for the second half of 1954; Obertreis, *Familienpolitik*, 116ff.; *Ehe und Familie in der DDR*, 8; Koch and Knöbel, *Familienpolitik der DDR*, 25; Helwig and Nickel, "Einleitung," 10; Linda Ansorg, "Die Erarbeitung des neuen Familienrechts—ein Beispiel für die Gesetzgebungspraxis der Deutschen Demokratischen Republik," *SR* 8 (1959): 736–47, esp. 738. For the decrees, see n. 58.

60. Markovits, "'The Road from "I" to "We."'" See the regular summary of key decisions in the leading legal journal, *Neue Justiz*; family matters take up an enormous amount of space. On the importance of the high court's decisions to the 1954 draft law, see Benjamin et al., *Zur Geschichte der Rechtspflege*, vol. 2, 103–4, 368; Toeplitz, "Die Vorbereitung des neuen Familienrechts durch die Rechtsprechung"; Benjamin, "Einige Bermerkungen zum Entwurf eines Familiengesetzbuches," esp. 350.

61. Toeplitz, "Die Vorbereitung"; Nathan, "Zur Neugestaltung," esp. n. 4.

62. "Die Entrechtung der Frau in der Sowjetzone," 1, 37. See also Hagemeyer, *Der Entwurf*, 7–9.

63. Grotewohl speech to the Volkskammer, 27 September 1950, reprinted in *Dokumente*, 177; see also Elli Schmidt's comments, Stenographische Niederschrift über den 3. Bundeskongreß des Demokratischen Frauenbundes Deutschlands, 21–24 April 1950 in Berlin, DFD/BV11, folio 41, SAPM-DDR-BA.

64. "Aus der Rede Otto Grotewohls zum 'Gesetz über den Mutter- und Kinderschutz und die Rechte der Frau' vor der provisorischen Volkskammer der DDR," 27 September 1950, reprinted in *Dokumente*, 179–91, esp. 182; Helmut Ostmann, "Welche prozeßrechtlichen Aufgaben stellt das neue Familienrecht?" *NJ* 9 (1955): 227–34; Eggers-Lorenz, "Zur Frage des Widerspruchs nach Par. 48 EheG bei leichtfertigem Verhalten zur Ehe"; Wilhelm Heinrich, "Die Rechtsprechung der Instanzgerichte zur Eheverordnung," *NJ* 10 (1956): 264–66, 522–56; Benjamin et al., *Zur Geschichte der Rechtspflege*, vol. 2, 376; Benjamin, "Die Kontinuität," 733. For later East German descriptions of the positive features of the socialist family, see Kuhrig and Speigner, "Gleichberechtigung der Frau," 56; Grandke, "Zur Entwicklung von Ehe und Familie," 230–31; Jansen, *Leitfaden des Familienrechts der Deutschen Demokratischen Republik*.

65. Benjamin, *Vorschläge zum neuen deutschen Familienrecht*, 13.

66. Such women were legally designated as women standing alone for purposes of benefits and preferred access to childcare.

67. Wilhelmine Schirmer-Fröscher's comments in Stenographische Niederschrift über den 3. Bundeskongreß des Demokratischen Frauenbundes Deutschlands, 21–24 April 1950, DFD/BV11, folios 69ff., here 73, SAPM-DDR-BA.

68. Goldman, *Women*.

69. Obertreis, *Familienpolitik*, 232–33; "Größere Sorgfalt bei der Abfassung von Scheidungsurteilen!" *NJ* 7 (1953): 556; Benjamin, "Einige Bemerkungen," 351.

70. H[ans] Nathan, "Kommentar," *NJ* 3 (1949): 171–73; Benjamin, "Die Ehe als Versorgungsanstalt." See also Wilhelm Heinrich, "Die Rechtsprechung des Obersten Gerichts auf dem Gebiete des Familienrechts," *NJ* 7 (1953): 537–42, esp. 537–38; Erika Th., "Arbeit, Gleichberechtigung und Unterhaltsansprüche der Frau im Spiegel der Rechtsprechung des Obersten Gerichts," *AS* 8 (1953): 214–15; Obertreis, *Familienpolitik*, 120–21.

71. OG Urteil vom 1. Dezember 1953—1 Zz 36/1950, *NJ* 5 (1951): 128–29. For West German criticism, see Schlicht, *Das Familien- und Familienverfahrensrecht*, 48.

72. *Ehe und Familie in der DDR*, 29.

73. Benjamin, "Die Ehe als Versorgungsanstalt," 209.

74. Ibid., 210; also Benjamin, *Vorschläge*, 9. On women's feelings of vulnerability, see also 15 November 1954, Berlin-Hohenschoenhausen, to DFD, DFD/BV505, SAPM-DDR-BA; Eggers-Lorenz, "Zur Frage"; "Zum Entwurf des neuen Familiengesetzbuches," *Fvh* 9/35 (August 1954): 10; Gerda Grube, "Zum Entwurf des neuen Familiengesetzbuches," *Fvh* 9/37 (September 1954): 10.

75. For consideration of "old marriages" in other matters related to divorce, see Friederike Kluge, "Gedanken einer Richterin zu Par. 48 FG," *NJ* 4 (1950): 16–17;

Schlicht, *Das Familien- und Familienverfahrensrecht*, 64; Helmut Ostmann, "Zur Richtlinien des Obersten Gerichts über die Voraussetzungen der Ehescheidung," *NJ* 11 (1957): 459–62; "Die Regelung des Unterhalts nach der Ehescheidung," *NJ* 8 (1954): 560–64; "Unter welchen Voraussetzungen steht der unschuldig geschiedenen Ehefrau ein Unterhaltsanspruch gegen den früheren Ehemann zu?" *NJ* 7 (1953): 555–56; Wilhelm Heinrich and Elfriede Göldner, "Die Rechtsprechung der Instanzgerichte zur Eheverordnung," *NJ* 10 (1956): 522–26.

76. See, for example, OG Urteil vom 12. Februar 1953—1 Zz 5/54, *NJ* 8 (1954): 178–79; Stadgericht Berlin, Urteil vom 25. September 1953—2 S 164/53, *NJ* 7 (1953): 663; OG Urteil vom 2. November 1953—1 Zz 127/53, *NJ* 7 (1953): 750–51; Obertreis, *Familienpolitik*, 121. On ideological motivations of judges, see Markovits, "'The Road from "I" to "We,"'" 487–95.

77. Obertreis, *Familienpolitik*, 127. Of 2,956 East Berlin women divorcing in 1961, 315 received awards of alimony of up to two years, and 14 for a longer period; "Ehelösungen nach der Unterhaltsverpflichtung des Mannes sowie nach der Zeit, in welcher die Frau berufstätig war 1961," *SJ-Berlin* (1963): 309.

78. 15 November 1954, report from Berlin-Hohenschönhausen to DFD, DFD/BV505, SAPM-DDR-BA; 10 October 1953, Eine Fürsorgerin to the Vorsitzende des DFD, DFD/BV556, folios 25–26, SAPM-DDR-BA; 11 August 1953, Ilse Thiele to Fr. H. W., DFD/BV556, folios 33–34, SAPM-DDR-BA; 29 October 1953, M. M. et al., DFD/BV556, folios 204–5, SAPM-DDR-BA; 3 October 1953 (received), Fr. N. to Herr Präsident, DFD/BV556, folio 308, SAPM-DDR-BA.

79. For summaries of benefits, see Leutwein, *Die sozialen Leistungen in der sowjetischen Besatzungszone* (1955), 70ff., 138, 142.

80. 5 October 1949, Anordnung zur Sicherung der rechtlichen Stellung der anerkannten Verfolgten des Naziregimes *(ZVOBl* I 765); Durchführungsbestimmungen zu der Anordnung zur Sicherung der rechtlichen Stellung der anerkannten Verfolgten des Naziregimes, *AS* 5 (1950): 141–44.

81. See, for example, FDGB Görlitz to Pieck, 29 November 1949, DQ2/3774, BAP.

82. 8 March 1954, Vorschläge zur Änderung bzw. Ergänzung der Anordnug zur Sicherung der rechtlichen Stellung der anerkannten VdN vom 5. Oktober 1949, IV 2/6.11/86, folios 39–44, here 40, SAPM-DDR-BA.

83. For welfare payments to victims of war in Berlin, see 5 March 1947, Magistrat von Groß-Berlin Hauptamt für Sozialwesen: Statistischer Bericht für das Jahr 1946, DQ2/105, folios 10–15, here 12, BAP.

84. Versorgung der Kriegsopfer: Überblick über die Regelung in den einzelnen Zonen, DQ2/3726, folios 239–45, here 239, BAP; on the reduction of civil servants' pensions to a minimum, see Leutwein, *Die sozialen Leistungen* (1955), 73.

85. 22 April 1947, Befehl Nr. 92 des Obersten Chefs der SMAD betr.: Maßnahmen zur Verbesserung der Sozialfürsorge für die deutsche Bevölkerung in der sowjetischen Besatzungszone Deutschlands, reprinted in *Jahrbuch Arbeit und Sozialfürsorge 1947/48*, 350–51. For a useful, if hostile, overview of the trend toward unified insurance in East Germany, see Leutwein, *Die sozialen Leistungen* (1955); for a sympathetic East German introduction, see S. Wiederhold, "Verbesserung der Sozialfürsorge nach Befehl 92," in *Jahrbuch Arbeit und Sozialfürsorge 1947/48*, 285–91. The Federal Republic's pension reform of 1957 equalized pensions for salaried employees and wage workers in the West German state.

86. "Verordnung über die Zahlung von Renten an Kriegsinvalide und Kriegshinterbliebene," *AS* 3 (1948): 345–46. A draft had included only mothers whose children could not be placed in an orphanage or in childcare; 18 November 1947, 2. Entwurf:

Verordnung über die Leistungsgewährung an Kriegsbeschädigte, Wehrmachtsbeschädigte und deren Hinterbliebene, DQ2/138, folios 38–41, BAP.

87. 21 April 1947, "Berechnung," DQ2/3726, folios 246–47, BAP.

88. Jenny Matern, remarks in Stenographische Niederschrift über die Sitzung des Frauensekretariats der Ostzone, 4–5 November 1947, IV 2/1.01/61, folios 3ff., here 65, SAPM-DDR-BA.

89. Protokoll der Arbeitskonferenz des FDGB-Bundesvorstandes über Fraueneinsatz, 13 June 1951, Halle/Saale, DY34/21505, SAPM-DDR-BA.

90. Jenny Matern, "Unser Beitrag zum 40. Internationalen Frauentag," *AS* 5 (1950): 97–98.

91. Verordnung über Sozialpflichtversicherung, 28 January 1947, *AS* 2 (1947): 99.

92. Leutwein, *Die sozialen Leistungen* (1955), 60; H. Schubert, "Der überwiegende Unterhalt bei Hinterbliebenenrenten," *AS* 9 (1954): 98–99.

93. H. Schubert, "Der Rentenanspruch unserer werktätigen Frauen," *AS* 8 (1953): 155; H. Hohaus, "Die Frau in der Sozialversicherung," *AS* 5 (1950): 114–16. For the effects of increasing female employment on women's reliance on widows' pensions in the later years of the GDR, see Berghahn, "Frauen, Recht und langer Atem—Bilanz nach über 40 Jahren Gleichstellungsgebot in Deutschland," 103–7.

94. Koch and Knöbel, *Familienpolitik der DDR*, 47; Leutwein, *Die sozialen Leistungen* (1955), 91. By official East German accounts, the number of job seekers was four times the number of recipients of unemployment compensation. West German estimates put the ratio at ten to one. Leutwein, *Die sozialen Leistungen in der sowjetischen Besatzungszone* (1957), vol. 1, 120–21.

95. For women's own complaints, see 15 March 1953, A. K. to Elli Schmidt, DFD/BV540, folio 251, SAPM-DDR-BA; 9 July 1953, E. L. to Elli Schmidt, DFD/BV555, SAPM-DDR-BA.

96. Leutwein, *Die sozialen Leistungen* (1955), 92.

97. The directive, which went into effect on March 1, 1953, is discussed in ibid., 55–59. In April 1953, the Bezirksverwaltung Potsdam extended this requirement to female welfare recipients; ibid., 92.

98. Werner Holling, "Zur Auslegung von Par. 54 VSV," *AS* 3 (1948): 268–80; "Zur Gewährung einer Hintebliebenenrente," *AS* 8 (1953): 733.

99. Leutwein, *Die sozialen Leistungen* (1955), 92; Leutwein, *Die sozialen Leistungen* (1957), vol. 1, 49–52, 79–84. See also Sozialversicherung Abt. Renten Direktive I/1953 (18 February 1953), reprinted in Leutwein, *Die sozialen Leistungen* (1957), vol. 1, 134–39.

100. Leutwein, *Die sozialen Leistungen* (1955), 63, 128, 133.

101. An additional 44,736 female heads of household drew on welfare for a portion of their income; Berichterstattung über die Sozialfürsorge, Berichtsmonat Juni 1954, DQ2/1374, folio 11, BAP. Overall, the number of welfare recipients dropped by half between 1947 and 1950, then by more than half again between 1950 and 1956. Leutwein, *Die sozialen Leistungen* (1955), 90; Mampel, *Das System der sozialen Leistungen in Mitteldeutschland und in Ost-Berlin*, 132.

102. Leutwein, *Die sozialen Leistungen* (1957), vol. 2, 73.

103. 30 September 1954, Ministerium für Arbeit, Abt. Sozialfürsorge, Untersuchungen und Vorschläge in der Sozialfürsorge, IV 2/6.11/84, folios 87–130, SAPM-DDR-BA.

104. For welfare payments, see 30 September 1954, Ministerium für Arbeit, Abt. Sozialfürsorge, Untersuchungen und Vorschläge in der Sozialfürsorge, IV 2/6.11/84,

folios 87–130, SAPM-DDR-BA. For social-insurance pensions, see Leutwein, *Die sozialen Leistungen* (1955), 139, 143.

105. Jahresbericht 1946, DQ2/3726, folios 1–26, here 3, BAP; Jenny Matern, remarks in Stenographische Niederschrift über die Sitzung des Frauensekretariats der Ostzone, 4–5 November 1947, IV 2/1.01/61, folios 3ff., here 61, 69–70, SAPM-DDR-BA; Käthe Kern, remarks, Sitzung des Bundesausschusses des DFD, 24 September 1948, DFD/BV95, folios 251–306, here 269, SAPM-DDR-BA; 25 November 1948, Bericht über die erste sächsische Landesschwerbeschädigten-Konferenz in Dresden, 29 October 1948, DQ2/3774, BAP; 29 November 1949, FDGB Görlitz an Wilhelm Pieck, DQ2/3774, BAP; Protokoll der Arbeitskonferenz des FDGB-Bundesvorstandes über Fraueneinsatz, 13 June 1951, Halle/Saale, DY34/21505, SAPM-DDR-BA; F. Bohlmann, "Die Versicherten haben das Wort," *AS* 4 (1949): 474–75.

106. Obertreis, *Familienpolitik*, 60; see also *Die Frau in der DDR*, 67; Krecker, Niebsch, and Günther, "Gesellschaftliche Kindereinrichtungen—eine Voraussetzung für die Vereinbarkeit von Berufstätigkeit und Mutterschaft," 263.

107. Gesetz der Arbeit zur Förderung und Pflege der Arbeitskräfte, 19 April 1950 (*GBl* 349ff).

108. 27 April 1955, G. W. and E. O. to the Sekretariat der Volkskammer, DFD/BV557, folio 209, SAPM-DDR-BA.

109. 13 November 1953, A. H. to the Präsident der DDR, DFD/BV556, folio 277, SAPM-DDR-BA.

110. 10 February 1953, G-W. P. to DFD, DFD/BV540, folios 186–87, SAPM-DDR-BA; see also 29 March 1955, E. K. to the Zentralvorstand des DFD, DFD/BV557, folio 186, SAPM-DDR-BA. For an official response, see 1 June 1955, Ilse Thiele to G. W. and E. O., DFD/BV557, folio 215, SAPM-DDR-BA.

111. 31 July 1956, Abt. Frauen: Sektor allg. Frauenarbeit: Information der Abt. Frauen to the Sekretariat des ZK zur Fragen des Hausarbeitstages (Entwurf), IV 2/17/32, folios 1–6, here 4, SAPM-DDR-BA.

112. Freizeitordnung vom 22. Oktober 1943, Ministerialrat Neitzel, Reichsarbeitsministerium, IV 2/17/31, folio 24, SAPM-DDR-BA.

113. Befehl #56 des Obersten Chefs der SMAD vom 17. Februar 1946, discussed in Käthe Kern, "Der Hausarbeitstag" [n.d.: 1946], IV 2/17/31 folio 10–11, SAPM-DDR-BA; Befehl 20 vom 3.6.1948, discussed in Sachse, "Ein 'heißes Eisen,'" 257.

114. Verordnung zur Wahrung der Rechte der Werktätigen und über die Regelung der Entlohnung der Arbeiter und Angestellten vom 20. Mai 1952 (*GBl* 377–83).

115. Verordnung über die weitere Verbesserung der Arbeits- und Lebensbedingungen der Arbeiter und der Rechte der Gewerkschaften, 10 December 1953.

116. Merkel, . . . *und Du*, 165–67.

117. 21 January 1952, Käthe Kern re. Gesetz über den Mutter- und Kinderschutz und die Rechte der Frau, DQ2/3887, folios 207–8, BAP; Zusammenstellung derjenigen Punkte, die in das Arbeitsgebiet der HA Gesundheitswesen fallen, DQ2/3887, folios 325–27, BAP.

118. 10 July 1953, FDGB Bundesvorstand, Beschluß des Sekretariats, DQ2/1800, BAP; 28 July 1953, Bundesvorstand des FDGB—Frauenabteilung—Sekretariatsvorlage. Entwurf zur Abänderung des Par. 34 der VO über die Wahrung der Rechte der Werktätigen und über die Regelung der Entlohnung der Arbeiter und Angestellten vom 20. Mai 1952, DQ2/1800, BAP; 25 August 1953, Friedel Malter, Ministerium für Arbeit, to the ZK der SED, Abt. Arbeit und Sozialwesen, DQ2/1800, BAP.

119. 31 July 1956, Abt. Frauen: Sektor allg. Frauenarbeit: Information der Abt.

Frauen an das Sekretariat des ZK zu Fragen des Hausarbeitstages (Entwurf), IV 2/17/32, folios 1–6, here 4, SAPM-DDR-BA; Arbeitsgruppe Frauen beim ZK der SED: Information über die Gewährung des Hausarbeitstages (n.d. [1956]), IV 2/17/32, folios 7–9, SAPM-DDR-BA.

120. 11 September 1959, Anträge und Vorschläge zum Entschliessungsentwurf, die die Frauenabteilung betreffen, DY39/106/5859, SAPM-DDR-BA; 20 November 1959, Frauensekretariat: Information betr: Anträge zum Hausarbeitstag an den 5. FDGB-Kongreß, DY39/85/5568, SAPM-DDR-BA.

121. "Hausarbeitstag," *AS* 8 (1953): 761; 1 June 1955, Ilse Thiele to the Frauenausschuß VEB Starkstrom-Anlagenbau Leipzig, DFD/BV557, folio 222, SAPM-DDR-BA; 1 June 1955, Ilse Thiele to E. K., DFD/BV557, folio 187, SAPM-DDR-BA; 5 February 1960, Auszug aus dem Bericht der Antragskommission, Koll. Otto Lehmann, Stellungnahme zum Hausarbeitstag am 5. FDGB-Kongreß, DY39/85/5568, SAPM-DDR-BA.

122. "Gute Freunde," *Fvh* 8/47 (1953): 3.

123. For the 1977 extention of the housework day, see Gerhard, "Die staatlich institutionalisierte 'Lösung' der Frauenfrage," 391.

124. 17 October 1951, Ministerium für Gesundheitswesen Hauptabteilung Mutter und Kind, Bericht über die Erfüllung des Gesetzes über den Mutter- und Kinderschutz und die Rechte der Frau vom 27. September 1950, DQ2/3887, folios 2–21, esp. 4, BAP; 3 July 1952, Ministerium für Arbeit und Berufsausbildung Hauptabteilung Mutter und Kind to the DFD Abt. Frauengesetz, Erfüllung des Gesetzes über den Mutter- und Kinderschutz und die Rechte der Frau vom 27. September 1950, DQ2/3887, folios 171–86, BAP; Einschätzung über die Entwicklung der Stellung der weiblichen Jugend in unserer Gesellschaft, IV 2/17/37, folios 42–56, SAPM-DDR-BA; 2 April 1959, FDGB Bundesvorstand Frauensekretariat, "Die Auslastung der Einrichtungen der Vorschulerziehung und Horte," IV 2/17/34, folios 2–8, SAPM-DDR-BA; 10 July 1959, Käthe Kern to the Ministerium für Gesundheitswesen der DDR, NY4145/66, folios 24–26, SAPM-DDR-BA; Krecker, Niebsch, and Günther, "Gesellschaftliche Kindereinrichtungen," 62, 157; Schmidt-Kolmer, *Verhalten und Entwicklung des Kleinkindes*.

125. Stenographische Niederschrift der Diskussion auf dem internationalen Frauenseminar über die Stellung der Frau in der Deutschen Demokratischen Republik, 19—26 January 1958, VI 2/1.01/426, folios 2ff., here 62–63, SAPM-DDR-BA.

126. Anordnung über materielle Hilfe für alleinstehende Mütter bei Erkrankung ihres Kindes, 19 January 1956 *(GBl* I 120); Käthe Kern, "Neuregelung der materiellen Hilfe für alleinstehende Werktätige," *AS* 15 (1960): 393–94.

127. 21 November 1953, Elfriede Gerber, DFD-Bundesvorstand, to A. H., DFD/BV556, folio 278, SAPM-DDR-BA.

128. 2. Verordnung zur Änderung der Besteuerung der Arbeitseinkommen vom 14. März 1957 (*GBl* I 190).

129. 19 November 1953, Parteisekretär der SED-Betriebsparteiorganisation des VEB Sächsische Kammgarnspinnerei Cossmannsdorf, DFD/BV556, folio 287, SAPM-DDR-BA.

130. 29 October 1953, M. M. et al., DFD/BV556, folios 204–5, SAPM-DDR-BA.

CHAPTER 8: WHAT'S THE DIFFERENCE?

1. *SJ-DR* (1941–42): 24; *SJ-BRD* (1953): 43; *SJ-BRD* (1962): 47; *SJ-DDR* (1955): 19; *Haushalte*, 300.

2. In 1960, the average age of first marriage for women was 23.7 in West Ger-

many and 22.5 in East Germany; *SJ-BRD* (1962): 59; SJ-DDR (1967): 553. In general, young marriage was more frequent in the postwar than in the prewar period, and in East Germany than in West Germany (Fig. A.1).

3. Of men aged thirty-five to thirty-nine, 84.9 percent were married in 1939. In 1950, 84.5 percent of West German and 83.7 percent of East German men of this age were married. By contrast, 91.6 percent of men aged thirty-five to thirty-nine were married in 1960 West Germany, and 93 percent (not counting residents of institutions) in 1964 East Germany. *SJ-DR* (1941–42): 24; *SJ-BRD* (1962): 47; *SJ-DDR* (1955): 19; *Haushalte nach Art, Größe, und Gebiet*, 300.

4. *SJ-BRD* (1962): 47; *SJ-BRD* (1953): 43; *SJ-DDR* (1955): 19; *Haushalte nach Art, Größe, und Gebiet*, 300.

5. Barthel, *Die wirtschaftlichen Ausgangsbedingungen*, 53–55; Reichling, *Die Heimatvertriebenen*, 15, 52–53. For East German women's testimony regarding their husbands' flight west, see "Die Aussprache," *Fvh* 3/5 (March 1948): 24; "Die Nächste, Bitte," *Fvh* 6/14 (April 1951): 22; 15 February 1953, C. F. to Elli Schmidt, DFD/BV540, folio 190, SAPM-DDR-BA. On the special appeal of settlement in the West for men of the war generation, see Zwahr, "Umbruch durch Ausbruch und Aufbruch," 448–49.

6. "Vertriebene und Deutsche aus der sowjetischen Besatzungszone und dem Sowjetsektor von Berlin am 6. Juni 1961 nach dem Jahr des Zuzugs in das Bundesgebiet," *WS* 17 (1966): 34ff., here 36. Approximately half a million Germans (53 percent male) moved in the other direction; the net increase for West Germany was 3,095,600 persons, of whom 47 percent were male. *SJ-BRD* (1963): 68.

7. Statistics regarding the marital status of refugees are not available, but the preponderance of young refugees means that single refugees were almost certainly overrepresented; *Statistik der BRD* 239: 27. See also Niethammer, "Erfahrungen und Strukturen," 99–100, 103; Wendt, "Die deutsch-deutschen Wanderungen—Bilanz einer 40-jährigen Geschichte von Flucht und Ausreise."

8. Malter, "Arbeitsfähige Sozialfürsorge-Unterstützungsempfänger wollen ihren Lebensunterhalt selbst verdienen"; 1 April 1953, Schreiben der Bezirksverwaltung Potsdam to the Referate Sozialwesen der Kreisverwaltung, cited in Leutwein, *Die sozialen Leistungen* (1955), 92; "Dank dem Beschluß unserer Regierung," *Fvh* 16/38 (22 September 1961): 22; Schlicht, *Das Familien- und Familienverfahrensrecht*, 71, 76. For evidence of welfare payments despite official policy, see 15 January 1955, V. K. to Ilse Thiele, DFD/BV557, folio 109, SAPM-DDR-BA.

9. Meyer and Schulze, *Von Liebe sprach damals keiner*, 178.

10. Minowsky, "Im Wohnungsbau auf das Neue orientieren!" 173.

11. "Hier spricht der Jurist," *Fvh* 6/44 (November 1951): 21.

12. 25 September 1953, A. G. to DFD, DFD/BV556, folios 120–21, SAPM-DDR-BA.

13. Alheit and Mühlberg, *Arbeiterleben in den 1950er Jahren*, 43. Euler, "Wohnverhältnisse, soziale und wirtschaftliche Situation der Untermieterhaushalte im Frühjahr 1960"; *Die Untermieten in der Bundesrepublik Deutschland nach der repräsentativen Nacherhebung vom 22.6.1951*.

14. Manfred Euler, "Die alleinlebenden Frauen—Wohnverhältnisse, soziale und wirtschaftliche Situation im Frühjahr 1960," *WS* 13 (1962): 390–94, here 391. "Die demographische Struktur der Haushalte und Familien," *WS* 16 (1965): 427–33, here 431. No statistics regarding subtenancy in East Germany are available.

15. Of all housing units, 47 percent had a bath. Euler, "Wohnverhältnisse," 15; Manfred Euler, "Die Qualität des Wohnungsbestandes," *WS* 12 (1961): 285–90; Alheit and Mühlberg, *Arbeiterleben*, 43.

16. Such complaints filled the pages of West German magazines for working women. See, for example, Inge Meyer-Sickendiek, "Die möblierte Dame," *FB* 2/10 (October 1952): 6.

17. "Krach im Haus," *Constanze* 9/16 (1956): 52; 29 April 1957, Bericht über die Erfüllung der Maßnahmen, die sich aus dem Volkswirtschaftsplan 1956 auf dem Gebiet der Wohnraumlenkung ergeben. Stand 31.12.1956, 16, DQ2/3950, BAP; Chwalczyk, Um den gerechten Wohnraum.

18. In 1960, every fifth leaseholder and nearly every third owner of an apartment in West German cities with over five hundred thousand people sublet rooms; Euler, "Wohnverhältnisse," 15.

19. K. Pankow, "Sondermaßnahmen in der Wohnraumbewirtschaftung in Thüringen," *AS* 6 (1951): 165–66; "Zur Wohnraumverteilung in Greifswald," *AS* 6 (1951): 486–87; Stutz, "Mündliche Wohnungsbeschwerden im Ministerium für Arbeit."

20. *Frauenstimme* 9/3–4 (December 1957): 4; "Spannkraft und Lebensfreude," *Frauenstimme* 5/5 (May 1953): 3–5. For West Germany, see also the series *Schriftenreihe für Frauenfragen*, which originated at the SPD Women's Conference in 1955; for example, Ostermeier, *Die wirtschaftlichen Probleme der alleinstehenden Frau*; Otto, *Beitrag zur psychologischen Situation der alleinstehenden Frau*; Swoboda, *Die alleinstehende Frau in der Sozialversicherung*. For East Germany, see Beschluß der 24. Bundesvorstandssitzung des FDGB, Berlin, 19 September 1956, reprinted in *Dokumente*, 206–11.

21. 29 April 1957, Bericht über die Erfüllung der Maßnahmen, die sich aus dem Volkswirtschaftsplan 1956 auf dem Gebiet der Wohnraumlenkung ergeben. Stand 31.12.1956, 16, DQ2/3950, BAP; Chwalczyk, "Um den gerechten Wohnraum."

22. Otto Mewes, "Soziale Forderungen im Wohnungsbau," *AS* 1 (1946): 121–23. See also Waterstradt, "Ernste Mängel in unserer bisherigen Wohnraumverteilung."

23. "Schützt die Familie! Schafft das familienrechte Heim!" Rede von Paul Lücke, 8 May 1954, Frankfurt am Main, II/272B 1 #23, PA. See also "Gebt der Familie Raum—Sichert das Familienheimgesetz!" Rede von Paul Lücke auf der Kundgebung der Vereinigten Familienorganisation in der Industrie- und Handelskammer, Cologne, 18 January 1956, II/272B 1 #21, PA; Hölzl, "Wohnungsbau ist Familienbau."

24. Franz-Joseph Würmeling, "Grundlage der Gesellschaft ist die Familie," *BPIB*, 21 November 1953, 1851–54, here 1852. The housing shortage was also blamed for abortions. See Bericht aus der Arbeit der Mütterhilfe in Hamburg, 1950, ADW, CAW 391, ADW-IM; Statistik über die Arbeit der Mütterhilfe vom 1.4.1952–31.3.1953, ADW, CAW 391, ADW-IM.

25. "Das Bundesministerium für Familienfragen im Urteil der Bevölkerung," *BPIB*, 10 April 1954, 598. See also "Liebe Frau von Heute," *Fvh* 6/33 (August 1951): 17.

26. 1. Wohnungsbaugesetz vom 24. April 1950 (*BGBl* I 83–88), par. 16. See also Ingeborg Jensen, "Wohnungsbau für Alleinstehende," *FB* 5/9 (September 1955): 59–60.

27. *Der hessische Wohnungsbau in den Jahren 1945–1960*, 8; 14 September 1955, Bundesministerium für Wohnungsbau I—3000/77/55, B134/ 3497, BAK; "Anteil der Einpersonenhaushalte an den Vergaben der Wohnungen des öffentlich geförderten sozialen Wohnungsbaues in den Jahren 1956 bis 1960 nach Ländern" (n.d. [1962]), B134/7004, BAK; Johannes Adams and Lothar Herberger, "Die demographische Struktur der Haushalte und Familien," *WS* 16 (1965): 427–33.

28. BMfW Frauenreferat, "Vermerk: Wohnungsbau für Alleinstehende," August 1955 (Entwurf), B134/3497, BAK; BMfW Frauenreferat, "Vermerk: Wohnungsbau für Alleinstehende," 7 November 1955, B134/3497, BAK; see also the petitions of the

Women's Conference of the Deutsche Gewerkschafts-Bund reprinted in *FA* 1 (April 1958): 10; "Bauen und Wohnen: I," *IF* 5 (April 1956): 13.

29. Kurzprotokoll über die gemeinsame Sitzung der Ausschüsse für Wiederaufbau und Wohnungswesen sowie für Bau- und Bodenrecht, 18 January 1956, DBT 2. Wahlperiode Protokoll Nr. 58 (32. Ausschuß), Protokoll Nr. 44 (33. Ausschuß), II/272A 5 #77, PA. See also Ingeborg Jensen, "Was interessiert die Alleinstehenden besonders am neuen Wohnungsbaugesetz?" *FB* 6/11 (November 1956): 75–76.

30. 2. Wohnungsbaugesetz (Wohnungsbau- und Familienheimgesetz) vom 27. Juni 1956 (*BGBl* I 523–58), pars. 14, 25, 27, 28.

31. Minowsky, "Im Wohnungsbau."

32. "Erfolge und Perspektiven der Arbeiterwohnungsbaugenossenschaften," *AS* 9 (1954): 543–44.

33. W. Stechert, "Hinweise zur Durchführung des Arbeiterwohnungsbaues," *AS* 9 (1954): 209–10.

34. The AWGs in the records I examined required from 200 to 800 hours, and most members of the AWG requiring only 200 hours performed 450 to 500 hours; Protokoll der Beratung der Frauenreferentinnen der Gewerkschaften zum Programm des FDGB zur weiteren Verbesserung der Lage der werktätigen Frau im Zentralkommittee, 5 October 1956, IV 2/17/33, folios 45–61, SAPM-DDR-BA; P. Gartner, "Der Start der Arbeiterwohnungsbaugenossenschaften im Bezirk Dresden," *AS* 10 (1955): 105.

35. Protokoll der Beratung der Frauenreferentinnen der Gewerkschaften zum Programm des FDGB zur weiteren Verbesserung der Lage der werktätigen Frau im Zentralkommittee, 5 October 1956, IV 2/17/33, folios 45–61, SAPM-DDR-BA; Beschluß der 24. Bundesvorstandssitzung des FDGB, Berlin, 19 September 1956, reprinted in *Dokumente*, 206–11; 16 April 1957, Kollegin Bombach, Referat für die Präsidiumssitzung über die Aufgaben der Gewerkschaften bei der Entwicklung des Genossenschaftlichen Wohnungsbaues, DY46/14/3969, SAPM-DDR-BA.

36. Housing projects outside the AWGs built more small apartments; *SJ-Berlin* (1963): 155.

37. Kolkmann and Schlißke, *Mütter allein*, 209; "Die Nächste, Bitte!" *Fvh* 9/3 (January 1954): 22.

38. "Wohnungsgesetz des Kontrollrates, Gesetz Nr. 18 vom 8.3.1946 über Erhaltung, Vermehrung, Sichtung, Zuteilung und Ausnutzung des vorhandenen Wohnraums," *AS* 1 (1946): 63–66; Rolf Helm, "Erläuterungen zum Wohnungsgesetz," *AS* 1 (1946): 340–41; Lange, "Neue Arbeitsmethoden des Wohnungsamtes," *AS* 6 (1951): 23; J[enny] Matern, "Zum Problem der Wohnraumverteilung," *AS* 5 (1950): 457–58.

39. K[arl] Jagodzinski, "Der Arbeitsplan eines großstädtischen Wohnungsamtes," *AS* 6 (1951): 94–95; A. Edel, "Das Ziel der Wohnraumlenkung," *AS* 6 (1951): 437–38; Waterstradt, "Ernste Mängel"; 29 April 1957, Bericht über die Erfüllung der Maßnahmen, die sich aus dem Volkswirtschaftsplan 1956 auf dem Gebiet der Wohnraumlenkung ergeben. Stand 31.12.1956, 5–6, DQ2/3950, BAP; 5 February 1951, Ministerium für Arbeit HA Arbeit SIII 34203/2 Ja/Di, Rundschreiben 1/51 betreff: Verbesserung der Arbeit der Wohnungsämter der Kreise und Gemeinden, DQ2/3963, BAP. For an exception, see 30 November 1956, "Wohnraumbedarfsplan der Stadt Dresden," DQ2/3950, BAP.

40. H. Stuhr, "Wohnraumbewirtschaftung in den Brennpunkten des Wohnraumbedarfs," *AS* 7 (1952): 411. For an earlier, less compulsory variant, see Karl Jagodzinski, "Das Wohngesetz und die Durchführungsverordnung für die sowjetische Besatzungszone," *AS* 1 (1946): 313–15.

41. "Zur Wohnraumverteilung in Greifswald," *AS* 6 (1951): 486–87; Stutz, "Mündliche Wohnungsbeschwerden"; 29 April 1957, Bericht über die Erfüllung der Maßnahmen, die sich aus dem Volkswirtschaftsplan 1956 auf dem Gebiet der Wohnraumlenkung ergeben. Stand 31.12.1956, 16, DQ2/3950, BAP; 1 September 1953, F. F. to Elli Schmidt, DFD/BV556, folio 46a, SAPM-DDR-BA; 26 February 1953, G. S. to Elli Schmidt, DFD/BV540, folio 239, SAPM-DDR-BA.

42. C.-H. Vaquette, "Die Wohnungsversorgung Alleinstehender in Hamburg," *Gemeinnütziges Wohnungswesen* 8 (October 1955): 463–64; "Wie wohnt die berufstätige Frau?" *Frauenwelt* (August 1951): 10.

43. Bundesministerium für Wohnungsbau, "Vermerk: Wohnungsversorgung Alleinstehender," 30 June 1955, B134/7004, BAK.

44. "Kinder und Jugendliche in Familien," 214, 194* (Tabellenteil).

45. *Statistik der BRD* 35/8: 28–32. For later in the decade, "Kinder und Jugendliche in Familien," 214, 194* (Tabellenteil). Parallel statistics are not available for East Germany; see, however, Pech, "Das Einkommen in Haushalten von Arbeitern und Angestellten"; Niethammer, "Erfahrungen und Strukturen," 102; Alheit and Mühlberg, *Arbeiterleben*, 80.

46. "Hinterbliebenenrente der unverheirateten berufstätigen Frau," *IF* 3 (June 1954): 5.

47. Bohne, *Das Geschick*, 22–23. See also Niethammer, von Plato, and Wierling, *Die volkseigene Erfahrung*, 429–40.

48. "Kinder erwerbstätiger Mütter ausserhalb der Land- und Forstwirtschaft nach Alter und Betreuung," *WS* 15 (1964): 458* (Tabellenteil); see also Groth, *Kinder ohne Familie*, 83.

49. "Wir diskutieren weiter," *Fvh* 16/21 (May 1961): 19; "Hilfsbereite Omas," *Fvh* 17/32 (August 1962): 21; Malter, "Arbeitsfähige"; *SJ-DDR* (1963): 452; *SJ-DDR* (1966): 452.

50. "Wir diskutieren: Mein Tagesplan," *Fvh* 6/41 (October 1951): 4. Grandmothers also provided childcare for their married children; see, for example, "Die Nächste, Bitte!" *FvH* 5/15 (June 1950): 22.

51. Bohne, *Das Geschick*, 25.

52. Spittel, *Ich habe keinen Menschen*, 7; "Ich bin Junggesellin . . . ," *Constanze* 9/17 (1956): 53.

53. Oe., Meyer and Schulze Interview Collection, Institut für Soziologie—TU-Berlin; Bohne, *Das Geschick*, 23–24; Niethammer, von Plato, and Wierling, *Die volkseigene Erfahrung*, 439; Wolf, "Noch eine Kategorie berufstätiger Frauen."

54. Wolf, "Noch eine Kategorie."

55. The figures on West Germany above were culled from a number of sources; no one of them presented straightforward data on the numbers of single women supporting adult dependents. In the case of East Germany, even fragmentary data are unavailable.

56. *Statistik der BRD* 35/8: 28–32.

57. "Kinderzahl der Haushaltungen am 13.9.1950 nach Bevölkerungsgruppe und Stellung im Beruf des Haushaltungsvorstandes," *SJ-BRD* (1956): 44; "Kinder und Jugendliche in Familien," 214; Hermann Schubnell, "Zahl und Struktur der Haushalte und Familien," *WS* 10 (1959): 593–601, here 598.

58. Pech, "Das Einkommen," 83.

59. See, for example, Niethammer, von Plato, and Wierling, *Die volkseigene Erfahrung*, 478–97; Co., Meyer and Schulze Interview Collection, Institut für Soziologie—TU-Berlin; Hagemann, *Frauenalltag*.

60. On the earlier history of the Law for the Protection of Mothers, see Bajohr, *Die Hälfte der Fabrik,* 298–309; Hagemann, *Frauenalltag,* 189–90. For an individual firm's provision of services for employed mothers, see Sachse, *Siemens.* For overviews of bourgeois and socialist feminists' programs, see Frevert, *Frauen-Geschichte;* Evans, *The Feminist Movement in Germany 1894–1933.*

61. Ruhl, *Verodnete Unterordnung,* 197.

62. Ibid., 197.

63. By contrast, divorced women, who did not draw pensions, increased their rate of employment from 53 to 69 percent as their children moved from the age category 0–3 to 3–6. Unwed mothers' rates of employment remained nearly constant, rising only from 77 to 78.5 percent. *Haushalte und Familie,* 127–28, 135, 137. For distinctions according to social class, see Alheit and Mühlberg, *Arbeiterleben,* 40–41.

64. *SJ-DDR* (1957): 170; *SJ-DDR* (1955): 19, 50.

65. Benjamin, "Wer bestimmt."

66. Koch and Knöbel, *Familienpolitik der DDR,* 50; Merkel, "Leitbilder und Lebensweisen," 369–70; Obertreis, *Familienpolitik,* 155.

67. *SJ-DDR* (1966): 452.

68. *Ergebnisse über die Struktur der wirtschaftlich tätigen Wohnbevölkerung,* 523. On women's continuing habit of leaving the labor force upon the birth of their first child, see Kurt Lungwitz, "Die Geborenen nach der Zugehörigkeit der Mütter zu sozialen Gruppen im Jahr 1959," *SP* (1961): 293–96.

69. The ratio of women to men in October, 1946, was as follows: Berlin, 146:100; Soviet zone, 135:100; French zone, 128:100; U.S. zone, 120:100; British zone, 119:100. *Volks- und Berufszählung vom 29. Oktober 1946 in den vier Besatzungszonen und Groß-Berlin.*

70. von Oertzen and Rietzschel, "Das 'Kuckucksei' Teilzeitarbeit"; Maier, "Zwischen Arbeitsmarkt und Familie," 270; Clemens, "'Die haben es geschafft,'" 62. On East German economic planners' resistance to creating part-time spots, see 20 March 1951, Heinz Rausch, "Hausarbeit—kein Hindernis für Ganztagsbeschäftigung der Frau," *Presse-Informationen: Amt für Information der DDR* Nr. 77, DQ2/3804, folios 77–78, BAP; K. Marks, "Zur Halbtagsbeschäftigung der Frauen," *AS* 6 (1951): 53; "Worauf es heute ankommt—zur Halbtagsbeschäftigung der Frauen," *AS* 6 (1951): 104–5; "Noch einmal zur Frage: Halbtagsbeschäftigung der Frauen," *AS* 6 (1951): 199–200; Margaret Bönheim, "Halbtagsbeschäftigung für Frauen," *AS* 6 (1959): 297–301.

71. The same was true of 16 percent of single mothers. Johannes Adams and Helga Gendriesch, "Familienstruktur und Frauenerwerbstätigkeit," *WS* 16 (1965): 703–9.

72. Margot Engelmann, "Der Verbrauch in Haushaltungen von Rentnern und Fürsorgeempfängern in den Jahren 1952 bis 1954," *WS* 6 (1955): 335–41, here 335; "Der Verbrauch in Haushaltungen von Rentnern und Fürsorgeempfängern in den Jahren 1955 und 1956," *WS* 8 (1957): 340–44, here 342.

73. Haas and Leutwein, *Die rechtliche und soziale Lage,* 120–22; Obertreis, *Familienpolitik,* 85.

74. Agnes Arndt, "Sind die weiblichen Angestellten mit ihrem Arbeitsplatz zufrieden?" *IF* 1 (April 1952): 8. West German women in salaried positions earned an average of DM 245 per month. Hildegard Bleyler, "Die berufstätige Frau in der Sozialversicherung," *FB* 6/4 (April 1956): 1; Margot Kalinke, "Sollen wir Frauen allein die Lasten tragen?" *FB* 4/7–8 (July-August 1954): 1–5.

75. Franke and Bazille, *Das tapfere Leben,* 39; for a critical discussion of this term (*milieugeschädigt*), see p. 47.

76. Most such books tried awkwardly to balance alarming passages with reassurances that single women could raise exemplary children. See, for example, Kolkmann and Schlißke, *Mütter allein*, 89–90; Wirtz, *Die Witwe*, 147–65; Franke and Bazille, *Das tapfere Leben*, 88ff.; "Die großen Töchter," *Constanze* 10/8 (1957): 44, 76.

77. Report of the Deutscher Fürsorgetag 1953 in Hannover, 15—17 October 1953, B153/739, folios 299–305, BAK. For social work journals, see, for example, Glücksmann-Lüdy, "Sollen Mütter erwerbstätig sein?"

78. Statistics concerning children under fifteen in female-headed households and numbers of youthful offenders are not strictly comparable since most youthful offenders were over the age of fifteen. "Kinderzahl der Haushaltungen am 13.9.1950 nach Bevölkerungsgruppe und Stellung im Beruf des Haushaltungsvorstandes," *SJ-BRD* (1956): 44.

79. For a useful survey of this genre of research, as well as a criticism of its methodologies, see Lehr, *Die Rolle der Mutter in der Sozialisation des Kindes*, 124–33. For contemporary criticism, see Krüger, "Die alleinstehende Frau als Erzieherin"; Oppens et al., *Die Frau in unserer Zeit*, 60.

80. Kolkmann and Schlißke, *Mütter allein*, 29ff., 49; "Väter müssen endlich her!" *Constanze* 10/19 (1957): 16–20.

81. Hofmann and Kersten, *Frauen zwischen Familie und Fabrik*, 148. See also Glücksmann-Lüdy, "Sollen Mütter erwerbstätig sein?"

82. Schmidt, "Im Vorzimmer," 206.

83. Franke and Bazille, *Das tapfere Leben*, 83; Krüger, "Die alleinstehende Frau"; "Kinder berufstätiger Mütter," *Sozialarbeit* 5 (1956): 326. For daughters' recollections, see Ilse Tolksdorf, letter to the editor, *Courage* (January 1979): 12; "Ängste, Zuneigung und Abgrenzung: Gespräch über unsere Mütter," *Courage* (October 1978): 12–31, esp. 16.

84. Franke and Bazille, *Das tapfere Leben*, 37; Kolkmann and Schlißke, *Mütter allein*, 76–77; Kroeber-Keneth, *Frauen unter Männern*, 115; Speck, *Kinder erwerbstätiger Mütter*, 107–18.

85. Kolkmann and Schlißke, *Mütter allein*, 142, 201; Franke and Bazille, *Das tapfere Leben*, 102ff. See also Meyer and Schulze, *Von Liebe sprach damals keiner*, 185–87, 217. For typical criticism of modern fathers, see Müller-Schwefe, *Die Welt ohne Väter*; "Es gibt keine richtigen Väter mehr!" *Constanze* 11/24 (1958): 14; Mitscherlich, *Auf dem Weg zur vaterlosen Gesellschaft*. For claims of men's increasing involvement in family life in the 1950s, see Harsch, "Public Continuity," 33; Niethammer, "Privat-Wirtschaft," 54–55.

86. Obertreis, *Familienpolitik*, 6; Mühlberg, "Überlegungen zu einer Kulturgeschichte der DDR," 83; Alheit and Mühlberg, *Arbeiterleben*, 68. On the inadequacy of even unpublished, archived data for reconstructing a social history of the 1950s in East Germany, see Niethammer, "Erfahrungen und Strukturen," 96–97.

87. *Studien zur Jugendkriminalität*; Müller and Seifart, "Jugendförderung und Jugendkriminalität," 15–41; Harria Harrland, "Jugendkriminalität und ihre Bekämpfung," *NJ* 10 (1956): 396–400; Bernd Murowski, "Die Rolle des Par. 7 JGG bei der Bekämpfung der Jugendkriminalität," *NJ* 9 (1955): 558–60. For a rare (and mild) exception, see Mannschatz, "Die Aufgaben der Jugendhilfe bei der Bekämpfung der Jugendkriminalität und des Rowdytums," 42–55.

88. "Unsere Vatis," *Fvh* 7/2 (1952): 2, reprinted in Merkel, . . . *und Du*, 166; "Der internationale Frauentag und unsere Männer," *Fvh* 10/9 (1955), reprinted in Merkel, . . . *und Du*, 165.

89. Biess, "'Pioneers of the New Germany.'" See, however, Merkel, . . . *und Du,* 166–67, for the early 1960s.

90. Anni Hanser, "Peter wird sein Wort halten," *Fvh* 9/2 (January 1954): 21; "Einzelkinder im Ferienlager," *Fvh* 6/31 (August 1951): 20–21.

91. Szepansky, *Die stille Emanzipation,* 168.

92. H. U. Behm, "Unser ganze Familie packt zu," *Fvh* 7/16 (April 1952): 9.

93. "Wir und unsere Kinder," *Fvh* 12/45 (November 1957): 19, 31. Voices favoring and opposing mothers' employment are found in "Die Frau von heute gibt Auskunft," *Fvh* 1/2 (March 1946): 20; Vera Giese, "So darf es nicht noch einmal sein!" *Fvh* 7/12 (March 1952): 21; Gerda Grenz, "Soll Mutter arbeiten?" *Fvh* 11/38 (September 1956): 3; Stockmann, "In der Familie beginnt die Erziehung"; "Darüber sollte man sprechen," *Fvh* 15/1 (January 1960): 4; Jutta Zimmermann, "Ich soll keine gute Mutter sein?" *FD* 1/9 (February 1963): 24–25; "Sie sprechen mit Stolz von ihrer Mutti," *FD* 1/9 (February 1963): 32. See also *Geschichte des DFD,* 135; Kuhrig and Speigner, "Gleichberechtigung der Frau," 54. On similar discussions in *Neues Deutschland* and *Eltern und Schule,* see Obertreis, *Familienpolitik,* 157.

94. See chapter 7.

95. "Die Nächste, Bitte," *Fvh* 7/28 (July 1952): 22; "Unsere Hausfrauen," *Fvh* 7/10 (March 1952): 17; "Ursel und Peter lernen gut," *Fvh* 8/44 (October 1953): 18; Walter Ulbricht, "Die Frauen—Mitgestalter der sozialistischen Gesellschaft," aus der Diskussionsrede auf der Konferenz der Frauenausschüsse, 21–22 January 1956 in Buna, in Ulbricht, *Zur Geschichte,* vol. 5, 600–6, esp. 602–3.

96. "Nur eine Hausfrau . . . ," *Fvh* 10/42 (October 1955): 9; "Wir und unsere Kinder," *Fvh* 12/45 (November 1957): 19, 31; Obertreis, *Familienpolitik,* 141–55.

97. See, for example, Stockmann, "In der Familie." In keeping with the GDR's downplaying of marital status, representations of such prototypes often left the woman's marital status unclear. See chapter 5; "Mein Werkzeug—Meine Drehbank—Mein Betrieb!" *Fvh* 6/38 (September 1951): 13; "Eine Fernstudentin erzählt," *Fvh* 9/50 (December 1954): 7; "Im Frauenbahnhof Pankow-Heinersdorf," *Fvh* 6/14 (April 1951): 5; Günther-Ottokar Braun, "Wally, wir sind stolz auf Dich," *Fvh* 7/41 (October 1952): 4; "Eine von ihnen," *Fvh* 15/42 (October 1960): 4–6. Interviews with women who fit this model appear in Clemens, "'Die haben es geschafft,'" and Szepansky, *Die stille Emanzipation,* 126–40.

98. Käthe Kern, "Vier Jahre Gesetz über den Mutter- u. Kinderschutz und das Recht der Frau," manuscript for *Presse der Volksdemokratien,* September 1954, NY4145/27, folios 49–55, here 49, SAPM-DDR-BA.

99. See the series "Zum Entwurf des neuen Familiengesetzbuches," which ran in *Frau von heute* from July to September 1954.

100. The East German figures include stillbirths; the West German figures do not. *SJ-DDR* (1965): 515; *SJ-BRD* (1965): 61. It is extremely difficult to draw conclusions about the desirability of unwed motherhood on the basis of illegitimacy rates since high illegitimacy rates can reflect lack of access to contraceptives or high rates of premarital abandonment rather than acceptance of unwed motherhood. Nevertheless, many factors affecting nonmarital childbearing were constant in the two Germanys. Abortion was illegal in both states; unwed women faced similar difficulties obtaining contraceptives; the demographic balance and improving economy favored marriage among young adults; so did preferred treatment for married couples on the housing market. An East German report estimated that there were seventy to one hundred thousand illegal abortions annually between 1950 and 1955; Harsch, "Society, the State, and Abortion," 59.

On the eve of the West German women's movement, illegal abortions were estimated at one million annually; Frevert, *Frauen-Geschichte,* 279.

101. Quoted in Szepansky, *Die stille Emanzipation,* 134.

102. "Mein Kind hat keinen Vater," Constanze 6/10 (May 1953): 16.

103. Helwig and Nickel, eds., *Frauen in Deutschland 1945–1992,* 12.

104. Spittel, *Ich habe keinen Menschen,* 11.

105. Be., 31, and Ni., 30, both in Meyer and Schulze Interview Collection, Institut für Soziologie—TU-Berlin.

106. See, for example, Gr., 27; Wu., 30; and Me., 47, all in Meyer and Schulze Interview Collection, Institut für Soziologie—TU-Berlin; Bohne, *Das Geschick,* 127ff.

107. Bohne, *Das Geschick,* 120.

108. Ibid., 41ff.; Hampele, "Arbeite mit, plane mit, regiere mit," 293; Niethammer, von Plato, and Wierling, *Die volkseigene Erfahrung,* 329–44; Hofmann and Kersten, *Frauen zwischen Familie und Fabrik,* 26–27; Kolkmann and Schlißke, *Mütter allein,* 193; Wirtz, *Die Witwe,* 135; Schmidt, "Im Vorzimmer," 192ff., 214; Clemens, "'Die haben es geschafft,'" 70–71.

109. Harsch, "Public Continuity," 45–47; "Direktive: Wie kann der DFD durch die Schaffung eines kulturellen Zentrums zum Anziehungspunkt für alle Frauen im Wohngebiet werden" (n.d. [1956]), IV 2/17/89, folios 42–56, SAPM-DDR-BA.

110. "Direktive: Wie kann der DFD durch die Schaffung eines kulturellen Zentrums zum Anziehungspunkt für alle Frauen im Wohngebiet werden" (n.d. [1956]), IV 2/17/89, folios 42–56, SAPM-DDR-BA.

111. Niethammer, von Plato, and Wierling, *Die volkseigene Erfahrung,* 112–35, 478–97.

112. Gr., Meyer and Schulze Interview Collection, Institut für Soziologie—TU-Berlin, 24.

113. Moeller, "'The Homosexual Man Is a "Man," the Homosexual Woman Is a "Woman."'" The decision is reprinted in part in Kokula, *Jahre des Glücks, Jahre des Leids,* 114–24.

114. "Briefe an Charlott," *Wir Freundinnen* 1/1 (October 1951): 24.

115. "Über einen Besuch," *Wir Freundinnen* 2/3 (March 1952): 4–5; "Briefe an Charlott," *Wir Freundinnen* 2/3 (March 1952): 25.

116. The Catholic moral watchdog organization, Volkswartbund, campaigned for criminalization of female homosexuality. Gatzweiler, *Das dritte Geschlecht.*

117. Sillge, *Un-Sichtbare Frauen,* 12.

118. Interview with "Lona V.," in Kokula, *Jahre,* 98.

119. von Friedeburg, *Die Umfrage in der Intimsphäre,* 87, 94. Only never-married women were questioned about current lesbian activity.

120. Kolkmann and Schlißke, *Mütter allein,* 61; Spittel, *Ich habe keinen Menschen,* 41.

121. Jutta Holtz, "Ich bin Junggesellin . . . ," *Constanze* 9/17 (1956): 53; Zu., 53, and Lu., 54, both in Meyer and Schulze Interview Collection, Institut für Soziologie—TU-Berlin; "Grundsatzerklärung der Hinterbliebenen," *VdK Mitteilungen* 8 (1958): 453; Bohne, *Das Geschick,* 13, 66, 120; Spittel, *Ich habe keinen Menschen,* 43ff.

122. "Die moderne Junggesellenküche," *WF* 13/6 (1958): 30–31; "Eine Junggesellin richtet sich ein," *Gleichheit* 2 (1952): 361; Hedwig Damaschke, "Die Wohnung der Alleinstehenden," *Gleichheit* 3 (1953): 129.

123. See also Fehrenbach, *Cinema in Democratizing Germany.*

124. Delille and Grohn, "Von leichten Mädchen, Callgirls und PKW-Hetären." The

novel is Erich Kuby, *Rosemarie—des deutschen Wunders liebstes Kind;* the film, "Das Mädchen Rosemarie," directed by Ernst Thiele.

125. "Wir wollen offen darüber sprechen," *Fvh* 7/48 (November 1951): 21.

126. "Wir wollen offen darüber sprechen," *Fvh* 7/50 (December 1951): 20; see also installations under the same title in *Fvh* 7/51 (December 1951): 21, and *Fvh* 8/6 (February 1952): 21.

127. Among men 24 percent approved of extramarital sex only in exceptional cases, such as a spouse's incurable illness; 10 percent of married women admitted to extramarital sex, and 58 percent of all women approved of it in certain circumstances. von Friedeburg, *Die Umfrage*, 82, 92.

128. "Vor unglücklichen Ehemännern wird gewarnt!" *Constanze* 11/23 (1958): [n. p.]; Spittel, *Ich habe keinen Menschen*, 37; "Wir wollen offen darüber sprechen," *Fvh* 7/50 (December 1951): 20.

129. von Friedeburg, *Die Umfrage*, 89.

130. Ni., 48; see also Wu., 48, both in Meyer and Schulze Interview Collection, Institut für Soziologie—TU-Berlin; Horst Fichtner, "Ehelosigkeit als kirchliches Problem," Kurzreferat gehalten am 4.1.1956 in der praktisch-theologischen Sektion des Deutschen Theologentages in Berlin-Spandau, 2, ADW-IM Bibliothek; Szepansky, *Die stille Emanzipation*, 134.

131. "Die Nächste, Bitte," *Fvh* 10/46 (November 1955): 22.

132. Bohne, *Das Geschick*, 95ff.

133. Ibid., 99, 150.

134. Among men 69 percent felt heterosexual sex was necessary for their happiness. von Friedeburg, *Die Umfrage*, 78.

135. Bohne, *Das Geschick*, 158–59.

136. Ibid., 176.

137. Ni., Meyer and Schulze Interview Collection, Institut für Soziologie—TU-Berlin, 30.

138. Spittel, *Ich habe keinen Menschen*, 11.

139. *SJ-BRD* (1962): 58; Manfred Ebert and Johannes Triller, "Die Entwicklung der Eheschließungen in der DDR von 1946 bis 1962," *SP* (1963): 252–55.

140. Spittel, *Ich habe keinen Menschen*, 15; Hofmann and Kersten, *Frauen zwischen Familie und Fabrik*, 128; "Aus der Statistik," *Die Innere Mission* 1 (1956): 24.

141. Bohne, *Das Geschick*, 80.

142. Ibid.

EPILOGUE: WHO'S MORE EMANCIPATED?

1. Ulrike Helwert, "Abschied vom feministischen Paradies—Zu den Schwierigkeiten der Annäherung zwischen Ost- und Westfrauen," in *WeibBlick* 2 (1992), quoted in Schenk and Schindler, "Frauenbewegung in Ostdeutschland—eine kleine Einführung," 138. See pp. 139–40 for a more explicit discussion of East German women's impressions that marriage, as understood in West Germany, is both exaggerated in importance and hopelessly outdated.

2. See, for example, Dahn, "Ein Tabu bei West-Frauen"; Kaiser, "Kinder waren uns so fremd wie Wesen vom anderen Stern."

3. On East and West German men's participation in housework and childcare, see Sass, "Väter." There is an extensive literature on the limits of women's equality in the

GDR; for examples dating from the eve of reunification and its immediate aftermath, see Dölling, "Culture and Gender"; Hampele and Naevecke, "Erwerbstätigkeit von Frauen in den neuen Bundesländern."

4. On social benefits and abortion law, see Berghahn and Fritzsch, *Frauenrecht in Ost und West Deutschland*, 82–84, 198–202. For summaries of shifts in childbearing, marriage, and employment following the period covered by the present study, see Kolinsky, *Women*; Frevert, *Frauen-Geschichte*, 244–87.

5. 10 February 1953, G-W. P. to DFD, DFD/BV540, folios 186–87, SAPM-DDR-BA; L. K. to Würmeling, 18 February 1955, B153/1113, folio 54, BAK.

Bibliography

ARCHIVAL COLLECTIONS

Abbreviations are those used in the notes.

Archiv der Arbeiterwohlfahrt (AW)

    Bibliothek

Archiv des Diakonischen Werkes—Innere Mission (ADW-IM)

ADW, BP	Brandenburger Provinz
ADW, CA	Central-Ausschuß
ADW, CA/GF	Central-Ausschuß—Gefährdeten Fürsorge
ADW, CAW	Central-Ausschuß—West
ADW, HGSt	Hauptgeschäftsstelle
ADW, NF	Nachlaß Detmold Fischer
ADW, ZB	Zentralbüro des Hilfswerkes
Bibliothek	

Berlin Documents Center (BDC)

    NS-Frauenschaft/Deutsches Frauenwerk

Bundesarchiv-Freiburg—Militärarchiv (BAF)

R17	Hauptvereinigungen
RH9	OKH/Heeresverwaltungsamt
RH12/23	Heeressanitätsinspektion
RH15	OKH/Allgemeines Heeresamt
RH19X	Oberkommandos der Heeresgruppen— Heeresgruppe C

RH20	Oberkommandos von Armeen und Armeeabteilungen
RH36	Kommandanturen der Militärverwaltung
RH50	Sanitätstruppen, Lazarette
RH55	Sanitätsdienststellen im Heimatkriegsgebiet
RL 14	Einheiten der Luftnachrichtentruppe
RL19	Territoriale Kommandobehörden
RW4	OKW/Wehrmachtsführungsstab
RW5	OKW/Amt Ausland/Abwehr
RW6	OKW/Allgemeines Wehrmachtamt
RW16	Wehrmacht Fürsorge- und Versorgungsdienststellen
RW19	OKW/Wehrwirtschaft- und Rüstungsamt

Bundesarchiv-Koblenz (BAK)

B105	Deutscher Städtetag, Verbindungsstelle Ffm
B106	Bundesministerium des Innern
B119	Bundesanstalt für Arbeitsvermittlung und Arbeitslosenversicherung
B134	Bundesministerium für Raumordnung, Bauwesen und Städtebau
B141	Bundesministerium für Justiz
B142	Bundesministerium für Gesundheitswesen
B148/V	Hauptamt für Soforthilfe
B149	Bundesministerium für Arbeit
B150	Bundesministerium für Vertriebene, Flüchtlinge und Kriegsbeschädigte
B153	Bundesministerium für Familie und Jugend
B208	Bundesgesundheitsamt
NL151	Nachlaß Marie-Elisabeth Lüders
NL219	Nachlaß Maria Probst
NS2	SS-Rasse- und Siedlungshauptamt
NS5	Deutsche Arbeitsfront
NS6	Partei-Kanzlei der NSDAP
NS7	Stellvertreter des Führers/Parteikanzlei
NS25	Hauptamt für Kommunalpolitik
NS32 II	SS Helferinnenschule Oberehnheim
NS44	NS-Frauenschaft
NSD54	NS-Kriegsopferversorgung
R2	Reichsfinanzministerium
R12	Reichsgruppe Industrie
R18	Staatssekretariat für das Gesundheitswesen
R22	Justiz
R36	Deutscher Gemeindetag
R41	Reichsarbeitsministerium
R43	Reichskanzlei
R58	Reichssicherheitshauptamt
Z5	Parlamentarischer Rat
ZSg1-156	Reichsbund der Kriegs- und Zivilbeschädigten, Sozialrentner und Hinterbliebenen

Bundesarchiv-Potsdam (BAP)

15.01	Reichsministerium des Innern
62.03	Deutsche Arbeitsfront—
	Arbeitswissenschaftliches Institut
DQ1	Ministerium für Gesundheitswesen
DQ2	Ministerium für Arbeit und Berufsausbildung
RAM	Reichsarbeitsministerium
	Reichslandbund-Pressarchiv
	Reichssicherheitshauptamt: Abt IV:
	Geheimes Staatspolizeiamt

Deutscher Caritas Verband—Archiv (DCV)

CA VIII	Frauenhilfe
319.4 SKF	Vereinsakten
329.1	Deutscher Nationalverband der katholischen
	Mädchenschutzvereine

Deutscher Gewerkschaftsbund—Archiv (DGB)

Bibliothek

Deutsches Hygiene-Museum, Dresden

Archiv

Generallandesarchiv Karlsruhe (GLK)

460	Arbeitsamt Karlsruhe
460	Arbeitsamt Tauberbischofsheim

Hessisches Hauptstaatsarchiv (HHA)

409/5	Frauenjugendgefängnis Frankfurt-Preungesheim
409/6	Frauenstrafgefängnis Frankfurt-Höchst
483	NSDAP Hessen-Nassau
502	Sozialminister und Eingaben an den MP
508	Sozialminister
520	Spruchkammer
521	Internierungs- und Arbeitslager Darmstadt
522	Internierungs- und Arbeitslager Darmstadt
649	OMG-Hessen
650	Regierungspräsident Hessen 1945–60
920	Statistisches Bundesamt Wiesbaden—Volkszählung
940	Landesarbeitsamt
942	Arbeitsamt Frankfurt
946	Arbeitsamt Wiesbaden

Institut für Geschichte und Biographie—Fern-Universität Hagen

Interview Collection

Institut für Sozialfragen, Berlin (SF)

Clippings Collection

Institut für Soziologie—TU-Berlin

Sibylle Meyer and Eva Schulze Interview Collection

National Archives (U.S.)—Suitland (NA-Suitland)

RG260	Office of Military Government
RG332	U.S. Forces European Theater

Nordrhein-Westfälisches Hauptstaatsarchiv (NRW)

LAA-BR	Landesarbeitsamt
LAA-NW	Landesarbeitsamt

Parlamentsarchiv des Deutschen Bundestages (PA)

Gesetzdokumentation

I/87	Bundesversorgungsgesetz
II/272	2.Wohnungsbaugesetz
III/394	Familienrechtsänderungsgesetz

Staatsarchiv der freien- und hanseatischen Stadt Hamburg (Sta HH)

Sozialbehörde I EF 70.24
Sozialbehörde I GF 00.11
Medizinkollegium II U 52-00

Stadtarchiv Darmstadt (SA-D)

ST23/12	Jüngere Melderegistratur
ST26.41	Hausakten des Städtischen Wohnungsamtes Darmstadt

Stadtarchiv Frankfurt (SA-F)

FK	Konzessionsakten
FLS	Luftschutz
FMAG	Magistrat

Stadtarchiv Hanau

E4	Steinheim

Stadtarchiv Wetzlar

Sozialamt

Stiftung Archiv der Partei und Massenorganisationen der Deutschen Demokratischen
Republik im Bundesarchiv (SAPM-DDR-BA)

IV 2/1.01	Konferenzen und Beratungen des Zentralkommittees der SED
IV 2/2	Politbüro
IV 2/2.027	Zentralkommittee der SED Bereich Gewerkschaften: Sekretariat Helmut Lehmann
IV 2/3	Protokolle der Sitzungen des Sekretariats
IV 2/6.11	Zentralkommittee der SED Bereich Gewerkschaften: Abt. Gewerkschaften und Sozialpolitik
IV 2/17	Zentralkommittee der SED: Abt. Frauen
DFD	Demokratischer Frauenbund Deutschland
DFD/BV	Demokratischer Frauenbund Deutschland— Bundesvorstand
DY34	FDGB Bundesvorstand
DY39	FDGB, IG Druck und Papier
DY46	FDGB, IG Metall
DY55/V278	Vereinigung der Verfolgten des Naziregimes
FDGB-Berlin	
NL3	Nachlaß Ernst Thälmann
NY4072	Nachlaß Franz und Käthe Dahlem
NY4106	Nachlaß Elli Schmidt
NY4145	Nachlaß Käthe Kern
NY4229	Nachlaß Elfriede Paul
NY4410	Nachlaß Gertrud Grothe
NY4440	Nachlaß Margarete Behm
NY4450	Nachlaß Frieda Krüger
NY4474	Nachlaß Erna Kuhn
NY4495	Nachlaß Friedel Malter

JOURNALS CONSULTED

Abbreviations are those used in the notes.
Arbeit und Sozialfürsorge (AS) (Soviet occupation, GDR)
Die Arbeiterwohlfahrt (FRG)
Archiv für Bevölkerungswissenschaft und Bevölkerungspolitik (ABB) (Reich)
Blätter der Wohlfahrtspflege
Bulletin des Presse- und Informationsamtes der Bundesregierung (BPIB) (FRG)
Bundesarbeitsblatt (FRG)
Bundesfrauenkonferenz des deutschen Gewerkschaftsbundes: Protokoll (FRG)
Bundesgesetzblatt (BGBl) (FRG)
Bundesversorgungsblatt (FRG)
Caritas (Reich, FRG)
Constanze (western occupation, FRG)

Courage (FRG)
Deutsche Jugendhilfe (Reich)
Deutsche Justiz (Reich)
Deutsche Kriegsopferversorgung (Reich)
Deutsches Recht (Reich)
Ehe und Familie im privaten und öffentlichen Recht: Zeitschrift für das gesamte Familienrecht (EF) (FRG)
Die Fackel (FRG)
Die Frau (Reich)
Frau im Beruf: Nachrichten des Verbandes der weiblichen Angestellten (FB) (FRG)
Die Frau von heute (Fvh) (Soviet occupation, GDR)
Frauen und Arbeit: Mitteilungsblatt der Hauptabteilung "Frauen" im DGB-Vorstand (FA) (FRG)
Frauenschaffen (Reich)
Frauenstimme (FRG)
Frauenwelt (U.S. occupation, FRG)
Für Dich (FD) (Soviet occupation, GDR)
Gemeinnütziges Wohnungswesen (FRG)
Gesetzblatt (Gbl) (GDR)
Gleichheit: Das Blatt der arbeitenden Frau (FRG)
Informationen für die Frau (IF) (FRG)
Die Innere Mission (Reich, U.S. occupation/Berlin, FRG)
Jugendwohl (Reich, FRG)
Ministerialblatt der inneren Verwaltung (MBLiV) (Reich)
Mitteilungen—Mitarbeiterorgan des Verbands der Kriegsbeschädigten, Kreigshinterbliebenen, und Sozialrentner Deutschlands (VdK Mitteilungen) (FRG)
Mitteilungen des deutschen Vereins für öffentliche und private Fürsorge (DVöpF) (Reich, U.S. occupation, FRG)
Monthly Report of the Military Government—US Zone (Monthly Report) (U.S. occupation)
Mutter und Volk (MV) (Reich)
Nachrichtendienst der Reichsfrauenführung (Reich)
Neue Berliner Illustrierte (NBI) (Soviet occupation, GDR)
Neue Justiz (NJ) (Soviet occupation, GDR)
Neues Beginnen (NB) (British occupation, FRG)
Neues Deutschland (GDR)
Neues Volk (Reich)
Official Gazette of the Control Council for Germany (occupation, all zones)
Die Praxis (FRG)
Reichsarbeitsblatt (Reich)
Reichsbund (FRG)
Reichsgesetzblatt (RGBl) (Reich)
Reichsministerialblatt der inneren Verwaltung (RMBliV) (Reich)
Sie (U.S. occupation/Berlin)
Sozialarbeit (FRG)
Soziale Fragen (FRG)
Soziale Praxis (Reich)
Soziale Welt (FRG)
Staat und Recht (SR) (GDR)

Stars and Stripes (SS) (U.S. military)
Statistik der Bundesrepublik Deutschland (Statistik der FRG) (FRG)
Statistische Praxis (SP) (GDR)
Statistisches Jahrbuch der Bundesrepublik Deutschland (SJ-FRG) (FRG)
Statistisches Jahrbuch der Deutschen Demokratischen Republik (SJ-DDR) (GDR)
*Statistisches Jahrbuch der Hauptstadt der Deutschen Demokratischen Republik—
Berlin (SJ-Berlin)* (GDR)
Statistisches Jahrbuch des Deutschen Reiches (SJ-DR) (Reich)
Verhandlungen des Deutschen Bundestages (VdBT) (FRG)
Volkswartbund (Reich, British occupation, FRG)
Die Welt der Frau (WF) (western occupation, FRG)
Wille und Weg (FRG)
Wir Freundinnen (FRG)
Wirtschaft und Statistik (WS) (Reich, FRG)
Zeitschrift für das Fürsorgewesen (FRG)
Zeitschrift für Haut- und Geschlechtskrankheiten (ZHGK) (Reich, FRG)
Zentralverordnungsblatt (ZVOBl) (GDR)

BIBLIOGRAPHY OF BOOKS AND ARTICLES
PUBLISHED BEFORE 1965, REFERENCE WORKS,
GOVERNMENT REPORTS, MEMOIRS, ORAL HISTORIES,
DOCUMENT COLLECTIONS

*10 Jahre im Dienste der Kriegsopfer 1950–1960: Bund deutscher Kriegsbeschädigter und
Kriegshinterbliebener e.V. Bonn.* Bonn: Bund deutscher Kriegsbeschädigter und
Kriegshinterbliebener, 1960.
Alfes, Georg. *Frauenseelsorge und Frauengemeinschaft.* Dusseldorf: Verbandsverlag
Weibliche Vereine, 1955.
Die alleinstehende Frau in der Sozialversicherung. Probleme der alleinstehenden Frau.
Bonn: SPD, 1957.
Arbeiten, arbeiten, arbeiten! Die "neuen Rechte" der Frau in der Sowjetzone. Bonn:
Bundesministerium für gesamtdeutsche Fragen, [1950].
Arndt, Klaus Dieter. *Wohnungsversorgung und Mietniveau in der Bundesrepublik.*
Berlin: Duncker and Humblot, 1955.
Arnold, Egon. *Angewandte Gleichberechtigung im Familienrecht: Ein Kommentar zu
der Rechtssituation seit dem 1.4.1953.* Berlin and Frankfurt am Main: Vahlen, 1954.
*Aufgaben der Fürsorge zur Überwindung der deutschen Volksnot: Bericht über den
deutschen Fürsorgetag in Frankfurt/Main des Deutschen Vereins für öffentliche und
private Fürsorge am 13. Mai 1946.* Berlin: Urban und Schwarzenberg, 1947.
Baldamus, Karl. *Frauen suchen ihr Recht: Schicksale und Gestalten vor dem Arbeits-
gericht.* Dusseldorf: Bund-Verlag, 1955.
Barsewisch, Elisabeth von. *Die Aufgaben der Frau für die Aufartung ihres Volkes.* Berlin:
Reichsausschuß für Volksgesundheitspflege, 1935.
Bartel, Walter, ed. *Die Deutsche Demokratische Republik auf dem Wege zum Sozialis-
mus: Dokumente und Materialien, Teil I (1945–1949).* Berlin: Volk und Wissen,
1959.
Bäumer, Gertrud. *Der neue Weg der deutschen Frau.* Stuttgart: Deutsche Verlags-
Anstalt, 1946.

Baumert, Gerhard. *Deutsche Familien nach dem Kriege.* Darmstadt: Eduard Röther Verlag, 1954.

——— . *Jugend der Nachkriegszeit.* Darmstadt: Eduard Röther Verlag, 1952.

Baumgart, Gertrud. *Frauenbewegung—Gestern und Heute.* Heidelberg: C. Winter, 1933.

Bebel, August. *Die Frau und der Sozialismus.* Zurich: Verlag der Volksbuchhandlung, 1879.

Bechmann, Annemarie, ed. *Das Leben meistern.* Regensburg: Pustet, 1954.

Becker, Howard. "German Families Today." In *Germany and the Future of Europe,* edited by Hans J. Morgenthau. Chicago: University of Chicago Press, 1951.

Behm, Hans Ulrich. *Gerda, Hilde und die anderen.* Berlin: Deutscher Frauenverlag, 1953.

Beitzke, Günther, and Konrad Hübner. *Die Gleichberechtigung von Mann und Frau.* Tübingen: Mohr, 1950.

Benjamin, Hilde. "Die Ehe als Versorgungsanstalt." *Neue Justiz* 3 (1949): 209–10.

——— . "Einige Bermerkungen zum Entwurf eines Familiengesetzbuches." *Neue Justiz* 8 (1954): 349–53.

——— . "Familie und Familienrecht in der DDR." *Einheit* 10 (1955): 448.

——— . "Die Kontinuität in der Entwicklung des Familienrechts der Deutschen Demokratischen Republik." *Wissenschaftliche Zeitschrift der Humboldt-Universität zu Berlin—Gesellschafts- und Sprachwissenschaftliche Reihe* 15/6 (1966): 731–39.

——— . *Vorschläge zum neuen deutschen Familienrecht.* Berlin, 1949.

——— . "Wer bestimmt in der Familie." *Neues Deutschland,* no. 28, supp. (1 February 1958).

Berger, Thomas, and Karl-Heinz Müller, eds. *Lebenssituationen 1945–48: Materialien zum Alltagsleben in den westlichen Besatzungszonen 1945–48.* Hannover: Niedersächsische Landeszentrale für politische Bildung, 1983.

Bergholtz, Ruth. *Die Wirtschaft braucht die Frau.* Darmstadt: Leske, 1956.

Bergler, Reinhold. *Kinder aus gestörten und unvollständigen Familien.* Berlin and Weinheim: Beltz, 1955.

Bericht des Kommittees für Leben und Arbeit der Frauen in der Kirche. Die Unordnung der Welt und Gottes Heilsplan, vol. 5. Tübingen: Furche, 1948.

Berlin nach dem Krieg—wie ich es erlebte: 28 Erlebnisberichte von älteren Berlinern aus dem Wettbewerb des Senators für Arbeit und Soziales. Berliner Forum, vol. 9. Berlin: Presse- und Informationsamt, 1977.

Bernhardt, Wolfgang. *Das Recht des unehelichen Kindes und dessen Neuregelung in beiden Teilen Deutschlands.* Bielefeld: Gieseking, 1962.

Die Beschäftigung Schwerbeschädigter. Ein Erfahrungsbericht der Bundesanstalt für Arbeitsvermittlung und Arbeitslosenversicherung über die Durchführung des SBG vom 16. Juni 1953. Nuremberg: Bundesanstalt für Arbeitsvermittlung und Arbeitslosenversicherung, 1955.

Beyer, Karl. *Familie und Frau im neuen Deutschland.* Langensalza, Berlin, and Leipzig: Beltz, 1936.

Biederich, Paul Heinrich. *Entgegen auf die Schrift "Das dritte Geschlecht" des Amtsgerichtsrats R. Gatzweiler.* Hamburg: Grieger, 1951.

Bier, Dora. *Der Mensch ohne Familie.* Cologne: Deutsches Gesundheitsmuseum, 1959.

Blieweis, Theodor. *Ehen, die zerbrachen: Bekenntnisse Geschiedener.* Vienna and Munich: Herold, 1960.

Boberach, Heinz, ed. *Meldungen aus dem Reich*. Herrsching: Pawlak Verlag, 1984.

Bodamer, Joachim. *Der Mann von heute—seine Gestalt und Psychologie*. Stuttgart: C. A. Schwab, 1956.

Boehmer, Gustav. *Die Teilreform des Familienrechts durch das Gleichberechtigungsgesetz vom 18. Juni 1957 und das Familienrechtsänderungsgesetz vom 11. August 1961*. Tübingen: Mohr, 1962.

Bohne, Regina. *Das Geschick der 2 Millionen: Die alleinlebende Frau in unserer Gesellschaft*. Dusseldorf: Econ-Verlag, 1960.

Böll, Heinrich. *Haus ohne Hüter*. 1954. Reprint, Frankfurt am Main: Ullstein, 1972.

Bönig, Heinrich. *Entwicklung und Bedeutung der Frauenarbeit*. Cologne: Zentralinstitut für Gesundheitserziehung, 1953.

Bonvech, Bernd et al., eds. *SVAG: Upravleniie propagandy (informatsii) I S.I. Tulpanov. 1945–1949. Sbornik dokumentov*. Moscow: Rossiia Molodaia, 1994.

Bordihn, Peter. *Bittere Jahre am Polarkreis: Als Sozialdemokrat in Stalins Lagern*. Berlin: LinksDruck, 1990.

Borgmann, Karl, ed. *Anruf und Zeugnis der Liebe: Beiträge zur Situation der Caritasarbeit*. Regensburg: Verlag Josef Habbel, 1948.

Bosch, Elisabeth. *Vom Kämpfertum der Frau*. Stuttgart: Alemannen-Verlag, 1938.

Bosch, Friedrich Wilhelm. *Familienrechtsreform*. Siegburg: Verlag Reckinger, 1952.

Boveri, Margret. *Tage des Überlebens: Berlin 1945*. Munich: R. Piper, 1968.

Bovet, Theodor. *Die Ehe: Ihre Krise und Neuwerdung. Ein Handbuch für Eheleute und ihre Berater*. Tübingen: Furche Verlag, 1949.

Bremme, Gabriele. *Die politische Rolle der Frau in Deutschland: Eine Untersuchung über den Einfluß der Frauen bei Wahlen und ihre Teilnahme in Partei und Parlament*. Göttingen: Vandenhoeck & Ruprecht, 1956.

Brendgen, Margarete. *Frau und Beruf: Beitrag zur Ethik der Frauenberufe unserer Zeit*. Cologne: Bachem, 1947.

Brückner, Günther. *Die Jugendkriminalität*. Hamburg: Verlag Kriminalstatistik, 1956.

Brühl, Günther. *Unterhaltsrecht: Grundbegriff und Praxis*. Bielefeld: Gieseking, 1960.

Brummert, Jakob, ed. *Alleinstehend—aber nicht vereinsamt: Die Chance der alleinstehenden Frau*. Friedberg bei Augsburg: Pallotti, 1965.

Bruns, Ingeborg. *Als Vater aus dem Krieg heimkehrte: Töchter erinnern sich*. Frankfurt am Main: Fischer, 1991.

Buerkner, Trude. *Der Bund Deutscher Mädel in der Hitlerjugend*. Berlin: Junker und Dünnhaupt, 1937.

Buresch-Riebe, Ilse. *Frauenleistung im Kriege*. Schriftenreihe der NSDAP, group 2, vol. 6. Berlin: Eher, 1941.

Die christliche Familie: Gemeinsamer Hirtenbrief der deutschen Bischöfe, Fulda 1946. Berlin: Morus Verlag, 1946.

Chwalczyk, Georg. "Um den gerechten Wohnraum." *Arbeit und Sozialfürsorge* 3 (1948): 29–31.

Cörper, Carl, Wilhelm Hagen, and H. Thomae, eds. *Deutsche Nachkriegskinder: Methoden und erste Ergebnisse der deutschen Längsschnittuntersuchung über die körperliche und seelische Entwicklung im Schulkindalter*. Stuttgart: Thieme, 1954.

von Crone, Eugen. *Erwerbsarbeit der verheirateten Frau*. Stuttgart: Flamberg, 1958.

Darius, Käte. "Die soziale und ökonomische Lage als Ursache der Prostitution." Diss., Johann Wolfgang Goethe Universität Frankfurt, 1957.

Deutscher Gewerkschaftsbund. Der Bundesvorstand. Hauptabteilung Frauen. *Ergebnisse einer Befragung über die Belastung der erwerbstätigen Frauen durch Beruf,*

Haushalt und Familie. Gewerkschaftliche Beiträge zur Frauen-Erwerbsarbeit, vol. 3. Cologne: Bund Verlag, 1961.

de Zayas, Alfred. *Zeugnisse der Vertreibung.* Krefeld: Sinus-Verlag, 1983.

Diehl, Guida. *Die deutsche Frau und der Nationalsozialismus.* Eisenach: Neulandverlag, 1933.

Dischner, Gisela, ed. *Eine stumme Generation berichtet: Frauen der dreissiger und vierziger Jahre.* Frankfurt am Main: Fischer Taschenbuch, 1982.

Dittmar, Louise. *Das Wesen der Ehe.* Lepizig, 1850.

Dokumentation der Vertreibung der Deutschen aus Ost-Mitteleuropa. Vol. I/1, *Die Vertreibung der deutschen Bevölkerung aus den Gebieten östlich der Oder-Neiße.* 1954. Reprint, Munich: DTV, 1984.

Dokumente der revolutionären Arbeiterbewegung zur Frauenfrage 1848–1974. Leipzig: Verlag für die Frau, 1975.

Donner, Wolf. *Die sozial- und staatspolitische Tätigkeit der Kriegsopferverbände. Ein Beitrag zur Verbandsdiskussion.* Berlin: Duncker und Humblot, 1960.

Drei Jahre Landeswohlfahrtsverband Hessen, 1953–56. Kassel: Landeswohlfahrtsverband Hessen, 1956.

Drewitz, Ingeborg. *Gestern war Heute: Hundert Jahre Gegenwart.* Dusseldorf: Classen, 1978.

Duevert, Helene. *Die Frau von heute: Ihr Weg und ihr Ziel.* Werningerode: G. Közle, 1933.

Duft, Carmen. *Gleicher Lohn für gleichwertige Arbeit.* Winterthur: Keller Verlag, 1958.

Dunckelmann, Hennig. *Die erwerbstätige Ehefrau im Spannungsfeld von Beruf und Konsum.* Tübingen: J.C.B. Mohr, 1961.

Eggener, Elfriede. *Die organische Eingliederung der Frau in den nationalsozialistischen Staat.* Leipzig: R. Noske, 1938.

Eggers-Lorenz, Ottegebe. "Zur Frage des Widerspruchs nach Par. 48 EheG bei leichtfertigem Verhalten zur Ehe." *Neue Justiz* 8 (1954): 135–37.

Ehe und Familie in der DDR: Einführung zum Entwurf des Familiengesetzbuches der Deutschen Demokratischen Republik. Berlin: Staatsverlag, 1965.

"Die Ehescheidungen im Bundesgebiet seit 1946." *Wirtschaft und Statistik* 2 (1950): 291–93.

Enderle, Irmgard. *Frauenüberschuß und Erwerbsarbeit.* Bielefeld: Gewerkschaftliches Zonensekretariat, n.d. [1947].

Engels, Friedrich. *The Origin of the Family, Private Property, and the State.* 1884. Reprinted in *The Marx-Engels Reader,* 2nd ed., edited by Robert C. Tucker. New York: Norton, 1978.

Engels, Friedrich. *Zur Wohnungsfrage.* Singen: Oberbadischer Verlag, 1947.

"Die Entrechtung der Frau in der Sowjetzone: Kommunistische Frauengesetzgebung in Propaganda und Wirklichkeit." Sopade Informationsdienst Denkschriften 49. Bonn: Vorstand der SPD, n.d. [ca. 1952].

Ergebnisse über die Struktur der wirtschaftlich tätigen Wohnbevölkerung. Ergebnisse einer zwanzigprozentigen Stichprobenaufbereitung. Berlin: Staatlicher Zentralverlag für Statistik, 1966.

"Erwerbstätige Mütter, Ausschnitte aus einer sozialempirischen Enquette in Westberlin." *Soziale Welt* 9/2 (1958): 106ff.

Eser, Wolfgang, Rolf Fröhner, and Maria von Stackelberg. *Familie und Ehe: Probleme in den deutschen Familien der Gegenwart.* Bielefeld: Maria von Stackelberg Verlag, 1956.

Euler, Manfred. "Wohnverhältnisse, soziale und wirtschaftliche Situation der Untermieterhaushalte im Frühjahr 1960." *Wirtschaft und Statistik* 13 (1962): 13–18.

Faber, Dorothea. *Die Wohnungswirtschaft in der sowjetischen Besatzungszone.* Bonn:
Bundesministerium für gesamtdeutsche Fragen, 1953.

Die Familie, ihre Krise und deren Überwindung. Vortragsreihe der 3. katholischen
sozialen Wochen 1951 in München. Augsburg: Winfried Werk, 1951.

Das Familienunterhaltswesen und seine praktische Handhabung. Leipzig: Lurche Verlag, 1940.

Feger, Gottfried. *Die unvollständige Familie und ihr Einfluß auf die Jugendkriminalität.*
Familie und Jugendkriminalität, vol. 1. Stuttgart: Ferdinand Enke Verlag, 1969.

Feldbinder, Else. "Zwischen Tanzbar und Gesundheitsamt." *Sie* 1 (20 October 1946): 9.

Fell, Anna Elisabeth. "Die Eigenart der in Frankfurt am Main venerologisch zwangsbe-
handelten Frauen 1948 und 1951: Untersuchungen und Vergleiche der sozialen
Struktur und sozialhygienischen Diagnostik." Diss., Johann Wolfgang Goethe Universität Frankfurt, 1952.

Fenske. *Von der sozialen Fürsorge zur demokratischer Sozialpolitik.* Dresden, 1945.

Fichtner, Horst. *Erfüllung der Ehelosigkeit: Lebenshilfe für ledige Frauen.* Berliner
Hefte zur Förderung der evangelischen Krankenseelsorge, vol. 4. Berlin: Evangelisches Konsistorium Berlin-Brandenburg—Generalkonvent für Krankenseelsorge,
1958.

Finckh, Renate. *Mit uns zieht die neue Zeit.* Baden-Baden: Signal Verlag, 1979.

Firkel, Eva. *Schicksalsfragen der Frau.* Vienna: Herder Verlag, 1954.

Fischer, Helmut Wolfgang. *Rechtsstellung des unehelichen Kindes.* Cologne: Örthen
Verlag, 1939.

Frank, Gertrud. *Sie brauchen Dich: Die alleinstehende, berufstätige Frau.* Munich: Verlag Ars Sacra, 1960.

Franke, Lothar, and Helmut Bazille, eds. *Das tapfere Leben: Lebensfragen alleinstehender Frauen und Mütter.* Cologne-Hoffnungsthal: Verlag Werner Scheuermann, 1957.

Frankenstein, Luise. *Uneheliche Kinder von ausländischen Soldaten mit besonderer
Berücksichtigung der Mischlinge.* Genf: Internationale Vereinigung für Jugendhilfe,
1953.

Die Frau im Beruf. Hamburg: Furche, 1954.

Eine Frau in Berlin: Tagebuchaufzeichnungen. Geneva and Frankfurt am Main: Verlag
Helmut Kossodo, 1959.

Die Frau in Kirche und Gesellschaft. Berlin and Hamburg: Lutherisches Verlagshaus,
1965.

Die Frau und ihre Rechte, gestern und heute. Frankfurt am Main: Deutscher Gewerkschaftsbund, 1961.

*Frauen finden ihren neuen Arbeitsplatz: Zusammenstellung und Arbeitsmöglichkeiten
für berufslose und berufsentfremdete Frauen aus der Vermittlungspraxis der Ar-
beitsämter.* Nuremburg: Bundesanstalt für Arbeitsvermittlung und Arbeitslosenversicherung, 1962.

Frauen für Frauen. Berlin: Zentraler Frauenausschuß, 1946.

Frauen gestern und heute. Berlin: Union, 1946.

*Frauen helfen—Frauen bauen auf! Referate der 2. Bundes-Frauenkonferenz des deut-
schen Gewerkschaftsbundes 12.–14. Mai 1955.* Dusseldorf: Bund, 1955.

Frauenarbeit. Frankfurt am Main: Industriegewerkschaft Metall, 1954.

Frei, Emil. *Mißbrauchte Mutterkraft oder die Erwerbsarbeit der Mütter und ihre Folgen.*
Winterthur: Genossenschaftsbuchhandlung, 1954.

Freier, Anna-Elisabeth, ed. *Frauenpolitik 1945–1949. Quellen und Materialien*. Dusseldorf: Schwann, 1985.

Freudenberg, Karl. *Die Sterblichkeit nach dem Familienstand in Westdeutschland 1949/1951*. Hamburg: Deutsche Akademie für Bevölkerungswissenschaft, 1957.

Frey, Virtue Ann. *Mütter und Männer: Ein Buch vom tapferen Herzen*. Stuttgart and Berlin: Truckenmüller, [1943].

———. *Tapfere Trauer. Ein Gedenken für unsere Gefallenen*. Stuttgart and Berlin: Truckenmüller, [1942].

Friedeburg, Ludwig von. *Die Umfrage in der Intimsphäre*. Beiträge zur Sexualforschung, vol. 4. Stuttgart: Enke Verlag, 1953.

Friese, Gerhard. *Das Ehegesetz*. Berlin: Reichsgesundheitsverlag, n.d.

Frobenius, Else. *Die Frau im Dritten Reich. Eine Schrift für das deutsche Volk*. Berlin: Huch Verlag, 1933.

Fröhner, Rolf. *Wie stark sind die Halbstarken?* Bielefeld: Maria von Stackelberg, 1956.

Fuchs, Dieter. "Die Zerrüttung der Ehe." Diss., Universität Köln, 1961.

Gatzweiler, Richard. *Das dritte Geschlecht: Um die Strafbarkeit der Homosexualität*. Cologne-Klettenberg: Volkswartbund, 1951.

Gerda Müller freut sich auf ihr Kind. Pössneck: Karl-Marx Werk, 1952.

Gesundheitswesen: Statistische Ergebnisse 1946–50. Stuttgart: Kohlhammer, 1952.

Gewerkschaftliche Beiträge zur Frauen-Erwerbsarbeit. DGB Frauenarbeit, vol. 2. Cologne-Deutz: Bund-Verlag, 1959.

Ein glückliches Familienleben—Anliegen des Familiengesetzbuches der DDR. Berlin: Staatsverlag, 1965.

Glücksmann-Lüdy, Elisabeth. "Sollen Mütter erwerbstätig sein?" *Neues Beginnen* 8 (1954): 148–50.

Gollwitzer, Helmut. *Und vergib uns unserer Schuld. Ein historisches Dokument 1945/48*, 2nd ed. Mainz: Hase & Köhler Verlag, 1965.

Görres, Ida Friederike. *Von Ehe und Einsamkeit*. Donauwörth: Cassianeum, [1949].

Greeven, Heinrich, ed. *Die Frau im Beruf: Tatbestände, Erfahrungen und Vorschläge zu drängenden Fragen in der weiblichen Berufsarbeit und in der Lebenshaltung der berufstätigen Frau*. Hamburg: Furche Verlag, 1954.

Grisebach, Agnes-Marie. *Eine Frau im Westen: Roman eines Neuanfangs*. Frankfurt am Main: Fischer, 1989.

———. *Eine Frau Jahrgang 13: Roman einer unfreiwilligen Emanzipation*. Frankfurt am Main: Fischer, 1988.

Gross, Walter. *Nationalsozialistische Rassenpolitik: Eine Rede an die deutschen Frauen*. Berlin: Rassenpolitisches Amt, 1934.

Groth, Sepp. *Kinder ohne Familie: Das Schicksal des unehelichen Kindes in unserer Gesellschaft*. Munich: Juventa Verlag, 1961.

Grotowohl, Otto. "Die Begründung des Gesetzes über den Mutter- und Kinderschutz und die Rechte der Frau vor der Provisorischen Volkskammer der Deutschen Demokratischen Republik am 28. September 1950." In *Gesetz über den Mutter- und Kinderschutz und die Rechte der Frau*. Berlin: Deutscher Zentralverlag, 1950.

———. *Gesunde Familie, Glückliche Zukunft*. Berlin: Deutscher Zentralverlag, 1950.

Grünig, Gerhard, and Emil Zellmer. *Arbeitsvorschriften für die erwerbstätige Frau und Mutter*. Cologne and Berlin: Heymann, 1953.

Guggemos, Maria. *Die alleinstehende Mutter und das heranwachsende Kind: Liesbeths Tagebuch*. Frankfurt am Main: Öffentliches Leben, 1956.

Günther, Hans. *Gattenwahl zu ehelichem Glück und erblicher Ertüchtigung.* 2nd ed. Munich: Lehmann, 1943.

Gutachten über die soziale und politische Stellung der Frau in Westdeutschland. Berlin: Nationale Front des demokratischen Deutschlands, 1962.

Haas, Gerhard, and Alfred Leutwein [pseud. Siegfried Mampel]. *Die rechtliche und soziale Lage der Arbeitnehmer in der sowjetischen Besatzungszone.* Bonn: Bundesministerium für gesamtdeutsche Fragen, 1954.

Haffter, Carl. *Kinder aus geschiedenen Ehen: Eine Untersuchung über den Einfluß der Ehescheidung auf Schicksal und Entwicklung der Kinder nach ärztlichen, juristischen und fürsorgerischen Fragestellungen.* Bern: Huber, 1948.

Hagemeyer, Hans, ed. *Frau und Mutter. Lebensquelle des Volkes.* Munich: Hohenreichen Verlag, 1942.

Hagemeyer, Maria. *Denkschrift über die zur Anpassung des geltenden Familienrechts an den Grundsatz der Gleichberechtigung von Mann und Frau (Art. 3 Abs. 2 GG) erforderlichen Gesetzesänderungen.* Cologne: Bundesanzeiger, [1951].

———. *Der Entwurf des Familiengesetzbuches der "Deutschen Demokratischen Republik."* Bonn: Bundesministerium für gesamtdeutsche Fragen, 1955.

———. *Zum Familienrecht in der Sowjetzone.* Bonn: Bundesministerium für gesamtdeutsche Fragen, 1956.

———. *Zum Familienrecht in der Sowjetzone.* Bonn: Bundesministerium für gesamtdeutsche Fragen, 1958.

Hagen, Wilhelm, Hans Thomae, and Anna Ronge. *10 Jahre Nachkriegskinder.* Munich: J. A. Barth, 1962.

Handbuch der Deutschen Demokratischen Republik. Berlin: Staatsverlag, n.d. [ca. 1964].

Hannsmann, Margarete. *Der helle Tag bricht an: Ein Kind wird Nazi.* Munich: Goldmann, 1982.

Harmsen, Hans. *Eheschließung Sterilisierter.* Berlin-Grunewald: Verlag Dienst am Leben, 1935.

Has, Franziska. *Das Verhältnis der unehelichen Eltern zu ihrem Kind.* Berlin: Duncker und Humblot, 1962.

Hasler, Hanni. *Unverheiratet bleiben—ein Unglück? Ein offener Brief an die ehelose Frau reiferen Alters.* St. Gallen: Valian, 1948.

Hasselblatt, Dora, ed. *Wir Frauen und die nationale Bewegung.* Hamburg: Agentur des Rauhen Hauses, 1933.

Haug, Theodor. *Ehescheidung oder Erneuerung der Ehe?* Evangelische Zeitstimmen, vol. 14. Hamburg: Reich und Heidrich evangelischer Verlag, 1947.

Haushalte nach Art, Größe und Gebiet. Vol. 2 of *Wohnbevölkerung und Haushalte in den Bezirken der DDR.* Halle: Bezirksstelle Halle [1966].

Haushalte und Familien: Ergebnisse einer 1% Sonderaufbereitung aus dem Mikrozensus vom Oktober 1957. Stuttgart: Kohlhammer, n.d.

Hausmann, Manfred. *Trost im Trostlosen.* Frankfurt am Main: Fischer, 1956.

Hegener, Heinz. *Welche Ansprüche haben die Kriegsbeschädigten und Kriegshinterbliebenen?* 2nd ed. Dortmund: Schmidt & Andernach, 1961.

Heiber, Helmut, ed. *Goebbels-Reden.* Vol. 2, 1939–45. Dusseldorf: Droste, 1972.

"Heimkehrer-Ehen." *Sie* 3/48 (28 November 1948): 4.

Helmreich, Karl, ed. *Ratgeber für entlassene Soldaten.* Munich and Berlin: Jehle Verlag, 1944.

Hemsing, Walter. "Der Heimkehrer und seine Ehe." *Caritas* 50 (September-October 1949): 198–208.

Hentig, Hans von. *Die Kriminalität der lesbischen Frau.* Beiträge zur Sexualforschung, vol. 15. Stuttgart: Enke Verlag, 1959.

Herrmann, Algard Hedwig. *Die ausserhäusliche Erwerbstätigkeit verheirateter Frauen: Eine sozialpolitische Studie.* Stuttgart: Enke Verlag, 1957.

Der hessische Wohnungsbau in den Jahren 1945–1960. Wiesbaden: Der hessische Minister des Innern, 1960.

Heuckeroth, Werner. *Die Aufgaben der Hauptfürsorgestelle des Landeswohlfahrtsverbandes Hessen.* Kassel: Landeswohlfahrtsverband Hessen, 1957.

Hildebrand, Ruth. *Frauenaufgaben im Krieg: Was die deutsche Frau heute wissen muß.* Berlin: Rödiger Verlag, [1939].

Hinze, Edith. "Die Eingliederung der Frauen und weiblichen Jugendlichen in das Arbeitsleben." *Arbeit und Sozialfürsorge* 1 (1946): 74–76.

Hinze, Edith, and Elisabeth Knospe. *Lage und Leistung erwerbstätiger Mütter: Ergebnisse einer Untersuchung in Westberlin.* Cologne: Carl Heymann Verlag, 1960.

Hippel, Franz von. *Recht, Sittlichkeit und Religion im Aufbau von Sozialordnung.* Tübingen: Mohr Verlag, 1958.

Hirschmann, Hans. "Die kirchliche Stellungnahme zur Familienrechtsreform in der Bundesrepublik." *Herder Korrespondenz* 6 (March 1953).

Hitler, Adolf. *Mein Kampf.* 2 vols. Munich: Verlag Franz Eher Nachf., 1927.

Hoffmann, Elisabeth. *Ungefreit: Von ledigem Weibestum.* Habelschwerdt: Franke, 1927.

Hoffmann, Ferdinand. *Sittliche Entartung und Geburtenschwund.* Politische Biologie: Schriften für naturgesetzliche Politik und Wissenschaft, vol. 4. Berlin and Munich: J. G. Lehmans, 1938.

Hofmann, Anton Christian, and Dietrich Kersten. *Frauen zwischen Familie und Fabrik: Die Doppelbelastung der Frau durch Haushalt und Beruf.* Munich: Pfeiffer, 1958.

Hollander, Walther von. "Der Mann als Ballast." *Constanze* 1/6 (May 1948): 7.

———. "Mütter ohne Männer." *Constanze* 1/6 (May 1948): 6.

———. "Zum Thema: Frauenüberschuß." *Sie* 2/48 (30 November 1947): 4; 2/49 (7 December 1947): 4; 2/50 (14 December 1947): 4.

———. "Ein zweites Mal nicht!" *Constanze* 1/9 (July 1948): 10.

Hölzl, Michael. "Wohnungsbau ist Familienbau." In *Der soziale Wohnungsbau der katholischen Kirche in Bayern seit 1945,* edited by Josef Thalhamer. Munich: Katholisches Wohnungsbau- und Siedlungswerk in Bayern, n.d. [ca. 1960].

Hubbard, William. *Familiengeschichte: Materialien zur deutschen Familie seit dem Ende des 18. Jahrhunderts.* Statistische Arbeitsbücher zur neueren deutschen Geschichte. Munich: Beck, 1983.

Huebner, Konrad. *Die künftige Rechtsstellung des unehelichen Kindes.* Berlin: De Gruyter Verlag, 1954.

Hueck, Alfred. *Die Bedeutung des Art. 3 des Bonner Grundgesetzes für die Lohn- und Arbeitsbedingungen der Frauen.* Cologne: Bundesvereinigung der deutschen Arbeitgeberverbände, 1951.

Hugeuenin, Elisabeth. *Die Frau und ihr Schicksal.* Zurich: E. Ösch, 1946.

Hymmen, Friedrich Wilhelm. *Briefe an eine Trauernde: Vom Sinn des Soldatentodes.* Sonderdruck für das Hauptkulturamt in der Reichspropagandaleitung der NSDAP. Stuttgart: J. Engelhorns Nachf. Adolf Spemann, 1942.

Ilse schafft für eine friedliche und glückliche Zukunft. N.p.: Baumwollspinnerei Riesa VEB, 1952.

Jahn, Bruno H. *Sinn und Sittlichkeit des Nationalsozialismus: Versuch einer vernunft-gemässen Begründung.* Stuttgart and Berlin: J. G. Cotta'sche Buchhandlung Nachf., 1934.

Jahrbuch Arbeit und Sozialfürsorge 1947/48. Berlin: Druck Neues Deutschland, 1948.

Jansen, Friedrich. *Leitfaden des Familienrechts der Deutschen Demokratischen Republik.* Berlin: Deutscher Zentralverlag, 1958.

Jörger, Kuno. *Caritaswerk der Witwen.* Freiburg: Deutscher Caritas Verband General Sekretär, 1956.

Jörissen, Luise. *Die Lage der Prostitution in Deutschland.* Sieburg: Weimar, 1957.

Jung, Carl G. *Die Frau in Europa.* 1929. Reprint, Zurich: Rascher, 1948.

Das junge Mädchen und die junge Frau in unserer Zeit. SPD Schriftenreihe für Frauenfragen. Hannover: Hannover'sche Druck- und Verlag Gesellschaft, 1959.

Kahle, Maria. *Die deutsche Frau und ihr Volk.* Warendorf: Heine Verlag, 1941.

Kaps, Johannes. *Martyrium und Heldentum ostdeutscher Frauen: Ein Ausschnitt aus der schlesischen Passion 1945/46.* Munich: Niedermayer und Miesgang, 1954.

Kardorff, Ursula von. *Berliner Aufzeichnungen: Aus den Jahren 1942–1945.* Munich: Nymphenburger, 1976.

Kätoch, Elke. *Langfristige Bestimmungsgründe fur die Erwerbstätigkeit verheirateter Frauen.* Cologne: Westdeutscher Verlag, 1965.

Kempf, Ludwig. *Der Haftungsgrund der unehelichen Vaterschaft.* Bielefeld: Deutscher Heimat Verlag, 1958.

Kern, Käthe. "Unsere eigene Sache..." *Die Frau von Heute* 3/10 (May 1948): 4.

———. *Die Wende im Leben der deutschen Frau.* Dresden: Büro des Präsidiums des Nationalrates der National Front des demokratischen Deutschland, 1950.

Kietz, Gabi, and Marita Schmidt. *Frauen unterm Hakenkreuz: Eine Dokumentation.* Berlin: Elefanten Press, 1985.

"Kinder und Jugendliche in Familien." *Wirtschaft und Statistik* 11 (1960): 214–18.

Klare, Rudolf. *Homosexualität und Strafrecht.* Hamburg: Hanseatische Verlagsanstalt, 1937.

———. "Zum Problem der weiblichen Homosexualität." *Deutsches Recht* 8 (1938): 503–7.

Köhler-Irrgang, Ruth. *Die Sendung der deutschen Frau in der deutschen Geschichte.* Leipzig: Von Hase und Köhler, 1940.

Kolkmann, Käthe, and Otto Schlißke. *Mütter allein: Lebens- und Erziehungshilfe.* Stuttgart: Kreuz, 1955.

KPD Zentralkommittee. *Die Frau im neuen Deutschland.* Berlin: Neuer Weg, [1946].

Kranz, Heinrich Wilhelm, and Siegfried Koller. *Die Gemeinschaftsunfähigen: Ein Beitrag zur wissenschaftlichen und praktischen Lösung des sog. "Asozialenproblems."* Giessen: Karl Christ, 1941.

Kriner-Fischer, Eva. *Die Frau als Richterin über Leben und Tod ihres Volkes.* Schriftenreihe des Reichsausschußes, vol. 12. Berlin: Reichsausschuß für Volksgesundheit, 1935.

Krockow, Christian Graf von. *Die Stunde der Frauen: Bericht aus Pommern 1944 bis 1947.* Munich: Deutscher Taschenbuch Verlag, 1991.

Kroeber-Keneth, Ludwig. *Frauen unter Männern: Grenzen und Möglichkeiten der arbeitenden Frau.* Dusseldorf: Econ-Verlag, 1955.

Krüger, Hildegard. "Die alleinstehende Frau als Erzieherin." *Informationen für die Frau* 9 (April 1960): 9–10.

Kuby, Erich. *Rosemarie—des deutschen Wunders liebstes Kind.* Stuttgart: H. Goverts, 1958.

Kurz, Karl. *Lebensverhältnisse der Nachkriegsjugend.* Bremen: Trijen Verlag, 1949.

Landeswohlfahrtsverband Hessen. *10 Jahre Sozialarbeit in Hessen 1953–1963.* Schriften des Landeswohlfahrtsverbandes Hessen, vol. 8. Kassel: Landeswohlfahrtsverband Hessen, 1964.

Laska, Vera, ed. *Women in the Resistance and in the Holocaust: The Voices of Eyewitnesses.* Westport, Conn.: Greenwood Press, 1983.

Laslowski, Ernst. *Dank an eine heimatvertriebene Frau.* Freiburg am Breisgau: Selbstverlag, 1959.

Leber, Annadore. "Der Heimgekehrte." *Die Frau von heute* 1/1 (February 1946): 20.

Leibl, Marianne. *Eine Frau über Frauen: Einsichten und Ratschläge einer erfahrenen Psychologin.* Stuttgart: Klett Verlag, 1951.

Leimbach, Herbert. *Die Aufgaben der Hauptfürsorgestelle des Landeswohlfahrtsverbandes Hessen.* Kassel: Meister Verlag, 1957.

Leutwein, Alfred [pseud. Siegfried Mampel]. *Die sozialen Leistungen in der sowjetischen Besatzungszone.* Bonn: Bundesministerium der gesamtdeutschen Fragen, 1955.

———. *Die sozialen Leistungen in der sowjetischen Besatzungszone.* 2 vols. Bonn: Bundesministerium der gesamtdeutschen Fragen, 1957.

Litt, Theodor. *Das Verhältnis der Generationen: Ehedem und heute.* Wiesbaden: Dieterich, 1947.

Lüders, Else. "Die Dientspflicht der Frau." *Soziale Praxis* 57 (15 November 1938): 1347–58.

Lüders, Marie-Elisabeth. *Fürchte Dich nicht! Persönliches und Politisches aus mehr als 80 Jahren.* Cologne and Opladen: Westdeutscher Verlag, 1963.

Lüdy, Elisabeth. *Erwerbstätige Mütter in vaterlosen Familien.* Deutsche Akademie für soziale und pädagogische Frauenarbeit. Berlin: Verlagsgesellschaft Müller, 1932.

Lund, Petra. "Möchten Sie 'auf Zeit' verheiratet sein?" *Constanze* 2/7 (March 1949): 3.

Lütge, Friedrich. *Sozialpolitik und Wohnungsbau.* Berlin: Schirmer, 1941.

Magnussen, Karin. "Krieg und Kriegsfolgen vom Standpunkt der Rassen- und Bevölkerungspolitik." *Archiv für Bevölkerungswissenschaft und Bevölkerungspolitik* 11 (1941): 145ff.

Malter, Friedel. "Arbeitsfähige Sozialfürsorge-Unterstützungsempfänger wollen ihren Lebensunterhalt selbst verdienen." *Arbeit und Sozialfürsorge* 8 (1953): 88–90.

Mampel, Siegfried. *Das System der sozialen Leistungen in Mitteldeutschland und in Ost-Berlin.* Bonn: Bundesministerium der gesamtdeutschen Fragen, 1961.

Mann und Frau in den Ordnungen von Ehe und Familie. Die Kirche in der Welt, vol. 34. Münster: Aschendorff, 1951.

Mannschatz, Eberhard. "Die Aufgaben der Jugendhilfe bei der Bekämpfung der Jugendkriminalität und des Rowdytums." In *Beiträge zur Bekämpfung der Jugendkriminalität.* Berlin: Deutscher Zentralverlag, 1961.

Maschmann, Melita. *Fazit: Kein Rechtfertigungsversuch.* Stuttgart: Deutsche Verlags-Anstalt, 1963.

———. *Das Wort hieß Liebe.* Heilbronn: Eugen Salzer, 1955.

Mayntz, Renate. *Die moderne Familie.* Stuttgart: Enke, 1955.

Merritt, Anna, and Richard Merritt. *Public Opinion in Occupied Germany: The OMGUS Surveys 1945–49.* Urbana: University of Illinois Press, 1970.

―――. *Public Opinion in Semisovereign Germany: The HICOG Surveys, 1949–55.* Urbana: University of Illinois Press, 1979.

Meyer-Ehlers, Grete. *Wohnerfahrungen: Ergebnisse einer Wohnuntersuchung.* Wiesbaden and Berlin: Bauverlag, 1963.

―――. *Wohnung und Familie.* Stuttgart: Deutscher Verlag, 1968.

Middendorf, Wolf. *Soziologie des Verbrechens.* Dusseldorf: E. Diederich, 1959.

Minowsky, Bruno. "Im Wohnungsbau auf das Neue orientieren!" *Statistische Praxis* (1960): 173–77.

Mitscherlich, Alexander. *Auf dem Weg zur vaterlosen Gesellschaft: Ideen zur Sozialpsychologie.* 1963. Reprint, Munich: R. Piper, 1973.

Moers, Martha. *Der Fraueneinsatz in der Industrie.* Berlin: Duncker und Humblot, 1943.

―――. *Frauenerwerbsarbeit und ihre Wirkungen auf die Frau.* Recklinghausen: Verlag Bitter, 1948.

Moser, Sigrid. *Bald nach Hause—Skoro domoi.* Berlin: Aufbau, 1991.

Moßhamer, Ottilie. *Wege der Frau.* Werkbuch der religiösen Mädchenbildung, vol. 2. Freiburg am Breisgau: Herder, 1952.

Müller, Werner, and Wolfgang Seifart. "Jugendförderung und Jugendkriminalität." In *Beiträge zur Bekämpfung der Jugendkriminalität.* Berlin: Zentralverlag, 1961.

Müller-Schwefe, Hans Rudolf. *Die Welt ohne Vater: Gedanken eines Christen zur Krise der Autorität.* Hamburg: Furche, 1957.

Myrdal, Alva, and Viola Klein. *Die Doppelrolle der Frau in Familie und Beruf.* Cologne: Kiepenheuer und Witsch, 1956.

Nathan, Hans. "Zur Neugestaltung des Familienrechts." *Neue Justiz* 3 (1949): 102–4.

Neues Unehelichenrecht in Sicht: Vorträge der Arbeitstagung in Coburg am 25., 26., und 27. Mai 1961. Heidelberg: Selbstverlag des deutschen Instituts für Vormundschaftswesen, 1961.

Neuordnung der Sozialversicherung. Special printing, *Arbeit und Sozialfürsorge.* Berlin: Druck Neues Deutschland, 1947.

Nipperdey, H. C. *Gleicher Lohn der Frau für gleiche Leistung.* Cologne: Bund, 1951.

Noelle-Neumann, Elisabeth, and Erich Peter Neumann, eds. *The Germans: Public Opinion Polls 1947–1966.* Bonn: Verlag für Demoskopie, 1967.

Nold, Liselotte. *Am Leben lernen: Ein Handbuch für Frauenarbeit.* Nuremberg: Laetare, 1959.

"Nur nicht heiraten!" *Constanze* 1 (August 1948): 5.

Oeter, Ferdinand, ed. *Familie im Umbruch.* Gütersloh: Gerd Mohn, 1960.

―――. *Familienpolitik.* Stuttgart: Friedrich Vorwerk, 1954.

Offenberg, Maria. "Die berufstätige alleinstehende Frau." *Frau, Kirche und Volk* (1950): 40–45.

Die ökonomischen Grundlagen der Familie in ihrer gesellschaftlichen Bedeutung. Berlin: Duncker und Humblot, 1960.

Oppens, Edith, et al., eds. *Die Frau in unserer Zeit: Ihre Wandlung und Leistung.* Oldenburg and Hamburg: Stalling, 1954.

Ostermeier, Elisabeth. *Die wirtschaftlichen Probleme der alleinstehenden Frau: Vortrag gehalten auf der SPD-Frauenkonferenz in Bad Hersfeld, Oktober 1955.* Bonn: Vorstand der SPD, 1955.

Otto, Eva. *Beitrag zur psychologischen Situation der alleinstehenden Frau: Vortrag gehalten auf der SPD-Frauenkonferenz in Bad Hersfeld, Oktober 1955.* Bonn: Vorstand der SPD, 1955.

Pauleser, P. Saturnin. *Die alleinstehende Frau: Gedanken für Ledige, Witwen und Geschiedene*. Miltenberg am Main: Christkönigsbund, 1955–56.

Pech, Siegfried. "Das Einkommen in Haushalten von Arbeitern und Angestellten." *Statistische Praxis* (1960): 81–83.

Peters, Karl. *Das Recht des unehelichen Kindes*. Bonn: Dümmlers, 1947.

Petersen, Käthe. "Sammelvormundschaft für gemeinschaftsfremde und gefährdete Frauen." *Mitteilungen des deutschen Vereins für öffentliche und private Fürsorge* 24 (1943): 38–40, 57–59.

Pfeil, Elisabeth. *Die Berufstätigkeit von Müttern: Eine empirisch-soziologische Erhebung an 900 Müttern aus vollständigen Familien*. Tübingen: Mohr, 1961.

———. *Fünf Jahre später: Die Eingliederung der Heimatvertriebenen in Bayern bis 1950 auf Grund der Untersuchung im Bayerischen Statistischen Landesamt*. Frankfurt am Main: W. Metzner, 1951.

"Der Pflichtabend im Juli. Thema: Der Einsatz der weiblichen Jugend für Familie und Volksgesundheit." *Reichsfrauenführung* 7 (June 1938): 219ff.

Picker, Henry. *Hitlers Tischgespräche im Führerhauptquartier*. Stuttgart: Seewalt, 1976.

Pilgert, Henry P. *Women in West Germany. With Special References to the Policies and Programs of the Women's Affairs Branch, Office of Public Affairs, Office of the US High Commission for Germany*. Bonn: Historical Division, Office of the Executive Secretary, US-HICOG, 1952.

Pius XII and Arbeitsgemeinschaft der katholischen deutschen Frauen, eds. *Zu den heutigen Aufgaben der Frau: Worte des Heiligen Vaters an die Frauen*. Cologne: Selbstverlag, 1953.

Planken, Helgard. *Die soziale Sicherung der nicht-erwerbstätigen Frau: Eine Untersuchung über die Lage der nicht-erwerbstätigen Frau in der BRD*. Berlin: Duncker und Humblot, 1961.

Portmann, Heinrich. *Das bedrohte Sakrament: Gedanken zur Ehekrise der Gegenwart*. Kevelaer: Butzon und Bercker, 1950.

———. *Das unauflösliche Band*. Münster, 1950.

———. *Der zerbrochene Ring: Aus dem Tagebuch eines Ehegerichts*. Kevelaer: Butzon und Bercker, 1951.

Präger, Lydia. *Keiner lebt allein: Vom Miteinander im Beruf und Leben*. Bad Salzuflen: MBK, 1961.

Preuß, Traute. *Starkes schwaches Geschlecht: Weg und Leistung der Frau*. Hamm: Grote, 1956.

Prinz, Friedrich, and Marita Krauß, eds. *Trümmerleben: Texte, Dokumente, Bilder aus den Münchner Nachkriegsjahren*. Munich: DTV, 1985.

Prollius, Helga. "Ein Königreich für einen Mann?" *Constanze* 1/8 (April 1948): 3.

Quardt, Robert. *Lebensschicksale unverheirateter Frauen*. Celle: Giesel Verlag, 1952.

Rationalisierungs kuratorium der deutschen Wirtschaft, ed. *Frauenarbeit: Ergebnisse einer Befragung*. Frankfurt am Main: Rationalisierungskuratorium der deutschen Wirtschaft, [1959].

Die Rechte der Arbeiter und ihre Verwirklichung im Osten und im Westen Deutschlands. Berlin: Deutscher Zentralverlag, 1957.

Redöhl, Hans. "Der Abstammungsnachweis bei unehelichen Kindern." *Neues Volk* 8 (February 1940): 24–25.

Rees, Hanna. *Frauenarbeit in der NS-Volkswohlfahrt*. Munich: Zentralverlag der NSDAP, 1938.

Reichenau, Irmgard. *Deutsche Frauen an Adolf Hitler*. Leipzig: A. Klein, 1934.

Reichling, Gerhard. *Die Heimatvertriebenen im Spiegel der Statistik.* Berlin: Duncker und Humblot, 1958.

Reichspropagandaleitung Hauptpropagandaamt. *Den Müttern und Frauen zum Muttertag 1944: Deutschland . . . kein Opfer . . . ist dafür zu groß!.* Berlin: Erasmusdruck, 1944.

Reimann, Georg. *Verehrt-verdammt-verraten? Jugend in Licht und Schatten.* Stuttgart: Decker, 1955.

Reinhardt, Lore. *Die deutsche Frau als Quelle völkischer Kraft und sittlicher Gesundung: Ein Beitrag zur Prägung eines neuen deutschen Frauentyps.* Leipzig: Klein, 1934.

Reinicke, Dietrich, and Elisabeth Schwarzhaupt. *Die Gleichberechtigung von Mann und Frau nach dem Gesetz vom 18.6.57.* Stuttgart: Kohlhammer, 1957.

Rheine, Thomas von. *Die lesbische Liebe: Zur Psychologie des Mannweibes.* Berlin-Charlottenburg: Arix & Ahrens, 1933.

Riebe, Ilse. "Das Dilemma der sieben Millionen." *Sie* 4/31 (31 July 1949): 11.

Rodnick, David. *Postwar Germans: An Anthropologist's Account.* New Haven, Conn.: Yale University Press, 1948.

Roquette, Hermann. *Das Recht des unehelichen Kindes: Stand vom 1. Juli 1943.* Berlin, Leipzig, and Vienna: Deutscher Rechtsverlag, 1943.

Rosenberg, Alfred. *Der Mythos des 20. Jahrhunderts.* Munich: J. G. Weiß'sche Buchdruckerei, 1934.

Roten, Iris von. *Frauen im Laufgitter.* Bern: Hallwag, 1958.

Ruhl, Klaus-Jörg, ed. *Die Besatzer und die Deutschen: Amerikanische Zone 1945–48.* Dusseldorf: Droste Verlag, 1980.

———, ed. *Deutschland 1945: Alltag zwischen Krieg und Frieden in Berichten, Dokumenten und Bildern.* Darmstadt: Luchterhand, 1984.

———, ed. *Frauen in der Nachkriegszeit 1945–1963.* Munich: DTV, 1988.

———, ed. *Neubeginn und Restauration: Dokumente zur Vorgeschichte der Bundesrepublik Deutschland 1945–49.* Munich: DTV, 1982.

———, ed. *Unsere verlorenen Jahre: Frauenalltag in Kriegs- und Nachkriegszeit 1939–1949.* Darmstadt: Luchterhand, 1985.

Rühland, Helmut. "Entwicklung, heutige Gestaltung und Problematik der Kriegsopferversorgung in der BRD." Diss., Universität Köln, 1957.

SBZ-Deutschland von 1955–1958. Bonn: Bundesminister für gesamtdeutsche Fragen, 1961.

SBZ-Handbuch. Munich: Oldenbourg, 1990.

Schaffner, Bertram. *Father Land: A Study of Authoritarianism in the German Family.* New York: Columbia University Press, 1948.

Schell, Annemarie von. "Gedanken zum Muttertag." *Reichsfrauenführung* 11 (May 1942): 57–59.

Schellenburg, Ernst. *Deine Sozialversicherung.* Berlin: Versicherungsanstalt Berlin, 1946.

Schelsky, Helmut. *Die skeptische Generation: Eine Soziologie der deutschen Jugend.* Dusseldorf: E. Diederich, 1963.

———. *Soziologie der Sexualität.* Hamburg: Rowohlt, 1955.

———. *Wandlungen der deutschen Familie in der Gegenwart: Darstellungen und Deutungen einer empirisch-soziologischen Tatbestandsaufnahme.* Stuttgart: Enke, 1954.

Scherer, Alice, ed. *Die Frau: Wesen und Aufgaben.* Freiburg am Breisgau: Herder, 1951.

Scherer, Alice, Robert Scherer, and Julius Dornreich. *Ehe und Familie.* Wörterbuch der Politik. Freiburg am Breisgau: Herder, 1956–59.

Schimmel, Winfried. "Ein Blick in die Prostitution der Nachkriegsjahre." *Berliner Gesundheitsblatt* 1 (special printing, 1950).

———. "Der Einfluß des Zweiten Weltkrieges auf die Prostitution in Berlin." *Berliner Gesundheitsblatt* 3 (special printing, 1952).

Schirach, Baldur von. *Anweisungen für die Jungen- und Mädellager.* Berlin: Dienststelle Reichsleiter, 1940.

———. *Die Hitlerjugend: Idee und Gestalt.* Leipzig: Köhler und Amelang, 1936.

———. *Ich glaubte an Hitler.* Hamburg: Mosaik, 1967.

Schlüter-Hermkes, Maria. *Wiege und Welt: Aufsätze und Reden über Frau, Ehe und Familie.* Münster: Regensberg, 1950.

Schmidt, Marita, and Gabi Dietz, eds. *Frauen unterm Hakenkreuz: Eine Dokumentation.* Munich: DTV, 1985.

Schmidt-Klevenow, Dr. "Das uneheliche Kind in der Volksgemeinschaft." *Deutsches Recht* 7 (1937): 148–52.

Schmidt-Kolmer, Eva. *Verhalten und Entwicklung des Kleinkindes.* Berlin: Akademie-Verlag, 1959.

Schmitz, Josef. *Die starkmütige Frau: Ein Buch von christlicher Witwenschaft.* Limburg: Lahn, 1952.

———. *Von christlicher Witwenschaft.* Münster: Regensberg, 1947.

Schmucker, Helga. *Die ökonomische Lage der Familie in der BRD.* Stuttgart: Encke, 1961.

Schneider, Michael. *Wohnungsbau für Minderbemittelte.* Berlin: Duncker und Humblot, 1956.

Scholtz-Klink, Gertrud. *Aufbau des deutschen Frauenarbeitsdienstes.* Leipzig: Die nationale Aufbau Verlagsgesellschaft, 1934.

———. "Einleitung." In *Frauen helfen siegen: Bilddokumente vom Kriegseinsatz unserer Frauen und Mütter.* Berlin: Zeitgeschichte, 1941.

———. *Die Frau im Dritten Reich: Eine Dokumentation.* Tübingen: Grabert, 1978.

Schönfeldt, Sybil Gräfin. *Sonderappell 1945: Ein Mädchen berichtet.* Munich: DTV, 1984.

Schönleiter, W[aldemar]. *Die Kriegsopferversorgung.* Stuttgart: Kohlhammer, 1961.

———. "Zweites Gesetz zur Änderung und Ergänzung des Bundesversorgungsgesetzes." *Bulletin des Presse- und Informationsamtes der Bundesregierung* 164 (29 August 1953): 1377–78.

Schottländer, Felix. *Die Mutter als Schicksal: Bilder und Erfahrungen aus der Praxis eines Psychotherapeuten.* Stuttgart: Klett, 1947.

Schreiner, Agnes. "Es geht um den Mann." *Sie* 4/46 (13 November 1949): 4.

Schroeder, Robert, ed. *Probleme der berufstätigen Frau.* Leipzig: Georg Thieme, 1957.

Schubert, Doris. *Frauen in der deutschen Nachkriegszeit.* Vol. 1, *Frauenarbeit 1945–49: Quellen und Materialien.* Dusseldorf: Schwann, 1984.

Schubert, Werner, ed. *Das Familien- und Erbrecht unter dem Nationalsozialismus.* Paderborn: Schoening, 1993.

Schulze, Emma. "Überlegungen zum Problem der 'Onkelehen.'" *Neues Beginnen* 9 (June 1955): 85.

Seiler, Hans. *Familienunterhalt.* Augsburg: Moser, 1940.

Sevenich, Maria. *Die Frau in der Verantwortung der Zeit.* Recklinghausen: Bitter, 1946.

Siber, Paula. *Die Frauenfrage und ihre Lösung durch den Nationalsozialismus.* Berlin and Wolfenbüttel: G. Kallmeyer, 1933.

Siegmund, Eduard, and Charlotte Siegmund-Krahmer, eds. *Kämpferin im Alltag: Von Frauen, die das Leben zwingen.* Leipzig: Klinkhardt, 1940.

Siemsen, Anna. *Der Weg ins Freie.* Frankfurt am Main: Büchergilde Gutenberg, 1950.

Simmat, William. *Prostitution und Öffentlichkeit: Soziologische Betrachtungen zur Affäre Nitribit.* Schmiden bei Stuttgart: Decker, 1959.

Sozialistische Einheitspartei Deutschlands. *Die Gleichberechtigung der Frau.* Berlin: Einheit, 1946.

Speck, Otto. *Kinder erwerbstätiger Mütter: Ein soziologisch-pädagogisches Gegenwartsproblem.* Stuttgart: Enke, 1956.

Spittel, Lydia. *Ich habe keinen Menschen: Probleme der ehelosen Frau.* Lahr: Ernst Kaufmann, 1959.

Spitz, Charlotte. *Mütter und Töchter: Ein Generationenproblem.* Schwarzenburg: Gerber Buchdruck, 1951.

Stämmler, Martin. *Rassenpflege im völkischen Staat.* Munich: Lehmann, 1934.

Ständer, Christine. *Von der Verantwortung der Frau: Ein Weckruf.* Warendorf: Schnell, 1947.

Steigertahl, Georg. *Fürsorgerliche, strafrechtliche und polizeiliche Maßnahmen gegenüber sozial-schwierigen und asozialen Personen.* Berlin: Deutscher Verein für öffentliche und private Fürsorge, 1938.

Steiner, Anna Maria, and Hans Sauerland. *Mütter: Gestalten und Schicksale.* Sieburg: Haus Michaelsberg, 1949.

Stellungnahme des deutschen Gewerkschaftsbundes zum Regierungsentwurf eines Gesetzes über die Gleichberechtigung von Mann und Frau. Dusseldorf: Bund, 1952.

Stern, Erich. *Die Unverheirateten.* Stuttgart: Enke, 1957.

Stockmann, Gisela. "In der Familie beginnt die Erziehung." *Die Frau von heute* 12/45 (November 1957): 8–9.

Straßner, Christina, ed. *Frauen an der Front.* Donauwörth: Auer, 1940.

Strecker, Gabriele. *100 Jahre Frauenbewegung in Deutschland.* Wiesbaden: Büro für Frauenfragen in der Gesellschaft zur Gestaltung öffentlichen Lebens, 1950.

———. *Überleben ist nicht genug.* Freiburg am Breisgau: Herder, 1981.

Stritt, Marie. "Rechtskämpfe." In *Handbuch der Frauenbewegung. II. Teil,* edited by Helene Lange and Gertrud Bäumer. Berlin: Beltz, 1901.

Studien zur Jugendkriminalität. Berlin: Staatsverlag, 1965.

Stutz, Lieselotte. "Mündliche Wohnungsbeschwerden im Ministerium für Arbeit." *Arbeit und Sozialfürsorge* 7 (1952): 107.

Swoboda, Grete. *Die alleinstehende Frau in der Sozialversicherung: Vortrag gehalten auf der SPD-Frauenkonferenz in Bad Hersfeld, Oktober 1955.* Bonn: Vorstand der SPD, [1957].

Thewes, Viktor. *Die Rechtsstellung der verlassenen Ehefrau.* Freiburg am Breisgau: Goldschagg, 1939.

Thilo, Hans-Joachim. *Der ungespaltene Mensch.* Göttingen: Vandenhoeck & Ruprecht, 1957.

Thudichum, Marina. *. . . die allein im Leben stehen.* Donauwörth: Cassianeum, 1956.

Thurnwald, Hilde. *Gegenwartsprobleme Berliner Familien: Eine soziologische Untersuchung an 498 Familien.* Berlin: Weidmann'sche Verlagsbuchhandlung, 1948.

Timerding, Heinrich Emil. *Das Problem der ledigen Frau.* Bonn: Marcus und Weber, 1925.

Többen, Heinrich. *Der Lebenswille der Frau.* Bonn: Dümmler, 1947.

Toeplitz, Heinrich. "Die Vorbereitung des neuen Familienrechts durch die Rechtsprechung." *Neue Justiz* 8 (1954): 658–63.

Torrel, U. "Auf ihren Schultern . . ." *Sie* 1/15 (17 March 1946): 6.

Träume werden Wirklichkeit. Berlin, 1959.

Tritz, Maria. *Die Frauenerwerbsarbeit in der Bundesrepublik.* Stuttgart: Kohlhammer, 1961.

Trode, Eduard, ed. *Die Mutterschaftshilfe in Deutschland.* Berlin: Langewort, 1937.

Ulbricht, Walter. *Zur Geschichte der deutschen Arbeiterbewegung. Aus Reden und Aufsätzen.* 10 vols. Berlin: Dietz, 1955–66.

The United States Strategic Bombing Survey. Vol. 1. New York: Garland, 1976.

Unruh, Trude. *Trümmerfrauen: Biografien einer betrogenen Generation.* Essen: Klartext, 1987.

Unsere Frauen und die Jugend im Luftschutz. Breslau: Frankes, n.d. [ca. 1939–40].

Die Untermieten in der Bundesrepublik Deutschland nach der repräsentativen Nacherhebung vom 22.6.1951. Stuttgart: Kohlhammer, n.d.

Untersuchungen zum Problem der Ehescheidung in Deutschland. Bad Godesberg: Gesellschaft für sozialwissenschaftliche Erhebungen und Analysen, 1955.

Värting, Mathilde Themis. *Die Frau in unserer Zeit.* Darmstadt-Eberstadt: Themis, 1952.

Vassiltchikov, Marie. *Berlin Diaries 1940–45.* New York: Vintage, 1988.

Verband der Kriegsbeschädigten, Kriegshinterbliebenen, und Sozialrentner Deutschlands. *Verwaltungsvorschriften und Rententabellen zum Gesetz über die Versorgung der Opfer des Krieges (BVG).* Neuwied: Strüder, 1951.

———. *Vom Wesen und Wirken des VdK Deutschlands.* Neuwied: Strüder, 1955.

———. *Was erwarten die Kriegsopfer vom neuen Bundestag?* Neuwied: Strüder, 1954.

Volks- und Berufszählung vom 29. Oktober 1946 in den vier Besatzungszonen und Groß-Berlin. Berlin: Duncker und Humblot, 1946.

Volksbund deutscher Kriegsgräberfürsorge. *Als die Sterbenden und siehe wir Leben: Ein Gedenkbuch für den Toten des Krieges.* Oldenburg: Stalling, 1950.

———. *Den Gefallenen: Ein Buch des Gedenkens und des Trostes.* Munich and Salzburg: Akademischer Gemeinschaftsverlag, 1952.

Walz, H. *Die Frau als Opfer des Fortschritts.* Hamburg: Furche, 1955.

Wandrey, Hanns. *Die gesetzliche Unterhaltspflicht unter Berücksichtigung der Gleichberechtigung von Mann und Frau.* 3rd ed. Bonn: Stollfuß, 1959.

Waterstradt, G. "Ernste Mängel in unserer bisherigen Wohnraumverteilung." *Arbeit und Sozialfürsorge* 5 (1951): 511.

Weber, Mina, and Gabriele Dolezich. *Die Alleinstehenden: Ihr Schicksal, ihre Würde und ihre Sendung.* Beuron: Hohenzollern, 1952.

Wegscheider, Hildegard. *An unsere Frauen. Die Frau im demokratischen Staat.* N.p.: Verlag das Volk, n.d. [1945].

Weichmann, Elsbeth. *Die Frau in der Wirtschaft: Entwicklung der deutschen Frauenarbeit von 1946–1951.* Hamburg: Club der berufstätigen Frauen, n.d. [1951].

Weiß, Wilhelm. *Das Gesundheitswesen in der sowjetischen Besatzungszone.* Bonn: Bundesministerium für gesamtdeutsche Fragen, 1952.

Wernicke, Kurt Georg, ed. *Parlamentarischer Rat 1948–49. Aktien und Protokolle.* Boppard am Rhein: Boldt, 1970.

Wie kommt die Frau zu ihrem Recht. Hamburg: Constanze-Verlag, 1951.

Wiedemann, Fritz. *Die Frau ohne Mann.* Wiesbaden: Wort und Bild Verlagsgesellschaft, 1952.

Wiener, Horst. *Anklage: Werwolf: Die Gewalt der frühen Jahre oder Wie ich Stalins Lager überlebte.* Reinbek: Rowohlt, 1991.

Wir wollen helfen. Freiburg am Breisgau: Deutscher Nationalverband der katholischen Mädchenschutzvereine, 1952.

Die wirtschaftliche Situation der alleinstehenden Frau. Probleme der alleinstehenden Frau. Bonn: SPD, 1956.

Wirtz, Hans. *Die Witwe: Leben in Leid und Neugestaltung.* Speyer: Pilger, 1951.

Wittwika, Ilse. *Was ich mit eigenen Augen sah.* Berlin, 1950.

Wohlenberg, Ursula. *Auch Sie, Frau Wendt.* Berlin: Deutscher Frauenverlag, 1953.

Die Wohnungsverhältnisse und der Wohnungsbedarf Alleinstehender. Münster: Westfälische Wilhelms-Universität Münster, n.d. [1962–63].

Wolf, Christa. *Kindheitsmuster.* Berlin and Weimar: Aufbau, 1976.

Wolf, Erna. "Noch eine Kategorie berufstätiger Frauen." *Gleichheit* 6 (1956): 123–25.

Wolf, Ernst, Gerhard Lücke, and Herbert Hax. *Scheidung und Scheidungsrecht: Grundfragen der Ehescheidung in Deutschland untersucht an Hand der Statistik.* Tübingen: Mohr, 1959.

Wollasch, Hans. "Familie in der Krise." In *Anruf und Zeugnis der Liebe: Beiträge zur Situation der Caritasarbeit,* edited by Karl Borgmann. Regensburg: Josef Habbel, 1948.

Wolle, Waldemar, and Hildegard Wolle-Egenolf. *Denkschrift des deutschen Frauenrings zum Kabinettsentwurf eines Gesetzes über die Gleichberechtigung von Mann und Frau auf dem Gebiete des bürgerlichen Rechts und über die Wiederherstellung der Rechtseinheit auf dem Gebiete des Familienrechts.* Berlin: Vorstand des deutschen Frauenrings, 1952.

Wulff, Annemarie. *Die uneheliche Mutter und ihr Kind.* Berlin: Deutscher Verein für öffentliche und private Fürsorge, 1935.

Würmeling, Franz-Joseph. *Familie—Gabe und Aufgabe.* Cologne: Luthe, 1963.

Wurzbacher, Gerhard. *Leitbilder gegenwärtigen deutschen Familienlebens.* Stuttgart: Enke, 1958.

Wuttke, Max. *Ratgeber für die Angehörigen unserer Soldaten.* Stuttgart: Kohlhammer, 1942.

Wuttke, Max, and Max Wenzel. *Handwörterbuch der Reichsversorgung mit Einbeziehung der Wehrmachtsfürsorge- und -versorgungsgesetze.* Stuttgart: Kohlhammer, 1942.

Zahn-Harnack, von, Agnes. "Wieder doppelte Moral?" *Sie* 1/50 (17 November 1946): 2.

Zarncke, Lilly. *Fragen aus der Bekämpfung der Geschlechtskrankheiten im Kriege—das Pflegeamt.* Berlin: Deutscher Verein für öffentliche und private Fürsorge, n.d. [1940].

———. *Mütter allein: Gespräche über Erziehungsfragen der Gegenwart.* Berlin: Morus, 1949.

———. *Zur Unterbringung asozialer Familien: Beiträge zur Kriegswohlfahrtspflege.* Frankfurt am Main: Heinrich Demuth, 1941.

Zillig, Maria. *Gefährdete weibliche Jugend unserer Tage.* Paderborn: Schöninghaus, 1951.

Ziskoven, Gertrud. "Sozialpädagogische Maßnahmen zur Bekämpfung von Geschlechtskrankheiten." *Volkswartbund* (November-December 1948): 2–9.

Zur Reform des Ehe- und Familienrechts. Münster: Aschendorff, 1952.

BIBLIOGRAPHY OF SECONDARY SOURCES, BOOKS,
AND ARTICLES PUBLISHED AFTER 1965

30 Jahre volkseigene Betriebe. Berlin: Dietz, 1976.

Abelshauser, Werner. *Wirtschaftsgeschichte der Bundesrepublik Deutschland 1945–80.* Frankfurt: Suhrkamp, 1983.

Alcoff, Linda. "Cultural Feminism versus Poststructuralism: The Identity Crisis in Feminist Theory." *Signs* 13 (1988): 405–36.

Alheit, Peter, and Dietrich Mühlberg. *Arbeiterleben in den 1950er Jahren.* Bremen: Universität Bremen, 1990.

Allen, Ann Taylor. *Feminism and Motherhood in Germany 1800–1914.* New Brunswick, N.J.: Rutgers University Press, 1991.

Aumueller-Roske, Ursula. "'Beteiligung und Widerstand': Thematisierung des Nationalsozialismus in der neueren Frauenforschung." *Feministische Studien* 2 (1990): 139–43.

Baird, Jay. *To Die for Germany: Heroes in the Nazi Pantheon.* Bloomington: Indiana University Press, 1990.

Bajohr, Stefan. *Die Hälfte der Fabrik: Geschichte der Frauenarbeit in Deutschland 1914 bis 1945.* Marburg: Arbeiterbewegung und Gesellschaftswissenschaft, 1979.

———. "Uneheliche Mütter im Arbeitermilieu: Die Stadt Braunschweig, 1900–1930." *Geschichte und Gesellschaft* 7 (1981): 474–506.

Barthel, Horst. *Die wirtschaftlichen Ausgangsbedingungen der DDR.* Berlin: Akademie-Verlag, 1979.

Baumann, Ursula. *Protestantismus und Frauenemanzipation in Deutschland, 1850–1920.* Frankfurt am Main: Campus, 1992.

Becker, Josef, Theo Stammen, and Peter Waldmann, eds. *Vorgeschichte der Bundesrepublik Deutschland: Zwischen Kapitulation und Grundgesetz.* Munich: Fink, 1979.

Benjamin, Hilde, et al., eds. *Zur Geschichte der Rechtspflege der DDR 1945–1949.* 3 vols. Berlin: Staatsverlag, 1976–86.

Benz, Wolfgang, ed. *Die Vertreibung der Deutschen aus dem Osten: Ursachen, Ereignisse, Folgen.* Frankfurt am Main: Fischer, 1985.

Bergen, Doris. *Twisted Cross: The German Christian Movement in the Third Reich.* Chapel Hill: University of North Carolina Press, 1996.

Berghahn, Sabine. "Frauen, Recht und langer Atem—Bilanz nach über 40 Jahren Gleichstellungsgebot in Deutschland." In *Frauen in Deutschland 1945–1992,* edited by Gisela Helwig and Hildegard Maria Nickel. Berlin: Akademie Verlag, 1993.

Berghahn, Sabine, and Andrea Fritzsche. *Frauenrecht in Ost und West Deutschland. Bilanz—Ausblick.* Berlin: BasisDruck, 1991.

Bessel, Richard. "The 'Front Generation' and the Politics of Weimar Germany." In *Generations in Conflict: Youth Revolt and Generation Formation in Germany 1770–1968,* edited by Mark Roseman. Cambridge: Cambridge University Press, 1995.

———. *Germany after the First World War.* New York: Oxford University Press, 1993.

———, ed. *Life in the Third Reich.* New York: Oxford University Press, 1987.

Bessel, Richard, and Ralph Jessen. "Einleitung: Die Grenzen der Diktatur." In *Die Grenzen der Diktatur: Staat und Gesellschaft in der DDR,* edited by Richard Bessel and Ralph Jessen. Göttingen: Vandenhoeck & Ruprecht, 1996.

———, eds. *Die Grenzen der Diktatur: Staat und Gesellschaft in der DDR.* Göttingen: Vandenhoeck & Ruprecht, 1996.

Bethlehem, Siegfried. *Heimatvertreibung, DDR-Flucht, Gastarbeiterzuwanderung.* Stuttgart: Klett-Cotta, 1982.

Biess, Frank. "'Pioneers of the New Germany': Returning POWs and the Making of East German Citizens, 1945–1955." Paper delivered at conference, *Geteilte Geschichte,* University of Washington, May 1997.

Blasius, Dirk. *Ehescheidung in Deutschland 1794–1945.* Göttingen: Vandenhoeck & Ruprecht, 1987.

Bock, Gisela. "Die Frauen und der Nationalsozialismus: Bemerkungen zu einem Buch von Claudia Koonz." *Geschichte und Gesellschaft* 15 (1989): 563–79.

———. "'Keine Arbeitskräfte in diesem Sinne'—Prostituierte im Nazi-Staat." In *"Wir sind Frauen wie andere auch"—Prostituierte und ihre Kämpfe,* edited by Pieke Biermann. Reinbeck bei Hamburg: Rohwohlt, 1980.

———. "Racism and Sexism in Nazi Germany: Motherhood, Compulsory Sterilization, and the State." In *When Biology Became Destiny: Women in Weimar and Nazi Germany,* edited by Renate Bridenthal, Atina Grossman, and Marion Kaplan. New York: Monthly Review Press, 1984.

———. *Zwangssterilisation im Nationalsozialismus: Studien zur Rassenpolitik und Frauenpolitik.* Opladen: Westdeutscher Verlag, 1986.

Bock, Gisela, and Pat Thane, eds. *Maternity and Gender Policies: Women and the Rise of the European Welfare States, 1880s–1950s.* London: Routledge, 1991.

Böhne, Kurt W. *Die deutschen Kriegsgefangenen in sowjetischer Hand. Eine Bilanz.* Bielefeld: Gieseking, 1966.

Böttger, Barbara. *Das Recht auf Gleichheit und Differenz: Elisabeth Selbert und der Kampf der Frauen um Art. 3 II Grundgesetz.* Münster: Verlag Westfälisches Dampfboot, 1991.

Boyer, Christoph, and Hans Woller. "Hat die deutsche Frau versagt? Die 'neue Freiheit' der Frau in der Trümmerzeit 1945–1949." *Journal für Geschichte* 2 (1983): 32–36.

Bridenthal, Renate. "Beyond Kinder, Küche, Kirche: Weimar Women at Work." *Central European History* 6 (1973): 148–66.

Bridenthal, Renate, Atina Grossman, and Marion Kaplan, eds. *When Biology Became Destiny.* New York: Monthly Review Press, 1984.

Bridenthal, Renate, Claudia Koonz, and Susan Stuard, eds. *Becoming Visible: Women in European History.* 2nd ed. Boston: Houghton Mifflin, 1987.

Broszat, Martin, ed. *Zäsuren nach 1945.* Munich: Oldenbourg, 1990.

Broszat, Martin, Klaus-Dietmar Henke, and Hans Woller, eds. *Von Stalingrad zur Währungsreform: Zur Sozialgeschichte des Umbruchs in Deutschland.* Munich: Oldenbourg, 1988.

Brown, Elsa Barkley, "'What Has Happened Here': The Politics of Difference in Women's History and Feminist Politics." *Feminist Studies* 18 (1992): 295–312.

Brownmiller, Susan. *Against Our Will: Men, Women, and Rape.* New York: Simon & Schuster, 1975.

Chambers-Schiller, Lee Virginia. *Liberty a Better Husband: Single Women in America: The Generations of 1780–1840.* New Haven, Conn.: Yale University Press, 1984.

Childers, Thomas, and Jane Caplan, eds. *Reevaluating the Third Reich.* New York: Holmes & Meier, 1993.

Clemens, Petra. "Frauen helfen sich selbst: Die Betriebsfrauenausschüsse der fünfziger Jahre in kulturhistorischer Sicht." *Jahrbuch für volksdeutsche Kulturgeschichte* 30 (1987): 107–42.

———. "'Die haben es geschafft, uns an unserem Ehrgeiz zu packen . . .' Alltag und

Erfahrungen ehemaliger Betriebsfrauenausschuß-Frauen in der Nachkriegs- und Aufbauzeit." In *So nah beieinander und doch so fern: Frauenleben in Ost und West,* edited by Agnes Joester and Insa Schoeningh. Pfaffenweiler: Centaurus, 1992.

Conze, Werner, and M. Rainer Lepsius, eds. *Sozialgeschichte der Bundesrepublik Deutschland: Beiträge zum Kontinuitätsproblem.* Stuttgart: Klett-Cotta, 1983.

Cramer, Alfons. *Zur Lage der Familie und der Familienpolitik in der Bundesrepublik Deutschland.* Opladen: Leske Verlag, 1982.

Crew, David. "German Socialism, the State and Family Policy, 1918–1933." *Continuity and Change* 1 (1986): 235–63.

Czarnowski, Gabriele. "Frauen als 'Mütter der Rasse.' Abtreibungsverfolgung und Zwangssterilisation im Nationalsozialismus." In *Unter anderen Umständen. Zur Geschichte der Abtreibung,* edited by Gisela Staupe and Lisa Vieth. Dresden and Berlin: Deutsches Hygiene Museum, 1993.

————. *Das kontrollierte Paar: Ehe- und Sexualpolitik im Nationalsozialismus.* Weinheim: Deutscher Studien Verlag, 1991.

————. "'The Value of Marriage for the *Volksgemeinschaft*': Policies towards Women and Marriage under National Socialism." In *Fascist Italy and Nazi Germany,* edited by Richard Bessel. New York: Cambridge University Press, 1996.

Dahn, Daniela. "Ein Tabu bei West-Frauen." In *Stiefschwestern: Was Ost-Frauen und West-Frauen voneinander denken,* edited by Katrin Rohnstock. Frankfurt am Main: Fischer, 1994.

Dammer, Susanne. *Mütterlichkeit und Frauendienstpflicht.* Weinheim: Deutscher Studien-Verlag, 1988.

Daniel, Ute. *Arbeiterfrauen in der Kriegsgesellschaft.* Göttingen: Vandenhoeck & Ruprecht, 1989.

Daum, Monika, and Hans-Ulrich Deppe. *Zwangssterilisation in Frankfurt/Main 1933–1945.* Frankfurt am Main: Campus, 1991.

Davis, Belinda. "Reconsidering Habermas, Gender, and the Public Sphere: The Case of Wilhelmine Germany." In *Society, Gender, and the State in Germany, 1870–1930,* edited by Geoff Eley. Ann Arbor: University of Michigan Press, 1996.

de Grazia, Victoria. *How Fascism Ruled Women: Italy, 1922–1945.* Berkeley: University of California Press, 1992.

Delille, Angela, and Andrea Grohn. *Blick zurück aufs Glück: Frauenleben und Familienpolitik in den 50er Jahren.* Berlin: Elefanten Press, 1985.

————, eds. *Perlonzeit: Wie die Frauen ihr Wirtschaftswunder erlebten.* Berlin: Elefanten Press, 1985.

————. "Von leichten Mädchen, Callgirls und PKW-Hetären." In *Hart und Zart: Frauenleben 1920–1970.* Berlin: Elefanten Press, 1990.

Dickinson, Edward Ross. *The Politics of German Child Welfare.* Cambridge, Mass.: Harvard University Press, 1996.

Diehl, James M. *The Thanks of the Fatherland.* Chapel Hill: University of North Carolina Press, 1993.

Dinter, Andreas. "Die Seuchen im Berlin der Nachkriegszeit 1945–1949." Ph.D. diss., Free University of Berlin, 1994.

Dollard, Catherine. "A Tool of Social Reform: The *Frauenüberschuß* of Late Imperial Germany." Master's thesis, University of North Carolina, 1992.

Dölling, Irene. "Between Hope and Helplessness: Women in the GDR after the 'Turning Point.'" *Feminist Review* 39 (1991): 3–15.

————. "Culture and Gender." In *The Quality of Life in the German Democratic*

Republic, edited by Marilyn Schattner Rueschemeyer and Christiane Lemke. New York: Sharpe, 1989.

Dröge, Annette. *In dieser Gesellschaft überleben: Zur Alltagssituation lesbischer Frauen*. Berlin: Lesbenstich Presse Verlag, 1982.

Drohsel, Petra. *Die Lohndiskriminierung der Frauen: Eine Studie über Lohn und Lohndiskriminierung von erwerbstätigen Frauen in der Bundesrepublik Deutschland, 1945–1984*. Marburg: SP-Verlag, 1986.

Dunskus, Petra, et al. "Zur Verwirklichung des Rechtes auf Arbeit für die Frauen." In *Zur gesellschaftlichen Stellung der Frau in der DDR*, edited by Herta Kuhrig and Wulfram Speigner. Leipzig: Verlag für die Frau, 1978.

Ebbinghaus, Angelika. "Helene Wessel und die Verwahrung." In *Opfer und Täterinnen: Frauenbiografien des Nationalsozialismus*, edited by Angelika Ebbinghaus. Nördlingen: Delphi, 1987.

———, ed. *Opfer und Täterinnen: Frauenbiographien des Nationalsozialismus*. Nördlingen: Delphi, 1987.

Eckert, Roland. *Familie und Familienpolitik: Zur Situation in der Bundesrepublik Deutschland*. Melle: Ernst Knoth, 1985.

Eiber, Ludwig. "Frauen in der Kriegsindustrie: Arbeitsbedingungen, Lebensumstände und Protestverhalten." Vol. 3, Herrschaft und Gesellschaft im Konflikt, Part B, *Bayern in der NS-Zeit*. Edited by Martin Broszat, Elke Fröhlich, and Anton Grossmann. Munich: Oldenbourg, 1981.

Eid, Volker, and Laszlo Vaskovics. *Wandel der Familie. Zukunft der Familie*. Mainz: Matthias Grünewald Verlag, 1982.

Eifert, Christiane, and Susanne Rouette, eds. *Unter allen Umständen: Frauengeschichte(n) in Berlin*. Berlin: Rotation, 1986.

Eldorado: Homosexuelle Frauen und Männer in Berlin 1850–1950. Berlin: Frölich und Kaufmann, 1984.

Epstein, Cynthia. *Deceptive Distinctions: Sex, Gender, and the Social Order*. New Haven, Conn.: Yale University Press, 1988.

Essner, Cornelia, and Eduard Conte. "'Fernehe,' 'Leichentrauung' und 'Totenscheidung': Metamorphosen des Eherechts im Dritten Reich." *Vierteljahrshefte für Zeitgeschichte* 44 (1996): 201–28.

Evans, Richard. *The Feminist Movement in Germany 1894–1933*. London: Sage Publications, 1976.

Das Familienrecht in beiden deutschen Staaten. Cologne: Heymann, 1983.

Fehrenbach, Heide. *Cinema in Democratizing Germany: Reconstructing National Identity after Hitler*. Chapel Hill: University of North Carolina Press, 1995.

———. "The Fight for the 'Christian West': German Film Control, the Churches, and the Reconstruction of Civil Society in the Early Bonn Republic." *West Germany under Construction: Politics, Society, and Culture in the Adenauer Era*, edited by Robert G. Moeller. Ann Arbor: University of Michigan Press, 1997.

Feuersenger, Marianne. *Die garantierte Gleichberechtigung: Ein umstrittener Sieg der Frauen*. Freiburg am Breisgau: Herder, 1980.

Fischer, Erica. *Aimee und Jaguar*. Cologne: Kiepenheuer & Witsch, 1994.

Fischer, Ursula. *Zum Schweigen verurteilt: Denunziert—verhaftet—interniert (1945–1948)*. Berlin: Dietz, 1992.

Fishman, Sarah. *We Will Wait: Wives of French Prisoners of War, 1940–1945*. New Haven, Conn.: Yale University Press, 1991.

Fraser, Nancy. "Rethinking the Public Sphere." *Social Text* 25–26 (1990): 56–80.

Die Frau in der DDR. Berlin: Staatsverlag der DDR, 1975.

Die Frau und die Gesellschaft. Leipzig: Verlag für die Frau, 1974.

Frauenalltag und Frauenbewegung 1890–1980: Ausstellungskatalog des historischen Museums Frankfurt. 4 vols. Basel: Strömfeld/Roter Stern, 1981.

Frauengruppe Faschismusforschung, ed. *Mutterkreuz und Arbeitsbuch: Zur Geschichte der Frauen in der Weimarer Republik und im Nationalsozialismus.* Frankfurt am Main: Fischer, 1978.

Frei, Norbert. "Wie modern war der Nationalsozialismus?" *Geschichte und Gesellschaft* 19 (1993): 367–87.

Freier, Anna-Elisabeth. "Frauenfragen sind Lebensfragen—Über die naturwüchsige Deckung von Tagespolitik und Frauenpolitik nach dem Zweiten Weltkrieg." In *"Das Schicksal Deutschlands liegt in der Hand seiner Frauen": Frauen in der deutschen Nachkriegsgeschichte,* edited by Anna-Elisabeth Freier and Annette Kuhn. Dusseldorf: Schwann, 1984.

Freier, Anna-Elisabeth, and Annette Kuhn, eds. *"Das Schicksal Deutschlands liegt in der Hand seiner Frauen": Frauen in der deutschen Nachkriegsgeschichte.* Dusseldorf: Schwann, 1984.

Frevert, Ute. *Frauen-Geschichte zwischen bürgerlicher Verbesserung und neuer Weiblichkeit.* Frankfurt am Main: Suhrkamp, 1986.

Fricke, Karl Wilhelm. "'Kampf dem Klassenfeind': Politische Verfolgung in der SBZ." In *Studien zur Geschichte der SBZ/DDR,* edited by Alexander Fischer. Berlin: Duncker und Humblot, 1993.

——— . *Politik und Justiz in der DDR: Zur Geschichte der politischen Verfolgung 1945–1968.* Cologne: Verlag Wissenschaft und Politik, 1979.

Ganßmüller, Christian. *Die Erbgesundheitspolitik des Dritten Reiches.* Cologne and Vienna: Böhlau, 1987.

Garner, Curt. "Public Service Personnel in West Germany in the 1950s." *Journal of Social History* 29 (1995–96): 25–80.

Gast, Gabrielle. *Die Politische Rolle der Frau in der DDR.* Dusseldorf: Bertelsmann, 1973.

Gellately, Robert. *The Gestapo and German Society: Enforcing Racial Policy 1933–1945.* Oxford: Clarendon Press, 1990.

Gerhard, Ute. "Die staatlich institutionalisierte 'Lösung' der Frauenfrage: Zur Geschichte der Geschlechterverhältnisse in der DDR." In *Sozialgeschichte der DDR,* edited by Hartmut Kaelble, Jürgen Kocka, and Hartmut Zwahr. Stuttgart: Klett-Cotta, 1994.

Gersdorff, Ursula von. *Frauen im Kriegsdienst 1919–1945.* Stuttgart: Deutsche Verlags Anstalt, 1969.

Geschichte des DFD. Leipzig: Verlag für die Frau, 1989.

Gimbel, John. *A German Community under American Occupation: Marburg, 1945–52.* Stanford, Calif.: Stanford University Press, 1961.

Goldman, Wendy. *Women, the State and Revolution: Soviet Family Policy and Social Life 1917–1936.* Cambridge: Cambridge University Press, 1993.

Gordon, Linda. "On 'Difference.'" *Genders* 10 (1991): 91–111.

——— , ed. *Women, the State, and Welfare.* Madison: University of Wisconsin Press, 1990.

Goschler, Constantin. *Wiedergutmachung: Westdeutschland und die Verfolgten des Nationalsozialismus 1945–1954.* Munich: Oldenbourg, 1992.

Gräfe, Marlis, and Bodo Ritscher. "Die Speziallager in der Sowjetischen Besatzungszone: Das Beispiel Buchenwald." In *Recht oder Rache? Buchenwald 1945–1950: Betroffene erinnern sich,* edited by Hanna Müller. Frankfurt am Main: Dipa, 1991.

Grandke, Anita. "Zur Entwicklung von Ehe und Familie." In *Zur gesellschaftlichen Stellung der Frau in der DDR*, edited by Herta Kuhrig and Wulfram Speigner. Leipzig: Verlag für die Frau, 1978.

Gravenhorst, Lerke, and Carmen Tatschmurat, eds. *TöchterFragen NS-Frauengeschichte*. Freiburg am Breisgau: Kore, 1990.

Grebing, Helga, Peter Pozorski, and Rainer Schulze. *Die Nachkriegsentwicklung in Westdeutschland 1945–1949*. 2 vols. Tübingen: Metzler, 1980.

Greven-Aschoff, Barbara. *Die bürgerliche Frauenbewegung in Deutschland 1894–1933*. Göttingen: Vandenhoeck & Ruprecht, 1981.

Gries, Rainer. *Die Rationengesellschaft*. Münster: Verlag Westphälisches Dampfboot, 1991.

Grossmann, Atina. "Feminist Debates about Women and National Socialism." *Gender and History* 3 (1991): 350–58.

———. "The New Woman and the Rationalization of Sexuality in Weimar Germany." In *Powers of Desire*, edited by Ann Snitow, Christine Stansell, and Sharon Thompson. New York: Monthly Review Press, 1983.

———. "A Question of Silence: The Rape of German Women by Occupation Soldiers." *October* 72 (April 1995): 43–63.

———. *Reforming Sex: The German Movement for Birth Control and Abortion Reform, 1920–1950*. New York: Oxford University Press, 1995.

Grunberger, Richard. *The 12-Year Reich: A Social History of Nazi Germany 1933–1945*. New York: Ballantine, 1971.

Guttmann, Barbara. *Weibliche Heimarmee: Frauen in Deutschland 1914–1918*. Weinheim: Deutscher Studien Verlag, 1989.

Gysi, Jutta, and Dagmar Meyer. "Leitbild: Berufstätige Mutter—DDR-Frauen in Familie, Partnerschaft und Ehe." In *Frauen in Deutschland 1945–1992*, edited by Gisela Helwig and Hildegard Maria Nickel. Berlin: Akademie, 1993.

Habermas, Jürgen. *Arbeit, Freizeit, Konsum*. Giessen: Gravenhage, 1973.

———. *The Structural Transformation of the Public Sphere*. Trans. Thomas Burger. Cambridge, Mass.: MIT Press, 1989.

Hachtmann, Rüdiger. "Industriearbeiterinnen in der deutschen Kriegswirtschaft 1936 bis 1944/45." *Geschichte und Gesellschaft* 19 (1993): 332–66.

Hagemann, Karen. *Frauenalltag und Männerpolitik: Alltagsleben und gesellschaftliches Handeln von Arbeiterfrauen in der Weimarer Republik*. Bonn: Dietz, 1990.

Hajnal, J. "European Marriage Patterns in Perspective." In *Population in History*, edited by D. V. Glass and D.E.C. Eversley. London: E. Arnold, 1965.

Hampele, Anne. "Arbeite mit, plane mit, regiere mit—Zur politischen Partizipation von Frauen in der DDR." In *Frauen in Deutschland 1945–1992*, edited by Gisela Helwig and Hildegard Maria Nickel. Berlin: Akademie, 1993.

Hampele, Anne, and Stefan Naevecke. "Erwerbstätigkeit von Frauen in den neuen Bundesländern—Lebensmuster unter Druck." In *Der lange Weg zur Einheit*, edited by Gert-Joachim Glaeßner. Berlin: Dietz, 1993.

Hansen, Eckhard. *Wohlfahrtspolitik im NS-Staat: Motivationen, Konflikte und Machtstrukturen im "Sozialismus der Tat" des Dritten Reiches*. Augsburg: Macro-Verlag, 1991.

Harsch, Donna. "Public Continuity and Private Change? Women's Consciousness and Activity in Frankfurt, 1945–1955." *Journal of Social History* 27 (1993): 29–58.

———. "Society, the State, and Abortion in East Germany, 1950–1972." *American Historical Review* 102/1 (1997): 53–84.

Harvey, Elizabeth. "'Die deutsche Frau in Osten': 'Rasse,' Geschlecht und öffentlicher Raum im besetzten Polen 1940–44." *Archiv für Sozialgeschichte* 38 (1998).

———. "Die Jugendfürsorge in der Endphase der Weimarer Republik." In *Soziale Arbeit und Faschismus*, edited by Hans-Uwe Otto and Heinz Sünker. Frankfurt am Main: Suhrkamp, 1989.

Hasenclever, Christa. *Jugendhilfe und Jugendgesetzgebung seit 1900*. Göttingen: Vandenhoeck & Ruprecht, 1978.

Hausen, Karin, ed. *Frauen suchen ihre Geschichte: Historische Studien zum 19. und 20. Jahrhundert*. Munich: Beck, 1983.

———. "The German Nation's Obligations to the Heroes' Widows of World War I." In *Behind the Lines: Gender and the Two World Wars*, edited by Margaret R. Higonnet et al. New Haven, Conn.: Yale University Press, 1987.

Heilig, Gerhard. "Die Heiratsneigung lediger Frauen in der Bundesrepublik Deutschland 1950–1985." *Zeitschrift für Bevölkerungswissenschaft* 11 (1985): 519–47.

Heineman, Elizabeth. "Complete Families, Half Families, No Families at All: Female-Headed Households and the Reconstruction of the Family in the Early Federal Republic." *Central European History* 29 (1996): 19–60.

———. "The Hour of the Woman: Memories of Germany's 'Crisis Years' and West German National Identity." *American Historical Review* 101 (1996): 354–95.

Helwig, Gisela, and Hildegard Maria Nickel. "Einleitung." In *Frauen in Deutschland 1945–1992*, edited by Gisela Helwig and Hildegard Maria Nickel. Berlin: Akademie, 1993.

———, eds. *Frauen in Deutschland 1945–1992*. Berlin: Akademie, 1993.

Hepp, Michael. "Vorhof zur Hölle: Mädchen im 'Jugendschutzlager' Uckermark." In *Opfer und Täterinnen: Frauenbiografien des Nationalsozialismus*, edited by Angelika Ebbinghaus. Nördlingen: Delphi, 1987.

Herbert, Ulrich. *Fremdarbeiter: Politik und Praxis des "Ausländer-Einsatzes" in der Kriegswirtschaft des Dritten Reiches*. Berlin: Dietz, 1985.

Herbst, Ludolf, ed. *Westdeutschland 1945–1955: Unterwerfung, Kontrolle, Integration*. Munich: Oldenbourg, 1986.

Herve, Florence, ed. *Geschichte der deutschen Frauenbewegung*. Cologne: Pahl-Rugenstein, 1987.

Higginbotham, Evelyn Brooks. "African-American Women's History and the Metalanguage of Race." *Signs* 17 (1992): 251–74.

Higonnet, Margaret R., et al., eds. *Behind the Lines: Gender and the Two World Wars*. New Haven, Conn.: Yale University Press, 1987.

Höhn, Maria. "Frau im Haus und Girl im Spiegel: Discourse on Women in the Interregnum Period of 1945–1949 and the Question of German Identity." *Central European History* 26 (1993): 57–90.

———. "GIs, Veronikas and Lucky Strikes: German Reactions to the American Military Presence in the Rhineland-Palatinate during the 1950s." Ph.D. diss., University of Pennsylvania, 1995.

Holmsten, Georg. *Kriegsalltag: 1933–1945 in Deutschland*. Dusseldorf: Droste, 1982.

Homze, Edward. *Foreign Labor in Nazi Germany*. Princeton, N.J.: Princeton University Press, 1967.

Hong, Young Sun. "Femininity as a Vocation: Gender and Class Conflict in the Professionalization of German Social Work." In *German Professions, 1800–1950*, edited by Geoffrey Cocks and Konrad H. Jarausch. New York: Oxford University Press, 1990.

Horbelt, Rainer, and Sonja Spindler. *Wie wir hamsterten, hungerten und überlebten: Zehn Frauen erzählen*. Frankfurt am Main: Eichborn, 1983.

Hörning, Erika. "The Myth of Female Loyalty." *Journal of Psychohistory* 16 (1988): 19–45.

Hudemann, Rainer. *Sozialpolitik im deutschen Südwesten zwischen Tradition und Neuordnung 1945–1953: Sozialversicherung und Kriegsopferversorgung im Rahmen französischer Besatzungspolitik.* Mainz: Verlag Hase und Köhler, 1988.

Jeffreys, Sheila. *The Spinster and Her Enemies.* London: Pandora, 1985.

Jellonnek, Burkhard. *Homosexuelle unter dem Hakenkreuz: Die Verfolgung von Homosexuellen im Dritten Reich.* Paderborn: Ferdinand Schöningh, 1990.

Jungwirth, Nikolaus, and Gerhard Kromschröder. *Die Pubertät der Republik: Die 50er Jahre der Deutschen.* Frankfurt am Main: Fricke, 1978.

Jurczyk, Karin. *Frauenarbeit und Frauenrolle: Zum Zusammenhang von Familienpolitik und Frauenerwerbstätigkeit in Deutschland von 1918–1975.* Frankfurt am Main: Campus, 1978.

Kaelble, Hartmut, Jürgen Kocka, and Hartmut Zwahr. "Einleitung." In *Sozialgeschichte der DDR,* edited by Hartmut Kaelble, Jürgen Kocka, and Hartmut Zwahr. Stuttgart: Klett-Cotta, 1994.

Kaiser, Hella. "Kinder waren uns so fremd wie Wesen vom anderen Stern." In *Stiefschwestern: Was Ost-Frauen und West-Frauen voneinander denken,* edited by Katrin Rohnstock. Frankfurt am Main: Fischer, 1994.

Kaplan, Marion A. *The Jewish Feminist Movement in Germany.* Westport, Conn.: Greenwood Press, 1979.

Kater, Michael. "Frauen in der NS-Bewegung." *Vierteljahreshefte für Zeitgeschichte* 31 (1983): 202–41.

Kaupen-Haas, Heidrun, ed. *Der Griff nach der Bevölkerung.* Nördlingen: Delphi, 1986.

Kershaw, Ian. *The "Hitler Myth": Image and Reality in the Third Reich.* Oxford: Oxford University Press, 1987.

———. *Popular Opinion and Political Dissent in the Third Reich: Bavaria, 1933–1945.* Oxford: Clarendon, 1983.

Kessler, Hannelore. *"Die deutsche Frau": Nationalsozialistische Frauenpropaganda im Völkischen Beobachter.* Cologne: Pahl-Rugenstein Verlag, 1981.

Kientopf, Anna. *Das friedensfeindliche Trauma: Die rote Armee in Deutschland 1945.* Lindhorst: Askania, 1984.

Kilian, Achim. *Einzuweisen zur völligen Isolierung: NKWD-Speziallager Mühlberg/Elbe 1945–1948.* Leipzig: Forum, 1993.

Kinz, Gabriele. *Der Bund Deutscher Mädel.* Frankfurt am Main: Peter Lang, 1990.

Klaus, Martin. *Mädchen im Dritten Reich: Der Bund Deutscher Mädel.* Cologne: Pahl-Rugenstein, 1983.

———. *Mädchen in der Hitlerjugend: Die Erziehung zur "deutschen Frau."* Cologne: Pahl-Rugenstein, 1980.

———. *Mädchenerziehung zur Zeit der faschistischen Herrschaft in Deutschland: Der Bund Deutscher Mädel.* Frankfurt am Main: Dipa Verlag, 1983.

Kleiber, Lore. "'Wo ihr seid, da soll die Sonne scheinen!': Der Frauenarbeitsdienst am Ende der Weimarer Republik und im Nationalsozialismus." In *Mutterkreuz und Arbeitsbuch,* edited by Frauengruppe Faschismusforschung. Frankfurt am Main: Fischer Taschenbuch, 1981.

Klessmann, Christoph. *Die doppelte Staatsgründung: Deutsche Geschichte 1945–55.* Göttingen: Vandenhoeck & Ruprecht, 1982.

———, ed. *Nicht nur Hitlers Krieg: Der Zweite Weltkrieg und die Deutschen.* Dusseldorf: Droste, 1989.

Klinksiek, Dorothee. *Die Frau im NS-Staat.* Stuttgart: Deutsche Verlags-Anstalt, 1982.

Klönne, Arno. *Die betrogene Generation.* Cologne: Pahl-Rugenstein, 1985.
———. *Jugend im Dritten Reich: Die Hitler-Jugend und ihre Gegner.* Munich: DTV, 1990.
Klonovsky, Michael, and Jan von Flocken. *Stalins Lager in Deutschland 1945–1950.* Berlin: Ullstein, 1991.
Koch, Petra, and Hans Günther Knöbel. *Familienpolitik der DDR im Spannungsfeld zwischen Familie und Berufstätigkeit von Frauen.* Pfaffenweiler: Centaurus, 1986.
Kocka, Jürgen. "Eine durchherrschte Gesellschaft." In *Sozialgeschichte der DDR,* edited by Hartmut Kaelble, Jürgen Kocka, and Hartmut Zwahr. Stuttgart: Klett-Cotta, 1994.
Kohli, Martin. "Arbeit, Lebenslauf und soziale Differenzierung." In *Sozialgeschichte der DDR,* edited by Hartmut Kaelble, Jürgen Kocka, and Hartmut Zwahr. Stuttgart: Klett-Cotta, 1994.
Kokula, Ilse. *Jahre des Glücks, Jahre des Leids: Gespräche mit älteren lesbischen Frauen.* Kiel: Verlag Christiane Gemballa, 1986.
———. "Lesbisch leben von Weimar bis zur Nachkriegszeit." In *Eldorado: Homosexuelle Frauen und Männer in Berlin 1850–1950. Geschichte, Alltag und Kultur.* Berlin: Frölich & Kaufmann, 1984.
———. "Zur Situation lesbischer Frauen während der NS-Zeit." *Beiträge zur feministischen Theorie und Praxis* 25–26 (1989): 29ff.
Kolinsky, Eva. *Women in Contemporary Germany: Life, Work and Politics.* Providence, R.I.: Berg, 1993.
König, Cosima. *Die Frau im Recht des Nationalsozialismus: Eine Analyse ihrer familien-, erb- und arbeitsrechtlichen Stellung.* Frankfurt am Main: Peter Lang, 1988.
König, Rene. "Familie und Autorität der deutschen Väter im Jahre 1955." In *Materialien zur Soziologie der Familie,* 2nd ed., edited by Rene König. Cologne: Kiepenheuer und Witsch, 1974.
Koonz, Claudia. "The Fascist Solution to the Woman Question in Italy and Germany." In *Becoming Visible: Women in European History,* 2nd ed., edited by Renate Bridenthal, Claudia Koonz, and Susan Stuard. Boston: Houghton Mifflin, 1987.
———. *Mothers in the Fatherland: Women, the Family, and Nazi Politics.* New York: St. Martin's Press, 1987.
Kopstein, Jeffrey. *The Politics of Economic Decline in East Germany, 1945–1989.* Chapel Hill: University of North Carolina Press, 1997.
Krecker, Margot, Gerda Niebsch, and Walter Günther. "Gesellschaftliche Kindereinrichtungen—eine Voraussetzung für die Vereinbarkeit von Berufstätigkeit und Mutterschaft." In *Zur gesellschaftlichen Stellung der Frau in der DDR,* edited by Herta Kuhrig and Wulfram Speigner. Leipzig: Verlag für die Frau, 1978.
Kreuzer, Margot. *Prostitution: Eine sozialgeschichtliche Untersuchung in Frankfurt a.M. von der Syphilis bis AIDS.* Stuttgart: Schwer, 1988.
Krüger, Dieter, and Gerhard Finn. *Mecklenburg-Vorpommern 1945 bis 1948 und das Lager Fünfeichen.* Berlin: Holzapfel, 1992.
Kuby, Erich. *Die Russen in Berlin 1945.* Munich: Scherz, 1965.
Kuckuc, Ina. *Der Kampf gegen Unterdrückung.* Munich: Frauenoffensive, 1975.
Kuhn, Annette. "Power and Powerlessness: Women after 1945, or the Continuity of the Ideology of Femininity." *German History* 7 (1989): 34–46.
———. "Die vergessene Frauenarbeit in der deutschen Nachkriegszeit." In *"Das Schicksal Deutschlands liegt in der Hand seiner Frauen": Frauen in der deutschen*

Nachkriegsgeschichte, edited by Anna-Elisabeth Freier and Annette Kuhn. Dusseldorf: Schwann, 1984.

Kuhn, Annette, and Valentine Rothe, eds. *Frauenarbeit und Frauenwiderstand im NS-Staat*. Dusseldorf: Schwann, 1982.

———, eds. *Frauenpolitik im NS-Staat*. Dusseldorf: Schwann, 1982.

Kuhrig, Herta, and Wulfram Speigner. "Gleichberechtigung der Frau—Aufgaben und ihre Realisierung in der DDR." In *Zur gesellschaftlichen Stellung der Frau in der DDR*, edited by Herta Kuhrig and Wulfram Speigner. Leipzig: Verlag für die Frau, 1978.

Langer, Ingrid. "In letzter Konsequenz . . . Uranbergwerk!" In *Perlonzeit*, edited by Angela Delille and Andrea Grohn. Berlin: Elefanten Press, 1985.

Lehmann, Albrecht. *Gefangenschaft und Heimkehr: Deutsche Kriegsgefangene in der Sowjetunion*. Munich: Beck, 1986.

Lehr, Ursula. *Die Rolle der Mutter in der Sozialisation des Kindes*. Darmstadt: Steinkopff, 1974.

Leiby, Richard. "Public Health in Occupied Germany 1945–49." Ph.D. diss., University of Delaware, 1985.

Lerner, Gerda. "Reconceptualizing Differences among Women." *Journal of Women's History* 1 (1990): 106–22.

Lewis, Jane, ed. *Women's Welfare, Women's Rights*. London: Croom Helm, 1983.

Lüdtke, Alf. "'Coming to Terms with the Past': Illusions of Remembering, Ways of Forgetting Nazism in West Germany." *Journal of Modern History* 65 (1993): 542–72.

Lueck, Margret. *Die Frau im Männerstaat: Die gesellschaftliche Stellung der Frau im Nationalsozialismus. Eine Analyse aus pädagogischer Sicht*. Frankfurt am Main: Lang, 1979.

Macciocchi, Maria Antoniette. *Jungfrauen, Mütter und ein Führer*. Berlin: K. Wagenbach, 1976.

Maier, Friederike. "Zwischen Arbeitsmarkt und Familie—Frauenarbeit in den alten Bundesländern." In *Frauen in Deutschland 1945–1992*, edited by Gisela Helwig and Hildegard Maria Nickel. Berlin: Akademie, 1993.

Markovits, Inga. "'The Road from "I" to "We"': Family Law in the Communitarian State." *Utah Law Review* 48 (1996): 487–536.

Mason, Timothy. "Women in Germany, 1925–1940: Family, Welfare and Work." *History Workshop* 1 (1976): 74–113; 2 (1976): 5–32.

May, Elaine Tyler. *Homeward Bound: American Families in the Cold War Era*. New York: Basic Books, 1988.

McClelland, Keith. "Rational and Respectable Men: Gender, the Working Class, and Citizenship in Britain, 1850–1867." In *Gender and Class in Modern Europe*, edited by Laura Frader and Sonya Rose. Ithaca, N.Y.: Cornell University Press, 1996.

Meister, Barbara, and Reinhard Langholf. "'Zweckmäßige Asozialenbehandlung': Entmündigung in der nationalsozialistischen Fürsorgepolitik." In *Opfer und Täterinnen: Frauenbiographien des Nationalsozialismus*, edited by Angelika Ebbinghaus. Nördlingen: Delphi, 1987.

Merkel, Ina. "Leitbilder und Lebensweisen von Frauen in der DDR." In *Sozialgeschichte der DDR*, edited by Hartmut Kaelble, Jürgen Kocka, and Hartmut Zwahr. Stuttgart: Klett-Cotta, 1994.

———. *. . . und Du, Frau an der Werkbank: Die DDR in den 50er Jahren*. Berlin: Elefanten Press, 1990.

Meyer, Sibylle, and Eva Schulze. *Auswirkungen des II. Weltkriegs auf Familien: Zum*

Wandel der Familien in Deutschland. Berlin: Institut für Soziologie der Technischen Universität Berlin, 1989.

———. *Von Liebe sprach damals keiner: Familienalltag in der Nachkriegszeit.* Munich: Beck, 1985.

———. *Wie wir das alles geschafft haben: Alleinstehende Frauen berichten über ihr Leben nach 1945.* Munich: Beck, 1984.

Meyer-Renschhausen, Elisabeth. *Weibliche Kultur und soziale Arbeit: Eine Geschichte der Frauenbewegung am Beispiel Bremens 1810–1927.* Cologne and Vienna: Böhlau, 1989.

Meyerowitz, Joanne J. *Women Adrift: Independent Wage Earners in Chicago, 1880–1930.* Chicago: University of Chicago Press, 1988.

Milton, Sybil. "Women and the Holocaust: The Case of German and German-Jewish Women." In *When Biology Became Destiny,* edited by Renate Bridenthal, Atina Grossman, and Marion Kaplan. New York: Monthly Review Press, 1984.

Mirrer, Louise, ed. *Upon My Husband's Death: Widows in the Literature and Histories of Medieval Europe.* Ann Arbor: University of Michigan Press, 1992.

Mitchell, Maria. "Materialism and Secularism: CDU Politicians and National Socialism, 1945–1949." *Journal of Modern History* 65 (1995): 278–308.

Mitscherlich, Alexander, and Margarete Mitscherlich. *Die Unfähigkeit zu Trauern: Grundlagen kollektiven Verhaltens.* Munich: R. Piper, 1967.

Mitterauer, Michael. *The European Family: Patriarchy to Partnership from the Middle Ages to the Present.* Chicago: University of Chicago Press, 1982.

———. *Ledige Mütter: Zur Geschichte illegitimer Geburten in Europa.* Munich: Beck, 1983.

Möding, Nora. "'Ich muß irgendwo engagiert sein—fragen Sie mich bloß nicht, warum': Überlegungen von Mädchen in NS-Organisationen." In *"Wir kriegen jetzt andere Zeiten": Auf der Suche nach der Volkserfahrung in nachfaschistischen Ländern,* edited by Lutz Niethammer and Alexander von Plato. Bonn: Dietz, 1985.

Moeller, Robert G. "'The Homosexual Man Is a "Man," the Homosexual Woman Is a "Woman"': Sex, Society, and the Law in Postwar West Germany." *Journal of the History of Sexuality* 4 (1994): 395–429.

———. *Protecting Motherhood: Women and Family in the Politics of Postwar West Germany.* Berkeley: University of California Press, 1993.

———. "Protecting Mother's Work: From Production to Reproduction in Postwar West Germany." *Journal of Social History* 22 (1989): 413–37.

———. "Reconstructing the Family in Reconstruction Germany: Women and Social Policy in the Federal Republic, 1949–1955." *Feminist Studies* 15 (1989): 137–69.

———. "War Stories: The Search for a Usable Past in the Federal Republic of Germany." *American Historical Review* 101 (1996): 1008–48.

Mosse, George. *Nationalism and Sexuality: Middle-Class Morality and Sexual Norms in Modern Europe.* Madison: University of Wisconsin Press, 1985.

Mühlberg, Dietrich. "Überlegungen zu einer Kulturgeschichte der DDR." In *Sozialgeschichte der DDR,* edited by Hartmut Kaelble, Jürgen Kocka, and Hartmut Zwahr. Stuttgart: Klett-Cotta, 1994.

Mühlfeld, Claus, and Friedrich Schönweiß. *Nationalsozialistische Familienpolitik.* Stuttgart: Enke, 1989.

Müller, Walter, Angelika Willms, and Johann Handl, eds. *Strukturwandel der Frauenarbeit 1880–1980.* Frankfurt am Main: Campus, 1983.

Naimark, Norman. *The Russians in Germany: A History of the Soviet Zone of Occupation 1945–1949*. Cambridge, Mass.: Harvard University Press, 1995.

Nave-Herz, Rosemarie, ed. *Wandel und Kontinuität der Familie in der Bundesrepublik Deutschland*. Stuttgart: Enke, 1988.

Nave-Herz, Rosemarie, et al. *Familiäre Veränderungen seit 1950. Eine empirische Studie*. 2 vols. Oldenburg: Institut für Soziologie, Universität Oldenburg, 1984.

Nawratil, Heinz. *Die deutschen Nachkriegsverluste unter Vertriebenen, Gefangenen und Verschleppten*. Munich: Herbig, 1986.

Neuman, Ursula. *Ohne Jeans und Pille—Als "man" noch heiraten mußte*. Stuttgart: Kreuz, 1994.

Neumann, Lothar F., and Klaus Schaper. *Die Sozialordnung der Bundesrepublik Deutschland*. 1982. Reprint, Frankfurt am Main: Campus, 1990.

Nicholson, Linda J., ed. *Feminism/Postmodernism*. New York: Routledge, 1990.

Nickel, Hildegard Maria. "'Mitgestalterinnen des Sozialismus'—Frauenarbeit in der DDR." In *Frauen in Deutschland 1945–1992*, edited by Gisela Helwig and Hildegard Maria Nickel. Berlin: Akademie, 1993.

Nienhaus, Ursula. *Berufsstand weiblich: Die ersten weiblichen Angestellten*. Berlin: Transit, 1982.

Niethammer, Lutz. *Entnazifizierung in Bayern: Säuberung und Rehabilitierung unter amerikanischer Besatzung*. Frankfurt am Main: Fischer, 1972.

———. "Erfahrungen und Strukturen. Prolegomena zu einer Geschichte der Gesellschaft der DDR." In *Sozialgeschichte der DDR*, edited by Hartmut Kaelble, Jürgen Kocka, and Hartmut Zwahr. Stuttgart: Klett-Cotta, 1994.

———, ed. *"Hinterher merkt man, daß es richtig war, daß es schiefgegangen ist": Nachkriegs-Erfahrungen im Ruhrgebiet*. Bonn: Dietz, 1983.

———, ed. *"Die Jahre weiß man nicht, wo man die heute hinsetzen soll": Faschismus-Erfahrungen im Ruhrgebiet*. Bonn: Dietz, 1983.

———. "Privat-Wirtschaft: Erinnerungsfragmente einer anderen Umerziehung." In *"Hinterher merkt man, daß es richtig war, daß es schiefgegangen ist": Nachkriegs-Erfahrungen im Ruhrgebiet*, edited by Lutz Niethammer. Bonn: Dietz, 1983.

Niethammer, Lutz, and Alexander von Plato, eds. *"Wir kriegen jetzt andere Zeiten": Auf der Suche nach der Volkserfahrung in nachfaschistischen Ländern*. Bonn: Dietz, 1985.

Niethammer, Lutz, Alexander von Plato, and Dorothee Wierling. *Die volkseigene Erfahrung: Eine Archäologie des Lebens in der Industrieprovinz der DDR*. Berlin: Rowohlt, 1991.

Obertreis, Gesine. *Familienpolitik in der DDR 1945–1980*. Opladen: Leske und Budrich, 1986.

Oertzen, Christine von, and Almut Rietzschel. "Das 'Kuckuckssei' Teilzeitarbeit. Die Politik der Gewerkschaften im deutsch-deutschen Vergleich." In *Frauen arbeiten: Weibliche Erwerbstätigkeit in Ost- und Westdeutschland nach 1945*, edited by Gunilla-Friederike Budde. Göttingen: Vandenhoeck & Ruprecht, 1997.

Otto, Hans-Uwe, and Heinz Sünker. *Politische Formierung und soziale Erziehung im Nationalsozialismus*. Frankfurt am Main: Suhrkamp, 1991.

———, eds. *Soziale Arbeit und Faschismus*. Frankfurt am Main: Suhrkamp, 1989.

Owings, Alison. *Frauen: German Women Recall the Third Reich*. New Brunswick, N.J.: Rutgers, 1993.

Pateman, Carole. *The Sexual Contract*. Stanford, Calif.: Stanford University Press, 1988.

Pedersen, Susan. *Family, Dependence, and the Origins of the Welfare State: Britain and France, 1914–1945.* New York: Cambridge University Press, 1993.

———. "Gender, Welfare, and Citizenship in Britain during the Great War." *American Historical Review* 95 (1990): 983–1006.

Peukert, Detlev J. K. *Grenzen der Sozialdisziplinierung: Aufstieg und Krise der deutschen Jugendfürsorge von 1878 bis 1932.* Cologne: Bund, 1986.

———. *Inside Nazi Germany: Conformity, Opposition, and Racism in Everyday Life.* Trans. Richard Deveson. New Haven, Conn.: Yale University Press, 1987.

———. *The Weimar Republic: The Crisis of Classical Modernity.* Trans. Richard Deveson. New York: Hill & Wang, 1992.

Peukert, Detlev J. K., and Jürgen Relecke, eds. *Die Reihen fast geschlossen: Beiträge zur Geschichte des Alltags unterm Nationalsozialismus.* Wuppertal: Hammer, 1981.

Phayer, Michael. *Protestant and Catholic Women in Nazi Germany.* Detroit: Wayne State University Press, 1990.

Plant, Richard. *The Pink Triangle: The Nazi War against Homosexuals.* New York: Henry Holt, 1986.

Plato, Alexander von, and Wolfgang Meinicke. *Alte Heimat—neue Zeit: Flüchtlinge, Umgesiedelte, Vertriebene in der Sowjetischen Besatzungszone und in der DDR.* Berlin: Verlagsanstalt Union, 1991.

Poiger, Uta G. "Rock 'n' Roll, Female Sexuality, and the Cold War Battle over German Identities." In *West Germany under Construction: Politics, Society, and Culture in the Adenauer Era,* edited by Robert Moeller. Ann Arbor: University of Michigan Press, 1997.

Polm, Rita. *"Neben dem Mann die andere Hälfte eines Ganzen zu sein?" Junge Frauen in der Nachkriegszeit.* Münster: Unrast, 1990.

Pore, Renate. *A Conflict of Interest: Women in German Social Democracy, 1919–1933.* Westport, Conn.: Greenwood, 1981.

Poutrus, Kirsten. "Von den Massenvergewaltigungen zum Mutterschutzgesetz. Abtreibungspolitik und Abtreibungspraxis in Ostdeutschland, 1945–1950." In *Die Grenzen der Diktatur: Staat und Gesellschaft in der DDR,* edited by Richard Bessel and Ralph Jessen. Göttingen: Vandenhoeck & Ruprecht, 1996.

Prinz, Friedrich, ed. *Trümmerzeit in München: Kultur und Gesellschaft einer deutschen Großstadt im Aufbruch, 1945–49.* Munich: Beck, 1984.

Proctor, Robert. *Racial Hygiene: Medicine under the Nazis.* Cambridge, Mass.: Harvard University Press, 1988.

Projektgruppe für die vergessenen Opfer des NS-Regimes in Hamburg, ed. *Verachtet—Verfolgt—Vernichtet: Zu den "vergessenen" Opfern des NS-Regimes.* Hamburg: VSA, 1986.

Pust, Carola, et al. *Frauen in der BRD: Beruf, Familie, Gewerkschaften, Frauenbewegung.* Hamburg: VSA, 1983.

Ramm, Thilo. *Grundgesetz und Eherecht.* Tübingen: Mohr, 1972.

———. *Das nationalsozialistische Familien- und Jugendrecht.* Heidelberg: Decker und Müller, 1984.

Rausch, Heinz. "Politisches Bewußtsein und politische Einstellungen im Wandel." In *Die Identität der Deutschen,* edited by Werner Weidenfeld. Munich: Hanser, 1983.

Recker, Marie-Luise. *Nationalsozialistische Sozialpolitik im Zweiten Weltkrieg.* Munich: Oldenbourg, 1985.

Reese, Dagmar, "The BDM Generation: A Female Generation in Transition from Dictatorship to Democracy." In *Generations in Conflict: Youth Revolt and Generation For-*

mation in Germany 1770–1968, edited by Mark Roseman. Cambridge: Cambridge University Press, 1995.

———— . *"Straff, aber nicht stramm—herb, aber nicht derb": Zur Vergesellschaftung von Mädchen durch den Bund Deutscher Mädel im sozialkulturellen Vergleich zweier Milieus.* Weinheim and Basel: Beltz, 1989.

Reich-Hilweg, Ines. *Männer und Frauen sind gleichberechtigt: Der Gleichberechtigungsgrundsatz (Art.3 Abs.2 GG) in der parlamentarischen Auseinandersetzung 1948–1957 und in der Rechtsprechung des Bundesverfassungsgerichts 1953–1975.* Frankfurt am Main: Europäische Verlagsanstalt, 1979.

Reichel, Peter. *Politische Kultur in der Bundesrepublik.* Opladen: Leske, 1981.

Reichel, Sabine. *What Did You Do in the War, Daddy? Growing Up German.* New York: Hill & Wang, 1989.

Reif, Heinz, ed. *Die Familie in der Geschichte.* Göttingen: Vandenhoeck & Ruprecht, 1982.

Reusch, Wolfgang. *Bahnhofsmission in Deutschland 1897–1987.* Frankfurt am Main: Peter Lang, 1988.

Richter, Hans, and Heinz Reichert. *Die materiellen staatlichen Leistungen der Sozialfürsorge der DDR.* Berlin: Staatsverlag, 1970.

Richter, Ulrike, et al. *Alltag im Nachkriegsdeutschland: Frauenleben und -schicksal nach dem Zweiten Weltkrieg in Hannover.* Hannover: Oberstadtdirektor, 1985.

Riley, Denise. *Am I That Name? Feminism and the Category of "Women" in History.* Minneapolis: University of Minnesota Press, 1988.

———— . "'The Free Mothers': Pronatalism and Working Women in Industry at the End of the Last War in Britain." *History Workshop Journal* 11 (1981): 58–118.

Ringelheim, Joan. "Women and the Holocaust: A Consideration of Research." *Signs* 19 (1985): 741–61.

Roberts, Mary Louise. *Civilization without Sexes: Reconstructing Gender in Postwar France, 1917–1927.* Chicago: University of Chicago Press, 1994.

Roberts, Ulla. *Starke Mütter—ferne Väter: Töchter reflektieren ihre Kindheit im Nationalsozialismus und in der Nachkriegszeit.* Frankfurt am Main: Fischer, 1994.

Roseman, Mark. "National Socialism and Modernisation." In *Fascist Italy and Nazi Germany*, edited by Richard Bessel. New York: Cambridge University Press, 1996.

Rosenthal, Gabriele, ed. *Die Hitlerjugend-Generation.* Essen: Die blaue Eule, 1986.

Rosenthal, Gabriele, and Christiane Grote, eds. *"Als der Krieg kam, hatte ich mit Hitler nichts mehr zu tun": Zur Gegenwärtigkeit des "Dritten Reiches" in Biographien.* Opladen: Leske und Budrich, 1990.

Rosenthal, Gabriele, et al. *1945—Ende oder Neuanfang? Lebenslaufrekonstruktionen von Angehörigen der "Hitlerjugendgeneration."* Berlin: Institut für Soziologie, Freie Universität Berlin, 1984.

Rösler, Jörg. "The Black Market in Post-War Berlin and the Methods Used to Counteract it." *German History* 7 (1989): 92–107.

Rothmaler, Christiane. "Die Sozialpolitikerin Käthe Petersen zwischen Auslese und Ausmerze." In *Opfer und Täterinnen: Frauenbiographien des Nationalsizialismus*, edited by Angelika Ebbinghaus. Nördlingen: Delphi, 1987.

———— . "Die 'Volksgemeinschaft' wird ausgehorcht und 'wichtiges Material der Zukunft' zusammengetragen." In *Verachtet—Verfolgt—Vernichtet*, edited by Projektgruppe für die vergessenen Opfer des NS-Regimes in Hamburg. Hamburg: VSA, 1988.

Rouette, Susanne. *Sozialpolitik als Geschlechterpolitik: Die Regulierung der Frauenarbeit nach dem Ersten Weltkrieg.* Frankfurt am Main: Campus, 1993.

Rüdiger, Jutta. *Die Hitler-Jugend und ihr Selbstverständnis im Spiegel ihrer Aufgabengebiete*. Lindenhorst: Askania, 1983.

———, ed. *Zur Problematik von Soldatinnen*. Lindenhorst: Askania, 1987.

Ruhl, Klaus-Jörg. *Verordnete Unterordnung: Berufstätige Frauen zwischen Wirtschaftswachstum und konservativer Ideologie in der Nachkriegszeit (1945–1963)*. Munich: Oldenbourg, 1994.

Rupieper, Hermann-Josef. "Bringing Democracy to the Frauleins: Frauen als Zielgruppe der amerkanischen Demokratisierungspolitik in Deutschland 1945–1952." *Geschichte und Gesellschaft* 17 (1991): 61–91.

Rupp, Leila. *Mobilizing Women for War: German and American War Propaganda, 1939–1945*. Princeton, N.J.: Princeton University Press, 1978.

———. "Mother of the Volk: The Image of Women in Nazi Ideology." *Signs* 3 (1977): 362–79.

Sachse, Carola. "'Ein 'heißes Eisen.' Ost- und westdeutsche Debatten um den Hausarbeitstag." In *Frauen arbeiten: Weibliche Erwerbstätigkeit in Ost- und Westdeutschland nach 1945*, edited by Gunilla-Friederike Budde. Göttingen: Vandenhoeck & Ruprecht, 1997.

———. *Siemens, der Nationalsozialismus und die moderne Familie: Eine Untersuchung zur sozialen Rationalisierung in Deutschland im 20. Jahrhundert*. Hamburg: Rasch und Röhring, 1990.

Saldern, Adelheid von. "Victims or Perpetrators? Controversies about the Role of Women in the Nazi State." In *Nazism and German Society*, edited by David Crew. London and New York: Routledge, 1994.

Sander, Helke, and Barbara Johr, eds. *BeFreier und Befreite: Krieg, Vergewaltigungen, Kinder*. Munich: Kunstmann, 1992.

Sanders-Brahms, Helma. *Deutschland, bleiche Mutter: Film-Erzählung*. Reinbek: Rowohlt, 1980.

Sass, Jürgen. "Väter: Eine Befragung in Ost und West." In *Stiefbrüder: Was Ostmänner und Westmänner voneinander denken*, edited by Katrin Rohnstock. Berlin: Elefanten Press, 1995.

Schenk, Christine, and Christiane Schindler. "Frauenbewegung in Ostdeutschland— eine kleine Einführung." *Beiträge zur feministische Theorie und Praxis* 16 (1993): 131–45.

Schenk, Herrad. *Die feministische Herausforderung: 150 Jahre Frauenbewegung in Deutschland*. Munich: Beck, 1980.

Scherer, Klaus. *"Asozial" im Dritten Reich: Die vergessenen Verfolgten*. Münster: Votum Verlag, 1990.

Schlicht, Goetz. *Das Familien- und Familienverfahrensrecht der DDR*. Tübingen and Basil: Horst Erdmann, 1970.

Schmacke, Norbert, and Hans-Georg Güse. *Zwangssterilisiert—Verleugnet— Vergessen*. Bremen: Brockkamp, 1984.

Schmackpfeffer, Petra. *Frauenbewegung und Prostitution: Über das Verhalten der alten und neuen deutschen Frauenbewegung zur Prostitution*. Oldenburg: Bibliotheks- und Informationssystem der Universität Oldenburg, 1989.

Schmidt, Margot. "Im Vorzimmer: Arbeitsverhältnisse von Sekretärinnen und Sachbearbeiterinnen bei Thyssen nach dem Krieg." In *"Hinterher merkt man, daß es richtig war, daß es schiefgegangen ist": Nachkriegs-Erfahrungen im Ruhrgebiet*, edited by Lutz Niethammer. Bonn: Dietz, 1983.

Schmidt-Harzbach, Ingrid. "Doppelt besiegt: Vergewaltigung als Massenschicksal." *Frankfurter Frauenblatt* (May 1985): 18–23.

———. "Die Lüge von der Stunde Null." *Courage* (1982): 33–40.

———. "Nun geht mal beiseite, ihr Frauen!" *Courage* (1982): 47–54.

———. "Eine Woche im April: Berlin 1945: Vergewaltigung als Massenschicksal." In *BeFreier und Befreite*, edited by Helke Sander and Barbara Johr. Munich: Kunstmann, 1992.

Schoenberg, Hans. *Germans from the East*. The Hague: Nijhoff, 1970.

Schoppmann, Claudia. *Nationalsozialistische Sexualpolitik und weibliche Homosexualität*. Pfaffenweiler: Centaurus, 1991.

———. *Zeit der Maskierung: Lebensgeschichten lesbischer Frauen im "Dritten Reich."* Berlin: Orlanda, 1993.

Schörken, Rolf. *Luftwaffenhelfer im Dritten Reich: Die Entstehung eines politischen Bewußtseins*. Stuttgart: Klett-Cotta, 1985.

Schröder, Michael, ed. *Auf geht's, Rama Dama! Frauen und Männer aus der Arbeiterbewegung berichten über Wiederaufbau und Neugebinn 1945–1949*. Cologne: Bund, 1984.

Schubert, Doris. "'Ehrfurcht vor dem Leben?' Zur Diskussion um die Reform des Par. 218 in der deutschen Nachkriegszeit." *Beiträge zur feministischen Theorie und Praxis* 14 (1985): 100ff.

Schubert, Friedel. *Die Frau in der DDR: Ideologie und konzeptionelle Ausgestaltung ihrer Stellung in Beruf und Familie*. Opladen: Leske, 1980.

Schubert, Werner. "Der Entwurf eines Nichtehelichengesetzes vom Juli 1940 und seine Ablehnung durch Hitler." *Zeitschrift für das gesamte Familienrecht* 31 (1984): 1–10.

———. *Die Projekte der Weimarer Republik zur Reform des Nichtehelichen-, des Adoptions- und des Ehescheidungsrechts*. Paderborn: Schöning, 1986.

Scott, Joan Wallach, "Gender: A Useful Category of Historical Analysis." *American Historical Review* 91 (1986): 1053–75.

———. *Gender and the Politics of History*. New York: Columbia University Press, 1988.

Seeler, Angela. "Ehe, Familie und andere Lebensformen in den Nachkriegsjahren im Spiegel der Frauenzeitschriften." In *"Das Schicksal Deutschlands liegt in der Hand seiner Frauen": Frauen in der deutschen Nachkriegsgeschichte*, edited by Anna-Elisabeth Freier and Annette Kuhn. Dusseldorf: Schwann, 1984.

Seidler, Franz W. *Blitzmädchen: Die Geschichte der Helferinnen der deutschen Wehrmacht im 2. Weltkrieg*. Koblenz and Bonn: Wehr & Wissen, 1979.

———. *Frauen zu den Waffen? Marketenderinnen, Helferinnen, Soldatinnen*. Koblenz and Bonn: Wehr & Wissen, 1978.

———. *Prostitution, Homosexualität, Selbstverstümmelung: Probleme der deutschen Sanitätsführung 1939 bis 1945*. Neckargemünd: Vorwinkel, 1977.

Shukert, Elfrieda Berthiaume, and Barbara Smith Scibetta. *War Brides of World War II*. Novato, Calif.: Presidio Press, 1988.

Siegele-Wenschkewitz, Leonore, and Gerda Stucklik, eds. *Frauen und Faschismus in Europa: Der faschistische Körper*. Pfaffenweiler: Centaurus, 1990.

Sillge, Ursula. *Un-Sichtbare Frauen. Lesben und ihre Emanzipation in der DDR*. Berlin: LinksDruck, 1991.

Skocpol, Theda. *Protecting Soldiers and Mothers: The Political Origins of Social Policy in the United States*. Cambridge, Mass.: Harvard University Press, 1992.

Smith, Arthur. *Heimkehr aus dem zweiten Weltkrieg: Die Entlassung der deutschen Kriegsgefangenen*. Stuttgart: Deutsche Verlags-Anstalt, 1985.

Sorge, Martin K. *The Other Price of Hitler's War: German Military and Civilian Losses Resulting from World War II*. New York: Greenwood Press, 1986.

Späth, Antje. "Vielfältige Forderungen nach Gleichberechtigung und 'nur' ein Ergebnis: Artikel 3 Absatz 2 GG." In *Das Schicksal Deutschlands liegt in der Hand seiner Frauen": Frauen in der deutschen Nachkriegsgeschichte*, edited by Anna-Elisabeth Freier and Annette Kuhn. Dusseldorf: Schwann, 1984.

Spieckermans, Anna. "Als Flakwaffenhelferin im Einsatz 1944/45: Ein Bericht." *Feministische Studien* 3/1 (1984): 27ff.

Steffens, Gerd. "Die praktische Widerlegung des Rassismus: Verbotene Liebe und ihre Verfolgung." In *Ich war immer gut zu meiner Russin": Zur Struktur und Praxis des Zwangsarbeitssystems im Zweiten Weltkrieg in der Region Südhessen*, edited by Fred Dorn and Klaus Heuer. Pfaffenweiler: Centaurus, 1991.

Stephenson, Jill. *The Nazi Organization of Women*. New York: Barnes & Noble Books, 1980.

———. "Triangle: Foreign Workers, German Civilians, and the Nazi Regime. War and Society in Württemberg, 1939–45." *German Studies Review* 15 (1992): 339–59.

———. "War and Society in Württemberg, 1939–1945: Beating the System." *German Studies Review* 8 (1985): 89–105.

———. *Women in Nazi Society*. New York: Harper & Row, 1975.

Stern, Frank. "The Historic Triangle: Occupiers, Germans and Jews in Postwar Germany." In *West Germany under Construction: Politics, Society, and Culture in the Adenauer Era*, edited by Robert Moeller. Ann Arbor: University of Michigan Press, 1997.

Sternheim-Peters, Eva. *Die Zeit der grossen Täuschungen: Mädchenleben im Faschismus*. Bielefeld: AJZ, 1987.

Stolten, Inge. *Das alltägliche Exil: Leben zwischen Hakenkreuz und Währungsreform*. Berlin: Dietz, 1982.

———, ed. *Der Hunger nach Erfahrung: Frauen nach '45*. Frankfurt am Main: Fischer, 1981.

Studienschwerpunkt "Frauenforschung" am Institut für Sozialpädagogik der TU Berlin, ed. *Mittäterschaft und Entdeckungslust*. Berlin: Orlanda, 1989.

Szepansky, Gerda. *Blitzmädel—Heldenmutter—Kriegerwitwe: Frauenleben im zweiten Weltkrieg*. Frankfurt am Main: Fischer, 1986.

———. *Die stille Emanzipation: Frauen in der DDR*. Frankfurt am Main: Fischer, 1995.

Theweleit, Klaus. *Männerphantasien*. 2 vols. Frankfurt: Roger Stern, 1977–78.

Thönnessen, Werner. *Frauenemanzipation: Politik und Literatur der deutschen Sozialdemokratie zur Frauenbewegung 1863–1933*. Frankfurt am Main: Europäische Verlagsanstalt, 1969.

Thürmer-Rohr, Christina. *Vagabundinnen: Feministische Essays*. Berlin: Orlanda, 1987.

Tobin, Elizabeth, and Jennifer Gibson. "The Meanings of Labor: East German Women's Work in the Transition from Nazism to Communism." *Central European History* 28 (1995): 300–42.

"Totalitäre Herrschaft und totalitäres Erbe." Special issue, *German Studies Review* 17 (1994).

Tröger, Annemarie. "Between Rape and Prostitution: Survival Strategies and Possibilities of Liberation of Berlin Women in 1945–48." In *Women in Culture and Politics: A Century of Change*, edited by Judith Friedlander, Alice Kessler-Harris, and Carol Smith-Rosenberg. Bloomington: Indiana University Press, 1986.

———. "The Creation of a Female Assembly-Line Proletariat." In *When Biology Became Destiny: Women in Weimar and Nazi Germany*, edited by Renate Bridenthal, Atina Grossmann, and Marion Kaplan. New York: Monthly Review Press, 1984.

Tumpek-Kjellmark, Katharina C. "From Hitler's Widows to Adenauer's Brides: Towards a Construction of Gender and Memory in Postwar Germany, 1938–1963." Ph.D. diss., Cornell University, 1994.

Um eine ganze Epoche voraus. Leipzig: Verlag für die Frau, 1970.

Usborne, Cornelie. "The New Woman and Generation Conflict: Perceptions of Young Women's Sexual Mores in the Weimar Republic." In *Generations in Conflict: Youth Revolt and Generation Formation in Germany 1770–1968,* edited by Mark Roseman. Cambridge: Cambridge University Press, 1995.

——— . *The Politics of the Body in Weimar Germany: Women's Reproductive Rights and Duties.* Ann Arbor: University of Michigan Press, 1992.

Vicinus, Martha. *Independent Women.* Chicago: University of Chicago Press, 1985.

Vogel, Ursula. "Property Rights and the Status of Women in Germany and England." In *Bourgeois Society in Nineteenth-Century Europe,* edited by Jürgen Kocka and Allan Mitchell. Providence, R.I.: Berg, 1993.

Vorländer, Herwart. *Die NSV: Darstellung und Dokumentation einer nationalsozialistischen Organisation.* Boppard am Rhein: Herald Boldt, 1988.

Walkowitz, Judith. *City of Dreadful Delight: Narratives of Sexual Danger in Late-Victorian London.* Chicago: University of Chicago Press, 1992.

——— . *Prostitution and Victorian Society: Women, Class and the State.* Cambridge: Cambridge University Press, 1980.

Weindling, Paul. *Health, Race, and German Politics between Unification and Nazism, 1870–1945.* Cambridge: Cambridge University Press, 1989.

Weingart, Peter, Jürgen Kroll, and Kurt Bayertz. *Rasse, Blut und Gene.* Frankfurt am Main: Suhrkamp, 1988.

Weitz, Eric D. *Creating German Communism, 1890–1990.* Princeton, N.J.: Princeton University Press, 1997.

Wendt, Hartmut. "Die deutsch-deutschen Wanderungen—Bilanz einer 40-jährigen Geschichte von Flucht und Ausreise." *Deutschland Archiv* 24 (1991): 386–95.

Weyrather, Irmgard. *Muttertag und Mutterkreuz: Der Kult um die "deutsche Mutter" im Nationalsozialismus.* Frankfurt am Main: Fischer, 1993.

Wiggershaus, Renate. *Frauen unterm Nationalsozialismus.* Wuppertal: Hammer, 1984.

——— . *Geschichte der Frauen und der Frauenbewegung in der Bundesrepublik Deutschland und in der Deutschen Demokratischen Republik nach 1945.* Wuppertal: Hammer, 1979.

Willenbacher, Barbara. "Zerrüttung und Bewährung der Nachkriegs-Familie." In *Von Stalingrad zur Währungsreform: Zur Sozialgeschichte des Umbruchs in Deutschland,* edited by Martin Broszat, Klaus-Dietmar Henke, and Hans Woller. Munich: Oldenbourg, 1988.

Windaus-Walser, Karin. "Gnade der weiblichen Geburt? Zum Umgang der Frauenforschung mit Nationalsozialismus und Antisemitismus." *Feministische Studien* 6 (1988): 102–15.

Winkler, Dörte. *Frauenarbeit im "Dritten Reich."* Hamburg: Hoffmann und Campe, 1977.

Winkler, Heinrich August, ed. *Politische Weichenstellungen im Nachkriegsdeutschland, 1945–53.* Göttingen: Vandenhoeck & Ruprecht, 1979.

Wittrock, Christiane. *Weiblichkeitsmythen: Das Frauenbild im Faschismus und seine Vorläufer in der Frauenbewegung der zwanziger Jahre.* Frankfurt am Main: Sendler, 1983.

Wobbe, Therese, ed. *Nach Osten: Verdeckte Spuren Nationalsozialistischer Verbrechen.* Frankfurt am Main: Verlag Neue Kritik, 1992.

Zumwalt, Ken. *The Stars and Stripes: World War II and the Early Years.* Austin, Tex.: Eakin Press, 1989.

Zur Wirtschaftspolitik der SED. Vol. 1, *1945 bis 1949.* Berlin: Dietz, 1984.

Zürn, Gaby. "Von der Herbertstraße nach Auschwitz." In *Opfer und Täterinnen: Frauenbiografien des Nationalsozialismus,* edited by Angelika Ebbinghaus. Nördlingen: Delphi, 1987.

Zwahr, Hartmut. "Umbruch durch Ausbruch und Aufbruch: Die DDR auf dem Höhepunkt der Staatskrise 1989. Mit Exkursen zu Ausreise und Flucht sowie einer ostdeutschen Generationenübersicht." In *Sozialgeschichte der DDR,* edited by Hartmut Kaelble, Jürgen Kocka, and Hartmut Zwahr. Stuttgart: Klett-Cotta, 1994.

Index

Abortion: in FRG, 241, 319n100; in GDR, 83, 198, 241, 319n100; in Nazi Germany, 34, 36–38; during military occupation, 127

Adoption, 130, 151

Adult dependents, 160, 216–17

Adultery: media reaction to, 128–31; men's, 2, 151, 128–29; by military wives, 54–56, 58–59, 95, 119, 122; policy and law on, 55–56; war widows' sexual activity perceived as, 173; wives' fear of, 131, 232–34; wives of POWs and, 115, 119

Alimony, 123, 138, 194–96, 201, 220, 224, 236–37, 295n23. *See also* Divorce

All German Women's Congress, 226

Allied Control Council, 90

American occupation. *See* Western Occupation Zone; Military occupation

Arbeiterwohungsbaugenossenschaften (AWG). *See* Workers' Building Cooperatives

"Asocials," 17–18, 26–31; definitions of, 18, 24, 28; illegitimate birth as indicator, 34; institutionalization of, 25, 27, 37; legal measures regarding, 26–27, 29–31; lesbians as, 28–29; male types , 28; prostitutes as, 29; unwed mothers as, 31–37; wives as, 44, 54

Auxiliary War Service, 64, 70–74, 275n114

Basic Law. *See* Laws and legislation, Basic Law

Bebel, August, 87, 146

Benjamin, Hilde, 177, 194

Berlin Wall, 211

Betriebsfrauenausschüsse (BFA). *See* Company Women's Commissions

Bigamy, 125, 129, 131

Birth rates, 6–7, 251

Births, nonmarital. *See* Children, nonmarital

Bismarck, Otto von, 142

Black Market, 84–87, 92, 97, 120, 122

Bock, Gisela, 12

Böll, Heinrich, 169

Bormann, Martin, 65, 70

Bund Deutscher Mädel (BDM). *See* League of German Girls

Bundestag: Civil Code reform, 145–50, 154

Caritas, 150–52

Catholicism: and politics, 142, 144; and social work, 144, 150–51

CDU in Soviet occupation zone, 190; housewifery, 146, 165; illegitimacy law, 144, 151; marriage and family, 143; money for children, 157–58; sexual morality, 105;

372 / *Index*

Soviet occupation: censorship in, 109, 129; compulsory labor in, 88–90, 94, 281n58; currency reform in, 94; and denazification, 113–14; DFD in, 183; and disrupted families, 189; flight West from, 211; and Housework Day, 203; KPD in, 179; labor in, 76, 87–88, 90–91, 94–95; missing men and, 111–12; prisoners of war and, 112–13; and rape, 77, 81–82, 95–97, 105–6; refugees in, 3, 83; and Saxon referendum, 180–82; and SED, 179–80; sexuality in, 95–97, 125, 128–29; unemployment in, 86. *See also* Military occupation

Soviet Union: abortion policy in, 181; collective housework measures in, 203; family policy in, 190; German exile in, 176; human reparations in, 89, 114, 118, 281n55; prisoner of war camps in, 112–18, 183; and sexual equality, 204; as victim, 243; war against, 79, 81, 184, 201. *See also* Soviet occupation

Sozialdemokratische Partei Deutschlands (SPD). *See* Social Democratic Party

Stars and Stripes, 100–101

Sterilization, 21–23, 25–27, 30, 37, 46, 78

Strecker, Gabrielle, 140–41

Surplus women. *See* Single women, demographics of

Third Reich. *See* Nazi Germany

Unemployment, 231; compensation for, 93, 199–200, 310n94; female, 86, 94, 160, 165, 185, 233; male, 7, 22, 38; statistical practices, 282, 75

Unwed motherhood, 53, 56, 117, 245, 265n301; "asociability" and, 31–37; avoidance of 38, 51, 127, 227, 239–40; demographics of, 127, 206, 209–10, 227, 251, 266n88, 302n23; "illegitimacy boom" and, 127, 245; law and policy on, 15, 31–38, 138, 143–

45, 150–56, 174, 190, 266n78, 270n42; media and, 127, 129, 227; Nazi promotion of, 72; popular attitudes toward, 6, 12, 129–30, 227–28, 319n100; social class and, 6, 12, 144. *See also* Children, nonmarital

Unwed partners, 148

Unwed women, 3, 5; attitudes of toward marriage, 50–51, 123–25, 235; and employment, 5, 40–42, 64–73, 156–57, 159, 201–5, 218–19; political activity of, 38–40, 66–67, 133–34, 141, 180–81, 239–40, 244–45; sex and, 6. *See also* Single women; Unwed motherhood

Veterans: employment of, 86, 166–67; pensions for, 197, 199, 299n81. *See also* Health, invalidism; Missing in Action; Prisoners of War

Victims of Fascism, 196–200

Victims of war. *See* Laws and legislation, Law to Aid Victims of War; Pensions, for widows; Veterans; War widows

Vocational training, 165, 178, 194, 226, 244. *See also* Education

Volkskammer, 202

War brides, 44–45, 72–73; emotional experience of, 51; family allowances for, 62–64; wartime employment of, 60, 63, 64, 73; widows' pensions for, 164. *See also* Marriage, wartime

War victims' associations, 166, 169

War widows, 1–3, 74, 216, 242; cohabitation of, 168–70; employment of, 165–68; low profile of in GDR, 189–91; and postmortem marriage, 47–48; and remarriage, 169; sexual lives of, 173–74; symbolic functions of, 51–52, 162, 173–75, 200, 243; World War I, 6, 38, 52, 241. *See also* War widows' pensions; Widows

War widows' pensions: in FRG; 138, 162–65, 168–71, 244; in GDR, 190, 196–201, 94; during military occu-